ⓕFrommer's®
Bahamas 2002

W9-AHI-729

Eleuthera is an island of gorgeous white- and pink-sand beaches. See chapter 8.
© *Bob Krist Photography.*

Paradise Island is home to the biggest, splashiest resort in The Bahamas, the Atlantis. See chapter 4. © Bob Krist Photography.

Some Paradise Island resorts boast multiple pools, tennis courts, golf courses, and waterfalls. See chapter 4 for more details.
© M. Timothy O'Keefe Photography.

The Atlantis Resort has an incredible marine park, where visitors can observe tropical fish, sharks, and stingrays from catwalks above and from glassed-in observatories below. See chapter 4. © Mark E. Gibson Photography.

The Bahamian parrot, a colorful local character. © Michael Defreitas Photography.

Old-fashioned horse-drawn surreys are a fun, leisurely way to explore Nassau. See chapter 3.
© Bob Krist Photography.

The spectacular sand of Paradise Island. See chapter 1 for details on the best beaches in The Bahamas. © Paul Barton/The Stock Market.

The Crystal Palace Casino on Cable Beach is one of the best places in The Bahamas to roll the dice or try your luck at the slot machines. If you're interested in gambling, head for Nassau, Cable Beach, Paradise Island, or Freeport/Lucaya (see chapters 3, 4, and 5). © Michael Ventura Photography.

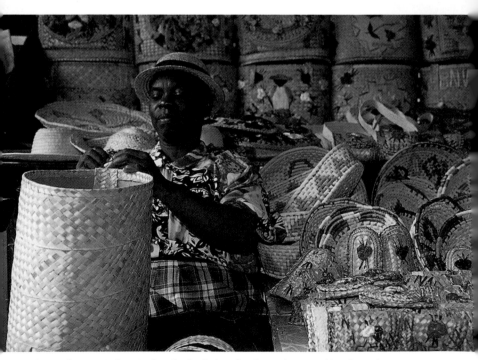

Nassau is a great place to shop for both duty-free luxury items and locally made handcrafts. See chapter 3. © Bob Krist Photography.

High energy Junkanoo parades and celebrations are held throughout the islands on December 26, and many of these activities are repeated on New Year's Day. See chapters 2 and 3 for details.
© Darrell Jones Photography.

Nassau is the scene of colorful Junkanoo festivals. See chapters 2 and 3.
© Michael Ventura/International Stock.

The Abacos are a world apart from the glitzy pleasures of Freeport/Lucaya, Nassau, or Paradise Island. See chapter 7. © Catherine Karnow Photography.

Shark Wall, off the coast of New Providence, is one of the most spectacular dive sites you'll ever explore. See chapter 3. © Jeff Rotman/Tony Stone Images.

The pirate Sir Henry Morgan is supposed to have buried a vast treasure at Morgan's Bluff, at the tip of North Andros. See chapter 6. © Darrell Jones Photography.

The 40-acre Lucayan National Park on Grand Bahama Island is filled with mangrove, pine, and palm trees. See chapter 5. © M. Timothy O'Keefe Photography.

The Bahamas is one of the best sportfishing destinations in the world.
© Darrell Jones Photography.

Lucky Bahamian schoolkids get to have recess on the beach! © Catherine Karnow Photography.

One of the most unforgettable adventures you can have in Lucaya is the chance to meet a friendly dolphin through UNEXSO's "Dolphin Experience." See chapter 5.
© M. Timothy O'Keefe Photography.

Development hasn't marred Cat Island, which boasts stunning, uncrowded beaches. See chapter 10. © Stephen Frink/WaterHouse Stock Photography.

See chapter 1 for details on the best dive sites throughout The Bahamas. © M. Timothy O'Keefe Photography.

The waters off the Abaco Islands are teeming with fish. See chapter 7.
© *Catherine Karnow Photography.*

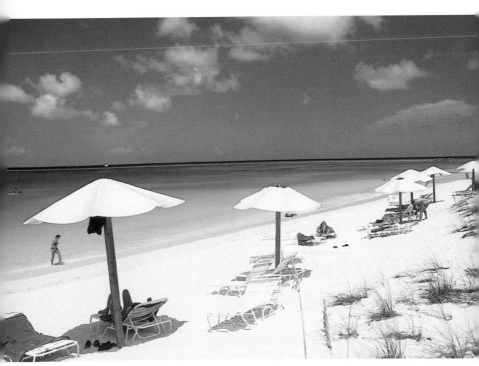

The Club Med on San Salvador boasts 2 miles of pristine white sands. See chapter 10.
© *Darrell Jones Photography.*

Full of colorful architecture, Nassau is the most historic city in The Bahamas. See chapter 3.

The Exumas are some of the loveliest islands in The Bahamas. See chapter 9 for details on snorkeling, beaches, sailing, and accommodations there.

Tens of thousands of pink flamingos nest in a nature preserve on Great Inagua Island. See chapter 10. © Bob Krist Photography.

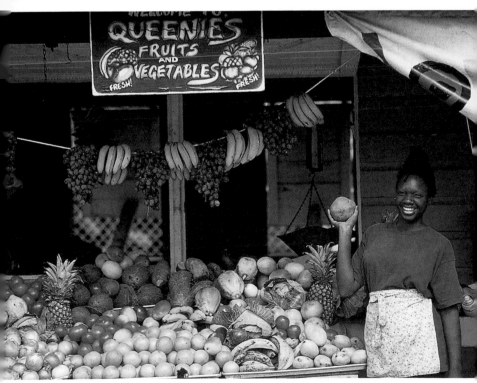

Lots of locally run farmstands offer a taste of The Bahamas. © Bob Krist Photography.

The Exumas boast gorgeous beaches, such as this stunning stretch of white sand on Stock Island, off George Town. See chapter 9. © Bob Krist Photography.

When should I travel to get the best airfare?

Where do I go for answers to my travel questions?

What's the best and easiest way to plan and book my trip?

frommers.travelocity.com

Frommer's, the travel guide leader, has teamed up with **Travelocity.com**, the leader in online travel, to bring you an in-depth, easy-to-use resource designed to help you plan and book your trip online.

At **frommers.travelocity.com**, you'll find free online updates about your destination from the experts at Frommer's plus the outstanding travel planning and purchasing features of Travelocity.com. Travelocity.com provides reservations capabilities for 95 percent of all airline seats sold, more than 47,000 hotels, and over 50 car rental companies. In addition, Travelocity.com offers more than 2,000 exciting vacation and cruise packages. Travelocity.com puts you in complete control of your travel planning with these and other great features:

> **Expert travel guidance from Frommer's** - over 150 writers reporting from around the world!

> **Best Fare Finder** - an interactive calendar tells you when to travel to get the best airfare

> **Fare Watcher** - we'll track airfare changes to your favorite destinations

> **Dream Maps** - a mapping feature that suggests travel opportunities based on your budget

> **Shop Safe Guarantee** - 24 hours a day / 7 days a week live customer service, and more!

Whether traveling on a tight budget, looking for a quick weekend getaway, or planning the trip of a lifetime, Frommer's guides and Travelocity.com will make your travel dreams a reality. You've bought the book, now book the trip!

A New Star-Rating System & Other Exciting News from Frommer's!

In our continuing effort to publish the savviest, most up-to-date, and most appealing travel guides available, we've added some great new features.

Frommer's guides now include a new **star-rating system.** Every hotel, restaurant, and attraction is rated from 0 to 3 stars to help you set priorities and organize your time.

We've also added **seven brand-new features** that point you to the great deals, in-the-know advice, and unique experiences that separate travelers from tourists. Throughout the guide look for:

Finds	Special finds—those places only insiders know about
Fun Fact	Fun facts—details that make travelers more informed and their trips more fun
Kids	Best bets for kids—advice for the whole family
Moments	Special moments—those experiences that memories are made of
Overrated	Places or experiences not worth your time or money
Tips	Insider tips—some great ways to save time and money
Value	Great values—where to get the best deals

We've also added a **"What's New"** section in every guide—a timely crash course in what's hot and what's not in every destination we cover.

Other Great Guides for Your Trip:

Frommer's Caribbean

Frommer's Caribbean Cruises & Ports of Call

Frommer's Caribbean Hideaways

Bahamas

2002

by Darwin Porter & Danforth Prince

Here's what the critics say about Frommer's:

"Amazingly easy to use. Very portable, very complete."
—*Booklist*

"The only mainstream guide to list specific prices. The Walter Cronkite of guidebooks—with all that implies."
—*Travel & Leisure*

"Complete, concise, and filled with useful information."
—*New York Daily News*

"Hotel information is close to encyclopedic."
—*Des Moines Sunday Register*

Hungry Minds™

Best-Selling Books • Digital Downloads • e-Books • Answer Networks •
e-Newsletters • Branded Web Sites • e-Learning
New York, NY • Cleveland, OH • Indianapolis, IN

About the Authors

Darwin Porter, while still a teenager, began writing about The Bahamas for the *Miami Herald* and has been a frequent visitor ever since. He is joined by Ohio-born **Danforth Prince,** formerly of the Paris bureau of *The New York Times,* who has coauthored numerous Frommer's best-sellers with Darwin, including our guides to the Caribbean, Bermuda, Puerto Rico, Jamaica, and the Virgin Islands. Together, they share their secrets, discoveries, and opinions about The Bahamas with you.

Published by:

Hungry Minds, Inc.

909 Third Ave.
New York, NY 10022

ISBN 0-7645-6440-4
ISSN 1068-9338

Editors: Olga Stavropoulos and Kimberly Perdue
Production Editor: Donna Wright
Cartographer: John Decamillis
Photo Editor: Richard Fox
Production by Hungry Minds Indianapolis Production Services

Front cover photo: On the beach in the Bahamas.
Back cover photo: The Mistral/Tudor Parasailing Finals.

Special Sales

For general information on Hungry Minds' products and services please contact our Customer Care department; within the U.S. at 800-762-2974, outside the U.S. at 317-572-3993 or fax 317-572-4002. For sales inquiries and reseller information, including discounts, bulk sales, customized editions, and premium sales, please contact our Customer Care department at 800-434-3422.

Manufactured in the United States of America

5 4 3 2

Contents

⑨ The Exuma Islands   251

⑩ The Southern Bahamas   270

⑪ Turks & Caicos   293

Appendix: The Bahamas in Depth   334

Index   339

List of Maps

An Invitation to the Reader

In researching this book, we discovered many wonderful places—hotels, restaurants, shops, and more. We're sure you'll find others. Please tell us about them, so we can share the information with your fellow travelers in upcoming editions. If you were disappointed with a recommendation, we'd love to know that, too. Please write to:

Frommer's Bahamas 2002
Hungry Minds, Inc. • 909 Third Avenue • New York, NY 10022

An Additional Note

Please be advised that travel information is subject to change at any time—and this is especially true of prices. We therefore suggest that you write or call ahead for confirmation when making your travel plans. The authors, editors, and publisher cannot be held responsible for the experiences of readers while traveling. Your safety is important to us, however, so we encourage you to stay alert and be aware of your surroundings. Keep a close eye on cameras, purses, and wallets, all favorite targets of thieves and pickpockets.

New! Frommer's Star Ratings & Icons

Every hotel, restaurant, and attraction listing in this guide has been ranked for quality, value, service, amenities, and special features using a star-rating scale. In country, state, and regional guides, we also rate towns and regions to help you narrow down your choices and budget your time accordingly. Hotels and restaurants in the Very Expensive and Expensive categories are rated on a scale of one (highly recommended) to three stars (exceptional). Those in the Moderate and Inexpensive categories rate from zero (recommended) to two stars (very highly recommended). Attractions, towns, and regions are rated according to the following scale: zero stars (recommended), one star (highly recommended), two stars (very highly recommended), and three stars (must-see).

In addition to the rating system, we also use seven icons to highlight insider information, useful tips, special bargains, hidden gems, memorable experiences, kid-friendly venues, places to avoid, and other useful information:

(Finds   (Fun Fact   (Kids   (Moments   (Overrated   (Tips   (Value

The following abbreviations are used for credit cards:

AE	American Express	DISC	Discover	V	Visa
DC	Diners Club	MC	MasterCard		

FROMMERS.COM

Now that you have the guidebook to a great trip, visit our website at **www.frommers. com** for travel information on nearly 2,000 destinations. With features updated regularly, we give you instant access to the most current trip-planning information available. At Frommers.com, you'll also find the best prices on air fares, accommodations, and car rentals—and you can even book travel online through our travel booking partners. At Frommers.com you'll also find the following:

- Daily Newsletter highlighting the best travel deals
- Hot Spot of the Month/Vacation Sweepstakes & Travel Photo Contest
- More than 200 Travel Message Boards
- Outspoken Newsletters and Feature Articles on travel bargains, vacation ideas, tips & resources, and more!

What's New in The Bahamas

Major developments in Paradise Island have taken the media heat while nearby Nassau and Cable Beach still peddle basically what they've had for a long time. There's talk of a renaissance for Grand Bahama Island (Freeport/Lucaya), which has begun to emerge from the doldrums it entered after the '60s and '70s.

NASSAU Accommodations The re-emergence of the once-decaying **British Colonial Hilton**, 1 Bay St. (© 800/HILTONS), after millions of dollars in renovations, has brought renewed life to the heart of Nassau. It is the first hotel in a decade or so to lure visitors away from Paradise Island and Cable Beach back to the heart of the Bahamian capital.

Dining The exclusive chateau **Graycliff**, W. Hill St. (© 800/688-0076), is generating a lot of buzz with its new restaurant, **The Humidor**, obviously appealing to cigar smokers. A team of on-site "rollers" produces the house brand of cigars. Fortunately, the food is great, too.

Sports Stuart Cove's Dive Bahamas, SW Bay St., South Ocean (© 800/879-9832), puts some excitement into the waters off the coast of Nassau. Stuart will take you 120 feet underwater to see both the freighter that sank for the James Bond movie *Never Say Never Again* and the Valkin bomber airplane used in another Bond film, *Thunderball*. He's also introduced a yellow submarine—actually individual self-contained, battery-powered jet bikes called "Scenic Underwater Bubbles." An air-fed bubble covers your head as these vehicles propel you through an underwater wonderland.

For complete details, refer to chapter 3, "New Providence (Nassau/Cable Beach)."

PARADISE ISLAND Accommodations Not satisfied with its $250-million transformation of the sprawling **Atlantis Paradise Island Resort & Casino**, Casino Dr. (© 800/ATLANTIS), Sun International, the developers, have also poured $100 million into renovations of the **Ocean Club**, Ocean Club Dr. (© 800/321-3000), making it once again the most exclusive resort on Paradise Island. Ocean Club also boasts the hottest new restaurant on the island and a newly created golf course (see below for both).

Dining French-born restaurant guru, Jean-Georges Vongerichten, has put his name and talent behind **Dune**, Ocean Club, Ocean Club Dr. (© 242/363-2000). Almost overnight, his restaurant, featuring signature dishes from his critically acclaimed New York City restaurants infused with a sophisticated Caribbean influence, has emerged as *the* cutting-edge culinary showcase in both Paradise Island and Nassau.

Sports Surfacing as the best golf course in the Greater Nassau area, **Ocean Club Golf Club**, Paradise Island Dr. (© 242/363-3925), is an 18-hole championship course, newly created by Tom Weiskopf from an old course. A par-72 course, it overlooks both the Atlantic Ocean and Nassau Harbour.

For complete details, see chapter 4, "Paradise Island."

GRAND BAHAMA (FREEPORT/ LUCAYA) Accommodations Although parts of it are still under construction, the massive resort **Our Lucaya,** Royal Palm Way, Lucaya (℃ **800/LUCAYAN**), is waking up tourism to Grand Bahama almost by itself. This megaresort is expected to draw visitors from all over the world, including those who shunned Grand Bahama Island in recent years because of declining standards, poor service, and decaying resort properties. But Our Lucaya isn't the whole story. Also on Grand Bahama Island, a cottage-style resort, **Old Bahama Bay,** West End (℃ **800/572-5711**), has taken a decaying Jack Tar Village 25 miles west of Freeport, added a marina, restored and rebuilt everything and turned it into a first-class resort.

Sports Golfers are flocking to the new kid on the block, the $5-million **The Reef Course,** Royal Palm Way, Lucaya (℃ **242/373-2002**), the first golf course to open in The Bahamas since 1969. It was designed by Robert Trent Jones Jr., who has described it as a "bit like a Scottish course but a lot warmer." The course boasts 6,920 yards of links-style playing grounds. For complete details, refer to chapter 5, "Grand Bahama (Freeport/Lucaya)."

ANDROS Accommodations The opening of small fishing lodges in one of the great bonefishing centers of the western world, the Bahamian archipelago of the Andros Islands, is generating excitement among fishermen flocking here by the hundreds. Their dinner is often their own catch of the day. Two of the best lodges to open include **Tranquility Hill** in Behring Point (℃ **242/368-4132**), which lies near miles of virgin flats

teaming with trophy-size bonefish. In Cargill Creek, the **Andros Island Bonefishing Club** (℃ **242/368-5167**) attracts Hemingway clones to the great barrier reef, which lies only 2 miles offshore. It's a real down-home place.

For complete details, see chapter 6, "Bimini, the Berry Islands & Andros."

THE EXUMAS Accommodations At long last, after a sleep of centuries, major tourism is on the way to the Southern Bahamas with the projected opening of the upmarket **Four Seasons Resort** (℃ **800/819-5053**). The Southern Bahamas has never seen the likes of anything like this, except for a Club Med on San Salvador island. A special feature will be an 18-hole golf course designed by Greg Norman. The complex is set to open sometime in 2002. For more details, see chapter 9, "The Exuma Islands."

TURKS & CAICOS Accommodations Only a few years ago the archipelago island nation was listed near the bottom of world countries in name recognition (Turks & what?). Today, its resort island of Provo has become a big-time player in the resorts sweepstakes, giving The Bahamas and the Caribbean some stiff competition.

The most heat and media attention focuses on **Parrot Cay** (℃ **649/946-7788**) on an offshore island facing the coast of Provo or Providenciales. It has now emerged as the Caribbean's number one celebrity haunt, outdistancing even Ocean Club on Paradise Island and the chic retreats on Anguilla and St. Barts in the Caribbean.

Back on Provo itself, the new boutique hotel, **Point Grace,** along Grace Bay (℃ **888/682-3705**), has lived up to the super hype it had at its opening. Almost overnight it has risen to become Provo's top choice for the discerning and well-heeled traveler. The fact that it opens onto one of the world's greatest beaches helps, too.

The capital of Turks & Caicos, the island of Grand Turk, is finally experiencing some hotel development of its own, attracting escapists who want to flee the hordes descending on Provo. **Arches of Grand Turk,** Lighthouse Rd. (*C* **649/946-2941**), is a newly constructed set of town houses a short walk from some beautiful white-sand beaches. The property is already attracting quality tourism to the island—that is, those who don't want to lodge at one of the long-standing but raffish inns.

1

The Best of The Bahamas

How would you like to spend your vacation in The Bahamas? Relaxed on a pink-sand beach, with an icy glass of rum in hand? Or stuck in a hotel that's not quite what you wanted and dining every night in restaurants that you suspect are just tourist traps? With this guide, you easily design the vacation that's right for you and discover the best of what the islands have to offer—we've done the work for you.

Below you'll find our carefully compiled and opinionated lists of fabulous beaches; the best spots for diving, snorkeling, fishing, and sailing; the best hotels (from modest inns to plush resorts) for honeymooners, families, and those who want to get away from it all; and the best restaurants, nightlife, and gambling. And if that's not enough, we'll even tell you how you can rent your own deserted island.

Since you're not likely to be island-hopping, this "best of" list can be an important resource in helping you plan the trip that's right for you. For more information on choosing the island that best suits your taste and provides the getaway you're looking for, refer to "The Islands in Brief," in chapter 2, "Planning Your Trip to the Bahamas." It'll give you a complete rundown on the pros and cons of each island in more detail.

1 The Best Beaches

- **Old Fort Beach** (New Providence Island): With pristine white sands and turquoise water, this is the least developed major beach on New Providence Island, near the relatively unpopulated western tip of The Bahamas's most crowded island. Many of its biggest fans are homeowners from nearby Lyford Cay, whose homes are among the priciest in The Bahamas. The beach is least crowded on weekdays, and windiest throughout the winter. There's great waterskiing in summer, when waters are the calmest. See chapter 3.
- **Cable Beach** (New Providence Island): The glittering shoreline of Cable Beach has easy access to shops, casinos, restaurants, water sports, and bars. It's a sandy 4-mile-long strip, with a great array of facilities and activities. See chapter 3.
- **Cabbage Beach** (Paradise Island): Think Vegas in the tropics. It seems as if most of the sunbathers dozing on the sands here are recovering from the previous evening's partying. It's likely to be crowded near the megahotels, but you can find a bit more solitude on the beach's isolated northwestern extension (Paradise Beach), which is accessible only by boat or on foot. Lined with palms, sea grapes, and casuarinas, the sands are broad and stretch for at least 2 miles. See chapter 4.
- **Xanadu Beach** (Grand Bahama Island): Grand Bahama has 60 miles of sandy shoreline, but

Xanadu Beach is most convenient to Freeport's resort hotels, several of which offer shuttle service to Xanadu. There's more than a mile of white sand and (usually) gentle surf. Don't expect to have Xanadu to yourself, but if you want more quiet and privacy, try any of the beaches that stretch from Xanadu for many miles in either direction. See chapter 5.

- **Tahiti Beach** (Hope Town, the Abacos): Since the beach is so isolated at the far end of Elbow Cay Island, you can be sure that only a handful of people will ever visit these cool waters and white sands. The crowds stay away because you can't drive to Tahiti Beach: To get there, you'll have to walk or ride a rented bike along sand and gravel paths from Hope Town. You can also charter a boat to get there, which isn't too hard, since the Abacos are the sailing capital of The Bahamas. See chapter 7.

- **Pink Sands Beach** (Harbour Island): Running the entire length of the island's eastern side, these pale pink sands stretch for 3 miles past a handful of low-rise hotels and private villas. A coral reef protects the shore from breakers, making for some of the safest swimming in The Bahamas. See chapter 8.

- **Ten Bay Beach** (Eleuthera): Ten Bay Beach lies a short drive south of Palmetto Point, just north of Savannah Sound. Once upon a time, the exclusive Cotton Bay Club chose to build here for a good reason; there may not be any facilities here, but since the hotel has closed, the white sands and turquoise waters are even more idyllic and private. See chapter 8.

- **Saddle Cay** (the Exumas): Most of the Exumas are oval-shaped islands strung end to end like the links of a 130-mile chain. One

notable exception is Saddle Cay, with a horseshoe-shaped curve near the Exumas's northern tip. It can be reached only by boat. Once you reach it, you'll find an unspoiled setting without a trace of the modern world and lots of other cays and islets where you can play Robinson Crusoe for a few hours. See chapter 9.

- **Stocking Island** (the Exumas): One of the finest white sandy beaches in The Bahamas lies off Elizabeth Harbour, the main harbor of the archipelago, close to the capital of George Town. A mile from the little town of George Town, Stocking Island is easily accessible by boat from Elizabeth Harbour. The sands of this offshore island are rarely crowded, and snorkelers and divers love to explore its gin-clear waters. In addition to its beach of powdery white sand, Stocking Island is known for its "blue holes" and for its coral gardens and undersea caves. See chapter 9.

- **Cat Island's Beaches:** The white sandy beaches ringing this island are pristine, opening onto crystal-clear waters and lined with coconut palms, palmettos, and casuarina trees—and best of all, you'll practically have the place to yourself. One of our favorite beaches here, near Old Bight, has a beautiful, lazy curve of white sand. Another fabulous beach lies 3 miles north of New Bight, site of the Fernandez Bay Village resort. This curvy white sandy beach is set against a backdrop of casuarinas, and is idyllic and unusually tranquil. A final good beach is the long, sandy stretch that opens onto Hawk's Nest Resort and Marina on the southwestern side. None of the Cat Island beaches has any facilities (bring anything you need from

The Bahamas

FLORIDA

BAHAMA ISLANDS

ATLANTIC OCEAN

TURKS & CAICOS ISLANDS

CUBA

CAYMAN ISLANDS

DOMINICAN REPUBLIC

VIRGIN ISLANDS

HAITI

JAMAICA

PUERTO RICO

Caribbean Sea

0   300 mi
0   300 km

0   50 Miles
0   50 Kilometers

ATLANTIC OCEAN

CAT ISLAND

Cockburn Town   SAN SALVADOR

Stella Maris   RUM CAY

Tropic of Cancer

LONG ISLAND

Deadman's Cay

CROOKED ISLAND

ACKLINS ISLAND

MAYAGUANA ISLAND

NORTH CAICOS   MIDDLE CAICOS

PINE CAY

PROVIDENCIALES

Grace Bay

EAST CAICOS

GRAND TURK ISLAND

CAICOS ISLANDS

SOUTH CAICOS

LITTLE INAGUA

SALT CAY   TURKS ISLANDS

GREAT INAGUA

your hotel), but they do have peace and quiet and seclusion. See chapter 10.

• **Grace Bay Beach** (Providenciales, Turks and Caicos Islands): These 12 miles of pale sands are the pride of Provo; Condé Nast has called this one of the world's best beaches. It's such a spectacular setting that increasing numbers of resorts, including Club Med, have sprung up along the shore. A couple of miles out from the northern shore, the beach is fringed by a reef with fabulous snorkeling. Back on land, there are plenty of places where you can rent watersports equipment. See chapter 11.

2 The Best Diving

• **New Providence Island:** Many ships have sunk near Nassau in the past 300 years, and all the dive outfitters here know the most scenic wreck sites. Other attractions are underwater gardens of elkhorn coral and dozens of reefs brimming with underwater life. The most spectacular dive site is the **Shark Wall,** 10 miles off the southwest coast of New Providence; it's blessed with incredible, colorful sea life and the healthiest coral offshore. You'll even get to swim with sharks (not as bait, of course). See chapter 3.

• **Grand Bahama Island:** The island is ringed with reefs, and dive sites are plentiful, including the Wall, the Caves (site of a long-ago disaster known as Theo's Wreck), and Treasure Reef. Other popular dive sites include Spit City (yes, that's right), Ben Blue Hole, and the Rose Garden (no one knows how this one got its name). What makes Grand Bahama Island a cut above the others is the presence of a world-class dive operator, **UNEXSO** (the Underwater Explorer's Society; ℂ **888/365-3483** or 242/373-1250). See chapter 5.

• **Andros:** Marine life abounds in the barrier reef off the coast of Andros, which is one of the largest in the world and a famous destination for divers. The reef plunges 6,000 feet to a narrow drop-off known as the Tongue of the Ocean. You can also explore mysterious blue holes, formed when subterranean caves fill with seawater, causing their ceilings to collapse and exposing clear, deep pools. See chapters 2 and 6.

• **Bimini:** Although Bimini is most famous for its game fishing, it boasts excellent diving, too. Three miles of offshore reefs attract millions of colorful fish. Even snorkelers can see black coral gardens, blue holes, and an odd configuration on the sea floor that is reportedly part of the lost continent of Atlantis (a fun legend, at any rate). Divers can check out the wreck of a motorized yacht, the *Sapona* (owned by Henry Ford), which sank in shallow waters off the coast in 1929. See chapter 6.

• **Eleuthera:** In addition to lovely coral and an array of colorful fish, divers can enjoy some unique experiences here, such as the "Current Cut," an exciting underwater gully that carries you on a swiftly flowing underwater current for 10 minutes. Four wrecked ships also lie nearby, at depths of less than 40 feet, including a barge that was transporting the engine of a steam locomotive in 1865, reportedly after the American Confederacy sold it to raise cash for its war effort. See chapter 8.

• **Long Island** (the Southern Bahamas): Snorkeling is spectacular on virtually all sides of the island. But experienced divers venturing into deeper waters offshore can visit underwater cages to feed swarms of mako, bull, and reef sharks. Dive sites abound, including the Arawak "green hole," a blue hole of incomprehensible depth. See chapter 10.

• **Turks and Caicos Islands:** These islands offer a rich assortment of relatively unexplored underwater sites, including sea lanes where boaters and divers often spot whales in April. A collection of unusual underwater wrecks includes the HMS *Endymion*, which sank during a storm in 1790. Miles of reefs house myriad kinds of colorful marine life. Right off Grand Turk, experienced divers love the many miles of "drop-off" diving, where the sea walls suddenly drop into the uncharted depths of blue holes more than 7,000 feet below sea level. Along the descent, you'll see colonies of black coral, rare forms of anemone, purple sponges, stunning gorgonia, endless forms of coral, and thousands of fish (with different species at different depths). See chapter 11.

3 The Best Snorkeling

• **New Providence Island/Paradise Island:** The waters that ring densely populated New Providence Island and nearby Paradise Island are easy to explore. Most people head for the Rose Island Reefs, the Gambier Deep Reef, Booby Rock Channel, the Goulding Reef Cays, and some easily seen, well-known underwater wrecks that lie in shallow water. Virtually every resort hotel on the island offers equipment and can book you onto a snorkel cruise to sites further offshore. See chapters 3 and 4.

• **Bimini:** Snorkelers are enthralled with the offshore black coral gardens, which are easily accessible from shore, and the colorful marine life around the island. Sometimes when conditions are right, snorkelers enjoy frolicking with a pod of spotted dolphins. Off North Bimini, snorkelers are attracted to a cluster of huge, flat rocks that jut from 20 to 30 feet out of the water at Paradise Point. The most imaginative snorkelers claim these rocks, which seem hand-hewn, are part of a road system that once traversed the lost continent of Atlantis. See chapter 6.

• **Long Island:** Shallow bays and sandy beaches offer many possibilities for snorkeling, and the staffs at both major resorts will direct you to the finest conditions near their stretches of beach. The southern end of the island is especially dramatic because of its unique sea cliffs. Many east-coast beach coves also offer fantastic snorkeling opportunities. See chapter 10.

• **Provo** (Turks and Caicos): Although this island is known primarily as one of the world's best dive sites, it also offers a number of snorkeling possibilities. The government has established the best snorkel trails at Smith's Reef and Bight Reef, right off of Provo's spectacular Grace Bay Beach. These reefs are right off the shoreline, and they provide easy access into the fragile but stunningly beautiful world of coral gardens, the most dramatic in the vast area immediately south of The Bahamas. See chapter 11.

4 The Best Fishing

- **Bimini:** All kinds of big-game fish flourish in the deep waters around Bimini, but the most sought-after trophy is the marlin, whose image appears on the Bahamian $100 bill. As many as 40 annual fishing tournaments are held every year in The Bahamas, many of which transform Bimini into a mini-Olympic village where fish are hunted by a daunting armada of well-equipped fishing boats. Bimini was Ernest Hemingway's favorite place to fish. See chapter 6.
- **Andros:** Bonefish thrive in the shallow, sunlit waters off Andros Island. It isn't the best-tasting fish in the islands (it's mostly cartilage and bones), but serious anglers say that it puts up one of the strongest fights of any fish in the world. Other islands good for bonefishing include Bimini, Walker's Cay, Abaco, Eleuthera, Exuma, and Long Island. See chapter 6.
- **The Abacos:** In the Marsh Harbour area, you'll find bonefish in the flats, marlin in the deep, and yellowtail on the reefs—and many of the world's greatest anglers will be in hot pursuit. In Elbow Cay, you can arrange to head out with the local fishermen. Another good place for deep-sea charters in the Abacos is Green Turtle Cay, which hosts a hugely popular fishing tournament each May. See chapter 7.

5 The Best Sailing

- **The Abacos:** Known among yachties for their many anchorages, sheltered coves, and plentiful marine facilities, the Abacos are considered one of the most perfect sailing areas in the world. You can charter boats of all shapes and sizes for a week or longer, with or without a crew. Major charter centers are in Marsh Harbour and Hope Town. Arrange for rentals with **The Moorings** (© **800/ 535-7289** or 242/367-4000), in Marsh Harbour. See chapters 2 and 7.
- **The Exumas:** Every April, the Exumas host the famed Family Island Regatta, the most popular sailing event in The Bahamas. Elizabeth Harbour is a mecca for yachties, who explore nearby deserted islands and cays, secluded bays, safe anchorage harbors, and secret coves. Even in winter, unless the weather turns unexpectedly bad (and foul weather is usually short-lived), the seas are balmy and the temperatures ideal. Yacht magazines praise the Exumas for having the finest cruising areas in The Bahamas. See chapters 2 and 9.

6 The Best Golf Courses

- **South Ocean Golf Course** (New Providence Island; © **242/362-4391**): This course, designed by Joe Lee with four challenging water holes, is so isolated from the congestion of Nassau that you can imagine yourself on a remote island. The rolling terrain is hilly and dotted with palm trees; from this relatively high elevation, you'll enjoy views over the "Tongue of the Ocean." We think this course is better and more demanding than the other major choice on New Providence Island at Cable Beach (see below). See chapter 3.
- **Cable Beach Golf Course** (New Providence Island; © **242/327-6000**): The oldest golf course in

The Bahamas, this par-72 green was the private retreat of British expatriates in the 1930s. Today, it's managed by a corporate namesake of Arnold Palmer and owned by Cable Beach casino marketers. Small ponds and water traps heighten the challenge, amid more than 7,000 yards of well-maintained greens and fairways. Despite these assets, however, we still prefer the competition: the Ocean Club Golf Club and the South Ocean Golf Course. See chapters 2 and 3.

• **Ocean Club Golf Club** (Paradise Island; © **242/363-3925**): Tom Weiskopf designed this 18-hole, par-72 course, and it's a stunner. With its own pitfalls, including the world's largest sand trap and water hazards (the Atlantic Ocean) on three sides, Jack Nicklaus and Gary Player have endorsed this course. For the best panoramic ocean view (good enough to take your mind off your game), play the par-3 14th hole. See chapters 2 and 4.

• **The Reef Course** (Grand Lucaya, Grand Bahama Island; © **242/373-2002**): Designed by Robert Trent Jones Jr., this is the first golf course to open in The Bahamas in some 3 decades. The course boasts 6,920 yards of links-style playing grounds. See chapter 5.

• **The Resorts at Bahamia** (Grand Bahama Island; © **242/350-7000**): This megaresort offers two golf courses, Bahama's Ruby and Bahama's Emerald, both of which are par 72, with rolling, sandy terrain. Dick Wilson designed both of these courses, but they're not as challenging as the South Ocean Golf Course. See chapter 5.

• **Provo Golf Club** (Turks and Caicos Islands; © **649/946-5991**): Designing a course on the arid surface of Provo was a major feat of landscape architecture. The design features a desert-inspired mixture of limestone and sand interspersed with greenery and relatively narrow fairways. The course is categorized as a challenging par 72. See chapter 11.

7 The Best Tennis Facilities

• **Paradise Island:** Paradise Island has the best courts and the best players in The Bahamas. If you're really serious about your game, consider checking into **Club Med Paradise** (© **242/363-2640**), which has the largest court complex on the island, with 20 clay composition courts (eight of them lit for night games), ball machines, a full staff of instructors who offer expert advice, and an instant-replay TV. The tennis complex at the **Atlantis** (© **242/**

363-3000) is more accessible to the general public, with a dozen asphalt courts, some lit for night games. See chapter 4.

• **Freeport** (Grand Bahama Island): Freeport is another top choice for tennis buffs. **The Resorts at Bahamia** (© **800/545-1300** or 242/350-7000) has 12 state-of-the-art courts, three of them clay and eight lit for night games. You don't have to be a guest to play here, but you should call ahead for a reservation. See chapters 2 and 5.

8 The Best Honeymoon Resorts

• **Sandals Royal Bahamian** (Cable Beach, New Providence Island; © **800/SANDALS** or 242/

327-6400): This Jamaican chain of couples-only, all-inclusive hotels is the honeymooners'

Eco-Tourism Highlights of The Bahamas

The Bahamas spreads over 100,000 square miles of the Atlantic Ocean and is home to countless natural attractions, including underwater reefs that stretch 760 miles from the Abacos in the northeast to Long Island in the southeast.

The Bahamas is the largest oceanic archipelago nation in the tropical Atlantic Ocean, with miles of crystal-clear waters rich with fish and other marine resources. Unlike Puerto Rico, Jamaica, Barbados, and other Caribbean island nations, The Bahamas has large areas of undeveloped natural land. The islands also have the most extensive systems of blue holes and limestone caves in the world.

Off the coast of Andros, The Bahamas has approximately 900 square miles of coral reefs, which makes it the third-largest barrier reef in the world. Rich with diverse marine life, the reef attracts green moray eels, cinnamon clownfish, and Nassau grouper. When officials realized that long-line fishing threatened this fragile ecology, The Bahamas became one of the first Caribbean countries to outlaw the sport.

Parliament also passed the Wild Birds Protection Act, in order to ensure the survival of all bird species throughout The Bahamas. Great Inagua Island shelters more than 60,000 pink flamingos, Bahamian parrots, and a large portion of the world population of reddish egrets. These birds live in the government-protected, 287-square-mile Inagua National Park.

The islands of The Bahamas are home to more than 1,370 species of plant life and some 13 species of mammals, the majority of them bats. Other mammals include wild pigs, donkeys, raccoons, and the Abaco wild horse. Whales and dolphins, including humpback and blue whales and the spotted dolphin, swim in the seas around the various islands.

The **Bahamas National Trust** administers 12 national parks and more than 240,000 acres of protected land. Its headquarters, with one of the finest collections of wild palms in the western hemisphere, are located in Nassau at **The Retreat on Village Road** (© **242/393-1317**). Guided 30-minute tours are conducted Tuesday through Thursday at noon and by appointment. Volunteers at The Retreat can also help arrange visits to the

favorite. The Bahamas's branch of the chain is more upscale than many of its Jamaican counterparts, and it offers 27 secluded honeymoon suites with semiprivate plunge pools. Enthusiastic staff members lend their experience and talent to on-site wedding celebrations; Sandals will provide everything from a preacher to flowers, as well as champagne and a cake. It's more expensive than most Sandals resorts, but you can usually get better rates through a travel agent or a package deal. See chapter 3.

• **Nassau Marriott Resort & Crystal Palace Casino** (New Providence Island; © **800/222-7466** or 242/327-6200): If you're bored with the idea of honeymooning in an isolated village, with just you, your loved one, the moon, and the stars, head to this flashy, high-tech megacomplex, where bright lights and a mind-boggling assortment national parks on the various islands, the best of which are previewed below. See chapter 3.

- **Lucayan National Park:** This park on Grand Bahama Island is the site of a 6-mile-long, underground, freshwater cave system, the longest of its type in the world. The largest cave contains spiral staircases that lead visitors into a freshwater world inhabited by shrimp, mosquito fish, fruit bats, freshwater eels, and a species of crustacean (*Spelionectes lucayensis*) that has never been found elsewhere. On the 40-acre preserve you'll find examples of the island's five ecosystems—pine forests, rocky coppice, mangrove swamps, whiteland coppice, and sand dunes. Pause to sunbathe on a lovely stretch of sandy beach, or hike along paths where you can spot orchids, hummingbirds, and barn owls. See chapter 5.

- **Pelican Cays Land and Sea Park:** Known for its undersea caves, seemingly endless coral reefs, and abundant plant and marine life, this park, 8 miles north of Cherokee Sound at Great Abaco Island, is a highlight for scuba divers. See chapter 7.

- **Exuma Cays National Land and Sea Park:** A major attraction of The Bahamas, this park is the first of its kind anywhere on the planet. The 22-mile-long, 8-mile-wide natural preserve attracts scuba divers to its 175 square miles of sea gardens with spectacular reefs, flora, and fauna. Inaugurated in 1958, it lies some 22 miles northwest of Staniel Cay or 40 miles southeast of Nassau and is accessible only by boat. See chapter 9.

- **Great Inagua:** This sleepy island in the Southern Bahamas is internationally famous for its colony of wild West Indian flamingos, the world's largest. In local dialect, these birds are sometimes called "fillymingos" or "flamingas." See chapter 10.

- **Union Creek Reserve:** This 7-square-mile enclosed tidal creek on Great Inagua serves as a captive breeding research site for giant sea turtles, with special emphasis on green turtles, which have been overhunted and are now an endangered species. See chapter 10.

of diversions will help you while away your time. See chapter 3.

- **Compass Point** (New Providence Island; ✆ **800/688-7678** or 242/327-4500): This choice is the charming and personalized statement of entrepreneur Christopher Blackwell; it's purely for those who shun megaresorts. The accommodations are found in floridly painted huts or cottages, some of which have kitchenettes and some of which are raised on stilts. Completely in harmony with its lovely natural setting, it's still state-of-the-art. See chapter 3.

- **Graycliff** (Nassau, New Providence Island; ✆ **800/688-0076** or 242/322-2796): This is the only member of the prestigious Relais and Châteaux chain in The Bahamas. The structure is at least 200 years old, and although many of the accommodations are much newer, they all still have old-fashioned charm. The setting, in a garden in the heart of downtown Nassau, lets you experience the everyday Bahamian life that you wouldn't see within the confines of a megaresort. You'll have lots of well-to-do vacationing corporate execs among your fellow guests. See chapter 3.

- **The Ocean Club** (Paradise Island; ✆ **800/321-3000** in the U.S., or 242/363-2501): It's elegant, low-key, and low-rise, and it feels exclusive. The guests are likely to include many older couples who might be celebrating second (or third) honeymoons. With waterfalls, fountains, reflecting pools, and a stone gazebo, the Ocean Club's formal terraced gardens were inspired by the club's founder (an heir to the A&P fortune) and are the most impressive in The Bahamas. At the center is a French cloister, with carvings from the 12th century. See chapter 4.

- **Xanadu Beach Resort & Marina** (Grand Bahama Island; ✆ **242/ 352-6782**): Despite its contemporary exterior, the public rooms of this resort contain many expensive decorative touches that might have been chosen by a reclusive billionaire. And sure enough, the builder of this resort was Howard Hughes, who lived in its penthouse for many years. The comfortable, contemporary bedrooms are suitable for an extended honeymoon; from here, you'll have easy access to the island's restaurants, beaches, and casinos. See chapter 5.

- **Green Turtle Club** (Green Turtle Cay, the Abacos; ✆ **242/365- 4271**): Honeymooners appreciate this resort's winning combination of yachting atmosphere and well-manicured comfort. The setting is small (31 rooms) and civilized in an understated way. The charming, clapboard-covered village of

New Plymouth is nearby, accessible by either motor launch or, even better, a 45-minute walk across windswept scrublands, which seem far removed from everything. See chapter 7.

- **Bluff House Club Beach Hotel** (Green Turtle Cay, the Abacos; ✆ **242/365-4247**): This place was named because of its location on an 80-foot-high cliff, above a pink-sand beach. Its 12 acres front the Sea of Abaco on one side and the harbor of White Sound on the other. The accommodations are very private, with a rustic, seafaring decor that has its own kind of elegance. In addition to rooms, the hotel offers beach and hillside villas, and colonial suites with private balconies that overlook the water. See chapter 7.

- **Pink Sands** (Harbour Island, Eleuthera; ✆ **800/OUTPOST** or 242/333-2030): You can have a spectacular getaway at this elite retreat on a 28-acre beachfront estate owned by Chris Blackwell, the famous founder of Island Records. Its location on a 3-mile stretch of private pink sand, sheltered by a barrier reef, is just one of its assets. You can ask for a bedroom that evokes an upscale bordello in Shanghai to put you in a romantic mood, and you can also enjoy the best meals on the island. See chapter 8.

- **Stella Maris Resort Club** (Long Island, the Southern Bahamas; ✆ **800/426-0466,** 242/338-2051, or 954/359-8236 in Fort Lauderdale): On the Atlantic, built on the grounds of an old plantation, Stella Maris has become a social hub on Long Island. Sailing is important here, as are diving and getting away from it all. Many of the guests hail from Germany, and they lend the place a European flair. This sleepy island itself is one of the most beautiful in The Bahamas, and honeymooners fit into the grand scheme of things perfectly. See chapter 10.

- **Point Grace** (Provo, Turks and Caicos; ℂ **800/858-2258** or 649/ 946-5555): One hundred years ago, a discerning woman found a honeymoon cottage here and, according to reports, had a blissful honeymoon as a prelude to a long and successful marriage. Today's honeymooners can also head here, booking a suite at one of the most elegant hotels in the country, which stands on a spectacular beachfront. With your bride or groom, you can wander about the complex in an Indonesian sarong before retreating to the utter privacy and seclusion of your honeymoon suite. See chapter 11.

9 The Best Family Vacations

- **Radisson Cable Beach Hotel** (Cable Beach, New Providence Island; ℂ **800/333-3333** or 242/327-6000): A family could spend their entire vacation on the grounds of this vast resort. There's a pool area that features the most lavish artificial waterfall this side of Tahiti; a health club at the nearby Crystal Palace that welcomes both guests and their children; Camp Junkanoo, with supervised play for children 3 through 12; and a long list of in-house activities that includes dancing lessons. See chapter 3.
- **The Atlantis Paradise Island Resort & Casino** (Paradise Island; ℂ **800/ATLANTIS** in the U.S., or 242/363-3000): This is one of the largest hotel complexes in the world, with endless rows of shops and water sports galore. Both children and adults will enjoy this 14-acre sea world with water slides, a lagoon for water sports, white sandy beaches, and underground grottoes, plus an underwater viewing tunnel and 800 feet of cascading waterfalls. Its children's menus and innovative, creative children's programs are the best in The Bahamas and perhaps even in the Caribbean, too. See chapter 4.
- **The Resorts at Bahamia** (Grand Bahama Island; ℂ **800/545-1300** or 242/350-7000): Many guests come here just to gamble and work on their tans, but others bring their kids. To divert them, the hotel maintains a pair of playgrounds and a swimming pool inspired by a tropical oasis, and offers children's platters in some of the restaurants. The architecture features lots of "Aladdin and His Lamp" accessories, such as minarets above a decidedly non-Islamic setting. See chapter 5.
- **Castaways Resort & Suites** (Grand Bahama Island; ℂ **242/ 352-6682**): Here's a good choice for families on a budget. The pagoda-capped lobby is set a very short walk from the ice-cream stands, souvenir shops, and fountains of the International Bazaar. Children under 12 stay free in their parents' room, and the in-house lounge presents limbo and fire-eating shows several evenings a month. The hotel offers a baby-sitting service and a free shuttle to Xanadu Beach. See chapter 5.
- **Regatta Point** (George Town, Great Exuma; ℂ **800/688-4752** in the U.S., or 242/336-2206): This resort offers efficiency apartments at moderate prices. On a palm-grove cay, it is family-friendly, with its own little beach. Bikes are available, and Sunfish can be rented. There is a grocery store nearby where you can pick up supplies.

Many units are suitable for families of four or five. See chapter 9.

• **Beaches Turks and Caicos Resort and Spa** (Provo, Turks and Caicos; ℂ **800/BEACHES** or 649/946-8000): This is the most family-friendly resort in the country (especially for the Rockefellers,

considering the prices). There's a professionally staffed children's center, and kids delight in all the activities the resort provides, including glass-bottom boat trips and a series of waterfalls on-site. See chapter 11.

10 The Best Places to Get Away from It All

• **Green Turtle Club** (Green Turtle Cay, the Abacos; ℂ **242/365-4271**): Secluded and private, this sailing retreat consists of tasteful one- to three-bedroom villas with full kitchens. It opens onto a small private beach with a 35-slip marina, which is the most complete yachting facility in the archipelago. Many rooms open onto poolside, and there's a dining room decorated in Queen Anne style. See chapter 7.

• **Dunmore Beach Club** (Harbour Island, off the coast of Eleuthera; ℂ **242/333-2200**): Dunmore is one of the less expensive all-inclusive resorts of The Bahamas. Because it's relatively small, the atmosphere feels like a private party in a New England summerhouse. Each of the dozen or so lodgings is positioned for privacy. For complete solitude, you can escape to the nether regions of the local beach. See chapter 8.

• **Club Med–Columbus Isle** (San Salvador, the Southern Bahamas; ℂ **800/CLUB-MED** or 242/323-8670): This was the first large resort to be built on one of The Bahamas's most isolated islands, site of Columbus's first landfall in the New World. It's unusually luxurious, and unusually isolated, for a Club Med, and it occupies a gorgeous beach. The sheer difficulty of reaching it adds to the

get-away-from-it-all mystique. See chapter 10.

• **Fernandez Bay Village** (Cat Island, the Southern Bahamas; ℂ **800/940-1905,** or 954/474-4821 in Plantation, Florida): The dozen stone and timber villas of Fernandez Bay Village are the closest thing to urban congestion Cat Island ever sees. There's a funky, thatch-roofed beach bar that'll make you feel like you're in the South Pacific, enjoying a cold beer each afternoon after you leave the stunning sands and turquoise waters behind for the day. There's only one phone at the entire resort, and your bathroom shower will probably open to a view of the sky. See chapter 10.

• **The Meridian Club** (Pine Cay, Turks and Caicos Islands; ℂ **800/331-9154** or 203/602-0300): This cluster of vacation homes is the only real development on an 800-acre island covered with shrubs and low trees; most of the island is devoted to nature conservation. You can drop out and disappear here, and many guests do. Communications with the outside world are deliberately limited (leave that cell phone behind!), and the only social life consists of saying an occasional hello to the occupants of the island's 30 or so privately owned homes. See chapter 11.

11 The Best Restaurants

• **Graycliff** (Nassau, New Providence Island; © **242/322-2796**): This is the most elegant restaurant on New Providence Island, with more class, style, and flair than anything found on Cable Beach. Bahamian seasonings add flair and zesty flavor to the continental cuisine. Place your order carefully, though—this is the most expensive restaurant in The Bahamas. After all, *someone* has to pay for the $8-million wine cellar, a sight worth seeing with 175,000 bottles. See chapter 3.

• **Sun And . . .** (Nassau, New Providence Island; © **242/393-1205**): On a par with Graycliff (and a bit cheaper to boot!), this is a favorite haunt of visiting celebrities. Most important, they serve top-notch food. As you cross a drawbridge to enter a soothing world with a fountain and rock pool, you'll begin to hear tantalizing sizzling sounds from the kitchen, which is always cooking up an array of vividly flavored fresh seafood, the hallmark of a master French chef. Try to save room for a soufflé—they can hold their own with anything this side of France. See chapter 3.

• **The Restaurant at Compass Point** (Love Beach, New Providence Island; © **242/327-4500**): The California/Caribbean cuisine here has made this a hot spot for savvy foodies—and one of The Bahamas's finest. The menu is innovative, with many exotic touches: Everybody in The Bahamas serves conch, but here it appears with agnolotti, sun-dried tomatoes, and spinach in a tomato-basil cream sauce. Or try a Bahamian maki roll with conch, mango, and cucumber served with wasabi and pickled ginger. See chapter 3.

• **Dune** (in the Ocean Club, Paradise Island; © **242/363-2000**): The most cutting-edge restaurant in either Paradise Island or Nassau is the creation of French-born restaurant guru, Jean-Georges Vongerichten. Every dish served here is something special—from shrimp dusted with orange powder to chicken and coconut milk soup with shiitake cakes. See chapter 4.

• **Five Twins** (in the Atlantis Paradise Island Resort and Casino, Paradise Island; © **242/363-3000**): This trendy, upscale restaurant has generated more excitement than any other that opened in the 1990s on this chic island across from Nassau. Featuring Pacific Rim cuisine, it serves flavorful dishes with a flair that even James Bond might have appreciated. (007 himself was seen dining on Paradise Island in *Thunderball.*) The chefs create refined dishes that justify the high prices. See chapter 4.

• **Villa d'Este** (in the Atlantis Paradise Island Resort and Casino, Paradise Island; © **242/363-3000**): This is the finest Italian restaurant on Paradise Island, with nothing in Nassau to top it, either. The setting is gracious, tasteful, and Old World, but it's the food that keeps them calling for reservations. All the old favorites are here, including veal parmigiana and fettuccine Alfredo as fine as what you'd find in Rome. Fresh herbs add zest to many dishes. The pasta dishes are particularly succulent. See chapter 4.

• **Mangoes** (Marsh Harbour, the Abacos; © **242/367-2366**): For the best and most authentic Bahamian food in the Abaco chain, head for this welcoming spot, where both visiting yachties and locals flock for the fine cuisine. Order up a "conch burger" for lunch, and in the evening you can return to enjoy the fresh catch of the day—straight from the sea and grilled to your specifications. The namesake mango sauce can really dress up a plate of grilled pork tenderloin. See chapter 7.

• **The Landing** (Harbour Island, Eleuthera; ℂ 242/333-2707): This attractive restaurant at the ferryboat dock has awakened the sleepy taste buds of Eleuthera. Brenda Barry and her daughter, Tracy, will feed you well from a choice international cuisine, often prepared with recipes they gathered during their world travels. Under mature trees in their garden, you can feast on succulent pastas, freshly made gazpacho, pan-fried grouper, or a warm duckmeat salad. See chapter 8.

• **Anacaona** (In the Grace Bay Club, Provo, Turks and Caicos; ℂ 649/946-5050): Both the setting and the Mediterranean/Caribbean cuisine are exquisite at this premier restaurant of the Grace Bay Club. As you're cooled by ceiling fans, lulled by the sounds of the ocean, your taste buds will suddenly be awakened by top-rate cuisine, prepared with the island's finest ingredients. The chef's grilled lobster alone commands a star, but he also prepares both the classics and innovative dishes exceedingly well. See chapter 11.

12 The Best Nightlife

• **Cable Beach:** Cable Beach has a lot more splash and excitement than Nassau, its neighbor on New Providence Island, and wandering around Cable Beach is also much safer than exploring the back streets of Nassau at night. The main attraction is the **Nassau Marriott Resort & Crystal Palace Casino** (ℂ 242/327-6200), with an 800-seat theater known for staging glitzy extravaganzas and a gaming room that will make you think you're smack dab in the middle of Vegas. One of the largest casinos on the islands, the Crystal Palace features 750 slot machines, 51 blackjack tables, nine roulette wheels, seven crap tables, and a baccarat table (we think the Paradise Island casino has more class, though). Despite all the glitter, you can still find cozy bars and nooks throughout the resort if you'd prefer a tranquil evening. See chapter 3.

• **Atlantis Paradise Island Resort & Casino:** Paradise Island has the flashiest nightlife in all of The Bahamas, hands down. Not even nearby Nassau and Cable Beach can come close. Nearly all of the action takes place at the incredible **Atlantis Paradise Island Resort & Casino** (ℂ 242/363-3000), where you'll find high rollers from Vegas and Atlantic City alongside grandmothers from Iowa who play the slot machines when family isn't looking. It's all gloss, glitter, and show biz, with good gambling (though savvy locals say the odds are better in Vegas). For a quieter night out, you can also find intimate bars, discos, a comedy club, and lots more in this sprawling behemoth of a hotel. See chapter 4.

• **Freeport:** Although the giant casino in **The Resorts at Bahamia** (ℂ 242/350-7000) ranks third behind Paradise Island and Cable

Beach, most of the nightlife in Freeport/Lucaya revolves around this glittering Moroccan-style palace, one of the largest casinos in either The Bahamas or the Caribbean. You get not only high- and low-stakes gambling, but also splashy Vegas- (or at least Reno-) style shows at the resort's **Casino Royale Showroom.** For real Bahamian entertainment, however, head for the **Yellow Bird Show Club,** in the **Castaways Resort** at the International Bazaar (© **242/352-6682**), for conga drums, steel drums, fire dances, and glass-eating. See chapter 5.

2

Planning Your Trip to The Bahamas

You can be in The Bahamas sipping a Goombay Smash after a quick 35-minute jet-hop from Miami. And it's never been easier to take advantage of great package deals that can make The Bahamas a terrific value.

1 The Islands in Brief

The Bahamian chain of islands, cays, and reefs stretches from Grand Bahama Island, 75 miles almost due east of Palm Beach, Florida, to Great Inagua, the southernmost island, which lies about 60 miles northeast of Cuba and fewer than 100 miles north of Haiti.

The most developed islands for tourism in The Bahamas are **New Providence Island,** site of Nassau (the capital) and Cable Beach; **Paradise Island;** and **Grand Bahama,** home of Freeport and Lucaya. If you're after glitz, gambling, bustling restaurants, nightclubs, and a beach-party scene, the big three islands are where you'll want to be. Package deals are easily found here.

Set sail (or hop on a short commuter flight) for one of the **Out Islands,** such as Andros, the Exumas, or the Abacos, and you'll find fewer crowds—and often lower prices, too. Though some of the Out Islands are sometimes accessible only by boat, it's worth your while to go the distance if you like the idea of having an entire beach to yourself. This is really getting away from it all.

Turks and Caicos (a completely separate country, near but not part of The Bahamas) are also relatively pristine, sleepy, and inexpensive—with the exception of Provo, which is undergoing a boom, with plenty of restaurants, entertainment options, sports facilities, and increasing numbers of tourists.

NEW PROVIDENCE ISLAND (NASSAU/CABLE BEACH) New Providence isn't the largest of the Bahamian Islands, but it's the historic heart of the nation, with a strong maritime tradition and the largest population in the country. Home to about 125,000 residents, it offers groves of pines and casuarinas; sandy, flat soil; the closest thing in The Bahamas to urban sprawl; and superb anchorages that are sheltered from rough seas by the presence of nearby Paradise Island. New Providence has the country's busiest airport and is dotted with hundreds of villas owned by foreign investors. Its two major resort areas are Cable Beach and Nassau, the capital.

The resort area of **Cable Beach** is a glittering beachfront strip of hotels, restaurants, and casinos; only Paradise Island has been more developed. Its center is the Marriott Resort & Crystal Palace Casino. Often, deciding between Cable Beach and Paradise Island isn't a choice of which island you prefer but a choice of which hotel you prefer. It's easy to sample the beaches, cuisine, nightlife, and gambling of both islands, since it takes only about 30 minutes to travel between the two.

Nassau, the Bahamian capital, isn't on a great stretch of shoreline and doesn't have as many first-rate hotels as either Paradise Island or Cable Beach—with the exception of the Bahama Hilton, which has a small private beach. The main advantages of Nassau are colonial charm and price. Its hotels may not be ideally located, but they are certainly cheaper; some offer very low prices even during the winter high season. You can base yourself here and commute easily to the beaches at Paradise Island or Cable Beach. Many non-beach types also prefer Nassau because it's the seat of Bahamian culture and history. It's also the shopping mecca of The Bahamas (many Floridians come here just to shop). Paradise Island and Cable Beach have shops, as well, but they can't compare to those in Nassau.

PARADISE ISLAND If high-rise hotels and glittering casinos are what you want, along with some of the best beaches in The Bahamas, there is no better choice than Paradise Island, directly off the coast of Nassau. It has the best food, the best entertainment, terrific beaches, casinos, and the best hotels. Its major drawbacks are that it's expensive and often overcrowded. Boasting a colorful history but also a host of unremarkable architecture, Paradise Island, inch for inch, is still probably the most intensely marketed piece of real estate in the world. The sands and shoals of this elongated and narrow island protect the wharves and piers of Nassau, which rise across a narrow channel only 600 feet away.

Owners of the 685-acre island have included brokerage mogul Joseph Lynch (of Merrill Lynch) and Huntington Hartford, heir to the A&P supermarket fortune. More recent investors have included Merv Griffin. The island today is a carefully landscaped residential and commercial complex with good beaches, lots of glitter (some of it tasteful, some of it way too over-the-top), and many diversions.

GRAND BAHAMA ISLAND (FREEPORT/LUCAYA) The island's name derives from the Spanish term *gran bajamar* ("great shallows"), which refers to the shallow reefs and sandbars that, over the centuries, have destroyed everything from Spanish galleons to English clipper ships on Grand Bahama's shores. (Although many of their onboard treasures were pillaged, others in deeper waters still await discovery by scuba divers.) Thanks to the tourist development schemes of U.S. financiers such as Howard Hughes, Grand Bahama boasts a well-developed tourist infrastructure. Sparely inhabited before the 1950s, it has experienced a population boom since the 1960s. Casinos, beaches, and restaurants are plentiful. Visitors can escape the island's towns and head across casuarina-dotted scrublands to explore the island's isolated western end.

Grand Bahama's **Freeport/Lucaya** resort area is another popular destination for American tourists, though we think it has a lot more tacky development than Paradise Island or Cable Beach. The compensation for that is a lower price tag on just about everything. Freeport/Lucaya offers plenty of opportunities for fine dining, entertainment, and gambling. Grand Bahama also offers the best hiking in The Bahamas and has some of the finest sandy beaches. Its golf courses attract players from all over the globe, and the island hosts major tournaments several times a year. You'll find some of the world's best diving here, as well as UNEXSO, the internationally famous diving school. Grand Bahama Island is especially popular with families.

BIMINI It's one of the smallest islands in The Bahamas, and it lies close enough to Miami (just 50 miles away) to be distinctly separate from the other islands of the archipelago. Bimini is divided into two islands, with a total area of 9 square miles. The smaller of these, North Bimini, is better developed than South Bimini. Luxurious yachts and fishing boats are always docked at the island's marinas.

Throughout Bimini, there's a slightly run-down Florida-resort atmosphere mingled with some small-town charm (think old-time Key West, before the cruise-ship crowds ruined the town). Because of its proximity to the Florida coast, Bimini is also a center for drug smuggling.

The setting for Ernest Hemingway's *Islands in the Stream,* Bimini attracts big-game fishers. For the casual sightseer, it has only minor appeal, but if you'd like to follow in the footsteps of such famous fishers as Zane Grey and Howard Hughes, Bimini is your island. Its sportfishing is among the best in the world. It's also an excellent center for yachting and cruising, and it offers some of the best scuba diving in The Bahamas.

THE BERRY ISLANDS Lying between Nassau and the coast of Florida, these islands, which cover only about 30 square miles of land, attract devoted yachties and serious fishermen. Composed of about 30 islets and cays and rows of barely submerged rocks, they have extremely limited tourist facilities and are geared mostly toward well-heeled anglers, many of whom hail from Florida. Most of the full-time population (about 700 people) lives on Great Harbour, the largest island, which measures only 6 by 2½ miles. We think the Berry Islands are a lot classier and far less dangerous and drug-infested than Bimini.

ANDROS Andros is actually two islands, connected by a series of canals and cays called *bights.* It's the largest landmass in The Bahamas (104 miles long and 40 miles wide). Andros

attracts divers and fishing enthusiasts, as well as casual sightseers.

The population numbers 8,180, although most of the island is uninhabited and unexplored. The main villages are Nicholl's Town, Andros Town, and Congo Town; all are accessible by frequent boat and plane connections from Miami and Nassau. Lodgings range from large resorts to small, plain guest houses that cater mainly to fishermen.

The world's third-largest barrier reef lies off the coast of Andros, and divers come from all over the world to explore it. The reef plunges 6,000 feet to a narrow drop-off known as the Tongue of the Ocean. Bonefishing here is among the best on earth, and Andros is also known for its world-class marlin and bluefin tuna fishing.

The natural wonders of the island have much to offer even those visitors who aren't interested in fishing or diving. Known as the "Big Yard," the central portion of Northern Andros is largely a dense forest of mahogany and pine where more than 50 varieties of orchids bloom. Southern Andros boasts a 40-square-mile forest and mangrove swamp—home to a variety of birds and animals, including the Bahamian parrot and the non-poisonous Bahamian boa constrictor, known as the "fowl snake." Any hotel can arrange a local guide to show you the attractions.

THE ABACO ISLANDS Though this "island" is often called Abaco, it is actually a cluster of islands and islets. With some 650 square miles of land, it is the second-largest grouping in The Bahamas. It is a mecca for yachties and other boaters who flock here year-round—particularly in July when the Regatta Time in Abaco race is held at the Green Turtle Yacht Club. (The Exumas, below, are also favorites with the yachting crowd.) For hundreds of years the residents of the Abacos have been boat builders, although tourism is now the main industry.

Moments Visiting a Loyalist Town

About a half-dozen Loyalist towns are scattered throughout The Bahamas: **Harbour Island, Spanish Wells, George Town,** and **Marsh Harbour** are notable examples. Each one was founded under difficult circumstances by disgruntled British colonists who did not cheer U.S. independence. The clapboard-sided houses they built still stand, resembling the saltbox cottages of New England, except for the bougainvillea climbing up the porch trellises. Life is gentle here, detached from the outside world, and charmingly old-fashioned.

Visitors will find everything from luxurious accommodations to rather bare-boned inns. With the exception of Harbour Island in Eleuthera, there is more New England charm here than anywhere else in The Bahamas. Loyalists who left New England after the American Revolution settled here and built Cape Cod–style clapboard houses with white picket fences. The best places to experience this old-fashioned charm are Green Turtle Cay and Elbow Cay, which are accessible from Marsh Harbour. Marsh Harbour itself houses an international airport and a shopping center, although its hotels aren't as good as those on Green Turtle Cay and Elbow Cay (Hope Town).

Many islands are undeveloped and uninhabited. For the best of both worlds, visitors can stay at resorts on Walker's, Green Turtle, and Treasure cays, and charter a boat to tour the more remote areas.

ELEUTHERA Long and slender, this most historic of the Out Islands (the first English settlers arrived here in 1648) is actually a string of islands that includes Spanish Wells and Harbour Island, a chic destination. The length of the island (110 miles) and the distances between Eleuthera's communities require access via three airports (Rock South, Governor's Harbour, and North Eleuthera). The island lies about 60 miles west of Nassau; frequent flights connect the two. Eleuthera is similar to Abaco, and

visitors are drawn to the miles of barrier reef and fabulous secluded beaches.

Gregory Town is the pineapple capital of the island chain. A bit farther south is Surfers Beach, one of the best surfing spots in The Bahamas. Several accommodations are available in this sleepy, slightly budget-oriented section of Eleuthera. The only major resort along the entire stretch of Eleuthera is Club Med at Governor's Harbour. Other inns are more basic.

At the southern end of the island, **Rock Sound** is in a slump, waiting to see whether the fabled Cotton Bay Club will ever reopen. Until this island and the nearby, once-exclusive enclave of Winderemere Island get going again, there's little reason to visit. Head for Harbour Island instead.

Off the coast of Eleuthera, **Harbour Island** offers excellent hotels and food, picket fences, and pastel-colored houses that evoke Cape Cod. The beaches on Harbour Island are famed for their pink sand, tinted that color by crushed coral and shells. Another offshore island near Eleuthera, **Spanish Wells** has extremely limited accommodations, and the residents—descendants of long-ago Loyalists—aren't as welcoming to visitors.

THE EXUMA ISLANDS Just 35 miles southeast of Nassau, this 365-mile-long string of islands and keys—most of them uninhabited—is the great yachting mecca of The

Moments **Taking the Slow Boat to the Out Islands**

Delivering goats, chickens, hardware, and food staples along with the mail, Bahamian mail boats greatly improve the quality of life for the scattered communities of the Out Islands. You can book passage on one to at least 17 different remote islands. All 30 boats leave from Nassau, and the round-trip takes a full day. For more information, consult an office of **The Bahamas Tourist Office** (see "Visitor Information," below) or the dockmaster at the Nassau piers at ℂ **242/393-1064**. See "Getting Around," later in this chapter, for additional details.

Bahamas, rivaling or even surpassing Abaco. These waters, some of the prettiest in The Bahamas, are also ideal for fishers (bonefishers especially). Many secluded beaches open onto tranquil cays. Daily flights service the Exumas from both Nassau and Miami.

Its center is **George Town** on **Great Exuma.** The Exuma National Land and Sea Park, which is protected by The Bahamas National Trust, encompasses much of the coastline. The park is accessible only by boat and is one of the major natural wonders and sightseeing destinations of The Bahamas, with an abundance of undersea life, reefs, blue holes, and shipwrecks. Portions of the James Bond thriller *Thunderball* were filmed at **Staniel Cay.** Each year in April, George Town hosts the interisland Family Island Regatta, a major event on the yachting calendar. A few good inns are centered mainly at George Town, and the locals are very hospitable. Otherwise, you'll practically have the archipelago to yourself.

THE SOUTHERN BAHAMAS
This cluster of islands on the southern fringe of The Bahamas is known for its remoteness and mostly undeveloped tourist industry. Most of the islands, however, have excellent beaches, good fishing, and dive sites. With an eel-like shape, **Cat Island** is only a few miles wide and 48 miles long. A lush, sleepy island in the southern Bahamian backwater, it's a great place to get away from it all. The most crowded time to

visit is during the annual Cat Island Regatta in summer, which attracts some of the top yachties from Florida and The Bahamas.

Tradition holds that **San Salvador** was the first landmass that Christopher Columbus reached during his voyage to the New World in 1492. (Modern scholars disagree, saying that Columbus landed somewhere more southeast.) Only 500 residents lived here before several new hotels were built (including a Club Med). With its newfound fame and good beaches, the island is sure to undergo further development.

The appropriately named **Long Island** stretches for 58 miles and despite a beautiful landscape that encompasses high cliffs in the north, wide and shallow beaches, historic plantation ruins, and native caves, it has remained thoroughly off the beaten track. It's not always easy to get here; there are two minor airports with arrivals from Nassau, but flights are not daily. Both the Stella Maris Resort Club and the luxurious Cape Santa Maria Beach, with its clubhouse and cottages set on a strip of gorgeous white sand, offer fishing and water sports.

Acklins Island & Crooked Island are hard to reach, have very limited tourist facilities, and appeal to people who want to escape civilization. The clear waters offshore offer good snorkeling and diving, and you'll have the fine sandy beaches almost all to yourself. The islands, which encompass about 190 square miles, are populated by a mere 1,000 souls. Accommodations are available on Crooked Island only.

Set very close to the eastern tip of Cuba, **Inagua Island** is the most southerly island of The Bahamas and the third largest in the nation. Pink flamingos thrive here. For the serious bird-watcher, there is no place like Inagua Island in the Caribbean. Inagua is hard to reach, but you can fly here. A handful of simple, no-frills inns provide overnight accommodations, but the island is a little lacking in terms of places to eat or get a drink.

TURKS & CAICOS Although these islands are actually part of the Bahamian archipelago—they are to the east of the southernmost islands of The Bahamas, directly north of Haiti and the Dominican Republic—they are governed separately.

Home of Cockburn Town, the capital of Turks and Caicos, **Grand Turk** nevertheless has a small-town atmosphere. The farthest island from Florida, it totals 9 square miles and houses 4,000 residents. Although Grand Turk is ringed by abundant marine life, most of the island's surface is flat, rocky, and dry. The diving here is world-class—the main draw for most visitors. Daily flights serve Grand Turk. Grand Turk has a relatively undeveloped tourist infrastructure, although it offers a scattering of inns and hotels. (The real tourist island of the Turks and Caicos, with first-class hotels, is Providenciales—or "Provo" for short. See below.)

With only 3½ square miles of surface, and very fine beaches, **Salt Cay** has experienced a recent influx of boaters and hotel owners. Salt Cay lies 9 miles southwest of Grand Turk; in recent years it has developed a corps of fans. The most famous resort on the island is the Windmills at Salt Cay.

Only a narrow saltwater channel separates **North Caicos** from Middle Caicos. Large, flat, and dotted with mangrove swamps and thriving vegetation, it offers good beaches and excellent bonefishing for the hardy souls who brave the inconvenience of getting here. Large sections of the island are protected as nature reserves. Unlike some of the virginal islands of Turks and Caicos, this one is at least blessed with some places to stay, including Club Vacanze/Prospect of Whitby Hotel, a resort that opens onto 7 miles of beach.

Middle (Grand) Caicos is the largest island (48 sq. miles) of the Turks and Caicos, although, ironically, it's home to only about 300 people. Few of the attempts to colonize the area were ever successful, although archaeologists are often intrigued by the artifacts that remain from long-since-vanished Lucayan Indians, marooned sailors, and stranded slaves. The island is only now beginning to awaken to tourism, and it remains relatively cut off from the outside world.

The surrounding reefs on **South Caicos** are treacherous, although Cockburn Town (the island's only port) is the best and largest natural harbor in the Turks and Caicos. Small fishing craft explore and fish in the island's numerous jagged coves. Other than Club Caribe Harbour & Beach Resort, there aren't many acceptable hotels here. Only about 1,400 residents (clustered around Cockburn Town) occupy this 8½-mile-long island. The island's airport accepts short-haul flights (and many privately owned aircraft) from Florida, the Turks and Caicos, and The Bahamas.

Part of the Caicos archipelago, **East Caicos** is almost completely uninhabited, with a uniformly low elevation above the sea and a landscape of scrubs and stunted trees. The island is accessible only by boat, and many visitors travel here for the 17-mile beach that stretches along the north coast. Some of the boaters who live on Middle Caicos will ferry passengers here for the day.

Providenciales' (Provo) 12-mile beach and pristine coastline were a tourist development waiting to happen. In the late 1970s, hotel megaliths such as Club Med poured money into increasingly popular low-rise eco-conscious resorts. Now Provo's tourist infrastructure far surpasses anything on Grand Turk. One of the larger islands of the Turks and Caicos, Provo is green but arid, with miles of scrubland and stunted trees covering the island's low, undulating hills. The population has grown in the past decade to around 6,000 persons, most of whom work in the tourist industry. Whatever the Turks and Caicos have to offer in organized sports is found here, including the nation's only golf course, boat tours, and diving excursions. The island also

has the best cuisine and the finest entertainment in the Turks and Caicos, but it's still much, much sleepier than the big developments of The Bahamas.

Pine Cay is the largest and most visible of the cays that stretch between North Caicos and Provo. Sparsely inhabited, with 800 acres and only about 35 carefully planned private homes under the administration of the Meridian Club, it's a relaxed but expensive enclave of European and North American investors. The island has its own landing strip, its own electrical generators, some remarkably good architecture, and sweeping stretches of beach. If you can afford it, 2½ miles of soft white sand plus a 500-acre nature reserve await you. The Meridian Club has a lot more class than any of the new and flashier resorts of Provo.

2 Visitor Information

This guidebook, of course, is your best tool for planning a successful vacation. The "Planning Your Trip Online" section that begins on p. 45 is packed with invaluable advice about how to search for late-breaking information on the Web.

Other good sources to try before you leave home are your travel agent or **The Bahamas Tourist Office** nearest you. They're on the Web at www. bahamas.com; or call **1-800-BAHAMAS,** and they have branch offices at the following locations:

Chicago: 8600 W. Bryn Mawr Ave., Suite 820, Chicago, IL 60631 (℡ **773/693-1500**)

Dallas: World Trade Center, 3102 Oaklawn Ave., Suite 700,

Dallas, TX 75210 (℡ **214/560-2280**)

Miami: 1 Turnberry Place, 19495 Biscayne Blvd. 809, Adventura, FL 33180 (℡ **800/688-4752,** or 305/932-0051)

Los Angeles: 3450 Wilshire Blvd., Suite 1204, Los Angeles, CA 90010 (℡ **800/439-6993**)

New York: 150 E. 52nd St., New York, NY 10022 (℡ **212/758-2777**)

Toronto: 121 Bloor St. E., Suite 1101, Toronto, ON M4W 3M5 (℡ **416/968-2999**)

United Kingdom: 3 The Billings, Walnut Tree Close, Guildford, Surrey GU1 4UL (℡ **01483/448900**)

3 Entry Requirements & Customs

ENTRY REQUIREMENTS

To enter The Bahamas, citizens of the United States coming in as visitors for

a period of less than 8 months need to bring proof of citizenship, such as a passport or a birth certificate with photo ID. (We strongly recommend that you bring a passport anyway, since you're traveling to a foreign country.) Onward or return tickets must be shown to immigration officials in The Bahamas.

The Commonwealth of The Bahamas does not require visas. On entry to The Bahamas, you'll be given an Immigration Card to complete and sign. The card has a carbon copy that you must keep until departure, at which time it must be turned in. You'll also have to pay a departure tax before you can exit the country (see "Taxes" under "Fast Facts," later in this chapter).

It's good policy to make copies of your most valuable documents, including your passport, before you leave home. Make a photocopy of the inside page of your passport, the one with your photograph. In case of loss or theft abroad, you should also make copies of your driver's license, airline tickets, hotel vouchers, and so on. You should also make copies of any prescriptions you take. Place one copy in your luggage and carry the original with you. Leave another copy at home.

CUSTOMS

Bahamian Customs allow you to bring in 200 cigarettes, 50 cigars, or 1 pound of tobacco, plus 1 quart of wine and a quart of "spirits" (that is, hard liquor). You can also bring in items classified as "personal effects," and all the money you wish.

Visitors leaving Nassau or Freeport/Lucaya for most U.S. destinations clear U.S. Customs and Immigration before departing The Bahamas. Charter companies can make special arrangements with the Nassau or Freeport flight services and U.S. Customs and Immigration for pre-clearance. No further formalities are required upon arrival in the United States once the pre-clearance has taken place in Nassau or Freeport.

Collect receipts for all the purchases you make in The Bahamas. *Note:* If a merchant suggests giving you a false receipt, misstating the value of the goods, beware—the merchant might be an informer to U.S. Customs. You must also declare all gifts received during your stay abroad.

If you purchased an item during an earlier trip abroad, carry proof that you have already paid Customs duty on the item at the time of your previous reentry. To be extra careful, compile a list of expensive carry-on items and ask a U.S. Customs agent to stamp your list at the airport before your departure.

Returning U.S. citizens who have been away for 48 hours or more are allowed to bring back, once every 30 days, $600 worth of merchandise duty-free. You'll be charged a flat rate of 10% duty on the next $1,000 worth of purchases. Be sure to have your receipts handy. On gifts, the duty-free limit is $100. You cannot bring fresh foodstuffs into the United States; canned or packaged foods, however, are allowed, and you can bring back 1 liter of alcohol. For more information, contact the **U.S. Customs Service**, 1301 Constitution Ave. (P.O. Box 7407), Washington, DC 20044 (© **202/927-6724**), and request the free pamphlet *Know Before You Go*. It's also available on the Web at **www.customs.ustreas.gov**.

U.K. citizens should contact **HM Customs & Excise Passenger Enquiries** (© **020/8910-3744**) or visit www.hmce.gov.uk.

For a clear summary of **Canadian** rules, visit the comprehensive Web site of the **Canada Customs and Revenue Agency** at **www.ccra-adrc.gc.ca**.

Citizens of **Australia** should request the helpful Australian Customs brochure *Know Before You Go*, available by calling © **1-300/363-263** from within Australia, or 61-02/ 921-32000 from abroad. For additional information, go online to **www. dfat.gov.au** and click on HINTS FOR AUSTRALIAN TRAVELERS.

For New Zealand customs information, contact the **New Zealand Customs Service** at ℂ **09/359-6655**, or go online to **www.customs.govt.nz**.

Check with your country's Customs or Foreign Affairs department for the latest guidelines—including information on items that are not allowed to be brought into your home country—just before you leave home.

4 Money

The currency is the **Bahamian dollar (B$1)**, which is pegged to the U.S. dollar so that they're always equivalent. (In fact, U.S. dollars are accepted widely throughout The Bahamas.) There is no restriction on the amount of foreign currency a tourist can bring into the country. Most large hotels and stores accept traveler's checks, but you may have trouble getting a personal check honored.

TRAVELER'S CHECKS

Traveler's checks are something of an anachronism from the days before the ATM made cash accessible at any time. These days, traveler's checks seem less necessary because most destinations, such as the major islands of The Bahamas, have 24-hour ATMs that allow travelers to withdraw small amounts of cash as needed—and thus avoid the risk of carrying a fortune around in an unfamiliar environment. Many banks, however, impose a fee every time a card is used at an ATM in a different city or bank. If you're withdrawing money every day, you might be better off with traveler's checks, as long as you don't mind showing identification every time you want to cash a check. It also makes sense to purchase traveler's checks if you plan to travel in the remote Out Islands, because ATMs will be scarcer there, if not altogether unavailable.

You can get traveler's checks at almost any bank. American Express offers denominations of $10, $20, $50, $100, $500, and $1,000. You'll pay a service charge ranging from 1% to 4%. You can also get **American Express**

traveler's checks over the phone by calling ℂ **800/221-7282**; by using this number, Amex gold and platinum cardholders are exempt from the 1% fee. AAA members can obtain checks without a fee at most AAA offices.

Visa offers traveler's checks at Citibank locations nationwide, as well as several other banks. The service charge ranges between 1.5% and 2%; checks come in denominations of $20, $50, $100, $500, and $1,000. **MasterCard** also offers traveler's checks through **Thomas Cook Currency Services;** call ℂ **800/223-7373** for a location near you.

If you opt to carry traveler's checks, be sure to keep a record of their serial numbers, *separately* from the checks of course, so you're ensured a refund in just such an emergency.

ATMS

ATMs are linked to a national network that most likely includes your bank at home. **Cirrus** (ℂ **800/424-7787;** www.mastercard.com/atm/) and **PLUS** (ℂ **800/843-7587;** www.visa.com/atms) are the two most popular networks; check the back of your ATM card to see which network your bank belongs to. Use the 800 numbers to locate ATMs in your destination.

If you're traveling abroad, ask your bank for a list of overseas ATMs. Be sure to check the daily withdrawal limit before you depart, and ask whether you need a new personal ID number.

CREDIT CARDS

Credit cards are invaluable when traveling. They are a safe way to carry

The U.S./Bahamian Dollars & the British Pound

The British pound trades at an average of around 67p = $1 U.S. or B$1, since the Bahamian and U.S. dollars are equivalent. Stated another way, $1.50 U.S. = £1. The chart below gives a rough approximation of conversion rates you're likely to find at the time of your trip, but confirm before you make transactions.

U.S./Bahamian$	U.K.£	U.S./Bahamian$	U.K.£
0.25	0.17	15	9.99
0.50	0.33	20	13.32
0.75	0.50	25	16.65
1.00	0.67	50	33.30
2.00	1.33	75	49.95
3.00	2.00	100	66.60
4.00	2.66	150	99.90
5.00	3.33	200	166.50
7.00	4.66	300	199.80
10.00	6.66	500	333.00

money and provide a convenient record of all your expenses.

You can also withdraw cash advances from your credit cards at any bank (though you'll start paying hefty interest on the advance the moment you receive the cash, and you won't receive frequent-flyer miles on an airline credit card). At most banks, you don't even need to go to a teller; you can get a cash advance at the ATM if you know your PIN number. (If you've forgotten your PIN number or didn't even know you had one, call the phone number on the back of your credit card and ask the bank to send it to you. It usually takes 5 to 7 business days, though some banks will provide the number over the phone if you tell them your mother's maiden name or pass some other security clearance.)

Almost every credit-card company has an emergency 800-number you can call if your wallet or purse is stolen. They may be able to wire you a cash advance off your credit card immediately, and in many places, they can deliver an emergency credit card in a day or two. Citicorp **Visa's** emergency number is ✆ **800/336-8472. American Express** cardholders should call ✆ **800/233-5432** to report a lost card, while traveler's check holders should call ✆ **800/221-7282** if they have a money emergency. **MasterCard** holders should call ✆ **800/307-7309.**

Odds are that if your wallet is gone, the police won't be able to recover it for you. However, after you realize that it's gone and you cancel your credit cards, it is still worth informing them. Your credit-card company or insurer may require a police report number.

5 When to Go

Throughout March and into mid-April, it's spring-break season for vacationing college and high-school students. This season is filled with beach parties, sports events, and musical entertainment, but if the idea of hundreds of partying fraternity kids doesn't appeal to you, beware. When you make your reservations, ask if your hotel is planning to host any big groups of kids.

THE WEATHER

The temperature in The Bahamas varies surprisingly little, averaging between 75°F and 85°F in both winter and summer, although it can get very chilly, especially in the early morning and at night. The Bahamian winter is usually like a perpetual May, so that's naturally the high season for North Americans who are dying to escape snow and ice in their own hometowns. Summer brings broiling hot sun and humidity, with a much greater chance of rain in the summer and fall.

The Tropic of Cancer crosses the Bahamian archipelago at about the halfway mark, passing through Great Exuma and the northern part of Long Island. Thus, there is some variation between the mean temperatures in the northernmost and southernmost islands, but the climate overall is mild. The Gulf Stream sweeps along the western shores with its clear, warm waters, and the prevailing trade winds blow steadily in from the southeast.

THE HURRICANE SEASON

The curse of Bahamian weather, the hurricane season, lasts (officially) from June 1 to November 30. But there is no cause for panic. More tropical cyclones pound the U.S. mainland than hurricanes devastate The Bahamas. Hurricanes are actually fairly infrequent in The Bahamas. However, when one does come, satellite forecasts generally give adequate warnings so that precautions can be taken.

If you're heading for The Bahamas during the hurricane season, you can call your nearest branch of the National Weather Service. In your phone directory, look it up under the U.S. Department of Commerce listing.

If you want to know how to pack just before you go, check the Weather Channel's online 5-day forecast at www.weather.com, or call © 1-900-WEATHER, for 95¢ per minute.

Average Temperatures & Rainfall (Inches) in The Bahamas

Note that these numbers are daily averages, so expect temperatures to climb significantly higher in the noonday sun and to cool off a good deal in the evening.

Month	Jan	Feb	Mar	Apr	May	June	July	Aug	Sept	Oct	Nov	Dec
Temp. °F	70	70	72	75	77	80	81	82	81	78	74	71
Temp. °C	21	21	22	24	25	27	27	28	27	26	23	22
Rainfall (in.)	1.9	1.6	1.4	1.9	4.8	9.2	6.1	6.3	7.5	8.3	2.3	1.5

THE BAHAMAS CALENDAR OF EVENTS

Many events in The Bahamas have no set dates from year to year. But once the event is announced, information becomes available to tourist offices. For specific events, you can call your nearest branch of The Bahamas Tourist Office (see "Visitor Information," above) at © 1-800-BAHAMAS or check their website at www.bahamas.com.

January

Junkanoo. This Mardi Gras–style festival begins 2 or 3 hours before dawn on New Year's Day. Throngs of cavorting, costumed figures prance through Nassau, Freeport/Lucaya, and the Out Islands. Jubilant men, women, and children wear elaborate headdresses and festive apparel as they celebrate their African heritage with music and dance. Mini-Junkanoos, in which visitors can participate, are regular events. Local tourist offices will advise the best locations to see the festivities, or call © 242/356-2691.

New Year's Day Sailing Regatta, Nassau and Paradise Island. Three dozen or more sailing sloops, ranging from 17 to 28 feet, converge off Montagu Bay in a battle for championship. Organized by The Bahamas Boat Owners Association. For information, contact the **Regatta Desk at the Ministry of Youth, Sports & Culture** (℡ 242/ 394-0445). January 2 and 3.

Annual Bahamas Wahoo Championships, the Abacos. Anglers from all over America take up the tough challenge to bait one of the fastest fish in the ocean reaching speeds up to 70 m.p.h. This fete takes place at Walker's Cay Hotel & Marina in the Abacos. For more information, call ℡ **800/WALKERS.**

February

The Mid-Winter Wahoo, Bimini. The Bimini Big Game Fishing Club draws Hemingway look-alikes and other anglers to this winter event that is heavily attended by Floridians. For more information, call ℡ **800/737-1007** or contact the tournament director, Raul Miranda, at the Big Game Fishing Club at ℡ **242/347-3391.** February 23 to 26.

Coca-Cola Junior Classic Golf, Grand Bahama Island. Young tennis pros square off in a highly competitive meet at the Country Club of the Resorts at Bahamia. The competition is open to visiting tennis players. Call the **Country Club of the Resorts at Bahamia** for more information (℡ **242/352-9661**). February 25 to 28.

March

Bacardi Billfish Tournament, Bimini. A prestigious weeklong tournament attracting the Who's Who of deep-sea fishing. Headquarters is the Bimini Big Game Fishing Club & Marina. For more information, call ℡ **800/737-1007** or 242/347-3391. March 18 to 23.

April

The Bahamas Family Island Regatta, George Town, the Exumas. Featuring Bahamian craft sloops, these celebrated boat races are held in Elizabeth Harbour. There's also a variety of onshore activities including basketball, a skipper's party, and a Junkanoo parade. Call ℡ **242/336-2430** for exact dates and information. Usually last week of April.

Bahamas Billfish North Abaco Championship, Walker's Cay in the Abacos. Six action-packed tournaments draw anglers in pursuit of the big one, and they are highly competitive. Call the **Bahamas Billfish Championship** at ℡ **954/ 920-5577** for more information. April to June.

May

Treasure Cay Billfish Championship, the Abacos. The Treasure Cay Hotel-Resort & Marina is one of the finest in the Out Islands, and its marina attracts fishing boats from throughout Florida, especially during this May billfish championship. Dates vary but you can call ℡ **242/365-8535** for more information.

Bimini Break Blue Marlin Rendezvous. This is a rendezvous off Bimini drawing anglers seeking an action-packed billfish tournament. The headquarters is the Bimini Big Game Fishing Club & Marina. For more information, call ℡ **800/ 737-1007** or 242/347-3391. May 12 to 15.

Bimini Billfish Championship. The same participants seem to show up year after year to the big-game-fishing capital of the world. Headquarters for the event is the **Bimini Big Game Fishing Club & Marina** at ℡ **800/737-1007** or 242/347-3391.

June

Eleuthera Pineapple Festival, Gregory Town, Eleuthera. This celebration devoted to the island's succulent pineapple features a Junkanoo parade, craft displays, dancing, a pineapple recipe contest, tours of pineapple farms, and a "pineathalon"—a ¼-mile swim, a 3½-mile run, and a 4-mile bike ride. For more information, call ⓒ **242/332-2142.** June 4 to 7.

Long Island Regatta, Salt Pond, Long Island, sees some 40 to 50 sailing sloops from throughout The Bahamas compete in three classes for trophies and cash prizes. Onshore, there are dancing to indigenous "rake and scrap" music, sporting events, and local food specialties for sale, all of which makes for a carnival-like atmosphere. For more information, call ⓒ **242/394-1535.** June 8 to 12.

Bahamas Summer Boating Fling/ Flotilla. Boating enthusiasts and yachtspeople make the 5-day crossing from Florida to The Bahamas (Port Lucaya's marina on Grand Bahama Island) in a flotilla of boats guided by a lead boat. All "flings" depart from the Radisson Bahia Mar Resort & Yacht Center in Fort Lauderdale. For more information, contact the **Bahamas Tourism Center** in Florida at ⓒ **800/ 327-7678** or 305/932-0051. June 21 to 25.

July

Annual Racing Time in Abaco, Marsh Harbour. This weeklong regatta features a series of five sailboat races in the Sea of Abaco. Onshore festivities include nightly entertainment, cocktail parties, beach picnics, cultural activities, and a grand finale party. For registration forms and information, contact **Dave or Kathy Ralph** at ⓒ **242/367-2677.** July 4 to 11.

Independence Week. Independence celebrations are marked throughout the islands by festivities, parades, and fireworks. It all culminates on Independence Day, July 10.

August

Emancipation Day. The first Monday in August commemorates the emancipation of slaves in 1834. A highlight of this holiday is an early-morning "Junkanoo Rushout" starting at 4am in Fox Hill Village in Nassau, followed by an afternoon of "cook-outs," cultural events such as climbing a greased pole, and the plaiting of the Maypole. First Monday in August.

Cat Island Regatta, Southern Bahamas. Sleepy Cat Island comes alive in the weekend of festive events, including sloop races, live "rake & scrape" bands, quadrille dancing, old-fashioned contests and games, and the sale of indigenous dishes. Contact the **Regatta Desk** at ⓒ **242/394-0445** in Nassau or **Allen Gilbert** at ⓒ **242/342-3011** on Cat Island. August 4 to 7.

September

Grand Bahama Junkanoo Carnival. This is an exciting weekend of cultural festivities, including a Junkanoo Carnival, a parade evocative of the famous carnival at Trinidad, and open-air concerts featuring the hottest bands. For more information, contact the **Grand Bahama Island Tourism Board** at ⓒ **242/352-8044.** September 21 or 24.

October

Discovery Day. The New World landing of Christopher Columbus, traditionally said to be the island of San Salvador, is celebrated throughout The Bahamas. Naturally, San Salvador town has a parade every year on this day, October 12.

North Eleuthera Sailing Regatta.
Native sailing sloops take to the
waters of North Eleuthera, Harbour
Island, and Spanish Wells in a weekend of championship races. For
information contact the **Eleuthera
Tourist Office** at © **242/332-2142**
or **Glenroy Aranha** at © **242/
333-2281.** Mid-October.

All Abaco Sailing Regatta. Local
sailing sloops rendezvous at Treasure Cay Harbour for a series of
championship races and onshore
festivities. Contact the **Regatta
Desk** in Nassau at © **242/394-
04445** or **Everette Hart** in Abaco
at © **242/367-2344.**

November

Guy Fawkes Day. The best celebrations are in Nassau. Nighttime
parades through the streets are held
on many of the islands, culminating
in the hanging and burning of Guy
Fawkes, an effigy of the British
malefactor who was involved in the
Gunpowder Plot of 1605 in London. It usually takes place around
November 5, but check with island
tourist offices.

**Bimini Big Game Fishing Club
All Wahoo Tournament.** Anglers
take up the tough challenge of bait-
ing one of the fastest fishes in the
ocean. Headquarters is the Bimini
Big Game Fishing Club &
Marina. For information, contact
© **800/737-1007** or **242/347-
3391.** November 15 to 18.

**Annual One Bahamas Music &
Heritage Festival.** This 3-day celebration is staged at both Nassau and
Paradise Island to celebrate national
unity. Highlights include concerts
featuring top Bahamian performing
artists. Events include "fun walks"
on the island and other activities.
For more information, contact the
**Nassau/Paradise Island Tourist
Office** at © **242/326-0633, ext.
4100).** November 24 to 26.

December

Junkanoo Boxing Day. High-
energy Junkanoo parades and
celebrations are held throughout
the islands on December 26. Many
of these activities are repeated on
New Year's Day (see "January,"
above).

6 Health & Insurance

STAYING HEALTHY

The Bahamas has excellent medical
facilities. Physicians and surgeons in
private practice are readily available in
Nassau, Cable Beach, and Freeport/
Lucaya. In the Out Islands there are 13
health centers. Medical personnel hold
satellite clinics periodically in small
settlements, and there are 36 other
clinics, making a total of 49 health
facilities throughout the outlying
islands. (We've listed the names and
telephone numbers of specific clinics
in the individual island coverage that
follows throughout this book.) If
intensive or urgent care is required,
patients are brought by the Emergency
Flight Service to Princess Margaret
Hospital in Nassau. Some of the big
resort hotels have in-house physicians
or can quickly secure one for you.

There is a government-operated
hospital, **Rand Memorial** (© **242/352-
6735**), in Freeport, plus government-
operated clinics on Grand Bahama
Island. Nassau and Freeport/Lucaya
also have private hospitals.

Dentists are plentiful in Nassau,
but somewhat less so on Grand
Bahama. You'll find two dentists on
Great Abaco Island, one at Marsh
Harbour, another at Treasure Cay, and
one on Eleuthera. Some of the remote
islands, especially those in the southern Bahamas, have no dentists at all,
though the staff at your hotel will
know where to send you for a serious
dental emergency.

> ## ⸝Tips⸜ The Smart Traveler
>
> If you're buying a package vacation or tour, don't buy your trip-cancellation insurance from your tour operator—talk about putting all of your eggs in one basket! Buy it from an outside vendor instead.

If you suffer from a chronic illness, consult your doctor before your departure. For conditions like epilepsy, diabetes, or heart problems, wear a **Medic Alert Identification Tag** (© 800/825-3785; www.medicalert. org), which will immediately alert doctors to your condition and give them access to your records through Medic Alert's 24-hour hotline. Membership is $35, plus a $15 annual fee.

Pack prescription medications in your carry-on luggage, not in luggage that you'll be checking. Carry written prescriptions in generic, not brand-name, form, and dispense all prescription medications from their original labeled vials. Also bring along copies of your prescriptions in case you lose your pills or run out.

INSURANCE

There are three kinds of travel insurance: trip cancellation, medical, and lost luggage coverage. (The airlines are usually liable for up to $2,500 if they lose your luggage on an overseas flight anyway, so most people will not require additional insurance.) Rule number one: Check your existing policies before you buy any additional coverage.

Trip-cancellation insurance is a good idea only if you've paid a large portion of your vacation expenses up front (say, by purchasing a cruise or a package tour). The other two types of insurance, however, don't make sense for most travelers.

Your existing **health insurance** should cover you if you get sick while on vacation (though if you belong to an HMO, you should check to see whether you are fully covered when away from home). If you need hospital treatment, most health-insurance plans and HMOs will cover out-of-country hospital visits and procedures, at least to some extent. However, most make you pay the bills up front at the time of care, and reimburse you after you've returned and filed all the paperwork. Members of **Blue Cross/Blue Shield** can now use their cards at select hospitals in most major cities worldwide (© 800/810-BLUE or www.bluecares. com for a list of hospitals).

Among the reputable issuers of travel insurance are **Access America** (© 800/284-8300; www.accessamerica.com), **Travel Guard International** (© 800/826-1300; www.noelgroup.com), and **Travelex Insurance Services** (© 800/228-9792; www.travelex-insurance. com). The **Divers Alert Network (DAN)** (©800/446-2671 or 919/684-8111;www.diversalertnetwork. org), insures scuba divers.

7 Tips for Travelers with Special Needs

FOR TRAVELERS WITH DISABILITIES

A disability shouldn't stop anyone from traveling. There are more resources out there than ever before.

Because the center of Nassau is relatively flat, it is fairly easy to get around, even for persons with minor disabilities.

A World of Options, a 658-page book of resources for travelers with disabilities, covers everything from biking trips to scuba outfitters. It costs $35 ($30 for members) and is available from **Mobility International USA,** P.O. Box 10767, Eugene, OR 97440 (© **541/343-1284,** voice and TDD; www.miusa.org). Annual membership for Mobility International is $35, which includes their quarterly newsletter, *Over the Rainbow.* In addition, **Twin Peaks Press,** P.O. Box 129, Vancouver, WA 98666 (© **360/694-2462**), publishes travel-related books for people with disabilities. **Moss Rehab ResourccNet (www. mossresourcenet.org**) is a great source for information, tips, and resources relating to accessible travel. You'll find links to a number of travel agents who specialize in planning trips for travelers with disabilities here and through **Access-Able Travel Source (www.access-able.com**), another excellent online source. You'll also find relay and voice numbers for hotels, airlines, and car-rental companies on Access-Able's user-friendly site, as well as links to accessible accommodations, attractions, transportation, tours, local medical resources and equipment repairers, and much more.

You can join the **Society for the Advancement of Travelers with Handicaps (SATH)**, 347 Fifth Ave., Suite 610, New York, NY 10016 (© **212/447-7284;** fax 212/725-8253; www.sath.org), to gain access to their vast network of connections in the travel industry. They provide information sheets on destinations and referrals to tour operators that specialize in traveling with disabilities. Their quarterly magazine, *Open World,* is full of good information and resources.

Travelers with disabilities may also want to consider joining a tour that caters specifically to them. One of the best operators is **Flying Wheels Travel,** 143 West Bridge (P.O. Box 382), Owatonna, MN 55060 (© **800/535-6790**). They offer various escorted tours and cruises, with an emphasis on sports, as well as private tours in minivans with lifts. Other reputable specialized tour operators include **Access Adventures** (© **716/889-9096**), which offers sports-related vacations; **Accessible Journeys** (© **800/TINGLES** or 610/521-0339), for slow walkers and wheelchair travelers; **The Guided Tour, Inc.** (© **215/782-1370**); **Wilderness Inquiry** (© **800/728-0719** or 612/379-3858); and **Directions Unlimited** (© **800/533-5343**).

Vision-impaired travelers should contact the **American Foundation for the Blind,** 11 Penn Plaza, Suite 300, New York, NY 10001 (© **800/232-5463**), for information on traveling with Seeing Eye dogs.

FOR FAMILIES

The Bahamas is one of the top family-vacation destinations in North America. The smallest toddlers can spend blissful hours on sandy beaches and in the shallow seawater or in swimming pools constructed with them in mind. There's no end to the fascinating pursuits offered for older children, ranging from boat rides to shell collecting to horseback riding, hiking, or even dancing. Some children are old enough to learn to snorkel and to explore an underwater

---

Tips **Finding an Accessible Hotel**

You can call the **Bahamas Association for the Physically Disabled** (© 242/322-2393) for information about accessible hotels in The Bahamas. This agency will also send a rented van to the airport to transport you to your hotel for a fee and can provide ramps.

Tips Escaping Your Kids

Many of the island's resorts realize that Mom and Dad's idea of fun may not be quite what the kids had in mind. So they offer extras like daily supervised children's activities, baby-sitters, family discounts, and kids' meals, helping your children to have a great vacation while their parents gain some freedom to relax, too.

---

wonderland. Some resorts will even teach kids to swim or windsurf.

Family Travel Times newsletter costs $40 (online only—www.familytraveltimes.com), and it's updated every 2 weeks. Subscribers also can call in with travel questions but only on Wednesday from 10am to 1pm Eastern Standard Time. Contact Family Travel Times, 40 Fifth Ave., New York, NY 10011 (© **888/822-4322,** or 212/477-5524).

Most families with kids head for New Providence (Nassau), Paradise Island, or Grand Bahama Island (Freeport). See the "Family-Friendly Hotels" boxes in those chapters for our recommendations of the best hotels for parents traveling with kids. See also "The Best Family Vacations," in chapter 1, for additional recommendations in the Out Islands.

FOR GAY & LESBIAN TRAVELERS

Think twice before choosing The Bahamas. Although many gay people visit or live here, the country has very repressive anti-homosexual laws. Relations between homosexuals, even if between consenting adults, are subject to criminal sanctions carrying prison terms. Sexual intercourse (either homosexual or heterosexual) in a public place (that would include a beach late at night) is punishable by up to 20 years in prison.

If you would like to make visiting gay beaches, gay bars, or gay clubs part of your vacation, consider Miami, Key West, or Puerto Rico instead.

Nevertheless, in the wake of the travel-industry disaster in which the government of the Cayman Islands refused a cruise ship permission to land with its gay passenger, government officials of The Bahamas took an opposite position. When word reached tourist authorities that protests were being organized against the arrival of gay cruises, some government officials actually went aboard to welcome these gay passengers to Nassau. Of course, cynics would claim they welcomed their dollars more than their sexual orientation, because the laws are still on the books. Yet we still applaud this welcoming attitude in the wake of the Cayman Islands debacle.

Nevertheless, The Bahamas cannot at all be considered a gay-friendly destination. Single gays or gay couples should travel here with great discretion.

FOR SENIORS

One of the benefits of age is that travel often costs less. Don't be shy about asking for discounts, but always carry some kind of identification, such as a driver's license, that shows your date of birth. Also, mention the fact that you're a senior citizen when you first make your travel reservations. Most airlines offer senior discounts.

Members of the **American Association of Retired Persons (AARP)**, 601 E St. NW, Washington, DC 20049 (© **800/424-3410** or 202/434-2277; www.aarp.org), get discounts not only on hotels but on airfares and car rentals, too. AARP offers members a wide range of special benefits, including *Modern Maturity* magazine and a monthly newsletter. **The National Council of Senior Citizens,** 8403 Colesville Rd., Suite 1200, Silver Spring, MD 20910 (✆ **301/578-8800;** www.ncsinc.org), a non-profit organization, offers a newsletter six times a year (partly devoted to travel tips) and discounts on hotel and auto rentals; annual dues are $13 per person or couple. **Sears Mature Outlook,** P.O. Box 9390, Des Moines, IA 50306 (✆ **800/336-6330**), began as a travel organization for people over 50, though it now caters to people of all ages. Members receive discounts on hotels and receive a bimonthly magazine. Annual membership is $19.95, which entitles members to discounts and, often, free coupons for discounted merchandise from Sears.

The Mature Traveler, a monthly 12-page newsletter on senior-citizen travel, is a valuable resource. It is available by subscription ($32 a year) from GEM Publishing Group, Box 50400, Reno, NV 89513-0400. GEM also

publishes *The Book of Deals,* a collection of more than 1,000 senior discounts on airlines, lodging, tours, and attractions around the country; it's available for $9.95 by calling ✆ **800/460-6676.** Another helpful publication is *101 Tips for the Mature Traveler,* available from Grand Circle Travel, 347 Congress St., Suite 3A, Boston, MA 02210 (✆ **800/221-2610** or 617/350-7500; fax 617/346-6700).

Grand Circle Travel is also one of the hundreds of travel agencies specializing in vacations for seniors (347 Congress St., Suite 3A, Boston, MA 02210; ✆ **800/221-2610** or 617/ 350-7500). Many of these packages, however, are of the tour-bus variety, with free trips thrown in for those who organize groups of 10 or more. Seniors seeking more independent travel should probably consult a regular travel agent. **SAGA International Holidays,** 222 Berkeley St., Boston, MA 02116 (✆ **800/343-0273**), offers inclusive tours and cruises for those 50 and older.

8 Package Deals

Before you start your search for the lowest airfare on your own, you may want to consider booking your flight as part of a package, since there are so many good-value packages often available to The Bahamas.

Package tours are not the same thing as escorted tours. They are simply a way to buy airfare and accommodations at the same time. For popular destinations like The Bahamas, they are a smart way to go, because in many cases, they can save you a lot of money. Often, a package that includes airfare, hotel, and transportation to and from the airport will cost you less than just the hotel alone would have, had you booked it yourself. That's because packages are sold in bulk to tour operators who resell

them to the public at a cost that drastically undercuts standard rates.

Packages, however, vary widely. Some offer a better class of hotels than others. Some offer the same hotels for lower prices. Some offer flights on scheduled airlines, while others book charters. In some packages, your choice of accommodations and travel days may be limited. Some packages let you choose between escorted vacations and independent vacations; others will allow you to add on just a few excursions or escorted day trips (also at lower prices than you could locate on your own) without booking an entirely escorted tour. Each destination usually has one or two packagers that are usually cheaper than the rest because they buy in even greater bulk.

It's important to spend a little time shopping around; just be sure to compare apples to apples, since the offerings can vary. You can use the reviews and rack rates given in this book to evaluate whether a package is really a good deal.

Here are a few tips to help you tell one package from another, and figure out which one is right for you:

• **Read this guide.** Do a little homework. Compare the rack rates that we've published to the discounted rates being offered by the packagers to see what kinds of deals they're offering—if you're actually being offered a substantial savings, or if they've just gussied up the rack rates to make their offer *sound* like a deal. If you're being offered a stay in a hotel we haven't recommended, do more research to learn about it, especially if it isn't a reliable franchise like Marriott or Hyatt. It's not a deal if you end up at a dump.

• **Read the fine print.** Make sure you know *exactly* what's included in the price you're being quoted, and what's not. Are hotel taxes and airport transfers included, or will you have to pay extra? Conversely, don't pay for a rental car you don't need. Before you commit to a package, make sure you know how much flexibility you have, say, if your kid gets sick or your boss suddenly asks you to adjust your vacation schedule. Some packagers require iron-clad commitments, whereas others will go with the flow, charging only minimal fees for changes or cancellations.

• **Use your best judgment.** Stay away from fly-by-nights and shady packagers. If a deal appears to be too good to be true, it probably is. Go with a reputable firm with a proven track record. This is where your travel agent can come in handy; he or she should be knowledgeable about different packagers, the deals they offer, and the general rate of satisfaction among their customers.

The best place to start your search is the travel section of your local Sunday newspaper. Also check the ads in the back of national travel magazines like *Travel & Leisure, National Geographic Traveler, Travel Holiday,* and *Condé Nast Traveler. Arthur Frommer's Budget Travel* always has lots of ads and frequent articles about good-value packages.

Liberty Travel (© 888/271-1584; www.libertytravel.com) is one of the biggest packagers in the Northeast, and it usually boasts a full-page ad in Sunday papers. You won't get much in the way of service, but you will get a good deal.

Another good resource is the airlines themselves, which often package their flights together with accommodations. Among the airline packagers, your options include **American Airlines Vacations** (© 800/321-2121;** www.aavacations.com), **Delta Vacations** (© 800/872-7786; www. deltavacations.com), and **US Airways Vacations** (© 800/455-0123; www. usairwaysvacations.com).

The biggest hotel chains and resorts also offer package deals. If you already know where you want to stay, call the resort itself and ask if it can offer land/air packages.

There's also **TourScan, Inc.** (© 800/962-2080 or 203/655-8091; www.tourscan.com), which researches the best value vacation at each hotel and condo. Two catalogs are printed each year. Each lists a broad choice of hotels on most of the islands in The Bahamas, in all price ranges. Catalogs cost $4 each, the price of which is credited to any TourScan vacation. Prices are based on travel from New York, Newark, Baltimore, Philadelphia, and Washington, D.C., although the company will arrange trips originating from any location in the United States or abroad on request.

For one-stop shopping on the Web, go to **www.vacationpackager.com,** a search engine that will link you to many different package-tour operators offering Bahamas vacations, often with a company profile summarizing the company's basic booking and cancellation terms.

Horizon Tours (© **202/393-8390;** www.horizontours.com) specializes in all-inclusive resorts on the islands of The Bahamas, plus other destinations in the Caribbean including Barbados, Jamaica, Aruba, St. Lucia, and Antigua.

Club Med (© **800/258-2633;** www.clubmed.com) has various all-inclusive options throughout the Caribbean and The Bahamas.

Frontiers International (© **800/ 245-1950,** or 724/935-1577 in Pennsylvania; www.frontierstrvl.com) features fly- and spin-fishing tours of The Bahamas and is a specialist in saltwater-fishing destinations.

FOR BRITISH TRAVELERS

Package tours to The Bahamas can be booked through **Harlequin Worldwide Connoisseurs Collection,** 2 North Rd., South Ockendon, Essex RM15 6QJ (© **01708/850-300).** This agency offers both air and hotel packages not only to Nassau, but to most of the Out Islands as well. The company also specializes in scuba-diving and golf holidays.

Another specialist is **Kuoni Travel,** Kuoni House, Dorking, Surrey RH5 4AZ (© **01306/742-222),** which offers both land and air packages to The Bahamas, including such destinations as Nassau and Freeport, and to some places in the Out Islands. They also offer packages for self-catering villas on Paradise Island.

9 Flying to The Bahamas

Nassau is the busiest and most popular point of entry (this is where you'll fly if you're staying on Paradise Island. From here, you can make connections to many of the more remote Out Islands. If you're headed for one of the Out Islands, refer to the "Getting There" section that appears at the beginning of each island's coverage later in this book for details. Freeport, on Grand Bahama, also has its own airport, which is served by flights from the U.S. mainland, too.

Flight time to Nassau from Miami is about 35 minutes; from New York, 2½ hours; from Atlanta, 2 hours and 5 minutes; from Philadelphia, 2 hours and 45 minutes; from Charlotte, 2 hours and 10 minutes; from central Florida, 1 hour and 10 minutes; and from Toronto, 3 hours.

THE MAJOR AIRLINES

From the U.S. mainland, about a half dozen carriers fly non-stop to the country's major point of entry and busiest airline hub, **Nassau International Airport.** Some also fly to the archipelago's second-most-populous city of Freeport. Only a handful (see below) fly directly to any of the Out Islands.

American Airlines's subsidiary **American Eagle** (© **800/433-7300;** www. aa.com) flies to Nassau non-stop from Miami, with more than a dozen daily departures. There is no non-stop flight between New York and Nassau on American (you'll have to fly to Miami and change planes there). American Eagle also offers about 10 daily flights between Miami and Freeport.

Delta (© **800/241-4141;** www. delta-air.com) has several connections to The Bahamas, with service from Atlanta, Fort Lauderdale, Orlando, and New York's LaGuardia.

The national airline of The Bahamas, **Bahamasair** (© **800/222-4262;** www.bahamasair.com), flies to

The Bahamas from Miami, landing at either Nassau (with seven non-stop flights daily) or Freeport (with three non-stop flights daily). **US Airways** (✆ **800/428-4322;** www.usairways.com) offers daily direct flights to Nassau from Philadelphia and Baltimore, with a brief stopover in Charlotte, North Carolina. **TWA** (✆ **800/221-2000;** www.twa.com) has one daily flight from New York's JFK to Nassau.

Smaller carriers include **Continental Connection** (✆ **800/231-0856**), with daily flights to North Eleuthera from both Fort Lauderdale and Miami, plus **Twin Air** (✆ **954/359-8266**), flying from Fort Lauderdale three times a week to Rock Sound and Governor's Harbour and four times a week to North Eleuthera. **Air Canada** (✆ **800/268-7240** in Canada, or 888/247-2262 in the U.S.; www.aircanada.ca) is the only carrier offering scheduled service to Nassau from Canada. A direct flight from Toronto leaves once weekly on Sunday; other flights from both Toronto and Montréal, as well as other Canadian cities, make connections in the U.S.

British travelers opt for transatlantic passage aboard **British Airways** (✆ **0845/773-3377** toll-free from anywhere in the U.K.; www.britishairways.com), which offers twice-weekly direct service from London to Nassau. The airline also has at least one flight daily to Miami. From here, a staggering number of connections are available to Nassau and many other points within the archipelago on several carriers.

FLYING TO THE OUT ISLANDS

Many frequent visitors to The Bahamas do everything they can to avoid the congestion, inconvenience, and uncertain connections of the Nassau International Airport. A couple of U.S.-based airlines offer service directly to some of the Out Islands. **American Eagle** (✆ **800/433-7300;** www.aa.com) offers frequent service from Miami's International Airport to the Abacos, Eleuthera, and the Exumas. **US Airways** (✆ **800/428-4322;** www.usairways.com) flies non-stop every day from Fort Lauderdale to Eleuthera, usually making stops at both Governor's Harbour and North Eleuthera. US Airways also flies every day from West Palm Beach to the Abacos, stopping in both Treasure Cay and Marsh Harbour.

Chalk's International (✆ **800/424-2557** or 242/363-1687) operates 17-passenger amphibious aircraft that take off and land in waters near the company's portside terminals. From the Florida mainland, a non-stop flight departs for Bimini from Miami's Watson Island Airport. The flight then continues on to Paradise Island. There's also a one-stop flight from Fort Lauderdale's Jet Center Airport to Bimini. (The airline also offers charter flights to virtually anywhere in The Bahamas.)

FLY FOR LESS: GET THE BEST AIRFARE

Be sure to read the section above on "Package Deals." Here are a few other easy ways to save:

1. Keep your eyes peeled for airfare **sales,** especially in the off-season. You'll almost never see a sale during the peak months of winter in The Bahamas, or during the Thanksgiving or Christmas seasons; but in periods of low-volume travel, you should find discounts. If your schedule is flexible, ask if you can secure a cheaper fare by staying an extra day or by flying midweek. (Many airlines won't volunteer this information, so be persistent and ask the reservations agent lots of questions.) If you already hold a

ticket when a sale breaks, it may even pay to exchange your ticket, which usually incurs a $50 to $75 charge.

2. **Consolidators,** also known as bucket shops, are a good place to find low fares. Consolidators buy seats in bulk from the airlines and then sell them back to the public at prices below even the airlines' discounted rates. Their small boxed ads usually run in the Sunday travel section at the bottom of the page. Before you pay a consolidator, however, ask for a record locator number and confirm your seat with the airline itself. Be prepared to book your ticket with a different consolidator—there are many to choose from—if the airline can't confirm your reservation. Also be aware that bucket-shop tickets usually are non-refundable or rigged with stiff cancellation penalties, often as high as 50% to 75% of the ticket price.

We've gotten great deals on many occasions from **Cheap Tickets** (✆ 800/377-1000; www. cheaptickets.com). **Council Travel** (✆ 888/COUNCIL; www. counciltravel.com) and **STA Travel** (✆ 800/781-4040; www. statravel.com) cater especially to young travelers, but their bargain-basement prices are available to people of all ages. **1800AIRFARE** (✆ 800/AIR-FARE; www. 1800airfare.com) was formerly owned by TWA but now offers the deepest discounts on many other airlines, with a 4-day advance purchase. Other reliable consolidators include **Lowest-fare.com** (✆ 888/278-8830; www.lowestfare.com); **Cheap Seats** (✆ 800/451-7200; www. cheapseatstravel.com); **1-800FLY-CHEAP** (www.flycheap.com);

TFI Tours International (✆ 800/745-8000 or 212/736-1140), which serves as a clearinghouse for unused seats; and "rebators" such as **Travel Avenue** (✆ 800/333-3335).

3. **Surf the Web** and save. For more information, see "Planning Your Trip Online," later in this chapter.

4. Book a seat on a **charter flight.** Discounted fares have pared the number available, but they can still be found. Most charter operators advertise and sell their seats through travel agents, thus making these local professionals your best source of information for available flights. Before deciding to take a charter flight, however, check the restrictions on the ticket: You may be asked to purchase a tour package, to pay in advance, to be amenable if the day of departure is changed, to pay a service charge, to fly on an airline you're not familiar with (this usually is not the case), and to pay harsh penalties if you cancel—but be understanding if the charter doesn't fill up and is canceled up to 10 days before departure. The most prominent charter operator is **Nassau/Paradise Island Express,** P.O. 1004, 284 Millburn Ave., Millburn, NJ 07041 (✆ 800/722-4262; fax 973/467-4933). The company contracts for the entire aircraft. No advance booking is required, and there are no restrictions on travel dates. You can stay for a day or as long as you like. The company contracts an entire Continental Airlines aircraft, which operates daily from both Newark and Houston. Airfare can be sold alone or in conjunction with hotel packages at New Providence, Paradise Island, and Freeport/Lucaya.

10 Cruises

Cruises to The Bahamas are usually either 3- or 4-day weekend getaways or weeklong itineraries in which the ship may stop at Nassau, Freeport, and/or one of several privately owned Bahamian islands for a day at the beach en route to Caribbean ports farther south. If you've never been to The Bahamas, consider a cruise to Nassau, where you can also enjoy Paradise Island and Cable Beach on the same visit. It has better shopping possibilities, better restaurants, and more entertainment than any other site in The Bahamas, including Freeport/Lucaya on Grand Bahama Island.

A brief summary of cruise lines that offer diversions in The Bahamas is outlined below, but for much more detailed information, and reviews of each of the ships spending significant time in either the Caribbean or The Bahamas, consider picking up a copy of *Frommer's Caribbean Cruises & Ports of Call 2002*.

Regardless of the ship you choose, there's a strong possibility that your cruise will depart from the cruise capital of the world, Miami. A handful of vessels also depart for Bahamian waters from Port Everglades (adjacent to Fort Lauderdale), Port Canaveral, and, in very rare instances, from New York. Many cruise-ship passengers combine a 3- or 4-day cruise with visits to Orlando's theme parks, Miami's South Beach, the Florida Everglades, or the Florida Keys and Key West.

Nearly all cabins aboard ships today have two twin beds that can be pushed together, plus storage space (of varying size), a shower and a toilet (ditto), and sometimes a TV showing a rotating stock of programs. If you want to keep costs to a minimum when booking, ask for one of the smaller, inside cabins (one without windows). If you're the type who likes to be active all day and then stay out late enjoying the ship's bars and nightclubs, you won't miss the sunshine anyway. On the other hand, passengers of means are being offered suites today that have an amazing array of pampering options (including hot tubs on their own private verandas!).

Because they buy in such bulk, cruise lines typically offer some of the best deals on airfare to your port of embarkation, and also typically offer extension packages that allow pre- or post-cruise stays at a hotel or resort.

Because getting around Freeport/Lucaya or Nassau is relatively easy, and the official shore excursions offered by most ships are dull and sometimes restrictive, it's best to decide what you want to do (shopping, swimming, snorkeling, or gambling) and head off on your own during your stop at each port of call. You'll certainly have time to relax at the beach if you choose, or to enjoy water sports (the chapters that follow will give you details on what companies or outfitters to contact for equipment, so you needn't feel dependent on the cruise line for everything). See chapter 3, for more details about sports in Nassau, or chapter 5, for information about sports in Freeport/Lucaya.

Tips **It's Not Easy Being Green**

Cabins situated on low decks in the middle of the ship are the most stable, and thus the best choices for those susceptible to seasickness. Various medications are also available, including Dramamine, Bonine, ginger capsules, and time-release Transderm patches (worn behind the ear), plus acupressure wristbands.

In Nassau, cruise ships anchor at piers along Prince George Wharf. Taxi drivers meet all arrivals and will transport you into the heart of Nassau, center of most shopping and sightseeing activities. Duty-free shops also lie just outside the dock area, but for that, you'd do better to go inside the city's commercial and historic core.

As you disembark, you'll find a tourist information office in a tall pink tower, where you can pick up maps of New Providence Island or of Nassau itself. One-hour walking tours are conducted from here if you'd like an overview of the city, with a guide pointing out historic monuments. Outside this office, an ATM will supply you with U.S. dollars if your cash is running low.

Here's a rundown of some major cruise lines that serve The Bahamas. Most of them focus on either Nassau or Freeport (or maybe both).

- **Carnival Cruise Line** (© **800/ 327-9501**; www.carnival.com): The cruise line everyone's heard of offers a big, loud, flashy cruise party with lots of gambling, glitz, and crowds, so if you're looking for some quiet, reflective time, this might not be your cup of rum. Carnival's best bet for The Bahamas is aboard the *Ecstasy,* a vessel that's been called "Vegas at Sea." It sails year-round on 3-night loops that depart from Miami on Friday, call briefly at Nassau, then spend almost an entire day, loaded with activities, at sea. The ship is very similar to another Carnival ship, the *Fantasy,* which sails on 3-night loops to Nassau and 4-night excursions to both Freeport and Nassau, and also manages to include the activity-loaded day at sea mentioned above. The *Fantasy,* however, departs throughout the year from Port Canaveral rather than from the more southerly port of Miami. The average on-board age of most passengers on these Bahamian jaunts is a relatively youthful mid-40s, although ages range from 3 to 95 and usually include lots of children.

- **Celebrity Cruises** (© **800/327-6700** or 305/539-6000; www.celebrity-cruises.com): Celebrity, a more upscale sibling company to Royal Caribbean, maintains six newly built medium- to large-size ships that offer Caribbean cruises of between 7 and 14 nights. If you always like to sail a line's newest and largest vessel, make it the *Millennium,* a real knockout of a megaship. They usually include stops at Key West, San Juan, Grand Cayman, Ocho Rios, Antigua, St. Thomas, and Curaçao, among others; in some cases, most notably aboard the *Century,* they'll stop for the day in Nassau. This line is unpretentious but classy, several notches above mass-market, but with pricing that's pretty competitive. Cabins are roomy and well-equipped, and the cuisine is among the best of any of the cruise lines.

- **Costa Cruise Lines** (© **800/462-6782** or 305/358-7325; www.costacruises.com): This old Italian cruise outfit offers virtually identical 7-night jaunts through the western and eastern Caribbean on two of its larger, newer ships (*CostaAtlantica* and *CostaVictoria*), departing from Fort Lauderdale. Of the two and if you have a choice, go for the *CostaAtlantica* (it debuted in 2000), a 2,112-passenger sleek megaship, which has balconies in three-fourths of its cabins. Ports of call during the eastern Caribbean itineraries of both vessels include stopovers in Nassau, as well as in such other ports as St. Thomas, San Juan, and Serena Cay (a private island known for its beaches off the coast of the Dominican Republic).

There's an Italian flair and lots of Italian design on board here, as well as an atmosphere of relaxed indulgence. The ships feature tame versions of ancient Roman Bacchanalia, as well as such celebrations as toga nights and focaccia and pizza parties by the pool.

• **Disney Cruise Line** (© 800/951-3532 or 407/566-7000; www.disney.go.com/DisneyCruise): Launched with lots of publicity in 1999, the *Disney Wonder* is saturated with the total Disney vibe and is specifically marketed to families. Megaship size at 85,000 tons, it succeeds in mingling state-of-the-art technology and audio-visuals with lots of Disney razzle-dazzle. Disney's ships also offer probably the best-designed family cabins of any cruise ship, the biggest children's facilities, and even a number of adults-only areas, including one swimming pool, a piano bar, a comedy club, and various social venues.

Disney Wonder itineraries begin and end in Port Canaveral, last between 3 and 4 days, and include daylong visits (8am to 3am) to Nassau and Castaway Cay (8am to 5pm), the latter a privately owned Bahamian island featuring extensive children's facilities, an adults-only beach area, a family beach area, and all the sports and recreation choices you could want. Most Disney cruises are sold as 7-night packages that include either 3 days at Disney World and 4 days at sea or vice versa. The 4-night cruise offers a full day at sea as well as visits to the ports.

• **Holland America Line—Westours** (© 800/426-0327; www.hollandamerica.com): HAL is the most high-toned of the mass-market cruise lines, with eight respectably hefty and good-looking ships serving a clientele of generally mature travelers. Late-night revelers and serious party people might want to book cruises on other lines, such as Carnival. Throughout the winter, four of these vessels include daylong stopovers in Nassau and/or full-day stopovers at the line's privately owned island (Half Moon Cay, in the Exumas) as part of 7- and 10-night cruises to such Caribbean ports as San Juan, St. Thomas, St. John, Antigua, Grand Cayman, Saint Maarten, Dominica, St. Kitts, Martinique, and St. Lucia. Fort Lauderdale is the point of embarkation for all three of the ships that make stops in The Bahamas.

• **Norwegian Cruise Line** (© 800/327-7030 or 305/436-4000; www.ncl.com): NCL offers 3-night Miami–Bahamas transits aboard the *Norwegian Sea,* visiting Nassau and either Great Stirrup Key (NCL's private island) or Key West. Generally inexpensive and emphasizing sports, NCL's ships attract a lot of active travelers in the 24-to-45 age bracket. Activities and cuisine are routine but adequate enough for short cruises. NCL's largest ship and corporate symbol (the *Norway,* built in 1961 as the famous *France*) offers better amenities and services but features only one Bahamian stopover (at Great Stirrup Cay) as part of 7-night eastern Caribbean cruises.

• **Royal Caribbean International** (© 800/327-6700 or 305/539-6000; www.royalcaribbean.com): Things run smoothly on this middle-of-the-road cruise line, which has a less frenetic atmosphere than that aboard Carnival's megaships but is more lively than Celebrity or Holland America. The company is well-run, and there are enough on-board activities to suit virtually any taste and age level. Though accommodations and facilities are more than adequate, they're not upscale, and cabins aboard some of the line's older vessels tend to be a bit more cramped than the industry norm. RCCL's fleet comprises some of the largest cruise ships in the world. The *Majesty of the* Seas sails from Miami, and the *Sovereign of the* Seas is launched from Port Canaveral. The 4-night cruises call at Nassau, Key West, and a private Bahamian island, CocoCay, which RCCL has loaded with facilities for beach barbecues and water sports. Three-night loops follow almost the same itinerary, calling at Nassau and CocoCay, but without a stopover in Key West. Other RCCL ships, such as *Enchantment of the Seas* and *Explorer of the Seas,* stop occasionally in either Nassau or Coco Cay as part of longer 7-day itineraries through either the eastern or western Caribbean.

11 Planning Your Trip Online

With a mouse, a modem, and a certain do-it-yourself determination, Internet users can tap into the same travel-planning databases that were once accessible only to travel agents. Sites such as **Travelocity, Expedia,** and **Orbitz** allow consumers to comparison shop for airfares, book flights, learn of last-minute bargains, and reserve hotel rooms and rental cars.

But don't fire your travel agent just yet. Although online booking sites offer tips and hard data to help you bargain shop, they cannot endow you with the hard-earned experience that makes a seasoned, reliable travel agent an invaluable resource, even in the Internet age. And for consumers with a complex itinerary, a trusty travel agent is still the best way to arrange the most direct flights to and from the best airports.

Still, there's no denying the Internet's emergence as a powerful tool in researching and plotting travel time. The benefits of researching your trip online can be well worth the effort:

• **Last-minute specials,** known as "E-savers," such as weekend deals or Internet-only fares, are offered by airlines to fill empty seats. Most of these are announced on Tuesday or Wednesday and must be purchased online. They are only valid for travel that weekend, but some can be booked weeks or months in advance. Sign up for weekly e-mail alerts at airline websites (see page 39) or check mega-sites that compile comprehensive lists of E-savers, such as Smarter Living (smarterliving.com) or WebFlyer (www.webflyer.com).

• Some sites will send you **e-mail notification** when a cheap fare becomes available to your favorite destination. Some will also tell you when fares to a particular destination are lowest.

• The best of the travel planning sites are now **highly personalized;** they track your frequent-flier miles, and store your seating and meal preferences, tentative itineraries, and credit-card information, letting you plan trips or check agendas quickly.

• All major airlines offer **incentives**— bonus frequent-flier miles, Internet-only discounts, sometimes even free cellphone rentals—when you purchase online or buy an e-ticket.

• Advances in mobile technology provide business travelers and other frequent travelers with **the ability to check flight status, change plans, or get specific**

directions from handheld computing devices, mobile phones, and pagers. Some sites will e-mail or page a passenger if a flight is delayed.

TRAVEL PLANNING & BOOKING SITES

The best travel planning and booking sites cast a wide net, offering domestic and international flights, hotel and rental-car bookings, plus news, destination information, and deals on cruises and vacation packages. Keep in mind that free (one-time) registration is often required for booking. Because several airlines are no longer willing to pay commissions on tickets sold by online travel agencies, be aware that these online agencies will either charge a $10 surcharge if you book a ticket on that carrier—or neglect to offer those air carriers' offerings.

The sites in this section are not intended to be a comprehensive list, but rather a discriminating selection to get you started. Recognition is given to sites based on their content value and ease of use and is not paid for—unlike some website rankings, which are based on payment. Remember: This is a press-time snapshot of leading websites—some undoubtedly will have

evolved or moved by the time you read this.

- **Travelocity** (www.travelocity.com or www.frommers.travelocity.com) and **Expedia** (www.expedia.com) are the most longstanding and reputable sites, each offering excellent selections and searches for complete vacation packages. Travelers search by destination and dates coupled with how much they are willing to spend.

- The latest buzz in the online travel world is about **Orbitz** (www.orbitz.com), a site launched by United, Delta, Northwest, American, and Continental airlines. It shows all possible fares for your desired trip, offering fares lower than those available through travel agents. (Stay tuned: At press time, travel-agency associations were waging an antitrust battle against this site.)

- **Qixo** (www.qixo.com) is another powerful search engine that allows you to search for flights and hotel rooms on 20 other travel-planning sites (such as Travelocity) at once. Qixo sorts results by price, after which you can book your travel directly through the site.

 Frommers.com: The Complete Travel Resource

For an excellent travel planning resource, we highly recommend **Arthur Frommer's Budget Travel Online** (www.frommers.com). We're a little biased, of course, but we guarantee you'll find the travel tips, reviews, monthly vacation giveaways, and online-booking capabilities thoroughly indispensable. Among the special features are: **"Ask the Expert"** bulletin boards, where Frommer's authors answer your questions via online postings; **Arthur Frommer's Daily Newsletter**, for the latest travel bargains and inside travel secrets; and Frommer's **Destinations archive**, where you'll get expert travel tips, hotel and dining recommendations, and advice on the sights to see for more than 200 destinations around the globe Once your research is done, the **Online Reservation System** (www.frommers.com/booktravelnow) takes you to Frommer's favorite sites for booking your vacation at affordable prices.

SMART E-SHOPPING

The savvy traveler is one armed with good information. Here are a few tips to help you navigate the Internet successfully and safely.

- **Know when sales start.** Last-minute deals may vanish in minutes. If you have a favorite booking site or airline, find out when last-minute deals are released to the public. (For example, Southwest's specials are posted every Tuesday at 12:01am Central Time.)
- **Shop around.** Compare results from different sites and airlines—and against a travel agent's best fare, if you can. If possible, try a range of times and alternate airports before you make a purchase.
- **Follow the rules of the trade.** Book in advance, and choose an off-peak time and date if possible. Some sites will tell you when fares to a particular destination tend to be cheapest.
- **Stay secure.** Book only through secure sites (some airline sites are not secure). Look for a key icon (Netscape) or a padlock (Internet Explorer) at the bottom of your browser before you enter credit card information or other personal data.
- **Avoid online auctions.** Sites that auction airline tickets and frequent-flier miles are the number-one perpetrators of Internet fraud, according to the National Consumers League.
- **Maintain a paper trail.** If you book an e-ticket, print out a confirmation, or write down your confirmation number, and keep it safe and accessible—or your trip could be a virtual one!

ONLINE TRAVELER'S TOOLBOX

Veteran travelers usually carry some essential items to make their trips easier. Following is a selection of online tools to bookmark and use.

- **Visa ATM Locator** (www.visa.com/pd/atm) or **MasterCard ATM Locator** (www.mastercard.com/atm). Find ATMs in hundreds of cities in the U.S. and around the world.
- **Foreign Languages for Travelers** (www.travlang.com). Learn basic terms in more than 70 languages and click on any underlined phrase to hear what it sounds like. *Note:* Free audio software and speakers are required.
- **Intellicast** (www.intellicast.com). Weather forecasts for all 50 states and cities around the world. *Note:* temperatures are in Celsius for many international destinations.
- **Mapquest** (www.mapquest.com). This best of the mapping sites lets you choose a specific address or destination, and in seconds, it will return a map and detailed directions.
- **Cybercafes.com** (www.cybercafes.com) or **Net Café Guide** (www.netcafeguide.com/mapindex.htm). Locate Internet cafes at hundreds of locations around the globe. Catch up on your e-mail and log onto the Web for a few dollars per hour.
- **Universal Currency Converter** (www.xe.net/currency). See what your dollar or pound is worth in more than 100 other countries.
- **U.S. State Department Travel Warnings** (www.travel.state.gov/travel_warnings.html). Reports on places where health concerns or unrest might threaten U.S. travelers. It also lists the locations of U.S. embassies around the world.

12 Getting Around

If your final destination is Paradise Island, Freeport, or Nassau (Cable Beach) and you plan to fly, you'll have little trouble in reaching your destination. However, if you're heading for one of the Out Islands, you face more exotic choices, not only of airplanes but also of other means of transport, including a mail boat, the traditional connecting link in days of yore.

As mentioned, each section on one of the Out Island chains has specific transportation information, but in the meantime, we'll give you a general overview.

See also section 13, "Chartering a Boat," below.

BY PLANE

The national airline of The Bahamas, **Bahamasair** (© 800/222-4262; www.bahamasair.com), serves 19 airports on 12 Bahamian islands, including Abaco, Andros, Cat Island, Eleuthera, Long Island, and San Salvador. Many of the Out Islands have either airports or airstrips, or are within a short ferry ride's distance of one. You can usually make connections to these smaller islands from Nassau.

BY MAIL BOAT

Before the advent of better airline connections, the traditional way of exploring the Out Islands—in fact, about the only way unless you had your own craft—was by mail boat. This service is still available, but it's recommended only for those who have lots of time and a sense of adventure. You may ride with cases of rum, oil drums, crawfish pots, live chickens, or even an occasional piano.

The boats—19 of them composing the "Post Office Navy"—under the direction of the Bahamian Chief of Transportation are often fancifully colored, high-sided, and somewhat clumsy in appearance, but the little motor vessels chug along, serving the 30 inhabited islands of The Bahamas. Schedules can be thrown off by weather and other causes, but most morning mail boats depart from Potter's Cay (under the Paradise Island Bridge in Nassau) or from Prince George Wharf. The voyages last from 4½ hours to most of a day, sometimes even overnight. Check the schedule of the particular boat you wish to travel on with the skipper at the dock in Nassau.

This is a cheap way to go. Many of the boats offer two classes of passenger accommodations, first and second. In first class you get a bunk bed; in second you may be entitled only to deck space. Actually, the bunk beds are usually reserved for the seasick, but first-class passengers sit in a fairly comfortable enclosed cabin, at least on the larger boats.

For information about mail boats to the Out Islands, contact the **Dockmasters Office** in Nassau, under the Paradise Island Bridge on Potter's Cay (© 242/393-1064).

BY TAXI

Once you've reached your destination, you'll find that taxis are plentiful in the Nassau/Cable Beach/Paradise Island area and in the Freeport/Lucaya area on Grand Bahama Island. These cabs, for the most part, are metered. See "Getting Around" in the chapters on each island that follow for further details.

In the Out Islands, however, it's not so easy. In general, taxi service is available at all air terminals, at least if those air terminals have "port of entry" status. They are also available near most marinas.

Taxis are usually shared, often with the local residents. Out Island taxis aren't metered, so you must negotiate the fare before you get in. (Expect to pay a rate of around $20 per hour.) Cars are often old and badly maintained, so be prepared for a bumpy ride over some rough roads if you've selected a particularly remote hotel.

BY RENTAL CAR

Many travelers don't really need to rent a car in The Bahamas, especially those who are coming for a few days of soaking in the sun at their resort's own beach. In Nassau and Freeport, you can easily rely on public transportation or taxis. In some of the Out Islands, there are a few car-rental companies, but most rental cars are unusually expensive and in poor condition (the roads are often in the same bad state as the rental cars).

Most visitors need transportation only from the airport to their hotel; perhaps you can arrange an island tour later, and an expensive private car won't be necessary. Your hotel can always arrange a taxi for you if you want to venture out.

You may decide that you want a car to explore beyond the tourist areas of New Providence Island, and you're very likely to want one on Grand Bahama Island. As for the Out Islands, turn to the relevant "Getting Around" sections of the chapters that follow to determine if you'll want a car (you may want one on Eleuthera, or to explore on Great Abaco Island); perhaps you'll stay put at your resort but rent a car for only 1 day of exploring.

The major U.S. car-rental companies operate in The Bahamas, but not on all the remote islands. There are also a handful of local car-rental companies, some of which may charge a few dollars less. We always prefer to do business with one of the major firms if they're present because you can call ahead and reserve from home via a toll-free number; they tend to offer better-maintained vehicles; and it's easier to resolve any disputes after the fact. Call **Budget** (℡ **800/ 472-3325;** www.budgetrentacar.com), **Hertz** (℡ **800/654-3001;** www. hertz.com), **Dollar** (℡ **800/800-4000;** www.dollarcar.com), or **Avis** (℡ **800/331-1084;** www.avis.com). Budget rents only in Nassau. Liability insurance is compulsory.

Road rules are much the same as those in the U.S., but *drive on the left.*

"Petrol" is easily available in Nassau and Freeport, though quite expensive. In the Out Islands, where the cost of gasoline is likely to vary from island to island, you should plan your itinerary based on where you'll be able to get fuel. The major towns of the islands have service stations. You should have no problems on New Providence or Grand Bahama Island unless you start out with a nearly empty tank.

Visitors may drive with their home driver's license for up to 3 months. For longer stays, you'll need to secure a Bahamian driver's license.

As you emerge at one of the major airports, including those of Nassau (New Providence) and Freeport (Grand Bahama Island), you can pick up island maps that are pretty good for routine touring around those islands. However, if you plan to do extensive touring in the Out Islands, you should go first to a bookstore in either Nassau or Freeport and ask for a copy of *Atlas of The Bahamas,* sponsored by the Ministry of Education in Nassau. It provides touring routes (outlined in red) through all the major Out Islands. Once you arrive on these remote islands, it may be hard to obtain maps.

13 Chartering a Boat

For those who can afford it, this is the most luxurious way to see The Bahamas. On your private boat, you can island-hop at your convenience. Well-equipped marinas are on every major island and many cays. There are designated ports of entry at Great Abaco (Marsh Harbor), Andros, the Berry Islands, Bimini, Cat Cay, Eleuthera, Great Exuma, Grand Bahama Island (Freeport/Lucaya), Great Inagua, New Providence (Nassau), Ragged Island, and San Salvador.

Vessels must check with Customs at the first port of entry and receive a cruising clearance permit to The Bahamas. Carry it with you and return it at the official port of departure.

You might buy *The Yachtsman's Guide to The Bahamas* (Tropic Isle Publishers), the only guide covering the entire Bahamas and Turks and Caicos islands. Copies of the book are available at major marine outlets and bookstores, and by mail direct from the publisher for $39.95, U.S. postpaid: Tropic Isle Publishers, Inc., P.O. Box 610938, North Miami, FL 33261-0938 (© **305/893-4277**).

Experienced sailors and navigators, with a sea-wise crew, can charter "**bareboat**" (a rental with a fully equipped boat but with no captain or crew). You're on your own, and you'll have to prove you can handle it before you're allowed to take out such a craft. Even if you are your own skipper, you may want to take along an experienced yachtsperson familiar with local waters, which may be tricky in some places.

Four to twelve people often charter yachts varying from 50 to more than 100 feet and split the cost. The Bahamas offers some of the most beautiful and romantic cruising grounds in the world, especially around such island chains as the Exumas, the Abacos, and Eleuthera.

Most yachts are rented on a weekly basis, with a fully stocked bar, plus equipment for fishing and water sports. People taking bareboat charters can save money and select menus more suited to their tastes by doing their own provisioning.

For information about bareboat charter companies, check with **Abaco Bahamas Charters** (© **800/626-5690,** or 242/366-0131), the **Moorings at Conch Inn** (© **800/535-7289,** or 242/367-4000), **Charter Cats of The Bahamas** (© **800/446-9441**), or **Tropical Diversions** (© **800/343-7256**).

14 The Active Vacation Planner

The more than 700 islands in the Bahamian archipelago (fewer than 30 of which are inhabited) are surrounded by warm, clear waters that are ideal for fishing, sailing, and scuba diving. (Detailed recommendations and the costs of these activities are previewed under the individual destinations listings.) The country's perfect weather and its many cooperative local entrepreneurs allow easy access to more than 30 sports throughout the islands. For sports-related information about any of the activities listed below, call © **800/32-SPORT.**

WATER SPORTS

FISHING The shallow waters between the hundreds of cays and islands of The Bahamas are some of the most fertile fishing grounds in the world. Even waters where marine traffic is relatively congested have yielded impressive catches. Grouper, billfish, wahoo, tuna, and dozens of other species thrive in Bahamian waters, and dozens of charter boats are available for deep-sea fishing. Reef fishing, either from small boats or from shorelines, is popular everywhere, with grouper, snapper, and barracuda being the most commonly caught species. Specialists, however, or serious amateurs of the sport, often head for any of the following destinations. The island of **Bimini** is known as the "Big-Game Fishing Capital of the World." Here anglers can successfully hunt for swordfish, sailfish, and marlin, and there are frequent tournaments (see the "Calendar of Events," earlier in this chapter). Bimini maintains its own Hall of Fame, where many a proud angler has had his or her catch honored. World records for the size of catches don't seem to last long here; they are usually quickly surpassed.

Walker's Cay in the Abacos and **Chub Cay** in the Berry Islands are famous for both deep-sea and shore fishing. Some anglers return to these cays year after year. Grouper, jacks, and snapper are plentiful. Even spearfishing without scuba gear is common and popular.

Andros boasts the world's best bonefishing. Bonefish (also known as "gray fox") are medium-size fish that feed in shallow, well-lit waters. Known as some of the most tenacious fish in the world, they struggle ferociously against anglers who pride themselves on using light lines from shallow-draft boats. **Andros Island Bonefishing Club** in North Andros (✆ 242/368-5167) specializes in fishing adventures off some of the most remote and sparsely populated coastlines in the country.

SAILING The Bahamas, rivaled only by the Virgin Islands and the Grenadines, is one of the top yachting destinations in the Atlantic. Its more than 700 islands and well-developed marinas provide a spectacular and practical backdrop for sailing enthusiasts, and there are frequent regattas (see the "Calendar of Events," earlier in this chapter). The mini-archipelago of the **Abacos** is called "The Sailing Capital of the World." You might think it deserves the title until you've sailed the **Exumas,** which we think are even better.

Don't be dismayed if you don't own a yacht. All sizes and types of crafts, from dinghies to blue-water cruisers, are available for charter, and crew and captain are optional. If your dreams involve experiencing the seagoing life for an afternoon or less, many hotels offer sightseeing cruises aboard catamarans or glass-bottomed boats, often with the opportunity to snorkel or swim in the wide-open sea.

The Abacos have many marinas. The best arrangements for boating can be made at **Abaco Bahamas Charters** (✆ 800/626-5690 or 242/366-0131) and at **The Moorings** (✆ 800/535-7289 or 242/367-4000). In the Exumas it's difficult to rent boats, because most yachties arrive with their own. However, take a chance and contact **Happy People Marina** (✆ 242/355-2008) on Staniel Cay.

SCUBA DIVING The unusual marine topography of The Bahamas offers an astonishing variety of options for divers. Throughout the more than 700 islands, there are innumerable reefs, drop-offs, coral gardens, caves,

---

⌒Tips A Warning to Poachers

It is illegal to take sponges or turtles from Bahamian waters. The Ministry of Agriculture, Fisheries, and Local Government also keeps a close eye on crayfish (spiny lobster) and prohibits the export of conch meat. Stone crab cannot be caught within 2 miles off Bimini or Grand Bahama.

Moments **Meet Flipper**

Oceanic Society Expeditions, Fort Mason Center, Building E, San Francisco, CA 94123 (© **800/326-7491** or 415/441-1106; www.oceanicsociety.org), organizes research trips involving close encounters with dolphins in the wild in the waters of The Bahamas.

---

and shipwrecks. In many locations, you may feel that you are the first human ever to explore the site. Since fewer than 30 of the Bahamian islands are inhabited, you can usually dive in pristine and uncrowded splendor. **Andros Island** boasts the third-largest barrier reef in the world. Chub Cay in the Berry islands, and Riding Rock, San Salvador, also offer premium spots to take a plunge in an underwater world teeming with aquatic life. The intricate layout of the Exumas includes virtually every type of underwater dive site, very few of which have ever been explored. The Abacos, famous for its yachting, and the extensive reefs off the coast of Freeport are also fabulous dive sites.

Freeport, incidentally, is home to the country's most famous and complete diving operation, **UNEXSO** (© **800/992-DIVE**). It offers an 18-foot-deep training tank where divers can work toward certification, and the popular "Dolphin Experience," in which visitors are allowed to pet, swim, snorkel, and dive with these remarkable animals.

The **Turks and Caicos** islands have some of the world's most magnificent underwater life. For years, divers and snorkelers have enjoyed immersing themselves in the countless varieties of brilliant coral and fish that thrive within TCI's nearly 500-mile, pristine reef system.

You can also easily learn to dive for the first time in The Bahamas. Lots of Bahamian hotels offer resort courses for novices, usually enabling a beginner to dive with a guide after several hours of instruction. You'll probably start out in the swimming pool for your initial instruction, then go out with a guide from the beach. A license proving the successful completion of a pre-designated program of scuba study is legally required for solo divers. Many resort hotels and dive shops offer the necessary training as part of a 5-day training course. Participants who successfully complete the courses are awarded PADI- or NAUI-approved licenses.

For useful information, check out the website of the Professional Association of Diving Instructors (PADI) at www.padi.com. You'll find a description of the best dive sites and a list of PADI-certified dive operators. *Rodale's Scuba Diving Magazine* also has a helpful website at www.scubadiving.com. Both sites list dive-package specials and display gorgeous color photos of some of the most beautiful dive spots in the world.

SEA KAYAKING If you want to explore the pristine Exumas National Land and Sea Park, a spectacular natural area consisting of 365 mostly uninhabited cays that may be more impressive than anything in the Caribbean, **Ecosummer Expeditions** is your best bet. They'll take you on sea-kayaking itineraries that will allow you lots of time to enjoy the area's white-sand beaches and numerous reefs. You can also snorkel along the way. A 1-week trip leaving from Nassau costs $1,445. The 2-week trip leaves from George Town, the capital of the Exumas, and goes for $2,095. For more information, call **Ecosummer Expeditions,** P.O. Box 1765, Clearwater, BC,

Canada V0E 1NO (② **800/465-8884**; www.ecosummer.com).

Another sea-kayaking outfit is **Ibis Tours**. They also take you through the Exumas, at $1,595 for an 8-day adventure, depending on the time of year. The trips include guides, all meals, the boat, equipment (including camping gear), and waterproof bags. The kayaks come with sails to shorten travel time and to make paddling easier. To make reservations, contact **Ibis Tours** at 5798 Sunpoint Circle, Boynton Beach, FL 33437 (② **800/525-9411;** www.ibistours.com). See chapter 9 for more information.

SNORKELING WITH THE PROS
Jean-Michel Cousteau, son of famed oceanographer Jacques Cousteau, has teamed up with the Out Islands of The Bahamas, American Airlines/American Eagle, and US Divers to create a snorkeling program that emphasizes marine conservation and education. Jean-Michel Cousteau's Out Islands Snorkeling Adventures, located in eight resorts on eight islands, takes visitors through Bahamian reefs from $99 a trip. The fee includes instruction, two guided tours, snorkeling gear, waterproof ID charts and reference books, and a T-shirt. They even send you a set of snorkeling gear after you've returned home. For more information, contact **The Bahamas Out Island Promotion Board** at ② **800/688-4752,** or 954/359-8099 in Fort Lauderdale.

OTHER ACTIVITIES
BIKE & SCOOTER RENTALS
Most biking or scooter riding is done either on New Providence Island (Nassau) or on Grand Bahama Island; both have relatively flat terrain. Biking is best on Grand Bahama Island because it's bigger, with better roads and more places to go. Getting around New Providence Island is relatively easy once you're out of the congestion of Nassau and Cable Beach. In Nassau many hotels will rent you a bike or motor scooter.

On Grand Bahama Island, you can rent bikes at most big hotels (see chapter 5, for phone numbers and addresses of hotels). You can also rent motor scooters starting at about $35 per day. The tourist office at Freeport/Lucaya will outline on a map the best biking routes.

In the Out Islands, roads are usually too bumpy and potholed for much serious biking or scooter riding. Bike-rental places are almost non-existent unless your hotel has some vehicles.

GOLF   The richest pickings are on Grand Bahama Island, home to three courses that have been designated as potential PGA tour stops. The **Bahamia** boasts two challenging and spectacular courses: the Princess Ruby and the Princess Emerald, site of The Bahamas National Open. The big news here is the opening of **The Reef Course,** the first new golf course to open in The Bahamas since 1969. Designed by Robert Trent Jones Jr., it features water along 13 of its 18 holes. The oldest course on Grand Bahama Island is the **Lucayan Park Golf & Country Club,** a heavily wooded course with elevated greens and numerous water hazards designed for precision golf. See chapter 5, for more information, and also refer to "The Best Golf Courses," in chapter 1.

Quality golf in The Bahamas, however, is not restricted to Grand Bahama Island. The **Cable Beach Golf Course,** part of the Radisson Cable Beach Hotel on New Providence, is the oldest golf course in the country, although not as good as the **South Ocean Golf Resort** in the secluded southern part of New Providence. The widely publicized **Ocean Club Golf Club** has unusual obstacles—a lion's den and a windmill—which have challenged the skill of both Gary Player and Jack Nicklaus. It also boasts the world's largest sand trap. After restoration, the course opened in 2000. See chapters 3 and 4, for more information, and also refer to "The Best Golf Courses," in chapter 1.

Golf is also available at a course in the Abacos on Treasure Cay. The design is challenging, with many panoramic water views and water obstacles. See chapter 7, for more information.

HIKING The Bahamas isn't the greatest destination for serious hikers. The best hiking is on Grand Bahama Island, especially in **Lucayan National Park,** which spreads across 40 acres and is located some 20 miles from Lucaya. A large map at the entrance to the park outlines the trails. The park is riddled with trails and elevated walkways. The highlight of the park is what may be the largest underground cave system in the world, some 7 miles long. Spiral steps let you descend into an eerie underground world.

Also on Grand Bahama Island, the **Rand Memorial Nature Centre** is the second-best place for hiking. It offers some 100 wooded acres that you can explore on your own or with a tour guide. A half mile of winding trails acquaints you with the flora and fauna that call Grand Bahama home, everything from a native boa constrictor to the Cuban emerald hummingbird, whose favorite food is the nectar of the hibiscus.

HORSEBACK RIDING The best riding possibilities are at Pinetree Stables on Grand Bahama Island (© 242/373-3600). Its beach rides are especially interesting. Both trail and beach rides are offered two times a day, Tuesday through Sunday; be sure to book rides a few days in advance. See chapter 5, for more information.

Virtually the only place on New Providence Island (Nassau) that offers horseback riding is **Happy Trails Stables,** Carl Harbour (© 242/362-1820), which features both morning and afternoon trail rides and requires a reservation. These tours include transportation to and from your hotel. The trail rides are guided through the woods and along the beach. See chapter 3, for more information.

Horseback riding is hardly a passion on the other islands.

TENNIS Most tennis courts are part of large resorts and are usually free during the day for the use of registered guests. Charges are imposed to light the courts at night. Non-guests are welcome but are charged a player's fee; they should call in advance to reserve. Larger resorts usually offer on-site pro shops and professional instructors. Court surfaces range from clay or asphalt to such technologically advanced substances as Flexipave and Har-Tru.

New Providence, with more than 80 tennis courts, wins points for offering the greatest number of choices. At least 21 of these lie on Paradise Island. Also noteworthy are the many well-lit courts at the Radisson Cable Beach Hotel. See chapters 3 and 4. After New Providence, Grand Bahama has the largest number of courts available for play—almost 40 in all. See chapter 5. Within the Out Islands, tennis courts are available on Eleuthera, the Abacos, the Berry Islands, and the Exumas. See chapters 6, 7, 8, and 9, for more information.

15 Tips on Accommodations

The Bahamas offers a wide selection of accommodations, ranging from small private guest houses to large luxury resorts. Hotels vary in size and facilities, from deluxe (offering room service, sports, swimming pools, entertainment, and so on) to fairly simple inns.

There are package deals galore, and they are always cheaper than "rack rates." (A rack rate is what an

What the Hotel Symbols Mean

As you're shopping around for your hotel, you may see the following terms used:

- **AP (American Plan):** Includes three meals a day (sometimes called full board or full pension).
- **EP (European Plan):** Includes only the room—no meals.
- **MAP (Modified American Plan):** Sometimes called half board or half pension, this room rate includes breakfast and dinner (or lunch instead of dinner if you prefer).

individual pays if he or she literally walks in from the street; these are the rates we've listed in the chapters that follow, though you can almost always do better at the big resorts.) So it's always good to go to a reliable travel agent to find out what, if anything, is available in the way of a land-and-air package before booking into a particular accommodation. See section 8, "Package Deals," earlier in this chapter, for details on a number of companies that usually offer good-value packages to The Bahamas.

There is no rigid classification of hotel properties in the islands. The word "deluxe" is often used (or misused) when "first class" might have been a more appropriate term. "First class" itself often isn't. For that and other reasons, we've presented fairly detailed descriptions of the properties so that you'll get an idea of what to expect. However, even in the deluxe and first-class resorts and hotels, don't expect top-rate service and efficiency. "Things," as they are called in the islands, don't seem to work as well here as they do in certain fancy resorts of California, Florida, or Europe. When you go to turn on the shower, sometimes you get water and sometimes you don't. You may even experience power failures.

The winter season in The Bahamas runs roughly from the middle of December to the middle of April, and hotels charge their highest prices during this peak period. Winter is generally the dry season in the islands, but there can be heavy rainfall regardless of the time of year. During the winter months, make reservations 2 months in advance if you can. You can't book early enough if you want to travel over Christmas or in February.

The off-season in The Bahamas—roughly from mid-April to mid-December (although this varies from hotel to hotel)—amounts to a sale. In most cases, hotel rates are slashed a startling 20% to 60%. It's a bonanza for cost-conscious travelers, especially for families who can travel in the summer. Be prepared for very strong sun, though, plus a higher chance of rain. Also note that hurricane season runs through the summer and fall.

THE ALL-INCLUSIVES

A hugely popular option in Jamaica, the all-inclusive resort hotel concept finally has a foothold in The Bahamas. At most resorts, everything is included—sometimes even drinks. You get your room and all meals, plus entertainment and many water sports (although some cost extra). Some people find the cost of this all-inclusive holiday cheaper than if they'd paid individually for each item, and some simply appreciate knowing in advance what their final bill will be.

The first all-inclusive resort hotel in The Bahamas was **Club Med** (© **800/258-2633**) at its property on Paradise Island. This is not a swinging-singles kind of place; it's popular with everybody from honeymooners to families with kids along. There's another mammoth Club Med at Governor's Harbour on Eleuthera. Families with kids like it a lot here, and the resort also attracts scuba divers. There's a third branch in San Salvador, in the southern Bahamas, which has more of a luxurious hideaway atmosphere.

The biggest all-inclusive of them all, **Sandals** (*©* **800/SANDALS**), came to The Bahamas in 1995 on Cable Beach. This Jamaican company is now walking its sandals across the Caribbean, having established firm beachheads in Ocho Rios, Montego Bay, and Negril. The most famous of the all-inclusives (but not necessarily the best), it caters only to male-female couples, having long ago rescinded its initial policy of "Any two people in love."

RENTAL VILLAS & VACATION HOMES

You might rent a big villa, a good-size apartment in someone's condo, or even a small beach cottage (more accurately called a cabana).

Private apartments come with or without maid service (ask up front exactly what to expect). This is more of a no-frills option than the villas and condos. The apartments may not be in buildings with swimming pools, and they may not have a front desk to help you.

Many cottages or cabanas ideally open onto a beach, although others may be clustered around a communal swimming pool. Most of them are fairly simple, containing no more than a plain bedroom plus a small kitchen and bathroom. In the peak winter season, reservations should be made at least 5 or 6 months in advance.

VHR Worldwide (*©* **800/633-3284** or 201/767-9393) offers the most comprehensive portfolio of luxury villas, condominiums, resort suites, and apartments for rent not only in The Bahamas, but also in the Caribbean, Mexico, the United States, and Europe.

Hideaways International (*©* **800/843-4433** in the U.S., or 603/430-4433; www.hideaways.com) publishes *Hideaways Guide*, a 148-page pictorial directory of home rentals throughout the world, with full descriptions so you know what you're renting. Rentals range from cottages to staffed villas to whole islands! On most rentals you deal directly with owners. At condos and small resorts, Hideaways offers member discounts. Other services include specialty cruises, yacht charters, airline ticketing, car rentals, and hotel reservations. Annual membership is $129; a 4-month trial membership is $49.

Sometimes local tourist offices will also advise you on vacation-home rentals if you write or call them directly.

THE BAHAMIAN GUEST HOUSE

The guest house is where many Bahamians themselves stay when they're traveling in their own islands. In The Bahamas, however, and to a very limited extent in the Turks and Caicos, the term "guest house" can mean anything. Sometimes so-called guest houses are really like simple motels built around swimming pools. Others are small individual cottages, with their own kitchenettes, constructed around a main building in which you'll often find a bar and restaurant serving local food.

In the Out Islands of The Bahamas, the guest houses are pretty no-frills. Those we've recommended are clean, decent, and safe for families or single women. Many of these guest houses are very basic. Salt spray on metal or fabric takes a serious toll, and chipped paint is commonplace. Bathrooms can fall into the vintage category, and sometimes the water isn't heated—but when it's 85°F to 92°F outside, you don't need hot water.

On the other hand, some of these places are quite comfortable. Some are almost luxurious; and in addition to giving you the opportunity to live with a local family, they boast swimming pools, private bathrooms in all rooms, and air-conditioning.

 FAST FACTS: The Bahamas

American Express Representing American Express in The Bahamas is **Playtours,** on Shirley Street (between Charlotte and Parliament streets), Nassau (© 242/322-2931). Hours are 9am to 5pm Monday through Friday. The travel department is also open Saturday 9am to 1pm. If you present a personal check and an AmEx card, you can buy traveler's checks here.

Business Hours In Nassau, Cable Beach, and Freeport/Lucaya, commercial banking hours are 9:30am to 3pm Monday through Thursday, 9:30am to 5pm on Friday. Hours are likely to vary widely in the Out Islands. Ask at your hotel. Most government offices are open Monday through Friday from 9am to 5pm, and most shops are open Monday through Saturday from 9am to 5pm.

Camera & Film Purchasing film in Nassau/Paradise Island or Freeport/Lucaya is relatively easy if a little expensive. But stock up if you're going to some of the remote Out Islands and need a special kind of film.

Car Rentals See "Getting Around," earlier in this chapter. We do not recommend renting a car in The Bahamas.

Climate See "When to Go," earlier in this chapter.

Crime See "Safety," below.

Currency See "Money," earlier in this chapter.

Drug Laws Importing, possessing, or dealing in unlawful drugs, including marijuana, is a serious offense in The Bahamas, with heavy penalties. Customs officers may at their discretion conduct body searches for drugs or other contraband goods.

Drugstores Nassau and Freeport are amply supplied with pharmacies (see individual island listings). However, if you're traveling in the Out Islands, it is always best to carry your prescribed medication with you, since pharmacies are harder to find.

Electricity Electricity is normally 120 volts, 60 cycles, AC. American appliances are fully compatible; British or European appliances will need both converters and adapters.

Embassies & Consulates The U.S. embassy is on Queen Street, P.O. Box N-8197, Nassau (© 242/322-4753), and the Canadian consulate is on Shirley Street Shopping Plaza, Nassau (© 242/393-2123). The British High Commission is in the BITCO Building (third floor), East Street, Nassau (© 242/325-7471).

Emergencies Throughout The Bahamas, the number to call for a medical, dental, or hospital emergency is © 919 or 911. To report a fire, however, call © 411.

Gambling   Casino gambling is legal in The Bahamas for visitors. Bahamians and Bahamas residents are prohibited from gambling, although they can enter the casinos in the company of friends from elsewhere. Games offered are dice, roulette, blackjack, baccarat, wheel of fortune, and slot machines. There is a casino at Cable Beach on New Providence and one on Paradise Island, and there are two at Freeport/Lucaya on Grand Bahama Island.

Holidays   Public holidays observed in The Bahamas are New Year's Day, Good Friday, Easter Monday, Whitmonday (7 weeks after Easter), Labour Day (the first Friday in June), Independence Day (July 10), Emancipation Day (the first Monday in August), Discovery Day (October 12), Christmas, and Boxing Day (the day after Christmas). When a holiday falls on Saturday or Sunday, stores and offices are usually closed on the following Monday.

Hospitals   See "Health & Insurance," earlier in this chapter.

Language   In The Bahamas, locals speak English, but sometimes with a marked accent that provides the clue to their ancestry—African, Irish, Scottish, or whatever. English is also the official language of the Turks and Caicos.

Liquor Laws   Liquor is sold in liquor stores and various convenience stores; it's readily available though not sold on Sundays. The legal drinking age is 18.

Mail & Postage Rates   Obviously, you'll need Bahamian (not U.S.) postage stamps to send postcards and letters. Most of the kiosks selling postcards also sell the stamps you'll need to mail them, so you probably won't need to visit the post office. Sending a postcard or an airmail letter (up to a half-ounce in weight) from The Bahamas to anywhere outside its borders (including the U.S., Canada, and the U.K.) costs 45¢ and 65¢, respectively, with 65¢ charged for each additional half-ounce of weight. Postcards and letters mailed within The Bahamas to anywhere else within The Bahamas cost 20¢ and 25¢ per half-ounce, respectively.

Mail to and from the Out Islands is sometimes slow. Airmail may go by air to Nassau and by boat to its final destination. If a resort has a U.S. or Nassau address, it is preferable to use it.

Newspapers & Magazines   Three newspapers are circulated in Nassau and Freeport: the *Nassau Guardian,* the *Tribune,* and the *Freeport News.* Circulation in the Out Islands is limited and likely to be slow.

You can find the *New York Times, Wall Street Journal, USA Today, The Miami Herald, Times of London,* and *Daily Telegraph* at newsstands in your hotel and elsewhere in Nassau, usually the day after they are published but sometimes later. Such U.S. magazines as *Time* and *Newsweek* are flown in from the mainland.

Passports   See "Entry Requirements," earlier in this chapter.

Pets   You'll have to get a valid import permit to bring any animal into The Bahamas. Application for such a permit must be made in writing, accompanied by a $10 processing fee and a $5 fax fee, to the **Director of Agriculture,** Department of Agriculture, P.O. Box N-3028, Nassau, The Bahamas (© **242/325-7413**), at least 4 weeks in advance.

Police   In Nassau, call the police at © **919**; in Freeport/Lucaya, dial © **911**.

Safety   When going to Nassau (New Providence), Cable Beach, Paradise Island, or Freeport/Lucaya, exercise the kind of caution you would if visiting Miami. Whatever you do, if people peddling drugs approach you, steer clear of them as if they had the bubonic plague. Americans and other foreigners have gotten into a world of trouble in The Bahamas by purchasing illegal drugs.

Women, especially, should take caution if walking alone on the streets of Nassau after dark, particularly if those streets appear to be deserted. Pickpockets (often foreigners) work the crowded casino floors of both Paradise Beach and Cable Beach. See that your wallet, money, or other valuables are secured.

If you're driving a rental car, always make sure your car door is locked, and never leave possessions in view in an automobile. Don't leave valuables, such as cameras and purses, lying unattended on the beach while you go for a swim. If you have valuables with you, especially jewelry, don't leave them unguarded in hotel rooms. Many of the bigger hotels will provide safes. Keep your hotel-room doors locked. Bahamian tourist officials often warn visitors, "If you've got it, don't flaunt it." This will minimize the possibility of your becoming a victim of crime.

You're less likely to get mugged in the Out Islands, where life is generally more peaceful. There are some resort hotels that, even today, don't have locks on the doors.

However, drug dealers frequent many of the Out Islands, especially Bimini, because of their proximity to Miami. Take special care if you plan to vacation here. Transporting illegal drugs between Bimini and the Florida coastline is so commonplace that every day the boating set sees bales of marijuana floating on the water as they make the crossing. The marijuana is dumped when vessels are spotted by the coast guard as they approach American territorial waters.

Taxes   Departure tax is $20 ($22 from Grand Bahama Island) for visitors ages 7 and up. International airline and steamship tickets issued in The Bahamas are subject to a nominal tax, which is written into the cost of the ticket. An 8% tax is imposed on hotel bills. There is no sales tax in The Bahamas.

Telephone   Communications have improved recently, although some of the Out Islands are still difficult to reach. In recent years, virtually every hotel in The Bahamas seems to have installed a fax machine. Direct long-distance dialing between North America and Nassau, Grand Bahama, the Abacos, Andros, the Berry Islands, Bimini, Eleuthera, Harbour Island, Spanish Wells, the Exumas, and Stella Maris on Long Island is available.

To call The Bahamas from the U.S. or Canada, dial 1-242 plus the 7-digit local number. From the U.K., dial 001-242 plus the local 7-digit number.

To make a direct international call from The Bahamas to the U.S. or Canada, dial 1 plus the area code and local number. To call other countries, dial 011 plus the country code (the U.K. is 44, for example), the area code, and the local number.

For local calls within The Bahamas, simply dial the 7-digit number. To call from one island to another within The Bahamas, dial 1-242 and then the 7-digit local number.

Note that the old coin-operated phones are still prevalent and still swallow coins. Each local call costs 25¢; you can use either Bahamian or U.S. quarters. Those old phones, however, are gradually being replaced by phones that use calling cards (debit cards), similar in appearance to a credit card, that come in denominations of $5, $10, $20, and $50. They can be bought from any office of BATELCO (Bahamas Telephone Co.).

BATELCO's main branch is on Kennedy Drive, Nassau (© **242/302-7000**), although a popular local branch lies in the commercial heart of Nassau, on East Street off Bay Street.

To get **directory assistance** within The Bahamas, dial © **916.** To reach an international or a domestic operator within The Bahamas, dial **0.** There is no distinction made in The Bahamas between the two types of operators.

To reach the major international services of **AT&T,** dial © **800/CALLATT** from any phone, or head for any phone with AT&T or USA DIRECT written on the side of the booth. Picking up the handset will immediately connect you with an AT&T operator. These phones are often positioned beside cruise-ship docks to help passengers disembarking on shore leave for the day. The number for **Sprint** is © **800/389-2111; MCI** can be reached at © **800/888-8000** or 800/624-1000.

Time   Eastern Standard Time is used throughout The Bahamas, and daylight saving time is observed in the summer.

Tipping   Many establishments add a service charge, but it's customary to leave something extra if service has been especially fine. If you're not sure whether service has been included in your bill, don't be shy—ask.

Bellboys and porters, at least in the expensive hotels, expect a tip of $1 per bag. It's also customary to tip your maid at least $2 per day—more if she or he has performed special services such as getting a shirt or blouse laundered. Most service personnel, including taxi drivers, waiters, and the like, expect 15% (20% in deluxe restaurants).

Tourist Offices   See "Visitor Information," earlier in this chapter, and also specific island chapters.

Water   Technically, tap water is drinkable throughout The Bahamas, and most local residents are accustomed to its slightly brackish taste. We opt for bottled because it tastes better, and because your holiday isn't worth being shortchanged by a queasy stomach. In some outlying places, water might be in short supply. Such populous islands as New Providence, Grand Bahama, and Marsh Harbour have ample pure water, filtered and chlorinated. Resorts tend to filter and chlorinate their water more aggressively than most other establishments on any particular island, and bottled water is available at all tourist facilities, stores, and supermarkets.

On many of the Out Islands, rainfall is a main source of water for drinking and other household uses. This is caught and kept in the cisterns that most houses have. Water from cisterns is always potentially dangerous. To avoid problems, it is best to stick to bottled water.

Weddings   You might prefer a wedding beneath a palm tree instead of a snowbound setting in your hometown. Any large resort in The Bahamas, as well as the Ministry of Tourism's People-to-People program, will help you arrange the details. Contact the **Ministry of Tourism** at P.O. Box N-3701, Nassau, The Bahamas (© **242/302-2034**).

Here's what's required: Both of you must be in The Bahamas at the moment you apply for your wedding license, the price of which is $40. If both of you are single and U.S. citizens, you must obtain an affidavit to that effect from the U.S. embassy in Nassau. The price of this is $10; you'll have to appear in person with proof of identity, such as a passport. If it's applicable, you'll also need to show proof of divorce. If all of the above-mentioned requirements are met, you can be married anytime after 24 hours of your arrival in The Bahamas. No blood test is necessary.

3

New Providence
(Nassau/Cable Beach)

One million visitors a year have cast their vote: They want to visit Nassau, adjoining Cable Beach, or Paradise Island (which is covered separately in chapter 4). This is the center of all the action: the best shopping, the best entertainment, the most historic attractions—plus some of the best beaches in The Bahamas.

The Out Islands, which we'll explore in the chapters ahead, are for people who want peace and quiet or those who'd like to pursue certain sports, such as sailing, diving, or big-game fishing, more seriously.

The capital of The Bahamas, the historic city of Nassau is a 35-minute flight from Miami. Despite the development and the modern hotels, a laid-back tropical atmosphere still hangs over the city, and it still offers a good dose of colonial charm. The commercial and banking hub of The Bahamas, as well as a mecca for shoppers, Nassau lies on the north side of New Providence, which is 21 miles long and 7 miles wide at its greatest point.

Cable Beach, a stretch of sand just west of the city, is lined with luxury resorts—in fact, the Nassau/Cable Beach area has the largest tourist infrastructure in The Bahamas, though there's another concentration of luxury hotels on Paradise Island. (If you want to stay right on the sands, don't choose a hotel in downtown Nassau itself. Head for Cable Beach or Paradise Island. You can easily reach the beach from a base in Nassau, but it won't be right outside your window.)

When you're based in Nassau/Cable Beach, you have an array of water sports, golf, tennis, and plenty of duty-free shopping nearby—and that's not to mention those fine, powdery beaches. In addition, the resorts, restaurants, and beaches of Paradise Island, discussed in the next chapter, are just a short distance away. (Paradise Island, which lies just opposite Nassau, is connected to New Providence Island by a toll bridge that costs $2 for cars, 25¢ for pedestrians; there's also frequent ferry and water-taxi service between Nassau and Paradise Island.)

As the sun goes down, Cable Beach and Paradise Island heat up, offering fine dining, glitzy casinos, cabaret shows, moonlight cruises, dance clubs, and romantic evening strolls. (We'd confine that evening stroll to Cable Beach or Paradise Island, though, and not the streets of downtown Nassau, which can be dangerous at night.)

The shops might draw a lot more business than the museums, but no city in The Bahamas is as rich in history as Nassau. You can take a "royal climb" up the Queen's Staircase to Fort Fincastle. These 66 steps lead to a fort said to have been cut in the sandstone cliffs by slaves in the 1790s. Other Nassau attractions include Ardastra Gardens, which feature 5 acres of landscaping and more than 300 exotic birds, mammals, and reptiles. (Most popular are the trained pink flamingos that march for audiences daily to their trainer's commands.)

New Providence Island

Blue Lagoon
Salt Cay
Hanover Sound
Athol Island
East End Point
Solomon's Lighthouse
Yamacraw Beach

Paradise Island
Cabbage Beach
Blackbeard's Tower
Fort Montagu
Montagu Beach
Paradise Island Bridge

ATLANTIC OCEAN

Sandilands Village
St. Augustine Monastery
Prince Charles Ave.
Long Point

Nassau
Paradise Beach
Rawson Square
Nassau Harbour

Soldier Rd.
East St.
Blue Hill Rd.
South Beach

Silver Cay
Arawak Cay
Nassau St.
Fort Charlotte

Long Cay

Saunders Beach
Cable Beach Golf Course
Harrold Rd.
Harold Pond
Fire Trail Rd.
Bonefish Pond
Boat Harbour
Cay Point

Discovery (Balmoral) Island
Cable Beach
Lake Cunningham
Gladstone Farms
Gladstone Rd.
Carmichael Village

Delaporte Point
John F. Kennedy Dr.
Gov't Experimental Farm
Cow Pen Rd.
Bacardi

Rock Point
The Caves
Lake Killarney
Carmichael Rd.
Millars Sound

Gambier Village
West Bay St.
Coral Harbour Rd.
Coral Sound
Coral Harbour

Love Beach
Tropical Gardens
Nassau International Airport
Northwest Point
Old Fort Beach
Old Fort (Ruins)
Western Rd.
Mount Pleasant
South Ocean Golf & Beach Resort
Adelaide Rd.
Adelaide Village

Lighthouse Creek
Lyford Cay
Goulding Cay
Clifton Cay
Clifton Bay
Clifton Point
Clifton Plantation (Ruins)
Southwest Rd.

2 Miles
2 Kilometers
0
0

N

BIMINI ISLANDS
GREAT HARBOUR CAY
BERRY ISLANDS
PARADISE ISLAND
NEW PROVIDENCE ISLAND
Nassau
Tongue of the Ocean
ANDROS ISLAND
Miami
FLORIDA
Straits of Florida

50 mi
50 km
0
0

Airport
Lighthouse

63

It's surprising that Nassau has retained its overlay of British colonial charm despite its proximity to Florida. It hasn't become Americanized; despite all the new development, traffic, and cruise-ship crowds, Nassau's a long way from becoming another Miami. Stately old homes and public buildings still stand, even though they exist side by side with modern high-rise buildings and bland government buildings. Tropical foliage lines streets where horse-drawn surreys still trot by, taking visitors for leisurely town tours. Police officers in immaculate white starched jackets and colorful pith helmets still direct traffic on the main streets.

1 Orientation

ARRIVING

BY PLANE   Planes land at **Nassau International Airport** (℗ 242/377-7281), which lies 8 miles west of Nassau by Lake Killarney.

There is no bus service from the airport to Cable Beach, Nassau, or Paradise Island. Your hotel may provide airport transfers if you've made arrangements in advance; these are often included in package deals. There are any number of car-rental offices here if you plan to have a car while on New Providence Island (see "Getting Around," below, though we don't really think you need one).

You can also take a taxi to your hotel. From the airport to the center of Nassau, expect to pay around $14; from the airport to Cable Beach, $8; from the airport to Paradise Island, $23 to $25 including toll. Drivers expect to be tipped 15%, and some will remind you should you "forget."

BY CRUISE SHIP   Nassau is one of the busiest cruise-ship ports in the world. (For details on cruise-ship travel, see "Cruises," in chapter 2.) In recent years, Nassau has spent millions of dollars expanding its port so that now 11 cruise ships can pull into dock at one time! Facilities in Nassau, Cable Beach, and Paradise Island become extremely overcrowded when major cruise ships dock. You'll have to stake out your space on the beach, and you will find shops and attractions overrun with visitors.

Cruise ships dock near Rawson Square, the very heart of the city and the shopping area, and the best place to begin a tour of Nassau. Unless you want to go to one of the beach strips along Cable Beach or Paradise Island, you won't need a taxi. You can go on a shopping expedition near where you dock: The Straw Market is nearby, at Market Plaza; Bay Street (the main shopping artery) is also close; and the Nassau International Bazaar is at the intersection of Woodes Rogers Walk and Charlotte Street.

VISITOR INFORMATION

The Bahamas Ministry of Tourism maintains a **tourist information booth** at the Nassau International Airport in the Arrivals terminal (℗ **242/377-6806**). Hours are from 8:30am to 11:30pm daily.

Information can also be obtained from the Information Desk at the **Ministry of Tourism's Office,** Rawson Square (℗ **242/328-7810**), which is open Monday through Friday from 9am to 5:30pm.

THE LAY OF THE LAND

Most of the hotels in Nassau are city hotels and are not on the water. If you want to stay right on the sands, choose a hotel in Cable Beach or on Paradise Island (see chapter 4).

Frommer's Favorite New Providence Experiences

Listening to the Sounds of Goombay. At some local joint, you can enjoy an intoxicating beat and such island favorites as "Goin' Down Burma Road," "Get Involved," and "John B. Sail."

A Ride in a Horse-Drawn Surrey. If you'd like to see Nassau as the Duke of Windsor did when he was governor, consider this unique form of transportation. It's elegant, romantic, and nostalgic. Surreys await passengers at Rawson Square, in the exact center of Nassau.

A Glass-Bottom Boat Ride. Right in the middle of Nassau's harbor, numerous boats wait to take you through the colorful sea gardens off New Providence Island. In the teeming reefs offshore, you'll meet all sorts of sea creatures that inhabit this underwater wonderland.

An Idyllic Day on Blue Lagoon Island. It's like an old Hollywood fantasy of a tropical island. Located off the eastern end of Paradise Island, this Blue Lagoon has seven sandy beaches. Boats from Nassau Harbour take you there and back.

Rawson Square is the heart of Nassau, lying just a short walk from **Prince George Wharf,** where the big cruise ships, usually from Florida, berth. Here you'll see the Churchill Building, which contains the offices of the Bahamian prime minister along with other government ministries.

Busy **Bay Street,** the main shopping artery, begins on the south side of Rawson Square. This was the street of the infamous "Bay Street Boys," a group of rich, white Bahamians who once controlled all political and economic activity on New Providence.

On the opposite side of Rawson Square is **Parliament Square,** with a statue of a youthful Queen Victoria. Here are more government houses and the House of Assembly. These are Georgian and neo-Georgian buildings, some dating from the late 1700s.

The courthouse is separated by a little square from the **Nassau Public Library and Museum,** which opens onto Bank Lane. It was the former **Nassau Gaol.** South of the library, across Shirley Street, are the remains of the **Royal Victoria Hotel,** which opened the year the American Civil War was launched (1861) and once hosted blockade runners and Confederate spies.

A walk down Parliament Street leads to the post office, and philatelists may want to stop in, since some Bahamian stamps are collector's items.

Going south, moving farther away from the water, Elizabeth Avenue takes you to the **Queen's Staircase,** one of the major landmarks of Nassau, leading to Bennet's Hill and Fort Fincastle.

If you return to Bay Street, you'll discover the **Straw Market,** where you can buy all sorts of souvenirs. At the intersection of Charlotte Street is another major shopping emporium, the **Nassau International Bazaar.**

If you continue east along Bay Street, you'll reach Paradise Bridge, which leads to **Paradise Island.** If you go west on Bay Street, you'll come to West Bay Street, the road that will take you to **Cable Beach** and the airport.

In Nassau, and especially in the rest of The Bahamas, you will seldom, if ever, find street numbers on hotels or other businesses. Sometimes in the more remote places, you won't even find street names. Get directions before heading somewhere in particular. Of course, you can always ask along the way, as Bahamians tend to be very helpful.

2 Getting Around

BY TAXI

You can easily rely on taxis and skip renting a car. The rates for New Providence, including Nassau, are set by the government. Working meters are required in all taxis, although you will also find gypsy cabs without meters. When you get in, the fixed rate is $2.20, plus 30¢ for each additional quarter of a mile. Each passenger over two pays an extra $2. Taxis can also be hired at the hourly rate of $20 to $23 for a five-passenger cab. Luggage is carried at a cost of 50¢ per piece, although the first two pieces are transported free. The radio taxi call number is ℂ 242/323-5111 for Bahamas Transport. You can also try **Taxi Cab Union** at ℂ 242/323-4555. It's also easy to get a taxi at the airport or at one of the big hotels.

BY CAR

You don't need to rent a car. It's a lot easier to rely on taxis when you're ready to leave the beach and do a little exploring.

However, if you choose to drive anyway, perhaps for a day of touring the whole island, some of the biggest U.S. car-rental companies maintain branches at the airport, downtown, and on Paradise Island. **Avis** (ℂ 800/331-1212; www.avis.com) operates at the airport (ℂ 242/377-7121 locally), and also has branches at the cruise-ship docks at Bay Street and Marlborough Street, behind the British Colonial Hilton (ℂ 242/326-6380), and in the Paradise Island Shopping Plaza (ℂ 242/363-2061). **Budget Rent-a-Car** (ℂ 800/527-0700; www.budgetrentacar.com) has a branch at the airport (ℂ 242/377-9000), and another on Paradise Island, at Hurricane Hole next to the police station (ℂ 242/363-3095). **Dollar Rent-a-Car** (ℂ 800/800-4000, or 242/377-7231 locally; www.dollarcar.com) rents at the airport. **Hertz** (ℂ 800/654-3131; www.hertz.com) has an airport location (ℂ 242/377-8684) and is also in downtown Nassau at East Bay (ℂ 242/393-0871).

Drive on the left!

BY JITNEY

The least-expensive means of transport is by jitney—medium-size buses that leave from the downtown Nassau area to outposts on New Providence. The fare

---

(Moments A Surrey with a Fringe on Top

The elegant, traditional way to see Nassau is in a horse-drawn surrey—the kind with the fringe on top and a wilted hibiscus stuck in the straw hat shielding the horse from the sun. Before you get in, you should negotiate with the driver and agree on the price. The average charge is $5 per person for a 25-minute ride. The maximum load is three adults plus one or two children under the age of 12. The surreys are available daily from 9am to 4:30pm, except when the horses are resting (that's 1 to 3pm from May to October, and 1 to 2pm from November to April). You'll find the surreys at Rawson Square, off Bay Street.

> **Tips On Your Own Sturdy Feet**
>
> This is the only way to see Old Nassau, unless you rent a horse and carriage. All the major attractions and the principal stores are close enough to walk to. You can even walk to Cable Beach or Paradise Island, although it's a hike in the hot sun. Confine your walking to the daytime, and beware of pickpockets and purse-snatchers. In the evening, avoid walking the streets of downtown Nassau, where muggings occur.

is 75¢, and exact change is required. They operate daily from 6:30am to 7pm. Some hotels on Paradise Island and Cable Beach run their own free jitney service. Buses to the Cable Beach area leave from the Navy Lion Road depot. Buses to the eastern area depart from the Frederick Street North depot, and buses to the malls leave from Marlborough Street East.

BY BOAT

Water taxis operate daily from 9am to 5:30pm at 20-minute intervals between Paradise Island and Prince George Wharf at a round-trip cost of $2 per person. There is also ferry service from the end of Casuarina Drive on Paradise Island across the harbor to Rawson Square for a round-trip fare of $2 per person. The ferry operates daily from 9:30am to 4:15pm, with departures every half hour from both sides of the harbor.

BY SCOOTER OR BICYCLE

Lots of visitors like to rent mopeds to explore the island. Unless you're an experienced moped rider, stay on quiet roads until you feel at ease. (Don't start out in all the congestion on Bay Street!) Many hotels have rentals on the premises. If yours doesn't, try **Knowles** (© **242/356-0741**), outside the British Colonial Hotel, which rents scooters for $50 per day. Included in the rental price are insurance and mandatory helmets for both drivers and passengers.

 FAST FACTS: New Providence

American Express The local representative is **Playtours,** 303 Shirley St., between Charlotte and Parliament streets, Nassau (© **242/322-2931**). Hours are Monday through Friday from 9am to 5pm, Saturday 9am to 1pm.

Climate See "When to Go," in chapter 2.

Dentist Try the dental department of the **Princess Margaret Hospital** on Sands Road (© **242/322-2861**).

Doctor For the best service, use a staff member of the **Princess Margaret Hospital** on Sands Road (© **242/322-2861**).

Drugstores Try **Lowes Pharmacy,** Palm Dale (© **242/322-8594**), open Monday through Saturday from 8am to 6:30pm. They also have two branches: **Harbour Bay Shopping Center** (© **242/393-4813**), open Monday through Saturday 8am to 8:30pm and Sunday from 9am to 5pm; and **Town Center Mall** (© **242/325-6482**), open Monday through Saturday 10am to 9pm and Sunday from 10am to 6pm. Nassau has no late-night pharmacies.

Embassies & Consulates   See "Fast Facts: The Bahamas," in chapter 2.

Emergencies   For any major emergency, call ✆ **911** or ✆ **919**.

Eyeglass Repair   The **Optique Shoppe,** 22 Parliament St. at the corner of Shirley Street (✆ **242/322-3910**), is convenient to the center of Nassau. Hours are Monday through Friday from 9am to 5pm and on Saturday from 9am to noon.

Hospitals   The government-operated **Princess Margaret Hospital** on Sands Road (✆ **242/322-2861**) is one of the major hospitals in The Bahamas. The privately owned **Doctors Hospital,** 1 Collins Ave. (✆ **242/ 322-8411**), is the most modern private health-care facility in the region.

Information   See "Visitor Information," above.

Laundry & Dry Cleaning   The **Laundromat Superwash** (✆ **242/323-4018**), at the corner of Nassau Street and Boyd Road, offers coin-operated machines; it's open 24 hours a day, 7 days a week. In the same building is the **New Oriental Dry Cleaner** (✆ **242/323-7249**). Another dry cleaner a short drive north of the center of town is the **Jiffy Quality Cleaner** (✆ **242/323-6771**) at the corner of Blue Hill Road and Cordeaux Avenue.

Photographic Needs   The largest camera store in Nassau is **John Bull,** Bay Street (✆ **242/322-3328**), a block east of Rawson Square.

Police   Dial ✆ **911** or ✆ **919**.

Post Office   The **Nassau General Post Office,** at the top of Parliament Street on East Hill Street (✆ **242/322-3344**), is open Monday through Friday from 8:30am to 5:30pm and on Saturday from 9am to 1pm. Note that you can buy stamps from most postcard kiosks.

Safety   Avoid walking in downtown Nassau at night, where there are sometimes robberies and muggings. (Most tourists are never affected, and Nassau is certainly safer than Kingston, Jamaica, or Port of Spain, Trinidad, but better safe than sorry.) Cable Beach and Paradise Island are much safer places to be in the evening.

Taxes   There is no sales tax, though there is an 8% hotel tax. All visitors leaving The Bahamas pay a $15 departure tax.

3 Where to Stay

In the hotel descriptions that follow we've listed regular room prices or "rack rates," but these are simply for ease of comparison. They are likely to be accurate for smaller properties, but you can almost always do better at the larger hotels and resorts. *Read the section "Package Deals" in chapter 2 before you book a hotel separately from your airfare,* and if you do book yourself, always inquire about honeymoon specials, golf packages, summer weeks, and other discounts. In many cases, too, a travel agent can get you a package deal that would be cheaper than these official rates.

Hotels add an 8% tax "resort levy" to your rate. Sometimes this is quoted as part of the price; at other times, it's added to your final bill. When you are quoted a rate, always ask if the tax is included. Many hotels also add a 15% service charge to your bill. Ask about these charges in advance so you won't be shocked when you receive the final tab.

Taxes and service are not included in the rates listed below. We'll lead off with a selection of hotels within the heart of Nassau, followed by accommodations in Cable Beach. Most visitors prefer to stay at Cable Beach since the resorts here are right on the sand. But it is possible to stay in Nassau and commute to the beaches at Cable Beach or Paradise Island; it's cheaper but less convenient. Those who prefer the ambience of Old Nassau's historic district and being near the best shops may decide to stay in town.

NASSAU
VERY EXPENSIVE
Grayclifff *A A A* A lovely, romantic place that stands across the street from Government House, the Graycliff is the grande dame of downtown Nassau hotels. Originally an 18th-century private home and a well-preserved example of Georgian colonial architecture, it's now an intimate inn, with an old-fashioned aristocratic atmosphere. For a few years, a bit of wear was beginning to show, but the management completed a renovation that has the hotel looking in fine form. And even though it isn't right on the beach, people who can afford to stay anywhere (especially honeymooners) often choose Graycliff because it epitomizes Nassau's old-world style and grace. Churchill, of course, can no longer be seen paddling around in the swimming pool with a cigar in his mouth, and the Beatles are long gone, but the three-story Graycliff remains a favorite with visiting celebs, well-heeled travelers with a sense of history, and business travelers who need to be near the center of town. Beach lovers usually head by taxi to either nearby Goodman's Bay or to the Western Esplanade Beach, nearly adjacent to Arawak Cay. The British Colonial Hilton is Graycliff's main competitor; they both have a rather staid, deliberately unflashy ambience. The Hilton is much bigger, and therefore much less personal, and doesn't have the romance and history of Graycliff.

Many guests opt for the historic garden rooms in the main house, which are large and individually decorated with antiques, though the better units are the more modern garden rooms. The Yellow Bird, Hibiscus, and Pool cottages are terrific choices (honeymooners especially like the privacy you get here), but the most luxurious accommodation of all is the Mandarino Suite, with Asian decor, a king-size bed, an oversize bathroom, and a private balcony overlooking the swimming pool. Bathrooms are spacious, with deluxe toiletries and robes.

The hotel boasts one of Nassau's finest, most elegant restaurants, also called Graycliff (see "Where to Dine," below). Always reserve well in advance. In 1999, the hotel added The Humidor, a casual bistro outfitted, with the fantasy cigar smoker in mind, with leather and lots of wood.

W. Hill St., P.O. Box N-10246, Nassau, The Bahamas. © **800/688-0076** in the U.S., or 242/322-2796. Fax 242/326-6110. www.graycliff.com. 18 units. Winter $290–$400 double, $310 poolside cottage for 2; off-season $200 double, $250 poolside cottage for 2. AE, MC, V. Free parking. Bus: 10 or 21A. **Amenities:** 2 restaurants, bar, 3 swimming pools, health club, Jacuzzi, sauna, room service (8am–11:30pm), concierge, laundry service, dry cleaning, baby-sitting, massage. *In room:* A/C, TV, minibar, hair dryer.

EXPENSIVE
British Colonial Hilton *A A* In the newly refurbished British Colonial Hilton, there's a palpable air of the long-ago days when The Bahamas was firmly within the political and social orbit of Britain. This landmark seven-story hotel has seen its share of ups and downs over the years. Plush and glamorous when it was built in 1900, it burned to the ground in 1920, and was rebuilt 3 years

Nassau Accommodations

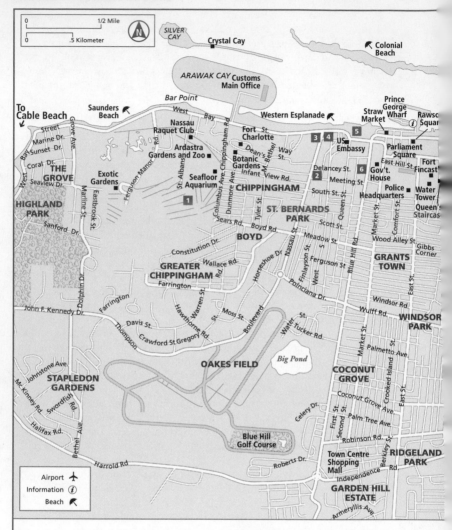

British Colonial Hilton **5**
Buena Vista Hotel **2**
Dillet's Guest House **1**
El Greco Hotel **4**

Graycliff **6**
Holiday Inn Junkanoo Beach **3**
Nassau Harbour Club **7**
Ocean Spray Hotel **4**

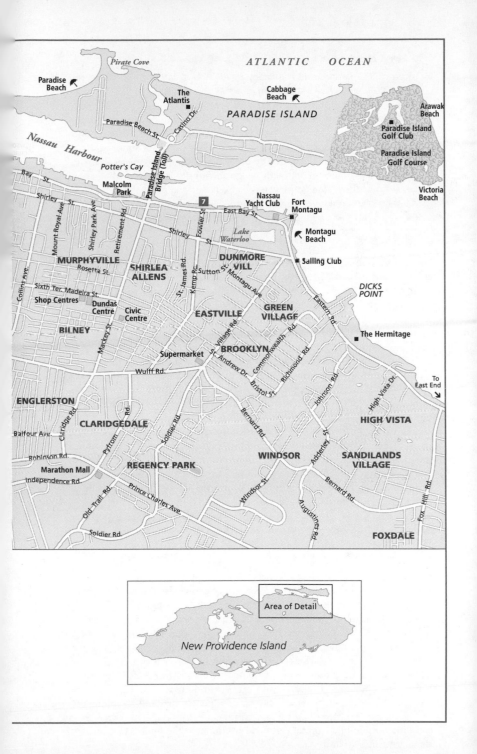

ATLANTIC OCEAN

Pirate Cove

Paradise
Beach

The
Atlantis

Cabbage
Beach

PARADISE ISLAND

Arawak
Beach

Paradise Beach St.

Casino Dr.

Paradise Island
Golf Club

Nassau Harbour

Paradise Island
Golf Course

Potter's Cay

Victoria
Beach

Bay St.

Malcolm
Park

Shirley St.

Paradise Island
Bridge (Toll)

7

Mount Royal Ave.

Shirley Park Ave.

Retirement Rd.

Fowler St.

East Bay St.

Nassau
Yacht Club

Fort
Montagu

Shirley St.

Lake
Waterloo

Montagu
Beach

MURPHYVILLE

Rosetta St.

SHIRLEA
ALLENS

DUNMORE
VILL

Sailing Club

St. James Rd.

Kemp Rd.

Sutton St.

Montagu Ave.

DICKS
POINT

Collins Ave.

Sixth Ter. Madeira St.

Shop Centres

Dundas
Centre

Civic
Centre

EASTVILLE

GREEN
VILLAGE

Eastern Rd.

BILNEY

Mackey St.

BROOKLYN

Village Rd.

Commonwealth Rd.

Richmond Rd.

The Hermitage

Supermarket

St. Andrew Dr.

Bristol St.

Wulff Rd.

Johnson Rd.

High Vista Dr.

To
East End

ENGLERSTON

Claridge Rd.

CLARIDGEDALE

Pyfrom Rd.

Soldier Rd.

Bernard Rd.

HIGH VISTA

Balfour Ave.

Robinson Rd.

Marathon Mall

Independence Rd.

REGENCY PARK

Prince Charles Ave.

Windsor St.

WINDSOR

Adelaide St.

Augustines Rd.

Bernard Rd.

SANDILANDS
VILLAGE

Fox Hill Rd.

Old Trail Rd.

Soldier Rd.

FOXDALE

Area of Detail

New Providence Island

Fun Fact In Suite Double O, A "License to Kill"

In both *Thunderball* and *Never Say Never Again*, James Bond, or secret agent 007, was served shaken martinis at the British Colonial. To commemorate that historic event, the Hilton-owned property now has a "Double-O" suite filled with Bond memorabilia, including posters, books, CDs, movie stills, and all the best Bond flicks, including *Goldfinger* and *Live and Let Die*. Guests can take a Bond book from the suite, perhaps *Tomorrow Never Dies*, and curl up on a chaise longue at the beach. The suite is a one-bedroom unit with living room and ocean views. When you get tired of the movie Bond, you can stroll over and meet the real Bond, namely, Sean Connery who is often at his island home on nearby Lyford Cay—that is, if 007 is kind enough to extend an invite.

---

later before deteriorating into a flophouse. Between 1996 and 1999, a Canadian entrepreneur poured $68 million into its restoration.

Don't expect the glitz and glitter of Cable Beach or Paradise Island here—the Hilton is after business travelers rather than the casino crowd. It also lacks the aristocratic credentials of Graycliff (see above). Nonetheless, it's a dignified and friendly, but rather sedate, hotel with a discreetly upscale decor (no Disney-style themes or gimmicks). Bedrooms are a bit on the small side, but capped with rich crown moldings and accessorized with tile or stone-sheathed bathrooms. The staff, incidentally, is superbly trained and motivated; we've found them upbeat and hardworking. There's a small beach a few steps away, but it's not very appealing (it's on the channel separating New Providence from Paradise Island, with no "cleansing" wave action at all).

The cuisine at the British Colonial is good standard fare, which doesn't even try to compete with the deluxe viands at Graycliff (see above). The most upscale restaurant is Wedgwood (see "Where to Dine," later in this chapter). Less formal is Portofino, a casual Italian trattoria. The Patio Grill offers light lunches beside the pool. A woodsy-looking bar, Blackbeard's Cove, evokes a private club in London, and attracts the local suit-and-tie crowd for after-work drinks.

1 Bay St., P.O. Box N-7148, Nassau, The Bahamas. ⓒ **800/HILTONS** in the U.S. and Canada, or 242/322-3301. Fax 242/322-2286. www.hilton.com. 291 units. Year-round $220–$295 double, from $305 suite. AE, DC, MC, V. Bus: 10. **Amenities:** 2 restaurants, 3 bars, pool, 3 tennis courts, health club, Jacuzzi, 24-hour room service, baby-sitting, laundry, bike rentals. *In room:* A/C, TV, minibar, coffeemaker, hair dryer.

MODERATE

Holiday Inn Junkanoo Beach   West of downtown Nassau and overlooking Junkanoo Beach, the hotel lies exactly between the Atlantis and Crystal Palace casinos. Although not as fine as Cable Beach, Junkanoo is also a safe beach with tranquil waters, white sands, and a lot of shells; the hotel offers lounge chairs on the beach but no waiter service for drinks. This place is a good value for those who don't want to pay the higher prices charged by the more deluxe hotels along Cable Beach. All the motel-style bedrooms have a view of either the beach or Nassau Harbour, and they come with extras you don't always find in a moderately priced choice, such as alarm clocks, two-line phones, and a working desk.

The on-site Bay Street Grille is not reason enough to stay here, although you can dine outside in a tropical courtyard overlooking the pool. There are many restaurants nearby, however.

W. Bay St. (P.O. Box SS-19055). **📞 800/465-4329** or 242/356-0000. Fax 242/323-1408. www.basshotels. com/holiday-inn. 117 units. Year-round $149 double, $179–$250 suite. AE, DC, DISC, MC, V. Bus: 10 or 17. **Amenities:** Restaurant, bar, heated swimming pool, fitness center, tour desk, laundry/valet, room service (7am–11pm). *In room:* A/C, TV, minibar, fridge, coffeemaker, hair dryer, iron/ironing board.

INEXPENSIVE

Buena Vista Hotel   Although this place really revolves around its restaurant (reviewed in "Where to Dine," below), it rents a few spacious bedrooms upstairs. It's a good bargain if you don't mind the lack of resort-style facilities. The building, with a pale pink facade, started out a century ago as a private home, and stands a half mile west of downtown Nassau. Expect a pastel decor, with a tasteful mix of antiques and reproductions. Each room comes with a small bath containing a shower unit. The staff might be a bit distracted because of the demands of the busy restaurant downstairs. Bus no. 16 carries you on a short eastbound trek into downtown Nassau, and you're about 10 minutes from the nearest beach.

Delancy and Augusta sts. (P.O. Box N-564), Nassau, The Bahamas. **📞 242/322-2811.** Fax 242/322-5881. www.buenavista-restaurant.com. 5 units. Mid-Apr to mid-Dec $70 double, $80 triple; mid-Dec to mid-Apr $100 double, $110 triple. AE, MC, V. Bus: 16. **Amenities:** Restaurant, bar, laundry. *In room:* A/C, TV, refrigerator, coffeemaker, hair dryer.

Dillet's Guest House 🍷 🅥ᵃˡᵘᵉ   This is New Providence's finest B&B. In the 1920s, a local contractor, Edward Dillet built a house just off West Bay and welcomed family, friends, and acquaintances to spend time here. Later, he expanded his home into a small inn. Now his daughter Iris invites travelers to do the same. Each room has amenities you don't usually find in guest houses, such as cable TV, a ceiling fan, a clock radio, a good bed, and a minibar stocked with soda (no alcohol) and chips. Five of the rooms have full kitchenettes, though the bathrooms tend to be small, each with a shower unit. The house is informal and homey — nothing fancy, but spotless and charming. The building's focal point is a gracefully appointed living room, with a large, striking coral-stone fireplace. No smoking.

The nearest public beaches are about a 7-minute walk away, and you can catch the no. 10 or 38 bus to Cable Beach for 75¢. You can also rent a bike at Dillet's and tour the area for $15 a day. A well-known artist, a relative of the Dillet family, John Cox, lives in a cottage in the garden, and he welcomes visits from guests to see whatever painting he's working on at the moment.

After a breakfast of freshly baked pastries, you can request an authentic Bahamian dinner that night for $30 per person, and Iris can even arrange a picnic for you to take to the beach. Afternoon tea is the highlight of the day here.

Dunmore Ave. and Strachan St., Chippingham, Nassau, The Bahamas. **📞 242/325-1133.** Fax 242/325-7183. www.islandeaze.com/dillets/. 7 units. Winter $105–$125 double; off-season $85 double. Extra person $25. Rates include continental breakfast. MC, V. Free parking. Bus: 10. **Amenities:** Dining room, laundry. *In room:* A/C, TV, minibar, fridge.

⟨Moments What to Do on a Rainy Day?

To cheer your spirits, head first for the **Pink Pearl** (see p. 83) and order local conch drizzled with a tamarind-flavored barbecue sauce. Hopefully, it'll be a weekend when a jazz combo plays on a side porch. Tearing yourself away, head over to the **Café Matisse** and ask for an order of apple semifreddo with kiwi sauce. After downing this touch of heaven, you'll be walking the streets outside *Singin' in the Rain*.

El Greco Hotel   Across the street from Lighthouse Beach, and a short walk from the shops and restaurants of Bay Street, El Greco is a well-managed bargain choice that attracts many European travelers. The Greek owners and staff genuinely seem to care about their guests—in fact, the two-story hotel seems more like a small European B&B than your typical Bahamian hotel.

The mid-size rooms aren't that exciting, but they're clean and comfortable, with decent beds and small tile bathrooms, containing shower units. After an extensive post-hurricane refurbishment in 1999, the bedrooms have a brighter decor—a sort of Mediterranean motif, each with two ceiling fans and carpeted floors. Accommodations are built around a courtyard that contains statues crafted in the Baroque Italian style, draped with lots of bougainvillea. There is no on-site restaurant, but you can walk to many places nearby for meals.

W. Bay St. (P.O. Box N-4187), Nassau, The Bahamas. © 242/325-1121. Fax 242/325-1124. www.bahamasnet. com. 27 units. Winter $129 double, $150 suite; off-season $89 double, $125 suite. AE, MC, V. Free parking. Bus: 10. **Amenities:** Pool, baby-sitting. *In room:* A/C, TV.

Nassau Harbour Club   Don't expect lush and sprawling gardens, or much peace and privacy here—this hotel is in the heart of Nassau's action and is usually overrun in March and early April with college kids on spring break. A compound of two-story pink buildings from the early 1960s arranged like a horseshoe around a concrete terrace, it occupies a bustling strip of land between busy Bay Street and the edge of the channel that separates New Providence from Paradise Island. From your room, you'll have views of yachts and boats moored at a nearby marina, and there is easy access to the shops, bars, and restaurants of downtown Nassau and within the Harbour Bay Shopping Centre, a few steps away. Throughout, it's down-to-earth and just a bit funky—a huge contrast with the glitter of such megaresorts as the Atlantis. Bedrooms are simple and small but comfortable, if a little worn and near the animated hubbub of the busy bar.

E. Bay St., P.O. Box SS-5755, Nassau, The Bahamas. © 242/393-0771. Fax 242/393-5393. www.thetrip. onlinevacationmall.com. 50 units. Winter $90–$120 double, $130 suite; off-season $80–$100 double, $110 suite. Extra person $25. AE, DISC, MC, V. Free parking. Bus: 11 or 19. **Amenities:** Restaurant, swimming pool, bar, laundry. *In room:* A/C, TV.

Ocean Spray Hotel   This modest four-story corner hotel is a short stroll from the shopping district and across the street from a good beach. Midsize bedrooms have comfortable twin beds, carpeting, and your basic Miami-motel decor. Although furnishings show some wear, they're clean and reasonably comfortable, though bathrooms are small, each with a shower unit. Students on spring break would be happy here.

This hotel is better known for its on-site restaurant and bar, Europe, than it is for its rooms.

W. Bay St. (P.O. Box N-3035), Nassau, The Bahamas. © 242/322-8032. Fax 242/325-5731. www. oceansprayhotel.com. 28 units. Winter $110 double; off-season $85 double. AE, MC, V. Free parking. Bus: 10. **Amenities:** Restaurant, bar, laundry. *In room:* A/C, TV, refrigerator.

CABLE BEACH

The glittering shoreline of Cable Beach, located west of Nassau, is topped only by Paradise Island (see chapter 4). It has loyal fans, many of whom think Paradise Island is too snobbish. Cable Beach has for years attracted visitors with its broad stretches of beachfront, a wide array of sports facilities, and great nightlife, including casino action. Deluxe or first-class resorts, two of which are all-inclusive, line the shoreline.

ACCOMMODATIONS ■
Breezes **13**
Clarion Resort South Ocean
Golf, Beach & Dive Resort **4**
Compass Point **12**

Nassau Marriott Resort
& Crystal Palace Casino **11**
Orange Hill Beach Inn **2**
Radisson Cable Beach Hotel **10**
Sandals Royal Bahamian Hotel **6**
West Wind II **3**

DINING ◆
The Beef Cellar **12**
The Black Angus Grile **11**
Café Johnny Canoe **12**
Capriccio **7**

Dickie Mo's **9**
The Poop Deck at Sandy Point **8**
The Restaurant at Compass Point **1**
Sole Mare **11**
Travellers Rest **5**

ATLANTIC OCEAN

BROWN'S POINT

Goodman's Bay

CABLE BEACH GOLF COURSE

PROSPECT RIDGE

NEW PROVIDENCE ISLAND

area of detail

West Bay St.
Devonshire St.
Rugby Ave.
Skyline Dr.
Poinciana Dr.
Sanford Dr.
Oak Hill Rd.
Lake Cunningham
Cable Beach Lagoon
West Bay St.
Hampshire St.
Yorkshire St.
Oxford Av.

1/4 Mile
.25 Kilometer

VERY EXPENSIVE

Breezes *☞* SuperClubs, which competes successfully with Sandals (see below) in Jamaica, spent $125 million transforming a tired old relic, the Ambassador Beach Hotel, into this all-inclusive resort. The nearby Sandals is more imposing, elegant, stylish, and upscale, with better amenities and views. Rowdier and more raucous, and located on a prime 1,500-foot beachfront along Cable Beach, Breezes attracts a more middle-of-the-road crowd; it's unpretentious and more affordable (though it ain't exactly cheap, and we think it's rather overpriced for what it is). This U-shaped beachfront resort has two wings of rooms plus a main clubhouse facing a large pool area. Except between March and May, when no one under 21 is admitted, both couples and single travelers over 16 are accepted here (unlike at Sandals, which accepts only heterosexual couples in love). Everything is included—the room, meals, snacks, unlimited wine (not the finest) with lunch and dinner, even premium brand liquor at the bars, plus activities and airport transfers.

The refurbished hotel rooms contain pastel-painted wooden furniture with Formica tops, and an air-conditioning system that actually works. Rooms, however, are not as luxurious as those at Sandals. Bathrooms are medium-size but well-equipped and are tiled with a shower and bathtub.

Diners can sample unremarkable international fare at the food court, although the Italian restaurant serves a better dinner. A beachside grill and snacks are available throughout the day. Entertainment includes a high-energy disco, a piano bar, and a nightclub. Karaoke is inevitable, but the professional "Junkanoo" live shows, which are presented every Saturday night, are better, and local bands often perform. The social centerpiece is a sometimes-overcrowded terrace with a swimming pool. The resort offers a first for The Bahamas—ice-skating in a 1,600-square-foot outdoor rink open 24 hours. Equipment is complimentary, and daily hockey matches are staged.

P.O. Box CB-13049, Cable Beach, Nassau, The Bahamas. © 800/GO-SUPER or 242/327-5356. Fax 242/327-5155. www.breezes.com. 391 units. Year-round $410–$505 double, $590–$780 suite. Rates include all meals, drinks, most activities, and airport transfers. No tipping allowed. AE, DISC, MC, V. Free parking. Bus: 10. No children under 16 year-round; no one under 21 Mar–May. **Amenities:** 2 restaurants, 4 bars, 5 pools, 3 tennis courts, fitness center, aerobics classes, non-motorized water sports, ice-skating. *In room:* A/C, TV, hair dryer.

Nassau Marriott Resort & Crystal Palace Casino *☞☞* This is the biggest and flashiest megaresort on the lovely sands of Cable Beach, and it's undergone a lot of changes since Marriott took it over from Carnival Cruise Lines. When Carnival ran it, it was shamelessly glitzy and nicknamed "The Purple Palace" because of its glaring color scheme. Although you still shouldn't expect understated elegance, Marriott has already toned it down a notch and has added touches of class. It's a great place for an action-packed honeymoon, complete with an excellent beach, swaying palm trees, and good snorkeling right offshore. It's so self-contained that you don't have to leave the premises during your entire stay. If you have a choice, stay here and not at Radisson's Cable Beach Hotel (see below), where food, service, and maintenance are not as good.

The complex incorporates five high-rise towers, a futuristic central core, and a cluster of gardens and beachfront gazebos—all connected with arcades, underground passages, and minipavilions. Bedrooms are modern, spacious, and comfortable, cozier and more low-key than the flashy exterior might lead you to believe. Most have ocean views. Units have one king-size bed or two doubles,

Moments   Junkanoo Festivals

No Bahamian celebration is as raucous as the Junkanoo (which is also the name of the music associated with this festival). The special rituals originated during the colonial days of slavery, when African-born newcomers could legally drink and enjoy themselves only on certain strictly predetermined days of the year. In its celebration, Junkanoo closely resembles Carnaval in Rio and Mardi Gras in New Orleans. Its major difference lies in the costumes and the timing (the major Junkanoo celebrations occur the day after Christmas, a reminder of the medieval English celebration of Boxing Day on December 26 and New Year's Day).

In the old days, Junkanoo costumes were crafted from crepe paper, often in primary colors, stretched over wire frames. (One sinister off-shoot of the celebrations was that the Junkanoo costumes and masks were used to conceal the identity of anyone seeking vengeance on a white or on another slave.) Locals have more money to spend on costumes and Junkanoo festivals today than they did in decades past. Today the finest costumes can cost up to $10,000 and are sometimes sponsored by local bazaars, lotteries, and charity auctions, though everyday folks from all walks of Bahamian life join in, too, usually with their own homemade costumes, many of which are sensual or humorous. The best time and place to observe Junkanoo is New Year's Day in Nassau, when throngs of cavorting, music-making, and costumed figures prance through the streets. Find yourself a good viewing position on Bay Street. Less elaborate celebrations take place in major towns on the other islands, including Freeport.

each with fine mattresses, along with tiny combination bathrooms (shower and tub) with spacious dressing areas and dual basins.

Aside from a massive casino (the largest in The Bahamas), the complex contains nine restaurants, and a cabaret theater (the Palace Theater, recommended under "New Providence After Dark," later in this chapter). The restaurants run a wide culinary gamut. The best and most expensive (also the most formal) is the Sole Mare, serving Italian food (see "Where to Dine," below). The Black Angus Grille (also see "Where to Dine") has some of the best steaks on Cable Beach.

W. Bay St. (P.O. Box N-8306), Cable Beach, Nassau, The Bahamas. ⓒ 800/222-7466 in the U.S., or 242/327-6200. Fax 242/327-6818. www.marriott.com. 867 units. Winter $189–$219 double, $299–$500 suite for 2; off-season $169–$199 double, $299–$500 suite for 2. AE, DC, DISC, MC, V. Free self-parking, valet parking $5. Bus: 10. **Amenities:** 5 restaurants, 5 bars, pool shaped like tropical lagoon, 10 tennis courts, 18-hole golf course, health club, gym, 24-hour room service, laundry/valet. *In room:* A/C, TV, minibar, hair dryer.

Radisson Cable Beach Hotel ⓕ ⓚⁱᵈˢ   Right in the middle of Cable Beach (its best asset) this high rise is connected by a shopping arcade to the Crystal Palace Casino. The nearby Nassau Marriott is glitzier and has better facilities, but the Radisson is still one of the most desirable choices for families, as it has the best children's programs in the area, and because many of its bedrooms contain two

(*Kids*) Family-Friendly Hotels

Nassau Beach Hotel *(see p. 79)*   This place actively caters to families, offering a large program of children's activities, including a play center with slides and swings, a video-game room, and a supervised recreation room.

Radisson Cable Beach Hotel *(see p. 77)*   A massive hotel on Cable Beach, dating from the 1980s, this has become a family favorite— largely because of its Camp Junkanoo, which offers daily supervised play for children 3 to 12.

West Wind II *(see p. 80)*   This is for families who want to set up housekeeping on Cable Beach. Time-share units containing two bedrooms and two bathrooms, each with a full kitchen, are rented out and are ideal for a family of four. There are two pools as well.

double beds, suitable for a family of four. The nine-story property has an Aztec-inspired façade of sharp angles and strong horizontal lines, built in a horseshoe-shaped curve around a landscaped beachfront garden. You'll think of Vegas when you see the rows of fountains in front, the acres of marble sheathing inside, and the four-story lobby with towering windows. Big enough to get lost in, but with plenty of intimate nooks, the hotel offers an almost endless array of things to do. Note, however, that readers constantly complain of staff attitude and slow service at this sprawling resort.

Bedrooms are modern and comfortable if rather standard, with big windows that open onto views of the garden or the beach. Units are equipped with one king-size bed or two doubles, along with phones with voice-mail, plus tiled combination baths (tub and shower).

The hotel contains six restaurants, the most glamorous of which is the Amici, serving a traditional Italian cuisine in a two-story garden setting. You can also spice up your evening at Tequila Pepe's Steakhouse-Cantina, which sometimes has karaoke and other entertainment. We try to avoid the overpriced Avocado's or Bimini's, both of which have poor service and an uninspired cuisine. The Mini-Market Grill serves Caribbean/continental breakfast and lunch buffets, and the Forge is a steak and seafood restaurant where guests are seated around a table-top grill to prepare their own steaks, seafood, or chicken. Beach parties and revues are often staged.

W. Bay St. (P.O. Box N-4914), Cable Beach, Nassau, The Bahamas. (℃) **800/333-3333** or 242/327-6000. Fax 242/327-6987. www.radisson.com. 700 units. Winter $275–$325 double; off-season $210–$290 double. Year-round $425–$1,275 suite. AE, DC, DISC, MC, V. Free parking. Bus: 10. **Amenities:** 6 restaurants, 2 bars, 3 pools, 18 tennis courts, 3 racquetball and 3 squash courts, room service (7am–10pm), concierge, baby-sitting at Camp Junkanoo for children 3–12, laundry, dry cleaning, beauty salon, boutiques. *In room:* A/C, TV, mini-bar, hair dryer.

Sandals Royal Bahamian Hotel *(℃(℃(℃*   This is the most upscale Sandals resort in the world. It's shockingly expensive, though you can often get special promotional rates that make it more reasonable. It originated as a very posh hotel, the Balmoral Beach, in the 1940s. In 1996, the Jamaica-based Sandals chain poured $20 million into renovating and expanding the property, which lies on a sandy beach a short walk west of the more glittery megahotels of Cable Beach. Everywhere, you'll find manicured gardens, rich cove moldings, hidden courtyards tastefully accentuated with sculptures, and many of the trappings of Edwardian England in the tropics. Only heterosexual couples, without children, are admitted, a politically incorrect policy discriminatory toward homosexuals and even offensive to many gay-friendly straight couples.

A favorite for honeymoon getaways, Sandals offers well-furnished and often elegant rooms, all classified as suites. Some are in the Manor House, while others are in outlying villas. Some have Jacuzzis and private pools, and some of the bathrooms are as spacious as many big-city apartments. The bedrooms have thick cove moldings, formal English furniture, excellent mattresses, and bathrooms loaded with perfumed soaps and cosmetics. The rooms that face the ocean offer small, curved terraces with ornate iron railings and views of an off-shore sand spit, Sandals Key.

Bahamian and international fare is offered in generous portions in the property's restaurants. In addition to spectacular buffets, the options include white-glove service and continental dishes in the Baccarat Dining Room. The two latest additions include Kimono's, offering Japanese cuisine, and Casanova, specializing in Italian fare. Other choices are The Royal Café for southwestern grilled specialties, and Spices, for upscale buffets at breakfast, lunch, and dinner. The pool here is one of the most appealing on Nassau, with touches of both Vegas and ancient Rome (outdoor murals and replicas of ancient Roman columns jutting skyward above the water). There is complimentary shuttle bus service to casino and nightlife options at the nearby Marriott Crystal Palace complex, plus concierge service in suites and upper-tier doubles.

W. Bay St., P.O. Box CB-13005, Cable Beach, Nassau, The Bahamas. © 800/SANDALS or 242/327-6400. Fax 242/327-6961. www.sandals.com. 405 units. Winter $4,620–$8,900 per couple for 7 days ($1,450–$2,710 per couple for 2 days); off-season $4,283–$8,540 per couple for 7 days ($1,260–$2,440 per couple for 2 days). Rates include meals, drinks, and activities. Always ask for special promotional rates or see what a travel agent can get you. AE, DISC, MC, V. Free parking. Bus: 10. Couples only; no children or singles allowed. **Amenities:** 8 restaurants, 7 bars, 5 pools, 2 tennis courts, exercise center, spa, water sports, access to golf facilities. *In room:* A/C, TV, hair dryer.

MODERATE

Nassau Beach Hotel *(Kids)* This place has been somewhat overshadowed by the glitzy properties a short walk away, but a crowd of loyal fans—often families—comes every year, enjoying a 3,000-foot white-sand beach. Guests here avoid the carnival at such neighboring megaresorts as the Nassau Marriott (although this place is now also part of the Marriott family). A good value, the Nassau Beach is a conservative, middle-of-the-road choice with a lively but restrained atmosphere.

The hotel was built in the 1940s, with three separate wings in a pink-and-white twin-towered design, and it features modified Georgian detailing and tile- and marble-covered floors. In the early 1990s, it was restored by new owners, and in 1999, $12 million was spent on upgrading the bedrooms and the public areas. Today, the place has been enhanced by new landscaping and touches that include ceiling fans and mahogany, English-inspired furniture. Each of the mid-size accommodations contains summery rattan pieces, comfortable beds, and a marble bathroom with a tub and shower combination.

On site are seven restaurants (including the Beef Cellar, which is reviewed under "Where to Dine," later in this chapter), plus entertainment in the evening (including live bands and dancing). It's also near the Crystal Palace Casino.

P.O. Box N-7756, Cable Beach, Nassau, The Bahamas. (C) 888/NASSAUB in the U.S., or 242/327-7711. Fax 242/327-8829. www.marriott.com. 400 units. Year-round $135–$300 double, $265–$485 1-bedroom suite, $370–$580 2-bedroom suite, $525–$700 2-bedroom penthouse. AE, DC, MC, V. Free parking. Bus: 10. **Amenities:** 7 restaurants, 3 bars, 6 tennis courts, health club, baby-sitting, water sports. *In room:* A/C, TV, hair dryer.

West Wind II *(Kids)*   Set on the western edge of Cable Beach's hotel strip, 6 miles from the center of Nassau, the West Wind II is a cluster of two-story buildings that contain two-bedroom, two-bathroom time-share units, each with a full kitchen (there's a grocery store nearby). The size and facilities of these units make them ideal for traveling families. These units are available to the public whenever they're not otherwise occupied by investors. All the diversions of the megahotels are close by and easily reached, but in the complex itself, you can enjoy a low-key, quiet atmosphere and privacy. (A masonry wall separates the compound from the traffic of West Bay Street and the hotels and vacant lots that flank it.) Each unit has a pleasant decor that includes white tiled floors, rattan furniture, and either a balcony or a terrace. Since units are identical, price differences depend on whether the units face the beach, the pool, or the garden. The manicured grounds feature palms, flowering hibiscus shrubs, and seasonal flower beds. Don't stay here if you expect any of the amenities or facilities of the nearby Nassau Beach Hotel (see above). West Wind II is more for do-it-yourself types.

W. Bay St. (P.O. Box CB-11006), Cable Beach, Nassau, The Bahamas. (C) **242/327-7019.** Fax 242/327-7529. www.westwindIIclub.com. 54 apts. Nov–Apr $1,490–$1,840 per week for up to 4 persons; May–Oct $1,240–$1,825 per week for up to 4 persons. MC, V. Bus: 10. **Amenities:** 2 swimming pools, 2 tennis courts, laundromat, baby-sitting. *In room:* A/C, TV, kitchen, refrigerator, coffeemaker.

WEST OF CABLE BEACH

Clarion Resort South Ocean Golf, Beach, and Dive Resort *(F)*   Set in an isolated position near the extreme western tip of New Providence, this is the only hotel in this area, which mostly consists of scrubland dotted with some upscale private villas. Centered around a well-known golf course, it's divided into two distinctly different sections. The larger and older of the two, with 152 rooms, lies across the coastal road from the sea, adjacent to the golf course, with low-rise, comfortable, but not particularly dramatic accommodations. Newer and better are the 111 oceanfront rooms, which seem like an upscale condominium complex built in Bahamian style, with large bathrooms containing whirlpool baths. Clients run the gamut here between young married couples and more sedate older folk. Most are relatively conservative, enjoying golf and the beach, and not minding the resort's isolation and lack of flashiness. A talented team of social directors keeps a stream of wholesome activities flowing, organizing lots of group activities like volleyball games on the beach.

Both sections of this resort have their own swimming pools, but other than the beach, most of the services for the hotel are in the older section, including two of the three restaurants. Most upscale of the lot is Papagayos; the others are alfresco snack bars and grills. There's live music most evenings; game nights are every Tuesday, with prize giveaways and trivia contests.

P.O. Box N-8191, South Ocean Rd. (C) **242/362-4391** or 877/766-2326. Fax 242/362-4810. www.clarionnassau.com. 263 units. Winter $165–$400 double; off-season $115–$175 double. AE, DC, MC, V. **Amenities:** 3 restaurants, 3 bars, 4 tennis courts, 2 pools, water sports, dive shop, baby-sitting. *In room:* A/C, TV.

Compass Point ℛℛ   Charming, personalized, and casually upscale, this is an alternative to the megahotels of Cable Beach, which lie about 6 miles to the east. It's part of the Island Records empire of music-industry mogul Chris Blackwell. Think British colonial hip, with guests straight out of Soho (either London or New York) and a smattering of music-industry types. The place isn't as snobby as Graycliff, but for those who want an intimate inn and like the vibrant Bahamian colors, there is no other place like it on the island. Scattered over 2 acres of some of the most expensive terrain in The Bahamas, the property lies beside one of the few sandy coves along the island's northwest coast, about 20 minutes from downtown Nassau and near a great snorkeling beach. The beach is very small, a sandy crescent that virtually disappears at high tide.

Each unit is a private, fully detached "hut" or cottage painted in pulsating, vivid colors. Everything larger than a studio has a kitchenette. Designed for privacy, all the units have exposed rafters, high ceilings with ceiling fans, and a half-dozen windows facing the ocean breezes. Some units are raised on stilts, others hug the ground. They all have king size beds with excellent mattresses covered in bright batik, private safes, sundecks, spacious bathrooms with herbal toiletries, CD players and a selection of music, and shower-only bathrooms (no tubs). Those few of the units without natural cross ventilation (about five) are air-conditioned. The most deluxe accommodations are the two-story cottages, each with a small outdoor kitchen and dining area. The Restaurant at Compass Point is recommended separately in "Where to Dine," below. There's also a bar that frequently hosts live music.

W. Bay St., Gambier, Love Beach, New Providence, The Bahamas. ℰ 800/688-7678 in the U.S., or 242/327-4500. Fax 242/327-3299. www.islandoutpost.com. 18 units. Winter $215 studio double, $275–$355 1-bedroom cottage, $425 2-bedroom cottage for 4. Rates are usually 20% lower in off-season. AE, DC, MC, V. Free parking. Bus: Western Bus. **Amenities:** Restaurant, bar, pool, tennis court. *In room:* TV, minibar, coffeemaker, iron/ironing board.

Orange Hill Beach Inn   This hotel, set on 3½ landscaped hillside acres, lies about 8 miles west of Nassau and 1 mile east of Love Beach, which has great snorkeling. It's perfect for those who want to escape the crowds and stay in a quieter part of New Providence Island; it's easy to catch a cab or jitney to Cable Beach or downtown Nassau. The welcoming owners, Judy and Danny Lowe, an Irish-Bahamian partnership, jokingly refer to their operation as "Fawlty Towers Nassau."

This place was built as a private home in the 1920s and became a hotel in 1979 after the Lowes added more rooms and a swimming pool. Rooms and apartments come in a variety of sizes, although most are small. However, each contains a good bed with a firm mattress. The bathrooms, likewise, are small but well-maintained, each with a shower unit. Each has a balcony or patio, and a few apartments are equipped with kitchenettes. Many of the guests are European, especially in summer.

On-site is a bar serving sandwiches and salads throughout the day, and a restaurant that offers simple but good dinners. Diving excursions to the rich marine fauna of New Providence's southwestern coast are among the most popular activities here.

W. Bay St. just west of Blake Rd., P.O. Box N-8583, Nassau, The Bahamas. ℰ 242/327-7157. Fax 242/327-5186. www.orangehill.com. 32 units. Winter $112–$117 double, $142 apt; off-season $81–$96 double, $116–$131 apt. AE, MC, V. Free parking. Bus: Western Bus. **Amenities:** Restaurant, bar, sea kayaks for rent, coin laundry. *In room:* A/C, TV. No phone.

4 Where to Dine

Nassau restaurants open and close with alarming regularity. Even if reservations aren't required, it's a good idea to call first just to see that a place is still functioning. European and American cuisine are relatively easy to find in Nassau. Surprisingly, it used to be difficult to find Bahamian cuisine, but in recent years, more places have begun to offer authentic island fare.

IN NASSAU
VERY EXPENSIVE
Buena Vista ☞ CONTINENTAL/BAHAMIAN/SEAFOOD   Although it's not quite up there with Graycliff or Sun And . . . , this is definitely third runner-up in Nassau's culinary sweepstakes. It's a block west of Government House (Delancy Street is opposite the cathedral close off St. Francis Xavier, and only a short distance from Bay Street). It opened back in the 1940s in a colonial mansion set on 5 acres of tropical foliage. Traditional elegance and fine preparations have always characterized this place.

You're likely to be shown to the main dining room, unless you request the cozy and intimate Victoria Room or, even better, the Garden Patio, which has a greenhouse setting and a ceiling skylight. The chef scours Nassau's markets to collect the freshest and finest ingredients, which he puts together in menus bursting with flavor and full of originality. Look for impromptu daily specials such as breaded veal chop or Long Island duckling. There is not only nouvelle cuisine here but also a respect for tradition. The rack of lamb Provençale is a classic, but you might want to try instead some of the lighter veal dishes. The cream of garlic soup has plenty of flavor but never overpowers. Instead of wildly fanciful desserts, Buena Vista sticks to the classics—say, cherries jubilee or baked Alaska flambé au cognac. Service is deft, efficient, and polite. Calypso coffee finishes the meal off nicely as you listen to soft piano music.

Delancy and Meeting sts. ℂ 242/322-2811. Reservations recommended. Main courses $35–$40; fixed-price dinner $40. AE, DC, MC, V. Mon–Sat 7–9:30pm. Bus: Western Bus.

Graycliff ☞☞☞ CONTINENTAL   We think Graycliff is simply the finest restaurant in The Bahamas. Part of the Graycliff hotel, an antiques-filled colonial mansion located opposite Government House, this restaurant is the domain of connoisseur and bon vivant Enrico Garzaroli. The chefs use local Bahamian products and delicacies whenever available and fashion them into a spicy and hearty cuisine. The chefs, while neither completely traditional nor regional, produce such innovative dishes as grouper soup in puff pastry, and plump, juicy pheasant cooked with pineapple grown on Eleuthera. Lobster is another specialty, with half in beurre blanc and the other side with a sauce prepared with the head of the lobster. The Grand Marnier soufflé alone is worth the trip. The wine list is the finest in the country, with more than 175,000 bottles. The collection of Cuban cigars here—almost 90 types—is said to be the most varied in the world.

W. Hill St. ℂ 242/322-2796. Reservations required. Jacket advised for men. Lunch main courses $17.75–$22.55; dinner main courses $32.50–$46. AE, DC, MC, V. Mon–Fri noon–2:45pm; daily 6:30–9:30pm. Bus: 10 or 17.

The Humidor ☞☞ INTERNATIONAL   Its theme derives from the growing popularity of cigars, and the way they mix well with people, liquors, beer, and food. You'll find it within a stone outbuilding of the previously recommended hotel, Graycliff, where two dining rooms and a highly accommodating bar area present a large selection of cigars from virtually everywhere. Part of the space is devoted to a factory, where a team of carefully trained "rollers" produced the house brand (Graycliff) of cigars. Drop in just for a drink and a smoke if you wish. Head to either of the two elegantly decorated dining rooms for a meal where patrons often puff away between courses. The cuisine is the kind of hearty fare types like Jackie Gleason or Frank Sinatra enjoyed back in the '50s—that is, well-prepared and unfussy selections of fresh fish and high-quality meat, even such bistro fare as lobster or crab cakes, tuna tartare, and a decent roast lamb with the inevitable mint sauce. Fresh oysters and clams—often washed down by champagne—are savory delights as well.

At the Graycliff Hotel, West Hill St. © 242/322-2796. Reservations recommended. Main courses $30–$43. AE, DC, MC, V. Tues–Sun dinner seatings at 7, 7:30, 9, and 9:30pm. Bar Tues–Sun 6:30–11pm. Bus: 10 or 21A.

Sun And . . . *©©* FRENCH/SEAFOOD   Near Fort Montagu, this place seems to have been here forever and can name-drop better than anyplace but Graycliff. Sun And . . . is the classic Nassau restaurant, a citadel of top-notch cuisine and service with a hearty dose of British colonial charm. To get to this hard-to-find place, you pass over a drawbridge between two pools and then enter a Spanish-style courtyard, complete with fountains. In this fine old Bahamian home, you can order drinks in the patio bar and then dine cozily inside or alfresco around the rock pool.

Start with the spicy conch chowder; there's none better in Nassau. The chef shines with ingeniously prepared dishes such as braised duckling with raspberry sauce. Sure, it's been done before, but it's prepared ever so well here. The grilled veal chop with portobello mushrooms is another of the more admirably executed dishes, as is the classic roast spring lamb, almost melt-in-your-mouth tender and perfectly seasoned without being overpowered with herbs and garlic. Local foodies always praise Ronny Deryckere's incomparable soufflés (even better than the Grand Marnier soufflé at Graycliff, and that's saying a lot). Our favorite is prepared with rum raisins and Black Label Bacardi. More than 100 wines complement the well-thought-out menu.

Lake View Rd., off Shirley St. © 242/393-1205. Reservations required. Jacket preferred for men. Main courses $32–$40. AE, DISC, MC, V. Tues–Sun 6:30–9:30pm. Closed Aug–Sept. Bus: 10 or 17.

EXPENSIVE

Pink Pearl *©* BAHAMIAN/CONTINENTAL   This winning restaurant is set across from the Nassau Yacht Haven Marina in a dark pink colonial building with a wraparound porch. Some of the restaurants nearby, such as the Poop Deck, do lots more business and become a lot more animated, but this place stands in stark contrast, simply because it's relatively uncrowded and relatively formal, though there's a live jazz band every Friday night. The menu mingles Bahamian staples with continental flair. The best examples include creamy conch chowder with chives; angel-hair pasta with crabmeat and fresh cream and green onions; grilled breast of duck with mango glaze and sweet mango mash; and fillet of snapper and plantain with sautéed spinach.

E. Bay St. © 242/394-6413. Reservations recommended. Main courses $23.95–$27.95. MC, V. Daily 11:30am–3:30pm and 6:30–10:30pm. Bus: 10.

Wedgwood Restaurant INTERNATIONAL   This is a very appealing relative newcomer to downtown Nassau, ensconced in a hotel that's known for a thoroughly British atmosphere. Hilton pays a royalty to England's Wedgwood

Nassau Dining

Avery's **1**
Bahamian Kitchen **13**
Buena Vista **4**
Café Matisse **14**
Café Skans **3**
Chippie's Wall Street Café **12**
Conch Fritters Bar & Grill **7**
Crocodiles Waterfront Bar & Grill **18**
Double Dragon **17**
East Villa Restaurant and Lounge **22**
Europe **6**

Gaylord's **15**
Graycliff **9**
The Humidor **8**
Mama Lyddy's Place **10**
Montagu Gardens **21**
Pink Pearl **20**
Poop Deck **19**
Shoal Restaurant and Lounge **2**
Sun and...**16**
Wedgwood Restaurant **5**

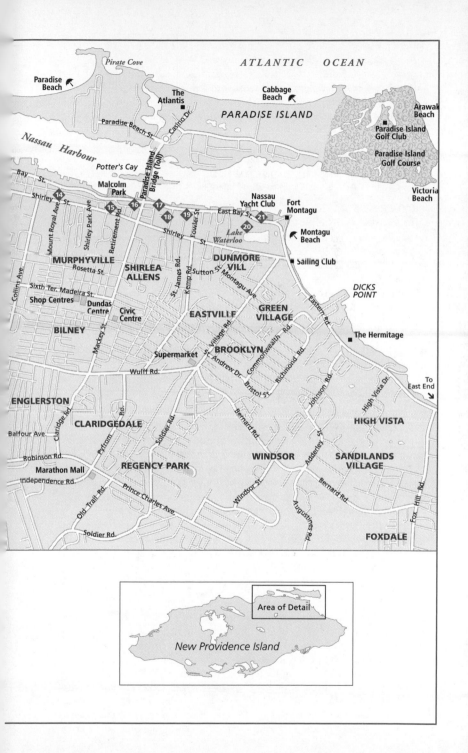

ATLANTIC OCEAN

Pirate Cove

Paradise
Beach

Cabbage
Beach

The
Atlantis

Arawak
Beach

PARADISE ISLAND

Paradise Island
Golf Club

Paradise Beach St.

Paradise Island
Golf Course

Nassau   Harbour

Potter's Cay

Victoria
Beach

Casino Dr.

Bay St.

Malcolm
Park

Paradise Island
Bridge (Toll)

Nassau
Yacht Club

Fort
Montagu

Shirley St.

14

Mount Royal Ave.

Shirley Park Ave.

Retirement Rd.

15

16

17

18

19

East Bay St.

21

Lake
Waterloo

20

Montagu
Beach

Shirley
St.

Fowler St.

Kemp Rd.

Sailing Club

MURPHYVILLE

Collins Ave.

Rosetta St.

SHIRLEA
ALLENS

St. James Rd.

Sutton St.

DUNMORE
VILL

DICKS
POINT

Sixth Ter. Madeira St.

Shop Centres

Dundas
Centre

Civic
Centre

Mackey St.

EASTVILLE

Montagu Ave.

GREEN
VILLAGE

Eastern Rd.

BILNEY

Supermarket

BROOKLYN

St. Andrew Dr.

Village Rd.

Commonwealth Rd.

Richmond Rd.

The Hermitage

Wulff Rd.

Bristol St.

Johnson Rd.

High Vista Dr.

To
East End

ENGLERSTON

Claridge Rd.

Pyfrom Rd.

Soldier Rd.

Bernard Rd.

Adderley St.

HIGH VISTA

Balfour Ave.

CLARIDGEDALE

WINDSOR

SANDILANDS
VILLAGE

Robinson Rd.

Marathon Mall

REGENCY PARK

Independence Rd.

Old Trail Rd.

Prince Charles Ave.

Windsor St.

Augustines Rd.

Bernard Rd.

Fox Hill Rd.

Soldier Rd.

FOXDALE

Area of Detail

New Providence Island

pottery company for the right to use the name and the right to outfit the place with a combination of gleaming mahogany and Wedgwood's trademark blue-gray color. Most of the guests here, many of them conducting business with local banks or manufacturers, begin their meal with a drink at the formal bar before heading into the dining room for seamless service and well-prepared food. Examples include tenderloin of beef, veal chop with exotic mushrooms, a succulent rock lobster with lime and garlic butter, and a savory loin of pork with onion marmalade. Everything here seems to taste better when it's accompanied by side orders like mushroom casserole with fresh chives.

In the British Colonial Hilton, 1 Bay St. 𝄞 **242/322-3301**. Reservations recommended. Main courses $19–$34. AE, MC, V. Daily noon–3pm and Mon–Sat 6–10:30pm. Bus: 10.

MODERATE

Café Matisse 🌶 INTERNATIONAL/ITALIAN   Set directly behind Parliament House, in a beige building that was built a century ago as a private home, this restaurant is on everybody's short list of downtown Nassau favorites. It serves well-prepared Italian and international cuisine to businesspeople, workers from nearby government offices, and all kinds of deal makers. There are dining areas within an enclosed courtyard, as well as on two floors of the interior, which is decorated with colorful Matisse prints. It's run by the sophisticated Bahamian-Italian team of Greg and Gabriella Curry, who prepare menu items that include an enticing cannelloni with lobster sauce; mixed grill of seafood; grilled rack of lamb with grilled tomatoes; a perfect osso buco Milanese; and a zesty curried shrimp with rice. There are also meal-size pizzas.

Bank Lane at Bay St., just north of Parliament Sq. 𝄞 **242/356-7012**. Reservations not necessary. Lunch main courses $12–$20; dinner main courses $17–$30. AE, MC, V. Mon–Sat noon–3pm and 6–10pm. Bus: 17 and 21.

East Villa Restaurant and Lounge CHINESE/CONTINENTAL   You might imagine yourself in Hong Kong during the 1980s in this well-designed modern house across the road from the headquarters of the Nassau Yacht Club. It's somewhat upscale, sometimes attracting rich Florida yachties to its dimly lit precincts, where aquariums bubble in a simple but tasteful contemporary setting. Zesty Szechuan flavors appear on the menu, but there are less spicy Cantonese alternatives, including sweet-and-sour chicken and steamed vegetables with cashews and water chestnuts. Lobster tail in the spicy Chinese style is one of our favorites. Dishes can be ordered mild, medium, or zesty hot.

E. Bay St. 𝄞 **242/393-3377**. Reservations required. Main courses $8.75–$29.50. AE, MC, V. Sun–Fri noon–3pm and daily 6–11pm. Bus: 11 or 19.

Europe GERMAN/CONTINENTAL   Attached to an inexpensive hotel, Europe offers the best German specialties in Nassau. Admittedly, that may not be the kind of food you came to Nassau for, and it's a little heavy for the tropics; but the dishes are properly rendered and politely served, and the price is fair. This is where you go when you think you can't stare another grouper or conch in the face. Robust flavors have traveled across the ocean rather well—at least the horde of German visitors on our last visit agreed. When the waiter suggests hearty soups to begin with, he means it—perhaps lima bean and sausage. Naturally, there is bratwurst and quite good sauerbraten. If you don't opt for the Wiener schnitzel, you might settle for a perfectly done pepper steak cognac. The chef will also prepare two kinds of fondue: bourguignonne and cheese.

Kids Family-Friendly Restaurants

Bahamian Kitchen *(see p. 88)*   For families who want to escape their hotel dining rooms and sample some real island specialties, this is one of the best places in the center of Nassau. The food is home cooked and reasonably priced to boot. If you're planning a picnic, they also do takeout here.

Double Dragon *(see p. 90)*   If your kids crave Chinese once a week back home, you can carry on that tradition by going to this Cantonese and Szechuan spot in the heart of Nassau. Prices are extremely reasonable and portions filling. You don't get a lot of atmosphere, but you do get well-cooked food with an Asian slant. Try their honey and garlic chicken!

Café Johnny Canoe *(see p. 93)*   Out on Cable Beach, this is one of the fun family restaurants along this tabled beachfront. If your kids love the likes of lobster, grouper fingers (tell them it's fish sticks), homemade soups, and some of the most well-stuffed sandwiches along the beach, they've come to the right place.

Everybody's favorite dessert is the meltingly moist German chocolate cake. All right, we said it was heavy. Diet tomorrow.

In the Ocean Spray Hotel, W. Bay St. © 242/322-8032. Lunch main courses $8–$14; dinner main courses $14–$24. AE, DISC, MC, V. Mon–Fri 8:30am–10pm. Bus: 10.

Gaylord's NORTHERN INDIAN   The Indian owners of this restaurant arrived in The Bahamas via Kenya and then England, and they are wryly amused at their success "in bringing India to The Bahamas." Within a room lined with Indian art and artifacts, you'll dine on a wide range of savory and zesty Punjabi, tandoori, and curried dishes. Some of the best choices are the lamb selections, although recently such concessions to local culture as curried or tandoori-style conch have cropped up on the menu. If you don't know what to order, consider a tandoori mixed platter, which might satisfy two of you with a side dish or two. Any of the korma dishes, which combine lamb, chicken, beef, or vegetables in a creamy curry sauce, are very successful. Take-out meals are also available.

Dowdeswell St. at Bay St. © 242/356-3004. Main courses $11.50–$25; fixed-price lunches $15.95–$18.95; fixed-price dinners $22.95–$46.50; vegetarian dinner $22.95. AE, MC, V. Mon–Fri noon–3pm and daily 6:30–11pm. Bus: 10 or 17.

Montagu Gardens STEAKS/SEAFOOD/CONTINENTAL   At the edge of Lake Waterloo, this restaurant is installed in an old mansion at the eastern end of Bay Street. The dining room is in a courtyard garden. The chefs get some of the best seafood and beef on the island, and they are especially noted for their Angus beef, which they carve into succulent T-bones, filet mignons, and rib eyes, all prepared to order. In addition, they also offer baby back ribs and, on most occasions, a perfectly seasoned and cooked rack of lamb. The stuffed lobster tail is a mite ordinary, but they do wonders with that old Bahamian standby, grouper, and also serve some moist and well-seasoned dolphinfish. If you eat too much here, you can dance the night away (and the calories) at the adjoining Club Waterloo.

E. Bay St. ℭ **242/394-6347**. Reservations recommended. Lunch main courses $4–$17; dinner main courses $12.50–$34. AE, MC, V. Mon–Sat 11:30am–3pm and 6–11pm.

Poop Deck BAHAMIAN/SEAFOOD   This is a favorite with yachties and others who find a perch on the second-floor, open-air terrace, which overlooks the harbor and Paradise Island. If you like your dining with a view, there is no better place in the heart of Nassau. At lunch, you can order conch chowder (perfectly seasoned) or some juicy beef burgers. The waiters are friendly, the crowd is convivial, and the festivities continue into the evening with lots of drinking and good cheer. Native grouper fingers served with peas 'n' rice is the Bahamian soul food dish on the menu. Two of the best seafood selections are the fresh lobster and the stuffed deviled crab. The creamy homemade lasagna with crisp garlic bread is another fine choice.

Nassau Yacht Haven Marina, E. Bay St. ℭ **242/393-8175**. Lunch $9.95–$34; main courses $13.95–$39. AE, MC, V. Daily noon–4pm and 5–10:15pm. Bus: 10 or 17.

Shoal Restaurant and Lounge BAHAMIAN   Many of our good friends in Nassau swear that this is the best joint for authentic local food. We're not entirely convinced this is true, but we rank it near the top. The place is a beehive of activity on Saturday morning when seemingly half of Nassau shows up for the chef's specialty, boiled fish and johnnycake. This may or may not be your fantasy, but if you're Bahamian, it is like pot liquor and turnip greens with cornbread to a Southerner. Far removed from the well-trodden tourist path, this restaurant is a real local favorite. After all, where can you get a good bowl of okra soup these days? Naturally, conch chowder is the favorite opener. Many diners follow that chowder with more conch, "cracked" this time. But you can also order more unusual dishes such as Bahamian-style mutton using native spices and herbs. The seafood platter, with lobster, shrimp, and fried grouper, is more international in appeal. Peas 'n' rice accompanies everything.

Nassau St. ℭ **242/323-4400**. Main courses $19–$25. AE, DISC, MC, V. Thurs–Tues 7:30am–12:30am.

INEXPENSIVE

Avery's Restaurant *(Finds)* BAHAMIAN   There is not a more authentic or native dining spot in all of New Providence. Occupying a pink-painted, two-story cinderblock house and set beside the main road passing through Adelaide Village, this is the hamlet's prominent bar and restaurant. Avery Ferguson, the owner, is likely to be tending bar or taking orders at the time of your arrival. Menu items focus on fresh seafood and imported meat items such as pork chops and steaks. Snapper and grouper are likely to be available either fried, grilled, or smothered (stewed) with onions, spices, and tomatoes. No one here will mind if you opt for a drink or two at any hour of the afternoon. The local brew (Kalik) is always available, as is virtually any drink you can think of that's made with Bahamian rum.

Adelaide Rd. ℭ **242/362-1547**. Reservations not necessary. Main courses $11–$28. MC, V. Daily noon–11pm.

Bahamian Kitchen *(Kids/Value)* BAHAMIAN   Next to Trinity Church, this is one of the best places for good Bahamian food at modest prices. Down-home dishes, full of local flavor, include lobster Bahamian style, fried red snapper, conch salad, stewed fish, curried chicken, okra soup, and pea soup and dumplings.

Most dishes are served with peas 'n' rice. You can order such old-fashioned Bahamian fare as stewed fish and corned beef and grits, all served with johnny-cake. If you'd like to introduce your kids to Bahamian cuisine, this is an ideal choice. There's take-out service if you're planning a picnic.

Trinity Place, off Market St. ☎ 242/325-0702. Reservations not needed. Lunches $3.50–$5; main courses $6.50–$11. AE, DC, MC, V. Mon–Sat 11:30am–1pm. Bus: 10 or 17.

Café Skans *(Value)* INTERNATIONAL This is a straightforward, Formica-clad diner with an open kitchen, offering flavorful food that's served without fanfare in generous portions. It's next door to the Straw Market, attracting local residents and office workers from the government buildings nearby. Menu items include Bahamian fried or barbecued chicken; souvlaki or gyros in pita bread; and burgers, steaks, and various kinds of seafood platters. This is where worka-day Nassau comes for breakfast.

W. Bay St., adjacent to the Straw Market. ☎ 242/322-2486. Reservations not accepted. Breakfast $3.45–$9.50; sandwiches $4.95–$8.95; main-course platters $5.95–$14. MC, V. Daily 8am–9pm.

Chippie's Wall Street Café INTERNATIONAL Its name derives from the owners' involvement with investments in the U.S.-based stock market, and part of its clientele comes here because of the trio of rentable computers that allow easy access to the Internet. (The price of access is $5.75 per 30-minute session.) Come here every Sunday to Thursday for light lunches and drinks that are served one flight upstairs from street level, and consider it an option for after-hours live music, drinking, and flirting during the extended hours every Friday and Saturday. Menu items include "the usual suspects"—grilled steaks and pork chops, salads, sandwiches, pastas, lobster, and chicken. Nothing is fancy here, but the food is quite satisfying. Your best bet is one of the daily specials when the cooks show more flair. Decor includes lots of Bahamian paintings, and wall murals that emulate some of the palms on a Bahamian beach.

Colony Place Shopping Arcade, Bay St. at George St. ☎ 242/356-2087. Reservations not necessary. Sand-wiches, salads, and platters $6.95–$19.95. AE, DC, DISC, MC, V. Sun–Thurs 9am–5pm; Fri–Sat food service 9am–10pm, bar service till 2am. Bus: 10.

Conch Fritters Bar & Grill BAHAMIAN/INTERNATIONAL A true local hangout with real island atmosphere, this light-hearted restaurant changes its focus several times throughout the day. In the morning, folks stop in for a quick breakfast before heading off to work in downtown Nassau. Lunches and dinners are high-volume, high-turnover affairs mitigated only by attentive staff who seem genuinely concerned about the well-being of their guests. Live music is presented every day except Monday from 7pm till closing, when the place trans-forms again into something of a singles bar. Seated on wicker furniture, beneath a blue mural of a Bahamian sky, you'll imagine yourself deep in the Out Islands. Food choices are rather standard but still quite good, including cracked conch, fried shrimp, grilled salmon, six different versions of chicken, blackened rib eye steak, burgers, and sandwiches. Specialty drinks from the active bar include a Goombay Smash.

Marlborough St. (across the street from the British Colonial Hilton). ☎ 242/323-8801. Reservations not nec-essary. Burgers, sandwiches, and platters $8.25–$24.95. AE, MC, V. Daily 7am–midnight.

Crocodiles Waterfront Bar & Grill INTERNATIONAL/BAHAMIAN One of the most appealing, funky bar/restaurants in Nassau lies about a 2-minute walk from the Nassau side of the Paradise Island Bridge, with a view over

Finds **Picnic, Anyone?**

Look no further than **Roscoe's,** at the Red Roof, on West Bay Street (© **242/322-2810**). Located in a graceful Victorian house, with a picket fence and lots of 19th-century charm, it sits a few steps west of the Paradise Island Bridge. Inside, you'll find more than 100 kinds of cheeses, smoked salmon, and cold cuts. You'll also find smoked meats from Germany, exotic rye breads from Canada, and daily take-out specials like chicken lasagna. There's a small cluster of tiny tables on a side porch if you prefer to eat in. Roscoe's is open Monday through Friday 8am to 4pm.

If you have a kitchenette, you might head for one of the fishing boats that moor beneath the Paradise Island Bridge and buy fresh lobster or conch to take home. You could also buy portions of johnnycake-to-go from the previously recommended Bahamian Kitchen (see above) or stock up on cold cuts and soda at any of Nassau's supermarkets.

Most of you will head straight for the beach, but another ideal spot for a picnic is Fort Charlotte, off West Bay Street on Chippingham Road (see below). After touring its dank dungeons, find a sunny spot on the grounds for your picnic. Others might prefer a picnic near the tropical foliage of the Botanical Gardens (see below).

---

the water. Set on a deck that's partially protected with thatched parasols but mostly open to the sky and a view of the channel, it's completely casual. (You'll recognize the place by the hundreds of stenciled crocodiles happily cavorting on the wall that separates the place from the dense traffic of East Bay Street.) After one of the rum concoctions from the bar, you might get into the swing of things. If you're hungry, order up cracked or grilled conch, a grilled 10-ounce sirloin steak, teriyaki-marinated salmon, grilled lobster tail, an island-inspired mango-glazed chicken breast, crab cakes, or a standard but creamy lasagna. A particularly good sandwich choice is blackened mahimahi. There's a nightclub on the premises with frequent live entertainment.

E. Bay St. © **242/323-3341.** Reservations not necessary. Main courses $10.75–$27.50. MC, V. Daily 11am–5pm and 6–10:30pm. Bus: 10 or 17.

Double Dragon *(Kids* CANTONESE/SZECHUAN   The chefs hail from the province of Canton in mainland China, and that's the inspiration for most of the food here. If you've ever really wondered about the differences between Cantonese and Szechuan cuisine, a quick look at the menu here will highlight the differences. Lobster, chicken, or beef, for example, can be prepared Cantonese style, with a mild black-bean or ginger sauce; or in spicier Szechuan formats of red peppers, chilis, and garlic. Honey-garlic chicken and orange-flavored shrimp are always popular and succulent. Overall, this place is a fine choice if you're eager for a change from grouper and burgers.

Bridge Plaza Commons, Mackey St. © **242/393-5718.** Reservations not necessary. Main courses $8–$13. AE, DISC, MC, V. Mon–Fri noon–10pm; Sat 4–11pm; Sun 5–10pm. Bus: 10 or 17.

Mama Lyddy's Place *(* *Value* BAHAMIAN/AMERICAN   This restaurant occupies the homestead of a Bahamian matriarch, Lydia Russell, who died in the 1980s and never had a hand in actually establishing the place. That honor belongs to her children, who used their extensive experience at a neighboring take-out place (**The Palm Tree Restaurant; ©** 242/322-4201) to re-create a sense of wholesomeness and The Bahamas the way it used to be. This place is set within a white-and-tangerine-colored stucco house in the heart of Nassau. Inside, you'll find lots of exposed wood, a color scheme of hot pink and black, and lots of local paintings inspired by Junkanoo. Menu items are as down-home as you can get (cracked conch, baked pork chops, fried or steamed grouper, minced or broiled lobster, and baked chicken) and are served with two of at least seven side dishes like potato salad, creamed corn, beets, coleslaw, macaroni and cheese, peas 'n' rice, or fried plantain.

Corner of Market St. at Cockburn St. © 242/328-6849. Reservations not necessary. Main courses $8–$20. No credit cards. Mon–Sat 8am–6pm; Sun 8am–3pm. Bus: 18.

CABLE BEACH
VERY EXPENSIVE
The Black Angus Grille *&* INTERNATIONAL/STEAKS/SEAFOOD   This is your best bet for dining if you're testing your luck at the Crystal Palace Casino nearby (and you may need to win to pay the hefty bill here). The Rotisserie in the Sheraton Grand Resort Paradise Island has the edge and is also more reasonably priced, but this is a close runner-up. Serving some of the best beef and steaks along Cable Beach, it's the favorite of hundreds of casino-goers. Set one floor above the gambling tables, it has a boldly geometric decor of brightly colored tilework and comfortable banquettes.

Although steaks are frozen and flown in from the mainland, they are well-prepared—succulent, juicy, and cooked to your specifications. The filet mignon is especially delectable, although the T-bone always seems to have more flavor. Prime rib is a nightly feature. The kitchen also prepares a number of sumptuous seafood platters, and Bahamian lobster tails here are fresh and flavorful.

In the Nassau Marriott Resort and Crystal Palace Casino, W. Bay St. © 242/327-6200. Reservations recommended. Main courses $28–$39.50. AE, DC, DISC, MC, V. Mon–Sat 6–11pm (though hours can vary, so call in advance). Bus: 10 or 38.

Sole Mare *&&* NORTHERN ITALIAN   This is our top choice for elegant dining along Cable Beach, and it also serves the best Northern Italian cuisine along the beach strip. The chefs are well-trained and inventive. A fillet of whatever fresh fish is available that day appears on the menu and is the keynote of many a delectable meal here. Many of the other ingredients have to be imported from the mainland, but the chefs still work their magic with them. Their apple-scented lobster bisque laced with cream and cognac is so velvety smooth it's worth the calorie overload. Veal sautéed with endive is something usually encountered in a little upmarket tavern in northern Italy, but it appears here perfectly prepared and with some extra flavor from white wine and capers. The dessert soufflés are hardly the equal of those served at Sun And . . . , but they're still excellent, especially when served with a vanilla sauce.

In the Nassau Marriott Resort & Crystal Palace Casino, W. Bay St. © 242/327-6200. Reservations required. Main courses $25–$39. AE, DC, DISC, MC, V. Wed–Sun 6–11pm (though hours can vary slightly, so call ahead). Bus: 10 or 38.

EXPENSIVE
The Beef Cellar *&* STEAKS/SEAFOOD   If you like steak, look no further on Cable Beach. The steaks here are juicy, succulent, and tender—and cooked just as you like. Located downstairs from the hotel's lobby, within a short walk

of the casino at the neighboring Nassau Marriott Resort, the Beef Cellar features a warmly masculine decor of exposed stone and leather, two-fisted drinks, and tables that have individual charcoal grills for diners who prefer to grill their own steaks. The prices here are more reasonable than those at the Black Angus Grille in the Marriott Resort.

In the Nassau Beach Hotel. ② 242/327-7711. Reservations not needed. Main courses $14.95–$32.50. AE, DC, MC, V. Daily 6–10:30pm. Bus: 10 or 38.

MODERATE

Capriccio ITALIAN/INTERNATIONAL   Set beside a prominent round-about, about a quarter mile west of the megahotels of Cable Beach, this restaurant lies within a grandly Italian building with Corinthian columns and an outdoor terrace. Inside, it's a lot less formal, outfitted like a luncheonette, but with lots of exposed granite, busy espresso machines, and kindly Bahamian staff who have been trained in their understanding of Italian culinary nuance. At lunch you get pretty ordinary fare such as fresh salads, sandwiches, and a few hot platters like cracked conch. But the cooks shine at night, offering dishes such as chicken breast with sage and wine sauce; spaghetti with pesto and pine nuts, and seafood platters.

W. Bay St. ② 242/327-8547. Reservations recommended. Lunch items $8.50–$14.50; dinner main courses $12.75–$21.75. MC, V. Mon–Sat 11am–10pm, Sun 5–10pm.

Dickie Mo's SEAFOOD/CONTINENTAL   Set on Cable Beach's main road, 2 blocks west of the Radisson Hotel, this restaurant is a well-maintained place that has managed to hold its own against the better-financed restaurants in the nearby megahotels. The decor is nautical, with fishnets, wide-plank flooring, weathered driftwood, and sailing memorabilia; there are three separate dining rooms plus an outside terrace. Enjoy such dishes as barbecued chicken or ribs, grilled salmon or mahimahi in garlic-flavored butter sauce, yellowfin tuna with onion and sweet-pepper sauce, and shark fillet. The most expensive items include stone crabs and broiled and stuffed lobsters. Good cooking, without fancy artifice, keeps diners coming back for more.

Next door, under the same ownership, is a red-and-black-fronted restaurant named **The Japanese Steak House,** which usually operates at about the same hours and prices.

Cable Beach Hwy., Cable Beach. ② 242/327-7854. Reservations not needed. Main courses $9.95–$35.95. AE, MC, V. Daily 4pm–midnight.

The Poop Deck at Sandy Point INTERNATIONAL/SEAFOOD   This is the largest and most imposing restaurant west of Cable Beach, convenient for the owners of the many upscale villas and condos that surround it. It's set within a pink concrete building that's highly visible from West Bay Street. But despite its impressive exterior, it's a little sterile-looking on the inside; it's a simple island restaurant that originally evolved from a roughneck bar that used to be here in the early 1970s. Lunch is usually devoted to well-prepared burgers, pastas, sandwiches, and salads. Dinners are more substantial, featuring filet mignon, surf-and-turf, cracked conch, and fried shrimp caught off the Bahamian Long Island. The house drink is a Bacardi splish-splash, containing Bacardi select, Nassau Royal Liqueur, pineapple juice, cream, and sugarcane syrup.

Poop Deck Dr., off W. Bay St. ② 242/327-DECK. Reservations recommended. Lunch main courses $11–$21; dinner main courses $18–$42. AE, MC, V. Tues–Sun noon–3pm and 5:30–11pm.

Finds **The Secret Garden**

The Retreat, Village Road (© **242/393-1317**), consists of 11 acres of the most unspoiled gardens on New Providence, even more intriguing than the Botanical Gardens. They're home to about 200 species of exotic palm trees. You'll think you've wandered into *1001 Arabian Nights* in this true oasis in the heart of Nassau. Half-hour tours of the grounds are given Tuesday through Thursday at noon. This is the home of The Bahamas National Trust, and the grounds (without the tours) can be visited Monday through Friday from 9am to 5pm for a $2 admission for adults or 50¢ for children.

INEXPENSIVE

Café Johnny Canoe *(Kids* INTERNATIONAL/BAHAMIAN There's absolutely nothing stylish about this place (it was originally a Howard John son's), but because of its good value and cheerful staff, it's almost always filled with satisfied families. Within a yellow-painted interior that's accented with junkanoo memorabilia, you can order filling portions of diner-style food with a Bahamian twist: cracked conch and lobster, grilled mahimahi, grouper fingers with tartar sauce, homemade soups, and fried fish. Sandwiches always come with one side order; platters always come with two. The place is named after the legend of a Bahamian slave who escaped in the canoe of a Junkanoo band. Every Friday night between 8 and 10pm, there's live junkanoo music, accented with goatskin drums and synchronized cowbells.

In the Nassau Beach Hotel, W. Bay St. © 242/327-3373. Breakfast $5–$7; salads, sandwiches, and lunch and dinner platters $8.95–$15.95. AE, MC, V. Daily 7:30am–midnight.

WEST OF CABLE BEACH

The Restaurant at Compass Point *(** CALIFORNIAN/CARIBBEAN/ INTERNATIONAL This is one of the best restaurants on New Providence, and the only one to join the stellar ranks of Graycliff and Sun And . . . in years. It's not as formal as either of those, but instead it has a low-key, casually hip style that attracts lots of entertainment-industry types and local foodies. The dining room is indoor/outdoor, outfitted in island colors; the interior is capped with slowly spinning ceiling fans.

The cuisine is a combination of California and Caribbean, with many innovative dishes, some of which even show a Thai influence. Lunch offerings include warm grilled-chicken sandwiches, salades Niçoise garnished with strips of grilled mahimahi, and tandoori fried calamari and jerk chicken salad. At night, many of the chef's dishes exhibit touches of whimsy, as in the case of agnolotti filled with conch (a masterful, original dish), snails in puff pastry, seafood fish cakes, a delectable rack of lamb with a guava-roasted garlic glaze, and grilled or blackened snapper. The risotto with a variety of mushrooms and fresh herbs is the best we've ever sampled on the island.

In the Hotel at Compass Point, W. Bay St., Gambier, Love Beach. © 242/327-4500. Reservations required. Lunch platters $6.75–$21; dinner main courses $18–$45. AE, MC, V. Daily 7am–10:30pm.

Travellers Rest *(* (*Value* BAHAMIAN/SEAFOOD Set in an isolated spot about 1½ miles west of the megahotels of Cable Beach, this restaurant feels far away from it all. Its owners will make you feel like you're dining on a remote

Out Island. Travellers Rest is set in a cozy cement-sided house that stands in a grove of sea-grape and palm trees facing the ocean. It was established by Winnipeg-born Joan Hannah in 1972, and since then has fed ordinary as well as famous folks like Stevie Wonder, Gladys Knight, spy novelist Robert Ludlum, Julio Iglesias, Eric Clapton, and Rosa Parks. You can dine outside, but if it's rainy (highly unlikely), you can go inside the tavern with its small bar decorated with local paintings. Many diners use the white-sand beach across from the restaurant; others pull up in their own boats. In this laid-back atmosphere, you can feast on well-prepared grouper fingers, barbecue ribs, curried chicken, steamed or cracked conch, or minced crawfish, and finish perhaps with guava cake, the best on the island. The conch salad served on the weekends is said to increase virility in men.

W. Bay St., near Gambier (9 miles west of the center of Nassau). ℂ 242/327-7633. Reservations not necessary. Lunch main courses $9–$22.50; dinner main courses $15–$24.50. AE, MC, V. Daily noon–10pm. Western Transportation bus to and from Nassau $1.75 each way.

5 Beaches, Water Sports & Other Outdoor Pursuits

One of the great sports centers of the world, Nassau and the islands that surround it are marvelous places for swimming, sunning, snorkeling, scuba diving, boating, waterskiing, and deep-sea fishing, as well as tennis and golf.

You can learn more about most of the available activities by calling **The Bahamas Sports and Aviation Information Center** (ℂ **800/32-SPORT** or 305/932-0051) from anywhere in the continental United States. Call Monday through Friday from 9am to 5pm, EST. Or write the center at 19495 Biscayne Blvd., Suite 809, Aventura, FL 33180.

HITTING THE BEACH

Lovely **Cable Beach** ℱℱ, is the most popular beach on New Providence Island, which offers all sorts of water sports, as well as easy access to shops, casino action, bars, and restaurants. The beach offers 4 miles of soft white sand, and the different types of food, restaurants, snack bars, and water sports offered at the hotels lining the waterfront are incredibly varied. You can arrange snorkeling or scuba diving, order fresh fruit juices or cold beer, or get your hair braided by one of the locals. The beach also functions as a kind of bazaar, with many Bahamians parading up and down, hawking various crafts. You'll need to hunt for a spot on the strip that's suitable for you. Waters can be rough and reefy, then calm and clear a little farther along the shore.

Cable Beach is far superior to the meager beach of Nassau, the **Western Esplanade** (also called **Junkanoo Beach**), which sweeps westward from the British Colonial. But if you're staying in a Nassau hotel and don't want to make the trip to Cable Beach, you might use the local beach instead; it has rest rooms, changing facilities, and a snack bar.

At some point in a visit, even Cable Beach beach buffs like to desert the sands here in favor of **Paradise Beach** on Paradise Island (see chapter 4). Paradise Beach is even more convenient to residents of Nassau hotels, because all they have to do is walk, drive, or take a boat to nearby Paradise Island. Paradise Beach can be reached by boat from the Prince George Wharf. Round-trip tickets cost $4 per person. It's also possible to drive to the beach across the Paradise Island Bridge for a toll of $2, or you can walk across for only 25¢.

To reach **Saunders Beach,** where many of the local people go on weekends, take West Bay Street toward Coral Island. This beach lies across from Fort Charlotte.

On the north shore, past the Cable Beach Hotel properties, **Caves Beach** lies some 7 miles west of Nassau. It stands near Rock Point, right before the turnoff along Blake Road that leads to the airport. Since visitors often don't know of this place, it's another good spot to escape the hordes. It's also a good beach with soft sands.

We often head for **Old Fort Beach** *(⁂* when we want to escape the crowds on weekdays, a 15-minute drive west of the Nassau International Airport (take West Bay Street toward Lyford Cay). This lovely sandy beach opens onto the turquoise waters of Old Fort Bay near the western part of New Providence. The least developed of the island's beaches, it attracts many homeowners from swanky Lyford Cay nearby. In winter the beach can be quite windy, but in summer it's as calm as the Caribbean Sea.

BOAT CRUISES

Cruises from the harbors around New Providence Island are offered by a number of operators, with trips ranging from daytime voyages for snorkeling, picnicking, sunning, and swimming, to sunset and moonlight cruises.

Barefoot Sailing Cruises, Sugar Reef Marina (© **242/393-0820**) runs the *Wind Dance,* which leaves for all-day cruises from this dock, offering many sailing and snorkeling possibilities. This is your best bet if you're seeking a more romantic cruise and don't want 100 people aboard. The cruises usually stop at Rose Island, which is a charming, picture-perfect spot, with an uncrowded white sandy beach and palm trees. You can also sail on a ketch, the 54-foot *Riding High,* which is bigger than the 41-foot *Wind Dance.* Another vessel, the 65-passenger catamaran *Big Foot,* has also joined the fleet. Cruise options are plentiful—including a half day of sailing, snorkeling, and exploring, for $34. A full day goes for $55. Champagne-and-cocktail cruises in the evening are also popular, for $35 per person. A private dinner cruise, lasting 3 moonlit hours, is a favorite with honeymooners who pay $480 for two.

If the cruise becomes a party, $480 is still charged for the first two people, then $55 for each additional person. All vessels are available for private charter.

Flying Cloud, Paradise Island West Dock (© **242/393-1957**), features catamaran cruises carrying 50 people on day and sunset trips, or a maximum of 30 for dinner. It's a good bet for people who want a more intimate cruise and shy away from the heavy volume carried aboard Majestic Tours catamarans (see below). Snorkeling equipment is provided free. A half-day charter costs $35 per person; a 2½-hour sunset cruise goes for $30. The 3½-hour dinner cruise at 7pm is $50 per person (half price for children). The 57-foot catamaran was designed and built by Gold Coast Yachts. Boats run daily, with departure times depending on the type of cruise. Round-trip transportation to the dock from your hotel is included.

Finds A Beach for Lovers

Continuing west along West Bay Street, you reach **Love Beach,** across from Sea Gardens, a good stretch of sand lying east of Northwest Point. Love Beach, although not big, is a special favorite with lovers. The snorkeling is superb, too. It's technically private, though no one bothers visitors who come, and locals fervently hope it won't ever become overrun like Cable Beach.

Majestic Tours Ltd, Hillside Manor (℃ **242/322-2606**), will book 3-hour cruises on two of the biggest catamarans in the Atlantic, offering views of the water, sun, sand, and outlying reefs. This is the biggest and most professionally run of the cruise boats, and it's an affordable option; but we find that there are just too many other passengers aboard. The *Yellow Bird* is suitable for up to 250 passengers, and the *Tropic Bird* carries up to 170. They depart from Prince George's Dock; ask for the exact departure point when you make your reservation. The cost is $15 per adult, $7.50 for children under 12, and snorkeling equipment is $10 extra. Departure days vary for both vessels; call for times, reservations, and more information. The outfitter has recently added another boat, the *Robinson Crusoe,* holding 350 passengers. This boat offers daily cruises from 10am to 4pm, costing $45 for adults or half price for children 11 and under. In addition, sunset dinner cruises Tuesday and Friday are launched at a cost of $45 per adult or half price for children.

FISHING

May through September are the best months for the oceanic bonito and the black-fin tuna; June and July for blue marlin; and November through May for the amberjack found in reefy areas.

Arrangements can be made at any of the big hotels, and unfortunately, there's a hefty price tag. Prices are usually $350 for a half-day boat rental for parties of two to six or $700 for a full day's fishing.

One of the most reliable companies, **Charter Boat Association** (℃ **242/ 363-2335**), offers a fleet of 8 to 10 vessels that can seat six comfortably; they can be rented for a half day ($350) or a full day ($700). Each additional person is charged $50 depending on boat size. Fishing choices are plentiful: You can troll for wahoo, tuna, and marlin in the deep sea or cast in the shallows for snapper, amberjack, grouper, and yellowtail. Anchoring and bottom fishing are calmer options. We recommend this charter because they offer so many types of fishing and give you a lot of leeway regarding where you want to fish and how much time you want to spend.

The best charter operator, **Nassau Yacht Haven** (℃ **242/393-8173**), has both a 35-foot boat and a 42-foot boat. Fishing is mainly close to shore. It takes 15 to 20 minutes to reach a drop-off where wahoo and barracuda abound. This charter is recommended not only for its quality fishing, but also for its convenience, since you don't have far to travel before you start fishing.

GOLF

Some of the best golfing in The Bahamas is found in Nassau. The following courses are open to the public, not just to guests of the hotels that operate the properties.

Cable Beach Golf Course *ƒƒ* on W. Bay Rd., Cable Beach (℃ **242/ 327-6000**), is a spectacular 18-hole, 7,040-yard, par-72 championship golf course, but it's not as challenging as the one at the South Ocean Golf Course (see below). The Cable Beach course is under the management of the Radisson Cable Beach Hotel, but it's often used by guests of the other hotels nearby. Greens fees are $40 for residents of Radisson, $100 for all other players. Carts can be rented for $60.

South Ocean Golf Course *ƒƒƒ* on SW Bay Rd. (℃ **242/362-4391**), the best course on New Providence Island and one of the best in The Bahamas, is a 30-minute drive from Nassau on the southwest edge of the island. The course has palm-fringed greens and fairways. Overlooking the ocean, the 6,706-yard beauty has some first-rate holes amid trees, shrubs, ravines, and undulating hills. The 18-hole, USPGA-sanctioned course has a par of 72. The lofty elevation of this course offers panoramic water views, including an area of the Atlantic called Tongue of the Ocean. Golf architect Joe Lee designed the course with four challenging water holes and made very effective use of the rolling terrain. Guests at the Clarion resort next to the course pay $75 for 18 holes; non-guests are charged $110 for 18 holes, plus $30 for anybody to rent a golf cart. It's best to phone ahead in case a golf tournament is scheduled for the day you had planned to play.

HORSEBACK RIDING

Happy Trails Stables, Coral Harbour, on the southwest shore (② 242/ 362-1820), offers a 1-hour-and-30-minute horseback trail ride for $85, including free transportation to and from your hotel. Riders must weigh less than 200 pounds. The stables are signposted from the Nassau International Airport, which is 2 miles away. Children must be 9 or older, and reservations are required, especially during the holiday season.

SNORKELING, SCUBA DIVING & UNDERWATER WALKS

There's great snorkeling off most of the beaches on New Providence, especially **Love Beach.** Most any of the hotels and resorts will rent or loan you snorkeling equipment. Several of the companies mentioned above under "Boat Cruises" also offer snorkel trips, as does Bahamas Divers, below. See also "Easy Side Trips to Nearby Islands," below, for additional snorkeling excursions.

There are more dive sites around New Providence than you can see in one visit, so we've included a few of our favorites. **Shark Wall** ⊕⊕ is the most intriguing, which is a diving excursion 10 miles off the coast; others include the Rose Island Reefs, the Southwest Reef, the Razorback, and Booby Rock Reef. All dive outfitters feature one or more of these sites.

Bahama Divers, E. Bay St. (② 242/393-5644), has packages that range from a half day of snorkeling to offshore reefs for $27 per person, to a half-day scuba trip with preliminary pool instruction for beginners, for $70 for two tanks or $45 for one tank, including all equipment. Half-day excursions for certified divers to deeper outlying reefs, drop-offs, and blue holes can be arranged.

Participants receive free transportation from their hotel to the boats. Children must be 12 or older, and reservations are required, especially during the holiday season.

Hartley's Undersea Walk, E. Bay St. (② 242/393-8234), offers an exciting and educational experience. They take you out from Nassau Harbour aboard the yacht *Pied Piper*. On the 3½-hour cruise, you're submerged for about 20 minutes, descending through shallow water until you walk along the ocean bottom through a "garden" of tropical fish, sponges, and other undersea life. As you're guided through the underwater world, you'll wear a helmet that allows you to see and breathe with ease. Entire families can go on this safe adventure, which costs $55 adults, $49 children. You don't even have to be able to swim. Two trips run per day, at 9:30am and 1:30pm, Tuesday through Saturday. Arrive 30 minutes before departures, and make reservations 2 to 3 days in advance.

Stuart Cove's Dive Bahamas, SW Bay St., South Ocean (P.O. Box CB13137, Nassau; ② 800/879-9832 in the U.S., or 242/362-4171), is about 10 minutes from top dive sites, including the coral reefs, wrecks, and an underwater airplane structure used in filming James Bond thrillers. The Porpoise Pen

---

Finds **Into the Murky Depths with James Bond**

Two James Bond flicks, _Thunderball_ and _Never Say Never Again_, were shot in and around Nassau. For Bond buffs, a thrill is to take a dive from Stuart Cove, who trained the Bond movie doubles, going down into the deep to see the freighter that was sunk for the movie _Never Say Never Again_ and the Valkin bomber airplane used in the flick _Thunderball_. Both wrecks are actual sets from the movies and lie beneath the water's surface at a depth of 210 feet. To get hooked up with this adventure, put yourself in the hands of the good folks at **Stuart Cove's Dive Bahamas** (see above).

Reefs, named for Flipper, and steep sea walls are also on the diving agenda. A two-tank dive in the morning costs $80, or an all-day program goes for $120. All prices for boat dives include tanks, weights, and belts. An open-water certification course starts at $695. Bring along two friends, and the price drops to $395 per person. Escorted boat snorkeling trips cost $40. A special feature is a series of shark-dive experiences priced from $125. In one outing, Caribbean reef sharks swim among the guests. In one dive, called "Shark Arena," divers kneel down while a dive master feeds the sharks off a long pole. Another experience, a "Shark Buoy" in 6,000 feet of ocean, involves a dive among silky-skinned sharks at about 30 feet. They swim among the divers while the dive master feeds them. Another popular outing is the Shark Wall dive along an 80-foot coral wall, with shark feedings at 50 feet.

The outfitter has recently generated much excitement with its introduction of yellow "submarines," actually jet bikes called Scenic Underwater Bubbles. An air-fed bubble covers your head as these self-contained and battery-powered jet bikes propel you through an underwater wonderland. The subs are popular with non-divers, and they're viewed as safe for kids as well (that is, those older than 12). An underwater armada is escorted along to view the reefs, all for a cost of $89. The whole experience, from pickup at your hotel or cruise ship to return, takes about 3 hours.

TENNIS

Courts are available at only some hotels. Guests usually play free or for a nominal fee, whereas visitors are charged.

Most of the courts at Cable Beach are under the auspices of the **Radisson Cable Beach Hotel,** West Bay Street (© **242/327-6000**), which offers 18 courts. Residents of Radisson play free until sunset. After that, illumination costs $15 per hour. Non-Radisson guests pay $15 per person.

Other hotels offering tennis courts include the **Nassau Beach Hotel,** West Bay Street, and Cable Beach (© **242/327-7711**), with six Flexipave night-lit courts.

6 Seeing the Sights

Most of Nassau can be explored on foot, beginning at Rawson Square in the center near the stalls of the Straw Market, the country's largest native market, which spills over to the waterfront. Here is where Bahamian fishers unload a variety of produce and fish—crates of mangoes, oranges, tomatoes, and limes, plus lots of crimson-lipped conch. To experience this slice of Bahamian life, go any morning Monday through Saturday before noon.

The best way to see some of the major public buildings of Nassau is to take our walking tour (see below), which will give you not only an overview of the historic sights, but also a feel for the city as a whole. Then you can concentrate on specific sights you'd like to take in, notably Ardastra Gardens and Coral Island Bahamas.

THE TOP ATTRACTIONS

Ardastra Gardens ☞   The main attraction of the Ardastra Gardens, almost 5 acres of lush tropical planting about a mile west of downtown Nassau near Fort Charlotte, is the parading flock of **pink flamingos.** The Caribbean flamingo, national bird of The Bahamas, had almost disappeared by the early 1940s but was brought back to significant numbers through the efforts of the National Trust. They now flourish in the rookery on Great Inagua. A flock of these exotic feathered creatures has been trained to march in drill formation, responding to the drillmaster's commands with long-legged precision and discipline. The Marching Flamingos perform daily at 11am, 2, and 4pm.

Other exotic wildlife at the gardens include boa constrictors (very tame), kinkajous (honey bears) from Central and South America, green-winged macaws, peacocks and peahens, blue-and-yellow macaws, capuchin monkeys, iguanas, hutias (a rat-like animal indigenous to the islands), ring-tailed lemurs, red-ruff lemurs, margays, brown-headed tamarins (monkeys), and a crocodile. There are also numerous waterfowl to be seen in Swan Lake, including black swans from Australia and several species of wild ducks.

You can get a good look at Ardastra's flora by walking along the signposted paths. Many of the more interesting and exotic trees bear plaques with their names.

Chippingham Rd. ☎ 242/323-5806. Admission $12 adults, $6 children. Daily 9am–5pm. Bus: 10.

Seaworld Explorer ☞   If you are curious about life below the waves but aren't a strong swimmer, hop aboard this submarine, which holds about 45 passengers. It's doubtful that the military will ever press this particular craft into service in wartime, but for a quick jaunt into the deep to see colorful fish and coral, it has no equal within The Bahamas. Tours last 90 minutes and include 45 minutes of actual underwater travel at depths of about 12 feet below the waves. Big windows allow big views of a protected ecology zone offshore from the Paradise Island Airport. About 20 minutes are devoted to an above-water tour of landmarks on either side of the channel that separates Nassau from Paradise Island.

Deveaux St. Docks. ☎ 242/356-2548. Reservations required. Tours daily at 11:30am year-round; additional departure at 1:30pm Dec–June. $33 adults, $19 children ages 2–12.

MORE ATTRACTIONS

Blackbeard's Tower   These crumbling remains of a watchtower are said to have been used by the infamous pirate Edward Teach in the 17th century. The ruins are only mildly interesting—there isn't much trace of buccaneering. What's interesting is the view: With a little imagination, you can see Blackbeard peering out from here at unsuspecting ships. Blackbeard also purportedly lived here, but this is hardly well-documented.

Yamacraw Hill Rd. (5 miles east of Fort Montagu). Free admission. Open all day. Reachable by jitney.

Finds **Going Over-the-Hill**

Few visitors take this trip any more, but it used to be a tradition to go "Over-the-Hill" to Nassau's most colorful area. Over-the-Hill is the actual name of this poor residential district, where the descendants of former slaves built compact, rainbow-hued houses, leaving the most desirable lands around the harbor to the rich folks. This, not the historic core of Nassau around Rawson Square, is truly the heart of Bahamian-African culture.

The thump of the Junkanoo-Goombay drum can be heard here almost any time of the day or night. The area never sleeps, or so it is said. Certainly not on Sunday morning, when you can drive by the churches and hear hell and damnation promised to all sinners and backsliders.

This fascinating part of Nassau begins a quarter of a mile south of Blue Hill Road, which starts at the exclusive Graycliff hotel. But once you're Over-the-Hill, you're a long way from the vintage wine and expensive Cuban cigars of Graycliff. Some people—usually savvy store owners from abroad—come here to buy local handcrafts from individual vendors. The area can be explored on foot (during the day only), but many visitors prefer to drive.

Botanical Gardens   More than 600 species of tropical flora are found in this 18-acre park, located within a former rock quarry near Fort Charlotte. The garden features vine-draped arbors, two freshwater ponds with lilies, water plants, tropical fish, and a small cactus garden. After viewing them, you can take a leisurely walk along one of the trails.

Chippingham Rd. © 242/323-5975. Admission $1 adults, 50¢ children under 12. Mon–Fri 8am–4pm; Sat–Sun 9am–4pm. Bus: 10 or 17.

Fort Charlotte   Begun in 1787, Fort Charlotte is the largest of Nassau's three major defenses, built with plenty of dungeons. It used to command the western harbor. Named after King George III's consort, it was built by Gov. Lord Dunmore, who was also the last royal governor of New York and Virginia. Its 42 cannons never fired a shot, at least not at an invader. Within the complex are underground passages and a waxworks, which can be viewed on free tours. Tour guides at the fort are free but are very happy to accept a tip.

Off W. Bay St. on Chippingham Rd. © 242/322-7500. Free admission. Mon–Sat 8:30am–4pm. Bus: 10 or 17.

Fort Fincastle   Reached by climbing the Queen's Staircase, this fort was constructed in 1793 by Lord Dunmore, the royal governor. You can take an elevator ride to the top and walk on the observation floor (a 126-foot-high water tower and lighthouse) for a panoramic view of the harbor. The tower is the highest point on New Providence.

Although the ruins of the fort can hardly compete with the view, you can walk around on your own. Be wary, however, of the very persistent young men who will try to show you the way here. They'll try to hustle you, but you really don't need a guide to see some old cannons on your own.

The so-called bow of this fort is patterned like a paddle-wheel steamer, the kind used on the Mississippi. It was built to defend Nassau against a possible invasion, though no shot was ever fired.

Elizabeth Ave. No phone. Free admission to fort, 50¢ for water tower. Mon–Sat 9am–4pm. Bus: 10 or 17.

Fort Montagu   Fort Montagu was built in 1741 and stands guard at the eastern entrance to the harbor of Nassau. It's the oldest fort on the island. The Americans captured it in 1776 during the War of Independence. Less interesting than Fort Charlotte and Fort Fincastle, the ruins of this place are mainly for fort buffs. Many visitors find the nearby park, with well-maintained lawns and plenty of shade, more interesting than the fort. Several vendors peddle local handcrafts in the park, so you can combine a look at a ruined fort with a shopping expedition if you're interested.

Eastern Rd. Free admission. No regular hours. Bus: 10 or 17.

Pirates of Nassau *(Kids)*   This museum celebrates the dubious "golden age of piracy" (from 1690 to 1720). Nassau was once a bustling and robust town where pirates grew rich from plundered gold and other goods robbed at sea. Known as a paradise for pirates, it attracted various rogues and the wild women who flooded into the port to entertain them—for a price, of course. This newly opened museum re-creates those bawdy, lusty days in a series of exhibits illustrating pirate lore. You can walk through the belly of a pirate ship (the *Revenge*) as you hear "pirates" plan their next attack. You can smell the dampness of a dungeon, and you'll even hear the final prayer of an ill-fated victim before he walks the gangplank. It's fairly cheesy, but fun for kids. Exhibits also tell the saga of Captain Woodes Rogers, who was sent by the English crown to suppress pirates in The Bahamas and the Caribbean.

Marlborough and George sts. © 242/356-3759. Admission $12 adults, $6 children 3–18, free 2 and under. Mon–Sat 9am–5pm. Bus: 10 or 17.

Pompey Museum   Vendue House was built of cut limestone blocks around 1769. The property served as the island's commodity market, where palm and coconut oil, lumber, dried fish, hardware, and slaves were bartered and sold. The slavery aspect of the place continued until 1834, when an act of Parliament outlawed the practice throughout the British Empire. Full emancipation was activated in 1838. Named after the leader of a 19th-century slave revolt in the Exumas, the museum houses an exhibition on Bahamian life and culture, including many mementos on what the museum refers to as "the enslavement experience," 19th-century agriculture and sea trading, and 19th-century Bahamian culture.

At Vendue House, Bay St. at George St. © 242/326-2566. Admission $1 adults, 50¢ children. Mon–Fri 10am–4:30pm, Sat 10am–1pm. Bus: 10 or 17.

Fun Fact **A Trimmed-Down, Sexy Queen Victoria**

When you've got nothing to do, stroll over to Parliament Square to gaze upon a statue of that sexy lady, Queen Victoria. The long-reigning queen is nearly always pictured bloated and plump, but the artist here abandoned the rotund figure and created a slimmer, more alluring young monarch. Artistic license, no doubt.

WALKING TOUR   HISTORIC NASSAU

Start	Rawson Square.
Finish	Prince George Wharf.
Time	2 hours.
Best Times	Monday through Saturday between 10am and 4pm.
Worst Times	Sunday when many places are closed, and any day lots of cruise ships are in port.

Begin your tour at:
❶ Rawson Square

The center of Nassau, Rawson Square lies directly inland from Prince George Wharf, where many of the big cruise ships dock. It is the crossroads of the city, and everyone seems to pass through here, from the prime minister to bankers and local attorneys, to cruise-ship passengers, to shoppers from Paradise Island, to Junkanoo bands. On the square is the Churchill Building, where the controversial prime minister Lynden Pindling conducted his affairs for 25 years before his ouster in 1992. The current prime minister and some other government ministries use the building today. Look for the statue of Sir Milo Butler, a former shopkeeper who became the first governor of The Bahamas after Britain granted independence in 1973.

Across Rawson Square is:
❷ Parliament Square

A statue of a youthful Queen Victoria dominates the square. To the right of the statue stand more Bahamian government office buildings, and to the left is the House of Assembly, the oldest governing body in continuous session in the New World. In the building behind the statue, the Senate meets; this is a less influential body than the House of Assembly. Some of these Georgian-style buildings date from the late 1700s and early 1800s.

The Supreme Court building stands next to the:
❸ Nassau Public Library and Museum

This 1797 building was once the Nassau Gaol (jail). If you want to pop in here for a look, you can do so Monday through Thursday from 10am to 8pm, Friday from 10am to 5pm, and

---

⟮*Moments* A Secret Look at Local Life

Although **Potter's Cay** is right in the heart of Nassau, lying under the bridge that leads to Paradise Island, it offers a unique opportunity to observe local life. Sloops from the Out Islands pull in here, hauling their fresh catch, with plenty of conch. You're likely to see the chef who will be preparing your fresh fish that night, buying it off the boat from one of these fishermen (unless he's using frozen fish from Miami). Freshly grown herbs and vegetables are also sold here, along with plenty of limes (the preferred seasoning for fish in The Bahamas). Tropical fruits such as paw-paw (papaya), pineapple (usually from Eleuthera), and bananas are also sold. Little stalls sell raw conch marinated in lime juice, conch salad, conch soup, and spicy conch fritters deep-fried in fat. Please be aware that if locals are trying to sell you something, such as handcrafts, they will welcome your visit. However, if you are visiting merely to rubberneck, they may view it as an intrusion on their privacy.

Nassau Harbour

Western Esplanade

Prince George Wharf

New Providence Island

Area of Detail

Marcus Bethel Dr.

West Bay St.

Nassau St.

Augusta St.

Marlborough St.

Queen St.

West St.

West Hill St.

Delancy St.

Meeting St.

Cumberland St.

George St.

Duke St.

Market St.

Frederick St.

Charlotte St.

East Hill St.

East St.

Sands Rd.

Elizabeth Av.

Bay St.

Shirley St.

Collins Av.

Woodes Rogers Walk

Parliament St.

Rawson Square

Parliament Square

start here

finish here

1/8 Mile
.125 Kilometer

† Church ⊠ Post Office ⓘ Information ☕ "Take a Break" stop

1 Rawson Square
2 Parliament Square
3 Café Matisse
4 Nassau Public Library and Museum
5 Royal Victoria Hotel

5 Nassau General Post Office
6 Queen's Staircase
7 Fort Fincastle
8 Prospect Ridge
9 Gregory Arch
10 St. Andrew's Kirk

11 Government House
12 Graycliff
13 St. Francis Romar Catholic Church
14 The British Colonial Hilton

15 Vendue House
16 Christ Church Cathedral
17 The Straw Market
18 Woodes Rogers Walk
19 Prince George Wharf

Saturday from 10am to 4pm. Chances are you will have seen greater libraries in your day. What's amusing is that the small prison cells are now lined with books. Another item of interest is the library's collection of historic prints and old documents dating from colonial days. It became the public library in 1873.

Across from the library on Shirley Street is the former site of the:

❹ Royal Victoria Hotel

In its day, the hotel was the haunt of Confederate spies, royalty, smugglers of all sorts, and ladies and gentlemen. Horace Greeley pronounced it "the largest and most commodious hotel ever built in the tropics," and many agreed with this American journalist. The hotel experienced its heyday during the American Civil War. At the Blockade Runners' Ball, some 300 guests reportedly consumed 350 magnums of champagne. Former guests have included two British prime ministers, Neville Chamberlain, and his replacement, Winston Churchill. Prince Albert, consort of Queen Victoria, also stayed here once. The hotel closed in 1971. After it was destroyed by fire, it was demolished and razed to the ground. Today, on its former site sits one of Nassau's showcase parking lots. Ironically, the parking lot seems to be such a source of pride to the city that it is unlikely the Royal Victoria will ever be rebuilt, at least in that spot.

After imagining the former splendor of the Royal Victoria, head south along Parliament Street.

TAKE A BREAK
If you'd like to relax, try **Café Matisse**, Bank Lane and Bay Street, behind Parliament Square (🕾 **242/356-7012**). Although this cafe is also a full-fledged restaurant, it's an ideal place to stop for a drink, especially during happy hour, Monday to Saturday from 5 to 7pm. The house specialty is pizza topped with *frutti di mare*, or fresh local seafood.

At the end of Parliament Street stands:

❺ Nassau General Post Office

If you're a collector, you may want to purchase Bahamian stamps, which can be valuable. You can also mail letters and packages.

Armed with your colorful purchases, walk east (right) on East Hill Street and turn left onto East Street, then right onto Shirley Street, and head straight on Elizabeth Avenue. This will take you to the landmark:

❻ Queen's Staircase

The stairway leads to Bennet's Hill. In 1793, slaves cut these 66 steps out of sandstone cliffs. They provided access from the center of Old Nassau to:

❼ Fort Fincastle

Lord Dunmore, who had a penchant for constructing unnecessary forts at great expense, built this fort in 1793. Designed in the shape of a paddlewheel steamer, the fort was a place to look out for marauders who never came. It was eventually converted into a lighthouse, because it occupied the highest point on the island. The tower is more than 200 feet above the sea, providing a panoramic view of Nassau and its harbor.

A small footpath leads down from the fort to Sands Road. Once you reach it, head west (left) until you approach East Street again, then bear right. When you come to East Hill Street (again), go left, because you will have returned to the post office.

Continue your westward trek along East Hill Street, which is the foothill of:

❽ Prospect Ridge

This was the old dividing line between Nassau's rich and poor. The rich people (nearly always white) lived along the waterfront, often in beautiful mansions. One estate belonged to Lord Beaverbrook, the British newspaper magnate. Black Bahamians went "over-the-hill" to work in these rich homes during the day but returned to Prospect Ridge to their own homes (most often shanties) at night. They lived in places like seedy Grant's Town, originally settled in the 1820s by freed slaves.

Near the end of East Hill Street, you come to:

❾ Gregory Arch

This tunnel was cut through the hill in 1850; after it opened, working-class black Bahamians didn't have to go "over-the-hill"—and steep it was—but could go through the arch to return to their villages.

At the intersection with Market Street, turn right. On your right rises:

❿ St. Andrew's Kirk (Presbyterian)

Called simply "the Kirk," the church dates from 1810 but has seen many changes over the years. In 1864, it was enlarged, and a bell tower was added along with other architectural features. This church had the first non-Anglican parishioners in The Bahamas.

On a steep hill, rising to the west of Market Street, you see on your left:

⓫ Government House

This house is the official residence of the governor-general of the archipelago, the queen's representative to The Bahamas. The post today is largely ceremonial, because an elected prime minister does the actual governing. This pink-and-white neoclassical mansion dates from the dawn of the 19th century. Poised on its front steps is a rather jaunty statue of Christopher Columbus. Sir James Carmichael Smyth, who became ruling governor in 1829, presented the statue to The Bahamas. Visitors aren't invited to call on the governor-general, but they can sign a guest book in a tiny guardhouse near the exit gate.

Opposite the road from Government House on West Hill Street rises:

⓬ Graycliff

A Georgian-style hotel and restaurant from the 1720s, this stamping ground of the rich and famous was constructed by Capt. John Howard Graysmith in

the 1720s. In the 1920s, it achieved notoriety when it was run by Polly Leach, a pal of gangster Al Capone. Later, Lord and Lady Dudley purchased it, erased the old memories, and furnished it with grand flair and taste. It attracted such famous guests as the Duke and Duchess of Windsor and Winston Churchill.

Upon leaving Graycliff, you will see a plaque embedded in a hill. The plaque claims that this site is the spot where the oldest church in Nassau once stood.

On the corner of West Hill Street and West Street is Villa Doyle, former home of William Henry Doyle, chief justice of the Bahamian Supreme Court in the 1860s and 1870s.

Opposite it stands:

⓭ St. Francis Roman Catholic Church

Constructed between 1885 and 1886, it was the first Catholic church in The Bahamas. The Archdiocese of New York raised the funds to construct it.

Continue along West Street until you reach Marlborough. Walk the short block that leads to Queen Street and turn right, passing the front of the American embassy. At the corner of Queen Street and Marlborough rises:

⓮ The British Colonial Hilton

Built in 1923, the most famous hotel in The Bahamas was once run by Sir Harry Oakes, who was at the time the most powerful man on the islands and a friend of the Duke of Windsor. Oakes's murder in 1943, still unsolved, was called "the crime of the century." An older hotel once occupied this spot, but it burned in 1922. The set for many James Bond thrillers, this historic location was also the site of Fort Nassau. In the summer of 1999, it became a Hilton.

One part of the hotel fronts George Street, where you'll find:

⓯ Vendue House

One of the oldest buildings in Nassau, Vendue House was once called the Bourse (Stock Exchange) and was the site of many slave auctions. It is now a museum.

Not far from Vendue House on George Street is:

16 Christ Church Cathedral

Dating from 1837, this Gothic Episcopal cathedral is the venue of many important state ceremonies, including the opening of the Supreme Court: a procession of bewigged, robed judges followed by barristers, accompanied by music from the police band.

If you turn left onto Duke Street and proceed along Market Street, you reach:

17 The Straw Market

The market opens onto Bay Street and is a favorite of cruise-ship passengers. You'll find not only straw products here, but all sorts of souvenirs and gifts as well. Bahamian women will weave you a basket or braid your hair with beads if you want.

Next, take the narrow little Market Range, leading to:

18 Woodes Rogers Walk

The walk was named for a former governor of the colony who was thrown into debtors' prison in London before coming back to Nassau as royal governor. Head east along this walk for a panoramic view of the harbor, with its colorful mail and sponge boats. Markets here sell vegetables, fish, and lots of conch. The walk leads to:

19 Prince George Wharf

The wharf was constructed in the 1920s, the heyday of American Prohibition, to provide more harbor space for the hundreds of bootlegging craft that defied the American blockade against liquor. It was named for the Duke of Kent (Prince George) in honor of his visit here in 1928. Its most aristocratic vessel is the yacht of Queen Elizabeth II, the HMS *Britannia*, which has been a frequent visitor over the years. Today the cruise ships dock here.

ORGANIZED TOURS

There's a lot to see in Nassau, and many tour options to suit your taste and take you through the colorful historic city and outlying sights of interest.

Goombay Guided Walking Tours, arranged by the Ministry of Tourism, leave from the Tourist Information Booth on Rawson Square at 10, 11:30am, 1, 2:30, and 3:45pm daily. Tours last for 45 minutes and include descriptions of some of the city's most venerable buildings, with commentaries on Nassau's history, customs, and traditions. The hour-long tours require advance reservations, as schedules may vary. The cost is $5, $2.50 for children under 12. Call ℂ 242/326-9772 to confirm that tours are on schedule.

Majestic Tours, Hillside Manor, Cumberland Street, Nassau (ℂ 242/ 322- 2606), offers a number of trips, both night and day, to many sites. A 2-hour city-and-country tour leaves daily at 2:30pm and goes to all points of interest in Nassau, including the forts, the Queen's Staircase, the water tower, and the Straw Market (passing but not entering it). The tour costs $20 per person, but ask for summer specials. An extended city-and-country tour also leaves daily at 2:30pm and includes the Ardastra Gardens. The charge is $28 per person, half price for children. Combination tours depart Tuesday, Wednesday, and Thursday at 10am and combine all the sights you see on the first tour listed above, plus the Retreat Gardens and lunch. It costs $36 per person, half price for children. Many hotels have a Majestic Tours Hospitality Desk in the lobby, for information about these tours, as well as for reservations and tickets. Other hotels can supply brochures and tell you where to sign up.

EASY SIDE TRIPS TO NEARBY ISLANDS

A short boat trip will take you to several small islands lying off the north coast of New Providence. One of these, **Blue Lagoon Island,** has become so popular that several cruise ships offer their passengers day trips here. Just 3 miles north of the Narrows at the eastern end of Paradise Island, Blue Lagoon has seven beaches. Although the name recalls images of Brooke Shields, barely clad, cavorting on a desert isle, the reality is quite different. Visitors can dance to a live band, dive with sea creatures at Stingray City, parasail, snorkel, kayak, shop, and lunch at a buffet, among many other things. They also have hammocks and a children's play area with toys.

Blue Lagoon Island has had several owners, including the British Navy, cartoonist John McCutcheon, and the author of *Sophie's Choice,* William Styron. McCutcheon built a watchtower in the 1940s to replace one that was destroyed by an earlier hurricane, and added his own special touch to the structure. He covered the walls of the first floor with his collection of rocks from famous places around the world, including a brick from the Great Wall of China.

Now Ludwig Meister owns the island, and **Nassau Cruises Ltd.** ✸✸✸, Paradise Island Bridge, (✆ **242/363-3333**) leases it and provides the transportation. Nassau Cruises maintains three motorized yachts, the *Calypso I,* the *Calypso IV,* and the *Islander.* These are the most luxurious cruises you can book. Their trip to uninhabited Blue Lagoon Island (see "Easy Side Trips to Nearby Islands," below) is reason enough just to sail with them. Equipped with bars, their yachts depart from a point just west of the tollbooth on the Paradise Island Bridge. Daytime trips depart every day for the scheduled beaches of Blue Lagoon Island, a 4-mile sail east of Paradise Island. The day sails leave at 10 and 11:30am and come back from the island at 1:30, 3, and 4:30pm. The Day Pass is $20 for adults and $10 for children and covers for the boat ride only. The all-inclusive Day Pass is $65 for adults and $35 for children (3 to 12) and covers transportation, the boat ride, lunch, two daiquiris for adults, and all non-motorized water sports, including snorkeling.

Remote **Rose Island** is a sliver of land poking up out of the sea northeast of the Prince George waterfront docks of Nassau. Shelling is one of the lures of this little islet. If you want to escape the crowds of Nassau, you can take a boat, the *Robinson Crusoe,* which leaves daily at 9am from Nassau and returns at 4:45pm. The cost is $45, $22.50 for children ages 5 through 11, and free for kids under 5. You can relax in a hammock, snorkel among the coral reefs, and enjoy the white-sand beach before and after your sizzling barbecue lunch with unlimited white wine (included in the price). Bookings for this island retreat trip are available through **Majestic Tours** (✆ **242/322-2606**).

If you want to see the Exuma island chain on a daylong excursion, try **The Fantastic Exuma Powerboat Adventure.** The name may sound silly, but the trip provides an excellent overview of the area. The boat departs Nassau Harbour at 9am and arrives in the Exuma Cays about an hour later. There are several stops, with snorkeling at a private cay (Ship Channel), a visit with the iguanas on Allan's Cay, feeding stingrays along the shore, and a barbecue lunch. A full bar is available all day, and the drinks are free. The cost is $175 per adult or $99 for children 2 through 12. For more information and prices, contact **Powerboat Adventures** (✆ **242/327-5385**).

7 Shopping

You can find a variety of bargains in Nassau—Swiss watches, Japanese cameras, French perfumes, Irish crystal and linens, and British china.

There are no import duties on 11 categories of luxury goods, including china, crystal, fine linens, jewelry, leather goods, photographic equipment, watches, fragrances, and other merchandise. Antiques, of course, are exempt from import duty worldwide. But even though prices are "duty-free," you can still end up spending more on an item in The Bahamas than you would back in your hometown. It's a tricky situation.

If you're contemplating a major purchase, such as a good Swiss watch or some expensive perfume, it's best to do some research in your hometown discount outlets before making a serious purchase in The Bahamas. While the alleged 30% to 50% discount off stateside prices might apply in some cases, it's not true in most cases. Certain cameras and electronic equipment, we have discovered, are listed in The Bahamas at, say, 20% or more below the manufacturer's "suggested retail price." That sounds good, except the manufacturer's suggested price might be a lot higher than what you'd pay in your hometown. You aren't getting the discount you think you are. Some shoppers even take along department-store catalogs from the States to determine if they are indeed getting a bargain.

A lot of price-fixing seems to be going on in Nassau. For example, a bottle of Chanel is likely to sell for pretty much the same price regardless of the store.

How much you can take back home depends on your country of origin. For more details, plus Customs requirements for some other countries, refer to "Customs," in chapter 2.

The principal shopping areas are **Bay Street** and its side streets downtown, as well as the shops in the arcades of hotels. Not many street numbers are used along Bay Street; just look for store signs.

ANTIQUES
Marlborough Antiques   This store carries the type of antiques you'd expect to find in a shop in London: antique books, antique maps and engravings, English silver (both sterling and plate), and unusual table settings (fish knives and so on). Among the most appealing objects are the store's collection of antique photographs of the islands. Also displayed are works by Bahamian artists Brent Malone and Maxwell Taylor. Corner of Queen and Marlborough sts. ⓒ 242/328-0502.

ART
Kennedy Gallery   Although many locals come here for custom framing, the gallery also sells original artwork by well-known Bahamian artists, including limited-edition prints, handcrafts, pottery, and sculpture. Parliament St. ⓒ 242/325-7662.

BRASS & COPPER
Brass and Leather Shop   With two branches on Charlotte Street, this shop offers English brass, handbags, luggage, briefcases, attachés, and personal accessories. Shop no. 2 has handbags, belts, scarves, ties, and small leather goods from such famous designers as Furla, Bottega Veneta, Pierre Balmain, and others. If you look and select carefully, you can find some good buys here. 12 Charlotte St., between Bay and Shirley sts. ⓒ 242/322-3806.

> ⌐Tips   **To Bargain or Not to Bargain**
>
> Don't try to bargain with the salespeople in Nassau stores as you would
> with merchants at the Straw Market (see "Markets," below). The price
> asked in the shops is the price you must pay, but you won't be pressed to
> make a purchase. The salespeople here are courteous and helpful in most
> cases.
>
> Stores in Nassau are generally open from 9am to 5 or 5:30pm Monday
> through Saturday. Most stores are closed on Sunday. Stores that are open
> on Sunday are noted below. The Straw Market does business 7 days a
> week.

CIGARS

Remember, U.S. citizens are prohibited from bringing Cuban cigars back home
because of the trade embargo. If you buy them, you're supposed to enjoy them
in The Bahamas.

Tropique International Smoke Shop   Many cigar aficionados come here to
indulge their passion for Cubans, which are handpicked and imported by
Bahamian merchants. The staff at this outlet trained in Havana, so they know
their cigars. In Nassau Marriott Resort & Crystal Palace Casino, W. Bay St. ℂ 242/327-7292.

COINS & STAMPS

Bahamas Post Office Philatelic Bureau   Here you'll find beautiful
Bahamian stamps slated to become collector's items. One of the most sought-
after stamps has a seashell motif. In the General Post Office, at the top of Parliament St. on
E. Hill St. ℂ 242/322-1112.

Coin of the Realm   This family-run shop is in a lovely building that was
hewn out of solid limestone over 200 years ago. The shop offers not only fine
jewelry, but also Bahamian and British postage stamps, mint and used, and rare
(and not-so-rare) Bahamian silver and gold coins. It also sells old and modern
paper Bahamian currency. Bahama pennies that were minted in 1806 and 1807
are now rare and expensive items. Charlotte St., just off Bay St. ℂ 242/322-4497.

FASHION

Barry's Limited   One of Nassau's more formal and elegant clothing stores,
this shop sells garments made from lamb's wool and English cashmere. Elegant
sportswear (including Korean-made Guayabera shirts) and suits are sold here.
Most of the clothes are for men, but women often stop in for a look at the fancy
handmade Irish linen handkerchiefs and the stylish cuff links, studs, and other
accessories. Bay and George sts. ℂ 242/322-3118.

Bonneville Bones   The name alone will intrigue, but it hardly describes
what's inside. This is the best men's store we've found in Nassau. You can find
everything here, from standard T-shirts and designer jeans to elegant casual
clothing, including suits. Bay St. ℂ 242/328-0804.

Cole's of Nassau   This boutique offers the most extensive selection of
designer fashions in Nassau. Women can be outfitted in everything from
swimwear to formal gowns, from sportswear to hosiery. Cole's also sells gift
items, sterling-silver designer and costume jewelry, hats, shoes, bags, scarves, and
belts. Parliament St. ℂ 242/322-8393.

Fendi   This is Nassau's only outlet for the well-crafted Italian-inspired accessories endorsed by this famous leather-goods company. With handbags, luggage, shoes, watches, cologne, wallets, and portfolios to choose from, the selection may well solve some of your gift-giving quandaries. Charlotte St. at Bay St. (C) 242/ 322-6300.

The Girls from Brazil   This is the best outlet for swimwear in Nassau. The walls alone are intriguing, featuring wooden cutouts of well-endowed Brazilians in bikinis. Prices are reasonable when compared to similar outlets in the Caribbean and Florida. The upper floor is devoted to a coffeehouse and cafe called Jitters, which serves light food, snacks, and cold drinks. Bay St. (C) 242/ 356-9381.

Mademoiselle, Ltd   The store specializes in the kinds of resort wear that looks appropriate at either a tennis club or a cocktail party. It features locally made batik garments by Androsia. Swimwear, sarongs, jeans, and halter tops are the rage here, as are the wonderfully scented soaps and lotions. Their on-site "Body Shop" boutique supplies all the paraphernalia you need for herbal massages and beauty treatments. Bay St. at Frederick St. (C) 242/322-5130.

HANDCRAFTS

Island Tings   Everything inside "Tings" pays homage to Bahamian artisans and their ability to craft worthwhile pieces from humble and sometimes-unlikely materials. Expect a minilibrary of books on the archipelago's culture and cuisine, as well as sculptures crafted from driftwood and conch shells, utilitarian jewelry, straw goods such as baskets, natural sea sponges, wall hangings, and Junkanoo masks made from all-natural traditional materials as well as new-fangled versions molded from fiberglass. The collection also includes aloe-based skin lotions and perfumes distilled from local plants and flowers. Bay St., between East St. and Elizabeth Ave. (C) 242/326-1024.

The Plait Lady   This outlet near The Sugar Reef Restaurant sells the finest handmade, 100% Bahamian straw wares in Nassau. Conch-shell mats, trays, and baskets, and many other handcrafts, are also sold here. Especially intriguing are the coiled baskets from Red Bays on Andros. Sometimes these are woven

---

(*Finds* Goin' Local—Coconut Gin and a Fish Fry

Locals call the small artificial island of **Arawak Cay** "Fish Fry." It lies right in the heart of Nassau, across West Bay Street (from the Botanical Gardens, walk back along Chippingham Road). Early in the day, you'll be able to buy ultra-fresh conch; vendors will crack the mollusk before your eyes (this isn't everybody's favorite attraction). They'll give you some hot sauce and tell you to chow down. Beginning around noon, you'll find at least a half-dozen simple bars and kiosks dispensing cracked conch, fried fish, and grits garnished with either spicy corned beef or tuna salad. With it, you can sample a favorite drink of the islands, coconut milk laced with gin (an acquired taste, to say the least, but you'll feel like a real Bahamian). It's at its most crowded and popular every Sunday night, beginning around 5pm until around midnight, when hundreds of Bahamians gather together next to bonfires to gossip, flirt, raise hell, and generally hang out.

with fabric from the famed Androsia Batik, also made on Andros. The Regarno Bldg., Victoria and Bay sts. © 242/356-5584.

Sea Grape Boutique   This is the finest gift shop on New Providence, with an inventory of exotic decorative items that you'll probably find fascinating. It includes jewelry crafted from fossilized coral, sometimes with sharks' teeth embedded inside, beadwork from Guatemala, Haitian paintings, silver from India, hairbrushes shaped like parrots, and clothing that's well-suited to the sometimes-steamy climate of The Bahamas. There's a second branch of this outfit, Sea Grape Too, in the Radisson Hotel's Mall, on Cable Beach (© 242/327-5113). West Bay Rd. (next to Travelers Restaurant). © 242/327-1308.

JEWELRY

John Bull   The jewelry department here offers classic selections from Tiffany & Co.; cultured pearls from Mikimoto; the creations of David Yurman, Stephen Lagos, Carrera y Carrera, and Sea Life by Kanbana; Greek and Roman coin jewelry; and Spanish gold and silver pieces. It's the best name in the business. The store also features a wide selection of watches, cameras, perfumes (including Estée Lauder, Chanel, and Calvin Klein offered at discount prices—though you should check carefully to make sure you're getting a bargain), cosmetics, leather goods, and accessories. It is one of the best places in The Bahamas to buy a Gucci or Cartier watch. The outlet has been the authorized agent for Rolex in The Bahamas for 30 years, and the store itself has been doing business since 1929. Corner of Bay and Charlotte sts. © 242/322-4253.

LEATHER

In addition to the stores mentioned below, another good store for leather goods is the **Brass and Leather Shop,** described under "Brass & Copper," above.

Gucci   This shop, opposite Rawson Square, is the best place to buy leather goods in Nassau. The wide selection includes handbags, wallets, luggage, briefcases, gift items, scarves, ties, casual clothes, evening wear for men and women, umbrellas, shoes, sandals, watches, and perfume, all by Gucci of Italy. Saffrey Sq., Bay St., corner of Bank Lane. © 242/325-0561.

Leather Masters   This well-known retail outlet carries an internationally known collection of leather bags, luggage, and accessories by Ted Lapidus, Lanvin, and Lancel of Paris; Etienne Aigner of Germany; and "i Santi" of Italy. Leather Masters also carries luggage by Piel and Marroquinera of Colombia, leather wallets by Bosca, and pens, cigarette lighters, and watches by Colibri. Silk scarves, neckties, and cigar accessories are also featured. Parliament St. © 242/322-7597.

LINENS

The Linen Shop   This is the best outlet for linens in Nassau. It sells beautifully embroidered bed linens, Irish handkerchiefs, hand-embroidered women's blouses, and tablecloths. Look also for the most exquisite children's clothing and christening gowns in town. Ironmongery Bldg., Bay St., near Charlotte St. © 242/322-4266.

MAPS

Balmain Antiques   This place offers a wide and varied assortment of 19th-century etchings, engravings, and maps, many of them antique and all reasonably priced. Other outlets have minor displays of these collectibles, but this outlet has the finest. Some items are 400 years old. It's usually best to discuss your interests with Mr. Ramsey, the owner, so he can direct you to the proper drawers. His specialties include The Bahamas, America during the Civil War, and black history. He also has a collection of military historical items. You'll find the shop on the second floor, three doors east of Charlotte Street. Mason's Bldg., Bay St., near Charlotte St. © 242/323-7421.

MARKETS

The **Nassau International Bazaar** consists of some 30 shops selling international goods in a new arcade. A pleasant place for browsing, the $1.8 million complex sells goods from around the globe. The bazaar runs from Bay Street down to the waterfront (near the Prince George Wharf). With cobbled alleyways and garreted storefronts, the area looks like a European village.

Prince George Plaza, Bay Street, is popular with cruise-ship passengers. Many fine shops (Gucci, for example) are found here. When you get tired of shopping, you can dine at the open-air rooftop restaurant that overlooks Bay Street.

The **Straw Market** in Straw Market Plaza on Bay Street seems to be on every shopper's itinerary. Even those who don't buy anything come here to look around. Bahamian craftspeople weave and pleat straw hats, handbags, dolls, placemats, and other items—including straw shopping bags to hold your purchases. You can buy items ready-made (often from Taiwan) or order special articles, perhaps bearing your initials. You can also have fun bargaining for the lowest price. The Straw Market is open daily from 7am to 7pm.

MUSIC

Cody's Music and Video Center   The finest record store in The Bahamas, Cody's specializes in the contemporary music of The Bahamas and the Caribbean. The father of owner Cody Carter was mentor to many of the country's first Goombay and Junkanoo artists. The store also sells videos, compact discs, and tapes. E. Bay St., corner of Armstrong St. © 242/325-8834.

PERFUMES & COSMETICS

Nassau has several good perfume outlets, notably **John Bull** and **Little Switzerland,** which also stock a lot of non-perfume merchandise.

The Beauty Spot   The largest cosmetic shop in The Bahamas, this outlet sells duty-free cosmetics by Lancôme, Chanel, YSL, Elizabeth Arden, Estée Lauder, Clinique, Prescriptives, and Biotherm, among others. It also operates facial salons. Bay and Frederick sts. © 242/322-5930.

Lightbourn's   A pharmacy 100 years ago, Lightbourn's is a family-owned and -operated business that today carries a wide selection of duty-free fragrances and cosmetics. It is known for the quality of its goods and its service. Bay and George sts. © 242/322-2095.

The Perfume Bar   This little gem has exclusive rights to market Boucheron and Sublime in The Bahamas. It also stocks the Clarins line (but not exclusively). Bay St. © 242/322-3785.

The Perfume Shop   In the heart of Nassau, within walking distance of the cruise ships, the Perfume Shop offers duty-free savings on world-famous perfumes. Treat yourself to a flacon of Eternity, Giorgio, Poison, Lalique, Shalimar, or Chanel. Those are just a few of the scents for women. For men, the selection

includes Drakkar Noir, Polo, and Obsession. Corner of Bay and Frederick Sts.
© 242/322-2375.

SPICES & SAUCES

Taste of the Islands   You can bring home spices from the Caribbean as well
as The Bahamas after a shopping jaunt here. If you want Blue Mountain coffee
from Jamaica (the best in the islands) or fiery hot sauce, you'll find it here. They
have all sorts of jerk seasoning, jams, spices, and even cigars. As for their rum
cake from the Cayman Islands, skip it and make your own! International Arcade.
© 242/356-7632.

STEEL DRUMS

Pyfroms   If you've fallen under the Junkanoo spell and want to take home
some steel drums, you've come to the right place. They'll always be useful if
island fever overtakes you after you return home. Bay St. © 242/322-2603.

8 New Providence After Dark

Gone are the days when tuxedo-clad gentlemen and elegantly gowned ladies
drank and danced the night away at such famous nightclubs as the Yellow Bird
and the Big Bamboo. You can still find dancing, along with limbo and calypso,
but for most visitors, the major attraction is gambling.

Cultural entertainment in Nassau is limited. The chief center for this is the
Dundas Center for the Performing Arts, which sometimes stages ballets, plays,
or musicals. Call © 242/393-3728 to see if a production is planned at the time
of your visit.

ROLLING THE DICE

Note that you also can easily head over to Paradise Island and drop into the massive, spectacular casino in the Atlantis resort. See chapter 4.

Nassau Marriott Resort & Crystal Palace Casino   This dazzling
casino—the only one on New Providence Island—is now run by Nassau
Marriott Resort. Although some experienced gamblers claim you get better
odds in Vegas, the Crystal Palace nevertheless stacks up well against all the
major casinos of the Caribbean. The 35,000-square-foot casino is filled with
flashing lights, and the gaming room features 750 slot machines in true Las
Vegas style, along with 51 blackjack tables, 9 roulette wheels, 7 craps tables, a
baccarat table, and a big six. W. Bay St., Cable Beach. © 242/327-6200. No cover.

THE CLUB & MUSIC SCENE

Club Waterloo   They've seen it all over the years at the Club Waterloo, located
in an old colonial mansion set beside a narrow saltwater estuary known as Lake
Waterloo. To qualify for the $5 cover charge, you can purchase a visitors' pass
from most taxi drivers, which will get you inside the door. If you're not registered
at a hotel, the cover charge is $15 Sunday to Thursday, going up to $40 on Friday and Saturday. But despite these high prices, you'll get the feeling that very few
people actually pay full price: It's management's way of screening out the bad
drunks. The main bar is open nightly from 8pm to 4am, and the sports bar is
open from midnight to 4am. Three other minor bars include the Shooters Bar,
where shots go for $2, an open-air pool bar, and a Bacardi Bar, which specializes
in its namesake. There's live entertainment on weekends, with DJs presiding on
weeknights. There are two separate dance floors here, one specializing in reggae

and calypso music, the other in old-fashioned rock and roll. There's also a kiosk-style snack bar where you can assuage the munchies. The crowd tends to be an eclectic mix of locals, Europeans, and American vacationers, both singles and couples. E. Bay St. ℂ **242/393-7324.** Cover $5–$40, including 1 or 2 drinks.

King & Knights   This is the only folkloric Bahamian show on New Providence. Its linchpin is Eric Gibson ("King Eric"), a talented musician and calypso artist from Acklins Island. He has functioned as the semi-official ambassador of Bahamian goodwill, conducting concert tours throughout North America, Europe, and Australia. A musical staple here since the late 1950s, his act includes a half-dozen musicians, four or five dancers, a "calypsonian" who might double as a comedian, and a limbo contortionist. The shows are a little short (only 75 min.), but end with a sequence that emulates the Junkanoo festival. If you opt for a dinner here, you can schedule it for whenever you want, before, during, or after the show. In the Nassau Beach Hotel, Cable Beach. ℂ **242/327-7711.** Reservations recommended. Cover charge $25, including 1 drink. Tues–Sun 8:30 and 10:30pm; Sun–Mon 8:30pm.

The Zoo   Set midway between Cable Beach and the western periphery of Nassau, this is the largest and best-known nightspot of its kind on New Providence. It's housed on two floors of what was once a warehouse, with five bars, an indoor/outdoor restaurant (Zoo Cafe), and a sometimes-crowded dance floor that attracts mainly an under-30 crowd. Each of the five bars has a different theme, including an underwater theme, a jungle theme, and a Gilligan's Island theme. The sports bar is complete with pool tables and wide-screen broadcasts. The most raucous area of the complex is on the street level, where a young crowd congregates to drink and dance. If you're looking for a respite from the brouhaha below, climb a flight of stairs to the "VIP Lounge," which offers stiff drinks and the chance for conversation. Most of the complex is open nightly from 8pm to 4am. W. Bay St. at Saunders Beach. ℂ **242/322-7195.** Cover $5–$40, sometimes including the 1st drink.

VEGAS-STYLE SHOWS

Palace Theater   This 800-seat theater is one of The Bahamas's major nightlife attractions. With fake palm trees on each side and lots of glitz, it's an appropriate setting for the Las Vegas–style extravaganzas that are presented on its stage.

Dinner is available within the resort, but it's not served in the theater itself. Guests actually prefer to dine in one of the resort's restaurants and arrive either before or after their meal to see the glittery shows. Two shows are presented every Tuesday, Wednesday, Friday, and Saturday, at 8:45 and 11pm. On Thursday and Sunday, only one show is presented, at 8pm. Except during periods of exceptionally heavy demand, the theater is usually closed on Monday. Advance reservations are recommended, especially for shows on Tuesday and Saturday, when many of the seats might be filled with cruise-ship passengers. In the Crystal Palace Casino, W. Bay St., Cable Beach. ℂ **242/327-6200.** Admission for show plus dinner in any of the resort's restaurants $59; admission to show with 2 drinks included but without dinner $39.

Rainforest Theater   Expect sequins, glitter, enough flesh to titillate (mildly) but never enough to offend within a family-friendly show that combines the Caribbean aesthetic with "Give My Regards to Broadway" razzmatazz. If you opt for dinner before the show, you'll be directed toward one of three on-site restaurants (Sole Mare, the Black Angus Steakhouse, or the seafood buffet) for dinners that will begin about 2 hours before the debut of the show. In the Nassau Marriott Resort, Cable Beach. © 242/327-6200, ext. 6861. Show with 1 drink, $39; show with fixed-price dinner, $59. Shows Tues 9:30pm; Wed, Fri, and Sun 9pm; Sat 8:30 and 11:15pm. Bus: 10.

THE BAR SCENE

Charlie's on the Beach/Cocktails 7 Dreams   The focus within this sparsely decorated club is local gossip, calypso and reggae music, and stiff drinks, all of which can combine into a high-energy night out in Nassau. At presstime, the setting was a simple warehouse-like structure a few blocks west of the British Colonial Hotel, although management warns that during some particularly active weekends (including spring break), the entire venue might move, short-term, to a larger, and as yet undetermined, location. Open only Wednesday and Friday to Sunday 8pm to 4:30am. West Bay St. near Long Wharf Beach. © 242/ 328-3745. Cover $10–$15.

Crocodiles Waterfront Bar & Grill   Look for the hundreds of crocodiles stenciled into the wall that shields this watering hole from busy East Bay Street, and venture into this funky bar for a rum drink. There's a relaxed vibe on the deck, which offers a bit of shade under thatched parasols. You can order up moderately priced steak, seafood, or sandwiches (this place is reviewed under "Where to Dine," earlier in this chapter). There's another wooden building on the premises that transforms into a high-energy nightclub, "The Last Quarter," every Wednesday, Friday, and Saturday from 10pm to 2am, with live music and a $10 cover that includes one drink. E. Bay St. (a 2-minute walk from the Nassau side of the Paradise Island Bridge). © 242/323-3341.

The Drop Off   Every harbor town has a rowdy, raucous, and sudsy dive with whiffs of spilled beer and ample doses of iodine from the nearby sea, and in Nassau, this is it. Most of its clients are either local residents, or workers aboard one of the fishing and cargo boats that bob at anchor in nearby Nassau Harbor (for example, the sheltered channel between New Providence and Paradise Island). The setting is a cavernous room lined with murals of underwater life, all within a cellar that's usually several degrees cooler than the baking sidewalks outside. There's live music some evenings after 11pm, and a short list of two-fisted plat-ters that includes grilled or fried snapper or grouper, steaks, burgers, and sandwiches. E. Bay St. at East St. © 242/322-3444.

Out Island Bar/The Beach Bar   These bars, both within the same hotel, are used primarily by its guests, but both of them are open to all, attracting everybody from newlyweds to those who married when Eisenhower was in office. The more central of the two is the Out Island Bar, set adjacent to the lobby and outfitted in a breezy wicker and rattan theme that goes well with the party-colored drinks that are its specialty. If you want a view, head for the thatch-covered beach bar, set directly on the sands of one of the best beaches in the area. In the Nassau Beach Hotel, Cable Beach. © 242/327-7711.

4

Paradise Island

Located just 600 feet off the north shore of Nassau, Paradise Island is a favorite vacation spot for East Coast Americans, who flee their icy winters for the stunning white sands of Paradise Beach. In addition to its gorgeous beaches, the island boasts beautiful foliage, including brilliant red hibiscus and a grove of casuarina trees sweeping down to form a tropical arcade.

Now the priciest real estate in The Bahamas, the island once served as a farm for Nassau and was known as Hog Island. Purchased for $294 by William Sayle in the 17th century, it cost A&P grocery chain heir Huntington Hartford $11 million in 1960. He decided to rename the 4-mile-long sliver of land Paradise before selling out his interests. Long a retreat for millionaires, the island experienced a massive building boom in the 1980s. Its old Bahamian charm is now gone forever, lost to the high rises, condos, second homes of the wintering wealthy, and gambling casino that have taken over. The centerpiece of Paradise Island is the mammoth Atlantis Paradise Island Resort & Casino, which has become a nightlife mecca and a sightseeing attraction in its own right.

For those who want top hotels, casino action, Vegas-type revues, some of the best beaches in The Bahamas, and a posh address, Paradise Island is the place to be. It's now sleeker and more upscale than Cable Beach, its closest rival, and Freeport/Lucaya. True, Paradise Island is overbuilt and overly commercialized, but its natural beauty still makes it a choice vacation spot, perfect for a quick 3- or 4-day getaway.

Although Paradise Island is treated as a separate entity in this guide, it is actually part of New Providence, to which it is connected by a bridge. (You must fly into Nassau to get to Paradise Island.) You can travel between the two on foot, by boat, or by car. So you have the option of staying in Nassau or Cable Beach and coming over to enjoy the beaches, restaurants, attractions, and casino on Paradise Island. You can also stay on Paradise Island and easily go into Nassau for a day of sightseeing and shopping. So view this section as a companion to chapter 3, on New Providence. Refer to the previous chapter for "Fast Facts: New Providence," transportation details, nearby sights, and a wider array of sports and recreation choices.

1 Orientation

ARRIVING

When you arrive at the **Nassau International Airport** (see chapter 3 for information on flying into Nassau), there is no bus service to take you to Paradise Island. Many package deals will provide hotel transfers from the airport. Otherwise, if you're not renting a car, you'll need to take a taxi. Taxis in Nassau are metered. It will usually cost you $23 to $25 to go by cab from the airport to your hotel. The driver will also ask you to pay the one-way $2 bridge toll.

VISITOR INFORMATION

Paradise Island does not have a tourist office of its own, so refer to the tourist facilities in downtown Nassau (see "Orientation," at the beginning of chapter 3). The concierge or the guest services staff at your hotel can also give you information about the local attractions.

ISLAND LAYOUT

Paradise Island's finest beaches lie on the Atlantic (northern) coastline; the docks, wharves, and marinas are located on the southern side. Most of the island's largest and glossiest hotels and restaurants, as well as the famous casino and a lagoon with carefully landscaped borders, lie west and north of the roundabout. The area east of the roundabout is less congested, with only a handful of smaller hotels, a golf course, the Versailles Gardens, the Cloister, the airport, and many of the island's privately owned villas.

2 Getting Around

You don't need to rent a car. Most visitors walk around Paradise Island's most densely developed sections and hire a taxi for the occasional longer haul. For information on renting a car, refer to "Getting Around," at the beginning of chapter 3.

The most popular way to reach nearby Nassau is to **walk across the toll bridge.** Pedestrians pay 25¢.

If you want to tour Paradise Island or New Providence by **taxi,** you can make arrangements with either the taxi driver or the hotel reception desk. Taxis wait at the entrances to all the major hotels. The going hourly rate is about $50 in cars or small vans.

If you are without a car and don't want to take a taxi or walk, you can take a **ferry to Nassau.** The ferry to Nassau leaves from the dock on Casino Drive every half hour, and the 10-minute ride costs $3 one-way. Quicker and easier than a taxi, the ferry deposits you right at Bay Street. Daily service is from 9:30am to 4:15pm.

Water taxis also operate between Paradise Island and Prince George Wharf in Nassau. They depart daily from 8:30am to 6pm at 20-minute intervals. Round-trip fare is $6 per person.

If you are a guest at one of the properties of Atlantis Paradise Island Resort & Casino, you can take a complimentary tour of the island, leaving Monday and Wednesday through Friday at 2pm.

Unlike New Providence, no public buses are allowed on Paradise Island.

3 Where to Stay

In the off-season (mid-Apr to mid-Dec), prices are slashed by at least 20%—and perhaps a lot more, though the weather isn't as ideal. But because Paradise Island's summer business has increased dramatically, you'll never see some of the 60% reductions that you might find at a cheaper property in the Greater Nassau area. Paradise Island doesn't have to lower its rates to attract summer business. For inexpensive accommodations, refer to the recommendations on New Providence Island (see chapter 3). Paradise Island ain't cheap!

Tips **Make a Deal Before You Go**

The rates given below are rack rates, and you should be able to avoid paying them. Always ask if special promotional rates are available, or see if a travel agent can help you do better. Package deals often greatly reduce the prices of these resorts, too. *Be sure to read the section on package deals in chapter 2 before you book a hotel yourself.*

VERY EXPENSIVE

Atlantis Paradise Island Resort & Casino *★★★* *(Kids)*   The megaresort of The Bahamas, the Atlantis is *massive*, opening onto a long stretch of white-sand beach with a sheltered marina. Think Vegas in the tropics, with a fairly interesting ancient mythology theme thrown in, and you'll get the picture. The advantage is that you'll never be bored; the downside is that it's sprawling and the service just can't keep up with the number of guests here. The Atlantis is a self-contained "water world," with the Lost Continent of Atlantis as its theme. It's a great choice for a family vacation, since kids love all the facilities and gimmicks, and the children's program is outstanding. Singles and young couples who want a lot of action like it, too, though some people find it too over-the-top and impersonal. The Atlantis proudly offers so many sports, dining, and entertainment options that many guests never set foot off the property during their entire vacation.

During 1998 and 1999, a $600-million face-lift was completed, adding more rooms and more wild design touches. A soaring "Royal Tower"—the tallest building in The Bahamas—was added, replete with decorative sea horses, winged dragons, and mega-size conch shells sprouting from cornices and rooflines. The casino and entertainment complex were moved to an area over the watery depths of a lagoon. The best and most plush accommodations are in this new Royal Tower. (Rooms in the Royal Tower's Imperial Club have a personal concierge and upgraded amenities.) But even in the older, less expensive sections, rooms have a comfortable tropical decor. Every one sports a balcony or terrace with water views, individually controlled air-conditioning, in-room movies, voice-mail, and modem access, plus roomy bathrooms with tubs and showers. The most deluxe accommodation is the "Bridge Suite," renting for $25,000 a day and sometimes occupied by Michael Jordan during his golfing holidays at the nearby links.

Any old hotel might sport tropical gardens, but the Atlantis goes one better by featuring the world's largest collection of outdoor open-air marine habitats, each of them aesthetically stunning. A few of these were conceived for snorkelers and swimmers, but most were designed so guests could observe the marine life from catwalks above and from glassed-in underwater viewing tunnels. Even folks who don't stay here—including thousands of cruise-ship passengers—come to check out these 11 distinctly different exhibition lagoons containing millions of gallons of water and at least 200 species of tropical fish. They include a shark tank, a stingray lagoon, and separate holding tanks for lobsters, piranhas, and underwater exotica. Swimmers can meander along an underwater snorkeling trail (Paradise Lagoon) and explore a five-story, Disney-style replica of a Mayan temple complete with 60-foot water slides. Scattered in between are a labyrinth of underground grottoes, cascading waterfalls, and replicas of what the uggglers, dancers and an assortment of acrobats fill the street.

She shoots you a wide-eyed look as a seven-foot cartoon character approaches.

What brought you here was wanting the kids

to see something magical while they still believed in magic.

America Online Keyword: Travel

With 700 airlines, 50,000 hotels and over 5,000 cruise and vacation getaways, you can now go places you've always dreamed of.

Travelocity.com
A Sabre Company
Go Virtually Anywhere.

"WORLD'S LEADING TRAVEL WEB SITE, 5 YEARS IN A ROW." WORLD TRAVEL AWARDS

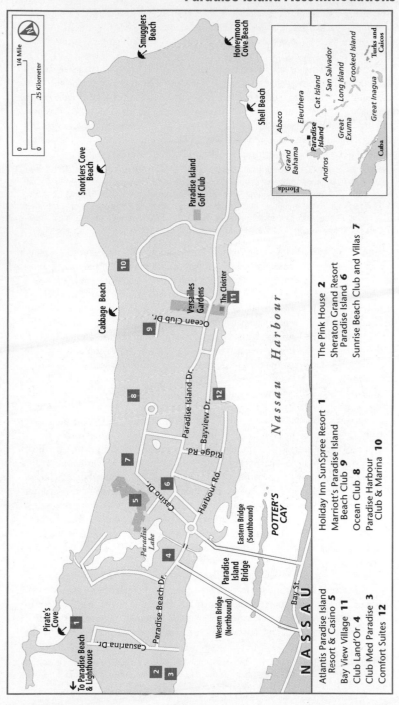

Paradise Island Accommodations

Smugglers Beach
Honeymoon Cove Beach
Shell Beach
Snorklers Cove Beach
Paradise Island Golf Club
Cabbage Beach
Versailles Gardens
The Cloister
Ocean Club Dr.
Paradise Island Dr.
Bayview Dr.
Ridge Rd.
Harbour Rd.
Eastern Bridge (Southbound)
POTTER'S CAY
Nassau Harbour
Paradise Lake
Paradise Island Bridge
Western Bridge (Northbound)
Bay St.
NASSAU
Casuarina Dr.
Paradise Beach Dr.
Pirate's Cove
To Paradise Beach & Lighthouse
Casino Dr.

1/4 Mile
.25 Kilometer

Florida
Grand Bahama
Abaco
Andros
Eleuthera
Cat Island
San Salvador
Paradise Island
Great Exuma
Long Island
Crooked Island
Great Inagua
Turks and Caicos
Cuba

Atlantis Paradise Island Resort & Casino **5**
Bay View Village **11**
Club Land'Or **4**
Club Med Paradise **3**
Comfort Suites **12**

Holiday Inn SunSpree Resort **1**
Marriott's Paradise Island Beach Club **9**
Ocean Club **8**
Paradise Harbour Club & Marina **10**

The Pink House **2**
Sheraton Grand Resort Paradise Island **6**
Sunrise Beach Club and Villas **7**

streets of Atlantis might have looked like before it was submerged underwater, as well as coral reefs. (But wait, there's more! You can also float along in an inner tube down the quarter-mile-long "Lazy River" that meanders through the grounds.)

The focal point of all this fun-in-the-sun is the massive **Paradise Island Casino,** the best-designed casino in The Bahamas. There are 13 bars, nightclubs, and lounges, including a cigar bar (see "Paradise Island After Dark," later in this chapter). The best of the hotel's 20 restaurants will be reviewed under "Where to Dine"; expect to pay a lot to dine in most all of these places. The superb, imaginative supervised children's program at Discovery Camp was developed for Atlantis in conjunction with the Discovery Channel.

Casino Dr. (P.O. Box N-4777), Paradise Island, The Bahamas. ⓒ 800/ATLANTIS in the U.S., or 242/363-3000. Fax 242/363-6300. www.atlantisresort.com. 2,349 units. Winter $295–$495 double, from $695 suite; off-season $185–$360 double, from $525 suite. Many package deals available. AE, DC, DISC, MC, V. Self-parking free, valet parking $5 day. **Amenities:** 20 restaurants, 13 bars, marina with 63 megayacht slips, 2 theaters, water sports, 14-acre water park, salon, spa, travel desk, 24-hour room service, 24-hour medical service, baby-sitting, laundry. *In room:* A/C, TV, minibar, refrigerator, hair dryer, iron/ironing board, safe.

✓ **Ocean Club** 𝕽𝕽𝕽   Sun International's Ocean Club is the most exclusive address on Paradise Island, with sky-high prices that match the pampering service (the best in The Bahamas) and refined ambience. The white-sand beach that lies adjacent to the hotel is the finest in the Nassau/Paradise Island area. This is also one of the best-developed tennis resorts in The Bahamas. In 1999, Sun International began a major expansion and renovation that was completed in 2000. A favorite honeymoon spot, it's more upscale than the megahotel Atlantis, which is really a fun family resort. Guests can revel in the casino and nightlife activities of Atlantis nearby, then retire to this more tranquil, secluded, and intimate retreat.

The tasteful and spacious rooms are plushly comfortable with safes, gilt-framed mirrors, dark-wood armoires, and one king-size or two double beds, each with state-of-the-art mattresses. The marble bathrooms in the suites are massive, and each contains a bidet, twin basins, and both a tub and shower.

The real heart and soul of the resort lies in the surrounding gardens, which were designed by the island's former owner, Huntington Hartford. This resort, in fact, was once his private home. Formal gardens surround a French cloister set on 35 acres of manicured lawns. The 12th-century carvings of the Cloister are visible at the crest of a hill, across a stretch of terraced waterfalls, fountains, a stone gazebo, and rose gardens. Larger-than-life statues dot the vine-covered niches on either side of the gardens. Begin your tour of the gardens at the large swimming pool, which feeds a series of reflecting pools that stretch out toward the cloister.

The exciting news for dining on Paradise Island is the resort's opening of Dune, the creation of culinary legend Jean-Georges Vongerichten. In addition, a pair of fountains illuminates the Courtyard Terrace at night. See "Where to Dine" later in this chapter for a review of both restaurants. Another option is a beachfront restaurant and bar where you can dine under cover but in the open air.

Ocean Club Dr. (P.O. Box N-4777), Paradise Island, The Bahamas. ⓒ 800/321-3000 in the U.S., or 242/363-2501. Fax 242/363-2424. www.oceanclub.com. 119 units, 5 private villas. Winter $635–$745 double, $1,130–$1,350 suite, $1,250–$1,350 villa; off-season $400–$715 double, $715–$830 suite, $810 villa. AE, DC, MC, V. Free parking. **Amenities:** 3 restaurants, 2 bars, pool, golf course, 9 tennis courts, spa and fitness center, baby-sitting, shuttle to casino. *In room:* A/C, TV, minibar, hair dryer, iron/ironing board, safe.

Moments **The Lost World**

A particularly stunning feature of the Atlantis resort is **"The Dig,"** an underwater site that's themed around an "archaeological excavation" of the mythical continent of Atlantis. Designed around a labyrinth of rooms and corridors, it's flanked with glass windows that overlook a designer's impression of the underwater remnants of a once-great city that was submerged by advancing floodwaters and sinking terrain. You'll see toppled columns, a map room, a stone-built calculator similar to an abacus, a decompression chamber, and a laboratory for inventions—all underwater, and populated with sharks, piranhas, bamboo sharks, and all manner of tropical fish, many of them color-coordinated for a spectacular decorative effect.

The effect of the site is so eerie and powerful that some visitors actually think this is a real excavation, and pepper the resort's tour guides and bartenders with questions about the "discovered" Lost Continent.

EXPENSIVE

Club Land'Or *ʁ*   Across the saltwater canal from Atlantis, these self-sufficient timeshare apartments are in three-story motel-like buildings set in a landscaped garden dotted with shrubs and reflecting pools. Although the club isn't located on the bay, the beach is a short drive away. There's a small freshwater swimming pool, as well as a walking path beside the canal where guests can take in a little salt air. If you're itching to try your luck at the casino, you'll have to drive there or take a taxi. Each of the accommodations includes a separate bedroom, a patio or balcony, a fully equipped kitchenette, and a living room. Bathrooms are utilitarian, with showers but no tubs. Some apartments are said to be suitable for four, but we think you'd really have to be into togetherness. The rates depend on the view (garden or water). Facilities include the Blue Lagoon restaurant (see "Where to Dine," below).

Paradise Dr. (P.O. Box SS-6429), Paradise Island, The Bahamas. ℂ 242/363-2400. Fax 242/363-3403. www.clublandor.com. (For reservations and information, contact the club's executive offices: 7814 Carousel Lane, Suite 200, Richmond, VA 23294; ℂ 800/552-2839 in the U.S.) 70 units. Winter $225–$250 apt for 2; off-season $165–$195 apt for 2. AE, DISC, MC, V. Free parking. **Amenities:** Restaurant, 2 bars, pool, activities program, baby-sitting, laundry. *In room:* A/C, TV, kitchen.

Club Med Paradise *ʁ*   This all-inclusive resort occupies 21 acres with lush gardens; its two wings of three-story pastel bungalows curve along 3 miles of white-sand beach. It appeals to visitors who like lots of activities and water sports. In 1996, Club Med began a $30-million renovation project that continued through 1998, turning the hotel into a "Finest Village," the most deluxe version of the club.

The mid-size rooms feature a mix of furniture and art from Asia and the Caribbean, and the bathrooms were redone in white marble. They're small, with twin beds (the norm for Club Meds—but why?), comfortable white-cane furniture, and little else. The theory is that you're going to be outdoors all day. In the middle of the complex stands a Georgian-style mansion housing public rooms and restaurant facilities. A walk through the landscaped garden brings members harborside and to the main restaurant. The resort accepts children under 12, but there are no special facilities for them. The place is mostly for people without children. It attracts lots of honeymooners and singles in their 30s. The biggest draw is the tennis facilities, which are among the best in The Bahamas.

Casuarina Dr. (P.O. Box N-7137), Paradise Island, The Bahamas. (C) 800/CLUB-MED in the U.S., or 242/363-2640. Fax 242/363-3496. www.clubmed.com. 360 units. Winter $160–$168 per person daily, $1,120–$1,175 per person weekly; off-season $158–$169 per person daily, $1,106–$1,183 per person weekly. Yearly membership of $50 per person. Prices are all inclusive. AE, DC, MC, V. Free parking. **Amenities:** Restaurant (both indoor and outdoor), pool, 18 tennis courts, fitness center, disco, beach bar, open-air theater/dance floor/bar complex, aerobics classes. *In room:* TV. No phone.

Holiday Inn SunSpree Resort (★   This older 12-floor property adjacent to the waters of Nassau Harbour opens onto a narrow beach but also has a very large swimming pool. It was rescued from oblivion in the late 1990s when a Florida-based investment group, Driftwood Ventures, renovated it. This group turned it into an all-inclusive resort, which lies just a short stroll away from the popular Atlantis and all its attractions. Bedrooms are mid-size with twins or king-size beds, plus well-maintained private bathrooms with tub and shower combinations. The decor is comfortable, airy and sunny, and outfitted with tropically inspired colors and upholsteries. All third-floor rooms and select units on the fourth floor are designated for non-smokers only.

Harbour Dr., P.O. Box SS-6249, Paradise Island. (C) 800/331-6471 in the U.S., or 242/363-2561. Fax 242/363-3803. holidayinn_paradiseisland@bahamas.net.bs. 246 units. Winter $380–$610 double; summer $380–$500 double. Rates include all drinks, meals, snacks, and most water sports. AE, DC, MC, V. **Amenities:** 2 restaurants overlooking the pool and harbor, poolside snackbar, lobby bar, tennis courts, exercise room, fitness center, supervised children's program, room service. *In room:* A/C, TV, refrigerator, coffeemaker, hair dryer, iron/ironing board, safe.

Marriott's Paradise Island Beach Club (★   Set near the eastern tip of Paradise Island, adjacent to a relatively isolated strip of spectacular beachfront, this two- and three-story time-share complex was built in 1985. Managed by Marriott, it's more of a self-catering condo complex than a full-fledged resort. Many guests cook at least some meals in their own kitchens and head elsewhere, often to bigger hotels, for restaurants, water sports, gambling, and entertainment.

(Kids Family-Friendly Hotels

Sheraton Grand Resort *(see p. 123)* A high-rise hotel with a panoramic view of the beach, the Sheraton offers family packages that reduce its regular rates substantially. In summer and during Easter and Christmas, activities for children from 5 through 13 are organized at Camp Caribbean.

Atlantis Paradise Island Resort & Casino *(see p. 118)* This waterworld extravaganza offers fun for all ages. Families are delighted with its innovative, activity-oriented Camp Paradise (ages 4 to 12), which operates year-round and is one of the best children's programs around (designed by the Discovery Channel).

Sunrise Beach Club and Villas *(see p. 123)* Some of the roomy apartments here are suitable for up to eight persons, so families of various sizes are accommodated comfortably. The resort has two swimming pools, one with a waterfall, plus a snack bar. Families also appreciate the fully equipped kitchens in each unit.

Views from the bedrooms are usually ocean panoramas; overall, the setting is comfortable and, at its best, even cozy. You'll feel like you have your own Florida apartment, with easy access to the beach. Apartments have two bedrooms, with wicker and rattan furnishings, and amenities that include double basins in each bathroom, plus a tub and shower.

On the premises are both a round and a triangular-shaped swimming pool, one with a simple snack bar that's open only at lunchtime. The entertainment and casino facilities of the more densely developed sections of Paradise Island are just a short walk away. The major drawback here is the service, which is very laissez-faire.

Garden View Dr. (P.O. Box N-10600), Paradise Island, The Bahamas. © **242/363-2814.** Fax 242/363-2130. www.marriott.com. 44 units. Year-round $300 for up to 6. AE, DC, MC, V. **Amenities:** Snack bar, 2 pools. *In room:* A/C, TV, kitchen.

Sheraton Grand Resort Paradise Island 🐾 *Kids* Opening onto a 3-mile stretch of sandy beach, the first Sheraton in either The Bahamas or the Caribbean, this hotel was radically rebuilt and renovated to the tune of $10 million after substantial damage during the 1999 hurricanes. This 14-story pink high rise offers some of the most comfortable recently renovated bedrooms on Paradise Island. This place is more understated than the Atlantis, a lot cheaper, and more user-friendly and manageable in terms of size and layout. Your kids will be happier with all the spectacular events at the Atlantis, but the Sheraton is a viable runner-up for the family trade. Guests can leave the shelter of the poolside terrace and settle almost immediately onto one of the waterside chaise longues at the beach. The hotel is within walking distance of the casino, restaurants, and nightlife facilities of the Atlantis Paradise Island Resort & Casino properties.

Welcoming drinks are served while you relax on comfortable chairs in the lobby bar amid palm trees and tropical foliage. All the spacious accommodations here are deluxe and tastefully decorated, and equipped with medium-size bathrooms containing tub and shower combos. Many have spacious balconies that afford sweeping water views. Two floors are no-smoking.

The premier restaurant is The Rotisserie, which serves excellent lobster, steak, and seafood. Other choices include the multilevel Verandah Restaurant, where you can have breakfast with a view of the sea. Julie's Ristorante Italiano is another good restaurant with moderate prices (see "Where to Dine," below).

Casino Dr., P.O. Box SS-6307, Paradise Island, The Bahamas. © **800/782-9488** in the U.S., or 242/363-3500. Fax 242/363-3500. www.sheratongrand.com. 340 units. Winter $240–$270 double, from $290 suite; off-season $255–$285 double, from $270 suite. AE, DC, MC, V. **Amenities:** 4 restaurants, 3 bars, pool, 4 lighted tennis courts, fitness center, room service, baby-sitting, valet, fleet of boats for various water pursuits such as parasailing or jet skiing, scuba and snorkeling lessons. *In room:* A/C, TV, minibar, coffeemaker, hair dryer, iron/ironing board, safe.

Sunrise Beach Club and Villas 🐾 *Kids* This cluster of Spanish-inspired low-rise town houses occupies one of the most desirable stretches of beachfront on Paradise Island. You'll find it midway between the Sheraton Grand and the Ocean Club, a short walk from the casino and a variety of sports and dining options. Accommodations are clustered within five separate groupings of red-roofed town houses, each with access to the resort's two swimming pools (one of which has a waterfall) and a simple snack bar. The hotel is usually full of lots of Germans, Swiss, and Austrians, many of whom stay for several weeks, preparing most of their own meals, since units have kitchens. Expect pastel colors, summery-looking furniture, and a private patio or veranda, plus king-size beds with good mattresses and floor-to-ceiling mirrored headboards, as well as average-size bathrooms with tub and shower. This is a good bet for "quieter" families who want a more subdued and relaxed vacation, and who want to avoid the "circus" going on 24 hours at the Atlantis.

P.O. Box SS-6519, Paradise Island, Nassau, The Bahamas. © 242/363-2250. Fax 242/363-2308. www.sunrisebeachvillas.com. 35 units. Winter $225 studio, $315–$470 1-bedroom apt for 1–4, $551 2-bedroom apt for 1–6, $859–$988 3-bedroom apt for 1–8; off-season $170 studio, $238 1-bedroom apt for 1–4, $416 2-bedroom apt for 1–6, $953–$1,097 3-bedroom apt for 1–8. AE, MC, V. **Amenities:** Restaurant, bar, 2 pools. *In room:* A/C, TV, kitchen.

MODERATE

Bay View Village ♋   More than 20 kinds of hibiscus and many varieties of bougainvillea beautify this 4-acre condo complex. If you get the right nest here, you'll find the accommodations better than those at the pricier Club Land'Or, its major competitor (see above). Although it is near the geographic center of Paradise Island, it's only a 10-minute walk to either the harbor or the white sands of Cabbage Beach (the complex has no beach of its own). The restaurants, nightlife, and casino of Atlantis are only a few minutes away.

We particularly recommend rooms near the center of the resort, because they are closest to the swimming pools and facilities. Each accommodation has its own kitchen with dishwasher, plus a patio or balcony and daily maid service. Some units open onto views of the harbor. A full-time personal cook can be arranged on request. The units come in a wide variety of sizes; the largest can hold up to six. Rates are slightly less for weekly rentals. Penthouse suites contain roof gardens that open onto views of the harbor. Bedrooms, with good firm mattresses, come with king-, queen-, or twin-size beds. Bathrooms are medium in size, well-maintained, and equipped with tub and shower combos.

Bayview Dr. (P.O. Box SS-6308), Paradise Island, The Bahamas. © 800/757-1357 in the U.S. and Canada, or 242/363-2555. Fax 242/363-2370. 30 units. www.bayviewvillage.com. Winter $290 1-bedroom suite for 2, $280 penthouse for 2, $330 town house for 4, $350–$385 villa for 4, $510 villa for 6; off-season $140 1-bedroom suite for 2, $200 penthouse for 2, $235 town house for 4, $245 villa for 4, $355 villa for 6. AE, MC, V. **Amenities:** Poolside cafe, 3 swimming pools, tennis court, baby-sitting, 2 coin-operated laundry rooms, minimarket. *In room:* A/C, TV, kitchen, hair dryer.

Comfort Suites *(Value*   A favorite with honeymooners and a good value, this three-story, all-suite hotel is across the street from the Atlantis. If the mammoth Atlantis seems too overpowering, Comfort Suites is a nice alternative. You get the splash and wonder of the Atlantis, but you don't have to stay there all night or when the cruise-ship crowds descend. Although there are both a pool bar and a restaurant on the premises, guests are granted signing privileges at each of the drinking-and-dining spots, as well as the pool, beach, and sports facilities of the nearby Atlantis. Accommodations are priced by their views, over the island, the pool, or the garden. The medium-size bathrooms have beach towels, and ample vanities. Bedrooms are standard motel size with two double beds or one king, each with a firm mattress.

Paradise Island Dr. (P.O. Box SS-6202), Paradise Island, The Bahamas. © 800/228-5150 or 242/363-3680. Fax 242/363-2588. www.comfortsuites.com/hotel/bs003. 228 units. Winter $260–$280 double; off-season $175–$225 double. Rates include continental breakfast. AE, DISC, MC, V. **Amenities:** Restaurant, bar, swimming pool, baby-sitting, laundry. *In room:* A/C, TV, minibar, coffeemaker, hair dryer, safe, refrigerator on request.

INEXPENSIVE

Paradise Harbour Club & Marina   The noteworthy thing about this place is its sense of isolation on heavily developed Paradise Island. Set near its extreme eastern tip, a few steps from the also-recommended Columbus Tavern, it was built in 1991. It's pale pink, with rambling upper hallways, terra-cotta tile floors, and clean, well-organized bedrooms. If available, opt for one of the top-floor accommodations so you can enjoy the view.

Paradise Island Dr. (P.O. Box SS-5804), Paradise Island, Nassau, The Bahamas. © 800/HOTEL-411 in the U.S., or 242/363-2992. Fax 242/363-2840. www.luxehotels.com. 22 units. Year-round $120–$220 double, $180–$300 jr. suite, $250–$360 1-bedroom apt for 4, $350-$550 2-bedroom apt. for 6. AE, DC, MC, V. **Amenities:** Restaurant, bar, pool, hot tub, tennis court, bikes for guests. *In room:* A/C, TV, kitchenette, minibar.

The Pink House ⋇ (Value) This place might remind you of a bed-and-breakfast in a verdant corner of England, thanks to its stately nature and the rigorous standards of its owner, Minnie Winn. It was built in the 1920s by Howard Major, the architect who designed many of the mansions of Palm Beach, Florida. Comfortable and commodious, it sports wide wraparound verandas, a brick facade, and a wood-paneled interior. Once part of an estate owned by the heirs to the Sears-Roebuck fortune, it sits on land that's now owned by Club Med (though neither Ms. Winn nor her house is associated with Club Med in any way). For access, you'll have to pass by a security guard at the entrance to the fenced-in Club Med Compound. And although Ms. Winn's establishment doesn't have any particular sports or entertainment facilities of its own, you can pay a fee between $35 and $50 per person for unlimited daylong access to Club Med's buffet tables, swimming pools, tennis courts, and water-sports facilities. Many guests of Ms. Winn, however, skip Club Med and swim on the beach (a 5-min. stroll across the narrow island), rest on one of the covered verandas where views extend out over the channel between Paradise Island and Nassau, and read in their simple but dignified and slightly worn mid-size bedrooms, each with a shower unit.

P.O. Box SS-19157, Casuarina Dr., Paradise Island, The Bahamas. © 242/363-3363. Fax 242/377-3383. www.bahamasnet.com/pinkhouse. 4 units. Dec–Apr $120 double; May–Nov $100 double. No credit cards. **Amenities:** Breakfast only, laundry. *In room:* A/C, TV.

4 Where to Dine

Paradise Island offers an array of the most dazzling, and the most expensive, restaurants in The Bahamas. If you're on a strict budget, cross over the bridge into downtown Nassau, which has far more reasonably priced places to eat. Meals on Paradise Island may be expensive, but they're often unimaginative. (Surf and turf appears on many a menu.) Unfortunately, you may not get what you pay for.

The greatest concentration of restaurants, all near the casino, is owned by Sun International. There are other good places outside this complex, however, including the Courtyard Terrace at the Ocean Club and The Rotisserie at the Sheraton Grand Resort, which is that hotel's showcase restaurant.

VERY EXPENSIVE

Bahamian Club ⋇ FRENCH/INTERNATIONAL Overall, this is our favorite restaurant at the Atlantis. With an upscale British colonial–era feel, it's a big but civilized and clubby spot, with spacious vistas, mirrors, gleaming mahogany, and forest green walls. The excellent food is served in two-fisted portions. Meat is king here, all those old favorites from roasted prime rib to Cornish hen, plus the island's best T-bone, along with a selection of veal and lamb chops. The retro menu also features the inevitable Dover sole, lobster, and salmon steak. All of these dishes are prepared only with top-quality ingredients imported from the mainland. Appetizers also harken back to the good old days, with fresh jumbo shrimp cocktail, baby spinach salad with a bleu cheese dressing, and onion soup. Side dishes are excellent here, especially the penne with fresh tomato sauce and the roasted shiitake mushrooms.

In the Atlantis. © 242/363-3000. Reservations required. Main courses $30–$44. AE, DC, DISC, MC, V. Daily 6:30–9:30pm.

Blue Lagoon ⊛ SEAFOOD Lying across the lagoon from Atlantis, this restaurant is located two floors above the reception area of the Club Land'Or. Come here to escape the glitter and glitz of the casino and the restaurants along Bird Cage Walk. Views of the harbor and Paradise Lake, and music from an island combo, will complement your candlelight meal. Many of the fish dishes, including stone crab claws or the Nassau conch chowder, are excellent. The chef even whips up a good Caesar salad for two. The ubiquitous broiled grouper amandine is on the menu, or try some of the other dishes such as steak au poivre with a brandy sauce, or duck a l'orange, or even chicken chasseur. Yes, you will probably have had better versions of these dishes elsewhere, but they are competently prepared and served here, even though the meats are shipped in frozen.

In the Club Land'Or, Paradise Dr. © 242/363-2400. Reservations required. Main courses $24–$43. AE, DC, MC, V. Daily 5–10pm.

Courtyard Terrace ⊛ CONTINENTAL/BAHAMIAN Okay, so the food isn't the island's finest, which it ought to be for these prices. The on-site Dune is better. But when the moon is right, an evening meal here can be heavenly for people who don't have to watch their wallets. You dine amid palms, flowering shrubs, and a fountain in a flagstone courtyard surrounded by colonial verandas. Live music wafts from one of the upper verandas to the patio below. This isn't the most glittering dining room, but it's the most sophisticated. Women should bring some kind of evening wrap in case it becomes chilly.

The menu includes a strong showing of the classics: beefsteak tartare, prime sirloin, lobster quiche, and chateaubriand. Such a menu also calls for rack of lamb; though the shrimp Provençale or the calves' liver lyonnaise, if featured, may have more zest. With candles flickering in the breeze, music floating down, and tables set with Wedgwood china and crisp linen, you might not even mind the slow service.

In the Ocean Club, Ocean Club Dr. © 242/363-3000. Reservations required. Jacket and tie required for men. Main courses $36–$70 (highest price for a Maine lobster; most dishes under $45). AE, MC, V. Daily 7–9pm.

Dune ⊛⊛⊛ INTERNATIONAL The most sophisticated and cutting-edge restaurant on Paradise Island lies in the west wing, lobby level, of the previously recommended Ocean Club. Created (and still owned) by French-born restaurant guru Jean-Georges Vongerichten, it has a charcoal-gray and black decor that looks like it was plucked directly from a chic enclave in Milan, a sweeping view of the ocean, a teakwood floor that evokes a yacht, and very attentive service. If you approach the place from the grounds, rather than from the interior of the hotel, you'll pass by the herb garden from which many of the culinary flavorings are derived. The chefs here invariably select the very finest ingredients, which are then handled with a razor-sharp technique. Every dish has a special something, especially shrimp dusted with orange powder and served with artichokes and arugula. A splendid choice is tuna spring rolls with soybean salsa. Also charming to the palate is a chicken and coconut milk soup served with shiitake cakes.

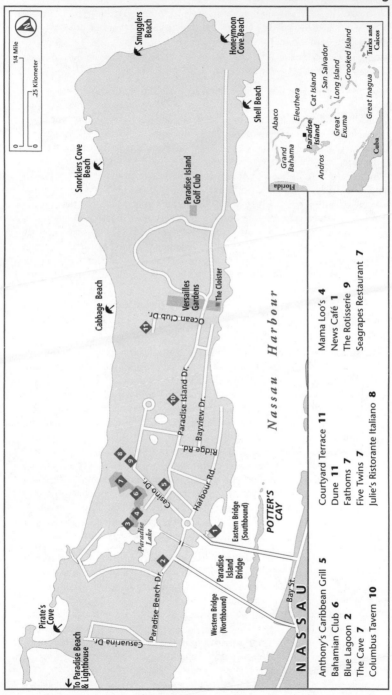

Paradise Island Dining

Anthony's Caribbean Grill **5**
Bahamian Club **6**
Blue Lagoon **2**
The Cave **7**
Columbus Tavern **10**

Courtyard Terrace **11**
Dune **11**
Fathoms **7**
Five Twins **7**
Julie's Ristorante Italiano **8**

Mama Loo's **4**
News Café **1**
The Rotisserie **9**
Seagrapes Restaurant **7**

The goat cheese and watermelon salad is an unexpected delight. Filet of grouper—that standard throughout The Bahamas—is at its savory best here when served with a zesty tomato sauce.

At the Ocean Club, Ocean Club Dr. (𝄐 242/363-2000, ext. 64739. Reservations required. Lunch main courses $13–$32; dinner main courses $20–$45. AE, DC, DISC, MC, V. Daily noon–3pm and 6–9:30pm.

Fathoms 𝄐 SEAFOOD   You'll feel as if you're dining under the sea in this very dark seafood palace, with menus printed on stainless-steel sheets and an almost-mystical decor. Illuminating its glossy, metallic interior and four enormous plate-glass windows, sunlight filters through the watery aquariums that surround The Dig, Atlantis's re-creation of an archaeological excavation of the underwater ruins of the Lost Continent.

At first you'll think the best appetizer is "Temple of Courage," a selection of raw seafood in season. But then you're tempted by the blackened sashimi flavored with red ginger as it passes by. The lobster gazpacho is the best on the island, and you can also dig into a bowl of steamy black mussels flavored with chardonnay, garlic, and tomato. The wood-grilled yellowtail appears perfectly cooked with a wasabi potato mash and caviar, and the grilled mahimahi is made extra inviting with its side dish of pumpkin ratatouille, a first for many diners. Save room for dessert, and make it a light, feathery soufflé—a different one is served every night.

In the Atlantis Aquarium. (𝄐 242/363-3000. Reservations recommended. Main courses $34–$59. AE, DC, MC, V. Daily 5:30–10pm.

Five Twins 𝄐 PACIFIC RIM   This is one of the most dramatic, cutting-edge, and upscale restaurants in the Atlantis. It's conspicuous consumption all the way, very plush, with a high-tech maritime decor that includes lots of wrought iron and tones of metallic silver and gold. Five Twins offers a cigar bar, ventilated well enough to keep non-smokers content, a satay and sushi bar, and an urban club-style setting with a DJ booth suspended 15 feet above the dance floor. Menu items fuse Indonesian satay with sushi and touches from California, Thailand, Japan, and other parts of the Pacific Rim.

Begin perhaps with the chilled oysters with apple slaw or pepper-cured salmon with vegetable tempura. The main courses are a savory kettle of goodies, especially the calamari noodles with endive or the steamed seabass with oven-baked eggplant given extra flavor by cardamom-carrot juice. The sweet and spicy lamb is delectable, appearing with red chard, white beets, and fresh spinach.

In the Casino and Entertainment Complex of the Atlantis Resort. (𝄐 242/363-3000. Reservations required. Main courses $28–$45. AE, DC, MC, V. Daily 6–10pm with a sushi and satay bar open daily 6:30pm–2am.

Villa d'Este 𝄐 ITALIAN   Paradise Island's most elegant Italian restaurant offers classic dishes prepared with skill and served with flair. It's become less oriented to Tuscan dishes and is more Americanized Italian now. Italian murals decorate the walls.

Main dishes have flair, including pan-fried chicken breast with artichokes and mushrooms in a lemon-laced white-wine sauce, or a whole roasted rack of lamb coated with red-wine sauce and rosemary potatoes. The freshly made fettuccine tomato sauce and basil is almost perfect. Salmon is quite delectable here, served with cannellini bean cream and resting under a basil crust.

In the Atlantis, Bird Cage Walk, Coral Tower, Casino Dr. (𝄐 242/363-3000. Reservations required. Main courses $33–$39. AE, DC, MC, V. Thurs–Tues 6–10pm.

(Kids) **Family-Friendly Restaurants**

The Cave *(see p. 131)* At the Atlantis, head here for lunchtime burgers, salads, and sandwiches. Kids love entering the simulated rock-sided tunnel lined with flaming torches. Later, they might return for an ice cream before the place closes at 5pm.

Seagrapes Restaurant *(see p. 131)* Off the lobby of the Atlantis, this tropical restaurant serves three meals a day. It's especially known for its low-price buffet lunches and dinners. Barbecued ribs, shrimp Creole, and apple pie appear on the menu.

EXPENSIVE

Mama Loo's *⊘* ASIAN Many people come here just to hang out in the bar, but if you're in the mood for a good Chinese meal, you'll be ushered to a table in a dining room with spinning ceiling fans, flaming torches from an overhead chandelier, and lots of potted palms. It evokes Shanghai during the British colonial age. The menu includes dishes from the Szechuan, Cantonese, Polynesian, and Caribbean repertoire. The best dish on the menu is Mama Loo's stir-fried lobster, beef, and broccoli with ginger. Two specialties we also like are shrimp in spicy chili sauce with a peanut sauce, and deep-fried chicken fillets with honey-flavored garlic sauce.

In the Coral Tower, Atlantis, Casino Dr. *©* **242/363-3000.** Reservations recommended. Main courses $21.75–$36.50. AE, DC, MC, V. Tues–Sun 6–10pm.

The Water's Edge *⊘* EURO/MEDITERRANEAN Three 15-foot waterfalls splash into an artificial lagoon just outside the dining room's windows. Huge chandeliers illuminate the room, which has views of an open kitchen, where a battalion of chefs work to create such dishes as paella Valencia or grilled salmon with French beans, potatoes, olives, and artichokes. The oak-smoked and spit-roasted duckling with figs and braised cabbage may win your hearts. Many guests come here just to sample the pizza and pasta specialties. The pizzas are standard, but some of the pastas have a bit of zest, including penne a l'arrabbiata, with a spicy tomato sauce. The chef pays special attention to the antipasti, which evokes the tangy flavors of the Mediterranean, especially the *soup au pistou* (vegetables with basil and roasted garlic). Depending on the night, some of these dishes are better than others. The main problem here is that the food has a hard time competing with the ambience.

At the Atlantis, Casino Dr. *©* **242/363-3000.** Reservations recommended. Main courses $22.50–$35. AE, DC, MC, V. Daily 7:30am–noon and 6:30–10pm.

MODERATE

Columbus Tavern CONTINENTAL/BAHAMIAN Far removed from the glitz and glamour of the casinos, the tavern seems relatively little known, even though Erika and Peter Kugler have been running it for years now. It deserves to be discovered, because it serves good food at reasonable (for Paradise Island) prices. The tavern has the typical nautical decor (don't come here for the setting), with tables placed both inside and outside overlooking the harbor. The bar is worth a visit in itself, with its long list of tropical drinks. You can go local by

---

Finds **Going Native with Conch**

Just once in your life, you've got to sample a Nassau conch salad. The best we could find on the island is at the **Sundeck Bar and Grille,** at the Sheraton Grand Resort on Casino Drive (✆ **242/363-3500).** The uncooked conch is marinated in Old Sour, a hot pepper sauce, to break down its tissue and to add an extra tangy flavor. It's served with diced small red or green peppers along with chopped onions. Sundeck chefs make it fresh daily but only on a limited basis. They warn, "When it's gone, it's gone." You'd better go early.

---

starting off with the conch chowder, or opt for cheese-stuffed mushrooms with foie gras. Even though they're imported frozen, both the chateaubriand and the rack of lamb are flawless. You can also order a decent veal cutlet and a quite good fillet of grouper with a tantalizing lobster sauce.

Paradise Island Dr. ✆ **242/363-2534.** Reservations required for dinner. Lunch main courses $8–$21; dinner main courses $15–$38. AE, MC, V. Daily 7am–3pm and 5:30–10pm.

Julie's Ristorante Italiano ⚜ *Value* ITALIAN   For moderately priced, down-home Italian cooking, check out this place. The gimmick is that you get to create your own pasta dish, choosing from a wide selection of pastas and sauces. Veal and chicken dishes dominate the menu, and most, especially the chicken parmigiana, are quite acceptable. A house specialty is Bahamian lobster tail with shrimp, scallops, and mushrooms topped with Alfredo sauce. You can also order fish, various shrimp dishes, or the ubiquitous grouper, appearing this time decorated with tricolor peppers.

In the Sheraton Grand Resort Paradise Island, Casino Dr. ✆ **242/363-2011.** Main courses $15.95–$32. AE, DC, DISC, MC, V. Daily 6–11pm.

The Rotisserie ⚜ AMERICAN   This place competes with the better-known steak houses on New Providence Island but does it at substantially lower prices. The setting includes lots of masculine dark paneling that's softened somewhat with a ring of hand-painted pink and red hibiscus borders. Enjoy sea views through the big open windows, or watch what's going on in the showcase-style glassed-in kitchen. Begin with a grilled chicken salad, conch fritters, or grouper coated with chopped plantain and served with a ginger-flavored butter sauce. Main courses include perfectly prepared roasted rack of lamb, spit-roasted chicken, filet mignon, and either sirloin or porterhouse steaks.

In the Sheraton Grand Resort Paradise Island, Casino Dr. ✆ **242/363-3500.** Reservations required. Main courses $17.95–$32.95. AE, DC, MC, V. Daily 6–11pm.

INEXPENSIVE

Anthony's Caribbean Grill AMERICAN/CARIBBEAN   Its owners think of this place as an upscale version of Bennigan's or TGI Fridays. But the decor is thoroughly Caribbean, thanks to psychedelic tropical colors, underwater sea themes, and jaunty maritime decorative touches. A bar dispenses everything from conventional mai-tais to embarrassingly oversized, 48-ounce "sparklers"— with a combination of rum, amaretto, vodka, and fruit punch that is about all most serious drinkers can handle. Menu items include burgers, pizzas capped with everything from lobster to jerk chicken, barbecued or fried chicken, ribs with coconut-mango sauce, and several meal-size salads.

Paradise Island Shopping Center, at the junction of Paradise and Casino drives. ✆ 242/363-3152. Reservations not necessary. Lunch platters and main courses $5.95–$14; dinner platters and main courses $11.95–$39.95. AE, MC, V. Daily 11:30am–11pm.

The Cave (Kids) BURGERS/SALADS/SANDWICHES   This burger-and-salad joint is near the Atlantis's beach, catering to the bathing-suit and flip-flops crowd, most often families. To reach the restaurant, you pass beneath a simulated rock-sided tunnel illuminated with flaming torches. The selection of ice cream will cool you off in the mid-afternoon sun.

At the Atlantis, Paradise Dr. ✆ 242/363-3000. Lunch platters $6–$9. AE, DC, MC, V. Daily 11am–6pm.

News Café DELI   Low-key and untouristy, this is where you'll find most of the island's construction workers, groundskeepers, and hotel staff having breakfast and lunch. They maintain a stack of the day's newspapers, so you can have something to read as you sip your morning cappuccino or latte. You can also stock up here on sandwiches for your beach picnic.

In the Hurricane Hole Shopping Centre, Paradise Island. ✆ 242/363-4684. Reservations not accepted. Pizzas, breakfast and lunch sandwiches, platters $5–$7. Assorted coffees $2–$3.25. No credit cards. Daily 7:30am–10pm.

Seagrapes Restaurant (Kids) INTERNATIONAL   Buffet lunches and dinners are the specialty of this pleasantly decorated tropical restaurant. This is the most affordable and family-oriented choice in the Atlantis, offering Cuban, Caribbean, and Cajun dishes. It's pretty straightforward fare, but you get a lot of food for not a lot of money—a rarity on pricey Paradise Island. The restaurant, which can seat 200 to 300 diners at a time, overlooks the lagoon and has a marketplace look, with buffet offerings displayed in little stalls and stations.

In the Atlantis, Casino Dr. ✆ 242/363-3000. Breakfast buffet $15.95; lunch buffet $15.95; dinner buffet $29.95. AE, DC, MC, V. Daily 7–11am, 12:30–3pm, and 5:30–10pm.

5 Beaches, Water Sports & Other Outdoor Pursuits

Visitors interested in something more than lazing on the beaches have only to ask hotel personnel to make the necessary arrangements. Guests at the **Atlantis** (✆ 242/363-3000), for example, can have access to a surprising number of diversions without so much as leaving the hotel property. They can splash in private pools; play tennis, Ping-Pong, and shuffleboard; ride the waves; snorkel; or rent Sunfish, Sailfish, jet skis, banana boats, and catamarans from contractors located in kiosks. Facilities are open to non-guests for $40 per day.

HITTING THE BEACH

For comments about Paradise Beach, refer to "Beaches, Water Sports & Other Outdoor Pursuits," in chapter 3. Paradise Island has a number of smaller beaches, as well. **Cabbage Beach** 🌴🌴 is among these, with broad sands that stretch for at least 2 miles. Casuarinas, palms, and sea grapes border it. It's likely to be crowded, but you can find a little more elbow room by walking on to the northwestern stretch of the beach.

FISHING

Anglers can fish close to shore for grouper, dolphinfish, red snapper, crabs, even lobster. Farther out, in first-class fishing boats fitted with outriggers and fighting chairs, they troll for billfish or giant marlin.

Frommer's Favorite Paradise Island Experiences

Catching a Dazzling Stage Show. In the Las Vegas tradition, show-biz extravaganzas are staged at the Atlantis showroom of the Paradise Island Casino.

Watching the Sunset at the Cloister. Here amid the reassembled remains of a 12th-century French stone monastery, once owned by William Randolph Hearst, you can enjoy one of the most beautiful pink and mauve sunsets in all The Bahamas.

A Day at Paradise Beach. It's one of the best beaches in the entire Caribbean. The beach is dotted with *chikees* (thatched huts) for when you've had too much of the sun.

A Night at the Casino. The Paradise Island Casino is one giant pleasure palace. Many visitors arrive on the island just to test their luck in this 30,000-square-foot casino. The nearby Bird Cage Walk is home to some of the finest restaurants in The Bahamas.

The best way to hook up with this pastime is to go to the activities desk of your hotel. All hotels have contacts with local charter operators who take their passengers out for a half or full day of fishing. For other possibilities, refer to "Beaches, Water Sports & Other Outdoor Pursuits," in chapter 3.

GOLF

Ocean Club Golf Club 𝒦𝒦 on Paradise Island Dr. (© **242/363-3925**), at the east end of the island, is an 18-hole championship golf course, designed by Tom Weiskopf, and overlooks both the Atlantic Ocean and Nassau Harbour. Attracting every caliber of golfer, the par 72 course is known for its Hole 17, which plays entirely along the scenic Snorkelers Cove. Greens fees, including cart, are $225 per player, and rental clubs and shoes are available.

Golfers who want more variety will find two other courses on New Providence Island (see "Beaches, Water Sports & Other Outdoor Pursuits," in chapter 3).

SNORKELING & SCUBA DIVING

For more scuba sites in the area, see "Snorkeling, Scuba Diving & Underwater Walks," in chapter 3.

Bahamas Divers, Sheraton Grand Resort, Casino Dr. (© **242/393-8724**), is the best all-around center for water sports on the island, specializing in scuba diving and snorkeling. A one-tank dive, all equipment included, costs $45; a two-tank dive goes for $70. Snorkeling reef trips depart daily at 10am and 2pm, costing $27 with all equipment included.

TENNIS

If you're a true tennis buff, you'll head for the previously recommended **Club Med** 𝒦𝒦 (© **242/363-2640**), which has the largest court complex on the island, a total of 18 clay composition courts. Six of these courts are lit for night games. There are ball machines, plus a full staff of instructors who offer expert advice. There's also instant-replay TV. Experienced tennis players who are residents of Club Med can sign up for the ATP (Advanced Tennis Player) program, where for a fee of $150 they'll be coached in tennis techniques for 6 hours a day over a period of 5 days. Non-guests who want to play tennis here should call ahead; they can buy an all-inclusive day pass ($40, valid any day from 10:30am to 6:30pm) and then combine as much tennis as they want with access to all of Club Med's facilities, including its buffets and bars.

Well-heeled tennis buffs check into **Ocean Club,** Ocean Club Drive (℗ **242/ 363-3000**). Many visitors come to Paradise Island just for tennis, which can be played day or night on the 10 Har-Tru courts near the Ocean Club. Guests booked into the cabanas and villas of the club can practically roll out of bed onto the courts. Although beginners and intermediate players are welcome, the courts are often filled with first-class competitors. At least two major tennis championships a year are played at the Ocean Club courts, drawing players from the world's top 20. Tennis is free for guests of the Ocean Club. Racket rentals cost $10 per hour for both residents and non-residents.

Other hotels with courts include the **Atlantis** ✦ (℗ **242/363-3000**), with nine hard-surface courts; and the **Sheraton Grand Resort** (℗ **242/363-2011**), with four night-lit Har-Tru courts and lessons available. These courts are open only to guests, with the Sheraton charging $15 per hour and the Atlantis $20 per hour.

6 Seeing the Sights

Most of the big hotels here have activity-packed calendars, especially for that occasional windy, rainy day that comes in winter. Hordes of Americans can be seen taking group lessons in such activities as backgammon, whist, tennis, and cooking and dancing Bahamian style. They're even taught how to mix tropical drinks, such as a Goombay Smash or a Yellow Bird. But to an increasing degree, hotels such as the Atlantis (see below) have configured themselves as destinations in their own right.

Atlantis Resort & Casino ✦✦   Regardless of where you're staying—even if it's at the most remote hotel on New Providence—you'll want to visit this lavish theme park, hotel, restaurant complex, casino, and entertainment center. It's Paradise Island's big attraction. You could spend all day here—and all night, too—wandering through the glitzy shopping malls; sampling the international cuisine of the varied restaurants; gambling at the roulette wheels, slot machines, and blackjack tables; or seeing Vegas-style revues. And once you're here, don't even think about leaving without a tour of "The Dig," a Disney-style attraction that celebrates the eerie and tragic legend of the lost continent of Atlantis. During the day you can dress casually, but at night you should dress up a bit, especially if you want to try one of the better restaurants.

The most crowded time to visit Atlantis is between 9am and 5pm on days when cruise ships are berthed in the nearby harbor. (That's usually every Tuesday and Saturday between 9am and 5pm.) The most crowded time to visit the casino is between 8 and 11pm any night of the week. There is no cover to enter: You pay just for what you gamble away (and that could be considerable), eat, and drink. The big shows have hefty cover charges, although some entertainment in the bars is free, except for the price of the liquor.

Casino Dr. ℗ **242/363-3000**. No cover. Open 24 hours.

The Cloister ✦   Located in the Versailles Gardens of the Ocean Club, this 12th-century cloister, originally built by Augustinian monks in southwestern

---

Moments **A Special Place of Beauty**

If you head up Paradise Island Drive, you'll reach Ocean Club Drive and a garden of tranquillity known as the **Versailles Gardens at the Ocean Club.** This is the loveliest spot on Paradise Island, far removed from the glitz and faux-glamour of the casinos. Its seven terraces frequently host weddings. Statues of some of Hartford's favorite people are found in the gardens, including Mephistopheles, Franklin D. Roosevelt, and even Napoléon. The gardens are open any time, day or night—and there's no admission.

France, was reassembled here stone by stone. Huntington Hartford, the A&P heir, purchased the cloister from the estate of William Randolph Hearst at San Simeon in California. Regrettably, after the newspaper czar originally bought the cloister, it was hastily dismantled in France for shipment to America, but the parts had not been numbered—they all arrived unlabeled on Paradise Island. The reassembly of the complicated monument baffled most conventional methods of construction, until artist and sculptor Jean Castre-Manne set about to reassemble it piece by piece. It took him 2 years, and what you see today, presumably, bears some similarity to the original. The gardens, which extend over the rise to Nassau Harbour, are filled with tropical flowers and classic statues. Unfortunately, although the monument retains a timeless beauty, recent buildings have encroached on either side, marring Huntington Hartford's original vision.

Ocean Club, Ocean Club Dr. © 242/363-3000. Free admission. Open 24 hours.

7 Shopping

For serious shopping, you'll want to cross over the Paradise Island Bridge into Nassau (see chapter 3). However, many of Nassau's major stores also have shopping outlets on Paradise Island.

The Shops at the Atlantis, in the Atlantis (© 242/363-3000), is the largest concentration of shops and boutiques on Paradise Island, rivaling anything else in The Bahamas in terms of size, selection, and style. The boutiques lie within the recently rebuilt Crystal Court Arcade within the sprawling Atlantis. Most of them are set adjacent to the resort's casino, in a well-appointed arcade that meanders between the Royal Tower and the Coral Tower; although a handful, as noted below, are scattered strategically throughout the resort. It's all very upscale and all about conspicuous consumption, so if you want to do more than browse, bring your platinum card.

There are two separate branches of **Colombian Emeralds** (one in the Crystal Court arcade, another closer to the beach within the Atlantis's Beach Tower), where the colored gemstones far outnumber the relatively limited selection of diamonds. Other choices include **Mademoiselle,** with branches in both the Beach Tower and the Coral Tower, where chic but simple clothing for women focuses on festive beach and resort wear.

The richest pickings lie within the **Crystal Court arcade.** Here, 35,000 square feet of merchandising space features **Lalique,** France-based purveyor of fine crystal and fashion accessories for men and women; **Cartier; Versace,** the late designer to the stars (this boutique also has a particularly charming house-wares division); **Armani,** whose clothes make almost any woman look like Michelle Pfeiffer and any man at least a bit thinner; **Façonnable,** youthful, sporty designer for young and beautiful club-hoppers; **Bulgari,** purveyor of the most enviable jewels in the world, as well as watches, giftware, and perfumes; and **Gucci** and **Ferragamo,** in case you forgot your dancing shoes. And if you want a bathing suit, **Coles of Nassau** sells swimwear by Gottex, Pucci, and Fernando Sanchez. Finally, **John Bull,** known for its Bay Street store in Nassau and as a pioneer seller of watches throughout The Bahamas, also has an interesting assortment of watches, jewelry, and designer accessories at this outlet.

8 Paradise Island After Dark

Paradise Island has the best **nightlife** in The Bahamas, and most of it centers around the Atlantis.

The Atlantis Resort's Casino and Discothèque   There's no other spot in The Bahamas, with the possible exception of the Crystal Palace complex on Cable Beach, with such a wide variety of after-dark attractions, and absolutely nothing that approaches its inspired brand of razzle-dazzle. Even if you stay in Nassau or Cable Beach, you'll want to drop into this artfully decorated, self-contained temple to decadence, even if gambling isn't really your passion. Whether you love it or hate it, this place is simply a jaw dropper.

The casino is the most lavishly planned, most artfully "themed" casino this side of Las Vegas. The only casino in the world built above a body of water, it was designed as an homage to the lost continent of Atlantis, and it appears to have risen directly from the waters of the lagoon. The illusion that it was until recently underwater is enhanced by water that gushes from illuminated fountains around its base, and by artfully positioned (artificial) cracks in its foundation, out of which thousands of gallons of water are constantly pumped, always for dramatic effect. During the day, sunlight floods the interior of the casino from the floor-to-ceiling windows that ring the complex, many of which offer views over the lagoon, the marina, the lavishly appointed water park, and the resort's gardens.

The casino is centered around buildings representing a Temple of the Sun and a Temple of the Moon with a painted replica of the zodiac overhead. Rising from key locations in and around the casino are five of the most elaborate sculptures in the world. Massive and complex, they were crafted by teams of artisans spear-headed by Dale Chihuly, the American-born resident of Venice whose glass-blowing skills are the most celebrated in the world. Other than the decor, the casino's gaming tables, open daily from 10am to 4am, provide the main attraction in this enormous place; in addition, about a thousand whirring and clanging slot machines operate 24 hours a day.

One side of the casino contains **Dragons,** a disco that manages to attract a few local hipsters as well as guests of the Atlantis. Come here anytime during casino hours for a drink. A sweaty, flirty crowd parties all night on the dance floor. Often, you can catch some of the best live music in The Bahamas, as bands take to the stage that's cantilevered above the dance floor. Live music begins around 9pm nightly. On Friday and Saturday, there's a cover charge of $25, payable by anyone not a guest of the Atlantis.

Ringing the casino are some 35,000 square feet of retail shopping space (see "Shopping," above) and an impressive cluster of hideaway bars and restaurants.

Also in the same Atlantis complex, **Joker's Wild** (© 242/363-3000) is the only real comedy club in The Bahamas, with a talented company of funny people who work hard to make their guests laugh. Show times are Tuesday through Sunday from 8:30 to 9:30pm and from 10:30pm to midnight. At least three comedians will appear on any given night, most of them hailing from The Bahamas, with occasional appearances of performers from London and New York. Midway between the Royal Tower and the Coral Tower. © 242/363-3000. No cover charge for casino, but cover charges apply to clubs and shows.

THE BAR SCENE

Dune Bar   Previously recommended as the number one restaurant on Paradise Island, this deluxe dining room is also the setting for the island's most elegant and sophisticated bar. It's increasingly popular as a plush and appealing, permissive singles bar. It's centered around a translucent white marble bar that's skillfully illuminated from behind. At the Ocean Club, Ocean Club Dr. © 242/363-2000, ext. 64722.

The Piranha Pub   Overall, this is the most unusual and interesting bar in the entire Atlantis Resort. This mystical-looking pub lies within the hotel's replica of the archaeological excavations of the lost continent of Atlantis. Schools of South America piranhas glare menacingly behind thick plate-glass windows a few inches from your face, darting through a forest of toppled columns, ruined arches, and scattered paving stones. The preferred drink here is a Miami Vice, something midway between a strawberry daiquiri and a piña colada. In theory, this place is open daily from 11am to midnight, but it closes whenever there isn't enough business, so call before you drop by. In The Dig, Atlantis Resort. © 242/363-3000.

Plato's Lounge   This is the hotel's most romantic bar, a sensual spot where you can escape the din of the slot machines. There's a glow from dozens of flickering candles set within lavish candelabras, and ocean views through the oversize windows. A pianist sets the mood during the cocktail hour and the early evening. In the morning, between opening and around noon, the site doubles as a cafe, serving pastries and snacks. On the lobby level of the Royal Towers, Atlantis Resort. © 242/363-3000.

5

Grand Bahama
(Freeport/Lucaya)

Big, bold, and brassy are the words that best describe Grand Bahama Island, where you'll find the resort area of Freeport/Lucaya. Though there's a ton of tourist development, it doesn't have the upscale chic of Paradise Island, but it does have fabulous white-sand beaches and a more reasonable price tag.

It may never return to its high roller days with the gloss and glitz of the '60s, when everybody from Howard Hughes to Frank Sinatra showed up, but recent renovations and massive development have brought a smile back to its face, which had grown wrinkled and tired over the latter part of the 20th century.

The second-most-popular tourist destination in The Bahamas (Nassau/Cable Beach/Paradise Island is first), Grand Bahama lies just 50 miles and less than 30 minutes by air off the Florida coast. That puts it just 76 miles east of Palm Beach, Florida. The island is the northernmost and fourth-largest landmass in The Bahamas (73 miles long and 4 to 8 miles wide).

Freeport/Lucaya was once just a dream—a low-lying pinewood forest that almost overnight in the 1950s turned into one of the world's major resorts. The resort was the dream of Wallace Groves, a Virginia-born financier who saw the prospect of developing the island into a miniature Miami Beach. Today, with the casino, the International Bazaar, high-rise hotels, golf courses, marinas, and a

bevy of continental restaurants, that dream has been realized.

The Lucaya district was developed 8 years later, as a resort center along the coast. It has evolved into a blend of residential and tourist facilities. As the two communities grew, their identities became almost indistinguishable. But elements of their original purposes still exist today. Freeport is the downtown area and attracts visitors with its commerce, industry, and own resorts, whereas Lucaya is called the "Garden City" and pleases residents and vacationers alike with its fine sandy beaches.

Grand Bahama is more than an Atlantic City clone, however. If you don't care for gambling at one of the island's two casinos, or if you're not interested in Vegas-style cabaret revues, there are alternatives. Because the island is so big, most of it remains relatively unspoiled. There are plenty of quiet places where you can get close to nature, including the Rand Memorial Nature Centre and the Garden of the Groves (see below). Lucayan National Park, with its underwater caves, forest trails, and secluded beach, is another major attraction. Just miles from Freeport/Lucaya are serene places where you can wander in a world of casuarina, palmetto, and pine trees. During the day, you can enjoy long stretches of open beach, broken by inlets and little fishing villages.

The reviews of Grand Bahama Island are definitely mixed. Some discerning travelers who could live anywhere have built homes here; others vow never to set foot on the island again, finding it "tacky" or "uninspired." Judge for yourself.

1 Orientation

For a general discussion on traveling to The Bahamas, refer to chapter 2.

ARRIVING

A number of airlines fly to Freeport from the continental United States, including **American Eagle** (© 800/433-7300; www.aa.com) and **Bahamasair** (© 800/222-4262; www.bahamasair.com), both with daily flights from Miami. **Lynx Air International, Inc.,** a Fort Lauderdale–based commercial carrier (© 888/596-9247), flies from Fort Lauderdale to Freeport. **GulfStream Continental Connection** (© 800/231-0856) flies to Freeport from both Fort Lauderdale and Miami. **TWA** (© 800/221-2000) flies in from New York's LaGuardia Airport about five times per week.

Many visitors arrive in Nassau, then hop a Bahamasair flight to Freeport. These 35-minute hops run about $128 round-trip.

No buses run from the airport to the major hotel zones. But many hotels will provide airport transfers, especially if you've bought a package deal. If yours does not, no problem; taxis meet arriving flights and will take you from the airport to one of the hotels in Freeport or Lucaya for about $11 to $14. The drive shouldn't take more than about 10 minutes.

VISITOR INFORMATION

Assistance and information are available at the **Grand Bahama Tourism Board,** International Bazaar in Freeport (© 242/352-6909). Another information booth is at the **Freeport International Airport** (© 242/352-2052). There's also a branch at the cruise-ship docks. Hours are 9am to 5pm Monday through Saturday.

ISLAND LAYOUT

Getting around Freeport/Lucaya is fairly easy because of its flat terrain. Although Freeport and Lucaya are frequently mentioned in the same breath, newcomers should note that Freeport is a landlocked collection of hotels and shops rising from the island's center, while Lucaya, about 2½ miles away, is a waterfront section of hotels, shops, and restaurants clustered next to a saltwater pond on the island's southern shoreline. Both were conceived as separate developments during their inception, but over the years, expansion has blurred their borders somewhat.

Freeport lies midway between the northern and southern shores of Grand Bahama Island. Bisected by some of the island's largest roads, it contains the biggest hotels, as well as two of the most-visited attractions in the country: the Resorts at Bahamia Casino, and the International Bazaar shopping complex. The local straw market, where you buy inexpensive souvenirs, lies just to the right of the entrance to the International Bazaar.

In addition to its hotels, Freeport has many banks, small local businesses, and government offices, most of which lie along East Mall Drive, a short walk from the bazaar. Most of these businesses and organizations are centered around Churchill Square. West of the International Bazaar, flanking both sides of West Sunrise Highway, are two of the island's four golf courses.

Grand Bahama Island

To reach **Port Lucaya** from Freeport, head east from the International Bazaar along East Sunrise Highway, then turn south at the intersection with Seahorse Road. Within about 2½ miles, it will lead to the heart of the Lucaya complex, Port Lucaya.

Set between the beach and a saltwater pond, Port Lucaya's architectural centerpiece is **Count Basie Square,** named for the great entertainer who used to have a home on the island. Within a short walk east or west, along the narrow strip of sand between the sea and the saltwater pond, rise most of the hotels of Lucaya Beach, as well as the headquarters of the famed Underwater Explorers Society.

Heading west of Freeport and Lucaya, the West Sunrise Highway passes industrial complexes such as The Bahamas Oil Refining Company. At the junction with Queen's Highway, you can take the road northwest all the way to **West End,** a distance of some 28 miles from the center of Freeport. Along the way you pass Freeport Harbour, where cruise ships dock. Just to the east lies Hawksbill Creek, a village known for its fish market. After passing this, you go through quaint villages with names like Eight Mile Rock and Bootleg Bay Village. West End used to be a haven for bootleggers running liquor to the United States during Prohibition.

Much less explored is the **East End** of Grand Bahama. It's located some 45 miles from the center of Freeport and is reached via the Grand Bahama Highway, which, despite its name, is rather rough in parts. Allow about 2 hours of driving time to reach the East End. The **Rand Memorial Nature Centre** lies about 3 miles east of Freeport. About 7 miles on is **Lucaya National Park.** Beyond the park is Gold Rock, a U.S. missile-tracking station. About 5 miles farther along the highway lies the hamlet of **Free Town.** East of Free Town is the village of **High Rock,** known for its Emmanuel Baptist Church. From here, the road becomes considerably rougher until it finally ends in **MacLean's Town,** which celebrates Columbus Day every year with a conch-cracking contest. From here, it's possible to take a water-taxi ride across Runners Creek to an exclusive club, Deep Water Cay, which caters to serious anglers.

In Freeport/Lucaya, but especially on the rest of Grand Bahama Island, you will almost never find a street number on a hotel or a store. Sometimes in the more remote places, you won't even find a street name. In lieu of numbers, locate places by prominent landmarks or hotels.

2 Getting Around

BY TAXI
The government sets the taxi rates, and the cabs are metered (or should be). If there's no meter, agree on the price with the driver in advance. The cost is $2 for the first three-quarters of a mile, plus 30¢ for each additional quarter mile.

Tips Island Hopping

If you'd like to visit some other islands while on Grand Bahama, you can do so aboard a small commuter-type airline, **Major's Airlines,** Freeport International Airport (© **242/352-5778**), which offers regular flights to Bimini for $100 round-trip, or to Abaco for $120 round-trip. Most of its carriers transport 9 to 15 passengers. Flights are not available every day, so call for schedules, reservations, and more information.

You can call for a taxi, although most taxis wait at the major hotels or the cruise-ship dock to pick up passengers. One major taxi company is **Freeport Taxi Company,** Old Airport Road (℃ **242/352-6666**), open 24 hours. Another is **Grand Bahama Taxi Union** at the Freeport International Airport (℃ **242/ 352-7101**), also open 24 hours.

BY BUS

There is public bus service from the International Bazaar to downtown Freeport and from the Pub on the Mall to the Lucaya area. The typical fare is 75¢ for adults, 50¢ for children. Check with the tourist office (see "Visitor Information," above) for bus schedules. There is no number to call for information.

BY CAR

If you plan to confine your exploration to the center of Freeport with its International Bazaar, and Lucaya with its beaches, you can rely on public transportation. However, if you'd like to branch out and explore the rest of the island (perhaps finding a more secluded beach), a rental car is the way to go. Try **Avis** (℃ **800/331-2112,** or 242/352-7666 locally; www.avis.com) or **Hertz** (℃ **800/ 654-3001,** or 242/352-9277 locally; www.hertz.com). Both of these companies maintain offices in small bungalows outside the exit of the Freeport International Airport.

One of the best local companies is **Star Rent-a-Car,** Old Airport Road (℃ **242/352-9325**), which rents everything from a Suzuki Swift to a Jeep Wrangler. Rates range from $49 per day with unlimited mileage, plus another $14 per day for a CDW (Collision Damage Waiver). Gas usually runs about $2.75 per gallon.

BY SCOOTER & BIKE

This is a fun way to get around as most of Grand Bahamas is flat with well-paved roads. Scooters can be rented at most hotels, or, for cruise-ship passengers, there are motor scooters for rent in the Freeport Harbour area. Helmets are required and provided by the outfitter. There are dozens of stands along the road in Freeport and Lucaya and also in the major parking lots. Rentals cost $40 per day, plus a $100 deposit, including insurance. Call ℃ **242/326-8329** for more information on scooters. Bikes, also available at most of these stands, rent for $20 per day, with a $50 deposit.

ON FOOT

You can explore the center of Freeport or Lucaya on foot, but if you want to venture into the East End or West End, you'll need to rent a car, hire a taxi, or try Grand Bahama's erratic public transportation.

 FAST FACTS: Grand Bahama

Climate   See "When to Go," in chapter 2.

Currency Exchange   Americans need not bother to exchange their dollars into Bahamian dollars, because the currencies are on par. However, Canadians and Brits will need to convert their money, which can be done at local banks or sometimes at a hotel, though hotels tend to offer less favorable rates.

Dentists   A reliable dentist is Dr. Larry Bain, Sun Alliance Building, Pioneer's Way, Freeport (☎ **242/352-8492**). Hours are Monday through Wednesday from 8:30am to 4pm and Thursday and Friday from 8:30am to noon.

Doctors   For the fastest and best service, just head to Rand Memorial Hospital (see "Hospitals," below).

Drugstores   For prescriptions and other pharmaceutical needs, go to Mini Mall, 1 West Mall, Explorer's Way, where you'll find **L.M.R. Prescription Drugs** (☎ **242/352-7327**), next door to Burger King. Hours are Monday through Saturday from 8am to 9pm and Sunday 8am to 3pm.

Embassies & Consulates   See "Fast Facts: The Bahamas," in chapter 2.

Emergencies   For all emergencies, call ☎ **911,** or dial 0 for the operator.

Eyeglass Repair   The biggest specialist in eyeglasses and contact lenses is the **Optique Shoppe,** 7 Regent Centre, downtown Freeport (☎ **242/352-9073**).

Hospitals   If you have a medical emergency, contact the **Rand Memorial Hospital,** East Atlantic Drive (☎ **242/352-6735,** or 242/352-2689 for ambulance emergency). This is a government-operated, 90-bed hospital.

Information   See "Visitor Information," earlier in this chapter.

Laundry & Dry Cleaning   Try **Jiffy Cleaners and Laundry,** West Mall at Pioneer's Way (☎ **242/352-7079**), open Monday through Saturday from 8am to 6pm.

Newspapers & Magazines   *The Freeport News* is a morning newspaper published Monday through Saturday except holidays. The two dailies published in Nassau, the *Tribune* and the *Nassau Guardian,* are also available here, as are some New York and Miami papers, especially the *Miami Herald,* usually on the date of publication. American newsmagazines, such as *Time* and *Newsweek,* are flown in on the day of publication.

Police   In an emergency, dial ☎ **911.**

Post Office   The main post office is on Explorer's Way in Freeport (☎ **242/352-9371**).

Safety   Avoid walking or jogging along lonely roads. There are no particular danger zones, but stay alert since Grand Bahama is no stranger to drugs and crime.

Taxes   All visitors leaving The Bahamas from Freeport must pay an $18 departure tax. There is no sales tax, but there's an 8% hotel tax.

Taxis   See "Getting Around," earlier in this chapter.

Weather   Grand Bahama, in the north of The Bahamas, has temperatures in winter that vary from about 60°F to 75°F daily. Summer variations range from 78 to the high 80s. In Freeport/Lucaya, phone ☎ **242/352-6675** for weather information.

3 Where to Stay

Your choices are the Freeport area, near the Bahamia Casino and the International Bazaar, or Lucaya, closer to the beach.

Remember: In most cases, a resort levy of 8% and a 15% service charge will be added to your final bill. Be prepared, and ask if it's already included in the initial price you're quoted.

FREEPORT

EXPENSIVE TO MODERATE

The Resorts at Bahamia *(R)* *(Kids)*   This is the faded, mass-market star of Freeport's hotels. It was built in the 1960s, and that design sensibility has become increasingly obvious as other, more dramatic hotels have been built. It strives for glitz and glitter, and it's been touched up frequently since its construction; but it still seems a bit dowdy.

In the late 1990s, it was acquired by the Florida-based Driftwood Hospitality Management Group, which immediately laid plans for a $42-million renovation of the resort and all its components. Although very few of these plans had been inaugurated at presstime for this guidebook, you can expect a radical renovation during the lifetime of this edition.

The resort doesn't have any beach of its own; it's slightly inland from the sea, with shuttle bus service making frequent connections. What does this mean for you? Bargains, if you don't mind commuting to the sands. Flanked by a pair of fine golf courses, and catering to the convention crowd, it's set on 2,500 acres of tropical grounds, about a mile from the nearest beach. Shuttle buses run every half hour to such competing beachfront resorts as the Xanadu and the Island Seas Resort.

There are in fact two "Bahamias": The Country Club at Bahamia and the slightly newer Tower at Bahamia. They jointly share one of the largest casinos in the country, a serviceable site that's functional but nowhere near as cutting edge as the Atlantis Casino on Paradise Island.

The Country Club at Bahamia attracts families, honeymooners, golfers, and others. The hotel's design is rather like an enormous low-rise wagon wheel, with a Disney-inspired minimountain at its core, surrounded by a swimming pool. The hotel is so spread out that guests often complain that they need ground transport to reach their bedrooms. Nine wings radiate from the pool. Some of the rooms have kitchenettes and are sold as timeshare units. Rooms in the 900 wing are the largest and best furnished, and are usually the ones that sell out first. Accommodations come in several classifications; however, even the standard rooms are well-equipped, albeit a bit faded, with two comfortable double beds, dressing areas, and full-size bathrooms. Both the Country Club and the Tower also rent out a number of suites that are furnished in summery fabrics and beachy but durable furniture.

The Tower, lying across the Mall from its larger sibling, is smaller and more tranquil, and a bit more posh, containing 19 suites and 318 luxuriously furnished large units. The Tower adjoins the Princess Casino and the International Bazaar. It rises 10 floors and stands on 7½ acres of grounds. The somewhat passé and even vaguely campy Arabic motif, the crowning glory of which is the Moorish-style tower (with turrets, arches, and a white dome), continues through the octagon-shaped lobby. Lots of conventioneers and folks on quick getaways from Florida tend to stay here.

The leading restaurant in the Country Club section is the upscale Rib Room (see "Where to Dine," below). There's also the Patio Coffee Shop and John B, both offering fine but rather ordinary lunch, dinner, and burgers.

Freeport/Lucaya Accommodations

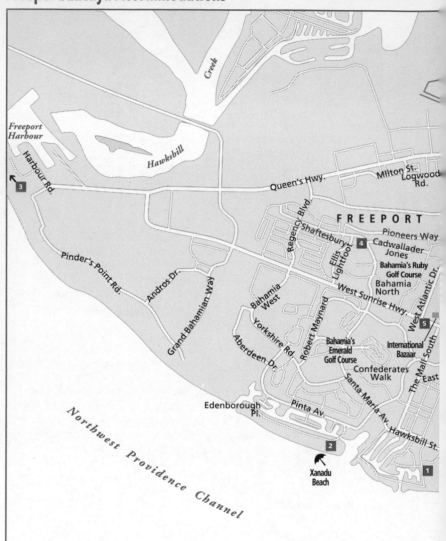

Castaways Resort & Suites **6**
Club Fortuna Beach **9**
Coral Beach **14**
Deep Water Cay Club **10**
Island Palm **8**
Lakeview Manor Club **4**
Old Bahama Bay **3**

Our Lucaya **11**
Pelican Bay at Lucaya **12**
Port Lucaya Resort & Yacht Club **13**
The Resorts at Bahamia **5**
Royal Islander **7**
Running Mon Marina & Resort **1**
Xanadu Beach Resort & Marina **2**

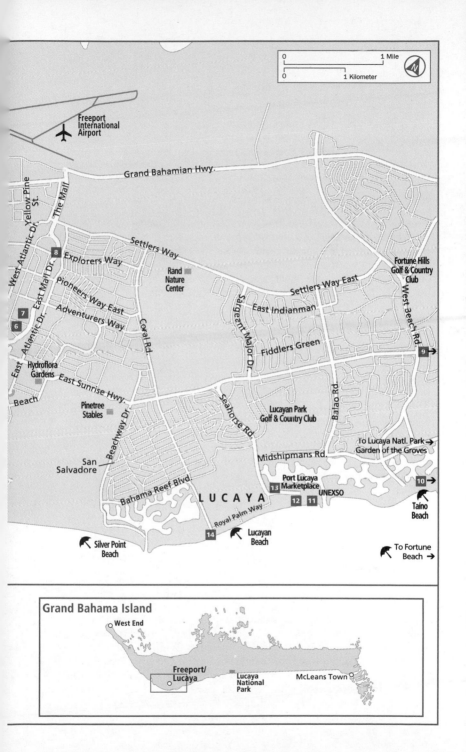

At the Tower, the best restaurants are the **Crown Room** (see "Where to Dine," below), plus **Morgan's Bluff** for seafood. Other dining options include the Lemon Peel and the outdoor La Terraza, which has a breakfast buffet in season. The Palm Pavilion offers a buffet dinner and floor show twice a week.

The Mall at W. Sunrise Hwy. (P.O. Box F-207), Freeport, Grand Bahama, The Bahamas. © **800/545-1300** in the U.S. and Canada, or 242/350-7000. Fax 242/350-7002. www.sunfinder.com. 965 units. Winter Country Club $$145–$155 double, $220 1-bedroom suite, $320 2-bedroom suite; Tower $165–$175 double, $360 1-bedroom suite, $470 2-bedroom suite. Off-season Country Club $98–$108 double, $180 1-bedroom suite, $240 2-bedroom suite; Tower $118–$128 double, $270 1-bedroom suite, $350 2-bedroom suite. Supplement for an all-inclusive plan including all meals and drinks $59–$79 per person. Up to 2 children under 12 stay free in parents' room. AE, DC, MC, V. **Amenities:** Restaurants, 2 pools; 2 18-hole championship golf courses nearby; 12 tennis courts (8 lit at night); Jacuzzi; nearby white-sand beach reached by shuttle-bus service; water sports, including deep-sea fishing; room service (7am to 10pm); baby-sitting; massage. *In room:* A/C, TV.

Xanadu Beach Resort & Marina 🕿 Once, the upper floors of this contemporary-looking tower were the refuge of reclusive billionaire Howard Hughes, who lived here for years without ever coming out. Since his death, this symmetrical 12-story tower has never recaptured its heady glamour. (In 1969, when it opened, Xanadu was an exclusive private club with members like Rat Packers Sammy Davis Jr. and Frank Sinatra.) Renovated in 1997 and 1998, it remains a viable but somewhat staid choice. We like it better than the anonymity and confusion of the Resorts at Bahamia, and it sits a 3-minute walk from a lovely, sandy beach (great for water sports), at the edge of a labyrinth of inland waterways and marinas, within a 10-minute drive of the international airport.

Carefully balanced with evenly spaced rows of carved balconies, the hotel sports a tropical pink exterior, and a contemporary 1960s design that doesn't look as dated as other Freeport architecture of similar vintage. The rooms may be a little worn here and there, but they're larger than you might expect, and they seem like upscale motel rooms in Florida. They're attractively and comfortably furnished, and housed in either the original 12-story tower or a three-story pool wing. All units have either one king-size bed or two doubles, with firm mattresses, and medium-size, well-maintained bathrooms.

The hotel offers the rather-standard Casuarina restaurant and the Ocean Front Bar and Grill. The cuisine is not a compelling reason to stay here.

Sunken Treasure Dr., P.O. Box F-42438, Freeport, Grand Bahama, The Bahamas. © **242/352-6782.** Fax 242/352-5799. www.bahamasvg.com/xanaduhotel.html. 184 units. Winter $125–$155 double, $170–$400 suite; off-season $94–$119 double, $129–$300 suite. AE, MC, V. Free parking. **Amenities:** Restaurant, grill, 3 bars, pool, 3 tennis courts, water sports, baby-sitting, room service, coin laundry, golf course nearby. *In room:* A/C, TV, minibar, hair dryer.

INEXPENSIVE

Castaways Resort & Suites 🕿 🕿 Castaways is a modest and unassuming hotel despite its platinum location adjacent to the International Bazaar and the casino. You stay here because of its location and the low price. It's not on the beach, but a free shuttle will take you to nearby Williams Town Beach or Xanadu Beach. Surrounded by gardens, the four-story hotel has a pagoda roof and an indoor/outdoor garden lobby with a gift shop, a clothing shop, a game room, and tour desks. Rooms are your basic motel style, and the best units are on the ground floor near the swimming pool.

The Flamingo Restaurant features unremarkable Bahamian and American dishes. There is a swimming-pool area with a wide terrace and a pool bar that offers sandwiches and cool drinks. The Yellow Bird Show Club (see "Grand

(Kids Family-Friendly Hotels

The Resorts at Bahamia *(see p. 143)*   This massive hotel does a lot of family business year-round, and it usually has bargain rates available for families on a budget. Two children's playgrounds with supervised activities are available.

Castaways Resort & Suites *(see p. 146)*   Located right at the International Bazaar, this family favorite lets children under 12 stay free in rooms with their parents. There's a large swimming pool plus a free shuttle to Xanadu Beach.

Running Mon Marina & Resort *(see p. 148)*   A children's playhouse and a playground are just part of the allure of this small resort that is a particular favorite of families who love boating. It lies on a 66-slip marina.

Bahama After Dark," later in this chapter) stays open until 3am and features limbo dancers and fire-eaters Monday through Saturday.

International Bazaar, P.O. Box F-42629, Freeport, Grand Bahama, The Bahamas. (℃) **242/352-6682.** Fax 242/352-5087. www.grand-bahama.com/castaways. 130 units. Winter $80–$105 double, $150[nd[$160 suites; off-season $75–$95 double, $130–$140 suites. Children under 12 stay free in parents' room. AE, MC, V. **Amenities:** Restaurant, night club, bar, pool, bike rentals, laundry, baby-sitting. *In room:* A/C, TV.

Island Palm   Set within the commercial heart of Freeport, this simple three-story motel, completely renovated in 1999, consists of four buildings separated by parking lots and greenery. Within an easy walk from virtually everything in town, and 1¼ miles from the International Bazaar, it offers good value in no-frills, eminently serviceable rooms that are often full of business travelers. Complimentary shuttle-bus service ferries anybody who's interested to nearby Williamstown Beach (also called Island Seas Beach), where you can use the beachfront facilities (including jet skis and snorkeling equipment) of its sibling resort, a time-share unit known as Island Sea. The Safari Restaurant, under separate management next door, is recommended separately (see "Where to Dine," below).

E. Mall Dr. (P.O. Box F-40200), Freeport, Grand Bahama, The Bahamas. (℃) **242/352-6648.** Fax 242/352-6640. 150 units. Year-round $89–$100 double. AE, DISC, MC, V. **Amenities:** Restaurant next door, bar, snack bar, pool, shuffleboard court. *In room:* A/C, TV.

Lakeview Manor Club   Today this 1970s-era resort is a time-share, but it was originally built as private apartments. It's a good bargain for those who want peace and privacy, but the staff seems a bit lax. Catering to self-sufficient types, it offers mid-size one-bedroom and studio apartments, each with tropical furniture, a private balcony, and a kitchenette, plus small bathrooms with shower stalls. The club overlooks the fifth hole of the PGA-approved Princess Ruby Golf Course. It's 5 miles from the beach, but it's ideal for golfers or for anyone to whom a sea view isn't important. A complimentary shuttle bus travels to International Bazaar and beach areas.

Cadwallader Jones Dr. (P.O. Box F-42699), Freeport, Grand Bahama, The Bahamas. (℃) **242/352-9789.** Fax 242/352-2283. www.bahamasvg.com/lakeview.html. 52 units. $75 double studio, $450 double studio weekly; $100 double 1-bedroom apt, $600 double 1-bedroom apt weekly. MC, V. Closed 1 week in Nov. **Amenities:** Pool, 2 tennis courts, reduced greens fees at nearby golf courses, laundry. *In room:* A/C, TV.

Royal Islander   Don't be fooled by the corny-looking, storm-battered exterior of this place. It was built during an unfortunate Disney-style period in Freeport's expansion, during the early 1980s, with an improbable-looking pyramidal roof inspired by a cluster of Mayan pyramids. Inside, it's a lot more appealing than you might think, with rooms arranged around a verdant courtyard that seems far, far removed from the busy traffic and sterile-looking landscape outside. Rooms have white-tile floors and bathrooms that are on the small side, with tiny sinks and shower stalls. Otherwise, the motif is Florida/tropical, with some pizzazz.

There's a coffee-shop-style snack bar on the premises, but other than that, you'll have to wander a short distance, perhaps to the International Bazaar just across the street, to find diversions and dining.

East Mall Dr., Freeport, Grand Bahama, The Bahamas. © 242/351-6000. Fax 242/351-3546. www.bahamasvg.com. 100 units. Winter $124 double; off-season $94–$104 double. AE, MC, V. **Amenities:** Coffee shop, pool, Jacuzzi, bar, laundry. *In room:* A/C, TV.

Running Mon Marina & Resort *(F (Kids*   Renovated in 2000, this is a small-scale, family-friendly resort that caters to yachties and anyone seeking peace and quiet. Originally built in 1991, it's ringed by canals and waterways, the focal point for which is a 66-slip marina. Rising two stories above a mostly flat landscape covered with sand, wispy trees, and scrub, it lies within a 5-minute drive east of the Xanadu Beach Hotel. All of the well-designed, mid-size bedrooms face the marina, and each is simply but comfortably outfitted with an unstocked refrigerator and wicker furniture, plus good beds and smallish bathrooms, each with a shower stall.

The complex includes a diving facility (if it's not opened in time for your arrival, the hotel will make alternative arrangements with an outside associate), plus a rather ordinary restaurant (the Mainsail) that's open for breakfast, lunch, and dinner. A free shuttle bus will take you to and from the International Bazaar and the beach near the Xanadu Hotel.

208 Kelly Court (P.O. Box F-42663), Freeport, Grand Bahama, The Bahamas. © 242/352-6834. Fax 242/ 352-6835. www.runningmonbahamas.com. 32 units. Winter $128 double, $249 suite; off-season $98 double, $198 suite. AE, MC, V. **Amenities:** Restaurant, 2 bars, children's playground, bike rentals, deep-sea fishing arranged. *In room:* A/C, TV, refrigerator.

LUCAYA
EXPENSIVE

Our Lucaya *(F/F/F*   This massive resort, one of the largest in The Bahamas, is firmly anchored at the center of two of the best white sandy beaches in The Bahamas—Lucayan Beach and Taino Beach. Expect nearly 8 acres of soft white sand. Freeport/Lucaya, which had been losing tourist business to Paradise Island, got a big boost in 1999 when this resort opened its doors. Prior to that, this was the site of two battered, past-their-prime hotels (the Atlantik Beach Hotel and the Lucayan Beach Resort & Casino). Accompanied by fireworks and brass bands, with the entire island looking on, the Atlantik Beach was imploded to make room for the vision of things to come. The Hong Kong–based Hutchison-Whampoa Group committed themselves to a total investment of at least $290 million. The radically redesigned resort was completed in 2000, when all three of its hotel components were fully operational and functional.

The first of the three sections was completed late in 1998 under the name **The Reef Village.** It's the only one of the three branches of Our Lucaya to focus exclusively on all-inclusive holidays, whereby all meals, drinks, and most activities are included in one set price. With a vague South Beach art-deco design, it's a massive, open-sided hexagon, with rooms facing the beach and the swimming pool. The resort is contemporary but relaxed; the developers have created a young vibe that draws a high number of families. Bedrooms are whimsical and fun, thanks to fabrics you'd expect on a loud Hawaiian shirt from the Elvis era and maple-veneered furniture, all put together with the kind of artful simplicity you'd expect in a California beach house.

In 2000, two newer subdivisions of Our Lucaya were opened, neither of which is marketed as an all-inclusive property. The smaller and somewhat more private of the two is **Lighthouse Pointe,** a 221-unit, low-rise complex that focuses specifically on an adult clientele. Its larger counterpart is the 550-unit **Breakers Cay,** a grand, 10-story, white-sided tower. The three sections stretch in a glittering profile along a narrow strip of beachfront, allowing residents to drop into any of the bars, restaurants, and gardens. A complex this big contains a staggering diversity of restaurants, each designed with a different theme and ambience. The best of the resort's 14 cuisine selections will be reviewed under "Where to Dine," later in this chapter. And consistent with the broad themes, each of the subdivisions has a dramatic and/or unconventional swimming pool. For example, the Reef Village's pool is designed around a replica of a 19th-century sugar mill, complete with an aqueduct that might be worthy of the ancient Romans. During the lifetime of this edition, look for the opening of a spa and fitness center, a quartet of tennis courts, a convention center, a state-of-the-art casino, and a shopping mall, and an increasing emphasis on golf, thanks to the opening of the spectacular Reef Course, which is separately recommended later in this chapter. Children aged 2 to 12 can be amused and entertained throughout daylight hours every day at Camp Lucaya, whose headquarters lie adjacent to the pool at the Reef Village.

P.O. Box F-42500, Royal Palm Way, Lucaya, Grand Bahama, The Bahamas. (*C*) 800/LUCAYAN in the U.S., or 242/373-1333. Fax 242/373-8804. www.ourlucaya.com. 1,350 units. For all-incusive Reef Village: year-round $420–$490 double, $35 extra per day for 3rd and 4th occupant. For EP (European Plan [no meals])residents of Lighthouse Pointe or Breakers Cay: year-round $155–$275 double, $30 extra for 3rd and 4th occupant. AE, DC, DISC, MC, V. **Amenities:** These will change as new additions open, but you can count on the following: 14 restaurants and lounges, 2 championship 18-hole golf courses, 3 pools, water sports, children's programs, room service, baby-sitting, laundry. *In room:* A/C, TV, minibar, iron. Suites: A/C, TV, kitchen, refrigerator, minibar, iron.

MODERATE

Pelican Bay at Lucaya ✿✿   Here's a good choice for travelers with champagne tastes and beer budgets, a hotel with more architectural charm than any other small property on Grand Bahama. It's built on a peninsula jutting into a labyrinth of inland waterways, with moored yachts on virtually every side. Pelican Bay evokes a Danish seaside village, with rows of "town houses," each painted a different color and sporting whimsical trim, and each overlooking the

---

(*Tips* Never Pay Top Price

Before you try to book your hotel on your own, be sure to read the section in chapter 2 on "Package Deals" and the tips on how to lower hotel costs. Never pay the rack rate! Use the rates given in this section as a point of comparison only.

harbor. The hotel opened in the fall of 1996 and later expanded with a new wing in 1999. Its location couldn't be better, right next to Port Lucaya Marketplace, where restaurants and entertainment spots abound. Lucayan Beach, one of the best stretches of white sand on the island, is just across the street, and Taino Beach, with equally good sands, lies immediately to the east of the hotel. UNEXSO, providing some of the best dive facilities in The Bahamas, is next door.

The spacious accommodations have Italian tile floors and whitewashed furniture, with either a king-size bed or twin beds with firm mattresses. The end rooms have cross ventilation and are the ideal choices for those who don't want to rely entirely on air-conditioning. No-smoking accommodations can also be requested. Each unit comes with a wet bar and satellite TV, as well as a balcony with a view of the nearby waterway and marina. Bathrooms, although of standard size, contain oversize cotton robes and tub and shower combos.

The hotel has one main restaurant, the Ferry House, which specializes in American and Bahamian food and serves breakfast, lunch, and dinner daily. The Yellow Tail Pool Bar offers drinks and snacks all day.

Royal Palm Way, P.O. Box F-42654, Lucaya, Grand Bahama, The Bahamas. (℃) 800/600-9192 in the U.S., or 242/373-9550. Fax 242/373-9551. www.grand-bahama.com. 69 units. Year-round $130–$170 double. AE, MC, V. **Amenities:** Restaurant, bar, pool, hot tub. *In room:* A/C, TV, refrigerator, coffeemaker, hair dryer, safe.

Port Lucaya Resort & Yacht Club ℱ   With its own 50-slip marina lying next to the Port Lucaya Marketplace, this is an even better choice than the Running Mon Marina & Resort, its major competitor. Opened in 1993, the resort consists of a series of pastel-colored two-story structures that guests reach via golf cart after checking in. The wings of guest rooms separate the piers—site of some very expensive marine hardware—from a verdant central green space with a gazebo-style bar and a swimming pool. All of this is in the heart of the Port Lucaya restaurant, hotel, and nightlife complex. Although set back inland on a waterway, Lucayan Harbour, this resort lies within a few minutes' walk of Lucayan Beach, one of the island's finest, and is also close to Taino Beach. Even though it's not right on the beach, it's such an easy walk that no one seems to complain. Some guests actually prefer the nautical, yachting look of the place and the nearness to Port Lucaya Marketplace.

The medium-size rooms have tile floors and are attractively and comfortably furnished with rattan pieces and big wall mirrors. The rooms are divided into various categories, ranging from standard to deluxe, and open onto the marina (preferred by yachtie guests), the Olympic-size swimming pool, or the well-landscaped garden. (If you don't want to hear the sounds coming from the lively marketplace, request units 1 through 6, which are more tranquil and away from the noise. Non-smokers can reserve a room in units 5 or 6.) Bathrooms with new showers are tidy and well-maintained, with adequate shelf space.

The hotel's restaurant, Tradewinds Cafe, offers standard Bahamian, American, and international dishes.

Bell Channel Bay Rd., P.O. Box F-42452, Lucaya, Grand Bahama, The Bahamas. (℃) 800/582-2921 or 242/373-6618. Fax 242/373-6652. www.portlucaya.com/resort. 163 units. Winter $100–$135 double; off-season $80–$110 double. Extra person $25. AE, MC, V. **Amenities:** Restaurant, 2 bars, pool, Jacuzzi, laundry. *In room:* A/C, TV.

INEXPENSIVE

Coral Beach   Built in 1965 as privately owned condominiums, this peacefully isolated property near a sandy beach sits amid gardens and groves of casuarinas

AT&T Direct® Service

1. Just dial the AT&T Access Number for the country you are calling from.
2. Dial the phone number you're calling.
3. Dial your card number.*

AT&T Access Numbers

Anguilla▲	1-800-USA-ATT1
Antigua (hotels)▲	1-800-USA-ATT1
Aruba▲	800-8000
Australia	**1-800-881-011**
Austria●	0800-200-288
Bahamas	**1-800-USA-ATT1**
Barbados▲	1-800-USA-ATT1
Belgium●	**0-800-100-10**
Bermuda▲	1-800-USA-ATT1
British V.I.▲	1-800-USA-ATT1
Canada	**1-800-CALL-ATT**
Cayman Islands▲	1-800-USA-ATT1
China, PRC▲	10811
Cook Islands	09-111
Costa Rica	0-800-0-114-114
Czech Republic▲	**00-42-000-101**
Denmark	**8001-0010**
Dominica▲	1-800-USA-ATT1
Dominican Republic▲	**1-800-USA-ATT1**
Egypt (Cairo)●	510-0200

For Access Numbers not listed, ask any operator for **AT&T Direct** Service.
In the U.S. call 1-800-222-0300 for **AT&T Direct** Service information.
Visit us at **www.att.com/traveler**
Bold-faced countries permit country-to-country calling.

▲ Available from select locations.

● Pay phones may require coin or card to place call.

✓ From N. Ireland, use U.K. Access Number.

▽ Includes "Lacatel" public phones.

★ From St. Maarten or phones at Bobby's Marina, use 1-800-USA-ATT1.

◖ Includes "Lenso" public phones.

* Credit card calling subject to availability. Payment terms subject to your credit card agreement.

When placing an international call *from* the U.S., dial 1-800-CALL-ATT.

AT&T

©3/01 AT&T

WW

AT&T Direct® Service

1. Just dial the AT&T Access Number for the country you are calling from.
2. Dial the phone number you're calling.
3. Dial your card number.*

AT&T Access Numbers

Fiji	004-890-1001
Finland●	0-8001-10015
France	0800-99-00-11
French Antilles▲	0800-99-00-11
Germany	0-800-2255-288
Greece●	00-800-1311
Grenada▲	1-800-USA-ATT1
Hong Kong	800-96-1111
Hungary	06-800-01111
Ireland✔	1-800-550-000
Israel	1-800-94-94-949
Italy●	172-1011
Jamaica▲	1-800-USA-ATT1
Jamaica▲	872
Japan ▲	005-39-111
Japan ▲	0066-55-111
Korea●	0072-911
Malaysia▲	1-800-80-0011
Mexico●▽	01-800-288-2872
Mexico ▽	001-800-462-4240

AT&T Direct® Service

1. Just dial the AT&T Access Number for the country you are calling from.
2. Dial the phone number you're calling.
3. Dial your card number.*

AT&T Access Numbers

Netherlands●	0800-022-9111
Neth. Antilles★ ▲	001-800-USA-ATT1
New Zealand●	000-911
Norway	800-190-11
Portugal▲	800-800-128
Puerto Rico/U.S. V.I.	1-800-CALL-ATT
St. Kitts/Nevis▲	1-800-USA-ATT1
St. Lucia▲	1-800-USA-ATT1
St. Vincent▲	1-800-USA-ATT1
Singapore	80-0001-0001
Singapore	800-0111-111
South Africa	0-800-99-0123
Spain	900-99-00-11
Sweden	020-799-111
Switzerland●	0-800-890011
Thailand◄	001-999-111-11
Trinidad & Tobago▲	1-800-USA-ATT1
Turkey●	00-800-12277
U.K.	0800-89-0011
U.K.	0500-89-0011

CENTRAL AMERICA   MIDDLE AMERICA

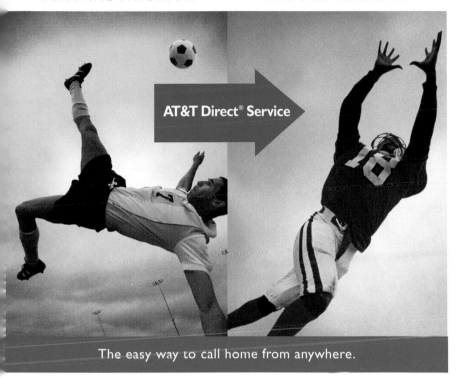

AT&T Direct® Service

The easy way to call home from anywhere.

Global
connection
with the AT&T
Network

AT&T
direct
service

For the easy way to call home, take the attached wallet guide.

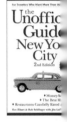

in a residential neighborhood. Some of the apartments and rooms have verandas, and four contain kitchenettes. More suitable for older travelers, the complex rents large but rather sparsely furnished units. The Garden Cafe provides
international food at reasonable prices and is open daily for breakfast and dinner. You're also within walking distance of the Port Lucaya Marketplace.

Coral Rd. at Royal Palm Way (P.O. Box F-42468), Lucaya, Grand Bahama, The Bahamas. © **242/373-2468.**
Fax 242/373-5140. 10 units. Winter $100 double, $105 triple; off-season $75 double, $80 triple. MC, V.
Amenities: Restaurant. *In room:* A/C, TV, minibar.

OUTSIDE FREEPORT/LUCAYA

Club Fortuna Beach 🏕   Think of this as an Italian Club Med. It caters to a
mostly European, relatively young crowd, who appreciate the 35 secluded acres
of beachfront and the non-stop sports activities that are included in the price.
Some guests like to go topless, not the norm in The Bahamas. Established in
1993, Club Fortuna lies 6 miles east of the International Bazaar in the southeastern part of the island, amid an isolated landscape of casuarinas and scrubland. Midsize bedrooms lie in a colorful group of two-story outbuildings. About
three-quarters have ocean views; the others overlook the garden. Each has a private balcony, a private safe, and two queen-size beds, with a small bathroom
with shower stalls. Singles can book one of these rooms, but they are charged
40% more than the per-person double-occupancy rate.

All meals, which are included in the rates, are served buffet-style in a pavilion
near the beach, and the Italian cuisine is actually some of the best on Grand
Bahama Island. In addition to the buffets, there is a casual Italian restaurant, La
Trattoria, where you can order sit-down dinners within a candlelit setting.
Bahamian and Italian performers provide nightly entertainment.

1 Dubloon Rd. (P.O. Box F-42398), Freeport, Grand Bahama, The Bahamas. © **242/373-4000.** Fax
242/373-5555. www.vivaresorts.com. 276 units. Winter $220–$236 double, $285–$438 triple, $352–$536
quad; off-season $200–$270 double, $261–$312 triple, $320–$432 quad. Children under 7 stay free. Children
7–11 50% off per day in parents' room (maximum of 2). Rates include meals, and land and water sports.
AE, MC, V. **Amenities:** 2 restaurants, bar, snack bar, Italian language lessons, baby-sitting, laundry, exercise
room, water sports, land sports, aerobics classes, outings to a nearby golf course, children's playground. *In
room:* A/C, safe. No phone.

Deep Water Cay Club 🏕 *Finds*   The ultimate hideaway, even more so than Paradise Cove, this is a secret address passed around privately by bonefish devotees.
Bahamian-style cottages are strung along a pristine beach of white sand on a private island. The bonefishing is first rate among these saltwater flats. The club has
been a tradition since it was established in 1958 by Gilbert Drake, a sportsman
and avid fisherman. The club continues today as the premier bonefishing lodge
in The Bahamas. Bonefish here average 4 to 5 pounds, and licensed guides head
a fleet of customized Dolphin Super Skiffs. Bedrooms are exceedingly spacious
and well-furnished, with private entrances and roomy bathrooms with tub and
shower. Some 22 guests at a time are housed here in an intimate, relaxed setting.

Everyone dines together on a well-prepared but simple continental and island
cuisine. Naturally the favorite dish is the catch of the day.

Deep Water Cay (1100 Lee Wagener Blvd., Suite 352, Fort Lauderdale, FL 33315). © **242/353-3073** or
954/359-0488. Fax 242/353-3095. www.deepwatercay.com/About.html. 9 units. Dec 1–Feb 28 $1,298 per
person double occupancy; Mar–Nov $1,375–$1,444 per person double occupancy. Rates all inclusive for
3 nights and 2½ days of fishing. No credit cards. **Amenities:** Dining room, self-service bar, pool, snorkeling,
boating, and fishing. *In room:* A/C, refrigerator, coffeemaker.

Old Bahama Bay 🏕   A cottage-style resort, this former Jack Tar Village is the
centerpiece of a 28-acre site with homesites and a marina. Its opening is hailed

as part of the overall renaissance of Grand Bahama Island. In an oceanfront set-ting, the resort has cottages adjacent to the marina complex; a private beach is only steps away. The colonial-style architecture graces a setting 25 miles west of Freeport, consisting of suites set in six two-story beach houses and three spacious buildings overlooking the marina. The living space is the most generous on the island, with custom-designed furnishings along with private beachfront terraces. Bathrooms are luxurious with deluxe toiletries, and a tub and shower combo. Conch Shack Eatery & Bar serves quite good Bahamian and American dishes at three meals a day.

West End, P.O. Box F-42546, Grand Bahama Island, The Bahamas. (C) 800/572-5711 in the U.S., or 242/346-6500. Fax 242/346-6546. 47 units. May–Dec 22 $250 double; Dec 23–Apr $275 double. $8 extra per child. AE, MC, V. **Amenities:** Restaurant, bar, 2 all-weather tennis courts, pool, exercise facilities, dive shop, water sports, snorkeling. *In room:* A/C, TV, fax and modem lines, refrigerator, coffeemaker.

4 Where to Dine

Foodies will find that the cuisine on Grand Bahama Island doesn't match the more refined fare served at dozens of places on New Providence (Nassau/Paradise Island). However, a few places in Grand Bahama specialize in fine din-ing; others get by with rather standard fare. The good news is that the dining scene is much more affordable here.

FREEPORT
EXPENSIVE
Crown Room *$* CONTINENTAL   The Crown Room offers stylish casino dining. It evokes an art-deco ocean liner, with pink-marble accents, brass-trimmed walls, and rose-colored mirrors. As you peruse the menu, light jazz is played in the background. Whatever you whisper to your dining partner is likely to be overheard, because tables are a little too closely placed. Prices are high for Freeport, but this Crown Room tries to be regal, and the service and the fine ingredients seem to justify the high tabs.

It's quite easy to fill up on the selection of hot and cold appetizers, ranging from pâté to smoked salmon to snow crab claws. The best of the main dishes is the perfectly roasted rack of lamb, with the medallions of veal coming in a close second. Pasta dishes are also quite succulent. Sometimes the chef will have some-thing more unusual on the menu, but for the most part, it's elegant country-club fare from a standard international repertoire.

In the Resorts at Bahamia, the Mall at W. Sunrise Hwy. (C) 242/352-6721. Reservations required. Jackets required for men. Main courses $19.95–$39.95. AE, DC, MC, V. Wed–Sat 6:30–11pm.

The Rib Room *$* SEAFOOD/STEAKS   The Rib Room serves the island's best steaks, in huge portions. Everything is served in the atmosphere of a British hunting lodge. If you don't want one of the steaks, opt instead for the blue-ribbon prime rib of beef with a passable Yorkshire pudding. Special praise goes to the broiled Bahamian lobster, but steer clear of the grouper. Shrimp can be succulent when it's not overcooked, and steak Diane, although rather fully fla-vored, is meltingly textured. The wine list is reasonably priced.

In the Resorts at Bahamia, the Mall at W. Sunrise Hwy. (C) 242/352-6721. Reservations recommended. Jack-ets required for men. Main courses $18.95–$31.95. AE, DC, MC, V. Thurs–Mon 6–11pm.

MODERATE
Morgan's Bluff *Kids* SEAFOOD   Families searching for a good moderately priced seafood restaurant often head to this spot in the Tower section of the

Resorts at Bahamia. Its high-tech pirate's lair decor is a little cheesy but will probably appeal to the kids. The captain's platter of mixed seafood is standard but filling. This is a good place to sample cracked conch (fried like Wiener schnitzel) if you haven't tried it before. Lobster is treated with care and respect here, appearing Thermidor-style or else in a bisque. Kids often go for the seafood crepes, although adults may prefer the clams Benedict instead. When the catch of the day (local or imported) is right, this place can be right on target, although some fish dishes can be pale and uninteresting.

In the Resorts at Bahamia, the Mall at W. Sunrise Hwy. ℰ 242/352-9661. Reservations recommended. Main courses $14.95–$18.95. AE, DC, MC, V. Wed–Sun 5:30–10:30pm.

Ruby Swiss Restaurant INTERNATIONAL   This place is an odd mix of alpine hospitality and Junkanoo friendliness. Despite the kitschiness, it attracts a rather staid clientele (lots of Europeans) who appreciate its large servings, its fine service, and the music that's presented every day during the dinner hour, from 7 to 10:30pm. Airy and high-ceilinged, it contains two bars (one, rescued from a Victorian building, is an antique) and two woodsy-looking dining rooms. The scope of the menu is staggering. Lunch might feature such standard fare as Reuben or club sandwiches, seafood or Caesar salads, or burgers. The house pâté, however, has the most flavor. For dinner, you can opt for the catch of the day, which is often grouper (rarely overcooked), zesty Creole-style shrimp, or such grand European classics as filet Richelieu (chateaubriand with hollandaise) or steak Diane, flambéed in cognac. Finish off with a Viennese strudel, the dessert specialty. After hours, the late-night snack menu, served until 5 or 6am daily, gives the place the air of a diner. Because it stays open almost until dawn, it's a good place to visit for a snack or a light meal after you've tired of the casinos.

W. Sunrise Hwy. (at W. Atlantic Ave.). ℰ 242/352-8507. Reservations required for dinner. Lunch main courses $5.75–$24.75; dinner main courses $5.75–$48.50; late-night main courses $7.75–$28. AE, DC, DISC, MC, V. Mon–Fri 11am–5am; Sat–Sun 6pm–6am.

INEXPENSIVE

Beckey's Restaurant BAHAMIAN/AMERICAN   This pink-and-white restaurant offers authentic Bahamian cuisine prepared in the time-tested style of the Out Islands. Go here to rev up before a day of serious shopping at the International Bazaar, which is right at hand. Owned by Beckey and Berkeley Smith, the place offers a welcome dose of down-to-earth non-casino reality. Breakfasts are either all-American or Bahamian and are available all day. Also popular are minced lobster, curried mutton, fish platters, baked or curried chicken, and conch salads. Stick to the local specialties instead of the lackluster American dishes.

E. Sunrise Hwy. and E. Beach Dr. ℰ 242/352-5247. Breakfast $3.50–$7.95; lunch items $6–$9; dinner main courses $7.95–$22. AE, MC, V. Daily 7am–11pm.

Geneva's BAHAMIAN/SEAFOOD   If you want to eat where the locals eat, head for Geneva's, where the food is made the old-fashioned way. This restaurant is one of the best places to sample conch, which has fed and nourished Bahamians for centuries. The Monroe family will prepare it for you stewed, cracked, or fried, or in a savory conch chowder that makes an excellent starter. Grouper also appears, prepared in every imaginable way. The bartender will get you into the mood with a rum-laced Bahama Mama.

Freeport/Lucaya Dining

Arawak Restaurant **13**
Barracuda's **12**
Beckey's Restaurant **3**
Cafe Michel **3**
Captain's Charthouse
    Restaurant **7**
China Temple **3**
Club Caribe **14**
Crown Room **2**

Fatman's Nephew **10**
Ferry House **11**
Geneva's **5**
Giovanni's Cafe **9**
La Dolce Vita **10**
Luciano's **10**
Morgan's Bluff **2**
Outrigger's Native Restaurant /
    White Wave Club **15**

The Pepper Pot **8**
Pisces **10**
The Pub on the Mall **6**
The Rib Room **2**
Ruby Swiss Restaurant **1**
Safari Restaurant **4**
Shenanigan's Irish Pub **10**
The Stoned Crab **16**

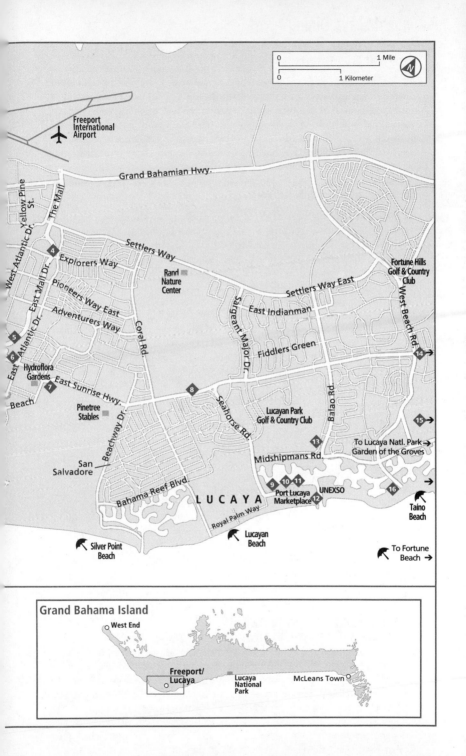

Freeport
International
Airport

Grand Bahamian Hwy.

Settlers Way

Explorers Way

Pioneers Way East

Adventurers Way

West Atlantic Dr.

Yellow Pine
St.

The Mall

East Mall Dr.

East Atlantic Dr.

Hydroflora
Gardens

Beach

East Sunrise Hwy.

Pinetree
Stables

Coral Rd.

Beachway Dr.

San
Salvadore

Bahama Reef Blvd.

Rand
Nature
Center

Settlers Way East

Fortune Hills
Golf & Country
Club

West Beach Rd.

Sargeant Major Dr.

East Indianman

Fiddlers Green

Seahorse Rd.

Lucayan Park
Golf & Country Club

Balao Rd.

Midshipmans Rd.

L U C A Y A

Royal Palm Way

Port Lucaya
Marketplace

UNEXSO

To Lucaya Natl. Park →
Garden of the Groves

Silver Point
Beach

Lucayan
Beach

Taino
Beach

To Fortune
Beach →

Grand Bahama Island

West End

Freeport/
Lucaya

Lucaya
National
Park

McLeans Town

Kipling Lane, the Mall at W. Sunrise Hwy. ℂ 242/352-5085. Lunch sandwiches and platters $4–$8; dinner main courses $8–$15.95. No credit cards. Daily 7am–11pm.

The Pepper Pot BAHAMIAN   This might be the only place on Grand Bahama that specializes in Bahamian take-out food. You'll find it after about a 5-minute drive east of the International Bazaar, in a tiny shopping mall. You can order take-out portions of the best guava puff on the island, as well as a savory conch chowder, the standard fish and pork chops, chicken souse (an acquired taste), cracked conch, sandwiches and hamburgers, and an array of daily specials. The owner is Ethiopian-born Wolansa Fountain.

E. Sunrise Hwy. (at Coral Rd.). ℂ 242/373-7655. Breakfast $3–$5; main courses $4–$7.50; vegetarian plates $1.50–$5. No credit cards. Daily 24 hours.

The Pub on the Mall INTERNATIONAL   Located on the same floor of the same building and under the same management, three distinctive eating areas lie across the boulevard from the International Bazaar and attract many locals. The **Prince of Wales** serves such Olde English staples as shepherd's pie, fish-and-chips, platters of roast beef or fish, and real English ale. One end of the room is devoted to the **Red Dog Sports Bar,** with a boisterous atmosphere and at least three TV screens blasting away for dedicated sports fans. **Silvano's** is an Italian restaurant serving lotsa pasta, usually with verve, as well as veal, chicken, beefsteaks, and such desserts as tiramisu. The Bahamian-themed **Islander's Roost** has a tropical decor of bright island color and a balcony overlooking the Bazaar. The food is good if not great; the main platters are a good value, usually very filling and satisfying. Menu items include sandwiches, salads, grilled fish, beefsteaks, and prime rib.

Ranfurley Circus, Sunrise Hwy. ℂ 242/352-5110. Reservations recommended. Main courses in Prince of Wales Pub and Red Dog $5.95–$29; main courses in Silvano's $12.25–$28.75; main courses in Islander's Roost $6.75–$29. AE, MC, V. Prince of Wales and Red Dog Sports Bar daily noon–2am. Silvano's Italian Restaurant daily noon–3pm and 5–11pm. Islander's Roost Mon–Sat 5:30pm–midnight.

Safari Restaurant INTERNATIONAL   At breakfast or lunch, you'll place your order at a kiosk-style snack bar and carry simple paper plates to an outdoor table near the pool. But at dinner, more formal meals are served in a large, conventional, sit-down restaurant, which has a bar and a stage for live music. The menu is full of straightforward staples like New York strip steaks, pork chops, hot roast beef, broiled or grilled snapper, broiled chicken, or seafood platters. After 10:30pm every Wednesday, Friday, Saturday, and Sunday, the place becomes a disco (with a $12 cover charge that includes the first drink). Locals often stop by for dinner and nightclubbing.

E. Mall Dr. ℂ 242/352-2805. American breakfast $4.95; lunch main courses $4–$8; dinner main courses $9.75–$22.95. AE, MC, V. Daily 7:30–11am, noon–4pm, and 5:30–9pm.

IN THE INTERNATIONAL BAZAAR

Cafe Michel BAHAMIAN/FRENCH   The name implies that you've found a real French bistro set amid the bustle of the International Bazaar, but alas, it turns out to be a mere coffee shop. Nevertheless, it's a good place for refueling when you're shopping the bazaar. There are about 20 tables outside, placed under red umbrellas and bistro-style tablecloths. Inside are about a dozen more. Local shoppers know to come here not only for coffee, but also for platters, salads, and sandwiches throughout the day. Both American and Bahamian dishes are served, including seafood platters, steaks, and, of course, grouper. The house specialty is a Bahamian lobster platter with all the fixings.

International Bazaar. ℭ 242/352-2191. Reservations recommended for dinner. Main courses $6.95–$28.95. AE, MC, V. Mon–Sat noon–8pm.

China Temple CHINESE   This is a Chinese joint—not a lot more—that also does takeout. Over the years it's proved to be the dining bargain of the bazaar. The menu is familiar and standard: chop suey, chow mein, and sweet-and-sour. It's certainly not gourmet Asian fare, but it's cheap; and it might hit the spot when you're craving something different.

International Bazaar. ℭ 242/352-5610. Lunch $6–$7.75; main courses $6.75–$32. AE, MC, V. Mon–Sat 10:30am–10pm.

LUCAYA

Arawak Restaurant INTERNATIONAL   Set in the clubhouse of one of Freeport's largest golf courses, and managed by the Reef Village (which is about a mile away), this restaurant boasts tall windows that overlook the fairways, lots of exposed wood, and an international menu that has occasional French touches. Lunch brings sandwiches, meal-size salads, and platters of grilled steaks and fish. Dinner is more substantial, with starters like a lobster-and-prawn cocktail, smoked salmon, and grilled portobello mushrooms with leeks and morels in Chablis sauce. Main courses such as breast of duck with honey sauce, surf and turf, rack of lamb, and chateaubriand are always popular and generally very well-prepared. Every Sunday from 11:30am to 3pm, there's a $35 brunch with unlimited champagne.

In the Lucaya Golf & Country Club, Bishop Lane. ℭ 242/373-1066. Reservations recommended for dinner. Lunch main courses $10–$16; dinner main courses $17–$31. AE, DISC, MC, V. Daily 11:30am–3pm and 6:30–10pm.

Barracuda's ℱ INTERNATIONAL   With high ceilings and big windows, this space is the size of an airplane hanger, and it's done up with playful art and a whimsical, hip decor that would be at home in Miami's South Beach. The kitchen turns out light international dishes that are loaded with flavor. Examples include lobster salad; tuna and white-bean salad; stone crab claws; leek tart with mozzarella and apples; chicken breast with fresh ginger; and all manner of steaks, seafood, and pastas. If you want to drink your dessert, consider a China Beach, a chocolate-laced affair that's made with crème de cacao, Kahlúa, and Carolans Irish cream.

In the Reef Village Hotel at the Lucayan Beach & Golf Resort, Royal Palm Way, Lucaya. ℭ 242/373-1333. Reservations not necessary. Main courses $9.50–$17. AE, DC, MC, V. Daily 11am–10:30pm.

Captain's Charthouse Restaurant INTERNATIONAL   In a casual, tree-top-level dining room, guests can select from a menu of 1950s favorites, such as prime rib of beef, teriyaki steak, and grouper fillet, along with some other good seafood dishes. You don't come here for New Wave cooking; this is the place for the old standards that mom and pop enjoyed. The chunky lobster Thermidor, baked in its shell, is a taste treat. Meals are served with tasty homemade bread and a do-it-yourself salad bar. Portions are large, but if you still have an appetite, the homemade desserts include key lime pie. A happy hour is held in the Mates Lounge from 5 to 7pm, with complimentary hors d'oeuvres. In winter, there's nightly entertainment and courtesy transportation to and from your hotel.

E. Sunrise Hwy. and Beach Dr. ℭ 242/373-3900. Early-bird dinner $10.95 (5–6:30pm); main courses $15.95–$28. AE, DISC, MC, V. Daily 5–9:30pm (last seating).

Kids Family-Friendly Restaurants

Morgan's Bluff *(see p. 152)*   This family restaurant, named after the 17th-century pirate Sir Henry Morgan, has a nautical decor and red neon "portholes." Casual dress is the rule.

Pier One *(see p. 172)*   In West End, children and their families "walk the plank" to reach this dining room resting on stilts above the water. A nearby shark pool thrills kiddies and grown-ups alike.

Ferry House *(see p. 158)*   A family favorite at Port Lucaya, this place has a real nautical atmosphere within the sheltered confines of the Port Lucaya Marina. Meal-size salads and thick stuffed sandwiches are a feature at lunch, giving way in the evening to grills, especially seafood platters, and succulent pastas.

The Stoned Crab ✶ SEAFOOD   Tired of frozen seafood shipped in from the mainland? Come here for the sweet stone crab claws and the lobster, both caught in Bahamian waters. There's none better on the island. You can's miss this place—a circa-1968 triple pyramid whose four-story wood and steel framework is strong enough to withstand any hurricane. Swiss-born Livio Peronino is the owner and chef, preparing a seafood platter with everything on it, including grouper, conch fritters, and all kinds of shellfish. The best pasta on the menu is linguine al pesto with lobster and shrimp. For starters, try the zesty conch chowder. Have a salad and home-baked raisin bread with your meal, and finish with Irish coffee.

At Taino Beach, Lucaya. ✆ 242/373-1442. Reservations recommended. Main courses $19–$38. AE, MC, V. Daily 5–10:30pm.

AT THE PORT LUCAYA MARKETPLACE

Fatman's Nephew ✶ BAHAMIAN   In another location, "Fatman" became a legend on Grand Bahama Island. Although he's no longer with us, the Fatman must have left his recipes and cooking skills to another generation of cooks. Today the place, which used to cater mainly to locals, has gone touristy, but much of the same traditional fare is still served with the same unflagging allegiance to Bahamian ways. The restaurant overlooks the marina at Port Lucaya from an eagle's-nest position on the second floor. You can enjoy drinks or meals inside, but we like to head out to an outdoor covered deck to watch the action below. There are usually at least eight kinds of game fish, including both wahoo and Cajun blackened kingfish, plus curried chicken, mutton, or beef. Bahamian-style shark soup, made from the flesh of hammerheads ("little tender ones," according to the chef), is sometimes featured on the menu.

Port Lucaya Marketplace. ✆ 242/373-8520. Main courses $8–$26. AE, DISC, MC, V. Daily 10am–midnight.

Ferry House ✶ Kids CONTINENTAL   This restaurant's bar floats on pontoons, beneath a canvas canopy, above the waters of Bell Channel, the waterway that funnels boats from the open sea into the sheltered confines of Port Lucaya Marina. On the waterside deck, you can order breakfast every day between 7 and 10am, joining a crowd of locals. Lunches are relatively simple affairs, consisting of sandwiches and meal-size salads. Dinner might feature a seafood platter laden with calamari, fish, and shrimp; a delectable broiled chicken breast stuffed with crabmeat or shrimp; coconut- or orange-flavored shrimp; and savory grilled veal chops with garlic sauce. Our favorite pasta is Rasta Pasta, linguine and chicken in a creamy vodka and tomato sauce.

Beside Bell Channel, Port Lucaya. © 242/373-1595. Reservations recommended for dinner, not needed at lunch. Lunch platters $7.25–$14.95; dinner main courses $18–$31. AE, MC, V. Daily 7–10am and 11am–11:30pm.

Giovanni's Cafe ITALIAN/SEAFOOD   Tucked away into one of the pedestrian thoroughfares of Port Lucaya Marketplace, you'll find a yellow-sided clapboard house that opens into a charming 34-seat Italian trattoria. The chefs (including head chef Giovanni Colo) serve Italian-influenced preparations of local seafood, specializing in seafood pasta (usually prepared only for two diners) and a lobster special. Giovanni stamps each dish with his Italian verve and flavor whether it be Bahamian conch, local seafood, or scampi. Dishes show off his precision and rock-solid technique.

In the Port Lucaya Marketplace. © 242/373-9107. Reservations recommended. Lunch main courses $6–$20; dinner main courses $11–$25. AE, DC, MC, V. Mon–Sat 11:30am–5pm and 5–10pm.

La Dolce Vita ✦ ITALIAN   Next to The Pub at Port Lucaya (see below) is a small upscale Italian restaurant with modern decor and traditional food. Enjoy freshly made pastas and Italian-style pizzas on a patio overlooking the marina or in the 44-seat dining room. Start with portobello mushrooms, fresh mozzarella with tomatoes, and a vinaigrette, or else carpaccio with arugula and spices. Homemade ravioli appears with different fillings such as cheese, lobster, or spinach. An excellent risotto flavored with black ink is served, or else you can order roast pork tenderloin or a crisp and perfectly flavored rack of lamb.

Port Lucaya Marketplace. © 242/373-8652. Reservations recommended. Main courses $15.95–$32. AE, MC, V. Daily 5–11pm. Closed Sept.

Luciano's ✦ CONTINENTAL   Its tables usually occupied by local government officials and deal makers, Luciano's is the grande dame of Freeport restaurants, with a very European atmosphere. It's the only restaurant in Port Lucaya offering caviar, foie gras, and bouillabaisse, all served with a flourish by a formally dressed waitstaff wearing black and white. You can go early and enjoy a cocktail in the little bar inside or on the wooden deck overlooking the marina. Lightly smoked and thinly sliced salmon makes a good opener, as do snails in garlic butter. Fresh fish and shellfish are regularly featured and delicately prepared, allowing their natural flavors to shine through, with no heavy, overwhelming sauces. Steak Diane is one of Luciano's classics, along with an especially delectable prime rib of beef.

Port Lucaya Marketplace. © 242/373-9100. Reservations required. Main courses $16.95–$29.95. AE, DISC, MC, V. Mon–Sat 5:30–10pm (last seating).

Outrigger's Native Restaurant/White Wave Club BAHAMIAN Cement-sided and simple, with a large deck extending out toward the sea, this restaurant was here long before the construction of the nearby Port Lucayan Marketplace, which lies only 4 blocks away. The restaurant area is the domain of Gretchen Wilson, whose kitchens produce a rotating series of dishes that include such lip-smacking dishes as lobster tails, minced lobster, steamed or cracked conch, pork chops, chicken, fish, and shrimp, usually served with peas 'n' rice and macaroni. Every Wednesday night, from 6pm to midnight, the restaurant is the venue for "Outrigger's Famous Wednesday Night Fish Fry," when as many as a thousand diners will line up for platters of fried or steamed fish, priced at $9 each, which are accompanied by live music. Drinks are served within the restaurant, but at any time of the week, you might consider stepping into the nearby ramshackle bar, the White Wave Club, which serves only drinks. Smith's Point. © 242/373-4811. Reservations not necessary. Main courses $8–$16. No credit cards. Daily noon–midnight.

Pisces *𝓕* BAHAMIAN/INTERNATIONAL   This is our favorite among the many restaurants in the Port Lucaya Marketplace, and we're seconded by a healthy mix of locals and yacht owners who pack the place every weekend. Decorated with Tiffany-style lamps and captain's chairs, it boasts the most charming waitstaff on Grand Bahama Island. Lunches are relatively simple affairs, with fish-and-chips, sandwiches, and salads. Pizzas are available anytime and come in 21 different types, including a version with conch, lobster, shrimp, and chicken. Dinners are more elaborate, with a choice of curries (including a version with conch); lobster in cream, wine, and herb sauce; all kinds of fish and shellfish; and several kinds of pasta.

Port Lucaya Marketplace. © 242/373-5192. Reservations recommended. Pizzas $14–$25; lunch main courses $6.95–$9.95; dinner main course $14.95–$25. AE, MC, V. Mon–Sat 11am–2am.

Shenanigan's Irish Pub CONTINENTAL   Dark and beer-stained from the thousands of pints of Guinness, Harp, and Killian's that have been served and spilled here, this is the premier Irish or Boston Irish hangout on Grand Bahama Island. Many visitors come just to drink, sometimes for hours at a time, soaking up the suds, and perhaps remembering to eventually order some food. If you get hungry, there's surf and turf, French-style rack of lamb for two, seafood Newburg, and several preparations of chicken.

Port Lucaya Marketplace. © 242/373-4734. Reservations not necessary. Main courses $12.95–$26.95. AE, DC, MC, V. Mon–Thurs 10:30am–midnight, Fri–Sat 10:30am–2am.

OUTSIDE FREEPORT/LUCAYA

Club Caribe AMERICAN/BAHAMIAN   Set about 7 miles east of the International Bazaar, beside a beach and an offshore reef that teems with underwater life, this restaurant is a funky and offbeat charmer. You can spend a day on the beach here, renting the club's snorkeling equipment, sunbathing or swimming, and perhaps enjoying one of the house-special cocktails (try a Caribe Delight, made with bananas, banana-flavored liqueur, and rum). When it's lunchtime, you might order up a heaping platter of cracked conch; barbecued ribs; snapper or grouper that's fried, steamed, or grilled; or a sandwich or salad. This place is simple, outdoorsy, and a refreshing change from the more congested parts of Grand Bahama.

Churchill Beach, Mather Town, off Midshipman Rd. © 242/373-6866. Reservations not necessary. Sandwiches and platters $4–$12.95. AE, DISC, MC, V. Tues–Sun 10:30am–6pm.

5 Beaches, Water Sports & Other Outdoor Pursuits

HITTING THE BEACH

Grand Bahama Island has enough beaches for everyone, the best ones opening onto Northwest Providence Channel at Freeport and sweeping east for some 60 miles to encompass Xanadu Beach, Lucayan Beach, Taino Beach, and others, eventually ending at such remote eastern outposts as Rocky Creek and McLean's Town. Once you leave the Freeport/Lucaya area, you can virtually have your

---

(*Moments*   Private White Sands for You Alone

Once you head east from Port Lucaya and Taino, you'll discover so many splendid white sandy beaches that you'll lose count. Although these beaches have names, you'll never really know what beach you're on unless you ask a local because they are unmarked. If you like seclusion and don't mind the lack of any facilities, you'll find a string of local favorites. Directly east of Taino is **Churchill's Beach,** followed by **Smith's Point, Fortune Beach,** and **Barbary Beach.** Fortune Beach is a special gem because of its beautiful waters and white sands.

---

pick of white sandy beaches all the way east. Once you're past the resort hotels, you'll see a series of secluded beaches used mainly by locals. If you like people, a lot of organized water sports, and easy access to hotel bars and rest rooms, stick to Xanadu, Taino, and Lucayan beaches.

Though there's fine snorkeling offshore, you should book a snorkeling cruise aboard one of the catamarans offered by Paradise Watersports (see below) to see the most stunning reefs.

Xanadu Beach *&& is one of our favorite beaches, immediately east of Freeport and the site of the famed Xanadu Beach Resort. The beach may be crowded at times in winter, but that's because of those gorgeous, soft, powdery white sands, which open onto tranquil waters. The beach is set against a backdrop of coconut palms and Australian pines. You can hook up here with some of the best water sports on the island, including snorkeling, boating, jet skiing, and parasailing.

Immediately east of Xanadu is **Silver Point Beach,** a little white sandy beach, site of a time-share complex where guests are out riding the waves on water bikes or playing volleyball on the beach. You'll see horseback riders from Pinetree Stables (see below) taking beach rides along the sands.

Most visitors will be found at **Lucayan Beach,** right off Royal Palm Way and immediately east of Silver Point Beach. This is one of the best beaches in The Bahamas, with miles of white sand. It might be crowded for a few weeks in winter, but in general there is beach-blanket space for all. At any of the hotel resorts along this beach, you can hook up with an array of water sports or get a frosty drink from a hotel bar. It's not for those seeking seclusion, but it's a fun beach-party scene.

Immediately to the east of Lucayan Beach is **Taino Beach,** a family favorite and a good place for water sports. This, too, is a fine, wide beach of white sands, opening onto generally tranquil waters.

Another choice not too far east is **Gold Rock Beach,** a favorite picnic spot with locals on weekends, although you'll usually have this beach to yourself on weekdays. Gold Rock Beach is a 12-mile drive from Lucaya. At Gold Rock you are at the doorstep to the **Lucayan National Park** (see below), a 40-acre park filled with some of the longest, widest, and most fabulous secluded beaches on the island.

BOAT CRUISES

Mermaid Kitty, Port Lucaya Dock (© **242/373-5880**), is supposedly the world's largest twin-diesel-engine glass-bottom boat. Any tour agent can arrange for you to go out on this vessel. You'll get a panoramic view of the beautiful underwater life that lives off the coast of Grand Bahama. Cruises depart from Port Lucaya behind the Straw Market on the bay side at 9:30, 11:15am, 1:15, and 3:15pm, except Monday and Friday, when only two tours leave at 9:30 and 11:15am. The tour lasts 1½ hours, costs $20 for adults and $12 for children 6 to 12, and is free for children 5 and under. When calling for a reservation, confirm the departure times mentioned above, because there may be seasonal variations.

The best sunset cruise on Grand Bahama island is offered by **Paradise Watersports,** Sunken Treasure Dr., Xanadu Beach (© **242/373-8681**). At $29 per person, the price includes dance music, unlimited Bahama Mamas (the drink, that is), wine, cheese, and crackers.

Superior Watersports, P.O. Box F-40837, Freeport (© **242/373-7863**), offers fun cruises around Grand Bahama on its *Bahama Mama,* a two-deck 72-foot catamaran. Its Robinson Crusoe Beach Party, offered daily from 11am to 4:30pm, costs $59 per person. There's also a sunset booze cruise that goes for $29. (In summer, these cruises are on Tuesday, Thursday, and Saturday night from 6:30 to 8:30pm. In the off-season, they are on the same nights but sail from 6 to 8pm.)

For an underwater cruise, try the company's semisubmarine, the *Seaworld Explorer.* The sub itself does not descend; instead, you walk down into the hull of the boat and watch the sea life glide by. The "sub" departs daily at 10, 11:30am, 1:30, and 3pm, and it costs $39 for adults and $25 for children 12 and under.

THE DOLPHIN EXPERIENCE
A pod of bottle-nosed dolphins is involved in a unique dolphin/human familiarization program at Dolphin Experience, located at **Underwater Explorers Society (UNEXSO),** next to Port Lucaya, opposite Lucayan Beach Casino (© **888/365-3483** or 242/373-1250). This "close encounter" program allows participants to observe these intelligent and friendly animals close up and to hear an interesting talk by a member of the animal-care staff. This project seems very eco-sensitive; this is the world's largest dolphin facility, so there are no cramped conditions. Dolphins can swim out to sea, and if they don't like the project, they could in theory never return to it. But they seem to enjoy interacting with humans and do return. You can step onto a shallow wading platform and interact with the dolphins; the experience costs $39 and is a highly educational, yet fun adventure for all ages. Children under 5 participate free. You'll want to bring your camera. An "Assistant Trainer" program is an all-day interactive experience in which a maximum of four people, ages 16 or older, learn

---

⟨Moments Land and Sea Ecotours

If you're a nature lover, escape from the casinos and take one of the **East End Adventures** (© **242/351-6250**) bush and sea safaris. You're taken through dense pine forests and along deserted beaches, going inland on hikes to such sites as blue holes, mangrove swamps, and underground caverns. You may even learn how to crack conch. A native lunch is served on a serene beach in Lightbourne's Cay, a remote islet in the East End. Most of the tour is laid-back, as you can snorkel in blue holes or shell hunt. Safaris are conducted daily between 8am and 5:30pm, costing adults $110 and kids $55.

about dolphins and marine mammals from behind the scenes. Participants help feed the animals and swim with them for a cost of $179. Dolphins also swim out from Sanctuary Bay daily to interact with scuba divers from UNEXSO in a "Dolphin Dive" program, costing $169.

FISHING

In the waters off Grand Bahama, you can fish for barracuda, snapper, grouper, yellowtail, wahoo, and kingfish, along with other denizens of the deep.

Reef Tours, Ltd., Port Lucaya Dock (© **242/373-5880**), offers one of the least expensive ways to go deep-sea fishing around Grand Bahama Island. Adults pay $70 if they fish, $40 if they only go along to watch. Four to six people can charter the entire craft for $300 to $460 per half day or $585 to $900 per whole day. Departures for the half-day excursion are at 8:30am and 1pm, 7 days a week. Bait, tackle, and ice are included in the cost.

GOLF

This island boasts more golf links than any other in The Bahamas. The courses are within 7 miles of one another, and you usually won't have to wait to play. All courses are open to the public year-round, and clubs can be rented from all pro shops on the island.

Bahamia's Emerald Golf Course, the Mall South, at the Resorts at Bahamia (© **242/350-7000**), was the site of The Bahamas National Open some years back, and more recently, in conjunction with the Ruby course (see below), it's the site of the annual January Grand Bahama Pro-Am Tournament. The course has plenty of trees along the fairways, as well as an abundance of water hazards and bunkers. The toughest hole is the ninth, a par 5 with 545 yards from the blue tees to the hole. In winter, greens fees to either of these courses are $75 per day, reduced to $65 in summer.

The championship course **Bahamia's Ruby Golf Course,** Sunrise Hwy., at the Resorts at Bahamia.(© **242/350-7000**), was designed by Joe Lee in 1968 and was the recent site of the Michelin Long Drive competition. For greens fees, see the Emerald Golf Course, above. It's a total of 6,750 yards if played from the championship blue tees.

Fortune Hills Golf & Country Club, Richmond Park, Lucaya (© **242/ 373-4500**), was originally intended to be an 18-hole course, but the back 9 were never completed. You can replay the front 9 for 18 holes and a total of 6,916 yards from the blue tees. Par is 72. Greens fees are $28 for 9 holes, $40 for 18. Electric carts cost $28 and $38 for 9 and 18 holes, respectively.

The best-kept and most-manicured course on Grand Bahama is the **Lucayan Park Golf & Country Club,** Lucaya Beach (© **242/373-1066**). Recently made over, it is quite beautiful and is known for a hanging boulder sculpture at its entrance. Greens are fast, and there are a couple of par 5s more than 500 yards long, totaling 6,824 yards from the blue tees and 6,488 from the whites. Par is 72. Greens fees are $67 for 18 holes. This includes a mandatory shared golf cart. We'll let you in on a secret: Even if you're not a golfer, sample the food at the club restaurant—everything from lavish champagne brunches to first-rate seafood dishes.

The first golf course to open in The Bahamas since 1969 made its premiere late in 2000. **The Reef Course** ⚐⚐ at Royal Palm Way, Lucaya (© **242/ 373-2002**), was designed by Robert Trent Jones Jr., who called it "a bit like a Scottish course but a lot warmer." The course requires precise shot-making to avoid its numerous lakes: There is water on 13 of its 18 holes and various types of long grass swaying in the trade winds. The course boasts 6,920 yards of links-style playing grounds. Residents of Our Lucaya, with which the course is associated, pay $100 for 18 holes or $66 for 9 holes. Non-residents are charged $120 for 18 holes, but the same price, $66, for 9 holes.

HORSEBACK RIDING

The **Pinetree Stables,** N. Beachway Dr., Freeport (© **242/373-3600**), are the best riding stables in The Bahamas, superior to rivals on New Providence Island (Nassau). Pinetree offers trail rides to the beach in winter Tuesday through Sunday at 9, 11am, and 2pm, but only at 9 and 11am off-season. The cost is $45 per person for a ride lasting 1½ hours.

SEA KAYAKING

If you'd like to explore the waters off the island's north shore, call **Kayak Nature Tours,** (© **242/373-2485**), who'll take you on trips through the mangroves, where you can see wildlife as you paddle along. The cost is $59 per person, and trips are offered daily from 9am to 4:30pm, with sandwiches included. Both single and double kayaks are used on these jaunts, and children must be at least 10 years of age.

SNORKELING & SCUBA DIVING

Serious divers are attracted to such Grand Bahama sites as the Wall, the Caves, Theo's Wreck, and Treasure Reef. Other sites frequented by UNEXSO include Spit City, Ben Blue Hole, and the Rose Garden. Keep in mind that UNEXSO's specialty is diving, while Paradise Watersports primarily entertains snorkelers.

Paradise Watersports, located at the Xanadu Beach Resort & Marina (© **242/352-2887**), offers a variety of activities. On the snorkeling trips, you cruise to a coral reef on a 48-foot catamaran. The cost is $25 per person. Kayaks rent for $8 for a half hour, $12 per hour, and waterskiing is priced at $20 for a 1½-mile ride. Parasailing costs $30 for a 4-minute ride. See "Boat Cruises," above, for their offerings.

The **Underwater Explorers Society (UNEXSO)** ☆☆☆ (© **888/365-3483** or 242/373-1250) is one of the premier dive outfitters in The Bahamas and the Caribbean. There are 12 dive trips daily, including reef trips, shark dives, wreck dives, and night dives. This is also the only facility in the world where divers can dive with dolphins in the open ocean (see "The Dolphin Experience," above).

A popular 3-hour learn-to-dive course is offered daily. Over UNEXSO's 30-year history, more than 50,000 people have successfully completed this course. For $99, students learn the basics in UNEXSO's training pools. Then, the same day, they dive the beautiful shallow reef with their instructor.

Several dive packages are offered to certified divers, including a three-dive package for $105, a four-dive package at $140, and a six-dive package at $210. For really serious divers, there is also a nine-dive package for $315. All equipment is included in the price, which covers a videotape of the experience.

There is one daily 2-hour snorkeling trip offered for $39, departing at 9am.

TENNIS

The Resorts at Bahamia ☆☆ at the Mall at West Sunrise Highway, has a near monopoly on tennis courts on Grand Bahama. **The Princess Country Club** (© **242/352-6721**) has six hard-surface courts, and the **Princess Tower** (© **242/352-9661**) has three. Guests and non-guests are charged $10 per hour, and lessons are also available. The courts are open daily from 9am to dusk. If you want to play at night, you have to call and reserve a special time. It costs $12 for the courts to be lighted.

Xanadu Beach Resort & Marina (Sunken Treasure Drive; ℭ **242/352-6782**) offers three clay courts (not lit for night play). The courts are free to both registered guests and non-guests, and are open to play at any time. Lessons run from $5 per group or from $15 to $25 for individuals.

6 Seeing the Sights

Several informative tours of Grand Bahama Island are offered. One reliable company is **H. Forbes Charter Co.**, the Mall at West Sunrise Highway, Freeport (ℭ **242/352-9311**). From headquarters in the lobby of the Bahamas Princess Country Club, this company offers half- and full-day bus tours. The most popular option is the half-day Super Combination Tour, priced at $30 per adult and $18 per child under 12. It includes guided visits to the botanical gardens, drive-through tours of residential areas and the island's commercial center, and stops at the island's deep-water harbor. Shopping and a visit to a wholesale liquor store are also included on the tour. Departures are Monday through Saturday at 9am and 1pm; the tour lasts 3½ hours.

See also "Beaches, Water Sports & Other Outdoor Pursuits," above, for details on UNEXSO's Dolphin Experience, and "Shopping," below, for coverage of the International Bazaar and the Port Lucaya Marketplace.

Parrot Jungle's Garden of the Groves   One of the island's major attractions is this 12-acre garden, which honors its founder, Wallace Groves, and his wife, Georgette. Seven miles east of the International Bazaar, this scenic preserve of waterfalls and flowering shrubs has some 10,000 trees. Tropical birds flock here, making this a lure for bird-watchers and ornithologists. There are free-form lakes, footbridges, ornamental borders, lawns, and flowers. Parrot Jungle of Miami, the new managers, have introduced a number of animals to the site, including macaws, cockatoos, pygmy goats, potbelly pigs, and American alligators. Other species introduced include the park's first Bahamian raccoons and the white crown pigeon, the latter on the endangered species list. The park also has a children's playground. A lovely little non-denominational chapel, open to visitors, looks down on the garden from a hill. **The Palmetto Café** (ℭ **242/ 373-5668**) serves snacks and drinks, and a Bahamian straw market is located at the entrance gate.

Midshipman Rd. and Magellan Dr. ℭ 242/373-5668. Admission $7.95 adults, $4.95 children 3–10; children under 3 free. Garden Mon–Sat 9am–4pm, Sun and holidays 10am–4pm. Palmetto Café daily 9am–4pm.

Hydroflora Gardens   At this artificially created botanical wonder, you can see 154 specimens of plants that grow in The Bahamas. A special section is devoted to bush medicine, which is widely practiced by Bahamians (who have been using herbs and other plants to cure everything from sunburn to insomnia since the native Lucayans were here centuries ago). Guided tours cost $6 per person.

On East Beach at Sunrise Hwy. ℭ 242/352-6052. Admission $3 adults, $1.50 children. Mon–Fri 9am–5pm, Sat 9am–4pm.

Lucayan National Park   This 40-acre park, filled with mangrove, pine, and palm trees, contains one of the loveliest, most secluded beaches on Grand Bahama, a long, wide, dune-covered stretch of sandy beach that you'll reach by following a wooden path winding through the trees. There's a coral reef offshore;

Finds **A Sudsy Look at Grand Bahama**

You don't think of Freeport as brewery country, but the island is known for its Hammerhead Ale, a favorite of connoisseurs. The Grand Bahama Brewing Co., Logwood Rd., Freeport (© 242/351-5191), offers tours Monday to Friday of its brewery at 10am, 12:30 and 4:40pm, and again on Saturday at 10:30am only. In addition to Hammerhead Ales, Lucayan Lager is also made here. Tours cost $5, but the fee is credited to any lager or ale purchases you might make.

---

bring your snorkeling gear along so you can glimpse the colorful creatures that live beneath these turquoise waters. As you wander through the park, you'll cross Gold Rock Creek, fed by a spring from what is said to be the world's largest underground freshwater cavern system. Two of the caves can be seen, because they were exposed when a portion of ground collapsed. The pools in the caves are composed of 6 feet of freshwater atop a heavier layer of saltwater. Spiral wooden steps have been built down to the pools, and there are 36,000 passages in the cavern system.

The freshwater springs once lured native Lucayans, those Arawak-connected tribes who lived on the island and depended on fishing for their livelihood. They would come inland to get fresh water for their habitats on the beach. Lucayan bones and artifacts, such as pottery, have been found in the caves, as well as on the beaches.

Midshipman Rd. © 242/352-5438. Admission $3; tickets are available only at the Rand Memorial Nature Centre (see below). Daily 9am–4pm. Drive east along Midshipman Rd., passing Sharp Rock Point and Gold Rock.

Rand Memorial Nature Centre   This 100-acre pineland sanctuary, located 2 miles east of the center of Freeport, is the regional headquarters of The Bahamas National Trust, a non-profit conservation organization. Nature trails highlight native flora and "bush medicine" and provide opportunities for bird watching; as you stroll, keep your eyes peeled for the lush blooms of tropical orchids or the brilliant flash of green and red feathers in the trees. Wild birds abound at the park, and a freshwater pond is home to a flock of West Indian pink flamingos, the national bird of The Bahamas. There is a bird-watching tour on the first Saturday of every month at 8am and a wildflower walk on the last Saturday of the month, also starting at 8am. Other features of the nature center include native animal displays, a replica of a Lucayan Indian village, an education center, and a gift shop selling nature books and souvenirs.

E. Settlers Way. © 242/352-5438. Admission $5 adults, $3 children 5–12; children under 5 free. Mon–Fri 9am–4pm. Guided tours at 10am Mon–Wed and Fri.

7 Shopping

Shopping hours in Freeport/Lucaya are 9:30am to 3pm Monday through Thursday, 9:30am to 5pm on Friday. Many shops are closed on Saturday and Sunday. However, in the International Bazaar, hours vary widely. Most places there are open Monday through Saturday. Some begin business daily at 9:30am; others don't open until 10am, and closing time ranges from 5:30 to 6pm.

THE INTERNATIONAL BAZAAR

One of the world's most unusual shopping complexes, the International Bazaar, at East Mall Drive and East Sunrise Highway, covers 10 acres in the heart of Freeport. Although it remains one of the most visited sites in The Bahamas, it frankly is a bit tarnished today and is due for a makeover. Looking better every day is its rising competitor, the Port Lucaya Marketplace (see below). There is a major bus stop at the entrance of the complex. Buses aren't numbered, but those marked INTERNATIONAL BAZAAR will take you right to the gateway. Visitors walk through the much-photographed Torii Gate, a Japanese symbol of welcome, into a miniature World's Fair setting (think of it as a kitschy Bahamian version of Epcot). Continental cafes and dozens of shops loaded with merchandise await visitors. The bazaar blends architecture and cultures from some 25 countries, each re-created with cobblestones, narrow alleys, and authentically reproduced architecture. True, it's more theme-park-style shopping than authentic Bahamian experience, but it's fun nevertheless. In the nearly 100 shops, you're bound to find something that is both unique and a bargain. Here you'll find African handcrafts, Chinese jade, British china, Swiss watches, Irish linens, and Colombian emeralds—and that's just for starters.

On a street patterned after the Ginza in Tokyo, just inside the entrance to the bazaar, is the Asian section. A rich collection of merchandise from the Far East can be found here, including cameras, handmade teak furniture, fine silken goods, and even places where you can have clothing custom-made.

To the left you'll find the Left Bank of Paris, or at least a reasonable facsimile, with sidewalk cafes where you can enjoy a cafe au lait and perhaps a pastry under shade trees. In the Continental Pavilion, there are leather goods, jewelry, lingerie, and gifts at shops with names such as Love Boutique.

A narrow alley leads you from the French section to East India, where shops sell such exotic goods as taxi horns and silk saris. Moving on from the India House, past Kon Tiki, you arrive in Africa, where you can purchase carvings or a colorful dashiki.

For a taste of Latin America and Iberia, make your way to the Spanish section, where serapes and piñatas hang from the railings, and imports are displayed along the cobblestoned walks.

Many items sold in the shops here are said to cost 40% less than if you bought them in the United States, but don't count on that. If you were contemplating a big purchase, it's best to compare prices before you leave home. You can have purchases sent anywhere you wish.

The **Straw Market,** next door to the International Bazaar, contains items with a special Bahamian touch—colorful baskets, hats, handbags, and place mats—all of which make good gifts or souvenirs from your trip. (As with the Straw Market in Nassau, some items sold here are actually made in Asia.)

Here's a description of the various shops in the bazaar.

ART

Flovin Gallery   This gallery sells original Bahamian and international art, frames, lithographs, posters, and Bahamian-made Christmas ornaments and decorated coral. It also offers handmade Bahamian dolls, coral jewelry, and other gift items. Another branch is at Port Lucaya Marketplace (see below). In the Arcade section of the International Bazaar. ℭ 242/352-7564.

CIGARS

You can get good Cuban cigars here, but remember that because of the U.S. trade embargo with Cuba, Americans are supposed to light them up while they're still abroad and not attempt to bring them home to the United States.

Bahamas Best   This shop sells "Castro's cigars," but also an assortment of fine smokes from Honduras, Jamaica, and the Dominican Republic. International Bazaar. (C) **242/352-4848.**

CRYSTAL & CHINA

Island Galleria   There's an awesome collection of crystal here. Fragile, breakable, and beautiful, it includes works of utilitarian art in china and crystal by Waterford, Aynsley, Lenox, Dansk, Belleek, and Swarovski. Anything you buy can be carefully packed and shipped. Another branch is located in the Port Lucaya Marketplace ((C) **242/373-8400**). International Bazaar. (C) **242/352-8194.**

FASHION

Tara Vao   This place specializes in French-designed 100% rayons made in Indonesia, especially Bali. Most of the garments are based on bold patterns of tropical flowers. Also look here for beaded belts, each laboriously fashioned in India from seashells and beads, a genuine bargain for around $20 each. International Bazaar. (C) **242/351-7198.**

HANDCRAFTS & GIFTS

Bahamian Souvenir Outlet   This place, just below the Ministry of Tourism, has lots of inexpensive souvenirs and gifts: the usual array of T-shirts, key rings, mugs, and all that stuff. International Bazaar. (C) **242/352-2947.**

Bahamian Things   This native art gallery sells an array of locally handcrafted items, including books on The Bahamas, Abaco ceramics, woodwork, and even handmade Christmas decorations. 15B Poplar Crescent, Freeport. (C) **242/352-9550.**

Caribbean Cargo   This is one of the island's best gift shops, specializing in such items as picture frames, candles, and clocks. In the Arcade section of the International Bazaar. (C) **242/352-2929.**

Far East Traders   Look for Asian linens, hand-embroidered dresses and blouses, silk robes, lace parasols, smoking jackets, and kimonos. There's a branch location inside the Island Galleria at the Port Lucaya Marketplace. International Bazaar. (C) **242/352-9280.**

The Old Curiosity Shop   Small but choice, this shop offers most esoteric and unusual gift and jewelry items: Lladró and Capodimonte Italian porcelain, porcelain flowers, Italian porcelain dolls, and unusual Dutch figurines in black bisque. The collection of Mexican and Italian silver chains is among the most appealing in Freeport. In the Arcade section of the International Bazaar. (C) **242/352-9280.**

Paris in The Bahamas   This shop contains the biggest selection of luxury goods under one roof in the International Bazaar. The staff wears couture black dresses like you might have expected in Paris, and everywhere there's a sense of French glamour and conspicuous consumption. There are both Gucci and Versace leather goods for men and women; crystal from Lalique, Baccarat, Daum, Kosta Boda, and Örrefors; and a huge collection of cosmetics and perfumes. International Bazaar. (C) **242/352-5380.**

Unusual Centre   Where else can you get a wide array of items made of eel skin or goods made from exotic feathers such as peacock? There's another branch at the **Port Lucaya Marketplace** (© 242/352-3994). International Bazaar. © 242/352-3994.

JEWELRY
Colombian Emeralds International   This is a branch of the world's foremost emerald jeweler, offering a wide array of precious gemstone jewelry and one of the island's best watch collections. Careful shoppers will find significant savings over U.S. prices. The outlet offers certified appraisals and free 90-day insurance. There are two branches at the Port Lucaya Marketplace (© 242/373-8400). South American Section of the International Bazaar. © 242/352-5464.

LEATHER GOODS
The Leather Shop   This is another good outlet, carrying a much more limited Fendi line, but also many other designers including Land and HCL. Additional leather goods include shoes and gift items. Additional locations include the Port Lucaya Marketplace (© 242/373-2323) and Regent's Centre (© 242/352-2895). International Bazaar. © 242/352-5491.

MUSIC
Intercity Music   This is the best music store on the island; you get not only Bahamian music, but soca, reggae, and all the music of the islands as well. CDs, records, and tapes are sold. You can also purchase Bahamian posters and flags, portable radios, Walkmans, and blank audio tapes, along with accessories for camcorders. There's a branch office at the Port Lucaya Marketplace (© 242/373-8820). International Bazaar. © 242/352-8820.

PERFUMES & FRAGRANCES
Les Parisiennes   This outlet offers a wide range of perfumes, including the latest from Paris, and it also sells Lancôme cosmetics and skin-care products. There's a branch office at the Port Lucaya Marketplace (© 242/373-2974). In the French section of the International Bazaar. © 242/352-5380.

The Perfume Factory Fragrance of The Bahamas   This is the top fragrance producer in The Bahamas. The shop is housed in a model of an 1800s mansion, in which visitors are invited to hear a 5-minute commentary and to see the mixing of fragrant oils. There's even a "mixology" department where you can create your own fragrance from a selection of oils. The shop's well-known products include Island Promises, Goombay, Paradise, and Pink Pearl (which has conch pearls in the bottle). The shop also sells Guanahani, a fragrance created to commemorate the 500th anniversary of Columbus's first landfall in the New World. (Guanahani was the Indian name for the southern Bahamian island of San Salvador, traditionally claimed to be the site of Columbus's landing.) Other perfumes and colognes include Sand, the number one Bahamian-made men's fragrance in the country. At the rear of the International Bazaar. © 242/352-9391.

STAMPS & COINS
Bahamas Coin and Stamp Ltd.   This is the major coin dealer on the island. It specializes in Bahamian coin jewelry, ancient Roman coins, and relics from sunken Spanish galleons. It also carries a vast selection of antique U.S. and English coins and paper money. International Bazaar. © 242/352-8989.

PORT LUCAYA MARKETPLACE
Port Lucaya Marketplace on Seahorse Road is a shopping and dining complex set on 6 acres. Free entertainment, such as steel-drum bands and strolling musicians,

adds to a festival atmosphere. A boardwalk along the water makes it easy to watch the frolicking dolphins.

The complex rose on the site of a former Bahamian straw market, but the craftspeople and their straw products are back in full force after having been temporarily dislodged.

The waterfront location is a distinct advantage. Many of the restaurants and shops overlook a 50-slip marina, home of a "fantasy" pirate ship featuring lunch and dinner/dancing cruises. A variety of charter vessels are also based at the Port Lucaya Marina, and dockage at the marina is available to visitors coming by boat to shop or dine.

Bandolera   The staff can be rather haughty here, but despite its drawbacks, this store carries a collection of chic women's clothing that's many, many cuts above the usual run of T-shirts and tank tops that are the norm within many of its competitors. Port Lucaya Marketplace. © 242/373-7691.

Coconits by Androsia   This is the Port Lucaya outlet of the famous batik house of Andros Island. Its designs and colors capture the spirit of The Bahamas. Fabrics are handmade on the island of Andros. The store sells quality, 100%-cotton resort wear, including simple skirts, tops, jackets, and shorts for women, and it also offers a colorful line of children's wear. Port Lucaya Marketplace. © 242/ 373-8387.

Flovin Gallery II   This branch of the art gallery located in the International Bazaar sells a collection of oil paintings (both Bahamian and international), along with lithographs and posters. In its limited field, it's the best in the business. It also features a number of gift items, such as handmade Bahamian dolls, decorated corals, and Christmas ornaments. Port Lucaya Marketplace. © 242/ 373-8388.

Jeweler's Warehouse   This is a place for bargain hunters looking for good buys on discounted, closeout 14-karat gold and gemstone jewelry. Discounts range up to 50%, but the quality of many of these items remains high. Guarantees and certified appraisals are possible. Port Lucaya Marketplace. © 242/373-8400.

Harley-Davidson of Freeport   This is one of only two registered and licensed Harley outlets in The Bahamas. You can special-order a motorcycle if you feel flush with funds from a casino, but it's more likely that you'll content yourself with T-shirts, leather vests, belts, caps, sunglasses, and gift items. Port Lucaya Marketplace. © 242/373-8269.

Photo Specialist   This is the best place on the island to purchase video and photo equipment, and it carries an extensive range of merchandise, including tapes and batteries. It has Sea & Sea 35mm underwater cameras for rent starting at $10 a day. They'll also repair cameras. Port Lucaya Marketplace. © 242/ 373-1244.

UNEXSO Dive Shop   This is the premier dive shop of The Bahamas. It sells everything related to the water—swimsuits, wet suits, underwater cameras, shades, hats, souvenirs, state-of-the-art diver's equipment, and computers. Port Lucaya Marketplace. © 242/373-1250.

8 Grand Bahama After Dark

Many resort hotels stage their own entertainment at night, and these shows are open to the general public.

Finds Bahamian Theater

Instead of one of those Las Vegas leggy showgirl revues, you can call the 450-seat **Regency Theater** (© **242/352-5533**), and ask if one of its performances is being scheduled. This is the home of two non-profit companies, The Freeport Players' Guild and Grand Bahama Players. The season runs from September to June, and you are likely to see works by both Bahamian and Caribbean playwrights. Some really intriguing shows are likely to be staged every year. Both groups are equally talented.

ROLLING THE DICE

The Casino at Bahamia   Most of the nightlife in Freeport/Lucaya centers around this glittering, giant, Moroccan-style palace, one of the largest casinos in The Bahamas and the Caribbean. Under this Moorish-domed structure, visitors play games of chance and attend Las Vegas–inspired floor shows. They can also dine in a first-class restaurant, the Crown Room (see "Where to Dine," above), which is the only restaurant within the sprawling Resort at Bahamia that requires jackets and neckties for men. Slot machines operate daily from 8:30am to 3am; table games are conducted daily from 10am to 3am. Entrance is free. In the Resorts at Bahamia, the Mall at W. Sunrise Hwy. © **242/350-7000.**

LIFE IS A CABARET

Casino Royale Showroom   The shows here come and go, but there are usually Vegas-inspired revues. Expect more than a dozen performers who cavort in Goombay-inspired colors with lots of glitter and a smattering of toplessness. Advance reservations are a good idea. Two shows a night are presented from Tuesday to Sunday, with the first at 8:30 and the second at 10:45pm. It's usually closed for 2 weeks during the month of September. In the Resorts at Bahamia, the Mall at W. Sunrise Hwy. © **242/350-7000.** Cover (including 2 drinks) $15.

THE CLUB & BAR SCENE

Located in the center of the **Port Lucaya Marketplace** waterfront restaurant and shopping complex, **Count Basie Square** contains a vine-covered bandstand where the best live music on the island is performed on Tuesday, Friday, and Saturday evenings from about 7:30 to 8pm. And it's free! The square honors the "Count," who used to have a grand home on Grand Bahama. Steel bands, small Junkanoo groups, and even gospel singers from a local church are likely to be heard performing here, their voices or music wafting across the 50-slip marina. There are several bars in the complex where you can sip a beer or a tropical rum concoction. (See "Where to Dine," earlier in this chapter, for details on a few of these, including **Fatman's Nephew** and **Shenanigan's Irish Pub.**)

Club 2000/The Ruthnell Deck   The setting is a sprawling green and white Bahamian-style house with a wraparound veranda, immediately adjacent to the International Bazaar. There's a large interior with a dance floor that offers a high-tech lighting system and lots of gyrating bodies, but lots of people gravitate to the wraparound deck, where beer and drinks are passed through open windows to the crowd outside. Frequent contests reward anyone who qualifies for the "sexiest black dress" or "most muscular male." It's open Tuesday to Sunday from 9pm till at least 1am. In the International Bazaar. © **242/352-8866.** $10 cover for men only; women admitted free.

Yellow Bird Show Club   This spot offers an evening of Bahamian entertainment, with steel drums, limbo, storytelling, conga drums, fire dancing, and glass eating. From Monday through Saturday, dinner is served at 6pm, with showtime at 9pm. There's a disco here after the show. In the Castaways Resort, International Bazaar. © 242/352-6682. Dinner shows $26–$32.

9 A Side Trip to West End

If you're looking for a refreshing escape from the plush hotels and casinos of Freeport/Lucaya, head to West End, 28 miles from Freeport. At this old fishing village, you'll get glimpses of how things used to be before package-tour groups began descending on Grand Bahama.

To reach West End, you head north along Queen's Highway, going through Eight Mile Rock, to the northernmost point of the island. West End has several good restaurants, so you can plan to make a day (or a night) of it.

A lot of the old village buildings are now dilapidated, but they still have some charm and some legend. Many old-timers remember when rum boats were busy and the docks buzzed with activity day and night. This was from about 1920 to 1933, when Prohibition rather unsuccessfully reigned in the United States. West End was so close to the U.S. mainland that rum-running became a lucrative business, with booze flowing out of West End into Florida at night. Al Capone is reputed to have been a frequent visitor.

Villages along the way to West End have colorful names, such as **Hawksbill Creek.** For a glimpse of local life, try to visit the fish market along the harbor here. You'll pass some thriving harbor areas, too, but the vessels you'll see will be oil tankers, not rumrunners.

Eight Mile Rock is a hamlet of mostly ramshackle houses that stretches along both sides of the road for—you guessed it—8 miles. At **West End,** you come to an abrupt stop. You can enjoy a meal here at the Buccaneer Club or Pier One before heading back to Freeport/Lucaya to catch the last show at the casino.

WHERE TO DINE

Buccaneer Club ⚓ CONTINENTAL/BAHAMIAN   The Buccaneer Club is a tropical version of a German beer garden and is the best place to eat in West End. Heinz Fischbacher and his Bahamian wife, Kitty, created the whimsical decor. The compound is ringed with stone walls; inside it, palm-dotted terraces and foot-stomping alpine music provide lots of fun for the yachting crowd that always packs this place. The collection of inner rooms contains mismatched crystal chandeliers and a beer-hall ambience that's unique in The Bahamas. Many of the dishes are from eastern Europe, including a decent Wiener schnitzel and an excellent veal Oskar. On Tuesday, the Fischbachers host Junkanoo beach parties, which cost $40 per person. The price includes transportation from hotels, an hour-long open bar, a buffet, a tequila-drinking contest, and limbo dancing.

Deadman's Reef. © 242/349-3794. Reservations required. Main courses $16–$30. AE, MC, V. Tues–Sun 5–11pm.

Pier One (Kids) BAHAMIAN/INTERNATIONAL   Many people head to this restaurant because it is close to the cruise-ship dock, and it's also an ideal place to sample some fresh seafood. It rises on stilts a few steps from the water's edge, and a footbridge leads to an interior loaded with nautical artifacts. The high-ceilinged bar is a nice spot for a round of drinks before your meal. There are several dining rooms, the most desirable of which overlooks schools of fish. The lunch fare includes a delectable cream-based clam chowder, and fresh oysters are also available. The house specialty is actually baby shark, prepared in a number of ways. (There's a shark pool on-site.) We prefer ours sautéed with garlic; the stuffed version, with cheese and crabmeat, tends to overpower the natural shark flavor. A fresh fish of the day is also featured.

Freeport Harbour. ℃ 242/352-6674. Reservations recommended for dinner. Lunch main courses $6–$18.50; dinner main courses $15.95–$40. AE, MC, V. Mon–Sat 10am–10pm.

6

Bimini, the Berry Islands & Andros

In this chapter we begin a journey through the Out Islands—a very different world from that found in the major tourist developments of Nassau, Cable Beach, Paradise Island, and Freeport/Lucaya.

In contrast, much larger Andros is located southwest of Nassau. In many ways Andros is the most fascinating, because it is actually a series of islands laced with creeks and dense forests, said once to have been inhabited by mysterious creatures.

Each of the three island chains attracts a different type of visitor. **Bimini,** just 50 miles off the east coast of Florida (and the setting for Hemingway's *Islands in the Stream*) lures the big-game fisher, the yachtie from Miami, and even the drug dealer from South Florida. (The proximity to the Florida mainland helps make drug smuggling big business here.) Bimini is home to world-famous sportfishing, excellent yachting and cruising, and some good scuba diving. Anglers will find seas swarming with tuna, dolphinfish, amberjack, white and blue marlin, swordfish, barracuda, and shark, along with many other varieties. Bonefish are also plentiful around the flats off the coast of Alice Town, the capital, but the blue marlin is the prize. (Bahamians think so highly of this fish that they even put it on their $100 bill.) Scuba divers can see black coral trees over The Bimini Wall and reefs off Victory Cay.

The **Berry Islands** are the kind of retreat that might attract weary Bill Gates or Steve Forbes types. It also draws fishermen, but this string of islands, which has only 700 residents, is mainly for escapists—*rich* escapists. The islands' very limited accommodations (some of which used to be private clubs) lie near the Tongue of the Ocean, home of the big-game fish.

Andros, the largest island in the nation, is mainly uninhabited. If The Bahamas still has an unexplored wilderness, this is it. The island's forest and mangrove swamps are home to a wide variety of birds and animals, including the non-poisonous Bahamian boa constrictor and the 6-foot-long iguana. The Bahamian national bird, the West Indian flamingo, can also be spotted during migration in late spring and summer. The waters off Andros are home to a wondrous barrier reef, the third largest in the world and a diver's dream. The reef plunges 6,000 feet to a narrow drop-off known as the Tongue of the Ocean. Andros's mysterious blue holes, another diver's delight, are formed when subterranean caves fill with seawater, causing the ceiling to collapse and expose clear, deep pools. Few come here anymore looking for Sir Henry Morgan's pirate treasure, said to have been buried in one of the caves off Morgan's Bluff on the north tip of the island. But Andros does attract anglers, because it is known for its world-class fishing for marlin and the bluefin tuna, and its bonefishing is perhaps the best in the world.

1 Bimini ★

Bimini is known as the big-game fishing capital of the world, and fishing is excellent throughout the year in flats, on the reefs, and in the streams. Ernest Hemingway came to write and fish, and here, he wrote much of *To Have and Have Not*. His novel *Islands in the Stream* put Bimini on the map.

Located 50 miles east of Miami, Bimini consists of a number of islands, islets, and cays, including North and South Bimini, the main tourist areas. You'll most often encounter the word "Bimini," but it might be more proper to say "The Biminis," since North Bimini and South Bimini are two distinct islands, separated by a narrow ocean passage. Ferry service shuttles between the two. The major development is on North Bimini, mostly in Alice Town. The western side of North Bimini is a long stretch of lovely beachfront.

Off North Bimini, in 30 feet of water, are some large hewn-stone formations that some people claim to be from the lost continent of Atlantis. Divers find the reefs laced with conch, lobster, coral, and many tropical fish.

Bimini's location off the Florida coastline is at a point where the Gulf Stream meets the Bahama Banks. This fact has made Bimini a favorite cruising ground for America's yachting set, who follow the channel between North and South Bimini into a spacious, sheltered harbor, where they can stock up on food, drink, fuel, and supplies at well-equipped marinas. From here, they can set off to cruise the cays that begin south of South Bimini. Each has its own special appeal, beginning with Turtle Rocks and stretching to South Cat Cay (the latter of which is uninhabited). Along the way, you'll pass Holm Cay, Gun Cay, and North Cat Cay.

Hook-shaped North Bimini is 7½ miles long, and combined with South Bimini, it makes up a landmass of only 9 square miles. That's why Alice Town looks so crowded. Another reason is that a large part of Bimini is privately owned; despite pressure from the Bahamian government, the landholders have not sold their acreage, and Bimini can't "spread out" until they do. At Alice Town, the land is so narrow that you can walk "from sea to shining sea" in just a short time. Most of Bimini's population of some 1,600 people lives in Alice Town; other hamlets include Bailey Town and Porgy Bay.

Although winter is usually high season in The Bahamas, visitors flock to Bimini's calmer summer waters, which are better for fishing. Winter, especially from mid-December to mid-March, is quieter, and Bimini has never tried to develop a resort structure that would attract more winter visitors. If you go to Bimini, you'll hear a lot of people mention **Cat Cay** (not to be confused with Cat Island, in the Southern Bahamas). You can stay overnight at Cat Cay's marina, which lies 8 miles off South Bimini. Transient slips are available to mariners. The island is the domain of **Cat Cay Yacht Club** (© **242/347-3565**), whose initiation fee is a cool $25,000. This is a privately owned island, attracting titans of industry and famous families. It is for the exclusive use of Cat Cay Club members and their guests, who enjoy a golf course, tennis, a large marina, white-sand beaches, and club facilities such as restaurants and bars. Many wealthy Americans have homes on the island, which has a private airstrip.

GETTING THERE

Note: A passport or a birth certificate with picture ID is required for entry to Bimini (bring your passport to be on the safe side), and an outbound (return) ticket also must be presented to Bahamian Customs before you will be allowed entry. Passengers returning from Bimini to the United States must pay a $15 departure tax.

BY PLANE   The island's only airstrip is at the southern tip of South Bimini, a time-consuming transfer and ferryboat ride away from Alice Town on North Bimini, site of most of the archipelago's hotels and yacht facilities.

The best way to avoid this transfer is to fly the small **Chalk's Ocean Airways,** based in Miami (© **800/424-2557**). The airline has a fleet of 17-passenger amphibious aircraft that land in the waters near Alice Town. Chalk's offers two daily flights from Miami, one of which originates in Fort Lauderdale. The 20- to 30-minute flights depart from the calm waters at Watson Island Terminal, near downtown Miami (about a $12 cab ride from Miami International Airport). Round-trip tickets start at $221. Chalk's sometimes flies in from Nassau; call the airline for more details. There is a baggage allowance of only 30 pounds per passenger; if you're carrying heavy travel or fishing gear, you'll be hit with overweight charges. *Note:* Chalk's doesn't allow any hand luggage on board— every piece of your luggage must be weighed and checked in.

Also, **Island Air** (© **800/444-9904** or 954/359-9942) flies five times a week from Fort Lauderdale to South Bimini.

BY BOAT   In the olden days, the traditional way to get from Nassau to Bimini was by a slow-moving boat; you can still do it, and it'll take you 12 hours. You can go by sea on the MV *Bimini Mack,* which leaves from Potter's Cay Dock in Nassau and stops at Cat Cay and Bimini. The vessel leaves Nassau weekly but with no set schedule. For details about departure, call the dockmaster at **Potter's Cay Dock** in Nassau (℡ **242/393-1064**).

GETTING AROUND

If you've taken our advice and traveled lightly to Bimini, you can walk to your hotel from the point where the seaplanes land in Alice Town. If not, a small minibus will transport you for $3 per person. If you arrive at the small airport on South Bimini, it is a $5 taxi and ferry ride to Alice Town.

You won't need a car on Bimini—in fact, there are no car-rental agencies. Most people walk to where they want to go (though your hotel may be able to arrange a minibus tour or rent you a bike or golf cart). The walk is up and down King's Highway, which has no sidewalks. It's so narrow that two automobiles have a tough time squeezing by. Be careful walking along this highway, especially at night when drivers might not see you.

This highway, lined with low-rise buildings, splits Alice Town on North Bimini. If you're a beachcombing type, stick to the side bordering the Gulf Stream. It's here you'll find the best beaches. The harborside contains a handful of inns (most of which are reviewed below), along with marinas and docks where supplies are unloaded. You'll see many Floridians arriving on yachts.

 FAST FACTS: Bimini

Banks   **The Royal Bank of Canada** has a branch office in Alice Town (℡ 242/347-3031), open Monday and Friday 9am to 3pm and Tuesday, Wednesday, and Thursday from 9am to 1pm.

Clothing   If you're going to Bimini in the winter months, you'd better take along a windbreaker for those occasional chilly nights.

Customs & Immigration   The Chalk's flight from Miami stops right near the Alice Town office of **Customs and Immigration** (℡ 242/368-2030) for The Bahamas. There's only one Immigration officer, plus another Customs official.

In Miami you will have been handed a Bahamian Immigration Card to fill out, and you must carry proof of your citizenship. Though it may be possible to use your voter-registration card or a birth certificate plus photo ID, we recommend that you just bring your passport to be on the safe side. Regrettably, many passengers cross over from Miami with only a driver's license, which will not be accepted by immigration. Customs may or may not examine your baggage.

Drugs   The rumrunners of the Prohibition era have now given way to those smuggling illegal drugs into the United States from The Bahamas. Because of its proximity to the U.S. mainland, Bimini, as is no secret to anyone, is now a major drop-off point for drugs, many of which have found their way here from Colombia. If not intercepted by the U.S. Coast Guard, these drugs will find their way to the Florida mainland and eventually to the rest of the United States.

Buying and/or selling illegal drugs, such as cocaine and marijuana, is an extremely risky business in The Bahamas. You may be approached by pushers on Bimini, but make sure you don't get into trouble, because there are undercover agents everywhere. If caught with any illegal drugs on Bimini, or elsewhere in The Bahamas, you will face immediate imprisonment.

Emergencies   To call the police or report a fire, dial ℭ **919**.

Mail   If you're sending mail back to the United States, we suggest you skip the Bahamian postal service entirely and drop your letter off at Chalk's airline's special basket. You can use U.S. postage stamps, and your mail will reach its mainland target far quicker than by the usual route.

Medical Care   There are nurses, a doctor, and a dentist on the island, as well as the **North Bimini Medical Clinic** (ℭ **242/347-2210**). However, for a serious medical emergency, patients are usually airlifted to either Miami or Nassau. Helicopters can land in the well-lit baseball field on North Bimini.

Special Events   The annual **Bacardi Rum Billfish** Tournament and the **Hemingway Billfish Tournament** bring world anglers to Bimini in March. Make hotel reservations well in advance. There are additional tournaments throughout the year; see "The Bahamas Calendar of Events," in chapter 2, for additional details. The Bahamas Tourist Office near you (see "Visitor Information," in chapter 2) can provide details if you'd like to enter a tournament.

Visitor Information   There's a branch of **The Bahamas Ministry of Tourism** in Bimini, located in the Government Building, Kings Highway, Alice Town (ℭ **242/347-3529**). It's open Monday to Friday from 9am to 5:30pm.

WHERE TO STAY

Accommodations in Bimini are extremely limited, and it's almost impossible to get a room during one of the big fishing tournaments unless you've reserved way in advance. Inns are cozy and simple; many are family-owned and -operated (chances are, your innkeeper's name will be Brown). Furnishings are often time-worn, the paint chipped. No one puts on airs here; the dress code, even in the evening, is very simple and relaxed. From wherever you're staying in Alice Town, it's usually easy to walk to another hotel for dinner or drinks.

Bimini Beach Hotel/Bimini Sands Condo Complex   There are two distinctly different aspects to this complex; both of which lie at the edge of a sandy beach, a 5-minute drive from South Bimini's international airport. The less well-accessorized and comfortable of the two is the two-story motel, half of whose rooms overlook the sea, the other half of which front a marina. Originally built in the 1970s, it was radically overhauled and renovated in 1999. Expect something akin to a roadside motel in Florida, but with a beach a few steps away. The condo complex is more elaborate, with many of the features you'd expect (balconies, patios, contemporary furniture, and so on) in a generic-looking apartment complex somewhere in South Florida. Like the motel section, half the rooms overlook the sea, the other half overlook a marina. Each of the two complexes has a bar, a restaurant, and a pool.

South Bimini. ℭ 242/347-3500. Fax 242/347-3501. 40 conventional motel rooms; 36 1- or 2-bedroom condos with kitchens. $120–$130 conventional double room in hotel section, $175–$200 1-bedroom condo with kitchen, $300 2-bedroom condo with kitchen. 2-night minimum is required in the condo complex. AE, MC, V. **Amenities:** 2 restaurants, 2 bars, 2 pools, volleyball court, tennis court. *In room:* A/C. No phone.

Bimini Big Game Fishing Club & Hotel ⚓   Run by the Bacardi Rum people, this is *the* place to stay on Bimini. Catering to anglers and yachties, it's a self-contained world with well-furnished guest rooms in the main building, surrounded by cottages and first-rate penthouse apartments, the latter often housing VIPs. The general manager, Curtis Carroll, is the most experienced hotelier on the island, and he will see to your requests and help ease your adjustment to Bimini, especially if you want to know anything about fishing. Usually the best anglers at the big-game fishing tournaments stay here, and during the tournaments, it's next to impossible to get a room without reservations long in advance.

Most of the accommodations are in its central structure; these units are large and equipped with two beds with firm mattresses. Everything is clean and comfortable, and the rooms have patios or porches opening onto a marina and the club's swimming pool. The ground-floor cottages are even more spacious than the standard bedrooms and have tiny kitchenettes with refrigerators. (Cooking, though, is strictly forbidden. If you want to charcoal-broil your catch of the day, you will have to use one of the outdoor grills.) The small bathrooms are well-maintained and come with shower stalls.

The hotel is the best place to go for food and entertainment on the island (see "Where to Dine" and "Bimini After Dark," below). The hotel will help you arrange all kinds of fishing charters.

King's Hwy. (P.O. Box 699), Alice Town, Bimini, The Bahamas, or P.O. Box 523238, Miami, FL 33152. © 800/737-1007 in the U.S., or 242/347-3391. Fax 242/347-3392. www.bimini-big-game-club.com. 35 units, 12 cottages, 4 penthouse apts. $158–$178 double, $208 cottage for 2, $315 penthouse. Extra person $25. AE, MC, V. **Amenities:** Restaurant, bar, pool, tennis court, laundry, baby-sitting, bike rentals. *In room:* A/C, TV, refrigerator.

Bimini Blue Water Resort Ltd.   This is essentially a resort complex for sportfishermen, with complete dockside services, containing 32 modern slips. It's one of the finest places of its kind in The Bahamas. The main building is a

---

ℭ Island in the Stream

Nevil Norton Stuart, a Bahamian, came to Bimini in the late 1920s and purchased the Fountain of Youth, a Prohibition-era bar, renaming it the **Bimini Big Game Fishing Club.** In 1940, Stuart reclaimed land in Bimini Harbor, constructed a marina, and added several cottages along with a desalination plant. Thus began the legend of one of the most highly publicized sportfishing meccas in the world.

Film stars, including Judy Garland and Sir Anthony Hopkins, among others, have lodged at the club, and Martin Luther King Jr., visited twice. Of course, no one immortalized the island as much as Hemingway, who called it "My Island in the Stream."

Today the complex has grown to more than 50 rooms, including cottages and penthouses, and it's owned by the rum maker Bacardi International. In the 100-slip marina, you'll find enormous sportfishing boats, costing more than several million dollars, proudly standing alongside simple outboard-powered runabouts.

The club hosts many fishing tournaments throughout the year, including the **Bacardi Rum Billfish Tournament** in March. This week-long world-class event attracts the biggest names in sportfishing and is regarded by many fishermen as the event of the year to win.

white-frame waterfront Bahamian guest house, the Anchorage, where Michael Lerner, the noted fisherman, used to live. It's at the top of the hill, with a dining room and bar from which you can look out onto the ocean (see "Where to Dine," below). The regular mid-size bedrooms contain double beds with good mattresses, wood-paneled walls, white furniture, and picture-window doors that lead to private balconies. Bathrooms are small with shower units.

The Marlin Cottage, although much altered, was one of Hemingway's retreats in the 1930s. He used it as a main setting in *Islands in the Stream*. It has three bedrooms, three bathrooms, a large living room, and two porches. In honor of his memory, the hotel sponsors the Hemingway Billfish Tournament every March.

King's Hwy. (P.O. Box 601), Alice Town, Bimini, The Bahamas. ℂ 242/347-3166. Fax 242/347-3293. 12 units. $90 double, $190 suite, $285 Marlin Cottage. AE, MC, V. **Amenities:** Dining room, bar, pool, marina. *In room:* A/C, TV.

Compleat Angler Hotel   Right on the main street, and affiliated with the Bimini Blue Water Resort, this small timeworn hotel was built in the 1930s, when big-game fishing was at its peak. The building is designed like an old country house, with Bahamian timber. The wood on the face of the building is from rum barrels used during the Prohibition era. Don't expect anything too fancy, but the Compleat Angler is loaded with island atmosphere. Ernest Hemingway made the hotel his headquarters on and off from 1935 to 1937 while he was stalking marlin, and the room in which he stayed is still available to guests. He penned parts of *To Have and Have Not* here. The small to mid-size rooms are tidily maintained and comfortable, with cramped bathrooms containing shower stalls. The best units are those in the front opening onto the encircling veranda, overlooking the courtyard bar and the street. You can swim, dine, shop, or fish right at your doorstep, and book fishing charters at the hotel. *Note:* Because of the famous, noisy bar on the premises (see "Bimini After Dark," below), this hotel is suitable only for night owls.

King's Hwy., P.O. Box 601, Alice Town, Bimini, The Bahamas. ℂ 242/347-3122. Fax 242/347-3293. 12 units. $67–$85 double. AE, MC, V. **Amenities:** 3 bars. *In room:* A/C.

Sea Crest Hotel & Marina   Built in 1981 and upgraded every year since, this hotel lies right on the main highway and was the first place to give the Bimini Big Game Fishing Club & Hotel some real competition. It's still not as good as that traditional leader, but the price is right. Rooms in this three-story hotel, which looks like a motel, are at their best on the third floor, because they have better ocean or bay views. Rooms don't have phones, and many are small, with rather cramped bathrooms, each with a shower stall, but they're comfortably furnished in a simple, traditional way. Accommodations open onto small balconies. Since the location is right in the heart of Alice Town, you can generally walk where you want to go. The Sea Crest is a family favorite, and children under 12 stay free. There's an on-site restaurant, Captain Bob's, which is independently operated and serves good seafood. The hotel is also a favorite of the boating crowd, because it offers a small 18-berth marina.

King's Hwy. (P.O. Box 654), Alice Town, Bimini, The Bahamas. ℂ 242/347-3071. Fax 242/347-3495. 12 units. $95.40 double. MC, V. **Amenities:** Restaurant, bar, marina. *In room:* A/C, TV.

WHERE TO DINE

Anchorage Dining Room   SEAFOOD/BAHAMIAN/AMERICAN   This dining room overlooks the harbor of Alice Town; you can see the ocean through picture windows. The modern, paneled room is filled with captain's chairs and

Formica tables. You might begin your dinner with conch chowder, then follow with one of the tempting seafood dishes, including spiny broiled lobster or perhaps a chewy cracked conch. They also do a good fried Bahamian chicken and a tender New York sirloin. The cooking is straightforward and reliable, never pretending to be more than it is.

In the Blue Hole Water Resort, King's Hwy., Alice Town. (€ 242/347-3166. Lunch items $4–$10; dinner main courses $12–$22. AE, MC, V. Daily 6–10pm.

Big Game Sports Bar SEAFOOD   This sports bar, always packed with serious fishermen from South Florida, is upstairs overlooking the marina. It offers standard fare, but the food is as reliable as the view. Menu items are displayed near the cash register. During lunch, the popular bar serves conch fritters, conch salad, conch chowder, and cracked conch, which is breaded like veal cutlet. But conch pizza is the specialty and is well worth the visit here. You can also order grouper fingers, barbecued back ribs, hamburgers, sandwiches, or a daily special.

In the Bimini Big Game Fishing Club & Hotel, King's Hwy., Alice Town. (€ 242/347-3391. Main courses $6–$12. AE, MC, V. Daily 11am–10pm.

Gulfstream Restaurant AMERICAN/CONTINENTAL/BAHAMIAN This place is the most upscale dining room on the island, with solid, simple cooking. Murals by Phil Brinkman depict scenes relating to the legend and lore of Bimini. A good wine list complements the island specialties, such as crisp homemade Bimini bread and freshly caught kingfish, along with broiled local lobster and grouper meunière. Instead of french fries, why not go Bahamian and order peas 'n' rice with your meal? If you're tired of fish, the kitchen will serve you a good steak, roast prime rib of beef, or lamb chops.

In the Bimini Big Game Fishing Club & Hotel, King's Hwy., Alice Town. (€ 242/347-3391. Reservations recommended for dinner. Main courses $16–$28. AE, MC, V. Daily 7:30–10:30am and 7–10pm. Closed Jan–mid-Feb.

Red Lion Pub BAHAMIAN   This centrally located restaurant is far larger than its simple façade would indicate. In a relaxed, friendly atmosphere, it's one of the best places on the island to retreat to after a day of fishing and sailing. It's one of the few non-smoking restaurants in the Out Islands. The dining room is in a large extension of the original pub and overlooks the marina in back. The well-prepared meals are local home-cooking: the local fish of the day, cracked conch, barbecued ribs, baked grouper in foil, followed by either key lime pie or banana cream pie. The price of the main course practically gets you a dinner unto itself.

King's Hwy., Alice Town. (€ 242/347-3259. Main courses $13–$23. No credit cards. Tues–Sun 6–10pm; pub Tues–Sun until 10:30pm.

WATER SPORTS & OTHER OUTDOOR ACTIVITIES
BEACHES
The beaches on Bimini are all clearly marked and signposted from the highways.

The beach that's closest to Alice Town is **Radio Beach,** the only one on Bimini with toilets, vendors, and snack bars. It's set adjacent to the piers and wharves of Alice Town, and consequently, it's the most popular and crowded beach on the island.

About 2 miles north of Alice Town, facing west, is **Spook Hill Beach.** Both it and its cousin, **Bimini Bay Beach,** about 2½ miles north of Alice Town, offer fewer crowds, good snorkeling, and lots of sunshine. Both are sandy-bottomed and comfortable on your feet. **Bimini Bay Beach,** wider than any other on the island, is the favorite of many local residents.

On South Bimini, the two favorites are the west-facing **Bimini Sands Beach,** a sandy-bottomed stretch that's immediately south of the channel that separates North from South Bimini; and the **Bimini Reef Club Beach,** south of the airport, where offshore snorkeling is worthwhile, thanks to very clear waters.

FISHING

Bimini 𝒜𝒜𝒜 is called the "Big Game Fishing Capital of the World," and more than anyone else, Ernest Hemingway made fishing here famous. But Zane Grey came this way, too, as did Howard Hughes. Richard Nixon used to fish here aboard the posh cruiser of his friend Bebe Rebozo. In the trail of Hemingway, fishermen still flock to cast lines in the Gulf Stream and the Bahama Banks. The annual **Bacardi Rum Billfish Tournament** and the **Hemingway Billfish Tournament** bring world anglers to Bimini in March.

Of course, everyone's after the big one, and a lot of world records have been set in this area for marlin, sailfish, swordfish, wahoo, grouper, and tuna. Fishing folk can spin cast for panfish and boat snapper, yellowtail, and kingfish. Many experts consider stalking bonefish, long a pursuit of baseball great Ted Williams, to be the toughest challenge in the sport.

Five charter boats are available in Bimini for big-game and little-game fishing, with some center-console boats rented for both bottom and reef angling. At least eight bonefishing guides are available, and experienced anglers who have made repeated visits to Bimini know the particular skills of each of these men who will take you for a half or full day of "fishing in the flats." Most skiffs hold two anglers, and part of the fun in hiring a local guide is to hear his fish tales and other island lore. If a guide tells you that 16-pound bonefish have turned up, he may not be exaggerating—catches that large have really been documented.

Reef and bottom fishing on Bimini are easier than bonefishing and can be more productive. There are numerous species of snapper and grouper to be found, as well as amberjack. This is the simplest and least expensive boat fishing, because you need only a local guide, a little boat, tackle, and a lot of bait. Sometimes you can negotiate to go out bottom fishing with a Bahamian, but chances are he'll ask you to pay for the boat fuel for his trouble. That night, back at your Bimini inn, the cook will serve you the red snapper or grouper you caught that day.

Most hotel owners will tell you to bring your own fishing gear to Bimini. A couple of small shops sell some items, but you'd better bring major equipment with you if you're really serious. Bait, of course, can be purchased locally.

At the **Bimini Big Game Fishing Club & Hotel,** King's Hwy., Alice Town (© **242/347-3391**), you can charter a 41-foot Hatteras at $700 to $800 for a full day of fishing, or $400 to $500 for a half day. A Bertram, either 28 or 31 feet, will also cost $700 to $800 for a full day or $400 to $500 for a half day. Although this outfitter is your best bet, you can also pick up a list of locals whose boats are available for charter at **Bimini Blue Water Marina,** King's Hwy., Alice Town (© **242/347-3166**). The average rate is around $400 to $500 per half day or $600 to $900 for a full day.

SCUBA DIVING & SNORKELING

There are black coral gardens and reefs to explore, plus wrecks and blue holes, plus a mysterious stone formation on the bottom of the sea that some people claim is part of the lost continent of **Atlantis** (it's 500 yd. offshore at Bimini Bay under about 20 ft. of water). Bimini waters are known for a breathtaking drop-off at the rim of the continental shelf, a cliff extending 2,000 feet down, a veritable underwater mountain.

⌒Finds Ruins of the Roaring '20s

A major attraction for both snorkelers and divers, not to mention rainbow-hued fish, is the *Sapona*, lying hard aground in 15 feet of water between South Bimini and Cat Cay ever since it was blown here by a hurricane in 1929. In the heyday of the Roaring Twenties, the ship, which was built by Henry Ford, served as a private club and speakeasy. You'll have to take a boat to reach the wreck site. Spearfishermen are attracted to the ruins, looking for the giant grouper, and dive operators on Bimini include the site in their repertoire. It's shallow enough that even snorkelers can see it.

The finest and most experienced outfitter is **Bimini Undersea**, King's Hwy., Alice Town (© 242/347-3089; www.biminiundersea.com).

The people to see here are Bill and Nowdla Keefe. Half-day snorkeling trips cost $29. Scuba rates are $49 for a one-tank dive, $89 for a two-tank dive, and $119 for a three-tank dive. Night dives Tuesday and Friday go for $49. All-inclusive dive packages are also available. For further information or reservations, the Keefes can be reached at © 800/348-4644 or 305/653-5572. You can also swim with dolphins in the wild two or three times a week, depending on demand. Most excursions take from 3 to 4 hours and cost $99 for adults or $69 for children 8 to 14 (free for children 7 and under).

TENNIS
You'll find hard-surface courts at the **Bimini Big Game Fishing Club & Hotel** (© 242/347-3391), King's Highway, which are complimentary and reserved for hotel guests and members. The courts are lit for night play, and you can purchase balls at the club. There are no public tennis courts.

EXPLORING THE ISLANDS: FOLLOWING IN THE FOOTSTEPS OF PONCE DE LEÓN & PAPA HEMINGWAY
At the southern tip of North Bimini, ramshackle **Alice Town** is all that many visitors ever see of the islands, since the major hotels are found here. You can see the whole town in an hour or two. The **Bimini Big Game Fishing Club & Hotel,** King's Highway, has some of the best duty-free liquor buys in town. If you're a souvenir collector, ask at the front office for T-shirts, sunglasses, coffee mugs, and Big Game Club hats.

If you're on the trail of Papa Hemingway, you'll want to visit **The Compleat Angler,** King's Highway in Alice Town (© 242/347-3122), where there is a museum of Hemingway memorabilia. The collection of prints and writings describes the times he spent in Bimini, mainly from 1935 to 1937. The prints are posted in the sitting room downstairs, and much of this memorabilia makes interesting browsing. There are a number of books by Hemingway in the library collection.

As you're exploring the island, you may want to stop off at the **Bimini Straw Market,** strike up a conversation with some islanders, and perhaps pick up a souvenir.

The **Queen's Highway** runs up the western side of North Bimini, and as you head north along it, you'll find it lined with beautiful beachfront. **King's Highway** runs through the town and continues north. It's lined with houses painted gold, lime, buttercup yellow, and pink that gleam in the bright sunshine.

At some point, you may notice the ruins of Bimini's first hotel, the **Bimini Bay Rod and Gun Club,** sitting unfinished on its own beach. Built in the early 1920s, it did a flourishing business until a hurricane wiped it out later in that decade. It was never rebuilt, though developers once made a never-finished attempt.

If you want to visit **South Bimini,** you can rent a taxi to see the island's limited attractions for about $15, which, regrettably, at least to our knowledge, does not include Ponce de León's legendary Fountain of Youth, as once rumored. There's not a lot to see, but you are likely to hear some tall tales worth the cab fare. You can also stop off at some lovely, uncrowded beaches.

BIMINI AFTER DARK

You can dance to a Goombay beat or try to find some disco music. Most people have a leisurely dinner, drink a lot in one of the local watering holes, and go back to their hotel rooms by midnight so they can get up early to continue pursuing the elusive "big one" the next morning. Every bar in Alice Town is likely to claim that it was Hemingway's favorite. He did hit quite a few of them, in fact. There's rarely a cover charge anywhere unless some special entertainment is being offered.

Beginning at midmorning and lasting until midnight at least, the bars at the **Bimini Big Game Fishing Club & Hotel,** King's Highway, Alice Town (© **242/347-3391**), are the place to hang out. Tall fish tales of the big one that got away fill the air. The **Big Game Sports Bar** (see "Where to Dine," above) starts serving its famed conch pizza at noon. No fewer than four TV sets are positioned for your favorite sports program, or you may want to enjoy a hand of cards. It's the best room in which to entertain yourself during those lazy days in Bimini. The poolside **Barefoot Bar,** open from midmorning to late afternoon, serves favorite island drinks and ice-cold beer. Off the main dining room of the Gulfstream Restaurant is the **Gulfstream Bar,** featuring Ratti, the island's best-known calypsonian, singing the songs of the island and strumming them on his guitar. Naturally, since Bacardi owns the place, all the rum punches are made with Bacardi rums.

Constructed of Prohibition-era rum kegs, the bar at **The Compleat Angler Hotel,** King's Highway, Alice Town (© **242/347-3122**), hosts an eclectic clientele who come to dance to the nightly calypso band and drink Goombay

---

⸢ Fun Fact Myths of Bimini

Bimini has long been shrouded in myths, none more far-fetched than the one claiming that the lost continent of **Atlantis** lies off the shores of North Bimini. This legend grew because of the weirdly shaped rock formations that lie submerged in about 30 feet of water near the shoreline. Pilots flying over North Bimini have reported what they envision as a "lost highway" under the sea. This myth continues, and many scuba divers are attracted to North Bimini to explore these rocks.

Ponce de León came to South Bimini looking for that legendary **Fountain of Youth.** He never found it, but people still come to South Bimini in search of it. Near the end of the 19th century, a religious sect reportedly came here to "take the waters." Supposedly, there was a bubbling fountain, or at least a spring, in those days. If you arrive on South Bimini and seem interested enough, a local guide (for a fee) will be only too happy to show you "the exact spot" where the Fountain of Youth once bubbled.

Moments   A Drink at the End of the World

Everybody eventually makes his or her way to the **End of the World Bar** (no phone) on King's Highway in Alice Town. When you get here, you may think you're in the wrong place—it's just a waterfront shack with sawdust or sand on the floor and graffiti everywhere. It was the late New York congressman Adam Clayton Powell who put this bar on the map in the 1960s. Between stints in Washington battling Congress and preaching at the Abyssinian Baptist Church in Harlem, the controversial congressman could be found sitting at a table here. While the bar doesn't attract the media attention it did in Powell's heyday, it's still a strong local favorite. Open daily from 9am to 3am.

Smashes. The bartender makes the best planter's punch in The Bahamas, challenging anyone to make it better. The place, as mentioned, is filled with Hemingway memorabilia, and it's open daily from 11am "until . . ."

2 The Berry Islands

A dangling chain of cays and islets on the eastern edge of the Great Bahama Bank, the unspoiled and serene Berry Islands begin 35 miles northwest of New Providence (Nassau), 150 miles east of Miami. This 30-island archipelago is known to sailors, fishermen, yachtspeople, Jack Nicklaus, and a Rockefeller or two, as well as to the beachcombers who love its pristine sands.

As a center of fishing, the Berry Islands are second only to Bimini. At the tip of the Tongue of the Ocean, a.k.a. TOTO, world-record-setting big-game fish are found, along with endless flats (the shallow bodies of water near the shore where bonefish congregate). In the "Berries," you can find your own tropical paradise islet, and enjoy—sans wardrobe—totally isolated white-sand beaches and palm-fringed shores. Some of the best shell collecting in The Bahamas is found on the beaches of the Berry Islands and in their shallow-water flats.

The main islands are, beginning in the north, Great Stirrup Cay, Cistern Cay, Great Harbour Cay, Anderson Cay, Haines Cay, Hoffmans Cay, Bond's Cay, Sandy Cay, Whale Cay, and Chub Cay. One of the very small cays, lying north of Frazer's Hog Cay and Whale Cay, has, in our opinion, the most unappetizing name in the Bahamian archipelago: Cockroach Cay.

The largest island within the Berry Islands is **Great Harbour Cay,** which sprawls over 3,800 acres of sand, rock, and scrub. Development here received a great deal of publicity when Douglas Fairbanks Jr., was connected with its investors. It became a multimillion-dollar resort for jet-setters who occupied waterfront town houses and villas overlooking the golf course or marina. There are 7½ miles of almost-solitary beachfront. Once Cary Grant, Brigitte Bardot, and other stars romped on this beach.

Bond's Cay, a bird sanctuary in the south, and tiny Frazer's Hog Cay (stock is still raised here) are both privately owned. An English company used to operate a coconut and sisal plantation on Whale Cay, also near the southern tip. Sponge fishermen and their families inhabit some of the islands.

BERRY ISLANDS ESSENTIALS

GETTING THERE   Great Harbour Cay is an official point of entry for The Bahamas if you're flying from a foreign territory such as the United States.

You can get here only via charter flights from South Florida, making these some of the most inconvenient islands to reach in all The Bahamas. **Tropical Diversions** (© **954/921-9084**) flies from Fort Lauderdale to Great Harbour Cay, usually in a five-passenger, twin-engine Piper Seneca; and **Island Express** (© **954/359-0380**) also operates charters from Fort Lauderdale, winging in to Chub Cay Airport.

If you're contemplating the **mail-boat** sea-voyage route, the **MV** *Captain Gurthdean* leaves Potter's Cay Dock in Nassau once a week on Thursday at 8pm, heading for the Berry Islands. Inquire at the **Potter's Cay Dock** for an up-to-the-minute report (contact the dockmaster at © **242/393-1064**).

FAST FACTS   The **Great Harbour Cay Medical Clinic** is at Bullock's Harbour on Great Harbour Cay (© **242/367-8400**). The **police station** is also at Bullock's Harbour (© **242/367-8344**).

GREAT HARBOUR CAY

An estimated 700 residents live on Great Harbour Cay, making it the most populated island of the Berry chain. Its main settlement is **Bullock's Harbour,** which might be called the "capital of the Berry Islands." The cay is about 1 ½ miles wide and some 8 miles long. There isn't much in town: a grocery store and some restaurants. Most visitors arrive to stay at the **Great Harbour Cay Yacht Club & Marina** (see below), outside of town.

Great Harbour Cay lies between Grand Bahama Island and New Providence (Nassau). It's 60 miles northwest of Nassau and 150 miles east of Miami, about an hour away from Miami by plane or half a day by powerboat. Unlike most islands in The Bahamas, the island isn't flat but contains rolling hills.

Deep-sea fishing possibilities abound here, including billfish, dolphinfish, king mackerel, and wahoo. Light-tackle bottom fishing is also good. You can net yellowtail, snapper, barracuda, triggerfish, and plenty of grouper. Bonefishing here is among the best in the world. The Great Harbour Cay marina is an excellent facility, with some 80 slips and all the amenities. Some of Florida's fanciest yachts pull in here.

When you tire of fishing, there are 8 miles of gorgeous white-sand beaches, a nine-hole golf course designed by Joe Lee, and four clay tennis courts.

ACCOMMODATIONS & DINING

Great Harbour Cay Yacht Club & Marina ⊛   The two-level waterfront town houses here overlook the marina (the staff will help you arrange fishing excursions). Each has its own private dock, topped off with a garage and patio. Other units are on the beach. Although privately owned, these accommodations are rented on a daily or weekly basis by the resort. Each unit is furnished individually by the owner. The town houses have a light, airy feeling, with some 1,600 square feet of living space. Each has two bedrooms and two and a half bathrooms and is suitable for up to six people. All have fully equipped kitchens, and some accommodations have TV. Beach villas, covered in cedar shakes, have tile floors and a Mediterranean-type decor. Units range from studio apartments (the cheapest rentals) to two-bedroom units, and daily maid service is included.

Dining facilities include the Wharf, serving breakfast and lunch, and the Tamboo Club, at the west end of the marina, open Wednesday through Monday for drinks and dinner only.

Great Harbour Cay, Berry Islands, The Bahamas (mailing address: 3512 N. Ocean Dr., Hollywood, FL 33019). © **800/343-7256** or 242/367-8838. Fax 242/367-8115. tdbahamas@aol.com. 18 units. $100–$175 double,

$500–$600 beach house or villa suitable for 5–6 guests. AE, MC, V. **Amenities:** 2 restaurants, bar, dock, snorkeling, fishing, bikes for guests. *In room:* A/C, TV. No phone.

CHUB CAY

Named after a species of fish that thrives in nearby waters, Chub Cay is well known to sportfishing enthusiasts. A self-contained hideaway with a devoted clientele, it's the southernmost of the Berry Islands, separating the mainland of South Florida from the commercial frenzy of Nassau.

Chub Cay's development began in the late 1950s as the strictly private (and rather spartan) enclave of a group of Texas-based anglers and investors. It was originally uninhabited, but over the years a staff was imported, dormitory-style housing was built, and the island's most famous man-made feature (its state-of-the-art, 90-slip marina) was constructed in the 979-acre island's sheltered lagoon.

After recovering from severe damage inflicted in 1992 by Hurricane Andrew, Chub Cay is today a tranquil, scrub-covered sand spit with awesome amounts of marine hardware, a dozen posh private homes, the marina, and a complex of buildings devoted to the **Chub Cay Club** (see below). Today, membership in the club begins at around $2,000 a year and grants reduced rates for marina slip rental, boat repairs, and hotel-room and villa rental. Non-members, however, are welcome to use the facilities, and rent rooms at the rates listed below.

There are a liquor store and a yachties' commissary on the island, an outlet for the sale of marine supplies, and a concrete runway for landing anything up to and including a 737. Most visitors reach Chub Cay by private yacht from the Florida mainland, but if you prefer to charter your fishing craft on Chub Cay, you'll find a mini-armada of suitable craft at your disposal. **Island Express Airlines** (© 954/359-0380) flies charter flights to Chub Cay from Fort Lauderdale. Charter flights can be arranged with the help of the Chub Cay Club's desk staff. If you opt to fly here, travel light; there's a baggage allowance of no more than 50 pounds per passenger.

The water temperature around Chub Cay averages a warm 80°F to 85°F year-round, even at relatively deep depths. There's only a small tidal change, and under normal conditions, there is no swell or noticeable current in offshore waters. The waters are incredibly clear, making for great snorkeling.

Many divers wax poetic over the dive spots of Chub Cay, including **Chub Wall** and **Mamma Rhoda Rock,** and the dozens of examples of rare coral that ring the island. The best scuba-dive outfitter is **Undersea Adventures** at the Chub Cay Club (© 800/327-8150 or 242/323-2412; www.nealwatson.com). Neal Watson, who founded Undersea Adventures, is one of the original pioneers of scuba diving, and he holds a number of world records. He has personally trained the staff here and selected the dive sites. From Chub Cay, you'll find some of the most diversified and exciting dive sites in either the Atlantic or the Caribbean, including **Dynamite Wall,** whose depth drops quickly from 80 to 6,000 feet. A two-tank dive costs $79, with half-day snorkeling trips going for $29.

ACCOMMODATIONS & DINING

Chub Cay Club *(F)* Breezy and comfortable, these air-conditioned accommodations are the only available option on all of Chub Cay. The place prides itself on its marina, freshwater swimming pools, and many nearby sandy beaches. Throughout the resort, there's a nautical, laid-back kind of feeling and a clubby atmosphere. Don't expect inspired architecture. None of the rooms has a phone, although a phone is available at the reception desk. The decor consists of modern wicker with firm beds, plus small, well-organized bathrooms with shower units. The remote feeling here is a welcome relief to many guests.

There's a restaurant (the Harbour House), with its own bar, as well as the Cay Bar set beside the pool, and the Hilltop Bar on the island's highest elevation. The latter offers a TV for sports broadcasts, pool tables, and occasional live music.

Chub Cay, Berry Islands, The Bahamas. ℂ 800/662-8555 or 242/325-1490. Fax 242/322-5199. (Or write to Chub Cay Club, P.O. Box 661067, Miami Springs, FL 33266.) www.chubcay.com. 34 units. $135–$170 double, $400 2-bedroom villa with kitchen, $500 3-bedroom villa with kitchen, $600 4-bedroom villa with kitchen. Discounts available for stays of a week or more. AE, MC, V. **Amenities:** Restaurant, 3 bars. *In room:* A/C, TV. No phone.

3 Andros ⭐⭐

The largest island in The Bahamas, Andros is one of the biggest unexplored tracts of land in the Western Hemisphere—and an excellent budget destination. Mostly flat, its 2,300 square miles are riddled with lakes and creeks, and most of the local residents, who still indulge in fire dances and go on wild boar hunts on occasion, live along the shore.

The most mysterious island in The Bahamas, Andros is 100 miles long and 40 miles wide. Its interior consists of a dense, tropical forest, really rugged bush, and mangrove country. The marshy and relatively uninhabited west coast is called the "Mud," and the east coast is paralleled for 120 miles by the second-largest underwater barrier reef in the world. The reef drops to more than a mile into the Tongue of the Ocean, or TOTO. On the eastern shore, this "tongue" is 142 miles long and 1,000 fathoms deep.

Lying 170 miles southeast of Miami and 30 miles west of Nassau, Andros is actually three major land areas: North Andros, Middle Andros, and South Andros. In spite of its size, Andros is very thinly populated (its residents number only around 5,000), although the tourist population swells it a bit. The temperature range here averages from 72°F to 85°F.

You won't find the western side of Andros written about much in yachting guides, because tricky shoals render it almost unapproachable by boat. The east coast, however, has miles of unspoiled beaches and is studded with little villages. Hotels that range from simple guest cottages to dive resorts to fishing camps have been built here. "Creeks" (we'd call them rivers) intersect the island at its midpoint. Also called "bights," they range in width from 5 to 25 miles, and they are dotted with tiny cays and islets.

The fishing at Andros is famous, establishing records for blue marlin caught offshore. Divers and snorkelers find that the coral reefs are among the most beautiful in the world, and everyone loves the pristine beaches.

A word of warning: Be sure to bring along plenty of mosquito repellent!

ESSENTIALS

GETTING THERE   Reaching Andros is not that difficult. **Bahamasair** (ℂ **800/222-4262** in the U.S.) has twice-daily 15-minute flights from Nassau to the airport at Andros Town in Central Andros (ℂ **242/368-2030**). There are also airports at San Andros in the north (ℂ **242/329-4224**); at Mangrove Cay (ℂ **242/369-0083**), and at Congo Town in South Andros (ℂ **242/369-2640**). Small carriers winging in to Andros include **Lynx Air International** (ℂ **888/596-9247**), coming from Fort Lauderdale to Congo Town 3 days a week.

Andros

To the Bimini Islands

To the Berry Islands

Morgan's Bluff

Nicholl's Town

Lowe Sound

Mastic Point

San Andros

Tongue of the Ocean

BARRIER REEF

Williams Island

ANDROS

Coakley Town
(or Fresh Creek)

Andros Town

Cargill Creek

Behring Point

North Bight

Moxey Town

Middle Bight

Mangrove Cay

Driggs Hill

Congo Town

Alcorine Cay

South Bight

Scuba Diving
Shipwreck
Reef
Airport

0   10 Miles

0   10 Kilometers

N

Florida

Abaco

Grand Bahama

Eleuthera

Paradise Island

Cat Island

Andros

San Salvador

Great Exuma

Long Island

Crooked Island

area of detail

Great Inagua

Turks and Caicos

Cuba

Make sure you know where you're going in Andros. For example, if you land at Congo Town on South Andros and you've booked a hotel in Nicholl's Town, you'll find connections nearly impossible at times (involving both ferryboats and a rough haul across a bad highway).

Andros's few available taxis know when the planes from Nassau are going to land, and they drive out to the airports, hoping to drum up some business. Taxis are most often shared. A typical fare from Andros Town Airport to Small Hope Bay Lodge is about $25.

Many locals, along with a few adventurous visitors, use the **mail boats** to get to Andros; the trip takes 5 to 7 hours across some beautiful waters. North Andros is serviced by the **MV Lisa J. II,** a mail boat that departs Potter's Cay Dock in Nassau heading for Morgan's Bluff, Mastic Point, and Nicholl's Town. It departs Nassau on Wednesday, returning to Nassau on Tuesday. The **MV Moxey** departs Nassau on Monday, calling at Long Bay Cays, Kemps Bay, and the Bluff on South Andros. It heads back to Nassau on Wednesday. For details about sailing and costs, contact the dockmaster at **Potter's Cay Dock** in Nassau (© **242/393-1064**).

ORIENTATION   Chances are your hotel will be in **North Andros,** in either Andros Town or Nicholl's Town. North Andros is the most developed of the three major Andros islands. **Nicholl's Town** is a colorful old settlement with some 600 people and several places serving local foods. Most visitors come to Nicholl's Town to buy supplies at a shopping complex. Directly to the south is **Mastic Point,** which was founded in 1781. If you ask around, you'll be shown to a couple of concrete-sided dives that offer spareribs and Goombay music. To the north of Nicholl's Town is **Morgan's Bluff,** namesake of Sir Henry Morgan, a pirate later knighted by the British monarch. **Andros Town,** with its abandoned docks, is another village, about 29 miles south of Nicholl's Town. Most visitors come to Andros Town to stay at the **Small Hope Bay Lodge** (see below) or to avail themselves of its facilities. The biggest retail industry, Androsia batik, is in the area, too. The scuba diving—minutes away on the barrier reef—is what lures much of the world to this tiny place; others come here just for the shelling. On the opposite side of the water is **Coakley Town.** If you're driving, before you get to Andros Town, you may want to stop and spend some restful hours on the beach at **Staniard Creek,** another old settlement on Andros that feels lifted from the South Seas.

Moving south to the second major landmass, **Central Andros** is smaller than either North or South Andros. The least developed of the three, the island is studded with hundreds upon hundreds of palm trees. The Queen's Highway runs along the eastern coastline, but the only thing about this road that's regal is its name. In some 4½ miles you can practically travel the whole island. It's truly sleepy, and for that very reason, many people come here to get away from it all. They don't find much in the way of accommodations, but there are some.

The third and last major land area, **South Andros** is the home of the wonderfully named **Congo Town,** where life proceeds at a snail's pace. The Queen's Highway, lined in part with pink-and-white conch shells, runs for about 25 miles or so. The island, as yet undiscovered, has some of the best beaches in The Bahamas, and you can enjoy them almost by yourself.

Another tiny island, undeveloped **Mangrove Cay** is an escapist's dream, attracting naturalists and anglers, as well as a few divers. It's separated from the northern and southern sections of Andros by bights. The settlements here only got electricity and a paved road in 1989. The best place for snorkeling and diving on Mangrove Cay is **Victoria Point Blue Hole** (any local can point you there if you're interested). Another village (don't blink as you pass through or you'll miss it) is **Moxey Town,** where you are likely to see fishermen unloading conch from the fishing boats. Ferries, operated free by the Bahamian government, ply back

---

(Fun Fact The Three-Toed, Red-Eyed Bahamian Elf

One of the legends of Andros island is that aborigines live in the interior. These were thought to be a lost tribe of native Arawaks—remnants of the archipelago's original inhabitants, who were wiped out by the Spanish centuries ago. Low-flying planes, looking for evidence of human settlements, have not turned up any indication to support this far-fetched theory. But who can dispute that *chickcharnies* (red-eyed Bahamian elves with three toes, feathers, and beards) live on the island? Even the demise of Neville Chamberlain's ill-fated sisal plantation was blamed on these mischievous devils.

The chickcharnie once struck terror into the hearts of superstitious islanders. They were supposed to live in the depths of the Androsian wilderness, making their nests in the tops of two intertwined palm trees. Tales are told of how many a woodsman in the old days endured hardship and misery because he thoughtlessly felled the trees that served as stilts for a chickcharnie nest. Like the leprechauns of Ireland, the chickcharnies belong solely to Andros. They are the Bahamian version of the elves, goblins, and fairies of other lands. Children are regularly threatened with them if they misbehave, and any business or domestic calamity is immediately attributed to their malevolent interference.

The origin of the legend is shrouded in mystery. One theory has it that the tales began in the late 19th century when a Nassau hunting enthusiast who wanted to protect his duck-hunting grounds in Andros invented the malicious elves to frighten off interlopers. Another claims that the myth was brought to The Bahamas in the early 1840s by bands of Seminoles fleeing Florida to escape white settlers (some of the Seminoles settled on the northern tip of Andros).

The most plausible explanation traces the chickcharnie to a now-extinct 3-foot-high flightless barn owl (*Tyto pollens*) that used to inhabit The Bahamas and West Indies. According to The Bahamas National Trust, the local conservation authority, such a bird, "screeching, hissing and clacking its bills in characteristic barn owl fashion, hopping onto its victims or pouncing on them from low tree limbs, would have been a memorable sight. And a frightening one."

The species may have survived here into historical times, and Andros, being the largest Bahamian landmass, was probably able to sustain *Tyto pollens* longer than the smaller islands. It is probable that the early settlers on Andros encountered such beasts, and it's possible that *Tyto pollens* was the inspiration for the chickcharnie. In any event, chickcharnie tales are still told in Andros, and there is no doubt that they will live on as a fascinating part of The Bahamas's cultural legacy.

and forth over the waters separating Mangrove Cay from South Andros. At the end of the road in North Andros, private arrangements can be made to have a boat take you over to Mangrove Cay.

GETTING AROUND   Transportation can be a big problem on Andros. If you have to go somewhere, it's best to use one of the local taxi drivers, though this can be a pricey undertaking.

The few rental cars available are in North Andros. These are few and far between, owing to the high costs of shipping cars to Andros. The weather also takes a great toll on the cars that are brought in (the salt in the air erodes metal), so no U.S. car-rental agencies are represented. Your best bet is to ask at your hotel to see what's available. It's not really recommended that you drive on Andros because roads are mainly unpaved and in bad condition, and gasoline stations are scarce. Outlets for car rentals come and go faster here than anybody can count. Currently, **AMKLCO Car Rental** at Fresh Creek (© 242/ 368-2056) rents a few cars, costing from $75 to $80 daily, with a $250 deposit required. Mileage is unlimited "unless you go too much."

You may want to rent a bike, but you'll experience the same bad roads you would in a rental car. Guests of the Small Hope Bay Lodge, Chickcharnie, and Mangrove Cay Inn can rent bikes at these hotels.

FAST FACTS   Banks are rare on Andros. There is one, the **Canadian Imperial Bank of Commerce** (© 242/329-2382), in San Andros, open Wednesday from 10am to 2pm.

The island has no big **post office,** although there is a post-handling office in the **Commissioner's Office** in Nicholl's Town on North Andros (© 242/ 329-2034). Hours are Monday through Friday from 9am to 4:30pm. Hotel desks will sell you Bahamian stamps. Make sure you mark cards and letters as airmail; otherwise, you'll return home before they do. Each little village on Andros has a store that serves as the post office.

Government-run clinics are at **North Andros** (© 242/329-2055) and at **Central Andros** (© 242/368-2038). Bring along whatever drugs (legal ones) or medicines you'll need while visiting Andros, because local supplies are very limited.

Call the **police** on **North Andros** at © 919; on **Central Andros** at © 242/ 368-2626; and on **South Andros** at © 242/369-0083.

WHERE TO STAY
At the hotels listed below, phone service is available only at the front desks.

IN ANDROS TOWN
Lighthouse Yacht Club & Marina   This complex lies at the mouth of Fresh Creek and features an 18-slip marina. A favorite of the yachting crowd, who needed such a place in Andros, the hotel rents comfortably furnished villas, each with a certain flair enhanced by Caribbean fabrics and ceiling fans. Accommodations open onto private patios and come with well-maintained private bathrooms with shower units. Scuba divers, snorkelers, and fishermen make ample use of the beach and the offshore waters, because the hotel lies near one of the world's largest barrier reefs and the deep Tongue of the Ocean.

The hotel has a good restaurant serving Bahamian and American dishes. Fishing charters are readily available, and scuba diving and snorkeling can easily be arranged through the hotel, which has a full dive shop on the premises. The package rates offered by the hotel, in addition to room and meals, include airport pickup.

Andros Town, Andros, The Bahamas. ℂ **242/368-2308.** Fax 242/368-2300. www.androslighthouse.com. 20 units. $120–$140 double, $140 villa. MAP (breakfast and dinner) $40 per person extra. Ask about dive packages. AE, DC, DISC, MC, V. **Amenities:** Restaurant, bar, dive shop, marina, pool, 2 clay tennis courts. *In room:* A/C, TV, refrigerator.

IN BEHRING POINT

Tranquility Hill   At the eastern entrance to north Bight, this is a fisherman's haven, lying just a short drive from Middle and South Bights. Newly constructed, the rustic inn lies near miles and miles of virgin flats teaming with trophy-size bonefish. Numerous creeks and lakes also are found in the area where record catches have been made of grey snapper, tarpon, and jacks. There are also three "Sunken Rocks," with large colonies of barracuda, Spanish mackerel, and mutton snapper. Nearby is the third largest reef in the world, with a sea of dolphins, kingfish, wahoo, marlin, and tuna. Bedrooms are spacious and well-furnished with comfortable beds and bathrooms with shower units. Units are equipped with double or king-size beds. Meals are prepared Bahamian-style, and guess what's on the menu? Enough fish and seafood to delight, although the cook will also prepare special requests. Meals are served family-style.

Behring Point, Andros, The Bahamas. ℂ or fax **242/368-4132.** www.bahamas-mon.com/hotels/tranquil/. 11 units. Winter $350 double; off-season $323 double. Rates include meals. MC, V. **Amenities:** Dining room. *In room:* A/C, TV.

IN CARGILL CREEK

Andros Island Bonefishing Club *ℱ*   If Hemingway were around today and wanted to go bonefishing, you'd invite him here. This rustic lodge lies at the confluence of Cargill Creek, the Atlantic Ocean, and the eastern end of North Bight. It fronts a small protected creek, a short distance from a wadeable flat, and fishing boats can dock directly in front of the lodge. Constructed in 1988, this is a modern but rather bare-bones facility that draws more repeat guests than any other hostelry in The Bahamas. More than two dozen fishermen can stay here at any time in accommodations with queen-size beds, ample dresser and closet space, and ceiling fans. Several rooms also have satellite TV, and some units also contain a refrigerator. The club is the domain of Captain Rupert Leadon, who knows more fishing stories than anybody else in Andros.

Food is hearty and plentiful, with an emphasis on fresh seafood, including Bahamian lobster and conch. Service is family-style.

Cargill Creek, Andros Island, The Bahamas. ℂ **242/368-5167.** Fax 242/368-5235. www.bahamas-mon.com/hotls/abone/. 12 units. Year-round $935 per person 3 nights, $1,675 per person 5 nights, $2,445 per person 7 nights. Rates include all meals, all-day fishing with boat and guide. Room only $165 per person. MC, V. **Amenities:** Dining room, honor bar, laundry. *In room:* A/C.

IN FRESH CREEK

Small Hope Bay Lodge *ℱℱ*   This is the premier diving and fishing resort of Andros, and one of the best in the entire Bahamas, with a white sandy beach right at its doorstep. It's an intimate and cozy beachside cottage colony, where tall coconut palms line a lovely beach and a laid-back atmosphere always prevails. Its name comes from a prediction (so far, accurate) from pirate Henry Morgan, who claimed there was "small hope" of anyone finding the treasure he'd buried on Andros. There is a spacious living and dining room where guests congregate for conversations and meals. Andros Town Airport is a 10-minute taxi ride from the lodge. Spacious cabins, cooled by ceiling fans, are made of coral rock and Andros pine and are decorated with Androsia batik fabrics. Honeymooners like to order breakfast served on their water bed.

For groups of three or more, the resort has a limited number of family cottages, featuring two separate rooms connected by a single bathroom. Single travelers have a choice of staying in a family cottage with private accommodations (which is the same as per-person double occupancy) or staying in a regular cottage with private bathroom, which is $45 extra per person nightly.

The bar is an old boat, dubbed the *Panacea*. The food is wholesome, plentiful, and good—conch chowder, lobster, and hot johnnycake. The chef will even cook your catch for you or make up a picnic lunch. Lunch is a buffet; dinner, a choice of seafood and meat every night. Children under 12 dine in the game room. Drinks are offered on a rambling patio built out over the sea. Nightlife is spontaneous—with dancing in the lounge or on the patio, underwater movies, and water slides. Definitely do not wear a tie at dinner. Diving is the lodge's specialty. The owners have been diving for more than 3 decades, and their well-respected dive shop has sufficient equipment, boats, and flexibility to give guests any diving experience they want, including a resort course for beginners. If you'd rather fish, the lodge can hook you up with an expert guide, especially for bonefishing.

Fresh Creek, Andros, The Bahamas (P.O. Box 21667, Fort Lauderdale, FL 33335). (C) **800/223-6961** in the U.S. and Canada, or 242/368-2013. Fax 242/368-2015. 20 units. www.smallhope.com. Year-round $350–$470 double. Rates include all meals. Ask about dive packages. AE, MC, V. **Amenities:** Dining room, hot tub, massage, bikes for guests, library, laundry. *In room:* Ceiling fans. No phone.

IN NICHOLL'S TOWN
Green Windows Inn   Kenny Robinson and her husband, Patrick, run this small, laid-back hotel set in a landscape of fruit trees and palms, where guests like to take their after-meal walks. The small rooms are on the second floor of the two-story inn, over the restaurant and bar. A recent improvement at the inn is the installation of tiny private bathrooms (shower stalls) in every bedroom along with both ceiling fans and air-conditioning. The restaurant caters only to hotel guests, with mainly seafood and local food cooked to order. The beach is a 10-minute walk from the inn, and the Robinsons can arrange bonefishing and snorkeling trips.

Rawfon St. (P.O. Box 23076), Nicholl's Town, Andros, The Bahamas. (C) **242/329-2194**. Fax 242/329-2016. 10 units. $90 double. AE, MC, V. **Amenities:** On-site small grocery store and car rental agency. *In room:* A/C, TV.

ON MANGROVE CAY
Mangrove Cay Inn   This pleasant, well-managed inn belongs to a native son, Elliott Greene, who returned with his wife Pat after years of cold-weather life in Syracuse, New York, to establish this breezy motel a short walk from the center of Grants, the third-largest village on Mangrove Cay (Moxey Town and Burnt Rock, though tiny, are still larger). Positioned amid scrubland, in the geographic center of the 9-mile-long island, the hotel was built in the early 1990s, 2 years after the inn was established as an easygoing and affable restaurant.

Separated from Grant's Beach by a brackish lake, with a mysterious blue hole positioned beside the path connecting the hotel to the beach, the accommodations have cozy but completely unpretentious furnishings. Each unit contains a small bathroom with a shower stall. How do guests spend their time here? Veranda-sitting on a porch that runs the length of the building and overlooks the water; riding on any of the bicycles that the hotel rents for a fee of around $10 a day; snorkeling with the hotel's equipment on the outlying reef (waters offshore are particularly rich in natural sponges and spiny Caribbean lobster); hiking; hill climbing; and looking for chickcharnies. And if you're interested in

fishing excursions, the Greenes can hire a local fishing guide for a full-day outing (parties of up to four can go for about $300 a day).

The wing that contains the bedrooms is attached to a restaurant that serves a
combination of Bahamian and American food with specialties of cracked conch,
grilled grouper and snapper, burgers, and steaks. (It's open for breakfast, lunch,
and dinner, at virtually any hour that passersby happen to show up.)

c/o General Post Office, Grants, Mangrove Cay, Middle Andros, The Bahamas. © 242/369-0069. Fax
242/369-0014. www.mangrovecay.com. 12 units. $105 double. No credit cards. **Amenities:** Restaurant. *In
room:* A/C. No phone.

SOUTH ANDROS

Emerald Palms By-the-Sea *⋆*   Lodging at this laid-back place, 2 miles
from the Congo Town airport, is a lot like staying at a beachside ranch. The
accommodations are set on 5 miles of beachfront on an island that contains
10,000 palm trees. The hotel is casual—a place to get away from urban life and
rest your jangled nerves on a white-sand beach. Guests are treated like members
of the family.

The rooms are large and comfortable, with well-laid-out bathrooms with
adequate shelf space and shower stalls. This resort has some of the fanciest decorations in Andros, and some of the most special amenities, including lanai-
style rooms and four-poster beds with mosquito netting—all in all, a relaxed,
tropical ambience.

Scattered over the palm-studded property are hammocks and a freshwater
swimming pool. The dining room features Bahamian seafood, and outdoor
steak barbecues and seafood buffets are sometimes held. South Bight marina is
1½ miles away, serving as a yacht anchorage for anyone who arrives by boat. The
hotel will rent you a car or bike.

Driggs Hill, P.O. Box 800, South Andros, The Bahamas. © 800/742-4276 or 242/369-2661. Fax
242/369-2667. www.bahamaoutislands.com. 20 units. Winter $110 double; off-season $100 double. MAP
(breakfast and dinner) $40 per person extra. AE, MC, V. **Amenities:** Restaurant, pool, tennis court, shuffle-
board, laundry. *In room:* A/C, TV, minibar.

WHERE TO DINE

Andros follows the rest of The Bahamas in its cuisine. Conch, in all its many
variations, is the staple of most diets, along with heaping portions of peas 'n' rice
and johnnycake, and pig or chicken souse.

The best places to dine are at the major hotels, including those previously recommended: the **Chickcharnie Hotel,** Fresh Creek, near Andros Town (© 242/
368-2025); and if you're in South Andros, **Emerald Palms By-the-Sea,** outside
Congo Town (© 242/369-2661). Most guests book into these hotels on the
Modified American Plan, which takes care of breakfast and dinner but frees
them to shop around for lunch. At any of these hotels, a dinner will run around
$25 to $30 per person.

If you're touring the island during the day, you'll find some local spots that
serve food. If business has been slow at some of these little places, however, you
might find nothing on the stove. You take your chances. On Mangrove Cay, try
Dianne Cash's Ultimate Delight, Main Rd. (© 242/369-0430), where you
can sample Dianne's version of baked crab backs served with peas and rice. Don't
plan on dropping by this place without some kind of advance notification.

BEACHES, WATER SPORTS & OTHER OUTDOOR PURSUITS

Golf and tennis fans should go elsewhere, but if you want some of the best bonefishing and scuba diving in The Bahamas, head to Andros.

HITTING THE BEACH

The eastern shore of Andros, stretching for some 100 miles, is an almost uninterrupted palm grove opening onto beaches of white or beige sand. There are several dozen access points that lead to the beach along the eastern shore. The roads are unmarked but clearly visible. The clear, warm waters offshore are great for snorkeling.

FISHING

Andros ⊕⊕⊕ is called the "Bonefish Capital of the World." The actual capital is Lowe Sound Settlement, a tiny hamlet with only one road, 4 miles north of Nicholl's Town. Anglers come here to hire bonefish guides. **Cargill Creek** is one of the best places for bonefishing on the island; nearby, anglers explore the flats in and around the bights of Andros (some excellent flats, where you can wade in your boots, lie only 75 to 125 yards offshore).

Whether you're staying in North, Central, or South Andros, someone at your hotel can arrange a fishing expedition, since there are many local guides and charter companies. In particular, the **Small Hope Bay Lodge,** in Andros Town on North Andros (© **242/368-2013**), is known for arranging fishing expeditions for both guests and non-guests; a guide will take you out for superb bonefishing. They also offer fly, reef, and deep-sea fishing, and provide tackle and bait.

SCUBA DIVING & SNORKELING

Divers from all over the world come to explore the **Andros barrier reef** ⊕⊕⊕, which runs parallel to the eastern shore of the island. It's one of the largest reefs in the world, but unlike Australia's Great Barrier Reef, which is miles off the coast, the barrier reef of Andros is easily accessible, beginning a few hundred yards offshore.

One side of the reef is a peaceful haven for snorkelers and novice scuba divers, who report that the fish are tame (often a grouper will eat from your hand, but don't try it with a moray eel). The water here is from 9 to 15 feet deep.

On the other side of the reef it's a different story. The water plunges to a depth of a full mile into the awesome **TOTO (Tongue of the Ocean)** ⊕⊕⊕. One diver reported that, as an adventure, diving in the ocean's "tongue" was tantamount to a flight to the moon.

Myriad, multicolored marine life thrives on the reef, and it attracts nature lovers from all over the world. The weirdly shaped coral formations alone are worth the trip. This is a living, breathing garden of the sea, and its caves feel like cathedrals.

For many years the U.S. Navy has conducted research at a station on the edge of TOTO. The research center is at Andros Town. It is devoted to oceanographic, underwater weapons, and antisubmarine research. Called **AUTEC (Atlantic Undersea Testing and Evaluation Centre),** this is a joint U.S. and British undertaking.

Fun Fact The Bahamian Loch Ness Monster

When the Atlantic Undersea Testing and Evaluation Centre (AUTEC) first opened, Androsians predicted that the naval researchers would turn up **"Lusca."** Like the Loch Ness monster, Lusca reportedly had been sighted by dozens of locals. The sea serpent was accused of sucking both sailors and their vessels into the dangerous blue holes around the island's coastline. No one has captured Lusca yet.

Among other claims to fame, Andros is known for its **"blue holes** ☞**,"** which rise from the brine. Essentially, these are narrow, circular pits that plunge as much as 200 feet straight down through rock and coral into murky, difficult-to-explore depths. Most of them begin under the level of the sea, although others appear unexpectedly—and dangerously—in the center of the island, usually with warning signs placed around the perimeter. Scattered at various points along the coast, they can be reached either in rented boats or as part of a guided trip. The most celebrated blue hole is Uncle Charlie Blue Hole, mysterious and fathomless, and once publicized by Jacques Cousteau. The other blue holes are almost as incredible.

One of these blue holes, called **Benjamin's Blue Hole,** is named after its discoverer, George Benjamin. In 1967, he found stalactites and stalagmites 1,200 feet below sea level. What was remarkable about this discovery is that stalactites and stalagmites are not created underwater. This has led to much speculation that The Bahamas are actually mountaintops, all that remains of a mysterious continent that sank beneath the sea (perhaps Atlantis?). Although Cousteau made a film—making the Blue Holes of Andros internationally famous—most of the blue holes, like most of the surface of the island itself, remain unexplored. Tour boats leaving from Small Hope Bay Lodge will take you to these holes.

As for snorkeling, you might head a few miles north of Nicholl's Town, where you'll find a crescent-shaped strip of white-sand beach, along with a headland, **Morgan's Bluff,** honoring the notorious old pirate himself. If you're not a diver, and can't go out to the Andros Barrier Reef off the shorefront at Fresh Creek and Andros Town, you can do the second-best thing and snorkel near a series of reefs known as "The Three Sisters." Sometimes, if the waters haven't turned suddenly murky, you can see about a dozen feet down—all the way to the sandy bottom. The schools of elkhorn coral are especially dramatic here.

Since **Mangrove Cay** is very underdeveloped, rely on the snorkeling advice and gear rentals you'll get from the dive shop at the **Seascape Inn** (☎ 242/ 369-0342). A two-tank dive costs $65 for guests of the hotel, or $75 for non-guests. Night dives are also possible ($50 for guests of the Seascape, or for non-guests).

Small Hope Bay Lodge, Fresh Creek, Andros Town, Central Andros (☎ 800/223-6961 in the U.S. and Canada, or 242/368-2013; www. smallhope.com), lies a short distance from the barrier reef, with its still-unexplored caves and ledges. A staff of trained dive instructors at the lodge caters to beginners and experienced divers alike. Snorkeling expeditions can be arranged, as well as scuba outings (visibility underwater exceeds 100 feet on most days, with water temperatures ranging from 72°F to 84°F). You can also rent gear here. To stay at the hotel here for 7 nights and 6 days, all-inclusive (meals, tips, taxes, airport transfers, and three dives a day), costs adults $1,585 or ages 12 to 17 $1,230. All guests are allowed access to the beachside hot-tub whirlpool, as well as to all facilities, such as free use of sailboats, Windsurfers, and bicycles.

EXPLORING THE ISLAND

Andros is largely unexplored, and with good reason—getting around takes some doing. With the exception of the main arteries, the few roads that exist are badly maintained and full of potholes. Sometimes you're a long way between villages or settlements, and if your car breaks down, all you can do is wait and hope that someone comes along to give you a ride to the next place, where you'll hope to find a skilled mechanic. If you're striking out on your own, make sure you have a full tank, because service stations are few and far between.

(Moments **What Would Tennessee Have Thought**

One custom in Andros is reminiscent of the Tennessee Williams drama *Suddenly Last Summer:* catching **land crabs,** which leave their burrows and march relentlessly to the sea to lay their eggs. The annual ritual occurs between May and September. However, many of the hapless crabs will never have offspring; both visitors and Androsians walk along the beach with baskets and catch the crustaceans before they reach the sea.

Not all of Andros can be explored by car, although there is a dream that as Andros develops, it will be linked by a road and causeways stretching some 100 miles or more. Most of the driving and exploring is confined to North Andros, and there, only along the eastern sector, going by Nicholl's Town, Morgan's Bluff, and San Andros.

If you're driving on Central or South Andros, you must stay on the rough **Queen's Highway.** The road in the south is paved and better than the one in Central Andros, which should be traveled only in an emergency or by a local.

Near Small Hope Bay at Andros Town, you can visit the workshop where **Androsia batik** is made (the same Androsia batik sold in the shops of Nassau and other towns). Androsia's artisans create their designs using hot wax on fine cotton and silk fabrics. The fabrics are then made into island-style wear, including blouses, skirts, caftans, shirts, and accessories. All hand-painted and hand-signed, the resort wear comes in dazzling red, blue, purple, green, and earth tones. You can visit the factory in Andros Town (© **242/368-2080**) Monday through Friday from 8am to 4pm.

Morgan's Bluff, at the tip of North Andros, lures men and women hoping to strike it rich. The pirate Sir Henry Morgan is supposed to have buried a vast treasure here, but it has eluded discovery to this day, although many have searched for it.

Bird-watchers are attracted to Andros for its varied **bird population.** In the dense forests, in trees such as lignum vitae, mahogany, Madeira, "horseflesh," and pine, lives a huge feathered population: many parrots, doves, and marsh hens. Ever hear a whistling duck?

Botanists are lured here by the **wildflowers** of Andros. It is said that some 40 to 50 species of wild orchids thrive here, some found nowhere else. New discoveries are always being made, as more and more botanists study the rich vegetation of Andros.

Red Bay Village is the type of discovery that continues to make Andros seem mysterious. An ancient tribe, headed by a chief and religiously following old rituals, was found living here as recently as a quarter of a century ago. The passage of time has made little difference to these people. Now the world comes to their door, and changes are inevitable; although the people still follow their ancient customs. The village, it is believed, was settled sometime in the 1840s by Seminoles and blacks fleeing slavery in Florida. The village is located off the northwestern coast of Andros. A causeway now connects the village to the mainland, and tourists can visit. You can reach Red Bay Village by road from Nicholl's Town and San Andros. You should be polite and ask permission before indiscriminately photographing these people.

7

The Abaco Islands

Called the "top of The Bahamas," the Abaco Islands compose the northernmost portion of the nation. This boomerang-shaped mini-archipelago is 130 miles long and consists of both Great Abaco and Little Abaco, as well as a sprinkling of cays. The islands are about 200 miles east of Miami and 75 miles north of Nassau.

People come here mainly to explore the outdoors, and the **sailing** ⊛⊛ and **fishing** ⊛⊛ are spectacular. The diving is excellent, too, and there are many lovely, uncrowded beaches. The Abacos are definitely a world apart from the glitzy pleasures of Freeport/Lucaya, Nassau, or Paradise Island.

Many residents of the Abacos descend from Loyalists who left New England after the American Revolution. Against a backdrop of sugar-white beaches and turquoise water, their pastel-colored clapboard houses and white-picket fences retain the Cape Cod architectural style of the first settlements on Abacos. One brightly painted sign in Hope Town says it all: SLOW DOWN. YOU'RE IN HOPE TOWN. The same could be said for all the Abacos.

The Abacos, with many first-rate resorts, are the most visited of the Out Islands. The weather is about 10°F warmer here than in southern Florida, but if you visit in January or February, remember that you're not guaranteed beach weather every day (remember, Miami and Fort Lauderdale, even Key West, can get chilly at times). When winter squalls hit, temperatures can drop to the high 40s in severe cases. Spring in the Abacos, however, is one of the most glorious and balmy seasons in all the islands. In summer it gets very hot around noon, but if you act as the islanders do and find a shady spot to escape the broiling sun, the trade winds will cool you off.

Yachties call the Abacos the "world's most beautiful cruising grounds" (though the Exumas are another serious contender). Excellent marine facilities, with guides, charter parties, and boat rentals, are available on Great Guana Cay, Green Turtle Cay, Hope Town, Marsh Harbour, Treasure Cay, and Walker's Cay. Sunfish, Sailfish, Hobie Cats, and Morgan bareboats are available. In fact, Marsh Harbour is the bareboat-charter center of the northern Bahamas. There you can rent a boat with everything but the crew. You may want to rent a small boat, pack a picnic (or have it done for you by any of the below-listed hotels that provide food service), and head for one of the uninhabited cays just big enough for two.

Anglers from all over the world come here to test their skill against blue marlin, kingfish, dolphinfish, yellowfin tuna, sailfish, wahoo, amberjack, and grouper. Fishing tournaments abound at Walker's Cay. There are plenty of Boston Whalers for bottom fishing and Makos for reef fishing and trolling, and you can also rent cruisers for deep-sea fishing.

Scuba divers can plumb the depths and discover the Abacos' caverns, inland "blue holes," coral reefs, and gardens, along with marine preserves and wrecks. Many scuba centers feature night dives. You can find top-rated outfits in Marsh Harbour, Hope Town, Treasure Cay, and Walker's Cay that offer NAUI/PADI instructors and a full line of equipment sales, rentals, and air fills.

ABACOS ESSENTIALS

GETTING THERE

BY PLANE   Three airports are found in the Abacos: **Marsh Harbour** (the major one, on Great Abaco Island), **Treasure Cay,** and **Walker's Cay.** The official points of entry are Marsh Harbour, Treasure Cay, Walker's Cay, and Green Turtle Cay (New Plymouth). Green Turtle Cay doesn't have an airstrip, but many members of the yachting crowd clear Customs and Immigration there.

Many visitors arrive from Nassau or Miami on **Bahamasair** (© 800/ 222-4262 or 242/367-2095). Flight schedules change frequently in The Bahamas, but you can usually get two to three daily flights out of Nassau, going first to Marsh Harbour, then on to Treasure Cay. If you're in West Palm Beach or Miami, you can often take a direct morning flight to Marsh Harbour and Treasure Cay.

Other connections include **American Eagle** (© 800/433-7300 or 242/367-2231), with two daily flights from Miami to Marsh Harbour; **Air Sunshine** (© 242/367-2800 in Marsh Harbour or 242/365-8900 in Treasure Cay), flying from Fort Lauderdale to both airports; and **Continental Connection** (© 800/231-0856 or 242/367-3415 in Marsh Harbour, 242/365-8615 in Treasure Cay), which flies to Marsh Harbour and Treasure Cay from several Florida locales. Smaller carriers include **U.S. Airways Express** (© 800/622-1015), winging into both airports from Palm Beach and Orlando, and **Twin Air** (© 954/359-8266), flying from Fort Lauderdale to both Treasure Cay and Marsh Harbour.

BY BOAT   The mail boat **MV *Captain Gurthdean*** sails on Tuesday from Nassau to Hope Town, Marsh Harbour, Turtle Cay, and Green Turtle Cay. It returns to Nassau on Friday. Trip time is 12 hours. **MV *Champion II*** leaves Nassau on Tuesday, arriving Wednesday at Sandy Point, Moore's Island, and Bullock Harbour, returning to Nassau on Thursday. For details on sailings (subject to change) and costs, contact the dockmaster at **Potter's Cay Dock** in Nassau (© 242/393-1064).

GETTING AROUND

BY TAXI   Unmetered taxis, which you often have to share with other passengers, meet all arriving flights. They will take you to your hotel if it's on the Abaco "mainland"; otherwise, they will deposit you at a dock where you can hop aboard a water taxi to one of the neighboring offshore islands, such as Green Turtle Cay or Elbow Cay. Most visitors use a combination taxi and water-taxi ride to reach the most popular hotels. From Marsh Harbour Airport to Hope Town on Elbow Cay, the cost is about $11 for the transfer. From the Treasure Cay Airport to Green Turtle Cay, the charge is about $14. Elbow Cay costs about $10 for the transfer.

It's also possible to make arrangements for a taxi tour of Great or Little Abaco. These, however, are expensive, and you don't really see that much either. It's better to sightsee on foot in one of the Loyalist settlements, such as New Plymouth, and there are lots of places where you can rent a bike.

BY FERRY   Mostly, you'll get around with **Albury's Ferry Service** (© 242/ 367-3147), which provides several ferry connections between Marsh Harbour and both Elbow Cay (Hope Town) and Man-O-War Cay, a 20-minute trip to

WALKER'S CAY

GRAND
CAY

STRANGER'S
CAY

Carter's Cay

Little Abaco
Island

SPANISH CAY

PENSACOLA CAYS

LITTLE
CAVE
CAY

CROSS
CAYS

Cooper's Town

GREEN TURTLE CAY

New Plymouth

Treasure Cay Airport

TREASURE
CAY

GREAT GUANA CAY

MAN
O' WAR
CAY

Marsh
Harbour

Tahiti Beach

THE MARIS

Marsh
Harbour Airport

Hope
Town

Elbow
Cay

MOORE'S ISLAND

Great Abaco
Island

Pelican Cays
Land & Sea Park

Pelican
Harbour

Casaurina
Point

Little Harbour

Cherokee

Eight Mile
Bay

GORDA CAY

Crossing Rocks

Sandy Point

Cross
Harbour

Bahamas National
Trust Sanctuary

Hole-in-the-Wall

0   15 Miles

0   15 Kilometers

N

Florida

Grand
Bahama

Abaco

area of detail

Eleuthera

Paradise
Island

Cat Island

Andros

San Salvador

Great
Exuma

Long Island

Crooked Island

Cuba

Great Inagua

Turks and
Caicos

✈ Airport

🐟 Scuba Diving

⚓ Shipwreck

either destination. The one-way fare is $8 adults, $4 children. (There are also ferries to Guana Cay.) The ferry docks are not far from the Marsh Harbour Airport; it's about a 10-minute, $14 cab ride for two passengers (plus $3 for each additional passenger).

For car-ferry service to Green Turtle Cay, see the Green Turtle Cay section below. There are ferries from Great Abaco Island to Green Turtle Cay, but those docks are a 35-minute $65 cab ride for up to four passengers from the Marsh Harbour Airport. It's better to fly to Treasure Cay rather than Marsh Harbour to do this, and then take a taxi to the ferry docks.

1 Marsh Harbour (Great Abaco Island)

The largest town in the Abacos, and the third largest in The Bahamas, Marsh Harbour lies on Great Abaco Island and is the major gateway to this island group.

Marsh Harbour is also a shipbuilding center, but tourism accounts for most of its revenues. Although the town doesn't have the quaint New England charm of either New Plymouth or Hope Town, Marsh Harbour has a shopping center and various other facilities not found in many Out Island settlements. The shoreline provides one of the finest anchorages in the Out Islands. There are good water-taxi connections, making this a popular place from which to explore some of the offshore cays, including Man-O-War and Elbow Cays.

We think of Marsh Harbour more as a refueling and transportation depot than as a true destination. However, because of its location—roughly in the center of the island—you may want to use it as a base, since it has a number of good inns. Several hotels will rent you a bike if you want to pedal around the town.

ESSENTIALS

GETTING THERE   See the introduction to this chapter. Marsh Harbour is the most easily accessible point in the Abacos from the U.S. mainland, with daily flights from Florida.

GETTING AROUND   You won't need a car to get around the town itself, but if you want to explore the rest of the island on your own, you can rent a car, usually for $70 a day or $350 per week (be prepared for bad roads, though). In Marsh Harbour call **A&P Rentals** at © 242/367-2655 or **Reliable Car Rentals** (© 242/367-3015) to see if any vehicles are available.

Rental Wheels of Abaco at Marsh Harbour (© 242/367-4643) will rent bikes at $8 a day or $35 a week, and also mopeds at $25 to $35 per day or $150 to $185 a week.

VISITOR INFORMATION   The **Abaco Tourist Office** is at Queen Elizabeth Drive in the commercial heart of town (© 242/367-3067). It's open Monday to Friday from 9am to 5:30pm.

FAST FACTS   There's a **Barclays Bank** on Don MacKay Boulevard (© 242/367-2152), plus several other banks and a **post office** (© 242/367-2571).

For medication, go to the **Chemist Shop Pharmacy,** Don MacKay Boulevard (© 242/367-3106), open Monday through Saturday 8:30am to 5:30pm. The best medical clinic in the Abacos is at the **Government Clinic,** Queen Elizabeth Road (© 242/367-2510); hours are Monday through Friday from 9am to 5pm. Dial © 242/367-2560 if you need the **police.**

SPECIAL EVENTS   In July, Marsh Harbour hosts **Regatta Week,** the premier yachting event in the Abacos, attracting sailboats and their crews from around the world. Every year, it's held sometime between Independence Day in the United States and Independence Day in The Bahamas (July 4 and July 10). A great number of the yachties participating in this event stay at the Green Turtle Club (see p. 220). For registration forms and more information, write to **Regatta Time in Abaco,** P.O. Box AB20551, Marsh Harbour, Abaco.

WHERE TO STAY

Abaco Beach Resort & Boat Harbour ⨏   This beachfront resort—the biggest and best in Marsh Harbour—is a good choice, especially if you're serious about diving or fishing. Extending over a sprawling acreage at the edge of town and fronting a small but lovely beach, it's a business with several different faces: the hotel, with handsomely furnished rooms that overlook the Sea of Abaco; the well-managed restaurant and bar; the Boat Harbour Marina, which has slips for 180 boats and full docking facilities; and a full-fledged dive shop.

Angler's Restaurant is one of Marsh Harbour's best (see separate recommendation under "Where to Dine," below). There's a swim-up bar and a beachfront bar serving light snacks and grog.

P.O. Box 20511, Marsh Harbour, Abaco, The Bahamas. ℭ **800/468-4799** in the U.S., or 242/367-2158. Fax 242/367-4154. www.abacobeachresort.net/. 82 units. Year-round $195–$275 double, $375 1-bedroom suite, $550 cottage for up to 4. AP (all meals) $60 extra per adult, $45 extra per child. AE, DISC, MC, V. To reach the place, you can take a taxi from Marsh Harbour Airport, a distance of 4 miles. A taxi will run you about $13, but be sure to agree on the price first with your driver. **Amenities:** Restaurant, 2 bars, 2 pools, 150-slip marina, 2 tennis courts, fitness center, laundry, fishing charters, full dive shop with dive master who arranges outings all over the Abacos, boat rentals, car and bicycle rentals, sightseeing tours. *In room:* A/C, TV.

Conch Inn Resort & Marina   Set at the southeastern edge of the harbor, this is a casual, one-story hotel leased on a long-term basis by one of the world's largest yacht-chartering companies, The Moorings. A number of small sandy beaches are within walking distance. Its motel-style, mid-size bedrooms are small, each with two double beds (roll-aways are available for extra occupants). Bathrooms are small but neatly kept with shower stalls. All units overlook the yachts bobbing in the nearby marina.

On the premises are an open-air swimming pool, fringed with palm trees, and a nearby branch of the Dive Abaco scuba facility. The on-site restaurant and bar (Bistro Mezzamare), under independent management, is recommended in "Where to Dine," below.

E. Bay St. (P.O. Box AB20469), Marsh Harbour, Abaco, The Bahamas. ℭ **242/367-4000.** Fax 242/367-4004. www.whatsonabaco.com. 9 units. $120 double. Extra person $10. MC, V. **Amenities:** Restaurant, bar, pool, dive shop, laundry, baby-sitting. *In room:* A/C, TV, refrigerator.

Lofty Fig Villas   This family-owned bungalow colony across from the Conch Inn overlooks the harbor. It doesn't have the services of a full-fledged resort, but it's good for families and self-sufficient types. Built in 1970, it stands in a tropical landscape with a freshwater pool and a gazebo where you can barbecue. Rooms have one queen-size bed and a queen-size hide-a-bed sofa, a fully tiled bathroom with shower, a dining area, a kitchen, and a private screened-in porch. Maid service is provided Monday through Saturday.

You're about a 10-minute walk from a supermarket and shops, and restaurants and bars lie just across the street. Marinas, a dive shop, and boat rentals are also close at hand. From the Lofty Fig, you have to walk, bike, or drive a mile east to a point near the Marsh Harbour ferryboat docks for access to a sandy beach and a snorkeling site (many visitors opt to go to Guana Cay for their day at the beach, via ferryboat).

P.O. Box AB20437, Marsh Harbour, Abaco, The Bahamas. ℂ and fax 242/367-2681. 6 villas. Dec 15–Sept 15 $120 daily or $780 weekly for 2. Extra person $25. Sept 16–Dec 14 $95 daily or $618 weekly for 2. Extra person $15. MC, V. *In-room amenities:* A/C, kitchen. No phone.

A NEARBY CHOICE

Nettie's Different of Abaco 𝒻 *(Finds)*　Set within the hamlet of Casuarina Point, 18 miles south of Marsh Harbour, this is a small family-managed bonefishing club surrounded by a wide deck and a garden. This ecologically conscious place was built at the edge of a saltwater marsh favored by a variety of birds, wild hogs, and iguana; it's a good choice for bird-watchers and superb for bonefishing enthusiasts. It's not luxurious, and it won't be to everyone's liking, but it's a peaceful place near good snorkeling and virgin beaches. The hotel is closely associated with several bonefishing guides in the neighborhood, any of whom can arrange full-day fishing excursions for around $275 per couple. (Not all equipment is included in this fee. Be sure you understand the arrangements thoroughly before you commit yourself.)

Each of the small to mid-size bedrooms has a screened-in porch, a ceiling fan, and simple furnishings, but only eight are air-conditioned. During your stay, you'll be in the midst of a closely knit, isolated community that's firmly committed to preserving the local environment and heritage. Nettie has created a living museum that takes you back through 100 years of the island's history.

There's a bar and restaurant where the staff will recite a selection of simple Bahamian fare to you before you sit down for your meal. Non-guests are welcome to drop in for two-course meals. The food is quite good.

Casuarina Point (P.O. Box AB20092), Abaco, The Bahamas. ℂ **242/366-2150.** Fax 242/327-8152. different@oii.net. 18 units. $1,314–$1,456 double for 4 nights, 3 days including bonefishing; $650–$800 double for 4 days, 3 days non-fishing. Rates include all meals. No credit cards. **Amenities:** Restaurant, bar, lap pool, Jacuzzi, boating, fishing, coin laundry, bikes for guests. *In room:* A/C. No phone.

WHERE TO DINE

If you'd like to go really casual, try **Island Bakery,** Don McKay Boulevard (ℂ **242/367-2129**), which has the best Bahamian bread and cinnamon rolls on the island, often emerging fresh from the oven. You might even pick up the makings for a picnic.

The best pizzas are sold at **Sapodilly's,** Queen Elizabeth Drive (ℂ **242/367-3498**); see below.

Angler's Restaurant 𝒻 BAHAMIAN/INTERNATIONAL　At the Boat Harbour, overlooking the Sea of Abaco, this is the main restaurant of the town's major resort. With a nautical theme and Bahamian decor, it showcases the cuisine of Austrian-born chef Dietmar Uiberreiter. Within a few steps of your seat, dock pilings rise from the water, yachts and fishing boats come and go, and the place is open and airy. The menu changes daily, but fresh seafood, which the chef prepares with finesse, is always featured, along with a well-chosen selection of meat and poultry dishes. Begin with spicy lobster bisque, or perhaps a timbale of grilled vegetables or crab Rangoon, served on bean-sprout slaw with a pineapple-coconut sauce. Main dishes often dance with flavor, notably the lobster stir in a mango chili sauce, or the guava-glazed charred lamb chops. The freshly caught red snapper we were recently served had just the right infusion of fresh basil.

In the Abaco Beach Resort & Boat Harbour, Marsh Harbour. ℂ **242/367-2158.** Reservations recommended for dinner. Main courses $14.50–$29.50. AE, MC, V. Daily 7:30–10:30am, 11:30am–2:30pm, and 6:30–10pm.

Bistro Mezzamare 𝒻 BAHAMIAN/ITALIAN　Only the Angler's Restaurant (see above) is more sophisticated and international than this winning choice. Set

Moments   A Taste of the Abacos

In Marsh Harbour, conch salad is sold right on the docks. "It'll make a man out of you," one local vendor tells everybody, even if the person is a woman. If you stick around long enough, you'll see Billy Thompson coming by in his little truck. He is said to make the world's best home-made soursop-and-mango ice cream.

adjacent to the Conch Inn and the upscale marina facilities of The Moorings, it attracts a lot of yachties and visiting professional athletes. The menu includes shrimp and crabmeat salad, lobster salad, seafood platters, at least four preparations of grouper and snapper, and just about everything a chef could conceivably concoct from a conch. The regulars don't even have to consult the menu; they just ask, "What's good?" on any given night. Many diners gravitate to the succulent pasta dishes, such as penne mirella (with shiitake mushrooms). If you're frittering away a few hours, drop in for a "Horny Conch," a rum-based drink with secret ingredients. The bar, set beneath an octagon gazebo near the piers, is a fine place to meet people.

At the Conch Inn (The Moorings), Bay St. © 242/367-4444. Lunch salads, sandwiches, and platters $7–$12; dinner main courses $14.75–$22.50. MC, V. Wed–Mon 8am–9:30pm, Tues 8am–3pm.

Flippers Restaurant BAHAMIAN/AMERICAN   This is a straightforward and uncomplicated diner-style restaurant, without the flair and pizzazz of Sapodilly's, Mangoes, or Wally's. It was established in the town's biggest shopping center in the late 1990s, with a well-scrubbed, no-nonsense decor that includes ceramic-tile floors, plastic-laminate bar tops, and half paneling. Menu items include burgers, sandwiches, and platters of grouper, shrimp, steak, chicken, and lobster.

Memorial Plaza. © 242/367-4657. Reservations not accepted. Lunch main courses $3.60–$5.75; dinner main courses $16–$21. AE, MC, V. Mon 8am–3pm, Tues–Sat 8am–9:30pm, Sun noon–3pm.

The Jib Room BAHAMIAN/AMERICAN   This funky restaurant/bar is a hangout for local residents and boat owners who savor its welcoming spirit. The Jib Room Restaurant is downstairs, and the canopied Jib Room Bar is upstairs. If you want the house-special cocktail, a Bilge Burner, get ready for a head-spinning combination of apricot brandy, rum, coconut juice, and vodka. Sunday night brings Jib's steak barbecue, when as many as 300 steaks are served. The only other dinner option is Wednesday, when grilled baby back ribs might be the featured dish of the day. Other choices include a seafood platter, New York strip steak, and broiled lobster—and yes, you've had it all before in better versions, but dishes are well-prepared. Go for the convivial atmosphere rather than the food.

Marsh Harbour Marina, Pelican Shores. © 242/367-2700. Lunch platters $5–$9 each; fixed-price dinners $18–$22. AE, MC, V. Thurs–Sat 11am–3pm; dinner Wed and Sun 7–11pm.

Mangoes Restaurant ✦ BAHAMIAN/AMERICAN   Set near the harbor-front, in one of the town's most distinctive buildings, Mangoes is the best, and certainly the most popular, restaurant on the island, attracting both yachties and locals. It boasts a cedar-topped bar and a cathedral ceiling that soars above a deck jutting out over the water. Somehow the chefs seem to try a little harder here, offering a typical grilled chicken breast, for example, but adding a hint of garlic and ginger. Pork tenderloin gets into the island spirit, coated with mango sauce, and the veal piccata in white wine and lemon juice shows continental flair. Our faithful friend, grilled grouper, is dressed up a bit with black olives, tomatoes, and onions Provençale-style, and barbecued baby back ribs and cracked conch make an appearance as well. Your best bet, as in nearly all Bahamian restaurants, is probably the fresh catch of the day. At lunch you can sample their locally famous "conch burger."

Front St. ✆ **242/367-2366.** Reservations recommended. Lunch $8.50–$12; main courses $18–$25. AE, MC, V. Mon–Sat 11:30am–2:30pm and 6:30–9pm. Bar daily 11:30am–midnight.

Mother Merle's Fishnet ✈ (Finds) BAHAMIAN   Many of the meals eaten aboard the yachts and sailing craft in the nearby harbor are prepared here. There's no dining room on the premises, so don't expect a place to sit and linger, although the well-prepared food, if you don't mind hauling it off to another venue, makes the limitations most palatable. The setting is a cement house on the town's main street. Inside, you'll find the gentle but aging matriarch Merle Williams, who is assisted by her able-bodied daughters, Angela and Shirley. As Mother Merle tells it, all Bahamian women are good cooks, a bit of an exaggeration, but you'll believe her words when you taste her family's three different preparations of chicken, all prepared by secret family recipes. Locals swear that Mother Merle makes the best cracked conch in the Abacos, and she's also known for her three different preparations of grouper.

Dundas Town. ✆ **242/367-2770.** Take-out service only. Main courses $11–$17. No credit cards. Mon–Sat 6:30–10:30pm.

Sapodilly's Bar & Grill BAHAMIAN   Marsh Harbour's newest restaurant occupies an open-air pavilion across the road from the harborfront, in an area of town known as "the tourist strip." Even if you eventually head into the high-raftered interior dining room, take time out for a drink or two on the covered open-air deck, surrounded by vibrant Junkanoo colors and a crowd of local hipsters, yacht owners, marina workers, and businessmen visiting from other parts of The Bahamas. Lunch might consist of grilled fish sandwiches, burgers, salads, and quiche. Dinners are more elaborate, with 12-ounce New York strip steak, a flavor-filled shrimp kebabs in teriyaki sauce, and zesty curried fillets of grouper. There's live music every Friday and Saturday from 8 to 11pm.

E. Bay St. ✆ **242/367-3498.** Reservations recommended. Lunch platters and sandwiches $5–$10; dinner main course $17–$24. AE, MC, V. Tues–Sun 11:30am–3pm and daily 6–9pm; bar daily 11am–midnight.

Wally's ✈ BAHAMIAN/INTERNATIONAL   This eatery occupies a tidy pink colonial villa on a lawn dotted with hibiscus, across the street from the water. There are an outdoor terrace, a boutique, and an indoor bar and dining area filled with Haitian paintings. The special drink of the house is a Wally's Special, containing four kinds of rum and a medley of fruit juices. The chef prepares the best Bahamian cracked conch at Marsh Harbour, as well as tender filet mignon, lamb chops, tarragon chicken, and an excellent version of smothered grouper. Main dishes come with a generous house salad and vegetables. The place really shines at lunchtime, when things can get very busy as hungry diners devour dolphinfish burgers, several kinds of chicken platters, and some well-stuffed sandwiches. Part of the style here comes courtesy of sisters Barbara and Maureen Smith, who head to Paris every fall and bring their culinary discoveries back to their enterprise in Marsh Harbour.

E. Bay St. ✆ **242/367-2074.** Reservations recommended for dinner. Lunch sandwiches and platters $9.50–$10.75; dinner main courses $19.75–$28.50. AE, MC, V. Mon–Sat 11:30am–3pm; Fri–Sat only 6–9pm, except between Mar and July when it's open Tues–Sat 6–9pm. Closed 6 weeks during Sept–Oct.

WATER SPORTS & OTHER OUTDOOR PURSUITS

All the innkeepers at Marsh Harbour can help fix you up with the right people or equipment for whatever sport you want to pursue, whether you just want to rent snorkel gear or you're looking for a full-day's fishing charter. For variety, you can also take the ferry over to Hope Town and check out the facilities and out-fitters there.

BOAT CHARTERS

Ask about the depth of the harbor before you rent, or even more importantly, before you attempt to navigate your way in or out of Marsh Harbour, since Hurricane Floyd changed the configuration of the channel. Yachts with deep drafts have reported trouble getting in and out of the port recently.

If you'd like to try bareboating in The Bahamas—seagoing without captain or crew—**Abaco Bahamas Charters,** 505 Beachland Blvd. (© 800/ 626-5690; fax 242/366-0151), can set you up; weekly charters of a 44-foot boat begin at $2,350, with a $1,000 deposit required. Only experienced sailors can rent.

The Moorings (© 800/535-7289 or 242/367-4000) is one of the leading charter sailboat outfitters in the world. It operates from an eagle's nest perch behind the Conch Inn Resort and Marina, overlooking a labyrinth of piers and wharves—at least 75 berths, with more on the way—where hundreds of upscale watercraft are tied up (many of them are for rent). With one of its vessels, you can enjoy short sails between the islands, stopping at white sandy beaches and snug anchorages. Yacht rentals generally range from $335 to $1,230 a day, with a skipper costing another $144 per day, and an onboard cook (if you want one) priced at an additional $124 per day.

For the more casual boater, **Sea Horse Boat Rentals,** at the Abaco Beach Resort (© 242/367-2513), offers some of the best rentals. An 18-foot Boston Whaler rents for $145 per day, and you can also book a 22-foot Privateer for $165 per day. Other vessels are also for rent, and all boats are equipped with a Bimini top, coolers, a compass, and a swimming platform, along with life jack-ets, a paddle, docking lines, and other equipment. Open daily from 8am to 5pm.

SNORKELING & SCUBA DIVING

Sea Horse Boat Rentals at the Abaco Beach Resort/Boat Harbour Marina (© 242/367-2513) also rents snorkel gear. One of the best places to snorkel, with a colorful reef, moray eels, and a plethora of beautiful rainbow-hued fish, is **Mermaid Beach.**

⟨Moments In Pursuit of the Rare Green Parrot

The Bahamian government set aside a 20,500-acre stretch of pine forest and scrubland as the **Abaco National Park** 🌠 in May of 1994. Its bound-aries are not marked with signs, but if you're driving, head south from Marsh Harbour, and after about 40 miles, follow the signs to HOLE IN THE WALL LIGHTHOUSE, which is the park's centerpiece. The sections of the park that are not pine forest resemble a sunbaked lunar landscape; there's no caretaker, no phone, and no visitors center. Despite its harshness, the park is a nesting ground for the colorful Bahamas parrot, a green fellow with additional markings of yellow, black, and red.

A Secret Hideaway: Little Harbour

In the Abaco gift and souvenir shops, you'll see a remarkable book, *Artist on His Island*, detailing the true-life adventures of Randolph and Margot Johnson, who lived a Swiss Family Robinson–type adventure with their three sons. Arriving on this southerly point of the Abacos aboard their old Bahamian schooner, the *Langosta*, they lived in one of the natural caves on the island until they eventually erected a thatched dwelling for themselves.

That was in 1951. Now the Johnsons, including son Pete, have achieved international fame as artists and sculptors—though they still live on their own Little Harbour Island, a cay shaped like a circle, with a white-sand beach running along most of it.

If you ask, your hotel in Marsh Harbour may arrange for you to visit the island, which is serviced by Albury's Ferry. This is the southernmost stop of the ferry line. Because the island is private property, you are asked to treat it as if it's someone's home you're visiting—as indeed it is.

On the island is a foundry in which Mr. Johnson, using an old "lost-wax" method, casts his bronze sculptures, many of which are in prestigious galleries today. Mrs. Johnson creates porcelain figurines of island life—birds, fish, boats, and fishers. She also works in glazed metals. They welcome visitors at their studio daily from 10 to 11am and from 2 to 3pm. It's also possible to purchase their art, which comes in a wide price range. Call (℃ **242/367-2720** for more information.

Scuba divers might try to check out the nearby **Pelican Cays Land and Sea Park** ⚓ nearby. There are no organized excursions, but Dive Abaco (see below) is the best source of information and might arrange a trip there. You can also drive down to the park by following the road immediately south of Marsh Harbour and then turning east at the sign leading toward the park. There are several areas here with small beaches suitable for swimming. The easiest jumping-off point is at Pelican Harbour.

Dive Abaco, Marsh Harbour (℃ **800/247-5338** in the U.S., or 242/367-2787), can provide services as simple as renting snorkel gear or as in-depth as offering full dive trips to tunnels and caverns in the world's third-longest barrier reef. There are resort courses for uncertified novice divers; these are all inclusive for $150. Two-tank dives, including tanks and weights for certified divers, are $70. Trips depart daily at 9:30am, and afternoon trips are dictated by demand. Shop hours are daily from 8:30am to 5pm; ask for owner-operator Keith Rogers.

SHOPPING

Solomon's Mines, Queen Elizabeth Drive, at the entrance to the Abaco Beach Resort (℃ **242/367-3191**), is a gem of a store that serves as a fine-gifts shop and a not-so-run-of-the-mill souvenir outlet. Its merchandise includes fine china and crystal from Waterford and Lenox, fine watches, perfumes, plus locally designed gold and silver Bahamian jewelry. There are souvenirs galore, as well as a boutique that features bathing suits and evening wear for women, and sportswear for men. Another possibility, **Cultural Illusions,** Memorial Plaza (℃ **242/**

367-4648), carries a collection of Androsia batik clothing, along with some local crafts. For that souvenir item, there is **Barefoot Gifts,** Queen's Hwy. (© **242/367-3596**).

2 Elbow Cay (Hope Town) 🌟

Elbow Cay is noted for its spectacular white-sand beaches. One of The Bahamas's best, **Tahiti Beach** 🌟🌟 lies in splendid isolation at the far end of Elbow Cay island, with sparkling waters and powdery white sands. Access is possible only on foot, by riding a rented bicycle across sand and gravel paths from Hope Town, or by private boat.

The cay's largest settlement is **Hope Town,** a little village with a candy-striped, 120-foot lighthouse, the most photographed attraction in the Out Islands. (You can climb to the top of the lighthouse for a sweeping view of the surrounding land and water.) Hope Town seems frozen in time. Like other off-shore cays of the Abacos, it was settled by Loyalists who left the new United States and came to The Bahamas to remain subjects of the British Crown. Its clapboard, saltbox cottages are weathered to a silver gray or painted in pastel colors, with white-picket fences setting them off. The buildings may remind you of New England, but this palm-fringed island has a definite South Seas flavor.

The island is almost free of cars. In exploring Hope Town, you can take one of two roads: "Up Along" or "Down Along," which runs along the water.

ESSENTIALS
GETTING THERE   You can reach Elbow Cay in about 40 minutes, via regularly scheduled ferry service from Marsh Harbour on Great Abaco. A one-way fare is $8, round-trip is $12, and service is three times daily. Call **Albury's Ferry Service** at © 242/365-6010 for more information.

FAST FACTS   Visitors and residents must go to Marsh Harbour for medical attention. There is a local **post office** (© 242/366-0098) at the head of the upper public dock, but expect mail sent from here to take a long time. Hours are Monday through Friday from 9am to 1:30pm and from 2:30 to 5pm.

WHERE TO STAY
Abaco Inn 🌟   A sophisticated little hideaway, set about 2 miles south of Hope Town, the Abaco Inn faces a lovely sandy beach on White Sound. It was radically overhauled and improved after the devastation of the 1990s hurricanes. It is more of a resort than its main rivals, Hope Town Hideaways and Club Soleil Resort and Marina. An informal barefoot elegance and a welcoming spirit prevail. The resort nestles on the narrowest section of Elbow Cay, between the crashing surf of the jagged eastern coast and the sheltered waters of White Sound and the Sea

---

Fun Fact Bahama Mama Malone

Malone seems to be the most popular name here. The founding mother of the town circa 1783 (perhaps 1775) was Wyannie Malone, who came here as a widow with four children. Her descendants are still a big part of the population of 500 full-time residents. A museum on Queen's Highway (no phone) is dedicated to Wyannie's memory and contains exhibits that trace the rich history of the cay. It's generally open from 10am to noon, but you can't be sure. Donations are welcome.

of Abaco to the west. From the cedar-capped gazebo, you can gaze out over the rocky tidal flats of the Atlantic. Excellent snorkeling is close at hand.

The mid-size accommodations are arranged in a crescent facing the beach. They're set amid palms and sea grapes, and each has its own hammock placed conveniently nearby for quiet afternoons of reading or sleeping. Your room will have a ceiling fan, a kitchenette, and a comfortable decor of white tile floors, sliding glass doors, and conservative furniture.

A modern, rambling clubhouse with a fireplace serves as both the social center and the most appealing restaurant/bar on the island (see "Where to Dine," below).

White Sound, Hope Town, Elbow Cay, Abaco, The Bahamas. (C) 800/468-8799 in the U.S., or 242/366-0133. Fax 242/366-0113. www.abacoinn.com. 22 units. Year-round $140–$165 double, $215 villas for 2. Extra person $25. AE, DISC, MC, V. **Amenities:** Restaurant, bar, pool, live entertainment, baby-sitting, coin laundry, bikes, airport shuttle, boating and fishing arranged. *In room:* A/C, kitchenette. No phone.

Club Soleil Resort   Abaco Inn may have better accommodations, but nothing surpasses the tranquillity of this inn. Because of its isolated position near the lighthouse on the western edge of Hope Town's harbor, the only way to get to this Spanish-style resort is by boat. Once there, you're just a short walk from some lovely sandy beaches. If you bring your own boat, you can moor it at this hotel's marina, but if you just happen to have left your boat at home, call the owners. They will quickly arrange a free waterborne transfer from any nearby coastline you designate. Mid-size rooms with shower units are contained in a two-story, Mediterranean-inspired annex, and they overlook a swimming pool and the boats that moor in the harbor. Each room contains two double beds and a clean and tasteful decor. Significant renovations and improvements have been made to this place since the hurricane damage of 1999. The restaurant is covered separately under "Where to Dine," below.

Western Harbourfront, Hope Town, Elbow Cay, The Bahamas. (C) 242/366-0003. Fax 242/366-0254. www. clubsoleil.com. 7 units. Year-round $115 double per night, $1,000 per week for 2-bedroom apt with kitchen. AE, MC, V. Closed Sept. **Amenities:** Restaurant, bar, pool, dock. *In room:* A/C, TV, coffeemaker, hair dryer, refrigerator.

Hope Town Hideaways *(*   These complete island homes let guests live like locals, or at least like second-home owners. These gingerbread-trimmed villas, across the harbor from where ferryboats arrive from the Great Abaco "mainland," within the shadow of the town's red-and-white striped lighthouse, are part of a larger complex of privately owned homes, surrounded by grounds that are dotted with bougainvillea, mangoes, and citrus trees. The spacious villas sleep one or two couples (the limit is six guests per villa). Each has a big kitchen, a dining room, a living area with two single daybeds, and two bedrooms with queen-size beds and separate entrances. Each bedroom includes custom built-in beds, dressers, makeup vanities, reading lamps, a private bathroom for each bedroom, and direct access to a private deck. Owners Chris and Peggy Thompson oversee housekeeping services and arrange rental boats, guided fishing trips, picnics, island-hopping excursions, and scuba or snorkeling trips.

When you first arrive, you'll have to call the hotel, which will send an employee for you in a putt-putt motorboat. (There's no access to this place by road from the center of Hope Town.) After that, you'll be assigned any of four putt-putt motorboats (included in the cost of your villa rental) as a means of getting from your rented home to anywhere else in Hope Town. Within about 24 hours, you'll become adept at lashing your boat to the piers, wharves, and pilings of Hope Town, and you'll even be able to navigate your way around the harbor at night.

Hope Town, Elbow Cay, Abaco, The Bahamas. © **242/366-0224.** Fax 242/366-0434. www.hopetown.com. 4 units. Year-round $190 double, $275 triple or quad. Rates include use of motorboat during your stay. DISC, MC, V. *In-room amenities:* A/C, kitchenettes.

Sea Spray Resort and Villas   On 6 acres of landscaped grounds, 3½ miles south of Hope Town and near the southernmost tip of Elbow Cay, these beach-front villas are owned and operated by Monty and Ruth Albury, who run them in a welcoming, personal way. In the aftermath of 1999's Hurricane Floyd, two of the original six units were literally blown away, but the remaining four were renovated and brought back into proper working order. They have full kitchens and decks that overlook the water. Villas are spacious and comfortably furnished, each with a small bathroom containing a shower unit. In 2000, the original pier and marina facilities were repaired, and many more slips and amenities were added. The Alburys and their hardworking staff are happy to share their vast experience of what to see and do on Elbow Cay and in the Abaco area: You can bike, sail, go deep-sea fishing, snorkel, go bonefishing, or explore nearby deserted islands.

Sea Spray also operates a restaurant serving well-prepared food at all three meals while diners enjoy a view of the crashing surf and a weathered gazebo. Non-guests are welcome, too; if you phone in advance for a reservation, man-agement will send a van to collect you from Hope Town.

White Sound, Elbow Cay, Abaco, The Bahamas. © **242/366-0065.** Fax 242/366-0383. www.seasprayresort. com. 4 units. Year-round $180 per night or $950 weekly 1-bedroom apt, $291 per night or $1,750 weekly 2-bedroom apt. MC, V. **Amenities:** Restaurant, unlimited use of Sunfish, barbecue pit, free boat dockage (up to 23 ft.), pool, bikes and snorkel gear for rent. *In room:* A/C, kitchenette.

Turtle Hill Vacation Villas 🏃   On the outskirts of Hope Town, a trio of lux-ury villas lie just steps from a vast secluded beach where sea turtles return to nest. Fruit trees and other tropical foliage make this a secluded getaway. Each house sleeps six persons comfortably in two large bedrooms, with a queen-size sleeper sofa in the living room, plus a full bathroom, well-equipped kitchen, a spacious living and dining area, and both central air-conditioning and ceiling fans. Linen is provided, and there is a private dock nearby.

Between Abaco Sea and Hope Town, Hope Town, Abaco, The Bahamas. © **800/339-2124** in the U.S., or 242/366-0557. Fax 242/366-0557. www.turtlehill.com. 3 units. Winter $280–$380; off-season $190–$270. AE, MC, V. **Amenities:** Freshwater pool and barbecue grills. *In room:* A/C, kitchen. No phone.

WHERE TO DINE

Abaco Inn 🏃 BAHAMIAN/AMERICAN   Flavor-filled food is served in a breezy, almost elegant waterfront setting. The chef prepares lunch dishes such as conch chowder, pasta primavera, and salads with delectable homemade dressings laced with tarragon and other herbs. The dinner menu changes frequently but usually features seafood, vegetarian, and meat dishes, each expertly seasoned and well-prepared. Typical meals are likely to begin with seafood bisque or vichys-soise, followed by coconut grouper (a house specialty), spinach fettuccine Alfredo, roasted lamb with herbs and mint sauce, or, our favorite, broiled red snapper with a light salsa. The key lime, crème brûlée, and coconut pies are delectable. The inn will send a minivan to pick you up from other parts of the island if you phone in advance.

About 2 miles south of Hope Town. © **242/366-0133.** Reservations required for dinner. Lunch sandwiches, salads, and platters $7–$14; dinner main courses $16–$35. DISC, MC, V. Daily 8–10:30am, noon–3pm, and 6:30–8:30pm.

Club Soleil Resort BAHAMIAN/SEAFOOD   This pleasant restaurant lies within a sunny Spanish-inspired building on the western side of Hope Town's harbor. To reach it from other points along Hope Town's harborfront, you'll either have to borrow or rent a motorboat, or phone the owners in advance to send a boat to meet you. Your choice of table is either inside the dining room or on a covered waterfront terrace. Lunch might include conch burgers, cheeseburgers, and an array of such salads as Niçoise and lobster.

The dinner menu usually features snapper, golden-fried grouper, or kingfish, cooked just right and with butter and garlic sauce. The broiled seafood platter served with lemon and garlic is another good choice. For those who don't want fish, either the rack of lamb Provençale or one of the excellent steaks should do the trick. The fixed-price Sunday brunch is always popular.

Western Harbourfront, Hope Town. ℭ 242/366-0003. Reservations recommended for dinner. Dinner main courses (including appetizers, salad, and soup) $13.95–$18.25; lunch main courses $7–$13. Tues–Sun 11:30am–2pm and 6–8:30pm.

Harbour's Edge ℱ BAHAMIAN Hope Town's best and most popular restaurant is set on piers above the water in a clapboard house. It's the island's lighthearted social center. The bar here has an adjacent waterside deck where you can moor if you arrive by boat, as many visitors do. Here and in the dining room as well, the crackle of VHF radio is always audible—boat owners and local residents often reserve tables on short-wave radio, channel 16.

Lunch includes such typical yet flavor-filled dishes as conch fritters, conch chowder, hamburgers, sandwiches, and conch platters. In the evening, dinners are also well-prepared—generous portions of chicken in white wine with potatoes, Greek or Caesar salad, pan-fried pork chops, char-grilled grouper, New York strip steak, fish in coconut milk, and more.

Hope Town, next to the post office. ℭ 242/366-0087. Reservations not accepted. Lunch main courses $8–$12; dinner main courses $19–$25. MC, V. Wed–Mon 11:30am–3pm and 6–9pm. Bar Wed–Mon 10am–midnight. Closed mid-Sept to mid-Oct.

Hope Town Harbour Lodge ℱ BAHAMIAN In one of the first lodges or inns ever built in Hope Town, this restaurant is still winning new friends, even those hard to please. At night, loving couples opt for a table on the cozy terrace with views of the harbor and the lights from the yachts. Menu items always taste better when preceded by one of those rum punches in the Wrecker's Bar overlooking the water. The menu is hardly inventive, but it's good, featuring the usual array of chicken, steaks, and pork chops. Occasionally a fisherman will bring in a big marlin that can be grilled to perfection. Bahamian lobster appears delightfully in a creamy fettuccine and the local grouper is fashioned into spring rolls, Chinese-style, and served with a mustard-laced chutney sauce. In the main dining area are found picture windows, rattan chairs, and nautical prints. During lunch, diners gravitate to the Reef Bar and Grill fronting the water.

Don't overlook the lodge as a possibility for rooms. It rents 19 comfortably furnished and air-conditioned doubles, with prices going from $120 to $160 all year. Accommodations lie on any of three floors, each with a patio or balcony, sliding glass doors, a small bathroom with shower stall, and wicker furnishings.

Hope Town. ℭ 242/366-0095. Reservations recommended for dinner. Lunch main courses $7–$15; dinner main courses $15–$35. MC, V. Daily 11:30am–2:30pm; Tues–Sun 6:30–9pm.

Rudy's Place ℱ ℱinds BAHAMIAN/AMERICAN Because of its isolated position, in a wooden house in a valley in the center of the island, this restaurant provides free transportation before and after dinner. It's owned by Rudy Moree, who prepares recipes handed down from his Bahamian grandmother. These, adapted to the tastes of his international clientele, might include crayfish tails

> ### *Finds* Exploring the Abacos by Boat
>
> The ideal way to explore the Abacos is by boat. **Island Marine,** Parrot Cay in Hope Town (✆ **242/366-0282;** fax 242/366-0282), will set you up. In one of its rental boats, you can cruise to the boatbuilding settlement of Man-O-War Cay, to artist Pete Johnson's bronze foundry-gallery in Little Harbour (see section 1, "Marsh Harbour (Great Abaco Island)," of this chapter), and to many uninhabited cays and deserted beaches where you can go shelling, exploring, and picnicking in peace.
>
> Small-boat rentals range from a 17-foot Boston Whaler to 23-foot Man-O-War boats, or even 22-foot Aquasports. Prices run from $90 to $135 per day or $500 to $800 per week. Island Marine is open daily from 8am to 5pm. It's a good idea to bring along documentation that shows you are qualified to handle a boat, although they're pretty casual about this. Island Marine will provide maps of the area.
>
> Resident Bahamian guides will also take you out in a rental boat or their own craft to enjoy bone-, reef-, or deep-sea fishing. Connections can be made through Island Marine or any of the island's hotel reception desks. Grouper, snapper, wahoo, yellowtail, dolphinfish, and kingfish abound in local waters.

baked with Parmesan and butter, a delectable broiled shrimp in a white wine and garlic sauce, or even a passable roasted duck in an orange sauce.

Center Line Rd. ✆ 242/366-0062. Reservations recommended. Fixed-price dinners $20–$30. MC, V. Mon–Sat 6:30–8:30pm (last order). Closed Sept–Oct.

SCUBA DIVING & OTHER WATERY ADVENTURES

Set about 20 steps south of Hope Town's post office, **Froggie's Out Island Adventure,** Harbour Road (✆ 242/366-0024), is the largest dive outfitter in the Abacos, with three boats (ranging from 35 to 55 ft. in length) that owner Tito Baldwin ("Froggie") uses to haul divers out to fabulous local dive sites. Beginners pay $90 for a half day, $100 for a full day, with a lesson included. Experienced divers with their own gear are charged $75 for a half-day excursion, $85 for a full-day excursion.

The company also organizes tours, from snorkel cruises to dolphin-watching trips. A full-day cruise out to Great Guana Cay costs $45 per person. An equivalent tour to Little Harbour, near the southernmost point of the Abacos, including visits to selected restaurants, bars, and an art gallery, also costs $45 per person. Froggie's Sunset Cruise, departing an hour before sunset and returning an hour after it's dark, costs $30 per person.

Dave's Dive Shop and Boat Rentals (✆ 242/366-0029) also rents boats and snorkel gear, and offers diving excursions.

SHOPPING

Of course, no one comes to Hope Town just to shop, but once you're here, you might want to pick up a souvenir. At **Kemp's Straw Market,** Hope Town, you can find some gift items made by local artisans.

The **Ebb Tide Gift Shop** (✆ 242/366-0088), the best-stocked gift shop in town, lies in a white clapboard house with yellow trim 1 block from the harbor.

Inside you'll find many treasures, including Androsia batiks made on Andros, costume jewelry, T-shirts, original watercolors, and fabrics sold by the yard.

3 Man-O-War Cay

Visiting here is like going back in time. The island has some lovely beaches, and many visitors come here to enjoy them—but it's best to leave your more daring swimwear at home. The people who call this island home are deeply religious and conservative. There is no crime—unless you bring it with you. No alcoholic beverages are sold on the island, although you can bring your own supply.

Like New Plymouth, Man-O-War is a Loyalist village, with similarities to a traditional New England town. The pastel clapboard houses, built by ships' carpenters and trimmed in gingerbread, are set off by freshly painted white-picket fences intertwined with bougainvillea.

The people here are basically shy, but they do welcome outsiders to their remote, isolated island. They are proud of their heritage, which includes a proud boat-building tradition, and many, especially the old-timers, have known plenty of hard times. Many of them are related to the "conchs" of Key West and, like them, are a tough, insular people who have exhibited a proud independence for many years.

Tourism has only just begun to infiltrate Man-O-War Cay. Because of the relative lack of hotels and restaurants, many visitors come over just for the day, often in groups from Marsh Harbour. If you do stay for a while, stop by the Man-O-War Marina to arrange your boat rentals and water sports; there's also a dive shop there.

GETTING THERE & GETTING AROUND

To reach Man-O-War Cay, you must cross the water from Marsh Harbour. **Albury's Ferry Service** (© **242/367-3147** in Marsh Harbour or **242/365-6010** in Man-O-War) leaves from a dock near the Abaco Beach Resort. The round-trip fare is $12 for adults and $6 for children ages 6 to 12. The ride takes about 45 minutes.

Except for a few service vehicles, Man-O-War Cay has almost no cars. If you want to explore farther than your own two feet will carry you, ask around and see if one of the locals will rent you a golf cart.

WHERE TO STAY

Schooner's Landing   Set in isolation on Man-O-War Cay's northeastern edge, this four-unit apartment complex is the only officially designated place to stay on the island. A seawall separates its lawns and hibiscus shrubs from the crashing surf, so swimmers and snorkelers meander a short distance down to the sands of a nearby beach. Each two-story unit contains a kitchen, ceiling fans, two private bathrooms, a TV that receives from an adjacent VCR machine only (you can rent videos at the hotel), and a summery decor of wicker and rattan furniture. Each comes with a small, tidily kept bathroom with a shower unit. There's no bar or restaurant, but either of two grocery stores on the island will deliver; most visitors opt to cook in, anyway.

Man-O-War Cay, Abaco, The Bahamas. © **242/365-6072.** Fax 242/365-6285. www.oii-net. 4 condos. $175 daily or $995 weekly. 3-day minimum stay required. AE, MC, V. **Amenities:** Private dock, barbecue grill, boating, fishing, laundry. *In room:* A/C, TV, VCR. No phone.

WHERE TO DINE

Man-O-War Marina Pavilion AMERICAN/BAHAMIAN   The sides of this wooden pavilion are open to the breezes and a view of the boats bobbing at the nearby harbor. A crowd of loyal boat owners and local residents is always here, enjoying the simple but savory cuisine of Marjorie Eldon. Monday to Thursday, the focus is on such time-favored staples as roasted chicken fingers, grilled fish, burgers, fried conch with peas 'n' rice, and steaks. On Friday and Saturday nights, however, many locals arrive for grilled lamb, fish, steaks, or chicken, and the place is practically transformed into a neighborhood block party. Though liquor isn't served, you can BYOB.

Harbour's Edge, Man-O-War Cay. ℂ 242/365-6185. Lunch main courses $7–$12; dinner main courses $10.50–$18.50. No credit cards. Mon–Sat 10:30am–2pm and 5:30–8:30pm. Closed Aug 15–Sept 30.

SHOPPING

Joe's Studio (ℂ 242/365-6082), on the harborfront, sells island-related odds and ends, like models of local sailing dinghies crafted from mahogany and mounted in half profile on a board. They're a great souvenir of your visit. Other items include original watercolors, handcrafted woodwork from native woods, and nautical souvenirs and gifts. Hours are Monday through Saturday from 9:30am to 5pm.

The most unusual store and studio on the island, **Albury's Sail Shop** (ℂ 242/365-6014) occupies a house at the eastern end, overlooking the water. The floor space is devoted to the manufacture and display of an inventory of brightly colored canvas garments and accessories. The 8-ounce cotton duck fabric once served as sailcloth for the community's boats. When synthetic sails came into vogue, four generations of Albury women put the cloth and their talents to use. Don't stop without chatting with the Albury women. Hours are Monday through Saturday from 7am to 5pm.

4 Great Guana Cay ✯

Longest of the Abaco cays, Great Guana, on the east side of the chain, stretches 7 miles from tip to tip and lies between Green Turtle Cay and Man-O-War Cay. The beachfront running the length of the cay is spectacular, one of the loveliest in The Bahamas. The reef fishing is superb, and bonefish are plentiful in the shallow bays.

The settlement stretches along the beach at the head of the palm-fringed Kidd's Cove, named after the pirate, and the ruins of an old sisal mill near the western end of the island make for an interesting detour. The island has about 150 residents, most of them descendants of Loyalists who left Virginia and the Carolinas to settle in this remote place, often called the "last spot of land before Africa."

As in similar settlements in New Plymouth and Man-O-War Cay, houses here resemble those of old New England. Over the years the traditional pursuits of the islanders have been boatbuilding, carpentry, farming, and fishing. It won't take you long to explore the village, because it has only two small stores, a one-room schoolhouse, and an Anglican church—that's about it.

GETTING THERE & GETTING AROUND

Albury's Ferry Service, Marsh Harbour (ℂ 242/365-6010), runs a twice-daily service to Great Guana Cay. A round-trip ticket costs $12 for adults, $6 for children.

Instead of driving around the island, most people get around in small boats. On the cay, boats are available to charter for a half day or a full day (or a month, for that matter). For example, a 23-foot sailboat, fully equipped for living and cruising, is available for charter, and deep-sea fishing trips can be arranged.

WHERE TO STAY

Dolphin Beach Resort ℱ   Set directly astride one of the best beaches in The Bahamas, a 15-minute walk north of Guana Cay's largest settlement (Guana Village), with miles of powder-soft sand in front of you, this resort offers informal but very comfortable lodgings. Four of the units are in the main house and have queen-size beds and ceiling fans, small refrigerators, and microwaves; three of them have private screened-in decks with teakwood furniture. The oceanfront cottages (six in all) also have queen-size beds, ceiling fans, air-conditioning, and full-size kitchenettes with stoves. Cottages can accommodate between two and four guests, depending on their size. The showers are placed outside but secluded and screened off by island flora. The place is private, intimate, and laid-back.

There's a restaurant on the premises, The Landing, with a "conch crawl," a Bahamian take on a lobster tank. Nippers, a beachfront bar and grill, is within a 5-minute walk.

Great Guana Cay, Abaco, The Bahamas (write to: Dolphin Beach Resort, 69 AB, P.O. Box 59-2548, Miami, FL 33159) ℂ **800/222-2646** or 242/365-5137. www.dolphinbeachresort.com. 10 units. Year-round $115–$155 double, $170 suite, $140–$225 cottage. AE, MC, V. **Amenities:** Restaurant, beachfront bar/grill, pool, bikes, kayaks, snorkeling. *In room:* A/C, coffeemaker, kitchenette.

WHERE TO DINE

For fun on the beach, head for **Nipper's Beach Bar & Grill** (ℂ **242/ 365-5143**), a dive where visitors hang out with the locals. Right on the sands, you sit in split-level gazebos and take in the surf, the most stunning seascape in the Abacos, with a snorkeling reef just 12 yards offshore. Burgers and well-stuffed sandwiches satisfy your hunger at lunch. But the best times to go are on a Wednesday, for one of the bonfires and fireworks displays, or on a Sunday night, for a boar roast. One guest is said to have consumed five "Nipper Trippers"—and lived to tell about it. This is the bartender's specialty, a mix of five different rums along with tropical juices. It's lethal.

5 Treasure Cay ℱ

Treasure Cay now contains one of the most popular and elaborate resorts in the Out Islands. On the east coast of Great Abaco, it boasts not only 3½ miles of spectacular sandy beach, widely recognized as one of the top-10 beaches in the world, but also one of the finest marinas in the Commonwealth, with complete docking and charter facilities.

Before the tourist complex opened, the cay was virtually unsettled. As a result, the resort has become the "city," providing its visitors, who number in the thousands, with everything they need, including medical supplies, grocery-store items (liquor, naturally), and even bank services. The real-estate office peddles condos, and the builders predict that they will one day reach a capacity of 5,000 guests. They hope that many visitors will like Treasure Cay so much that they'll buy into it.

See "Getting There" under "Abacos Essentials," at the beginning of this chapter, for details on flying to Treasure Cay. Some direct service is available to the island from Florida. You could also fly into Marsh Harbour (see section 1, "Marsh Harbour (Great Abaco Island)," of this chapter) and take a 20-mile taxi ride north along the paved but bumpy Sherben A. Boothe Highway.

Treasure Cay also hosts one of the most popular fishing tournaments in The Bahamas: the **Treasure Cay Billfish Championship** in May.

WHERE TO STAY

Banyan Beach Club Resort *❋*   Although it doesn't have the scale or amenities of the much larger Treasure Cay Resort, about a half mile away, this well-maintained compound of apartments, each with a kitchenette, has a slightly lower price tag and an idyllic location on the sands of a stunning beach. It was built in the 1970s, but because of a radical renovation that was completed in the 1990s, it looks much newer. The apartments are simple, streamlined, and modern, with small bathrooms equipped with shower units. Those with water views are larger and a bit more expensive. This is a good place for a quiet vacation of swimming, reading, and relaxing. The new Tiki Bar is the setting for weekly cocktail parties.

P.O. Box AB 22158, Treasure Cay, Abaco, The Bahamas. ℂ **888/625-3060** or 242/365-8111. Fax 242/365-8112. www.banyanbeach.com. 22 units. Winter $175–$200 1-bedroom suite, $275–$300 2-bedroom suite; off-season $125–$150 1-bedroom suite, $225–$250 2-bedroom suite. MC, V. **Amenities:** Bar, wading pool, golf carts for rent, snorkeling. *In room:* A/C, TV, kitchenette.

Treasure Cay Hotel Resort & Marina *❋*   One of the biggest of the Out Island resorts, this property attracts boaters, golfers, fishers, and divers, as well as yachties and escapists seeking a remote yet rather-luxurious retreat. The foundation for this resort was laid in 1962, when a group of international investors recognized the potential of the property. The vast majority of the peninsula (1,200 acres), as well as the marina facility, all of the villas, 80 privately owned condominiums, the tennis courts, and several blocks of other housing, remains under the ownership of the original investors. Guests sometimes rent electric golf carts (priced at around $35 a day) or bicycles to explore the far-flung palm and casuarina groves of this sprawling compound.

Guests of the resort appreciate the *House and Garden* look of the architecture, the tropical plantings, the spectacular beachfront, an excellent golf course, and the marina facilities. Simply furnished in conservatively modern tropical motifs, most accommodations overlook the dozens of sailing craft moored in the marina. The recently renovated villas are very attractive, with full kitchens, two bedrooms, and washer/dryers, plus a mid-size bathroom with a shower unit.

The restaurant, the Spinnaker, serves good international cuisine, and two bars dispense tropical drinks.

Treasure Cay, Abaco, The Bahamas. ℂ **800/327-1584** or 242/365-8535. Fax 954/525-1699. www.treasure-cay.com. (For reservations, contact Treasure Cay Services, Inc., 2301 S. Federal Hwy., Fort Lauderdale, FL 33316; ℂ 954/525-7711.) 95 units. Winter $250 double, $395 villa for up to 4; off-season $180 double, $325 villa for up to 4. MAP (breakfast and dinner) $39 per person extra. AE, DISC, MC, V. **Amenities:** Restaurant, 2 bars, 18-hole golf course, 6 tennis courts, boat rentals, fishing guides, snorkeling, 150-slip marina, scuba charters, golf-cart rentals, water sports. *In room:* A/C, TV, kitchenette.

WHERE TO DINE

For "serious" dining, head for the **Treasure Cay Hotel Resort & Marina** (see above). If you'd like to sample the fare at a local joint, however, call **Touch of Class,** Queen's Highway at Treasure Cay Road (ℂ **242/365-8195**), which will send a shuttle bus to pick you up for the 10-minute drive north of the resort. The menu changes every night, but count on tasty island cuisine, often made with homegrown ingredients. No credit cards are accepted.

WATER SPORTS & OTHER OUTDOOR PURSUITS

Treasure Cay Golf Club (ℂ **242/365-8535**), designed by Dick Wilson, Treasure Cay, offers 6,985 yards of fairways, though it's hardly the best course this famed golf architect ever designed. Greens fees are $75 for 18 holes. This is the only golf course in the Abacos, and it lies half a mile from the center of the resort.

Treasure Cay Marina (© **242/365-8250**) offers full-service facilities for a variety of water sports. Fishing boats with experienced skippers will guide anglers to tuna, marlin, wahoo, dolphinfish, barracuda, grouper, yellowtail, and snapper. Treasure Cay's own bonefish flats are just a short cruise from the marina. A full day of bonefishing costs $325. A sportfishing boat goes for $320 for a half day, $450 for a full day. In addition, you can arrange to rent a sailboat, a Hobie Cat, windsurfing boards, and snorkeling gear. The marina has showers, fish-cleaning facilities, 24-hour weekday laundry service, and water and electricity hookups.

Deep-sea fishing is arranged through the reception desk of the **Treasure Cay Resort and Marina** (© **242/365-8535**), which will also arrange for you to hire a bonefishing guide. The same resort has six of the best tennis courts in the Abacos, four of which are lit for night games. Fees are $14 hourly for the hard courts or $16 hourly for the clay courts.

The best diving is provided by **Divers Down** (© **242/365-8465**), which rents equipment and takes scuba divers to some of the best sites in the Abacos where the marine life down below is spectacular in all its rainbow-hued glory. Whale Cay and No Name Cay are some of the best sites for viewing Bahamian marine life. Divers are also taken to the site of the 1865 wreck of *San Jacinto*, a steamship freighter that went down. If you're not a serious diver but want a close encounter with the water, call **C & C Boat Rentals** (© **242/365-8585**) which can take you on $55 snorkeling and island-exploring trips that feature a cookout on the beach.

6 Green Turtle Cay (New Plymouth) ★★

Three miles off the east coast of Great Abaco, Green Turtle Cay is the jewel of the archipelago, a little island with an uneven coastline, deep bays, sounds, and good beaches, one of the best stretching for 3,600 feet. Here you can roam through green forests, gentle hills, and secluded inlets. The island is 3½ miles long and half a mile across, lying some 170 miles due east of Palm Beach, Florida.

Water depths seldom exceed 15 to 20 feet inside the string of cays that trace the outer edge of the Bahama Bank. Coral gardens teem with colorful sea life, making for fabulous snorkeling. Shelling on the lovely beaches and offshore sandbars is among the finest in The Bahamas. If you have a boat, you can explore such deserted islands as Fiddle Cay to the north and No Name Cay and Pelican Cay to the south of Green Turtle Cay.

New Plymouth, at the southern tip of the cay, is an 18th-century settlement that has the flavor of an old New England sailing port. Much of the original masonry was made from lime that was produced when conch shells were broken up, burned, and sifted for cement (records say that the alkali content was so high that it would burn the hands of the masons who used it). Clapboard houses with gingerbread trim line the narrow streets of the little town, which once had a population of 1,800 people, now shrunk to 400. Green Turtle Cay became known for the skill of its shipbuilders, although the industry, like many others in the area, failed after slaves were totally emancipated in The Bahamas in 1838.

Parliament is the village's main street, and you can walk its entire length in just 10 minutes, acknowledged only by a few clucking hens. Many of the houses have front porches, which are occupied in the evening by people enjoying the breezes.

ESSENTIALS

GETTING THERE   Fly to **Treasure Cay Airport,** where a taxi will take you to the ferry dock for departures to Green Turtle Cay (New Plymouth). At the dock, you may have to wait a while for the ferry. It's about a 15- to 20-minute ride to Green Turtle Cay from the dock. The ferry will take you directly to the Green Turtle Club, if you're staying there, or to New Plymouth. This land-and-sea transfer costs $16 per person round-trip.

FAST FACTS   **Barclay's Bank PLC** operates a branch (✆ **242/365-4144**) open only from 10am to 1pm on Tuesday and Thursday.

If you need medical attention on **Green Turtle Cay,** there is a government clinic (✆ **242/365-4028**) run by a nurse.

You enter Green Turtle Cay's **post office** (✆ **242/365-4242**) through a pink door. It has a public telephone. Hours are Monday through Friday from 9am to 5pm.

As for safety, there's no crime in New Plymouth, unless you import it yourself. There is a little jail made of stone, which makes visitors chuckle. No one can remember when, if ever, it held a prisoner.

SPECIAL EVENTS   One event that draws visitors in droves is the **Green Turtle Club Fishing Tournament,** held in May. In 1984, the winner hooked a 500-pound blue marlin that was so heavy that the competing participants from other boats generously came aboard the winning craft to bring the fish in. For more information, contact one of the Bahamian Tourist Offices or the **Green Turtle Club Hotel** (✆ **242/365-4271**), which is more or less the official head-quarters, when the tournament is held.

WHERE TO STAY

Bluff House Club Beach Hotel ⟨⟨   One of the most famous and legendary hotels in the Out Islands, Bluff House originated in the 1950s when it was the private home of C. Pearce Cody III and his wife, Kitty. When friends of their friends asked if they could pay for a few days'stay, the Codys reinvented their home as the first hotel in the Out Islands. It's welcomed some extremely famous guests in the intervening years, including a well-heeled "same time next year" group. Bluff House occupies one of the most desirable pieces of real estate in The Bahamas, 10 acres on the highest point in the Abacos with panoramic views; it fronts the Sea of Abaco on one side and the sheltered harbor of White Sound on the other. A romantic spot, it has a lovely nautical charm with British colonial overtones. Against a backdrop of palm, oak, and pine-forested jogging trails, it lies within a 5-minute boat ride from the village of New Plymouth. Likewise, the hotel's boat hauls guests to the village 3 mornings a week for sightseeing and shopping and also for a Saturday-night dance.

The hotel offers villas and hotel rooms in a variety of configurations and sizes, either set beside the beach or cantilevered into the steep hillside facing the sheltered harbor; all have lovely views and some have kitchens. The best accommodations are the spacious colonial-style suites, with cathedral ceilings and balconies that overlook the Sea of Abaco. Inside, decors include floral bed covers and tropical furniture. Each comes with a small tidy bathroom containing a shower unit.

Breakfast and dinner (including complimentary wine) are served in the main Club House, where drinks and fresh hors d'oeuvres are offered before a candlelit dinner that features local conch, grouper, snapper, and lobster, as well as roast duck à l'orange. (See "Where to Dine," below.) The bar/lounge in the hotel's main building is one of our favorite rooms in The Bahamas, with sweeping vistas out across Green Turtle Cay; the blue-and-white, cypress-paneled interior is cozy and comfortable, with simple good taste. Peace and prosperity prevail among nautical memorabilia and a flickering fire within an iron stove as slow-whirling tropical fans, wicker furnishings, and polished wooden floors create an upscale and highly appealing ambience. The daytime bar and grill, the Bluff House Mama, specializes in light meals. Most Thursdays, dinner is served as part of an elaborate beachfront barbecue that's accompanied by music from a live local band.

Green Turtle Cay, Abaco, The Bahamas. © 242/365-4247. Fax 242/365-4248. www.bluffhouse.com. 30 units. $115–$250 double, $210–$325 1-bedroom villa, $299–$410 2-bedroom villa, $399–$495 3-bedroom villa. MAP (breakfast and dinner) $36 per person extra. AE, DISC, MC, V. **Amenities:** Restaurant, bar; 45-slip marina with boats for rent; pool; tennis court; free use of rackets, balls, and snorkeling equipment; arrangements for reef fishing, deep-sea fishing, and bonefishing; baby-sitting; laundry. *In room:* A/C. No phone.

Coco Bay Cottages   On the north end of Green Turtle Cay, at a point where 500 feet of land separate the Atlantic from the Sea of Abaco, this cottage complex opens onto a beach on the Atlantic side of the island and another sandy beach on the more tranquil bay. It is ideal for those who'd like to anchor in for a while (literally—lots of folks arrive by private boat, which you can moor here free, or otherwise you come directly by water taxi from the airport dock). It enjoys a 70% repeat clientele. Furnished in a refreshing style of Caribbean furnishings and pastel colors, the oceanfront property occupies 5 acres, dotted with some 50 tropical fruit trees. Each of the cottages has two bedrooms, a living room, a dining room, and a fully equipped kitchen with microwave, plus a small bathroom with a shower unit. Rebuilt in 1988 and renovated in 1996, the spacious cottages have improved over the years. Linens and kitchen utensils are provided (there are three shops in New Plymouth where you can stock up), and ceiling fans and trade winds cool the rooms.

P.O. Box AB22795, Green Turtle Cay, Abaco, The Bahamas. © 800/752-0166 or 242/365-5464. Fax 242/365-5465. www.cocabaycottages.com. 4 cottages. $175–$225 daily or $1,000–$1,400 weekly. MC, V. *In-room amenities:* Kitchenette.

Deck House   These cottages lie on the leeward side of the island at the entrance to White Sound. Rented weekly as a complex, it can house up to six people. It consists of two bedrooms and two bathrooms, each with a shower stall, plus a small guest house for two with bathroom—in other words, it houses three couples "with privacy." There is a living room, plus a kitchen, and linens and all utensils are provided. Out back is a sundeck. Owners A. V. and Dorothy Lang prefer bookings from Saturday noon to the following Saturday noon, and only one group at a time can rent the site. Incidentally, a maid comes in Saturday to put things in order.

White Sound, Green Turtle Cay, Abaco, The Bahamas. © 513/821-9471 in Cincinnati, OH (for information, write to Dorothy Lang, 535 Hickory Hill Lane, Cincinnati, OH 45215). 2 units. $850 weekly for 4, $1,140 weekly for 6. No credit cards. **Amenities:** Free use of boat and Sunfish. *In room:* No phone.

Green Turtle Club ⟨⟨   An outstanding choice for laid-back luxury, a bit more elegant than Bluff House, this resort attracts honeymooners and snorkelers. But it is a superb choice if you're a serious angler, boater, or diver, because there's an excellent full-service marina and dive shop on the premises. Although it sustained heavy damage during the 1999 hurricanes, the Green Turtle Club immediately undertook major renovations and repair work, and it emerged into the new millennium in tip-top shape. It is spread across 80 acres of low-lying scrubland. The waters around the resort are shallow enough that from a position on shore, you can spot schools of fish and sometimes even a green turtle paddling along above the sandbanks. Today the inn's ambience is very much that of a clubhouse, lodge, and country club; the courteous staff offers assistance yet doesn't intrude on anyone's peace and privacy.

The Green Turtle Yacht Club, host of the prestigious Bahama Cup Around the Island Race, has its base here. It's associated with the Birdham Yacht Club, one of the oldest in England, and with the Palm Beach Yacht Club. Members have their own villas right on the water, often with private docks, although temporary guests will be lodged in spacious bungalows (usually two accommodations to a building) set within a gently sloping, carefully landscaped garden. Rooms are among the most upscale and luxurious in the Out Islands. Think England in the tropics, for the bedrooms boast Sheraton-style mahogany furniture, four-poster beds, French-inspired draperies, oak floors, terra-cotta-tiled patios, and wicker or rattan furniture. Each comes with an immaculate mid-size bathroom with shower stalls and generous shelf space.

The flag-festooned bar is the social center of the resort, where there's occasionally live music. There's an unmistakable British note to evenings here, beginning with predinner cocktails beside a roaring fire in the bar's iron stove (in chilly weather only, of course), before everyone adjourns to the pine-paneled dining room for well-prepared dinners. Breakfast and lunch are usually served on a veranda.

Green Turtle Cay, Abaco, The Bahamas. ℭ 242/365-4271. Fax 242/365-4272. www.greenturtleclub.com. 31 units. Year-round $190–$230 double, $260–$270 suite, $325–$540 villa for up to 4. Prices higher at Christmas. Children under 12 stay free in parents' room. Extra person $20. MAP (breakfast and dinner) $41 per adult extra, $26 per child extra. AE, DISC, MC, V. Most guests arrive at Treasure Cay Airport, then take a taxi (there are usually plenty there) to the ferry dock, where a water taxi will take you to the club for a fee of about $8 each way. **Amenities:** Restaurant, bar, pool, water sports, marina, dive shop, laundry. In room: A/C, VCR, refrigerator. No phone.

New Plymouth Inn ℱ   This two-story inn, a mix of New England and Bahamian styles, stands next door to the former home of Neville Chamberlain, the prime minister of Great Britain on the eve of World War II. It's more like a guest house or a big B&B than either the Green Turtle Club or Bluff House. In the heart of New Plymouth Village, the inn has colonial charm, a Loyalist history, cloistered gardens, and a patio pool. It was one of the few buildings in town to survive the 1932 hurricane. The inn is run by Wally Davies, an expert diver and swimmer, who has turned New Plymouth Inn into a charming oasis, refurbishing the 120-year-old building with taste and care.

The inn has wide, open verandas, intricate cutout wooden trim, and an indoor A-frame dining room. The comfortable hammock on the front porch is constantly fought over. The light and airy rooms are kept spotlessly clean; some units are air-conditioned, and each comes with a bathroom containing a shower unit. Many of the same guests have come back every year since the inn opened in 1974.

Out on the veranda, you can smell night-blooming jasmine mixing with fresh-baked island bread. Dinners of fresh native lobster, snapper, conch, and vintage wines are served by candlelight. Roasts, steaks, chops, and imported beer in frosty steins are also part of the menu. The bar and lounge are the social center. Sunday brunch is the most popular on the island.

New Plymouth, Green Turtle Cay, Abaco, The Bahamas. ℭ 242/365-4161. Fax 242/365-4138. 9 units. $130 double. Rates include breakfast and dinner. MC, V. Closed Sept–Oct. **Amenities:** Restaurant, pool, fishing, snorkeling. In room: A/C. No phone.

WHERE TO DINE

The previously recommended hotels have the best food on the island, but consider one of the local spots as well.

The Club House Restaurant ☞ INTERNATIONAL   You can drop in here at midday for a burger, sandwich, or salad, but a note of elegance emerges at dinner, which is always kicked off at the cocktail hour in what we think is the most beautiful and appealing bar in the Bahamian Out Islands. Lined with limed cypress, trimmed in cerulean blue, and beautifully proportioned, it includes sweeping views out over two shorefronts from the highest point in the Abacos. Dinner is served within a Queen Anne–style dining room. It's always a set menu, with items that change every night, but the cuisine is invariably excellent. You might start with something like Waldorf salad or smoked salmon, followed by grilled and mango-flavored chicken breast or lobster tail that's simply broiled with lemon and butter. Triple chocolate cheesecake or key lime pie makes a soothing dessert.

At the Bluff House Club Beach Hotel, Green Turtle Cay. ℂ 242/365-4247. Reservations required. Lunch platters $6–$10; fixed-price dinners $31 per person. AE, DISC, MC, V. Daily 11:30am–2pm and daily at 7:30pm, with hors d'oeuvre service (included in the price) beginning at 6:30pm.

Laura's Kitchen BAHAMIAN/AMERICAN   On the main street of town, across from the Albert Lowe Museum, this family-owned spot occupies a well-converted white Bahamian cottage. Laura Sawyer serves up lunch and dinner in a simple, homey decor. The menu changes nightly, depending on what's at the market, but she always serves the old reliables her family has eaten for generations: fried grouper, fried chicken, and a tasty cracked conch.

King St. ℂ 242/365-4287. Reservations recommended for dinner. Lunch $4–$8.50; dinner $12–$18. MC, V. Daily 11am–3pm and 5:30–9pm. Closed Sept.

Plymouth Rock Liquors & Café BAHAMIAN/AMERICAN   This place has the best selection of wines and liquors for sale in New Plymouth, including at least 60 kinds of rum, plus Cuban cigars. Part of its space is set aside for a pleasant and attractive luncheonette run by hardworking co-owners Kathleen and David Bethell. They serve up a tasty conch chowder, sandwiches, split pea soup, beef souse, and cracked conch with cucumber slices and potato salad. There's also an art gallery on the premises, featuring works by about 50 artists, many of whom specialize in local themes.

Parliament St., Green Turtle Cay. ℂ 242/365-4234. Sandwiches and platters $3.50–$6.50. DISC, MC, V. Café Mon–Sat 9am–5pm; liquor store Mon–Thurs 9am–6pm, Fri–Sat 9am–9pm.

Rooster's Rest Pub and Restaurant BAHAMIAN   Just beyond the edge of town, Rooster's, the local dive, serves good Bahamian food, including lobster, conch, and your best bet, fresh fish. It's casual through and through, the way The Bahamas used to be; nouvelle cuisine hasn't washed up on these shores yet. All main courses in the evening are served with peas 'n' rice, coleslaw, and potato salad. The cook also prepares some tasty ribs.

Gilliam's Bay Rd. ℂ 242/365-4066. Reservations recommended for dinner. Lunch burgers and snacks $5–$7; main courses $10–$16. MC, V. Mon–Sat 11:30am–9:30pm.

The Wrecking Tree Bar & Restaurant BAHAMIAN   This funky wooden place is recognized by its coral and terra-cotta colors, and by the much-mangled casuarinas tree that grows next to its foundation. The hearty menu is as simple as can be, featuring mostly peas 'n' rice, conch, grouper fingers, chicken souse,

Finds **Miss Emily's Blue Bee Bar**

Our favorite bar in the Out Islands is **Miss Emily's Blue Bee Bar,** on Victoria Street in New Plymouth (© **242/365-4181**). This simple bar is likely to be the scene of the liveliest party in the Out Islands at any time of day; even normally buttoned-up types find themselves flirting or dancing before long. You never know what will be going on here. Until rising waters from the 1999 hurricanes washed some of them away, most of its walls were covered with the business cards of past guests and celebrities. Only some now remain, but stop by and see how many replacements have been plastered up. The Goombay Smash, the specialty here, has been called "Abaco's answer to atomic fission." Its recipe includes secret proportions of coconut rum, "dirty" rum, apricot brandy, and pineapple juice. Miss Emily (Mrs. Emily Cooper) was a legend in these parts. She's gone now, but her memory lives on: Her daughter, Violet Smith, knows her secret recipe for The Goombay Smash, as well as a potent version of a rum punch. Tips at the bar go to St. Peter's Anglican Church. No food is ever served here, but the bar is open Monday to Saturday from 11am until late.

and burgers. Come here for a simple lunch, a midday beer, and a view over the boats in the nearby harbor.

The Harbourfront. No phone. Main courses $5–$10. No credit cards. Daily 11am–3pm.

WATER SPORTS & OTHER OUTDOOR PURSUITS

If you want to go deep-sea fishing, the people to see are the Sawyer family, father and son. Referrals are usually made through the **Green Turtle Club** (© **242/ 365-4271**), or you can call directly at © **242/365-4173**. A half day of fishing costs $240; a full day is $340. These costs can be divided among four people. If you want to go bonefishing, the charge is $140 per half day or $240 for a full day.

You can make scuba-diving arrangements with **Green Turtle Club Divers** (© **242/365-4271**), which has a full-service dive shop right at the hotel. Both divers and snorkelers get a 15% discount if they are registered at the hotel. **Brendal's Dive Shop** (© **242/365-4411;** www.brendal.com) also has a good reputation, and they can organize memorable outings. Both places will rent you snorkel gear.

Call **Lincoln Jones** at © **242/365-4223,** and he'll arrange a snorkeling adventure for you—probably on some deserted beach that only he knows about. Prices are to be negotiated, of course, but a lunch of fresh conch or lobster is a fine addition to any day.

You can usually rent a boat through **Donny's Boat Rentals** at © **242/ 365-4119.** You'll find everything for rent from 14-foot Whalers to 25-foot Makos. The Bluff House and the Green Turtle Club both have full-service marinas.

There's a tennis court at **Bluff House** (© **242/365-4247**), where everyone plays free.

EXPLORING THE ISLAND: A JOURNEY TO THE 18TH CENTURY

New Plymouth celebrated its bicentennial in 1984 by establishing a memorial that honors American Loyalists and also some of their notable descendants, including Albert Lowe, a pioneer boatbuilder and historian. The garden, complete with busts of notable islanders, is designed in the pattern of the Union Jack and lies across from the New Plymouth Inn.

There isn't much shopping, but consider a visit to the Ocean Blue Gallery, adjoining the **Plymouth Rock Café** on Parliament Street (© **242/365-4234**). This two-room outlet has one of the best collections of local artwork in the Abacos: some sculptures, some paintings, but all originals.

Albert Lowe Museum   More than anything else we've seen in The Bahamas, this museum gives a view of the rawboned and sometimes-difficult history of the Out Islands. You could easily spend a couple of hours reading the fine print of the dozens of photographs that show the hardship and the valor of citizens who changed industries as often as the economic circumstances of their era dictated.

There's a garden in the back of the beautifully restored Loyalist home; the caretaker will give you a guided tour of the stone kitchen, which occupants of the house used as a shelter when a hurricane devastated much of New Plymouth in 1932. Inside the house, a narrow stairway leads to three bedrooms that reveal the simplicity of 18th-century life on Green Turtle Cay. Amid antique settees, irreplaceable photographs, and island artifacts, you'll see a number of handsome ship models, the work of Albert Lowe, for whom the museum was named.

The paintings of Alton Lowe, son of the former boatbuilder and founder of the museum, are also on display. Cherub-faced and red-haired, Alton, who usually resides in Miami now, has for some time been one of the best-known painters in The Bahamas. His works hang in collections all over the world. Many of his paintings have been used as the background for Bahamian postage stamps, blowups of which are displayed in the museum. Your guide on your tour might open the basement of the house for you, as well, where you'll see some of Alton's paintings for sale, along with work by other local artists.

Parliament St. © 242/365-4094. Admission $3 adults, $2 children. Mon–Sat 9am–noon and 1–4:30pm.

NEW PLYMOUTH AFTER DARK
Ask at your hotel if the local junkanoo band, the *Gully Roosters,* are playing their reggae- and calypso-inspired sounds. They're the best in the Abacos and often appear at various spots on island.

See the note on **Miss Emily's Blue Bee Bar** earlier in this section, too. You might catch a live band, and you'll certainly enjoy a wonderful setting for a drink in the bars at the **Bluff House** and the **Green Turtle Club** (see "Where to Stay," above). **Rooster's Rest Pub and Restaurant** (see "Where to Dine," above) is another option.

7 Spanish Cay
Set 12 miles northwest of Green Turtle Cay, this island was named after a pair of Spanish galleons that sank offshore during the 17th century. Originally owned by Queen Elizabeth II, the island was purchased in the 1960s by Texas-based investor (and former owner of the Dallas Cowboys) Clint Murchinson. After his death in the early 1980s, two successive Florida conglomerates poured time, money, and landscaping efforts into developing the island as a site for upscale private homes.

Although its vegetation began with little more than stunted shrubs and sea grapes, today the narrow, 3-mile-long, 185-acre island is forested with 6,000 palms, descendants of the original 800 specimens Murchinson planted in the 1970s. Unusual among the coral-and-sand islands of the northern Bahamas,

Spanish Cay is relatively vertiginous, rising to a panoramic altitude of 65 feet above sea level. The little island has 5 beaches and about 7 miles of shoreline. Most guests of the inn (see below) and the residents of the island's private homes maneuver their way along the island's paved roads on electric-powered golf carts.

The island contains a 75-slip, state-of-the-art marina, private homes, and a collection of garden suites available to overnight guests. The island also has a pair of restaurants (each with its own bar). The Wrecker's Raw Bar, the more upscale of the two, is built on stilts above the tidal flats of the island's Atlantic shore. The island also boasts a 5,000-foot airstrip, a complete PADI-certified dive shop, a handful of sailing vessels for excursions above the coral reefs of the Sea of Abaco, and a congenial staff, which for the most part ferries in every day from the nearby community of Cooper's Town. A one-way trip costs $10.

Most visitors arrive by private boat or chartered aircraft from Fort Lauderdale. You can also fly to Treasure Cay on **Bahamasair** (© **800/222-4262** or 242/ 367-2095), then have the inn arrange water transportation from there.

WHERE TO STAY & DINE

The Spanish Cay Resort & Marina ℱ   Recent renovations and improved transportation have made this property better and more accessible. Bedrooms have been improved and completely refurbished to accommodate more than two guests per room. All the suites are roomy and spacious, with a double bed, a foldout sofa bed, and a small refrigerator, plus a tidy bathroom with a shower stall. The apartments, of course, are even more spacious, with both king-size beds and twins in their two bedrooms, plus a full kitchen, living room, dining room, and deck overlooking the marina. A one-bedroom apartment can sleep up to four people; a two-bedroom accommodates six.

Two on-site restaurants serve Bahamian fare such as conch, but also chicken, fish, steak, and even lobster on occasion. Dinners are reasonably priced, and the chef always offers fresh fish, which is caught and cooked on the same day.

Cooper's Town, Abaco, The Bahamas. © **888/722-6474** or 242/365-0083. Fax 242/365-0453. 9 units. Winter $250–$275 double, $375 2-bedroom condo; off-season $200–$220 double, $300 2-bedroom condo. MC, V. **Amenities:** Restaurant, 4 tennis courts, snorkeling, scuba gear. *In room:* Refrigerator. No phone.

8 Walker's Cay

Lying at the edge of the Bahama Bank, this is the northernmost, the outermost, and one of the smallest islands in the Abaco chain. The cay produces its own fresh water and electricity. Coral reefs surround this island, dropping off to depths of some 1,000 feet. It's known around the world as one of the best deep-sea fishing resorts.

Ponce de León reportedly stopped here in 1513 in search of fresh water—just 6 days before he "discovered" Florida. From the 17th century, this was a place known to pirates, who stored their booty here. It became a bastion for blockade-runners during the American Civil War, and later it was a hideout for rumrunners in the days of U.S. Prohibition.

To get here, prospective guests should call the Walker's Cay Hotel and Marina at © **800/WALKERS** and make arrangements for a flight from Fort Lauderdale.

WHERE TO STAY & DINE

Walker's Cay Hotel & Marina ℱ   Established in the 1930s and a legend among sports fishermen ever since, this resort occupies all 100 acres of a private island that contains the largest and most elaborate full-service marina in The

Abacos. Each year, it runs at least two of the country's biggest deep-sea fishing tournaments. Come here for the fishing, for the marina and its charter boats, and for the way that sports (especially fishing and scuba) permeate the air, but not necessarily for the luxury of the accommodations. These are rather-standard motel-style units, which benefited in 1999 from a complete renovation. Each accommodation contains a small bathroom with a shower stall.

Meals are generally adequate and are served in both the Lobster Trap and the Conch Pearl Restaurants. Both have their own bars and a hearty roster of American/Bahamian fare that includes lots of steak and fresh fish.

Walker's Cay, Abaco, The Bahamas. ℂ **800/WALKERS** in the U.S. and Canada, or 954/359-1400 in Fort Lauderdale. Fax 954/359-1414. Address mail to 700 SW 34th St., Fort Lauderdale, FL 33315. Local phone in the Abacos: 242/353-1252. Mar 1–Sept 3 $150–$160 double, $325–$373 2-bedroom villa (without kitchen); Sept 4–Feb 28 $110–$120 double, $300–$325 2-bedroom villa (without kitchen). Supplement per person for MAP, $37.50 per day. AE, DISC, MC, V. **Amenities:** 2 restaurants, 2 bars, 2 tennis courts, laundry, baby-sitting, water sports, freshwater and saltwater swimming. *In room:* A/C. No phone.

8

Eleuthera

A sort of Bahamian Plymouth Rock, Eleuthera Island was the first permanent settlement in The Bahamas, founded in 1648. A search for religious freedom drew the Eleutherian Adventurers from Bermuda here, to the "birthplace of The Bahamas." The long narrow island they discovered and colonized still bears the name "Eleuthera"—Greek for freedom. The locals call it "Cigatoo."

These adventurers found an island of white- and pink-sand beaches framed by casuarina trees, high, rolling green hills, sea-to-sea views, dramatic cliffs, and sheltered coves, and they're still here, unspoiled, waiting for you to discover today. More than 100 miles long but merely 2 miles wide (guaranteeing that you're never far from the beach), Eleuthera is about 70 miles east of Nassau (a 30-min. flight). The population of 10,000 is largely made up of farmers, shopkeepers, and fishermen who live in old villages of pastel-washed cottages. The resorts here are built around excellent harbors, and roads run along the coastline, though some of them are inadequately paved.

Eleuthera and its satellite islands, **Spanish Wells** and **Harbour Island,** offer superb snorkeling and diving amid coral gardens, reefs, drop-offs, and wrecks. Anglers come to

Eleuthera for bottom-, bone-, and deep-sea fishing, testing their skill against the dolphinfish, the wahoo, the blue and the white marlin, the Allison tuna, and the amberjack. Charter boats are available at Powell Point, Rock Sound, Spanish Wells, and Harbour Island. You can also rent Sunfish, sailboats, and Boston Whalers for reef fishing.

Eleuthera rivals the Abacos in terms of popularity among foreign visitors, although boaters are more drawn to the Abacos and the Exumas. Along with the Abacos, Eleuthera has the largest concentration of resort hotels outside of the major developments of Nassau/Paradise Island and Freeport/Lucaya.

In many ways, we love gorgeous **Harbour Island,** with its charming Dunmore Town, even more than New Plymouth or Hope Town in the Abacos; it's almost a Cape Cod in the tropics. Of the 10 destinations recommended in this chapter, Harbour Island gets our vote as the number-one choice.

Spanish Wells is another small island just off the north end of Eleuthera. Spanish galleons put sailors ashore to fill the ships' casks with fresh water after long sea voyages—hence the present-day name of the island.

ELEUTHERA ESSENTIALS

GETTING THERE

BY PLANE Eleuthera has three main airports. **North Eleuthera Airport** (© 242/335-1242), obviously, serves the north along with the two major offshore cays, Harbour Island and Spanish Wells. **Governor's Harbour Airport** (© 242/332-2321) serves the center of the island, and **Rock Sound International**

Airport (© 242/334-2171) handles traffic to South Eleuthera. Make sure, when making your reservations, that your flight will arrive at the appropriate airport; one visitor flew into Rock Sound Airport, only to face a $100 taxi ride and a water-taxi trip before reaching his final destination of Harbour Island in the north.

Bahamasair (© 800/222-4262) offers daily flights between Nassau and the three airports, North Eleuthera, Governor's Harbour, and Rock Sound.

In addition, several commuter airlines, with regularly scheduled service, fly from the Florida mainland with either non-stop or one-stop service. Many private flights use the North Eleuthera Airport, with its 4,500-foot paved runway. It is an official Bahamian port of entry, and a Customs and Immigration official is on hand.

USAir Express (© 800/428-4322) operates what might be the most popular way of reaching two of Eleuthera's airports directly from the mainland of Florida. Flights depart once a day from Miami flying non-stop to North Eleuthera, then continue on, after briefly unloading passengers and baggage, to Governor's Harbour.

American Eagle (© 800/433-7300) offers daily flights from Miami to Governor's Harbour. Usually there is only one flight a day, but if demand merits it, there can be two flights on Friday and three on Saturday and Sunday, since most visitors fly over for the weekend.

Small carriers include **Twin Air** (© 954/359-8266), flying from Fort Lauderdale three times a week to Rock Sound and Governor's Harbour and four times a week to North Eleuthera.

BY FERRY   A new inter-island link, **Bahamas Fast Ferries** (© 242/323-2166), originates in Potter's Cay, beneath the Paradise Island Bridge, and fans out at regular intervals to Harbour Island, North Eleuthera, and Governor's Harbour. Round-trip fares are $90 for adults, $50 for children under 12.

BY MAIL BOAT   Several mail boats visit Eleuthera from Nassau, leaving from Potter's Cay Dock. Weather conditions often cause their schedules to change. For details about sailings, consult the dockmaster at **Potter's Cay Dock** in Nassau (© 242/393-1064).

MV _Current Pride_ goes from Nassau to Current Island, serving lower and upper Bogue. It departs Nassau at 7am Thursday and returns on Tuesday.

The **_Bahamas Daybreak III_** departs on Monday for South Eleuthera, stops at Rock Sound, and returns to Nassau on Tuesday. It then leaves from Nassau on Thursday for The Bluff and Harbour Island, with a Sunday return scheduled.

The **_Eleuthera Express_** sails from Nassau to Spanish Wells and Governor's Harbour on Monday and Thursday, and returns to Nassau on Sunday and Tuesday.

GETTING AROUND

It's virtually impossible to get lost on Eleuthera—there's only one road that meanders along the entire length of its snake-shaped form, and you'll stray from it only very rarely. Because it's so easy to tour the island, most visitors rent a car at least for 1 day (prices are usually around $70 a day). This can be arranged simply by asking your hotel or any of the taxi drivers lined up either outside the North Eleuthera Airport or at the ferryboat docks heading to Harbour Island.

The front desk of any hotel will help you make arrangements for a car rental if you don't choose to go with Fine Threads.

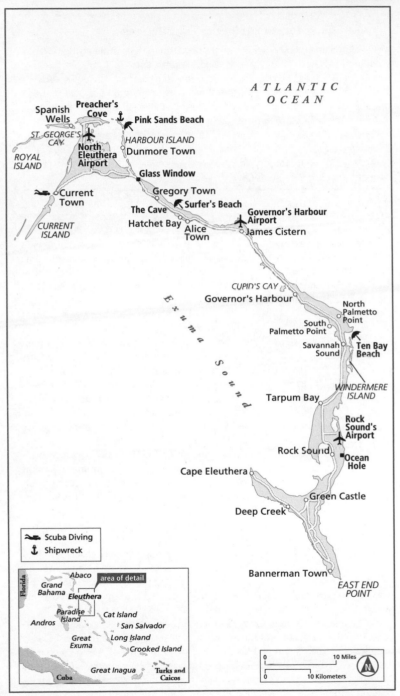

Eleuthera

ATLANTIC OCEAN

Spanish Wells
Preacher's Cove
Pink Sands Beach
ST. GEORGE'S CAY
ROYAL ISLAND
HARBOUR ISLAND
Dunmore Town
North Eleuthera Airport
Glass Window
Current Town
CURRENT ISLAND
Gregory Town
Surfer's Beach
The Cave
Hatchet Bay
Alice Town
Governor's Harbour Airport
James Cistern

Exuma Sound

CUPID'S CAY
Governor's Harbour
North Palmetto Point
South Palmetto Point
Savannah Sound
Ten Bay Beach
WINDERMERE ISLAND
Tarpum Bay
Rock Sound's Airport
Rock Sound
Ocean Hole
Cape Eleuthera
Green Castle
Deep Creek
Bannerman Town
EAST END POINT

Scuba Diving
Shipwreck

Florida
Grand Bahama
Abaco
area of detail
Eleuthera
Paradise Island
Andros
Cat Island
San Salvador
Great Exuma
Long Island
Crooked Island
Great Inagua
Turks and Caicos
Cuba

| 0 | | 10 Miles |
| 0 | | 10 Kilometers |

Finds **An In-Depth Look with Fine Threads**

There's no one who knows Eleuthera better than the people at the North Eleuthera–based **Fine Threads Taxi, Rental Cars & Tours** (© 242/ 359-7780). Here, owner Frederick Neely (nicknamed "Fine Threads" because of his well-tailored clothes) will either rent you your own rental car or take you on a private island tour (available for up to six people). An 8-hour experience will cost $250; a 4-hour experience will cost $130. Tours usually begin at 9:30am and take in a series of bars, restaurants, and geological or historical attractions in Rock Sound, Lower Bogue, Palmetto Point, and Gregory Town. If you negotiate with your driver, you might also visit Preacher's Cave.

---

1 Rock Sound

Located in South Eleuthera, Rock Sound is a small shady village, the island's main town and once its most exclusive enclave. The closing of two old-time landmark resorts, the Cotton Bay Club and the Windermere Club, has at least for now halted the flow of famous visitors, who once included everybody from the late Princess Diana to a parade of CEOs. No reopenings are yet in sight, but at least that means that you can have many of South Eleuthera's best beaches practically to yourself.

Rock Sound opens onto Exuma Sound and is located to the south of Tarpum Bay. The town is at least 2 centuries old, and it has many old-fashioned homes with picket fences out front. Once notorious for wreckers who lured ships ashore with false beacons, it used to be known as "Wreck Sound."

The main reason to come here is to play the **Robert Trent Jones Jr. Course** at the Cotton Bay Club on Rock Sound (© **242/334-6156**), a par-72, 18-hole, 7,068-yard course. Greens fees are $75, but you must call ahead to reserve a tee time.

Divers flock to **South Eleuthera Divers** (© **242/334-2221**), where divemaster Tim Riley operates the only dive outfitter in the southern part of Eleuthera. He knows all those hard-to-find reefs and will take you to wrecks off Rock Sound and Cape Eleuthera teeming with marine life. Call well in advance of your visit to make reservations.

After leaving Rock Sound, head south, bypassing the remains of the Cotton Bay Club, and continue through the villages of Green Castle and Deep Creek. At this point you take a sharp turn northwest along the only road leading to **Cape Eleuthera.** Locals call this "Cape Eleuthera Road," though you won't find any markings other than a sign pointing the way. If you continue to follow this road northwest, you'll reach the end of the island chain, jutting out into Exuma Sound.

Now relatively deserted, Cape Eleuthera was once home to a chic resort and yacht club that drew some of the movers and shakers from America's East Coast, including Richard Nixon and his pal Bebe Rebozo; some of the top golfers in America played its Bruce Devlin–Bob van Haage 18-hole course, which winds its way along the water. They're all gone now, but the splendid **white sandy beaches**—three of them—remain the same, and locals claim the deep-sea fishing is as fine as it ever was.

ESSENTIALS

Rock Sound itself boasts a shopping center and a bank in addition to its airport, but not a lot else. Many residents who live in South Eleuthera come here to stock up on groceries and supplies.

A doctor and four resident nurses form the staff of the **Rock Sound Medical Clinic** (© 242/334-2226). Office hours are daily from 9am to 1pm; after that, the doctor is always available to handle emergency cases.

If you need the police, call © **242/334-2244.**

WHERE TO STAY & DINE

Sammy's Place BAHAMIAN   Hot gossip and cheap, juicy burgers make Sammy's the most popular hangout in Rock Sound—come here for a slice of local life. Sammy's is on the northeastern approach to the settlement, in a neighborhood that even the owner refers to as "the back side of town." Sammy Culmer (who's assisted by Margarita, his daughter) will serve you drinks (including Bahama Mamas and rum punches), conch fritters, Creole-style grouper, breaded scallops, pork chops, and lobster. If you drop in before 11am, you might be tempted by a selection of egg dishes or omelets.

This is primarily a restaurant and bar, but Sammy does rent four rooms with air-conditioning and satellite TV, plus two efficiency cottages containing two bedrooms with a kitchen. These accommodations can be yours for $83 per night, double occupancy.

Albury's Lane, Rock Sound. © 242/334-2121. Reservations recommended only for special meal requests. Bahamian breakfasts $7; lunch $3–$9; main courses $8–$20. MC, V. Daily 7:30am–10pm.

2 Tarpum Bay

If you're looking for an affordable vacation on high-priced Eleuthera, head here. This charming waterfront village, some 9 miles north of Rock Sound, is good for fishing and has a number of simple, inexpensive guest houses. This tiny settlement with its many pastel-washed, gingerbread-trimmed houses is a favorite of artists, who have established a small colony here with galleries and studios.

Gaulding's Cay, north of town, has a lovely beach with exceptional snorkeling.

WHERE TO STAY & DINE

Cartwright's Ocean Front Cottages   Cartwright's is a cluster of simple cottages right by the sea, with fishing, snorkeling, and swimming at your door. This is one of the few places where you can sit on your patio and watch the sunset. The small cottages, most recently renovated in 1996, are fully furnished, with utensils, stove, refrigerator, pots and pans, and maid service provided. Each unit comes with a small bathroom containing a shower stall. You'll be within walking distance of local stores and restaurants.

Fun Fact A "Hole" in the Ocean

The **Ocean Hole,** which is about 1¼ miles east of the heart of Rock Sound, is said to be bottomless. This saltwater lake that eventually meets the sea is one of the most attractive spots on Eleuthera. You can walk right down to the edge of the water. Many tropical fish can be seen here; they seem to like to be photographed—but only if you feed them first.

Bay St., Tarpum Bay, Eleuthera, The Bahamas. © 242/334-4215. cartwrights@hotmail.com. 3 units. $90 1-bedroom cottage, $120 2-bedroom cottage, $170 3-bedroom cottage. No credit cards. No phone.

Hilton's Haven Motel and Restaurant Across the road from the beach and a short drive from the Rock Sound airport, this Bahamian two-story structure with covered verandas is modest and completely unpretentious, with decent prices. Comfortably furnished apartments, each with a private sun patio and bathroom with shower stalls, come with either air-conditioning or ceiling fans. What makes this place special is Mary Hilton herself, everybody's "Bahama Mama." In fact, as a professional nurse, she has delivered some 2,000 of Eleuthera's finest citizens. She started Hilton's Haven to provide retirement income for herself. "Hilton is my God-given name," she says. "I never met Conrad."

The main tavern-style dining room, with a library in the corner, provides well-cooked food daily; the emphasis is on freshly caught fish. You can order grouper cutlets with peas 'n' rice, steamed conch, and the occasional lobster.

Tarpum Bay, Eleuthera, The Bahamas. © 242/334-4231. Fax 242/331-4020. hilhaven@batelnet.bs. 11 units. $80 double, $100 triple, also $100 apt for 4. MAP (breakfast and dinner) $17 per person extra. No credit cards. **Amenities:** Restaurant, bar. *In room:* Some with A/C. No phone.

3 Windermere Island

Windermere is a very tiny island, connected by ferry to "mainland" Eleuthera. It is midway between the settlements of Governor's Harbour and Rock Sound.

This island couldn't be more discreet. "We like to keep it quiet around here," one of the staff at the presently closed Windermere Island Club once told us. Regrettably, that wasn't always possible for this once-deluxe and snobbish citadel. When Prince Charles first took a pregnant Princess Diana here in the 1980s, she was photographed by paparazzi in her swimsuit. Much to the horror of the club, the picture gained worldwide notoriety.

Even without its posh hotel, Windermere Island is worth a day trip. **Savannah Sound,** with its sandy sheltered beaches and outstanding snorkeling, is particularly appealing (bring your own gear). There are also excellent beaches for shelling and picnicking, and there is good bonefishing, with some catches more than 10 pounds.

West Beach, a good place for sunning and swimming (great for children), is about a 10-minute walk from the shut-down Windermere Club. The beach is on Savannah Sound, the body of calm, protected water separating Windermere from the main island of Eleuthera.

Visitors can enjoy a number of activities, from bonefishing to windsurfing. The dockmaster at West Beach is well-qualified to guide and advise about bonefishing, or perhaps you'd like to go deep-sea fishing for white marlin, dolphinfish, grouper, wahoo, Allison tuna, and amberjack. Since there is no permanent outfitter, you have to ask around locally about who can take you out.

4 Palmetto Point

On the east side of Queen's Highway, south of Governor's Harbour, North Palmetto Point is a little village where visitors rarely venture (although you can get a meal there). This laid-back town will suit you if you want peace and quiet off the beaten track.

The Eleutherian Adventurers

Long before the first English colonists arrived, Eleuthera was inhabited by native Lucayans. However, around the mid-16th century, Spaniards came this way, captured this peaceable people, and shipped them to the Caribbean as slaves.

Pirates plied the waters off Eleuthera and its adjacent islands, but after the Lucayans were forced out, there were no inhabitants here for a century—until Capt. William Sayle led the "Eleutherian Adventurers" here from Bermuda to start a new life. The founding party, consisting of about 70 people, had a rough time of it. Their ship and cargo were lost on dangerous reefs on the north coast of the island. Trapped, they had to live off the land as best they could, initially inhabiting a cave (for a description, see "The Current," below). Many of them nearly starved, but they nevertheless drew up their own constitution, promising justice for all. Help came from Virginia colonists, who sent food to the little band of adventurers.

Life on Eleuthera eventually proved too difficult for many of the founding party. Many, including Captain Sayle, later returned to Bermuda. Soon, however, both Bermuda and England sent reinforcements, including some slaves, and a permanent settlement was founded. Freed slaves also came to this island and established settlements. The next wave of settlers was Loyalists fleeing the new United States to continue living under the British Crown. They settled principally in two offshore cays, Harbour Island and Spanish Wells.

Ten Bay Beach &&& is one of the best beaches in The Bahamas, with its sparkling turquoise water and wide expanse of soft white sand. The beach lies a 10-minute drive south of Palmetto Point and just north of Savannah Sound. There are no facilities, only idyllic isolation.

WHERE TO STAY

Palmetto Shores Vacation Villas   This is a good choice if you want your own apartment and value independence and privacy over hotel services. Asa Bethel rents villas suitable for two to four guests. Units are built in a plain Bahamian-style, with living rooms, kitchens, small bathrooms with shower units, and wraparound balconies that open directly onto your own private beach. Furnishings are simple but reasonably comfortable, VCRs are included, and the villas lie within walking distance of local shops and tennis courts.

P.O. Box EL25131, Governor's Harbour, Eleuthera, The Bahamas. © **888/688-4752** or 242/332-1305. Fax 242/332-1305. www.ivacation.com/p6835.htm. 10 units. Winter $100–$180 1-, 2-, and 3-bedroom villas for 2; off-season $90–$180 1-, 2-, and 3-bedroom villas for 2. Year-round $180 2-bedroom villa for 4. Extra person $20–$30 summer, $30 winter. MC, V. **Amenities:** Deep-sea fishing, free Sunflower sailboats, snorkeling, car rentals. *In room:* A/C, TV, VCR.

Unique Village   Located on a steep rise above the Atlantic coast of Eleuthera, this hotel is the creative statement of a Palmetto Point businessman who also owns the local hardware store (Unique Hardware). Built in 1992, the hotel offers accommodations in several configurations (everything from conventional single or double rooms to a one-bedroom apartment with a kitchenette to two-bedroom villas with full kitchens). Each comes with a small bathroom with a shower stall. A flight of wooden steps will bring you to the beach, where a reef breaks up the Atlantic surf and creates calm waters on this sandy cove. There's a bar and restaurant, also called Unique Village, on-site (see "Where to Dine," below), but few other amenities. Although there is no sailing, scuba, or tennis on-site, the staff can direct you to other facilities that lie within a reasonable drive (you'll probably want a car here).

N. Palmetto Point, The Bahamas (send mail to P.O. Box EL25187, Governor's Harbour, Eleuthera, The Bahamas). ℂ 800/688-4752 or 242/332-1830. Fax 242/332-1838. uniqvil@grouper.batelnet.bs. 13 units. Winter $120–$140 double, $160 1-bedroom apt for 2, $190 2-bedroom apt for up to 4; off-season $90–$110 double, $130 1-bedroom apt, $160 2-bedroom apt for up to 4. Extra person $25. MAP (breakfast and dinner) $35 per person per day. MC, V. **Amenities:** Bar, restaurant. *In room:* A/C, TV.

WHERE TO DINE

Mate & Jenny's Pizza Restaurant & Bar BAHAMIAN/AMERICAN   This popular restaurant, known for its conch pizza, has a jukebox and a pool table. It's the most popular local joint, completely modest and unassuming. In addition to pizza, the Bethel family will prepare pan-fried grouper, cracked conch, or light meals, including snacks and sandwiches. Lots of folks come here just to drink. Try their Goombay Smash, Rumrunner, or piña colada, or just a Bahamian Kalik beer.

S. Palmetto Point, right off Queen's Hwy. ℂ 242/332-1504. Pizza $6–$24; main courses $12–$25. No credit cards. Wed–Sat and Mon 11am–3pm and 5:30–9:30pm.

Muriel's Home Made Bread and Restaurant 🏵 *(Finds)* BAHAMIAN   Muriel Cooper's operation runs a bakery and a take-out food emporium. Her rich and moist pineapple and coconut cakes are some of the best you'll find in the Out Islands. A limited menu of true local cooking includes full dinners, such as chicken with chips, cracked conch, conch chowder, and conch fritters. If you want a more elaborate meal, you'll have to stop by in the morning to place your order. This is an ideal arrangement if you're staying in a cottage or villa nearby.

N. Palmetto Point. ℂ 242/332-1583. Main courses $7–$10. No credit cards. Mon–Sat 10am–6pm.

Unique Village Restaurant & Lounge BAHAMIAN/AMERICAN   This is the best place for food in the area, offering the widest selection. You can drop in for a Bahamian breakfast of boiled or stewed fish served with johnnycakes, or steamed corned beef and grits ("regular" breakfasts, including hearty omelets, are also available). Lunch offerings include zesty conch chowder and an array of salads. Burgers are served, along with what the kitchen calls "Bahamian belly pleasers," including the steamed catch of the day. At night the choices grow, and you'll find the best New York sirloin available in mid-Eleuthera, ranging in size from 8 to 16 ounces. Cracked conch fried in a light beer batter is one of the better renderings of this dish on the island.

In the Unique Village, N. Palmetto Point. ℂ 242/332-1830. Main courses $13.95–$32. MC, V. Daily 7:30–11:30am, noon–5pm, and 6–10pm.

5 Governor's Harbour

At some 300 years old, Governor's Harbour is the island's oldest settlement, reportedly the landing place of the Eleutherian Adventurers. The largest town on Eleuthera after Rock Sound, it lies midway along the 100-mile-long island; its airport is likely to be your gateway to the island.

The town today has a population of about 1,500, with some bloodlines going back to the original settlers, the Eleutherian Adventurers, and to the Loyalists who followed some 135 years later. Many old homes line the streets amid the bougainvillea and casuarina trees. **Brenda's Boutique,** Haynes Avenue (© 242/332-2089), is a two-room store occupying a clapboard-sided building a few steps away from the only traffic light in Eleuthera. Inside is a large selection of T-shirts, sundresses, bathing suits, and Bahamian souvenirs like conch jewelry. Hours are Monday to Saturday 9am to 5:30pm.

Leaving Queen's Highway, you can take a small bridge, thought to be about 150 years old, to Cupid's Cay. As you're exploring, you'll come upon one of the most interesting buildings in the area, an old Anglican church with its tombstone-studded graveyard.

ESSENTIALS

GETTING THERE   See the beginning of this chapter for details. The town airport is one of the island's major gateways, with daily flights arriving from Nassau and Florida.

VISITOR INFORMATION   The **Eleuthera Tourist Office** is on Queens Highway (© 242/332-2142); it's generally open Monday to Friday 9am to 5pm.

FAST FACTS   If you're staying outside the town in a cottage or an apartment, you may find services and supplies in Governor's Harbour or at nearby Palmetto Point.

Governor's Harbour has a branch of **Barclays Bank International** on Queen's Highway (© 242/332-2300).

Also on Queen's Highway is the **Governor Harbour's Medical Clinic** (© 242/332-2001), open Monday through Friday from 9am to 5:30pm. The clinic is also the site of a dentist's office. The dentist is here from 9:30am until 3pm, Monday through Wednesday and Friday only. Call for an appointment before going here.

If you need the police, call © **242/332-2111.**

There's a **post office** on Haynes Avenue (© 242/332-2060).

WHERE TO STAY

Buccaneer Club   This three-story farmhouse, built more than a century ago, offers views over the harbor. Today, it sports yellow-painted plank siding, white trim, and an old-fashioned design. The beach lies within a 10-minute stroll. Bedrooms are comfortable, unpretentious, well-maintained, clean, and outfitted with simple but colorful furniture, plus a small bathroom with shower stall. Your host and hostess are Michelle and Dwight Johnson, an Indian/Bahamian entrepreneurial team who foster a calm, quiet atmosphere.

Lunch and dinner are served daily in an airy, newly built annex with island murals. Specialties include Bahamian and American standbys: steaks, burgers, club sandwiches, cracked conch, grilled grouper with lemon butter sauce, and chili.

Haynes Dr. at Buccaneer Dr. (P.O. Box 86), Governor's Harbour, Eleuthera, The Bahamas. © 242/332-2000. Fax 242/332-2888. 5 units. Mid-Dec to mid-Apr $99 double; mid-Apr to mid-Dec $88 double. DISC, MC, V. **Amenities:** Restaurant, bar, pool. *In room:* A/C, TV.

Duck Inn and Orchid Gardens ☞ (*Finds*)   The accommodations you'll rent here are larger, plusher, more historic, and more charming than what you'd expect in a conventional hotel. All come with kitchenettes. The complex consists of three clapboard-sided houses, each built between 80 and 175 years ago, and each almost adjacent to another, midway up a hillside overlooking the sea. Nassau-born John (J.J.) Duckworth and his Michigan-born wife, Emily, along with their son John Lucas, are your hosts. Much of their time is spent nurturing a sprawling collection of beautiful orchids being cultivated for export to Europe and the U.S. The collection of orchids, some 4,000 strong, is one of the largest in North America.

Queen's Hwy., Governor's Harbour, Eleuthera, The Bahamas. (C) 242/332-2608. www.theduckinn.com. 3 units. $121 studio for 2, $242 4-bedroom cottage for up to 8. MC, V. *In-room amenities:* A/C, kitchenette. No phone.

Laughing Bird Apartments   These simple apartments lie near the edge of town on a beach in the center of Eleuthera and are a good bet if you want to set-tle in for a week or so. Efficiencies come with a living/dining/sleeping area, with a separate kitchen and a separate bathroom with shower stall. Apartments front the beach on an acre of landscaped property. The units are bright, clean, and airy.

Haynes Ave. and Birdie St. (P.O. Box EL25076), Governor's Harbour, Eleuthera, The Bahamas. (C) 800/ 688-4752 or 242/332-2012. Fax 242/332-2358. www.sundial.net. 4 units. $85–$105 double, $110–$115 triple, $120–$125 quad. DISC, MC, V. **Amenities:** Room service, laundry, bike rentals, a garden, tables and chairs for outdoor eating, and a garden barbecue. Arrangements made for waterskiing, surfing, fishing, sail-ing, tennis, golf, and snorkeling. *In room:* A/C.

WHERE TO DINE
Pammy's BAHAMIAN   Tile-floored and Formica-clad, this is just a little cubbyhole with a few tables. Lunchtime brings sandwiches, and dinner features platters of cracked conch, pork chops, and either broiled or fried grouper. Don't expect anything fancy, 'cause this definitely ain't it. It's a true local joint serving up generous portions of flavor-filled food.

Queen's Hwy. at Gospel Chapel Rd. (C) 242/332-2843. Reservations not accepted. Breakfast platters $4–$5.50; lunchtime platters $4–$8; dinner main courses $11–$20. No credit cards. Mon–Sat 8am–9pm.

HITTING THE BEACH
Near the center of town are two sandy beaches known locally as the **Buccaneer Public Beaches;** they're adjacent to the Buccaneer Club, on the sheltered west-ern edge of the island, facing Exuma Sound. Snorkeling is good here—it's best at the point where the pale turquoise waters near the coast deepen to a dark blue. Underwater rocks shelter lots of marine flora and fauna. The waves at these beaches are relatively calm.

On Eleuthera's Atlantic (eastern) side, about a half mile from Governor's Har-bour, is a much longer stretch of mostly pale pink sand, similar to what you'll find in Harbour Island. Known locally as the **Club Med Public Beach,** it's good for bodysurfing and, on days when storms are surging in the Atlantic, even con-ventional surfing.

Don't expect any touristy kiosks selling drinks, snacks, or souvenirs at any of these beaches, because everything is very pristine and undeveloped.

GOVERNOR'S HARBOUR AFTER DARK
Ronnie's Smoke Shop & Sports Bar, Cupid's Cay ((C) 242/332-2307), is the most happening night spot in central Eleuthera, drawing folks from miles in either direction. It's adjacent to the cargo depot of Cupid's Cay, in a connected cluster of simple buildings painted in combinations of black with vivid Junkanoo colors. Most folks come here just to drink Kalik beer and talk at either

of the two bars. But if you want to dance, there's an all-black room just for disco music on Friday and Saturday nights. There's also the only walk-in cigar humidor on Eleuthera. If you get hungry, order up a plate of barbecue, a pizza, chicken wings, or popcorn. The place is open daily from 10am till at least 2am, and sometimes 5am, depending on business.

6 Hatchet Bay

Twenty-five miles north of Governor's Harbour, Hatchet Bay was once known for a sprawling British-owned plantation that had 500 head of dairy cattle and thousands of chickens. Today, that plantation is gone, and this is now one of the sleepiest villages on Eleuthera, as you can see if you veer off Queen's Highway onto one of the town's ghostly main streets, Lazy Shore Road or Ocean Drive.

WHERE TO STAY & DINE

Rainbow Inn ✆ Two miles south of Alice Town, and near a sandy beach, the Rainbow Inn is a venerable survivor in an area where many competitors have failed. Quirky and appealing to guests who return for quiet getaways again and again, it's an isolated collection of seven cedar-sided octagonal bungalows. The accommodations are simple but comfortable, spacious, and tidy; each has a kitchenette, lots of exposed wood, a ceiling fan, a small bathroom with a shower unit, and a porch. There's a sandy beach a few steps away.

One of the most appealing things about the place is its bar and restaurant, a destination for residents far up and down the length of Eleuthera. It's an octagon with a high-beamed ceiling and a thick-topped woodsy-looking bar where guests down daiquiris and piña coladas amid nautical trappings. It has live Bahamian music twice a week and one of the most extensive menus on Eleuthera. The owners take pride in the fact that the menu hasn't changed much in 20 years, a fact that suits its loyal fans just fine. Local Bahamian food includes fish, conch chowder, fried conch, fresh fish, and Bahamian lobster. International dishes feature French onion soup, escargots, and steaks, followed by key lime pie for dessert. Table no. 2, crafted from a triangular teakwood prow of a motor yacht that was wrecked off the coast of Eleuthera in the 1970s, is a perpetual favorite.

P.O. Box EL25053, Governor's Harbour, Eleuthera, The Bahamas. ✆ **800/688-0047** in the U.S., or 242/335-0294. Fax 242/335-0294. www.rainbowinn.com. 5 units. $115–$140 studio, $175–$200 2- or 3-bedroom villas. MAP (breakfast and dinner) $40 per person extra. MC, V. Closed Sept 7–Nov 15. **Amenities:** Restaurant, bar, pool, tennis court (free tennis balls and rackets provided), snorkeling gear, bikes, rental cars. *In room:* A/C.

7 Gregory Town

Gregory Town stands in the center of Eleuthera against a backdrop of hills, which break the usual flat monotony of the landscape. A village of clapboard cottages, it was once famed for growing pineapples. Though the industry isn't as strong as it was in the past, the locals make a good pineapple rum out of the fruit, and you can visit the Gregory Town Plantation and Distillery, where it's produced. You're allowed to sample it, and we can almost guarantee you'll want to take a bottle home with you.

WHERE TO STAY

The Cove Eleuthera On a private sandy cove 1½ miles northwest of Gregory Town and 3 miles southeast of the Glass Window, this year-round resort is

---

Finds For a Drop-Dead Pineapple Tart

Follow the smell of fresh-baked goods to **Thompson's Bakery,** Johnson Street (© **242/335-5053**), which is open Monday to Saturday 8:30am to 6pm. Run by two local sisters, Monica and Daisy Thompson, this simple bakery occupies a wooden lime-green building near the highest point in town (next to the largest building in town, also painted lime green). Although it churns out lots of bread, including raisin, whole-wheat, and coconut bread, every day, its fresh pineapple tarts, priced at $1 each, are among the best we've ever tasted. You might also find fresh-baked doughnuts and cinnamon rolls.

---

set on 28 acres partially planted with pineapples; it consists of a main clubhouse and seven tropical-style buildings, each containing four units, nestled on the oceanside. The resort was devastated during the hurricanes of 1999, and a radical rebuilding program was needed. By late 2000, rooms were back in shape. Each one has tile floors and a porch, with no TVs or phones to distract you. All accommodations are equipped with a small bathroom with shower stalls.

The restaurant (see below) serves three meals a day, and the lounge and the Pineapple Patio, poolside, are open daily for drinks and informal meals. Kayaks, bicycles, two tennis courts, and a small freshwater pool compete with hammocks for your time. There's fabulous snorkeling right off the sands here, with colorful fish darting in and out of the offshore reefs.

Queen's Hwy. (P.O. Box GT1548), Gregory Town, Eleuthera, The Bahamas. © 800/552-5960 in the U.S. and Canada, or 242/335-5142. Fax 242/335-5338. www.thecoveeleuthera.com. E-mail: ann@thecoveeleuthera. com. 26 units. Winter $109–$139 double; $149 triple; off-season $89–$119 double, $99–$129 triple. 1 child under 12 stays free in parents' room. MAP (breakfast and dinner) $33 per person extra. AE, MC, V. **Amenities:** Restaurant, bar, tennis courts, pool, kayaks, bikes, snorkeling. *In room:* A/C. No phone.

WHERE TO DINE

Cambridge Villas BAHAMIAN   This is one of the few choices in town, occupying a large cement-sided room on the ground floor of a battered hotel (the accommodations aren't as appealing as the restaurant). Harcourt and Sylvia Cambridge, the owners, serve conch burgers, conch chowder, and sandwiches, usually prepared by Sylvia herself. It's just a simple spot, where you might be entertained by the continually running soap operas broadcast from a TV over the bar.

Main St. © **242/335-5080.** Reservations not accepted. Sandwiches and platters $3.50–$9. MC, V. Daily 7:30am–9pm.

The Cove BAHAMIAN/CONTINENTAL   In the previously recommended hotel 1½ miles north of Gregory Town, this spacious dining room is your best bet in the area. It's nothing fancy but good homemade local fare. The restaurant is decorated in a light, tropical style. Lunch begins with the inevitable conch chowder; we recommend you follow it with a conch burger, a generous patty of ground conch blended with green pepper, onion, and spices. Conch also appears several times in the evening, including the best cracked conch in town, which has been tenderized and dipped in a special batter and fried to a golden perfection. The kitchen serves the best fried chicken in the area. People travel from miles around to attend the Saturday-night $25 buffet—the smoked dolphinfish dip is reason enough to stop in. They also offer a vegetarian buffet for $17.25.

Queen's Hwy. ℂ **242/335-5142.** Reservations not necessary. Breakfast $4.50–$9; lunch $6–$12; main courses $10–$32. AE, MC, V. Daily 8–10:30am, noon–2:30pm, and 6:30–8:30pm.

Cush's Place BAHAMIAN   Macushla Scavella (Cush, for short) is the owner of this big yellow stucco-sided building set about a half mile south of Gregory Town. Inside the somewhat sterile-looking interior, you'll find a jukebox, a pool table, and a bartender named Walter. Generous portions of Bahamian food are (slowly) served throughout the day and evening. Pork chops and chicken a la Cush (fried chicken) are ongoing staples, along with sandwiches, lobster tail, and steamed conch with black-eyed peas and corn on the cob. Come here to hang out with the locals, perhaps over drinks and a platter of food.

Queen's Hwy. ℂ **242/335-5301.** Reservations not necessary. Sandwiches $2.75–$4; lunch and dinner main courses $9–$18. No credit cards. Daily 10am–midnight.

EXPLORING THE AREA: THE GLASS WINDOW & BEYOND

On Queen's Highway in the heart of town, behind a colorful facade, is the **Island Made Gift Shop** (ℂ **242/335-5369**), with an outstanding inventory that owes its quality to the artistic eye and good taste of owner Pamela Thompson. Look for one-of-a-kind paintings on driftwood or crafted on the soles of discarded shoes, handmade quilts from Androsian fabrics, Abaco ceramics, and jewelry made from pieces of glass found on the beach. There are extraordinary woven baskets from the descendants of Seminole Indians and escaped slaves living in remote districts of Andros Island. Especially charming are bowls crafted from half-sections of conch shells.

Dedicated surfers have come here from as far away as California and Australia to test their skills at **Surfer's Beach,** a couple of miles south of town on the Atlantic side. The waves are at their highest in winter and spring; even if you're not brave enough to get out there, it's fun to watch.

South of town on the way to Hatchet Bay are several caverns worth visiting, the largest of which is called simply **the Cave.** It has a big fig tree out front, which the people of Gregory Town claim was planted long ago by area pirates who wanted to conceal the cave because they had hidden treasure in it.

Local guides (you have to ask around in Gregory Town or Hatchet Bay) will take you into the interior of the cave, where the resident bats are harmless (even though they must resent the intrusion of tourists with flashlights). At one point the drop is so steep—about 12 feet—that you have to use a ladder to climb down. Eventually you reach a cavern studded with stalactites and stalagmites. At this point, a maze of passageways leads off through the rocky underground recesses. The cave comes to an abrupt end at the edge of a cliff, where the thundering sea is some 90 feet below.

After leaving Gregory Town and driving north, you come to the famed **Glass Window,** Eleuthera's chief sight and narrowest point. Once a natural rock arch bridged the land, but it's gone now, replaced by an artificially constructed bridge. As you drive across it, you can see the contrast between the deep blue ocean and the emerald green shoal waters of the sound. The rocks rise to a height of 70 feet. Often, as ships in the Atlantic are being tossed about, the crew looks across the narrow point to see a ship resting quietly on the other side. Hence the name Glass Window. Winslow Homer was so captivated by this spot that he once captured it on canvas.

GREGORY TOWN AFTER DARK

The place to be in Gregory Town, especially on a Saturday night, is **Elvina** on Main Street (✆ **242/335-5032**). Owners Ed and Elvina Watkins make you feel right at home and practically greet you at the door with a cold beer. Although they won't be hired by the queen to decorate Buckingham Palace, they have given their place a funky charm, with local artwork, license plates, and surfboards. Surfers and locals alike flock here to chow down on burgers, Bahamian dishes, and Cajun grub, served daily from 10am to "whenever we close." Elvina's husband, "Chicken Ed," is from Louisiana, and does he ever know how to make a great jambalaya. Incidentally, you can bring your dirty clothes here as well, because the couple also runs the washeteria next door.

8 The Current

The inhabitants of the Current, a settlement in North Eleuthera, are believed to have descended from a tribe of Native Americans. A narrow strait separates the village from Current Island, where most of the locals make their living from the sea or from plaiting straw goods.

This is a small community where the people often welcome visitors. There are no crowds and no artificial attractions. Everything focuses on the sea, a source of pleasure for the visiting tourists, but a way to sustain life for the local people.

From the Current, you can explore some interesting sights in North Eleuthera, including **Preacher's Cave,** where the Eleutherian Adventurers found shelter in the mid-17th century when they were shipwrecked with no provisions. (Note that your taxi driver may balk at being asked to drive there; the road is hard on his expensive tires.) If you do reach it, you'll find a cave that seems like an amphitheater. The very devout Eleutherian Adventurers held religious services inside the cave, which is pierced by holes in the roof, allowing light to intrude. The cave is not far from the airport, in a northeasterly direction.

Another sight is **Boiling Hole,** which is in a shallow bank that seems to boil at changing tides.

WHERE TO STAY

Sandcastle Apartments   For escapists seeking a location far removed from the usual tourist circuit, this utterly plain but airy accommodation is a good bet. The on-site kitchen, the easy access to a simple grocery store within a 5-minute walk, and the self-contained nature of this extremely modest accommodation often appeal to families. There are a double bed in the bedroom, a queen-size pullout bed in the living room, and a view over shallow offshore waters, where children can wade safely for a surprisingly long distance offshore. The accommodation comes with a small bathroom with a shower stall. The unit lies just across the road from the sea, and if you want to explore, bicycles are available.

The Current, Eleuthera, The Bahamas. ✆ 242/335-3244. Fax 242/393-0440. 1 unit. $75–$90 double. Extra person $10. No credit cards. *In-room:* A/C.

9 Harbour Island 🌟🌟🌟

One of the oldest settlements in The Bahamas, founded before the United States was a nation, Harbour Island lies off the northern end of Eleuthera, some 200 miles from Miami. It is 3 miles long and half a mile wide.

Affectionately called "Briland," Harbour Island is studded with good resorts. The spectacular **Pink Sands Beach** 🌟🌟🌟 runs the whole length of the island on its eastern side. The famous beach is protected from the ocean breakers by an outlying coral reef, which makes for some of the safest swimming in The Bahamas. Except for unseasonably cold days, you can swim and enjoy water sports year-round. The climate averages 72°F in winter, 77°F in spring and fall, and 82°F in summer. Occasionally, evenings are cool, with a low of about 65°F from November to February.

For years, local residents made their livings from farming, shipbuilding, fishing, and sponge diving. Farms still operate today on the main body of Eleuthera, on land that Andrew Devereaux, a colonel in the British army, gave to the Brilanders in 1783. The Civil War in the United States brought an economic boom to the area, as the Brilanders prospered by defying the blockade that the Union had placed on shipping to and from the Confederate States.

By 1880, Dunmore Town had become the second-most-important town of The Bahamas. It not only was a port of entry, but it also had a major shipyard (turning out vessels as large as four-masted schooners) and three sugar mills. Eventually, the town fell on bad times, but Prohibition in the United States brought another brief economic boom as rum-running became a major source of income. Times were hard after Prohibition was repealed, an event followed by the Great Depression and World War II. But in recent decades, the tourist industry discovered the beautiful sands of Harbour Island, and prosperity is back.

ESSENTIALS

GETTING THERE   To reach Harbour Island, take a flight to the **North Eleuthera airstrip,** which is only a 1½-hour flight from Fort Lauderdale or Miami and a 30-minute flight from Nassau (see the beginning of this chapter for details on which airlines provide service). From there, it's a 1-mile taxi ride to the ferry dock. The taxi costs $4 per person if you share the expense with other passengers. From the dock, you'll take a 2-mile motorboat ride to Harbour Island. There's usually no waiting, because a flotilla of high-powered motorboats makes the crossing whenever at least two customers show up, at a cost of $4 per person. (If you're traveling alone and are willing to pay the $8 one-way fare, the boat will depart immediately, without waiting for a second passenger.)

GETTING AROUND   Once they reach Harbour Island, most people don't need transportation. They walk to where they're going, rent a pedal bicycle (check your equipment carefully before you rent it, since some bicycles rented to tourists on Harbour Island are way past their prime), or putt-putt around the island on an electric golf cart. Most hotels offer these for rent, or at least will arrange for a cart or bicycle; usually, they'll be delivered directly to your hotel.

If you want to go some distance on the island, call **Reggie's Taxi** at © 242/333-2116 or **Big M Taxi Service** at © 242/333-2043.

Michael's Cycles on Colebrook Street (© 242/333-2384) is the best place to go if you want some mobility other than your own two feet. The shop is open daily from 8am to 8pm. Bikes rent for $10 per day, and you can also rent two-seater motorbikes for $30 a day, or even a two-seater golf cart for between $40 and $48 per day, depending on the model.

VISITOR INFORMATION   The **Harbour Island Tourist Office** is on Bay Street (© 242/333-2621); it's generally open Monday to Friday 9am to 5pm.

FAST FACTS   The **Royal Bank of Canada** is just up the hill from the city dock (© 242/333-2250).

The **Harbour Island Health Centre,** South Street, Dunmore Town (© **242/ 333-2227**), handles routine medical problems. Hours are Monday through Friday from 9am to 5pm. The on-call doctor can be reached at © **242/333-2822. Harbour Pharmacy Health Care and Prescription Service** can be found on the waterfront near the corner of King Street (© **242/333-2174**). It sells health-and-beauty aids, fills prescriptions, and offers over-the-counter drugs Monday to Saturday 8am to 9pm.

The police can be reached at either © **919** or © **242/333-2111.**

WHERE TO STAY
VERY EXPENSIVE
Dunmore Beach Club ⓕⓕⓕ   This formal and very exclusive colony of cottages is the quintessentially elegant hideaway, with 8 acres of well-manicured grounds along the island's legendary 3-mile pink-sand beach. It's not as elaborate or sleek as its nearest rival, Pink Sands, but it's cozier and, in a way, more posh. Renovations in 1999 brought it up to the standards of the very best accommodations in Harbour Island; huge showers and whirlpool tubs are all-new and the air-conditioning system is state-of-the-art. The Bahamian-style bungalows attractively combine traditional furnishings and tropical accessories, with no phones or TVs to distract you. Overall, the feeling is dignified, comfortable, and very pleasant.

Breakfast is offered on a garden terrace under pine trees with a view of the beach. Dinner is served, at one sitting, at 8pm; men must wear jackets (ties are optional). Superb Bahamian and international cuisine is served formally in a dining room with a beamed ceiling, louvered doors, Villeroy & Bosch china, and windows with views over the blue Atlantic. A clubhouse is the focal point for socializing. A living room with a library and a fireplace provides additional cozy nooks, as does the ocean-view bar-lounge.

Colebrook Lane (P.O. Box EL27122), Harbour Island, The Bahamas. © **877/891-3100** or 242/333-2200. Fax 242/333-2429. www.dunmorebeach.com. 12 units. Nov–Apr $465 double, $495 suite; off-season $415 double, $440 suite. Winter rates include all meals; off-season rates includes MAP (breakfast and dinner). MC, V. Closed Sept–Oct. **Amenities:** Restaurant, bar/lounge, laundry, baby-sitting, bike rentals, tennis court. *In room:* A/C. No phone.

Pink Sands ⓕⓕⓕ   This is a posh and sophisticated hideaway, just the place to sneak away to with that special (wealthy) someone, adjacent to a 3-mile stretch of pink sand beach, sheltered by a barrier reef. It's an elegant, relaxed retreat on a 28-acre beachfront estate; it feels a bit like a pricey private club, but it's less snobbish and a lot more hip than the Dunmore Beach Club. Its owner is Chris Blackwell, the founder of Island Records, who is increasingly known as a hotel entrepreneur and who spared no expense here. The resort's outrageous clubhouse is the most beautifully and imaginatively decorated room in the Out Islands.

The airy, spacious bedrooms have either an ocean or a garden view. Smaller units contain art-deco touches straight out of Miami's South Beach; larger, more expensive units have Indonesian (especially Balinese) furnishings and art, and huge decks. All rooms have kitchenettes or kitchens, central air-conditioning, pressurized water systems, walk-in closets, satellite TVs, CD players and a CD selection, wet bars, private patios with teak furnishings, and beautifully tiled bathrooms with tubs and showers. The interior design features marble floors with area rugs, oversize Adirondack furnishings, local artwork, and batik fabrics.

The rooms have dataports, and fax machines and cellular phones can be supplied if you need them.

Hotel guests get some of the best meals on the island, an ABC fusion of Asian, Bahamian, and Caribbean cuisine. Dinner is a four-course nightly affair, included in the MAP price for guests and priced at $70 per person, without drinks, for non-guests who phone ahead for reservations. Lunches are much less formal, served in the Blue Bar, a post-modern pavilion beside the beach.

Chapel St., Harbour Island, The Bahamas. © 800/OUTPOST or 242/333-2030. Fax 242/333-2060. www.islandoutpost.com. 25 units. Winter $625–$725 1-bedroom cottage, $1,100–$2,000 2-bedroom cottage; off-season $475–$575 1-bedroom cottage, $875–$1,225 2-bedroom cottage. Rates include MAP (breakfast and dinner). AE, MC, V. **Amenities:** Restaurant, bar, freshwater pool, 3 tennis courts, room service (breakfast 7:30–10:30am, dinner 7–9pm), personal laundry services, gym, clubhouse, beach palapa/tiki bar. *In room:* A/C, TV, VCR, coffeemaker, hair dryer, safe.

Romora Bay Club ⊛   This is one of the quirkiest, most cosmopolitan hotels on Harbour Island. It's more akin to the whimsy and music-industry celebrity chic of Pink Sands than anything else, but here the price tag's lower, there's a stronger French flavor, and the design isn't as self-conscious. It was originally developed as a private club for reclusive millionaires. Later, Lionel Rotcage, the French-born son of Paris's leading nightlife impresario (Régine), rebuilt all rooms with the flair of Morocco, central Africa, or Italy—and sometimes all three, always with lots of post-modern whimsy, unusual tile work, and bold colors. The guests tend to range in age from 25 to 50 and tend to view it as a private club, where hanging out with a chic international crowd is part of the entertainment. The social center is a dramatic living room with oversize art (one piece is a Picasso). Thanks to a cooperative arrangement with a local dive outfit, the place is a favorite spot for divers (see "Beaches & Water Sports," below). Bungalows and villas are spacious and newly refurbished, with bright Caribbean colors, and comfortable king-size or twin beds. Most of the units come with a large bathroom with tub or shower combos. Check into numbers 7, 8, or 9 for the most panoramic views.

Lunches in the hotel's Restaurant Ludocris tend to be buffet-style, featuring light-textured but elegant salads and warm-weather foods. Dinners are more formal, prepared by a young French-born chef, Christophe Micou, whose previous training included stints with French culinary superstars Roger Verger and Paul Bocuse. See "Where to Dine," below. All flights are met at the airport by taxis for the 1-mile drive to the ferry dock, and there's a 2-mile ferry ride direct to the club's private dock.

Colebrook St., Harbour Island, The Bahamas. © 800/688-0425 in the U.S., or 242/333-2325. Fax 242/333-2500. www.romorabay.com. 31 units. Winter $310–$400 double, $540–$580 suite; off-season $220–$320 double, $440–$480 suite. Rates include breakfast and lunch. AE, MC, V. **Amenities:** Restaurant, fitness center, pool, tennis courts, Sunfish rentals, deep-sea fishing, garden, access to sandy beach. *In room:* A/C.

EXPENSIVE

Coral Sands ⊛⊛   The hotel, whose exterior is painted a soft coral pink, stands on 9 hilly acres overlooking the beach and within walking distance of the center of Dunmore Town. Coral Sands is a longtime favorite that does a big business with happy repeat visitors. Originally built with an airy design that featured big-windowed loggias and arcades, it opens directly onto the 3-mile pink-coral-sand beach for which the town is famous. Casual elegance, with ample doses of personal charm and friendliness, permeates every aspect of this hotel. Recent renovations and improvements have revitalized the property and freshened up the decor. Many rooms have private verandas or terraces, all are eminently comfortable, and all allow you to fall asleep to the soothing sounds of waves breaking on the shore. The owners are Latex Foam Products (LIS, Inc.) of Ansonia, Connecticut, so all beds have the antibacterial, dust-mite-resistant latex mattresses produced by this company. Bathrooms are mid-size and well-kept, mostly with shower and tub combos.

The hotel's restaurant, The Poseidon, offers the finest cuisine on Harbour Island (see "Where to Dine," below). Simpler, less elaborate food is also offered at the beachfront Commander's Beach Bar & Restaurant, which is dramatically cantilevered high above the pale pink sands.

Chapel St., Harbour Island, The Bahamas. ☎ 800/468-2799 in the U.S. and Canada, or 242/333-2350. Fax 242/333-2368. www.coralsands.com. 27 units. Winter $210–$260 double, $335–$430 1-bedroom suite, $430–$620 2-bedroom suite; off-season $155–$195 double, $260–$325 1-bedroom suite, $325–$475 2-bedroom suite. MAP (breakfast and dinner) $50 per person extra. AE, DC, MC, V. Closed U.S. Labor Day–Oct 28. **Amenities:** Restaurant, beach bar & restaurant, free-form swimming pool, 2 tennis courts, boogie boards, windsurfing, snorkeling equipment, cabanas, rentable sailboats. *In room:* A/C, coffeemaker.

Runaway Hill Club Small and intimate, this conservative, comfortable hotel overlooks acres of pink sandy beachfront. It has a huge lawn and is separated from Colebrook Street by a wall. The building's original English colonial dormers are still prominent, as are many of its original features. In winter, a crackling fire is sometimes built in the hearth near the entrance. The social center is a cheerfully decorated lounge/dining room/bar/reception area painted in joyful island colors with a sense of Bahamian whimsy. Each of the bedrooms is different, giving the impression that you are lodging in a private home—as indeed this used to be. Only two of the rooms at this place are in the original house, and these are accessible via the building's original 18th-century staircase. The others are within comfortable annexes built during the 1970s and 80s. Bathrooms are small but well-maintained, and seven contain tub and shower combos, the rest showers.

Dinners are served on the breeze-filled rear porch overlooking the swimming pool, and non-guests are welcome (see "Where to Dine," below).

Colebrook St. (P.O. Box EL27031), Harbour Island, The Bahamas. ☎ 800/728-9803 in the U.S., or 242/333-2150. Fax 242/333-2420. www.cpscaribnet.com/ads/runaway/runa.htm. 10 units. Winter $240–$250 double; off-season $205–$215 double. MAP (breakfast and dinner) $60 per person extra. AE, MC, V. Closed Sept 5–Nov 15. No children under 17 accepted. **Amenities:** Restaurant, pool, bike rental, fishing trips, water sports. *In room:* A/C. No phone.

MODERATE
The Landing ⏶ This intimate inn is understated, tasteful, and lovely. Virtually destroyed by a hurricane in 1999, it was well-restored by its owners, Tracy and Brenda Barry, the latter a former Miss Bahamas. The first doctor on Harbour Island built the house in the 1850s as his private residence. It's set within a pair of stone and clapboard-sided buildings constructed in 1800 and 1820, respectively, very close to the piers where ferryboats arrive from Eleuthera. A veranda looks out over the harbor. Accommodations are breezy, airy, and high-ceilinged, and they open onto wraparound verandas, which seem to expand the living space within. Expect bold, cheerful island colors, and design touches that evoke the seafaring days of old Harbour Island. The bathrooms are large and tiled, with tubs and showers.

Bay St. (P.O. Box 190), Harbour Island, The Bahamas. ☎ 242/333-2707. Fax 242/333-2650. www.harbourislandlanding.com. 7 units. Mid-Dec to mid-Apr $190–$295 double. Rates are 10% lower off-season. Rates include breakfast. MC, V. **Amenities:** Restaurant, bar. *In room:* A/C. No phone.

INEXPENSIVE

Bahama House Inn *⋆* *Finds*   This is the only true B&B, with the owners living on-site, on Harbour Island. The setting is a pink-sided clapboard house that was built between 1798 and 1800 by the island's first justice of the peace, Dr. Johnson. In 1999, Denver-born owners John and Joni Hersh bought a 1950s-era house next door for future expansions. Mid-size rooms are artfully old-fashioned, low-key, and comfortable, and they are usually accessible via gracious verandas that wrap around the upper and lower floors. Bathrooms are tiled, beautifully maintained, and come with shower stalls. Everything shows a personal touch here, including the beautiful gardens. The beach is a 5-minute walk away, and the house's living room has satellite TV.

At the corner of Dunmore and Hill sts., Harbour Island, The Bahamas. © 242/333-2201. Fax 242/333-2850. www.bahamahouseinn.com. 5 units. Winter $125–$155 double; off-season $105–$130 double. MC, V. Closed Sept–Oct. *In-room:* Ceiling fans. No phone.

Tingum Village   This is a simple, no-frills choice, but it does the trick at bargain prices and draws a loyal repeat business. It lies just off the main street, a 3-minute walk to the beach. Set in a steamy tropical garden, Tingum Village offers basic accommodations in small cement-sided bungalows. Each of the rooms has air-conditioning, ceiling fans, and a patio with plastic furniture, plus a small bathroom with a shower stall. Rooms aren't the most comfortable, and you'll really wish they'd improve the wattage in the reading lamps, and that the ceiling fans wouldn't squeak. But it has its charming moments as well. The cottage is meant for six to eight people, though it can hold up to 10 (but that would be very cramped).

The hotel's restaurant, Ma Ruby's, overlooks the garden and offers standard Bahamian and American food (see "Where to Dine," below).

P.O. Box 61, Colebrook St., Harbour Island, Eleuthera, The Bahamas. © 242/333-2161. Fax 242/333-2161. www.wherestay.com/island/resorts/030/html. 18 units. Winter $95–$135 double, $95–$145 triple, $250 cottage; off-season $75–$125 double, $85 triple, $225 cottage. AE, MC, V. **Amenities:** Restaurant. *In room:* A/C. No phone.

WHERE TO DINE

If you don't want to dress up for lunch, you can head for **Seaview Takeaway** (© 242/333-2542), at the foot of the ferry dock. Here you can feast on all that good stuff: pig's feet, sheep-tongue souse, and most definitely cracked conch. Everything tastes better with fungi or rice 'n' peas. Daily specials range from $3 to $8, and service is Monday to Saturday 9am to 5pm.

Finds Ma Ruby's Conch Burger

If you'd like to sample some real local fare, head to **Ma Ruby's** on Colebrook Street (© 242/333-2161). Some islanders claim you will get the best meal in Eleuthera if Ma Ruby (the cook and owner) is personally in the kitchen. Her conch burger is certainly worthy of an award. She's been stewing chicken, baking grouper, and serving hearty meals in a trellised courtyard for a long while, and she's got a lot of devoted fans. The place is well-known for its cheeseburgers, which the manager says were ranked as one of the 10 best in the world by "Mr. Cheeseburger in Paradise" himself, Jimmy Buffett. The prices range from $6 to $18 for the a la carte menu; a four-course fixed-price Bahamian dinner costs $18 to $35. The restaurant is open daily 8am to midnight.

Tips **Pack a Picnic**

The **Dunmore Deli,** at the corner of King and Princess streets
(② 242/333-2644), shares its premises with a liquor store but won its
fame by serving thick-stuffed sandwiches of tuna, chicken salad, smoked
salmon, or Black Angus roast beef. There's also a good selection of pâtés,
specialty cheeses, exotic coffees, and salads. You can eat your food at a
table on the building's front veranda or haul it off to a beach or your
boat.

Sybil's Bakery, Dunmore and Duke streets (② 242/333-3024), has
thrived through two generations of owners and is a municipal monument. Food is dispensed in Styrofoam containers that are easy to take
away. The cinnamon rolls, fresh-baked every morning, are the clear
favorites. Lunch focuses on chef's salads, peas 'n' rice, and macaroni and
cheese. It's all very informal, laid-back, and flavorful.

EXPENSIVE

The Landing *℘* INTERNATIONAL   This restaurant occupies the ground
floor and most of the garden of the previously recommended hotel, a stately
looking antique building that's just to the right of the dock as your ferryboat
pulls into Harbour Island. Designed and built with a combination of thick stone
walls and clapboards in 1800, with an annex that's only 20 years younger, it's the
domain of Brenda Barry and her daughter and son-in-law Tracy and Toby Tyler.
Their cuisine derives from the talent of Aussie-born Jennifer Learmonth, who
blends her natural talents with international training.

The menu changes with the availability of fresh ingredients but might include
conch and sweet-corn chowder, or fettuccine with anchovies and capers. One of
the best pastas is cappellini with lobster, braised romaine, chili, and lime juice.
Other pleasing choices include linguine with pesto and mozzarella, fried squid
with aïoli, and Angus tenderloin with green peppercorns.

Bay St. ② 242/333-2707. Reservations recommended. Lunch main courses $12–$22; dinner main courses
$15–$40. MC, V. Sun 9am–2pm, Thurs–Tues 7–10pm.

The Poseidon *℘* INTERNATIONAL   This is one of the finest restaurants in
The Bahamas, thanks to executive chef Susan Neff, a passionate devotee of her
craft, who has a high-energy, highly humorous approach to cuisine and life. She's
usually on hand to greet diners before or after their meal. Start off with the
house drink (a version of Pimm's Cup called Commander's Choice) at the bar,
and then you'll be seated on a terrace overlooking the sea. Signature dishes
include Poseidon lobster, served with a sauce made from Italian asiago cheese
and sauvignon blanc. White conch chowder is as superb as it is unusual, based
as it is on New England–style clam chowder but not seen as often as you'd think.
Yellowfin tuna in an Asian marinade carries the aromas of ginger, soy, Eleutherian honey, fresh tangerines, and sesame seed. Dessert might be an amaretto
chocolate mousse. Many of the herbs used to flavor Ms. Neff's dishes are grown
a few steps from the kitchen.

In the Coral Sands hotel, Chapel St. ② 242/333-2350. Reservations recommended. Main courses $20–$30.
AE, MC, V. Daily 7–9pm.

Restaurant Ludocris FRENCH/INTERNATIONAL   The French-inspired
meals at the Dunmore Beach Club are traditional, impeccably orchestrated

affairs, but the Romora Bay Club's restaurant, its leading competitor, is all sleek French chic. The trendiness doesn't detract from what might be a charming meal—it just means that you should be prepared for the unpredictable. You'll dine on a covered terrace. The menu changes according to the season and the chef's inspiration, but it might include a tartine of potatoes with foie gras, grouper or red snapper cooked in a salt crust (the flavor is flaky and delicious), and mahimahi with red-wine sauce and vegetable-based tagliatelle. Dessert might consist of a slice of chocolate cake, with the moist chocolate artfully arranged to seem half-melted.

In the Romora Bay Club, Colebrook St. ⓒ **242/333-2325.** Reservations recommended. Fixed-price 4-course menu $50. AE, MC, V. Daily 7:30–9:30pm.

Runaway Hill Club ⓐ BAHAMIAN/AMERICAN/INTERNATIONAL The dining room here enjoys a sweeping view over the beachfront. Inside, the decor is brightly painted in strong, whimsical colors, with wicker and rattan furniture and a fine collection of watercolors the owner has spent years collecting. The kitchen is known for such well-prepared dishes as rack of veal with a sherry-flavored caper sauce and noodles, conch marinara, crabmeat soup with scotch, spicy lobster bisque, beef tenderloin, and many versions of local fish.

Colebrook St. ⓒ **242/333-2150.** Reservations required. Fixed-price dinner from $60. AE, MC, V. Mon–Sat dinner at 8pm. Closed Sept 5–Nov 15.

MODERATE

The Harbour Lounge INTERNATIONAL This old clapboard-sided building is the first place you're likely to see as you step off the ferryboat arriving from the "mainland" of Eleuthera. Built in the early 1800s, it's one of the most satisfying and authentic choices on the island. Sometimes dining here is like attending an island dinner party. These might be followed with such menu items as marinated blackened grouper, soft-shell or stone crabs, lobster tail, different preparations of conch, and a combination of feta cheese and shrimp marinara. Overall, it's a charming place, and the veranda will give you a front-row seat for all the goings-on of Harbour Island.

Bay St. ⓒ **242/333-2031.** Reservations recommended for dinner. Lunch salads, sandwiches, platters $10–$12.50; dinner main courses $18–$35. MC, V. Daily 11am–4pm and 6–9:30pm.

INEXPENSIVE

Angela's Starfish Restaurant BAHAMIAN/AMERICAN This is the local joint where many of the islanders go themselves, and it serves the most authentic Eleutherian cuisine. Residents as well as visitors plan their Sunday around an evening meal here, although it's equally crowded on other nights. Run by Bahamians Angela and Vincent Johnson, the house sits on a hill above the channel in a residential section somewhat removed from the center of town. Angela can often be seen in the kitchen baking. Cracked conch and an array of seafood are specialties, and chicken potpie and pork chops are also favorites. You can dine on the palm-dotted lawn with its simple tables and folding chairs, although for chilly weather there's an unpretentious dining room inside near the cramped kitchen. It can get quite festive at night, after the candles are lit and the crowd becomes jovial.

Dunmore and Grant sts. ⓒ **242/333-2253.** Reservations required. Breakfast $3–$6.50; lunch $4–$10; main courses $13–$25. No credit cards. Daily 8am–8:30pm.

Avery's Restaurant & Grill BAHAMIAN From the moment you enter, you'll get the immediate sense that this is a simple, friendly, family-run restaurant. It occupies a tiny wooden house, painted in pastel tones of purple, green, and pink, near Tingum Village. Inside, you'll find a clean, white-tiled room with no more than four tables, and a deck with three more. Gaylean Cleare and her daughter, Avery, are the owners. Their breakfasts provide nourishment to city employees around town. The rest of the day, sandwiches and platters of seafood and steaks emerge steaming from the kitchens in an unending stream.

Colebrook St. (℃ 242/333-2093. Reservations not accepted. Breakfast and lunch platters $2–$8; dinner main courses $10–$12. No credit cards. Daily 7am–midnight.

BEACHES & WATER SPORTS

Pink Sands Beach is our favorite beach in all The Bahamas; its sands stretch for 3 uninterrupted miles. Although the beach is set against a backdrop of low-rise hotels and villas, it still feels tranquil and pristine. The sun is best in the morning (afternoons start to become shadowy), and waves are generally gentle, owing to an offshore reef that breaks the waves coming in from the Atlantic. There are many good places for snorkeling, and this also is the best place on the island for a long, leisurely morning stroll.

Big Red Rentals (℃ 242/333-2045) rents boats and snorkel gear, and offers various snorkel cruises and other outings.

The **diving** in this part of The Bahamas is among the most diverse in the region, with visibility in midsummer reaching as far as 200 feet on good days. A 197-foot steel freighter, the *Carnarvon*, sank in 1917 and is today one of the region's highlights. Nearby are the badly rusted chassis of a half-dozen railway boxcars reportedly captured by Confederate soldiers from the Union army during the Civil War and sold to the owner of a sugar plantation in Cuba. Hit by a hurricane during their southbound transit, the barge containing them sank, scattering the boxcars along the sea bottom. Today, only the wheelbases remain visible above the reef fish and kelp that have made the site their home.

The most spectacular dive site of all, however, judged among the 10 top dives in the world, is the **Current Cut Dive** 𝓡𝓡𝓡. One of the fastest (9 knots) drift dives in the world, it involves descending into the fast-moving current racing between the rock walls that define the underwater chasm between Eleuthera and Current Island. Swept up in the currents with schools of stingrays, mako sharks, and reef fish, divers are propelled along a half mile of underwater distance in less than 10 minutes. The dive may be one of the highlights of your whole life.

Valentine's Dive Center, Harbourfront (℃ 800/383-6480 or 242/333-2142), maintains a full range of dive activities. The dive center is in a wooden building near the entrance to Valentine's Marina. Lessons in snorkeling and scuba diving for beginners are given daily at 9:30am. Snorkeling from a boat costs $20 for a half-day tour. A full certification course for scuba is taught for $525. Single-tank dives, daily at 9:30am and 2pm, cost $45; two-tank dives go for $70; and night dives (four divers minimum) are $45 per person. Underwater cameras, with film included, rent for $35 for both a half day and a full day. The guides at Valentine's are proud to point out the wreck of the *Carnarvon* (mentioned above). Cave and cavern dives are also conducted.

SHOPPING

Miss Mae's Tea Room and Fine Things, Dunmore Street (℃ 242/333-2002), lives up to its billing. It's one of the island's finest boutiques, with not only standard T-shirts and bathing suits, but also antique furniture, jewelry, books, and even cups and dishes.

Works by local artists are for sale at the **Sugar Mill** (© **242/333-2173**), which also sells Bahamian coin jewelry and shell objects gathered in Eleuthera.

Briland's Ambrosia (© **242/333-2342**) sells the best selection of bathing suits, with bright batik fabrics printed on the island of North Andros.

Finally, check out **Princess Street Gallery** (© **242/333-2788**), where Charles Carey has restored an ancestral home and uses it as a showcase to display works by local artists.

HARBOUR ISLAND AFTER DARK

Unpretentious **Gusty's,** Coconut Grove Avenue (© **242/333-2165**), boasts sweeping sea and sunset views. Inside, you'll find a sand-covered floor, while the outdoor veranda is sometimes the scene of lighthearted fashion shows sponsored by local dressmakers. Virtually everyone in Harbour Island has been here at one time or another, and it's one of the best places to meet locals. Live music is featured on some nights, with recorded bar music the rest of the week.

Seagrapes, Colebrook Street (© **242/333-2439**), is another favorite place of the locals, where you can hoogie down to the sounds of disco or catch a live band. Expect to be jostled and crowded on a Saturday night, because everyone on the island comes here for a wild Bahamian hoedown.

Vic-Hum Club, Barracks Street (© **242/333-2161**), established in 1955, is the quintessential Harbour Island dive. It's pure lighthearted Bahamian kitsch and charm. The walls have been layered with the covers of hundreds of record albums and sports posters that music-industry and basketball buffs find fascinating. The Vic-Hum is open 24 hours a day, catering to breakfasting construction workers in the morning, and locals meeting friends for a beer all afternoon. Some of them play basketball on an indoor court that's transformed later in the evening into a dance floor (disco music begins at 10pm every Fri and Sat).

10 Spanish Wells

Called a "quiet corner of The Bahamas," Spanish Wells is a colorful cluster of houses on St. George's Cay, half a mile off the coast of northwest Eleuthera. It is characterized by its sparkling bays and white beaches, sleepy lagoons, excellent diving, and fine fishing colony.

The Eleutherian Adventurers were the first people to inhabit St. George's Cay after the Spanish had exterminated the original residents, the Arawaks (Lucayans). It was prominent on the charts of Spanish navigators, however, as the final landfall for galleons heading home from the New World laden with plunder. The Spaniards sank a well here to replenish their potable water before setting off across the Atlantic—hence the name "Spanish Wells." Ponce de León noted this stopover, where he was able to get water (if not the youth-preserving liquid for which he was searching).

After the American Revolution, Loyalists joined the descendants of the Eleutherian Adventurers at Spanish Wells. Some, particularly those from southern plantations in America, did not stay long on St. George's Cay, however, because the Spanish Wellsians were adamantly opposed to slavery. Hoping to start island plantations, the new wave of immigrants had brought slaves with them and were forced to move on to other parts of The Bahamas with their African bondsmen. The people of Spanish Wells still have strong religious beliefs, and there's a bounty of churches on the island.

The towheaded, blue-eyed people of this little town number fewer than 1,500 souls. More than half the people on the island are named Pinder. As the saying goes, "We was Pinders before we married, and we're Pinders now." The names Albury, Higgs, Sawyer, and Sweeting are also prominent. The islanders' patois blends 17th-century English with the accents of others who have settled on the island over the centuries. For years they have been known as good seamen and spongers, and some of them are farmers. Because of the infertile soil on St. George's Cay, however, they have to do their planting on "mainland" Eleuthera.

Over the centuries, the Spanish Wellsians have tried their hand at many economic ventures, from growing cotton and pineapples for export, to shipbuilding, lumbering, and fishing. Of these, fishing and some agriculture have been lasting moneymakers, joined today by tourism. Many have grown rich on harvesting spiny lobster.

You can walk or bicycle through the village, looking at the houses, some more than 200 years old, which have New England saltbox styling but bright tropical coloring. You can see handmade quilts in many colors, following patterns handed down from generations of English ancestors. Homeowners display these quilts on their front porches or out their windows, and they are for sale. No one locks doors here or removes ignition keys from cars.

GETTING THERE

To reach the island, you can fly to the **airstrip on North Eleuthera,** from which taxis will deliver you to the ferry dock. Regardless of the time of day you arrive, a ferryboat will be either waiting for passengers or about to arrive with a load of them.

A boat runs between Gene's Bay in North Eleuthera to the main pier at Spanish Wells. The ferries depart whenever passengers show up, and the cost is $10 per person round-trip.

WHERE TO STAY

The Adventurer's Resort   Since the 1999 hurricane demolished all the competition, this has emerged as the most appealing, most solid-looking, and most recommendable hotel in Spanish Wells. It occupies a two-story, pale lavender-colored building in a well-tended garden about a quarter mile west of the town center. There's no restaurant or bar on-site, but the staff member will direct you to nearby eateries and to the beach, which lies about a half mile away. The small bedrooms have simple, durable furniture with tropical upholstery; six of the units are apartments with kitchenettes. Each comes with a shower unit. Maid service is provided when you rent the regular double room, but not the apartments.

Harbourfront (P.O. Box EI 27498), Spanish Wells, The Bahamas. ℂ 242/333-4883. Fax 242/333-5073. mapleleaf@batelnet.bs. 18 units. Year-round $75 double, $100 1-bedroom apt with kitchenette, $165 2-bedroom apt with kitchenette. AE, MC, V. *In room:* A/C, TV.

WHERE TO DINE

Jack's Outback BAHAMIAN   Decent, unpretentious, and well-scrubbed, this little place stands along the waterfront in the heart of town. There's a hint of funkiness here, in its luncheonette-style combination of wood, plastic, and Formica, and its color scheme of pink and blue. Known for its home-cooking, it offers the usual array of sandwiches and cheeseburgers, as well as Bahamian foods like cracked conch, conch burgers, and conch chowder. There are also steaks, barbecued ribs, and cheesy shrimp poppers. The interior is air-conditioned, with views of the sea.

Harbourfront. ℂ 242/333-4219. Sandwiches $2.50–$6.50; main courses $9–$24. MC, V. Daily 9am–11pm.

9

The Exuma Islands

The Exumas are some of the prettiest islands in The Bahamas. Shades of jade, aquamarine, and amethyst in deeper waters turn to transparent opal near sandy shores: The water and the land appear almost inseparable. Sailors and their crews like to stake out their own private beaches and tropical hide-aways, and several vacation retreats have been built by wealthy Europeans, Canadians, and Americans.

A spiny, sandy chain of islands, the Exumas, which begin just 35 miles southeast of Nassau, stretch more than 100 miles from Beacon Cay in the north to Hog Cay and Sandy Cay in the south. These islands have not been developed like the Abacos and Eleuthera, so they are relatively inexpensive. But they still have much to offer, with crystal-clear waters on the west around the Great Bahama Bank and the 5,000-foot-deep Exuma Sound on the east, uninhabited cays ideal for picnics, rolling hills, ruins of once-great plantations, and coral formations of great beauty. Although they're crossed by the Tropic of Cancer, the islands have average temperatures ranging from the mid-70s to the mid-80s.

Most of our resort recommendations are in and around George Town, the pretty, pink capital of the Exumas, on Great Exuma. A community of some 900 residents, it was once considered a possible site for the capital of The Bahamas because of its excellent **Elizabeth Harbour** (see below).

Nearly all the other cays are uninhabited or sparsely populated. Over the years, remote accommodations have come and gone on these islands. Today the only resort hotels, which attract mostly the yachting set, are found at Staniel Cay and Sampson Cay.

The cruising grounds around the Exumas, which are scattered over an ocean area of 90 square miles, are among the finest to be found in the western hemisphere, if not in the world, for both sail- and powerboats. The **sailing** rivals both those of the Grenadines in the Caribbean and the Abacos in The Bahamas. Which one yachties prefer depends on personal taste; each is paradise, if you're a boater. If you don't come in your own craft, you can rent one here, from a simple little Daysailer to a fishing run-about, with or without a guide. The annual regatta in April in Elizabeth Harbour has attracted such notables as Prince Philip and the ex-king of Greece, Constantine. The Exumas are often referred to by yachting people as "where you go when you die if you've been good."

Snorkeling and scuba-diving opportunities draw aficionados from around the world to the **Exuma Cays National Land and Sea Park** ☆☆☆, a vast underwater preserve, and to the exotic limestone and coral reefs, blue holes, drop-offs, caves, and night dives. Dive centers in George Town and Staniel Cay provide air fills and diving equipment.

Fishing is superb here, and the "flats" on the west side of Great Exuma are famous for bonefishing.

Finds **Saddle Cay: The Perfect Beach**

For years boaters have known of a special beach, **Saddle Cay,** whose horseshoe-shaped curve lies near the northern tip of the small archipelago. The only way to reach it is by private boat; there are no organized excursions or tours (the Exumas are much too laid-back for that). However, if you own a boat, head for Saddle Cay, and you won't be disappointed when you see this totally unspoiled beach of white sands and tranquil waters. The cay is perfect for beachcombers, bird-watchers, and snorkelers—but don't expect facilities.

You can find (if you're lucky) blue marlin on both sides of Exuma Sound, as well as sailfish, wahoo, and white marlin, plus numerous others. Other popular activities include tennis, boardsailing, and waterskiing.

The Exumas are among the friendliest islands in The Bahamas; the people are warmhearted and not (yet) spoiled by tourism. They seem genuinely delighted to receive and welcome visitors to their shores. They grow a lot of their own food, including cassava, onions, cabbages, and pigeon peas, on the acres their ancestors worked as slaves. Many fruits grow on the cays, including guavas, mangoes, and avocados. You can watch these fruits being loaded at Government Wharf in George Town for shipment to Nassau. The sponge industry is being revived locally; this product of the sea is found in shallow waters and creeks to the south side of the Exumas.

On most maps this chain is designated as the "Exuma Cays," but only two of the main islands—Great Exuma and Little Exuma—bear the name *cay.* A single-lane bridge connects those two cays, where the major communities are concentrated.

EXUMAS ESSENTIALS

GETTING THERE

BY PLANE The Exumas' major commercial airport—the **Exuma International Airport**—is 10 miles from George Town, the capital. The most popular way to visit the Exumas is to fly there aboard **Bahamasair** (© 800/222-4262), which has daily service from Nassau to George Town. A flight usually leaves Nassau in the morning sometime between 8:45 and 9:15am, depending on the day. There are also midafternoon flights on Monday, Friday, and Saturday. In addition, Bahamasair flies directly from Miami to George Town on Thursday and Sunday, but call ahead because flight schedules are subject to change.

American Eagle (© 800/433-7300) serves Exuma from Miami daily.

Other minor carriers servicing the archipelago include **Lynx Air International** (© 888/596-9247), with air links from Fort Lauderdale. **Air Sunshine** (© 800/327-8900 or 954/434-8900) flies from three Florida cities, Fort Lauderdale, Sarasota, and St. Petersburg, but only on Tuesday and Thursday. Returns are possible aboard this airline on Monday, Wednesday, and Friday.

For flights to the private airstrip at Staniel Cay, refer to section 4 of this chapter.

BY MAIL BOAT Several mail boats leave from Potter's Cay Dock in Nassau, stopping at various points along the Exumas.

The **MV *Grand Master*** goes from Nassau to George Town. Departures are on Tuesday at 2pm with a return to Nassau on Friday morning.

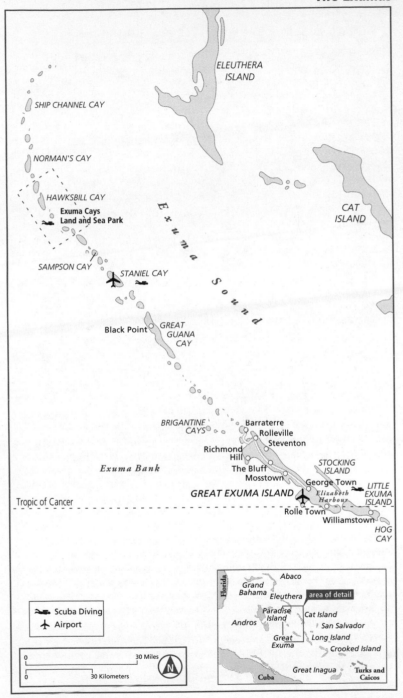

ELEUTHERA
ISLAND

SHIP CHANNEL CAY

NORMAN'S CAY

HAWKSBILL CAY

**Exuma Cays
Land and Sea Park**

CAT
ISLAND

E x u m a

SAMPSON CAY

STANIEL CAY

S o u n d

Black Point

GREAT
GUANA
CAY

BRIGANTINE
CAYS

Barraterre

Rolleville

Steventon

Richmond
Hill

Exuma Bank

The Bluff

Mosstown

STOCKING
ISLAND

George Town

LITTLE
EXUMA
ISLAND

GREAT EXUMA ISLAND

*Elizabeth
Harbour*

Tropic of Cancer

Rolle Town

Williamstown

HOG
CAY

Scuba Diving

Airport

0   30 Miles

0   30 Kilometers

N

Florida

Grand
Bahama

Abaco

Eleuthera

area of detail

Paradise
Island

Cat Island

Andros

San Salvador

Great
Exuma

Long Island

Crooked Island

Great Inagua

Turks and
Caicos

Cuba

Finds   **In Search of the Red-Legged Thrush**

Under the protection of The Bahamas National Trust, **Exuma Cays National Land and Sea Park,** in the northern reaches of the Exuma chain, begins at Conch Cut and extends northward to Wax Cay Cut, encompassing Halls Pond Cay, Warderick Wells, Shroud Cay, Hawksbill Cay, Cistern Cay, and Bell Island, as well as numerous other small uninhabited islands. It lies to the northwest of Staniel Cay. You can reach the park only by chartered boat or seaplane, and it's very expensive to visit.

The park is some 22 miles long, and much of it is a sea garden with reefs, some only 3 to 10 feet beneath the water's surface.

Before 1986, visitors were allowed to fish for spiny lobster, hog fish, conch, and such; but the park is now designated a marine replenishment nursery, and it's against the law to remove any plant, marine, or bird life.

Many bird-watchers visit the park, looking for the red-legged thrush, the nighthawk, and even the long-tailed "Tropic Bird," plus many, many more winged creatures.

This was once the home of the Bahamian iguana, which is now found only on Allan's Cays, a tiny island group just north of Highborne Cay. The government is taking belated steps to protect this creature, which is found nowhere else in the world.

Ibis Tours (© 800/525-9411) offers kayaking expeditions to the park. There is no more adventurous way to see the scattered beaches, rolling scrublands, and coral reefs of the entire island chain than by kayak. The 8-day adventure costs $1,595 per person, double occupancy. This cost includes transportation to and from Nassau. Another company featuring a week of kayaking and camping on remote islands, at $1,445 per person, is **Ecosummer Expeditions,** 1516 Duranleau St., Vancouver, BC, Canada V6H 3S4 (© 800/465-8884).

Since hours and sailing schedules are subject to change because of weather conditions, it's best to check with the dockmaster at **Potter's Cay Dock** in Nassau (© 242/393-1064).

GETTING AROUND

After your arrival at the airport in George Town, chances are you'll meet Kermit Rolle. Kermit, who runs things up in Rolleville, knows as much about the Exumas as anyone else (maybe more). You can stop in at **Kermit's Airport Lounge,** Exuma International Airport (© 242/345-0002), which is just across from the airport terminal building. If you're lucky, Kermit will be free, and you can negotiate a deal with him to take you in his car for a tour.

BY TAXI   If your hotel is in George Town, it will cost about $24 to get here in a taxi from the airport. Rides often are shared. The island has only a few taxis, and most of them wait at the airport. Hotels can usually get you a taxi if you need to go somewhere and don't have a car. For a taxi, call **Leslie Dames** at © 242/357-0015.

BY CAR   It's also possible to rent a car during your stay, though the major North American companies aren't represented here. Try **Exuma Transport,**

Main Street, George Town (℃ **242/ 336-2101**). They have cars to rent for $60 per day and up, or $300 per week. A $200 deposit is required. Your hotel can also usually arrange a rental car for you through a local firm.

1 George Town

The Tropic of Cancer runs directly through George Town, the capital and principal settlement of the Exumas, located on the island of Great Exuma. Some 900 people live in this tranquil seaport village, which opens onto a 15-mile-long harbor. George Town, partly in the tropics and partly in the temperate zone, is a favorite port of call for the yachting crowd. Its one road runs parallel to the shoreline of the harbor.

Sometimes the streets of George Town are nearly deserted, except when the mail boat from Nassau arrives at Government Wharf, bringing everybody out. If you've rented a housekeeping unit on the Exumas, you can come here to buy fresh fish when the fishermen arrive with their catches.

If you need to stock up on supplies, George Town is the place to go, since it has more stores and services than any other spot in the Exumas. It has dive centers, marinas, markets, a doctor, and a clinic. George Town often doesn't bother with street names, but it is so small that everything is easy to find.

ESSENTIALS

GETTING THERE   Flights from Nassau and Miami come into nearby Exuma International Airport, 10 miles away. See the beginning of this chapter for details on airlines and taxis.

FAST FACTS   A branch of the **Bank of Nova Scotia,** Queen's Highway (℃ **242/336-2651**), is open Monday through Thursday from 9:30am to 3pm, on Friday from 9:30am to 5pm.

If you come to the Exumas aboard your own boat, **Exuma Docking Services,** Main Street, George Town (℃ **242/336-2578**), has slips for 52 boats, with water and electricity hookups. There's a restaurant on the premises, and you can replenish your liquor stock from the store here. They also have a Laundromat, a fuel dock, land-based fuel pumps, and a store with supplies for boats and people.

The government-operated **medical clinic** can be reached by phone at ℃ **242/ 336-2088.** To call the **police** in George Town, dial ℃ **242/336-2666,** but only for an emergency or special services.

SPECIAL EVENTS   In April, the **Family Island Regatta** (℃ **800/ 32-SPORT** for more information) draws a yachting crowd from all over the world to Elizabeth Harbour. It's a rollicking week of fun, song, and serious racing when the island sloops go all out to win. It's said that some determined skippers bring along extra crewmen to serve as live ballast on windward tacks, then drop them over the side to lighten the ship for the downwind run to the finish. The event, a tradition since 1954, comes at the end of the crawfish season.

WHERE TO STAY
EXPENSIVE
Hotel Higgins Landing 🌟🌟   The beach at this resort is spectacular, the stuff of tropical fantasies. The only hotel on undeveloped Stocking Island, this is one of the first eco-resorts in The Bahamas, and it has taken great care to preserve the natural beauty of its surroundings on this gorgeous island. This solar-powered

---

(*Tips*) **Big Boom Tourism on the Horizon**

After a sleep of centuries, Great Exuma is heading for major development. One of the largest resort developments in the history of the Out
Islands has been announced, with the development of a 235-room **Four
Seasons Resort** at Emerald Bay. It overlooks a mile-long stretch of sandy
beach, and, as a special feature will have at its centerpiece, an 18-hole
golf course designed by Greg Norman. By the time you arrive in The Exumas, the 6,873-yard golf course may be operational. Norman is already
telling the press that his course at Emerald Bay will be "one of the finest
oceanfront courses in the world." For a report on the latest developments, call 800/819-5053.

---

hideaway is one of the self-billed great escapes of The Bahamas. It's bordered by
Elizabeth Harbour and the Atlantic on one side, and the crystal blue waters of
Turtle Lagoon, with the colorful reefs, on the other.

Cottages are exquisitely decorated with antiques, mirrors, and the Higgins
family heirlooms. Accommodations are furnished with queen-size beds, and
each unit is given an island accent with cool tile floors and ceiling fans, plus a
well-maintained private bath with shower stalls.

The landscaped grounds are as colorful as your imagination, attracting many
types of wildlife, ranging from herons and hummingbirds to green sea turtles.
The island is reached by hotel ferry service from George Town.

Rates include a full breakfast and a candlelit first-rate dinner (non-guests are
welcome, too, with advance reservations). The open-air bar overlooks the water.

Stocking Island, Box EX29146, George Town, Exuma, The Bahamas. (*C*) **888/688-4752** in the U.S., or (*C*) and
fax 242/336-2460. http://higginslanding.com/fast.htm. 5 units. $385 double, $580 triple, $670 quad. MAP
(breakfast and dinner) included. AP (also with lunch) $20 extra. Minimum stay of 3 nights required; 50%
deposit required to secure reservation. MC, V. No children under 18. Dec 15–Apr 15. **Amenities:** Restaurant,
bar, library, water sports, rowing boats. *In room:* Ceiling fans. No phone.

Peace & Plenty Bonefish Lodge *&*   Miles south of George Town, this is
one of three Peace & Plenty properties in the Exumas—and the poshest of them
all. It caters almost exclusively to fishermen and their companions. In a setting
of young palms, the two-story inn is built of concrete and stone and lies on a
peninsula enveloped by crystal-clear waters and sandy flats. This is the most elegant bonefishing inn in The Bahamas—you can fish all day and come back to
be pampered in luxury.

The lobby is inviting, with tile floors and rattan pieces. From many of the mid-
size rooms opening onto the wraparound balcony, you'll have a great view of the
turquoise waters, or perhaps you'd rather doze in a hammock. Accommodations
are furnished in bright floral spreads and prints, with air-conditioning and ceiling fans, along with spacious, immaculate bathrooms and shower units. You
don't have to be an angler to stay here—but it helps. If you don't fish, you may
be left out of the conversation at night.

The food served in the clubby dining room is excellent, with a well-trained
chef who not only knows how to grill your steak to perfection, but can whip up
a vegetarian platter, too. Of course, the finest way to dine here is on fish caught
that same day by the chef himself or one of the other guests. After cleaning the
fish, the chef tosses scraps to the resident sharks in the adjoining waters. This is

the chief evening entertainment, although there are an honor bar and a lobby lounge upstairs with TV and VCR.

Queens Hwy. (P.O. Box EX29173), George Town. ☎ 242/345-5555. Fax 242/345-5556. www.peace&plenty. com. 8 units. $929 per person 3 nights, 2 days; $1,287 per person 4 nights, 3 days. Rates are all-inclusive. MC, V. **Amenities:** Restaurant, bar, free shuttle to Stocking Island, van to George Town, snorkeling, bonefishing, bikes, laundry. *In room:* A/C. No phone.

MODERATE

Club Peace & Plenty This attractive, historic waterside inn, though not as luxurious as the Coconut Cove Hotel (see below), is a classic island hotel in the heart of George Town. Once a sponge warehouse and later the home of a prominent family, it was converted into a hotel in the late 1940s, making it the oldest in the Exumas. The two-story pink and white hotel has dormers and balconies opening onto a water view. The grounds are planted with palms, crotons, and bougainvillea. Peace and Plenty fronts Elizabeth Harbour, which makes it a favorite of the yachting set, including former visitor Prince Philip. This branch of the Peace and Plenty family is more of a beach and boating resort, not quite as oriented toward bonefishing as the others, although the staff can make arrangements for you if you'd like.

The mid-size units are all tastefully furnished, although there is still a lingering 1950s vibe. A recent refurbishment has freshened things up a bit, though, with bright print spreads and draperies, and furnishings in white wicker or rattan. All rooms have queen, double, or twin beds, and a tiled bathroom with shower only. Many also contain balconies opening onto harbor views; of course, the oceanfront rooms are the most desirable.

You can dine either indoors or outside, with calypso music on the terrace (see "Where to Dine," below) and continental, Bahamian, and American specialties available. There are also two cocktail lounges, one of which was converted from an old slave kitchen and is now filled with nautical gear, including lanterns, rudders, and anchors. The hotel faces Stocking Island and maintains a private beach club there, offering food and bar service, as well as miles of sandy dunes. A boat, free for hotel guests ($5 one-way for non-guests), makes the run to Stocking Island.

Queen's Hwy. (P.O. Box EX29055), George Town, Great Exuma, The Bahamas. ☎ 800/525-2210 in the U.S. and Canada, or 242/336-2551. Fax 242/336-2550. Pandp@peace&plenty.com. 35 units. Winter $150–$165 double; off-season $115–$125 double. MAP (breakfast and dinner) $36 per person per day. Ask about bonefishing packages. AE, MC, V. **Amenities:** On-site restaurant, 2 bars, offshore beach club with food and drink, free boat, pool. *In room:* A/C, TV.

Coconut Cove Hotel 🏖 Set on a calm bay with good snorkeling all around, this 10-unit hotel began its life as the private home of Thomas Chimento and his wife, Pamela Predmore. Built as a home in the mid-1980s, its main building is a long (96-feet), single-story, rectangular bungalow, with one side composed almost entirely of sliding glass doors that face the ocean. Inside, mahogany doors and panels glow; many were constructed by Tom himself. It's a great value, offering luxury and a wonderful setting at a much more reasonable price than many of the nearby resorts. The spectacular sands of Stocking Island are a 5-minute boat ride offshore.

The upscale accommodations all have private terraces; some are beachfront, whereas others overlook a pond and tropical gardens. These also have private terraces. The Paradise Suite, a favorite with honeymooners, is the special place to stay, with a private hot tub on the terrace. All the accommodations have queen-size beds, refrigerators, bathrobes, toiletries, shower-only bathrooms, and both air-conditioning and ceiling fans.

The club also has a modest beachfront freshwater pool, plus a "Sandbar" for poolside drinks. The hotel operates a good restaurant, The Coconut Cove, serving fine Bahamian and American dishes, plus seafood and Italian selections.

Queen's Hwy. (P.O. Box EX29299; a mile west of George Town), George Town, Great Exuma, The Bahamas. ℭ 888/688-4752 in the U.S., or 242/336-2659. Fax 242/336-2658. www.exumabahamas.com. 13 units. Winter $140–$250 double; off-season $100–$200 double. AE, DISC, MC, V. **Amenities:** Restaurant, bar, fishing and diving outings, dive shop, laundry. *In room:* A/C, TV, hair dryer. No phone.

The Palms at Three Sisters

In 1994, this low-key resort opened on an isolated spot 7 miles from its nearest neighbor, on a 1,200-foot stretch of lovely white sand. Rooms lie within a two-story, motel-like building and have English colonial details and simple, summery furniture. It's a great place for privacy and seclusion. The resort, incidentally, is named after a trio of rocks (the Three Sisters) with a composition that differs radically from the coral formations throughout the rest of the Exumas. They jut about 15 feet above sea level just offshore from the beach. Bedrooms are comfortable, containing small bathrooms with shower units.

Meals and drinks are served in a low-slung annex, with views stretching out over the Atlantic (see "Where to Dine," below). Live music is presented every Friday on a flowering patio.

Queen's Hwy., Bahama Sound Beach (P.O. Box EX29215; 9 miles northwest of George Town), George Town, Great Exuma, The Bahamas. ℭ 888/688-4752 or 242/358-4040. Fax 242/358-4043. seaoats@batelnet.bs. 14 units. Winter $110 double, $130 triple, $125 cottage; off-season $80 double, $95 triple, $100 cottage. Extra person $20. MC, V. **Amenities:** Restaurant, snorkeling, tennis court (lit for night play), swimming pool, bikes. Boat outings nearby to a sandy cay offshore for picnics. *In room:* A/C, TV. No phone.

Peace & Plenty Beach Inn *(Kids)*

This tranquil inn is a world-class bonefishing resort, opening onto 300 feet of white-sand beach. Its sibling, the Peace and Plenty Bonefish Lodge, is more posh, but the price tag here compensates. This is also a favorite resort for snorkelers, offering a special Jean-Michel Cousteau snorkeling program. The inn contains first-class, well-furnished double rooms, plus small bathrooms with shower stalls. The bedrooms have Italian tile floors, as well as balconies overlooking Bonefish Bay and Elizabeth Harbour. For some action, and additional activities and facilities, you can go over to the Club Peace and Plenty (there are shuttles between all the Peace and Plenty properties).

An adjacent structure housing the attractive bar and restaurant was designed to reflect the colonial flavor of George Town. Very good meals are served here.

Harbourfront (P.O. Box EX29055), George Town, Great Exuma, The Bahamas. ℭ 800/525-2210 in the U.S. and Canada, or 242/336-2250. Fax 242/336-2253. http://207.151.58.81. 16 units. Winter $155–$180 double; off-season $135–$145 double. Up to 2 children under 13 stay free in parents' room. AE, MC, V. **Amenities:** Restaurant, bar, shuttle bus to George Town, ferry to Stocking Island, freshwater pool, boat rentals, scuba diving, snorkeling, and fishing excursions arranged. *In room:* A/C. No phone.

Regatta Point *(F)*

This inn lies on a small cay just across the causeway from George Town, opening onto a small sandy beach. The cay used to be known as Kidd Cay, named after the notorious pirate. Overlooking Elizabeth Harbour, the present complex consists of six efficiency apartments, which are not air-conditioned, although the cross ventilation is good. Ceiling fans help, too. Each of the pleasantly furnished, summery units has its own kitchen and maid service, plus a small bathroom containing shower stalls. This is a good choice for families. Those guests who don't want to cook for themselves can have dinner at one of the previously mentioned hotels in town, or at a local restaurant. Nearby grocery stores are fairly well-stocked if you feel like cooking.

Finds **Life on a Houseboat**

The most offbeat way to live in the Exumas is on a brightly decorated floating houseboat. Each boat is like a hotel suite that can be used to explore Elizabeth Harbour and the coast of the Exumas. In between moving your houseboat from anchorage to anchorage, you can go fishing, snorkeling, scuba diving, or just beachcombing. Brand new in 1999, each houseboat is fully equipped, sleeping 6 to 8, with air-conditioning, hot and cold running water, a marine radio, an inflatable dinghy, a fully equipped galley, all linens, purified water, and a propane barbecue grill. Boats range from a one-bedroom 35-footer to a two-bedroom 43-footer. It doesn't take a special license or even much experience to operate one of these boats, and all boat dwellers are given instruction about safety and cruising routes. We know of no better way than to explore the isolated coves of the Exumas with this much comfort. For reservations, write to **Bahamas Houseboats**, P.O. Box EX 29031, Government Dock, George Town, Exuma, The Bahamas (© **242/336-BOAT**; fax 242/336-2629; www.bahamahouseboats.com/accommodations.htm). Daily rentals (3-day minimum) range from $275 to $350, with a security deposit of $500 required. Rentals can be paid by MasterCard or Visa.

This little colony hums with action in April during the Family Island Regatta. Your hostess, American Nancy Bottomley, does much to ease your adjustment into the slow-paced life of the Exumas. In 1963, she discovered this palm-grove cay—which is really bush country—and opened the little colony of efficiencies in 1965. She even had to build the causeway herself. Mrs. Bottomley will help arrange water sports and outings. Sunfish and bicycles are available at no extra charge.

Regatta Point, Kidd Cove (P.O. Box 6), George Town, Great Exuma, The Bahamas. © **800/688-4752** in the U.S., or 242/336-2206. Fax 242/336-2046. www.exumabahamas.com. 6 units. Winter $148–$164 double, $210 2-bedroom apt for up to 4; off-season $114–$132 double, $172 2-bedroom apt for up to 4. Extra person $15. No credit cards. *In-room:* Kitchenette. No phone.

INEXPENSIVE

Two Turtles Inn   Set opposite the village green, midway between the harborfront and a salt-water estuary known as Victoria Pond, this two-story hotel is as popular for its bar and restaurant as for its plain accommodations. Originally built of stone and stained planking in the early 1960s, it's arranged around a courtyard. Each room has a ceiling fan, plus a somewhat cramped bathroom with a shower stall. For hitting the beach or enjoying water sports, head to Peace and Plenty, a short walk away, where both guests and non-guests can rent equipment. Tennis, sailing, boating, snorkeling, and scuba diving can be arranged through other nearby hotels.

Main St. (P.O. Box EX29251), George Town, Great Exuma, The Bahamas. © **888/688-4752** in the U.S. or 242/336-2545. Fax 242/336-2528. 13 units. Winter $118 double; off-season $106 double. Children under 12 stay free in parents' room. MC, V. *In-room:* A/C, TV.

(*Finds* **Fresh, Sexy Conch**

The best conch salad is found at **Big D's Conch Spot No. 2,** Government Dock (no phone). "Fresh, sexy conch," as it's called here, is served daily. They'll make it right in front of you, so you know what's going into your salad. For some reason, they're open only on Monday, Wednesday, and Friday.

WHERE TO DINE

With a few exceptions, the best places to take meals in George Town are in the main hotels reviewed above.

There are several casual joints in George Town where you can grab a quick meal. **Towne Cafe,** Marshall Complex (✆ **242/336-2194**), serves one of the best breakfasts in George Town. It's really the town bakery. If you'd like to drop in any day but Sunday, you can also enjoy a lunch of local Exuman specialties, including stewed grouper or chicken souse. Their grilled fish and seafood sandwiches are worth the trip here.

A former school bus was recycled and turned into **Jean's Dog House,** along Queen's Highway in George Town. Here you'll find the island's best lobster burger in a cramped but spotless kitchen on wheels. Instead of eating in the hotel dining room, we like to go here for breakfast and order the "MacJean," a robust sandwich with sausage or bacon, plus cheese, on freshly baked bread. Of course, she's also noted for her "dogs," or frankfurters. The owner is a well-loved personality known only as Jean. Visit her only from 7am to 3pm, and don't bother taking your credit card.

Coconut Cove Hotel Restaurant ✺✺ INTERNATIONAL   This is the hot dining ticket on the island. Lying 1 mile west of the capital of George Town, it is the culinary domain of Thomas Chimento and Pamela Predmore. Retiring here from New York City, they have awakened the sleepy tastebuds of the Exumians with their excellent fare. We'd walk a mile for their signature pizza—one made with salmon, crème fraîche, onions, capers, and fresh dill. Their shrimp and lobster combo is a delight, as is their grilled chicken with artichokes, tomatoes, and mushrooms bathed in a pesto sauce. The Bahamian stone crab claws are just as good as those served on Miami Beach, except Pamela steams them with onions, leeks, and fresh herbs—all served with a hot mustard sauce.

Queen's Hwy. ✆ **242/336-2659.** Reservations required. Main courses $29.95–$34.95. AE, DC, DISC, MC, V. Tues–Sun 6–9pm.

MODERATE

Club Peace & Plenty Restaurant CONTINENTAL/BAHAMIAN/ AMERICAN   Go here for the finest island dining, with plentiful, good home-cooking that leaves everyone satisfied. You might begin with conch salad or one of the salads made with hearts of palm or artichoke hearts, then follow with local lobster. Bahamian steamed grouper regularly appears on the menu (of course), simmered with onions, sweet pepper, tomatoes, and thyme. But you can also order such special dishes as an herb-flavored Cornish game hen that is juicy and perfectly roasted and flavored. Lunch options include homemade soups, conch burgers, a chef's salad, or deep-fried grouper. Breakfast offerings range from traditional French toast or scrambled eggs and sausage to the truly Bahamian boiled fish and grits.

You sit under ceiling fans, looking out over the harbor. Windows on three sides and candlelight make it particularly nice in the evening. And who knows who will be at the next table? A celeb or two, or a crowd of yachties providing conversation and amusement.

In the Club Peace & Plenty, Queen's Hwy. ℂ **242/336-2551.** Reservations required for dinner. Breakfast $7.50; lunch $7.50; main courses $16.50–$29. AE, DC, DISC, MC, V. Daily 7:30am–9:30pm.

The Palm INTERNATIONAL   Set beside a sandy, isolated beach, 9 miles northwest of the Exuma capital, this airy, oceanfront restaurant is associated with one of the island's best resorts. Breakfasts are hearty steak-and-egg fare, although you can also get Bahamian coconut pancakes. Lunches include lobster salads, conch chowder, grouper fingers, burgers, and sandwiches. Dinners are more formal. Although the food is familiar, it's well-prepared. Flame-broiled grouper might be your best and freshest choice.

At the Palms at Three Sisters hotel, Queen's Hwy., Bahama Sound Beach (9 miles northwest of George Town). ℂ **242/358-4040.** Breakfast $3–$11; lunch platters and sandwiches $5.95–$13; dinner main courses $16–$22; sunset specials $12–$14. MC, V. Daily 7am–10pm.

Sam's Place BAHAMIAN/INTERNATIONAL   If Bogie were alive today, he'd surely head for this laid-back second-floor restaurant and bar overlooking the harbor in George Town. Sam Gray, the owner, offers breakfasts to catch the early boating crowd. Lunches could include everything from freshly made fish chowder to spaghetti with meat sauce. You'll also be able to order an array of sandwiches throughout the day. The dinner menu changes daily, but you're likely to find such well-prepared main courses as Exuma lobster tail, roast lamb, Bahamian steamed chicken, and pan-fried wahoo. Of course, you can always get native conch chowder. At dinner, the talk here is of one of everybody's dreams— owning a private utopia, one of those uninhabited cays still remaining in the Exuma chain.

Main St. ℂ **242/336-2579.** Breakfast and lunch $4–$7.50; dinner main courses $11–$22.50. MC, V. Daily 7:30am–10pm.

INEXPENSIVE
Eddie's Edgewater BAHAMIAN   Victor and Andrea Brown, who provide good, traditional Bahamian food, run this popular restaurant overlooking Lake Victoria. The place is unpretentious and unfussy. Among the choices are conch chowder, okra soup, grouper, and the endangered turtle steak. On Monday nights, a local band plays from 7:30 to 11pm. The place is very casual, and it doesn't close until the last person staggers out, which sometimes is as late as 2am.

Charlotte St., George Town. ℂ **242/336-2050.** Main courses $6–$16. MC, V. Mon–Sat 7am–midnight.

Kermit's Airport Lounge BAHAMIAN   Owned by one of the island's most entrepreneurial taxi drivers, Kermit Rolle, this simple but appealing place lies across the road from the entrance to the airport. It's the semiofficial waiting room for most of the island's flights, and it might make your wait more convenient and fun. The cook will fry you some fish, and there's always beans and rice around. Johnnycake and sandwiches are also available, along with burgers and an array of tropical drinks. Until an airplane flies you to a better restaurant, this place might come in handy.

Exuma International Airport. ℂ **242/345-0002.** Beer $3; cheeseburgers $5–$7; platters from $5. No credit cards. Daily 7am–5pm.

BEACHES, WATER SPORTS & OTHER OUTDOOR PURSUITS

STOCKING ISLAND 🏝

Stocking Island, which lies in Elizabeth Harbour, faces the town across the bay, less than a mile away. This long, thin barrier island has some of the most gorgeous white-sand beaches in The Bahamas. Snorkelers and scuba divers come here to explore the blue holes, and it is also ringed with undersea caves and coral gardens. Boat trips leave daily from Elizabeth Harbour heading for Stocking Island at 10am and 1pm. The cost is $8 per person one-way. However, guests of Club Peace and Plenty ride free.

If you'd like to go shelling, walk the beach that runs along the Atlantic side of Stocking Island.

The island has a beach club run by **Club Peace & Plenty** (℗ 242/336-2551). (Stocking Island used to be a private enclave for guests at Club Peace and Plenty, but now all visitors use it.) Here you can rent kayaks for only $25 per day or Sunfish for $35 a day; snorkel gear goes for $10 a day. Visibility is great in these waters, and there are many kinds of colorful fish to see.

BOATING, SEA KAYAKING & SAILING

Landlocked **Lake Victoria** covers about 2 acres in the heart of George Town. It has a narrow exit to the harbor and functions as a diving-and-boating headquarters.

Exuma Dive Centre (℗ 242/336-2390) rents 17-foot sea kayaks for $57.50 for a half day or $80 for a full day.

On Stocking Island, you can go to the kiosk there that's operated by Peace and Plenty Beach Club.

If you come to the Exumas aboard your own boat, **Exuma Docking Services,** Main Street, George Town (℗ 242/336-2578), has slips for 52 boats, with water and electricity hookups. You can stock up on supplies here, get fuel, and do laundry.

FISHING

Many visitors come to the Exumas just to go bonefishing. Arrangements for outings can be made at **Club Peace and Plenty,** Queen's Highway (℗ 242/345-5555), the central office for the Peace and Plenty properties. The Exumas offer miles of wadable flats (shallow bodies of water), and trained guides accompany you. Fly fishing instruction and equipment are also offered.

SNORKELING

The best snorkeling within easy reach of George Town is on Stocking Island (see above).

You can also rent snorkeling equipment for $8 a day at **Minns Water Sports** in George Town (℗ 242/336-3483).

SCUBA DIVING

Divers should head for the **Exuma Dive Center** in George Town (℗ 800/874-7213 or 242/336-2390), which features dives to "walls," coral heads, and blue holes. They also offer resort courses. Most reefs lie only 20 minutes by boat from the outfitter's dive shop. Dives start at $60, with basic scuba instruction costing $395. The center can also arrange dive and hotel packages for you if you call.

Mystery Cave is a famous dive site, tunneling for more than 400 feet under the island.

Fun Fact Why Everyone Is Named Rolle

By the late 17th century, Great Exuma had become a major producer of salt, and permanent settlers began to arrive. Pirates constantly harassed the salt merchants' sailing vessels, but some families from Nassau must have looked on this as the lesser of two evils. On New Providence they were subjected to the terrorism inflicted by both the pirates and the Spanish, and in the latter part of the 17th century and the first of the 18th, they fled to the relative peace of the Exumas.

In 1783, a handful of Loyalist families fled the newly established United States of America after British defeat and came to the Exuma Cays. In the 18th century, cotton and salt were kings on the Exumas. English plantation owners brought in many slaves to work the fields, and many of today's Exumians are direct descendants of those early slaves, who were mostly of African origin. The "kings" did not stay long on the throne. Insects went for the cotton, and salt lands such as those of the Turks and Caicos Islands proved much too competitive for those of the Exumas, so the British eventually abandoned these pursuits.

Most of the white owners went back to where they came from, but the slaves, having no such option, stayed on, subsisting by working the land abandoned by their former owners, and took the names of those owners as their own. A look through the George Town directory turns up such names as Bethel, Ferguson, and especially Rolle, the same as those of the long-gone whites.

At one time, Lord John Rolle held much of the Exumas under a grant from the British Crown, giving him hundreds of acres. He is reported to have owned 325 slaves who worked this acreage, but Lord Rolle never set foot on his potentially rich plantation. Stories vary as to what happened to the slaves—whether they were, as some claim, freed by Lord Rolle and given land, or whether, upon being released from bondage by the United Kingdom Emancipation Act in 1834, they took over the land, with or without Rolle's approval. Whichever, descendants of those same slaves are important Exumians today.

Today it seems that every other person is named Rolle. One elderly woman, sitting in front of her little shanty painted in florid tricolors, and wearing a Bahama Mama T-shirt, confided, "You're born a Rolle, all your cousins are called Rolle, you marry a Rolle and have children called Rolle, and you are a Rolle and all the mourners at your funeral, related or not, are called Rolle." She claimed that since everyone in the Exumas keeps track of their blood relatives, the locals know which Rolles are "real family" and which are not related by blood. "That's got to be kept in mind," she said, "when it comes time to get married."

EXPLORING GEORGE TOWN

There isn't much to see here in the way of architecture except the confectionery pink and white **Government Building,** which was "inspired" by the Government House architecture in Nassau. Under an old ficus tree in the center of town, there's a **straw market** where you can talk to the friendly Exumian women and perhaps purchase some of their handcrafts.

George Town has a colorful history, despite the fact that it appears so sleepy today. (There's so little traffic, there is no need for a traffic light.) Pirates used its deep-water harbor in the 17th century, and those called the "plantation aristocracy," mainly from Virginia and the Carolinas, settled here in the 18th century. In the next 100 years **Elizabeth Harbour,** the focal point of the town, became a refitting base for British man-of-war vessels, and the U.S. Navy used the port again during World War II.

There's not too much shopping, but there are a few places where you can purchase souvenirs and gifts. **Exuma Liquor and Gifts,** Queen's Highway (© 242/336-2101), is the place to stock up on liquor, wine, and beer. The **Peace and Plenty Boutique,** Queen's Highway (© 242/336-2551), stands next to the Sandpiper and across the street from the previously recommended Club Peace and Plenty, which owns it. Its main draw is a selection of Androsia batiks for women, and Androsia cloth is sold by the yard. You can also find such practical items as film and suntan oil. They also have a large selection of men and women's sportswear.

The Sandpiper, Queen's Highway (© 242/336-2084), stands across from Club Peace and Plenty. Its highlights are the original serigraphs by Diane Minns, but it also offers a good selection of Bahamian arts and crafts, along with such items as Bahamian straw baskets (or other handcrafted works), sponges, ceramics, watches, and postcards. Diane designs and silk-screens T-shirts here in the shop, and she welcomes anyone to watch her at work.

One of the offshore sights in Elizabeth Harbour is **Crab Cay,** which can be reached by boat. This is believed to have been a rest camp for British seamen in the 18th century.

GEORGE TOWN AFTER DARK

The best place to head for some after-dark diversion is **Club Peace and Plenty** (see above). Although summer nights are slow here, there's usually something happening in winter, ranging from weekly poolside bashes to live bands that keep both locals and visitors jumping up on the dance floor. You might also check out the action at the previously recommended **Two Turtles Inn.** If it's a Monday night, head over to **Eddie's Edgewater** (see above) for a Rake 'n' Scrape evening, featuring cowbells, goatskin drums, and other musical instruments.

EXPLORING FARTHER AFIELD

Queen's Highway, which is still referred to as the "slave route," runs the length of Great Exuma, and you can travel it in either a taxi or a rented car to take in the sights in and around George Town.

Twenty-eight miles north of George Town, **Rolleville,** named after Lord Rolle, is still inhabited by descendants of his freed slaves. It is claimed that his will left them the land. This land is not sold but is passed along from one generation to the next.

As you travel along the highway, you'll see ruins of plantations. This land is called **"generation estates,"** and the major ones are **Steventon, Mount Thompson,** and **Ramsey.** You pass such settlements as Mosstown (which has working farms), Ramsey, the Forest, Farmer's Hill, and Roker's Point. Steventon is the last settlement before you reach Rolleville, which is the largest of the plantation estates. There are several **beautiful beaches** along the way, especially the one at **Tarr Bay** and **Jimmie Hill.**

Some visitors may also want to head south of George Town, passing Flamingo Bay and Pirate's Point. In the 18th century Captain Kidd is said to have anchored at **Kidd Cay.** You, however, can stay at the previously recommended Regatta Point.

Flamingo Bay, the site of a hotel and villa development, begins just half a mile from George Town. It's a favorite rendezvous of the yachting set and bonefishers.

WHERE TO DINE

Iva Bowe's Central Highway Inn Restaurant & Bar BAHAMIAN   This roadside tavern, operated by Mrs. Lorraine Bowe-Lloyd, specializes in very tender cracked conch. The conch is marinated in lime, pounded to make it tender, and then fried with her own special seasonings. It's the best in the Exumas. You might also try her crawfish salad or shrimp scampi. This is good Bahamian cookery.

Queen's Hwy. (¼ mile from the entrance to the International Airport and about 6½ miles northwest of George Town). ② 242/345-7014. Lunch $6–$10; main courses $10–$20. No credit cards. Mon–Sat 10am–10pm.

Kermit's Hilltop Tavern BAHAMIAN   Originally built in the 1950s by members of the Rolle family, this stone-sided restaurant sits atop the highest point in Rolleville, with a view over the rest of the town. Today, it's open as a tavern and general meeting place for almost everyone in town, as well as for people passing through. Lunch and drinks are served continuously throughout the day and early evening, but more formal meals of chicken, fish, or lobster should be arranged by phone in advance. Try Kermit's curried mutton, steamed conch, or pan-fried grouper. This is one of the most authentic places for true Bahamian cuisine. "They cook the way my mama used to," one diner told us, "and that's why we come here." Call it Bahamian soul food—some of the produce comes fresh from Kermit's farm. The place lies about 20 miles north of George Town.

Rolleville. ② 242/345-6006. Reservations required for dinner. Lunch platters $7–$10; 3-course dinners $12–$20. No credit cards. Lunch and snacks daily 9am–closing varies; dinner by prior arrangement only.

2 Little Exuma ⟨⋆⟩

This is a faraway retreat, the southernmost of the Exuma Cays. It has a subtropical climate, despite that it's in the tropics, and lovely white-sand beaches. The waters are so crystal-clear in some places that you can spot the colorful tropical fish more than 60 feet down. The island, about 12 square miles in area, is connected to Great Exuma by a 200-yard-long bridge. It's about a 10-mile trip from the George Town airport.

Less than a mile offshore is **Pigeon Cay,** which is uninhabited. Visitors often come here for the day and are later picked up by a boat that takes them back to Little Exuma. You can go snorkeling and visit the remains of a 200-year-old wreck, right offshore in about 6 feet of water.

On one of the highest hills of Little Exuma are the remains of an old pirate fort. Several cannons are located nearby, but documentation is lacking as to when it was built or by whom. (Pirates didn't leave too much data lying around.)

Coming from Great Exuma, the first community you reach on Little Exuma is called **Ferry,** so named because the two islands were linked by a ferry service before the bridge was built. See if you can visit the private chapel of an Irish family, the Fitzgeralds, erected generations ago.

Along the way, you can take in **Pretty Molly Bay,** site of the now-shuttered Sand Dollar Beach Club. Pretty Molly was a slave who committed suicide by

---

Fun Fact   **A Romantic Legend**
_____

On the road to Little Exuma, you come to the hamlet of **Rolle Town,** which is another of the generation estates that was once, like Rolleville in the north, owned by Lord Rolle and is populated today with the descendants of his former slaves. This sleepy town has some 100-year-old houses.

In an abandoned field, where goats frolic, you can visit the Rolle Town Tombs, burial ground of the McKay family. Capt. Alexander McKay, a Scot, came to Great Exuma in 1789 after he was granted 400 acres for a plantation. His wife joined him in 1791, and soon after, they had a child. However, tragedy struck in 1792 when Anne McKay, who was only 26, died along with her child. Perhaps grief stricken, her husband died the following year. Their story is one of the romantic legends of the island.

The village claims a famous daughter, Esther Rolle, the actress. Her parents were born here, but they came to the United States before she was born.

---

walking into the water one night. The natives claim that her ghost can still be seen stalking the beach every night.

Many visitors come to Little Exuma to visit the **Hermitage,** a plantation constructed by Loyalist settlers. It is the last surviving example of the many that once stood in the Exumas. It was originally built by the Kendall family, who came to Little Exuma in 1784. They established their plantation at **Williamstown** and, with their slaves, set about growing cotton. But they encountered so many difficulties having the cotton shipped to Nassau that in 1806 they advertised the plantation for sale. The ad promised "970 acres more or less," along with "160 hands" (referring to the slaves). Chances are you'll be approached by a local guide who, for a fee, will show you around. Also ask to be shown several old tombs in the area.

Also at Williamstown (look for the marker on the seaside), you can visit the remains of the **Great Salt Pond.**

If you really have to see everything, maybe you can get a local to take you over to **Hog Cay,** the end of the line for the Exumas. This is really just a spit of land, and there are no glorious beaches here. It's visited mainly by those who like to add obscure islets at the very end of the road to their list of explorations. Hog Cay is privately owned, and it is farmed. The owner seems friendly to visitors. His house lies in the center of the island. There is also an old lookout tower with a 5-foot cannon at its base. At one time it stood guard for ships coming and going into Elizabeth Harbour.

3 Barraterre

For years linked to the world only by boat, Barraterre was connected to "mainland" Great Exuma by a road in the 1980s. The area is now open for development, but no one here expects that to happen anytime soon. The place is no more than a sleepy hamlet, and everybody seems to be named McKenzie. To reach Barraterre, head north on Queen's Highway, but instead of continuing to "end of the line" Rolleville, turn left in the direction of Stuart Manor. Pass through Alexander and keep going until you reach the end of another road— here lies little Barraterre, snoozing in the sun. For the boating crowd, it is the gateway to the **Brigantine Cays,** which stretch like the beads of a necklace to the northwest.

Here you'll see how the "life of the cays" is lived—the biggest event is the arrival of the mail boat, a vital link to the outside world. No one, not even any of the McKenzies, is absolutely certain how the place got its name. Perhaps it came from the French, bar terre, or "land obstruction."

The Barraterrians live in a hilly community, with vividly painted houses (many in decay).

4 Staniel Cay ✦

Staniel Cay lies 80 miles southeast of Nassau at the southern end of the little Pipe Creek archipelago, which is part of the Exuma Cays. It's an 8-mile chain of mostly uninhabited islets, sandy beaches, coral reefs, and bonefish flats. There are many places for snug anchorages, making this a favorite yachting stopover in the mid-Exumas. Staniel Cay, known for years as "Stanyard," has no golf course or tennis courts, but it's the perfect island for "the great escape."

An annual bonefishing festival is sponsored here on August 5, during the celebration of Bahamian Independence Day. **The Happy People Marina (© 242/ 355-2008)** arranges sportfishing trips with local guides, as well as snorkeling trips.

About 100 Bahamians live on this island, and there's a local **straw market** where you can buy handcrafts, hats, and handbags. The little cay was settled in the mid-18th century, and its oldest building is a 200-year-old shell.

Before the coming of the airplane, it took days to reach the island from Miami or Nassau, but now there's a 3,000-foot paved airstrip. Today, some of the vacation homes on Staniel Cay are owned by pilots. A telecommunications center links the island with both The Bahamas and the United States.

Visitors to this island arrive by private boat or a chartered flight. To arrange a possible flight, contact **Executive Air Travel** and speak to Capt. Dennis Rotolo (© 954/224-6022) in Fort Lauderdale.

WHERE TO STAY & DINE

Happy People Marina   Exumian, Kenneth Rolle operates this marina. His mother was the regionally famous Ma Blanche, who had a mail boat named for her. Guests who check in here are interested mainly in boating, as this place is

---

⟨Moments Never Say Never Again at Thunderball

Just off Staniel Cay is the **Thunderball Grotto,** one of the most beautiful diving and snorkeling sites in The Bahamas. Some scenes from the James Bond movie *Thunderball* were filmed here. Another James Bond flick, *Never Say Never Again,* also featured scenes shot at this grotto, as did the comedy *Splash.* Divers can explore the grotto, though it's a preserve under the protection of The Bahamas National Trust. At low tide, it's possible to swim or snorkel here and spot gorgeous tropical fish; a blowhole in the roof illuminates the cave.

just a decent motel to spend the night. Rooms are small and utterly basic, adjoined by a little bathroom with a shower stall. There are a meager private beach and dockage facilities, but there's no service or fuel for the majority of the island's visiting yachts. The prevailing atmosphere is casual, and all of the rooms face the waterfront. A recently added apartment features a full kitchen, two bedrooms, two bathrooms, and a living room.

Meals and drinks are served in a separate building closer to the center of town, within a minute of the marina. Known as the Royal Entertainer Lounge, it sometimes welcomes local bands and serves meals according to a flexible schedule.

Staniel Cay, the Exumas, The Bahamas. ℂ 242/355-2008. 9 units. $90 double, $200 apt. No credit cards. In-room: A/C. No phone.

Staniel Cay Yacht Club Staniel Cay is a great getaway, and the Staniel Cay Yacht Club is the place to get away to. Although once famous in yachting circles, drawing celebrities like Malcolm Forbes, it fell off for several years before bouncing back. Now it once again welcomes the yachting world to its location near a white sandy beach. Guest cottages, each with a small shower unit, have been completely remodeled and refurbished and are quite charming. Each cottage is painted a different color and has different decorative features. The cottages also have west-facing balconies, which make for unimpeded views of the sun setting over the water. This is one of the few guarantees each day on Staniel Cay. Since the island is only a mile wide, you can easily walk to the local village, which has a grocery store, straw market, church, and post office.

An on-site clubhouse offers American/Bahamian cuisine for breakfast, lunch, and dinner, with a menu featuring steaks and seafood, nothing too foreign or experimental. The club can rent you boats for activities, from a 13-foot Boston Whaler including fuel for $85, to something smaller, plus scuba and snorkeling gear.

Staniel Cay, the Exumas, The Bahamas. ℂ 954/467-8920 in the U.S., or 242/355-2024. Fax 242/355-2044. www.stanielcay.com. For information, write 2233 S. Andrews Ave., Fort Lauderdale, FL 33316. 6 units. Winter $125 double; off-season $95 double. Extra person $25–$35. MC, V. In-room: A/C, minibar. No phone.

5 Sampson Cay

Tiny Sampson Cay, directly northwest of Staniel Cay and just to the southeast of the Exuma Cays National Land and Sea Park, has a certain charm. It has a full-service marina, as well as a small dive operation. Other than Staniel Cay, Sampson Cay has the only marina in the Central Exumas. To fly here, you'll need to go to Staniel Cay first. However, most visitors arrive in their own boats. Local guides take out sportfishers for the day. Sampson Cay lies 67 nautical miles southeast of Nassau and is one of the safest anchorages in the Exumas and a natural "hurricane hole." The cay lies near the end of Pipe Creek, which has been called a "tropical Shangri-La."

Yachties used to find food and lodging here at Sampson's Cay Colony, but at presstime it was closed and its future uncertain. Check locally if you're passing through.

6 Norman's Cay

Throughout the Exumas, you'll see islands with NO TRESPASSING signs posted. In some cases this is meant with a vengeance. In the early 1980s, at least on one island, you could have been killed if you had gone ashore!

On a summer day long ago, our boat sailed by Cistern Cay. Back then, our guide told us that Robert Vesco owned part of that island. "He likes to keep it very, very private here," he cautioned, heading for friendlier shores. (Vesco, of course, was the financier much wanted by the U.S. government.) Even though the fugitive is long gone (under arrest in Cuba), people around here still like to keep it quiet.

Perhaps the most bizarre Out Islands episode in all The Bahamas was centered around Norman's Cay, one of the northernmost islands in the Exumas, 44 nautical miles southeast of New Providence Island. At one time when we stayed at the former hotel here, Norman's Cay Club, this was a South Seas island–type outpost. Reportedly it was once the retirement home of the pirate Norman.

Located adjacent to the Exuma Cays National Land and Sea Park, this was always a very special cay. Sections rise as high as 50 feet above sea level, and it is heavily wooded with lignum vitae, royal poinciana, palmetto, tamarind, and casuarina. This is a bird-watcher's paradise, and snorkeling and scuba diving on the coral heads are among the best in the Exumas, with vertical drop-offs, black-coral forests, spectacular cuts, and wrecks.

In the old days you might have run into Ted Kennedy, Walter Cronkite, or William F. Buckley Jr. enjoying the pleasures of Norman's Cay. The remote outpost enjoyed great popularity with a Harvard/Boston clique.

However, in the 1980s, the situation changed drastically when a German-Colombian, Carlos Lehder (pronounced "Leader") Rivas purchased most of the island. The story of his purchase of Norman's Cay was mentioned in the 1985 *Newsweek* article "Empire of Evil," documenting the horrors of cocaine smuggling. A short time after Lehder, as he is known, purchased the property, the Colombian flag was flying over Norman's Cay, and many of the wintering wealthy fled in horror from the island when they returned to find their second homes broken into and trashed.

Norman's Cay, experts have stated, became the major distribution point for drug export to the United States. Millions of dollars worth of cocaine was flown from Colombia and deposited in hangars at Norman's Cay before being smuggled into the United States. It is estimated that some 30 pilots crashed attempting to fly in their illegal cargoes. You can still see the wreckage of a C-46 that went down in the bay.

When an undersecretary of state arrived from Washington and landed on the island, a Colombian commando ordered him off at gunpoint. He left, but when he returned to the U.S. capital, he launched a major protest. Apparently, the U.S. government applied strong pressure on the Bahamian government to clean up Norman's Cay.

Lehder fled Norman's Cay for further adventures in Colombia, where he was captured and extradited to the United States. He was later tried, convicted, and imprisoned.

Norman's Cay may one day realize its tourist potential again, but for the moment it remains relatively abandoned, visited only by a stray yachting party or perhaps one of the American Canadian Caribbean Cruise Line's vessels, which explore the backwaters of The Bahamas and call here because of the good beaches and snorkeling possibilities.

10

The Southern Bahamas

This cluster of islands on the southern fringe of The Bahamas is one of the last frontier outposts that can be reached relatively quickly from the U.S. mainland. Their remoteness is one of the most compelling reasons to visit them—that, and a chance to see life in The Bahamas the way it used to be. Some of the islands are proud to proclaim that "we are as we were when Columbus first landed here," an exaggeration that nonetheless contains a kernel of the truth.

The Southern Bahamas have a colorful history. In the 18th century, Loyalists from the Carolinas and Virginia came here with slave labor and settled many of the islands. For about 20 years they had thriving cotton plantations until a blight struck, killing crops and destroying the industry. In 1834, the United Kingdom Emancipation Act freed slaves throughout the British Empire. When the Loyalists moved on to more fertile ground, they often left behind the emancipated blacks, who then had to eke out a living as best they could.

With some notable exceptions, such as Long Island, tourism developers have stayed clear of these islands, although they have enormous potential, as most of them have excellent beaches, good fishing, and fine dive sites.

If you consider visiting any of these islands, be forewarned that transportation is inconvenient, and except for two or three resorts, accommodations are limited. For these and other reasons, the boating and yachting crowd has composed the majority of visitors up to now.

Many changes are in the wind for the Southern Bahamas. Right now, however, there's almost no traffic, no banks, no lawyers. There are, however, mosquitoes. You may want to plan ahead and bring a good insect repellent and a long-sleeved shirt for protection.

1 Cat Island

Untainted by tourism, lovely Cat Island is the sixth-largest island in The Bahamas. The fishhook-shaped island—some 48 miles long and 1 to 4 miles wide—lies about 130 miles southeast of Nassau and 325 miles southeast of Miami. (Don't confuse Cat Island with Cat Cay, which is a little private island near Bimini.)

Cat Island (named after the pirate Arthur Catt) is located near the Tropic of Cancer, between Eleuthera and Long Island. It has one of the best climates in The Bahamas, with temperatures in the high 60s during the short winters, rising to the mid-80s in summer, with trade winds making the place even more comfortable. It is home to some 2,000 residents, some of the friendliest in The Bahamas.

With its pristine virgin **beaches,** Cat Island ⊛ is one of the most beautiful islands in The Bahamas, and it is so little visited that it's inexpensive and still feels undiscovered.

area of detail

Florida
Grand Bahama
Abaco
Eleuthera
Paradise Island
Andros
Cat Island
San Salvador
Great Exuma
Long Island
Crooked Island
Great Inagua
Cuba
Turks and Caicos

0   60 Miles
0   60 Kilometers

N

Arthur's Town
CAT ISLAND
Arthur's Town Airport
Moss Town

Exuma Sound

Cockburn Town
SAN SALVADOR
CONCEPTION ISLAND

ATLANTIC OCEAN

RUM CAY
Port Nelson

Stella Maris Airport
Simms

Tropic of Cancer

LITTLE EXUMA ISLAND
LONG ISLAND
Deadman's Cay Airport
Clarence Town

JUMENTO CAYS

Samana Cay

Colonel Hill
CROOKED ISLAND
Chesters Bay
Landrail Point
ACKLINS ISLAND
FORTUNE ISLAND
The Bight of Acklins
Snug Corner
Pirates Well
Spring Point
MAYAGUANA ISLAND

Duncan Town
RAGGED ISLAND

Crooked Island Passage

Windward Passage

Caicos Passage

CASTLE ISLAND

Hogsty Reef

LITTLE INAGUA

GREAT INAGUA

Inagua National Park
Matthew Town

CUBA

🤿 Scuba Diving
✈ Airport

Many local historians claim that Cat Island residents were the first to see Columbus. The great explorer himself was believed by some to have been welcomed here by the peaceful Arawaks. Regardless of whether Columbus stopped here, the island has a rich history of adventurers, slaves, buccaneers, farmers, and visionaries of many nationalities. Cat Island remains mysterious to some even now. It's known as a stronghold of such strange practices as obeah (West Indian witchcraft) and of miraculously healing bush medicines.

A straight asphalt road (in terrible shape) leads from the north to the south of the island. Along the way you can select your own beach—and chances are you'll have complete privacy. These beaches offer an array of water sports, and visitors can go swimming or snorkeling at several places. **Fernandez Bay** is a picture-postcard, white-sand beach set against a turquoise blue sea and lined with casuarina trees. The island's north side is wild, untamed shoreline. Boating and diving are among the main reasons to go to Cat Island, and diving lessons are available for novices.

Arthur's Town, in the north, is the major town and the boyhood home of actor Sidney Poitier. (He has many relatives still living on the island, including one or two amazing look-alikes we recently spotted.) Poitier shared memories of his childhood home in his book *This Life.*

ESSENTIALS

GETTING THERE   A commercial flight on **Bahamasair** (© **800/222-4262** in the U.S.) leaves Nassau for Arthur's Town on Tuesday, Thursday, and Sunday at 11:45am. There is also an airport near the **Bight,** the most scenic village on the island. Other minor carriers serving the island include **Air Sunshine** (© **800/327-8900**), flying to New Bight from Fort Lauderdale, and **Lynx Air International Launches** (© **888/596-9247**), which has service between Fort Lauderdale and Cat Island two times a week.

Cat Island is also serviced by **mail boat.** The **MV *North Cat Island Special*** (© 242/393-1064) departs Potter's Cay Dock in Nassau weekly, heading for Bennett's Harbour and Arthur's Town. It leaves on Tuesday at 2pm and returns to Nassau on Thursday. Another vessel, **MV *Sea Hauler*** (© 242/393-1064), departs Potter's Cay in Nassau on Tuesday at 2pm, going to Old and New Bight, and returns on Sunday.

GETTING AROUND   No taxi service is available on Cat Island. Hotel owners, if notified of your arrival time, will have someone drive to the airport to pick you up. You can, however, rent a car from **Russell Brothers,** Bridge Inn, New Bight (© **242/342-3014**), to go exploring on your own. Prices begin at $80 daily, with unlimited mileage. A special rate of $70 daily is offered to guests of Bridge Inn. Hours are Monday through Saturday from 8am to 6pm.

FAST FACTS   There are three medical clinics, each of which is among the simplest in The Bahamas. They are found in the settlements of Arthur's Town, Old Bight, and Smiths Bay, and they're not always open. In case of an emergency, notify your hotel staff immediately. Someone will try to get in touch with a medical person. Serious cases are flown to Nassau. If you're not in good health and might require medical assistance on vacation, Cat Island is not the island to choose. There is no central number to call for help.

SPECIAL EVENTS   The island's annual **Three-Day Regatta** takes place every summer, usually at the end of July. It attracts the largest collection of visitors to Cat Island; the inns prove inadequate to receive them. Call your local Bahamas Tourist Office (see chapter 2) for more information.

WHERE TO STAY & DINE

Bridge Inn Lying 300 yards from a beach, the relaxed and casual Bridge Inn is owned by Cat Islander Allan Russell, who is ably assisted by a group of family members. The inn offers baby-sitting services so that parents can play tennis or go diving, boardsailing, snorkeling, jogging, bicycling, fishing, or just sightseeing with the knowledge that their youngsters are being carefully tended and are having fun, too. Bedrooms are modest and small, motel-style affairs, and each unit can house three to four guests. Each of the high-ceilinged units comes with a private bath containing a shower stall.

On the premises you'll find a full bar and a restaurant that serves a rather simple Bahamian and international cuisine. Local jam sessions ("rake and scrape") are easily arranged for your entertainment, usually on Friday night.

New Bight, Cat Island, The Bahamas. (C) **888/688-4752** or 242/342-3013. Fax 242/342-3041. www. outisland.com. 12 units. $110 double, $125 triple. MC, V. **Amenities:** Restaurant, bar, room service, laundry, baby-sitting. *In room:* A/C, TV, minibar.

Fernandez Bay Village (A) Opening onto Fernandez Bay, this is the best resort on the island. Although rustic, it has a certain charm, mainly because of its position on a curvy white sandy beach set against casuarinas blowing in the trade winds. The beach, or anywhere else for that matter, is never crowded on Cat Island. Go here only if you really want to get away from it all; this place is far too laid-back for full hotel service. Things get done, but it takes time around here—and no one's in a hurry. Fernandez Bay Village has been in the Armbrister family since it was originally established on a plantation in 1870. Its rusticity and seclusion are part of its charm, and yet, if you wish, you can get acquainted with other guests with similar interests (or even watch videos). Yachtspeople, who moor in the water offshore (there are no marina facilities), often visit the resort to take advantage of the general store's fresh supplies. Nearby Smith's Bay is one of the best storm shelters in the region—even the government mail boats take refuge here during hurricanes.

The "village" consists of full housekeeping villas, each of which sleeps up to six people, as well as three double-occupancy cottages, built of stone, driftwood, and glass. Each unit comes with a private garden bathroom with a shower stall.

Meals are served in a clubhouse decorated with antiques and Haitian art. The clubhouse, which opens onto a view of the beach and sea, also features a sitting library area, a stone fireplace, and overhead fans. Dinners are served on a beach terrace adjacent to a thatched-roof tiki bar that runs on the honor system. On many nights a blazing bonfire near the water becomes a focal point for guests who want to listen to island music.

3 miles north of New Bight, Cat Island, The Bahamas. (C) **800/940-1905** or 242/342-3043, or 954/474-4821 in Plantation, FL. Fax 242/342-3051, or 954/474-4864 in Plantation, FL. 12 units. www.fernandezbayvillage. com. Winter $280–$295 villa for 4, $170–$180 cottage for 2; off-season $255–$270 villa for 2, $160–$170 cottage for 2. Half-board $45 per person. AE, MC, V. The resort will supply air transportation from Nassau on request (usually in the private plane owned and operated by the manager himself) for $200. Flights land at the nearby New Bight Airport. **Amenities:** Restaurant, bar, kayaks, bikes, snorkeling, waterskiing, scuba, flyfishing, car rentals, laundry, baby-sitting. *In room:* Kitchen. No phone.

Greenwood Beach Resort & Dive Center The location on an 8-mile stretch of the Atlantic, bordered by pink sands, is always idyllic, and there's good snorkeling right offshore. Since 1992, a German family has run this beach resort and dive center, constantly making improvements. This group of modern buildings on the most isolated section of the island has a private sandy beach and a freshwater pool. It's better run and equipped than the Bridge Inn, and it attracts mostly divers. The small ocean-view double rooms are all equipped with full bathrooms and showers and their own terraces. There is an all-purpose bar and a dining room.

The hotel's dive center is the best on the island. The inn has a 40-foot motor-boat for diving excursions, and its Tabaluga Diving Base has complete equipment for 20 divers at a time. A two-tank dive is $65, and equipment is $5 to $10 extra depending on your needs. The resort also has two fishing boats available for both bonefishing ($150 for a half day, $200 for a full day) and deep-sea fishing ($200 for a half day, $300 for a full day). The staff greets each arriving Bahamasair flight.

Port Howe, Cat Island, The Bahamas. © 877/228-7475 in the U.S., or 242/342-3053. Fax 242/342-3053. www.greenwoodbeachresort.com. 20 units. Nov–Apr $99 double; May–Oct $85. Free meals for children under 7. AE, MC, V. **Amenities:** Dining room, bar, pool, dive center, fishing boats, baby-sitting, laundry, bike rental. *In room:* Ceiling fans. No phone.

Hawk's Nest Resort & Marina   This remote getaway and marina lies on the southwestern side of Cat Island, fronting a long, sandy beach and containing its own runway for charter flights and private planes, plus an eight-slip marina attracting the yachting crowd. This intimate resort is set near the village of Devil's Point, lying some 10 miles west of Columbus Point close to the ruins of the once-flourishing but now-abandoned Richman Hill and Newfield Plantation. Bedrooms, with either two queen-size beds or a king-size bed, are well-furnished and brightly decorated, each with a shower unit. Each room features a patio for those late-afternoon toddies overlooking the sunset. If you bring the family, you may want to look at the two-bedroom house on the beach, separate from the other structures. The clubhouse, the rooms, and the main house are spacious and inviting.

They serve full breakfasts (cooked to order), sandwiches for lunch, and a buffet-style dinner, with the unannounced fare changing nightly. The club can rent out snorkeling equipment for as little as $10 per day, or you can go scuba diving for $45 for a one-tank dive. A 24-foot hydrosport boat is also made available to guests for a charge of $450 for a half day or $675 for a full day. Golf carts are available free of charge, which can make a sightseeing trip around the small island rather easy.

Devil's Point, Cat Island, The Bahamas. © 800/688-4752 or 242/342-7050. Fax 242/342-7051. www. hawks-nest. com. 10 units, 1 2-bedroom house. $140 daily double. MAP (breakfast and dinner) $50 per person extra. MC, V. **Amenities:** Restaurant, pool, 2 tennis courts, laundry, dive shop, snorkel gear, bike rental. *In room:* A/C, TV, coffeemaker, hair dryer.

Pigeon Cay Beach Club   This B&B lies at the north end of the island, about a 15-minute ride from the airport and fronting a tranquil bay. The main building consists of a trio of separate but attached units, a small store, and the check-in office. Each accommodation comes with a fully equipped kitchen. In addition, there are some light and airy cottages, ranging from one bedroom to three bedrooms. Cottages are built of stucco and coral stone with beamed ceilings, along with Mexican tile floors. Each unit comes with a shower stall.

North End, Cat Island, The Bahamas. © 242/354-5084. Fax 242/354-2091. www.pigeoncaybahamas.com. 7 units. Year-round $140 1-bedroom unit, $210 2-bedroom unit, $320 3-bedroom unit. AE, MC, V. *In-room:* Kitchen, ceiling fans. No phone.

EXPLORING THE ISLAND: PLANTATIONS, PEAKS & A HERMITAGE

There's an interesting Arawak cave at Columbus Point on the southern tip of the island. In addition, you can see the ruins of many once-flourishing plantations.

Some old stone mounds are nearly 200 years old. Early planters, many of them Loyalists, marked their plantation boundaries with these mounds. These include the Deveaux Mansion, built by Col. Andrew Deveaux of the fledgling U.S. Navy, who recaptured Nassau from the Spanish in 1783. The plantation's heyday was during the island's short-lived cotton boom. Yet another mansion, Armbrister Plantation, lies in ruins near Port Howe.

You can hike along the natural paths through native villages and past exotic plants. Finally, you reach the peak of Mount Alvernia, the highest point in The Bahamas, at 206 feet above sea level, where you will be rewarded with a spectacular view. The mount is capped by the **Hermitage,** a religious retreat built entirely by hand by the late Father Jerome, the former "father confessor" of the island, who was once a mule skinner in Canada. Curiously, the building was scaled to fit his short stature (he was a very, very short man). Formerly an Anglican, this Roman Catholic hermit priest became a legend on Cat Island. He died in 1956 at the age of 80, but his memory is kept very much alive here.

The **dive center at the Greenwood Beach Resort** (© **242/342-3053**) will take you out on diving or snorkeling excursions, or will rent you snorkel gear and other water toys.

2 San Salvador ✛

This may be where the New World began. For some years it has been believed that Christopher Columbus made his first footprints in the western hemisphere here, although some scholars strongly dispute this. The easternmost island in the Bahamian archipelago, San Salvador lies 200 miles southeast of Nassau. It is some 63 square miles in area, much of which is occupied by water. There are 28 landlocked lakes on the island, the largest of which is 12 miles long and serves as the principal route of transportation for most of the island's population of 1,200. A badly maintained 40-mile road circles the perimeter of San Salvador.

The tiny island keeps a lonely vigil in the Atlantic. **The Dixon Hill Lighthouse** at South West Point, about 165 feet tall, can be seen from 90 miles away. The light is a hand-operated beacon fueled by kerosene. Built in the 1850s, it is the last lighthouse of its type in The Bahamas. The highest point on the island is **Mount Kerr** at 138 feet.

Except for the odd historian or two, very few people ever used to visit San Salvador. Then **Club Med–Columbus Isle** opened, and the joint's been jumping ever since—at least at the Club Med property. Away from here, San Salvador is as sleepy as it ever was, although it's been known for years as one of the best dive sites in The Bahamas. The snorkeling, fishing, and lovely white-sand beaches are equally good.

ESSENTIALS

GETTING THERE   Club Med (see below) solves transportation problems for its guests by flying them in on weekly charter planes from Miami or Eleuthera. Otherwise, **Riding Rock Inn** (see below) has charter flights every Saturday from Fort Lauderdale. You can also rely on public transportation by land or sea, but if you do, you'll have to wait a long time before getting off the island.

Bahamasair (© **800/222-4262**) has lots of flights to the island because of the Club Med. Departure times from Nassau are constantly changing, so check with the airline for a schedule.

From Nassau, the mail boat **M/VT *Lady Francis*** leaves Tuesday heading for San Salvador and Rum Cay. The trip takes 18 hours under uncomfortable

Fun Fact **The Columbus Question**

In 1492, a small group of peaceful Lucayan natives (Arawaks) were going about their business on a little island they called Guanahani, where they and their forebears had lived for at least 500 years. Little did they know how profoundly their lives would change when they greeted the arrival of three small strange-looking ships bearing Columbus and his crew of pale, bearded, oddly costumed men. It is said that when he came ashore, Columbus knelt and prayed—and claimed the land for Spain.

Unfortunately, the event was not so propitious for the reportedly handsome natives. Columbus later wrote to Queen Isabella that they would make ideal captives—perfect servants, in other words. It wasn't long before the Spanish conquistadors cleared the island, as well as most of The Bahamas, of Lucayans, sending them into slavery and early death in the mines of Hispaniola (Haiti) in order to feed the Spanish lust for gold from the New World.

But is the island now known as San Salvador the actual site of Columbus's landing? Columbus placed no lasting marker on the sandy, sun-drenched island of his landfall, and the result has been much study and discussion during the past century or so as to just where he actually landed. Some say that it was on one of the cays of the Turks and Caicos Islands; others claim that it was on Cat Island.

In the 17th century, an English pirate captain, George Watling, took over the island and built a mansion to serve as his safe haven. The island was listed on maps for about 250 years as Watling's (or Watling) Island.

conditions. For details about sailing, contact the dockmaster at **Potter's Cay Dock** in Nassau (© **242/393-1064**).

GETTING AROUND   Taxis meet arriving planes and will take you to **Riding Rock Inn** (see below), where you can rent a car from $85 a day to explore the island on your own. You can also rent bicycles here at $10 a day. The latter are the most popular means of transport for visitors.

FAST FACTS   The **San Salvador Medical Clinic** (© **242/331-2105**) serves the island's residents, but serious cases are flown to Nassau. The clinic is open Monday through Friday from 9am to 5pm, and only emergencies are handled on Saturday and Sunday.

To call the police, dial © **919.** (Phones are rare on the island, but the front desk at Riding Rock Inn will place calls for you.)

WHERE TO STAY & DINE

Club Med–Columbus Isle *⋆⋆*   This is one of the most ecologically conscious, and one of the most luxurious, Club Meds in the western hemisphere. Set at the edge of one of the most pristine beaches in the archipelago (2 miles of white sand), about 2 miles north of Cockburn Town, the resort is the splashiest place in the entire Southern Bahamas. Its promoters estimate that more than 30% of the island's population works within the club.

In 1926 the Bahamian legislature formally changed the name of the island to San Salvador, feeling that enough evidence had been brought forth to support the belief that this was the site of Columbus's landing. Then in 1983, artifacts of European origin (beads, buckles, and metal spikes) were found here together with a shard of Spanish pottery, and Arawak pottery and beads. It is unlikely that the actual date of these artifacts can be pinned down, although they are probably from about 1490 to 1560. However, the beads and buckles fit the description of goods recorded in Columbus's log.

National Geographic published a meticulously researched article in 1986 written by its senior associate editor, Joseph Judge, with a companion piece by the former chief of the magazine's foreign editorial staff, Luis Marden, setting forth the belief that Samana Cay, some 65 miles to the southeast of the present San Salvador, was Guanahani, the island Columbus named San Salvador when he first landed in the New World. The question may never be absolutely resolved, but there will doubtless be years and years of controversy about it. Nevertheless, history buffs still flock here every year hoping to follow in the footsteps of Columbus.

Whether or not it was actually on this island, Columbus and his men did hit land at around 2am on the moonlit night of October 12, 1492. The native population, probably awakened from a sound sleep, called these strange creatures "men from Heaven." Perhaps "men from Hell" would have been a better description. The Spanish discovery of this island and others led to a holocaust, as the Spanish wiped out the native populations.

Most of the prefabricated buildings were barged to the site in 1991. The resort is built around a large free-form swimming pool with tiles that tint the water exactly the same color as the nearby ocean. The public rooms are some of the most lavish and cosmopolitan in the country, with art and art objects imported from Asia, Africa, Oceania, the Americas, and Europe, and assembled by a battalion of designers. Bedrooms each contain a private balcony or patio, furniture that was custom-made in Thailand or the Philippines, sliding glass doors, and feathered wall hangings crafted in the Brazilian rain forest by members of the Xingu tribe. Rooms are large (among the most spacious in the entire chain). Most have twin beds, but you might be able to snag one of the units with a double or a king-size bed if you're lucky. Each comes with a mid-size bathroom with shower stall. Dozens of multilingual GOs (guest relations organizers, or *gentiles organizateurs*) are on hand to help initiate newcomers into the resort's many diversions. Unlike many other Club Meds, this one does not encourage children and deliberately offers no particular facilities for their entertainment.

The main dining room, where meals are an ongoing series of buffets, lies in the resort's center. Two specialty restaurants offer Italian and grilled food, respectively. Non-fat, low-calorie, and vegetarian dishes are also featured. Nightly entertainment is presented in a covered, open-air theater and dance floor behind one of the bars.

2 miles north of Cockburn Town, San Salvador, The Bahamas. (✆ **800/CLUB-MED** or 242/331-2000. Fax 242/ 328-0940. www.clubmed.com. 270 units. Winter $1,379–$2,079 per person double; off-season $1,134–$1,379 per person double. No discounts for children. Rates include all meals, drinks during meals, and most sports activities. AE, MC, V. Children under 12 not recommended. **Amenities:** 3 restaurants, bar lounge, 10 tennis courts (3 lit for night play), pool, fitness center, largest scuba facility in the Club Med chain, wind-surfing, kayaking and kayak-scuba diving, mini-armada of Hobie Cats and other sailing craft. *In room:* A/C, TV, refrigerator.

Riding Rock Inn Resort & Marina   San Salvador's second resort is the motel-style Riding Rock Inn, catering largely to divers. Its simple ambience is a far cry from the extravagant Club Med. Each accommodation faces either a pool or the open sea. The most recent improvement to the inn is an 18-room oceanfront building, where the bedrooms are decorated in a tropical decor, with two double beds, satellite TV, a refrigerator, a telephone, ceiling fans, and air-conditioning. Each unit is equipped with a mid-size bathroom with shower stall.

The resort specializes in weeklong packages that include three dives a day, all meals, and accommodations. Packages begin and end on Saturday and, if a client pays a $300 supplement, can include specially chartered round-trip air transportation from Fort Lauderdale. Although most of the guests are already experienced and certified divers, beginners can arrange a $105 resort course for the first day of their visit and afterward participate in most of the community's daily dives. Full PADI certification can also be arranged for another supplement of $400.

An island tour is included in the rates, but after that, most folks rent a bike or scooter from the hotel. On the premises are a restaurant serving routine Bahamian specialties and a bar with a seating area that juts above the water on a pier.

Cockburn Town, San Salvador, The Bahamas. (✆ **800/272-1492** in the U.S., or 954/359-8353 in Florida. Fax 242/331-2020. www.ridingrock.com. 42 units. $114–$141 double, $156–$188 triple, $194 quad. Dive pack-ages available. MC, V. **Amenities:** Restaurant, bar, pool, dive shop, fishing, tennis court. *In room:* A/C, TV, refrigerator. No phone.

BEACHES, WATER SPORTS & OTHER OUTDOOR PURSUITS

The beaches of San Salvador, miles and miles of sandy shores with rarely another person in sight, are ideal for shelling, swimming, or snorkeling. Try **Bamboo Point, Fernandez Bay, Long Bay,** or **Sandy Point.**

Associated with the Riding Rock Inn (see above), **Guanahani Dive Ltd.** (✆ **242/331-2631**) offers dive packages, as well as snorkeling, fishing, and boat-ing trips. Year-round divers can book a getaway package for 5 days and 4 nights that costs from $654 to $710 per diver, including meals, transportation, diving, rental gear, and a charter flight. Prices are based on double occupancy.

Riding Rock Inn also has a tennis court where guests can play for free.

Bonefishers are attracted to **Pigeon Creek,** and some record catches have been chalked up here.

EXPLORING THE ISLAND: COMMEMORATING COLUMBUS

Among the settlements on San Salvador are Sugar Loaf, Pigeon Creek, Old Place, Holiday Track, and Fortune Hill. United Estates, which has the largest population, is a village in the northwest corner near the Dixon Hill Lighthouse. The U.S. Coast Guard has a station at the northern tip of the island.

Except for the party people at Club Med, San Salvador is mainly visited by the boating set, who can live aboard their craft. If you're exploring for the day, you'll find one or two local cafes that serve seafood.

The attractions listed below charge no admission and may be viewed at any time. If a preponderance of monuments is anything to go by, this would have to be the San Salvador Columbus visited and named.

The Chicago Herald installed the **Chicago Herald Monument** on Crab Cay to the explorer in 1892, but it is highly unlikely—in fact, almost impossible—that any landing was made at this site. It opens onto reefs along the eastern shore, surely a dangerous place for a landing.

At Long Bay, the **Olympic Games Memorial** to Columbus, located 3 miles south of Cockburn Town, was erected in 1968 to commemorate the games in Mexico. Runners carrying an Olympic torch circled the island before coming to rest at the monument and lighting the torch there. The torch was then taken to Mexico on a warship for the games. Another marker is underwater, supposedly where Columbus dropped anchor on his *Santa Maria*.

Jut north of the Olympic Games Memorial stands the **Columbus Monument.** On December 25, 1956, Ruth Durlacher Wolper Malvin, a Columbus scholar and widow of Hollywood producer David L. Wolper, established a simple monument commemorating the landfall of Columbus in the New World. Unlike the spot marked by the *Chicago Herald* monument, this is actually supposed to be the place where Columbus and his men landed.

At French Bay, **Watling's Castle,** also known as Sandy Point Estate, has substantial ruins that are about 85 feet above sea level. The area is located some 2½ miles from the "Great Lake," on the southwestern tip of the island. Local "experts" will tell you all about the castle and its history. Only problem is each "expert" we've listened to (three in all, at different times) has told a different story about the place. Ask around and perhaps you'll get yet another version; they're entertaining, at least. One of the most common legends involves a famous pirate who made his living either by salvaging the wreckage from foundered ships or by attacking ships for their spoils.

Once plantations—all doomed to failure—were scattered about the island. The most impressive ruins of this former life are **Farquharson's Plantation,** west of Queen's Highway, near South Victoria Hill. In the early part of the 19th century, some Loyalist families moved from the newly established United States to this island, hoping to get rich from farmland tended by slave labor. That plan collapsed when the United Kingdom Emancipation Act freed the slaves in 1834. The plantation owners moved on, but the former slaves stayed behind.

A relic of those times, Farquharson's Plantation is the best-known ruin on the island. People locally call it "Blackbeard's Castle," but it's a remnant of slavery, not piracy. You can see the foundation of a great house, a kitchen, and what is believed to have been a punishment cell (jail).

COCKBURN TOWN

San Salvador's capital, Cockburn (pronounced "Coburn") Town, is a harbor village that takes its name from George Cockburn, who is said to have been the first royal governor of The Bahamas to visit this remote island. That was back in 1823.

Look for the town's landmark: a giant almond tree. Major events in San Salvador, like the Columbus Day parade held every October 12, generally take place here.

New World Museum   This museum, located 3½ miles north of Riding Rock Inn, has relics dating from Indian times, but you'll have to ask until you find someone with a key if you want to go inside. The museum lies just past

Bonefish Bay in the little village of North Victoria Hill. Part of a large estate, called Polaris-by-the-Sea, it's owned by Ruth Durlacher Wolper Malvin.

North Victoria Hill. No phone. Free admission. Open anytime during the day.

Holy Saviour Roman Catholic Church   The very first Christian worship service in the New World was Catholic. It thus seems fitting that the Roman Catholic Diocese of The Bahamas in 1992, on the eve of the 500th anniversary of the Columbus landfall, dedicated a new church on San Salvador.

Cockburn Town. Free admission. Services Sun at 10am.

DISCOVERING RUM CAY & CONCEPTION ISLAND

"Where on earth is Rum Cay?" you ask. (That's pronounced "key," of course.) Even many Bahamians have never heard of it. Located midway between San Salvador and Long Island, this is another cay, like Fortune Island (see below), that time forgot.

That wasn't always the case, though. The very name conjures up images of swashbucklers and rumrunners. Doubtless, it was at least a port of call for those dubious seafarers, as it was for ships, as well, to take on supplies of salt, fresh water, and food before crossing the Atlantic or going south to Latin America. The cay's name is supposed to have derived from a rum-laden sailing ship that wrecked upon its shores.

Like many other Bahamian islands, this one once attracted British Loyalists fleeing the new United States of America. They were drawn here by the hope of establishing themselves as farmers and plantation overlords, but even those brave and homeless immigrants abandoned the island as unproductive. Salt mines were the mainstay of the island's economy before they were wiped out by a hurricane at the turn of the 19th century. After that, most of the inhabitants migrated to Nassau, so that by the 1970s the population of Rum Cay stood at "80 souls."

The well-known underwater cinematographer Stan Waterman once described Rum Cay as the "unspoiled diving jewel of The Bahamas." For that reason, a diving club was opened here in 1983, but it closed, regrettably, in 1990. Port Nelson, the island's capital, is where most of Rum Cay's 100 inhabitants live.

Some maintain that Rum Cay was the next island where Columbus landed after he found and named San Salvador. He dubbed that second island Santa Maria de la Concepcion. However, many students of history and navigation believe that the second stop was at the island today called Conception, which lies northwest of Rum Cay and about the same distance northeast of Long Island. You'll have to go here in a private boat.

Joseph Judge, a writer whose articles have appeared in *National Geographic,* believes that neither of these islands was Columbus's second stop. He holds that, based on modern computer science and knowledge of the ocean bottom and currents, the island the discoverer named Santa Maria de la Concepcion has to be Crooked Island.

The uninhabited Conception Island is under the protection of The Bahamas National Trust, which preserves it as a sea and land park. It's a sanctuary for migratory birds. The most esoteric divers find excellent dive sites here, and the rapidly diminishing green turtle uses its beaches as egg-laying sites. Park rules are strict about littering or removing animal or plant life.

With the demise of the Rum Cay Club, tourist traffic to the island came to a halt except for the odd yachting party or two. But with the increased interest in tourism that followed the 1992 Columbus celebrations, the area is gaining renewed interest. At present, you can arrange for boaters on San Salvador to take you to see these islands, which remain frozen in time.

3 Long Island

The Tropic of Cancer runs through this long, thin sliver of land, located 150 miles southeast of Nassau. The island stretches north to south for some 60 miles. It's 1½ miles wide on average, and only 3 miles wide at its broadest point.

Long Island is characterized by high cliffs in the north, wide and shallow sand beaches, historic plantation ruins, native caves, and Spanish churches. It is also the site of the saltworks of the **Diamond Crystal Company.** The island's present population numbers some 3,500 people.

The famed **diving sites** ✪ are offshore, such as the Arawak "green" hole, a "bottomless" blue hole of stunning magnitude. The best beach bets include Deal's Beach, Cape Santa Maria Beach, Salt Pond Beach, Turtle Cove Beach, and the South End beaches, the latter offering miles of waterfront with powdery white or pink sands.

Most historians agree that Long Island, which has only recently emerged as a minor tourist resort, was the third island Columbus sailed to during his first voyage of discovery. The Lucayans (Arawaks) who lived here at the time, and who had come from South America via Cuba, called their island Yuma, but Columbus renamed it Fernandina, in honor of King Ferdinand, and claimed it for Spain.

Loyalist plantation owners came here from the Carolinas and Virginia in the 18th century, and brought with them their slaves and their allegiance to the British Crown. There was a brief cotton boom, but when the slaves were freed in 1834, the owners abandoned the plantations and left the island. Inhabited by the former slaves, Long Island slumbered for years, until German resort developers began investigating its resources in the 1960s.

ESSENTIALS

GETTING THERE   There are two airstrips here, connected by a bad road. The **Stella Maris strip** is in the north, and the other, called **Deadman's Cay,** is in the south, north of Clarence Town (it's highly unlikely that you'll land here, and this one is a very expensive cab ride from most of the island's accommodations). **Bahamasair** (✆ **800/222-4262** in the U.S.) flies direct and daily from Fort Lauderdale, landing at the Stella Maris airport, which is near most of the hotels.

From Nassau, a mail boat sails weekly to Clarence Town on the southern end of Long Island. Departures are on Tuesday, and the trip takes a grueling 18 hours. For information contact the dockmaster at **Potter's Cay Dock,** Nassau (✆ **242/393-1064**).

GETTING AROUND   The **Stella Maris Resort Club** (✆ **242/338-2051**) can make arrangements to have you picked up at the airport upon arrival and can also arrange for a rental car. Otherwise you can contact **Taylor's Rentals** (✆ **242/338-7002**). This outfitter also rents scooters for $46 per day.

FAST FACTS   The **police** can be reached by calling ✆ **242/337-0999** or 242/337-0444.

The **Bank of Nova Scotia** (✆ **242/338-2002**) operates a small currency-exchange facility at the Stella Maris Resort. Hours are only on Tuesday and Thursday from 9:30am to 2pm, and Friday from 9:30am to 5pm.

SPECIAL EVENTS   In June, Long Island sailors participate in the big event of the year, the 4-day **Long Island Regatta.** They've been gathering since 1967 at Salt Pond for this annual event. In addition to the highly competitive sailboat races, Long Island takes on a festive air with calypso music and reggae and lots of drinking and partying. Many expatriate Long Islanders come home at this time, usually from Nassau, New York, or Miami, to enjoy not only the regatta but rake-and-scrape music. Call your local Bahamas Tourist Office (see chapter 2) for more information.

WHERE TO STAY

Cape Santa Maria Beach Resort 𝒢   This cozy nest has become the most luxurious resort on the island, taking over the position long held by the Stella Maris Resort Club. Cottages with two rooms are centered around a clubhouse, and the entire complex opens onto a stunning 4-mile strip of white sand. All units are only 60 feet from the beach, which offers great snorkeling. Although the accommodations don't have phones or TVs, each room is air-conditioned and also has ceiling fans, plus a small bathroom with shower stall. Bedrooms have a light, tropical, and airy feeling, with marble floors and tasteful rattan furniture. There's also a screened-in porch with ceiling fans so you can enjoy the outdoors without the mosquitoes, the curse of the Southern Bahamas.

The place is ideal for families, and several accommodations are configured so that children will have a separate room.

The hotel's 65-seat restaurant is also good, serving a tasty Bahamian, North American, and seafood cuisine.

Cape Santa Maria, off Queen's Hwy., Long Island, The Bahamas. ℭ 800/663-7090 or 242/338-5273. Fax 242/338-6013. www.capesantamaria.com. 20 units. Winter $1,040 per room 4 nights, $1,820 per room 7 nights; off-season $780 per room 4 nights, $1,365 per room 7 nights. Extra person $50. All meals $75 per person extra. AE, MC, V. **Amenities:** Restaurant, health club, water sports, bike rental, car rental, snorkeling gear, sailboats. *In room:* A/C, coffeemaker, hair dryer. No phone.

Lochabar Beach Lodge   One of the most remote retreats in this guide, this lodge offers escapist studios for those fleeing from the civilized world. You step from your studio to a pristine beach of white sand 75 feet away, surrounding a "blue hole" in a natural cove. The only acceptable lodgings in the southern part of Long Island, these guest studios measure 600 or 1,200 square feet each. In lieu of ceiling fans, the studios were built to take advantage of the trade winds. Guests keep their Bahama shutters and double screen doors open to capture those breezes. Each studio comes with a small bathroom containing a shower stall. Studios have kitchenettes, and a member of the staff will drive you to a nearby store to stock up on provisions.

Big Blue Hole, 1 mile south of Clarence Town, Long Island, The Bahamas. ℭ 242/327-2567. Fax 242/327-2567. www.bahamasvg.com/lochabarbeach.html. 2 units. Year-round $115–$150 double. Extra person $20. MC, V. **Amenities:** Snorkeling, bonefishing excursions, car rentals. *In room:* Kitchenette, ceiling fan. No phone.

Stella Maris Resort Club𝒢   Situated on a ridge overlooking the Atlantic, the Stella Maris Resort Club stands in a palm grove on the grounds of the old Adderley's Plantation. Although you can swim here, the beach isn't the best, so the hotel maintains a cabana at Cape Santa Maria, a gorgeous white sandy beach directly north, and offers shuttle service for its guests.

Accommodations vary widely—rooms, studios, apartments, and cottages with one to four bedrooms. Each accommodation has its own walk-in closet and fully equipped bathroom. Some are directly on the water. All of the buildings, including the cottages and bungalows, are set around a central clubhouse and a trio of pools. The resort makes a great honeymoon destination; everything is relaxed and informal.

The inn serves a good Bahamian cuisine, as well as continental specialties. There are rum-punch parties, cave parties, barbecue dinners, Saturday dinners, and dancing. Numerous water sports include complete diving facilities. Divers and snorkelers can choose from coral head, reef, and drop-off diving along the protected west coast of the island, at the north, and all along the east coast, around Conception Island and Rum Cay. Waterskiing and bottom and reef fishing are also offered; there are three good bonefishing bays close by. Some 12-foot Scorpion and Sunfish sailboats are free to hotel guests.

Ocean View Dr., P.O. Box LI30105, Long Island, The Bahamas. © 800/426-0466 or 242/338-2051, or 954/359-8236 for the Fort Lauderdale booking office. Fax 242/338-2052. www.stellamarisresort.com. 45 units. Winter $145 double, $165 1-bedroom cottage, $290–$555 bungalow or villa; off-season $120 double, $140 1-bedroom cottage, $240–$495 bungalow or villa. AE, MC, V. **Amenities:** Restaurant, bar, pools, water sports, boats. *In room:* Refrigerator, some units with private pools. No phone.

Thompson Bay Inn Located at Salt Pond, 12 miles south of Stella Maris, Thompson Bay Inn is a modest two-story stone inn. You can't get much simpler than this place, but some escapists seek it out, finding the two properties recommended above either too expensive or too elaborate. The small rooms are simply furnished, and the inn's four bathrooms with shower stalls are shared.

The inn's combination bar, lounge, dance hall, and restaurant serves plain but good Bahamian dishes, including conch, grouper, and peas 'n' rice.

Main Rd., Thompson Bay (P.O. Box LI30123), Stella Maris, Long Island, The Bahamas. © 242/338-0052. 8 units. Winter $65 double; off-season $55 double. No credit cards. **Amenities:** Restaurant, bar. *In room:* Ceiling fans. No phone.

WHERE TO DINE

All the inns above serve food, but you should call for a reservation. In addition, you can try some local joints. Try **Kooters,** Queen's Highway, Mangrove Bush (© 242/337-0340), which couldn't be more casual or laid-back, but is known for serving the best conch burger on Long Island. You can also drop in for sandwiches, and the cook does a mean batch of home fries. They also do daily specials such as fresh grilled fish or barbecue baby back ribs.

Another joint worth checking out is **The Forest,** Queen's Highway, Miley's (© 242/337-3287), lying south of Clarence Town. Its cracked conch is the island's finest, and you can also order the standard grouper fingers or even barbecued chicken. Spicy wings and potato skins are also served. The bar is made of seashells. On Friday nights a live band plays for dancing, and The Forest becomes an island hot spot.

EXPLORING THE ISLAND

There isn't much shopping, but you can visit **Wild Tamarind,** lying half a mile east of Queen's Highway at the hamlet of Petty's (© 242/337-0262). Here Denis Knight makes the best ceramics on the island. You might want to carry off one of his ceramic sculptures or at least a bowl or vase.

Most of the islanders live at the unattractively named **Deadman's Cay.** Other settlements have equally colorful names: Roses, Newfound Harbour, Burnt Ground, Indian Head Point, and, at the northern tip of the island, Cape Santa Maria, generally believed to be the place where Columbus landed and from where he looked on the Exumas (islands that he did not visit). Our favorite

---

(*Finds* The Old Hamlet of Simms

At a point 8 miles south of Stella Maris, you come to the hamlet of Simms, oldest on the island. Here the inhabitants of the little pastel-colored shacks live pretty much as they did a half century ago.

If you're here for lunch, try one of the roadside eateries serving conch salad. Our favorites are **Jeraldine's Jerk Pit** (no phone) along Queen's Highway. You can order even more substantial food, especially grouper fingers and fresh crayfish, at **Mario's Blue Chip,** Queen's Highway (© 242/ 338-8964). Leave your credit cards at home, of course, and don't anticipate regular opening hours.

---

name, however, is Hard Bargain. No one seems to know how this hamlet got its name. **Hard Bargain,** now a shrimp-breeding farm, lies 10 miles south of Clarence Town.

Try to visit **Clarence Town,** located 10 miles south of Deadman's Cay, along the eastern coastline. It was here that the stubby little priest, Father Jerome, who became known as the "father confessor" of the islands, built two churches before his death in 1956—**St. Paul's,** an Anglican house of worship, and **St. Peter's,** a Roman Catholic church. The "hermit" of Cat Island (you can visit his Hermitage there) was interested in Gothic architecture. He must also have been somewhat ecumenical, because he started his ministry as an Anglican but embraced Roman Catholicism along the way.

Many of the ruins recall the days when local plantation owners figured their wealth in black slaves and white cotton. The remains of **Dunmore's Plantation** at Deadman's Cay stand on a hill with the sea on three sides. There are six gateposts (four outer and two inner), as well as a house with two fireplaces and wall drawings of ships. At the base of the ruins is evidence that a mill wheel was once used. It was part of the estate of Lord Dunmore, for whom Dunmore Town on Harbour Island was named.

In the village of Grays stand the ruins of **Gray's Plantation,** where you'll see the remnants of at least three houses, one with two chimneys. One is very large, and another seems to have been a one-story structure with a cellar.

Adderley's Plantation, off Cape Santa Maria, originally occupied all the land now known as Stella Maris. The ruins of this cotton plantation's buildings consist of three structures that are partially intact but roofless.

Two underground sites that can be visited on Deadman's Cay are **Dunmore's Caves** and **Deadman's Cay Cave.** You'll need to hire a local guide to explore these. Dunmore's Caves are believed to have been inhabited by Lucayans and later to have served as a hideaway for buccaneers. The cave at Deadman's Cay, one of two that lead to the ocean, has never been fully explored. There are two native drawings on the cavern wall.

A lot of savvy anglers come here to fish instead of the more famous places, such as Andros. The secret of the good fishing found here is the presence of a major current stream, called the **North Equatorial Current,** which originates in the Canary Islands. This stream washes the shores of Long Island. In its wake the current transports huge schools of blue marlin, white marlin, sailfish, rainbow runners, yellowfin tuna, blackfin tuna, wahoo, and dolphinfish. Wahoo is best hunted from September through November. Catches weigh from 10 to 90 pounds, and some yellowfin have weighed up to 150 pounds. The small black-fin tuna (July through Dec) weigh from 10 to 30 pounds. In addition, there are miles and miles of reef fishing, with hundreds of species, including snapper or grouper that have been known to weigh 100 pounds. A jewfish caught here weighed 500 pounds. Inshore fishing for bonefish is also possible. These fish can be caught from an anchored boat, from the beach, or while wading in foot-deep water.

Although there are no water-sports outfitters on Long Island, the two major resorts, the **Stella Maris Resort Club** and the **Cape Santa Maria Beach Resort** (see above) fill the void and offer more water sports than you can do in a week. Both offer bonefishing at a rate of $200 to $250 per day for up to two people; reef fishing is from $350 per day for up to four people; deep-sea fishing is $600 to $650 per day for up to four people. **Snorkeling** off the beach is complimentary at both resorts. However, boat excursions can be as little as $10 per hour at Cape Santa Maria; on Wednesday and Saturday, these excursions are complimentary at the Stella Maris. Both resorts offer scuba diving ranging from $75 to $95 per person per day, with equipment rentals ranging from $17.50 to $25. Both also offer complimentary Hobie Cats, boogie boards, Windsurfers, and bicycles; the Stella Maris even offers waterskiing at a cost of $40 per person.

4 Acklins Island & Crooked Island

These little tropical islands, approximately 240 miles southeast of Nassau, make up an undiscovered Bahamian frontier outpost. Columbus came this way looking for gold. Much later, Acklins Island, Crooked Island, and their surrounding cays became hideouts for pirates who attacked vessels in the Crooked Island Passage (the narrow waterway Columbus sailed), which separates the two islands. Today a well-known landmark, the **Crooked Island Passage Light,** built in 1876, guides ships to a safe voyage through the slot. Also known as the Bird Rock Lighthouse, it is a popular nesting spot for ospreys, and the light still lures pilots and sailors to the **Pittstown Point Landing Resort.** A barrier reef begins near the lighthouse, stretching down off Acklins Island for about 25 miles to the southeast.

Although Acklins Island and Crooked Island are separate, they are usually mentioned as a unit because of their proximity to one another. Together, the two islands form the shape of a boomerang. Crooked Island, the northern one, is 70 square miles in area, whereas Acklins Island, to the south, occupies 120 square miles. Both islands, which have good white-sand beaches and offer fishing and scuba diving, are inhabited mainly by fishermen and farmers.

In his controversial article in *National Geographic* in 1986, Joseph Judge identified Crooked Island as the site of Columbus's second island landing, the one he named Santa Maria de la Concepcion.

It is estimated that by the end of the 18th century, there were more than three dozen working plantations on these islands, begun by Loyalists fleeing mainland North America in the wake of the Revolutionary War. At the peak plantation period, there could have been as many as 1,200 slaves laboring in the 3,000 "doomed" acres of cotton fields (which were later wiped out by a blight). The people who remained on the island survived not only by fishing and farming, but also, beginning in the mid-18th century, by stripping the Croton cascarilla shrub of its bark to produce the flavoring for Campari liquor.

ESSENTIALS

GETTING THERE   There's an airport at Colonel Hill on Crooked Island and another airstrip at **Spring Point,** Acklins Island.

Bahamasair (© **800/222-4262** in the U.S.) has two flights a week from Nassau, on Wednesday and Saturday, to Crooked Island and Acklins Island, with returns to Nassau scheduled on the same day.

There is also mail-boat service, with the **MV *United Star,*** leaving Potter's Cay Dock in Nassau and heading for Acklins Island, Crooked Island, Fortune Island (Long Cay), and Mayaguana Island each week. Check the schedule and costs with the dockmaster at **Potter's Cay Dock** in Nassau (© **242/393-1064**).

A government-owned **ferry** service connects the two islands; it operates daily from 9am to 4pm. It links Lovely Bay on Acklins Island with Browns on Crooked Island. The one-way fare is $4.

Once you arrive at Crooked Island, a **taxi** service is available, but because of the lack of telephones, it's wise to advise your hotel of your arrival—they'll probably send a van to meet you.

FAST FACTS   There are two government-operated clinics. Phones are scarce on the islands, but your hotel desk can reach one of these clinics by going through the operator. The clinic on Acklins Island is at **Spring Point and Chesters Bay,** and the one on Crooked Island is at **Landrail Point.**

The **police** station on Crooked Island can be reached by dialing © **242/ 344-2599.**

WHERE TO STAY & DINE

Pittstown Point Landing   Located on a beach at the extreme northwestern tip of Crooked Island, this hotel is so isolated you'll forget all about the world outside. For most of the early years of its life, it was a well-guarded secret shared mostly by the owners of private planes who flew in from the mainland of Florida for off-the-record weekends. Even today, about 80% of the clients arrive by one- or two-engine aircraft that they fly themselves as part of island-hopping jaunts around The Bahamas. The island maintains its own 2,300-foot, hard-surface landing strip, which is completely independent from the one used for the twice-per-week flights from Nassau on Bahamasair.

In 1994, a group of investors upgraded the place, taking great care not to alter its funky appeal. Surrounded by scrub-covered landscape at the edge of a turquoise sea, it lies 2½ miles north of the hamlet of Landrail Point (population 60) on a sandy peninsula. Within easy access are some of the weirdest historic sites in The Bahamas, including the sun-baked ruins of a salt farm (Marine Farms Fortress) that was sacked by American-based pirates in 1812.

Spartan accommodations with shower-only bathrooms lie within three low-slung, cement-sided buildings. They lie directly on the beach, usually with screened-in porches facing the sea. Because of the constant trade winds blowing in, the bedrooms don't have air-conditioning, only large paddle-shaped ceiling fans. The entire resort shares only one telephone/fax, which is reserved for emergency calls.

Meals are served in a stone-sided building that was originally erected late in the 1600s as a barracks for the British West Indies Naval Squadron and later was the region's post office. The restaurant serves seafood and North American and Bahamian specialties. Guests always take the meal plan, but they're joined by a scattering of yacht owners or aviators who drop in spontaneously for drinks and dinner.

Finds **The Ghost Island of Fortune**

Lying off the coast of Crooked Island, **Fortune Island** is truly a place that time forgot. Your hotel can put you in touch with a boater on Crooked Island who will take you here. Experts believe, based on research done for *National Geographic*, that Fortune Island (sometimes confusingly called Long Cay) is the one Columbus chose to name Isabella, in honor of the queen who funded his expedition. Its only real settlement is Albert Town, which is classified as a ghost town, but officially isn't—some hardy souls still live here. Fortune Hill, visible from 12 miles away at sea, is the local landmark. Hundreds of Bahamians came here in the 2 decades before World War I and would wait to be picked up by oceangoing freighters, which would take them to seek their fortunes as laborers in Central America—hence, the name Fortune Hill.

Landrall Point, Crooked Island, The Bahamas. © **800/PLACE-2-B** or 242/344-2507. www.pittstown.com. (For reservations and information, contact Pittstown Point Landing, 238A Airport Rd., Statesville, NC 28677.) 12 units. Year-round $150–$180 double. AP (all meals). $60 per person extra. AE, MC, V. **Amenities:** Restaurant. *In room:* Ceiling fans. No phone.

EXPLORING THE ISLANDS: UNCOVERING A PIRATE HIDEOUT & MORE

Crooked Island opens onto the **Windward Passage,** the dividing point between the Caribbean Sea and The Bahamas. Whatever else he may have named it, it is said that when Columbus landed at what is now Pittstown Point, he called it Fragrant Island because of the aroma of its many herbs. One scent was cascarilla bark, used to flavor **Campari liquor** as well as the native **Cascarilla Liqueur,** which is exported. For the best view of the island, go to **Colonel Hill,** if you didn't arrive at the Crooked Island Airport (also known as the Colonel Hill Airport), with the same vantage.

Guarding the north end of this island is the **Marine Farms Fortress,** an abandoned British fortification that saw action in the War of 1812. It looks out over Crooked Island Passage and can be visited (ask your hotel to make arrangements for you).

Hope Great House is also on the island, with orchards and gardens that date from the time of George V of England.

Other sights include **French Wells Bay,** a swampy delta leading to an extensive mangrove swamp rich in bird life, and the **Bird Rock Lighthouse,** built a century ago.

At the southern end of Acklins Island lies **Castle Island,** a low and sandy bit of land where an 1867 lighthouse stands. Pirates used it as a hideout, sailing forth to attack ships in the nearby passage.

Acklins Island has many interestingly named villages—Rocky Point, Binnacle Hill, Salina Point, Delectable Bay, Golden Grove, Goodwill, Hard Hill, Snug Corner, and Lovely Bay. Some Crooked Island sites have more ominous names, such as Gun Point and Cripple Hill.

5 Mayaguana Island

Sleepy Mayaguana seems to float adrift in the tropical sun at the remote extremities of the southeastern edge of The Bahamas. It occupies 110 square miles and has a population of about 500. It's a long, long way from the development of Nassau and Paradise Island.

Standing in the Windward Passage, Mayaguana is just northwest of the Turks and Caicos Islands. It's separated from the British Crown Colony by the Caicos Passage. Around the time of the American Civil War, inhabitants of Turks Island began to settle in Mayaguana, which before then had dozed undisturbed for centuries.

Acklins Island and Crooked Island lie across the Mayaguana Passage. Mayaguana is only 6 miles across at its widest point, and about 24 miles long. Its beaches are enticing, but you'll rarely see a tourist on them, other than the occasional German. A few tourism developers have flown in to check out the island, but so far no activity has come about. Because of its remote location, the United States has opened a missile-tracking station here.

The island's southern location makes it ideal in winter. And certainly if you come to Mayaguana to escape a harsh winter back home, no one will ever think of looking for you here. Summers are scorchingly hot, however.

GETTING THERE

Bahamasair (© **800/222-4262** in the U.S.) flies in here to a little airstrip. Flights arrive from Nassau Monday and Friday at 8am.

From Nassau, a **mail boat,** going also to Crooked Island, Acklins Island, and Fortune Island (Long Cay), makes a stop at Mayaguana. For information, check with the dockmaster at **Potter's Cay Dock** in Nassau (© **242/393-1064**).

WHERE TO STAY & DINE

Few other outposts in The Bahamas are as remote as Mayaguana, which is the main reason why many visitors come—to get away from everything. Many visitors arrive by boat and just ask around for availability at one of the ultra-simple lodgings here. Some locals are willing to house you in one of their spare bedrooms for a rate that can be negotiated up or down to almost anything. But if you're interested in the best on the island, head for either of the two properties; neither has a phone.

The less formal of the two is the somewhat-ramshackle **Mayaguana Inn Guest House,** a five-room, cement-and-wood-sided flat-roofed inn with a shared sitting area and five battered and very simple accommodations. A few steps away lie the **Paradise Villas,** a cottage complex in the center of town, where each of eight units has a private bathroom, and the common room has a satellite TV. Each charges between $60 and $70 for a double room, including breakfast, but, of course, these rates must be negotiated on the spot.

Be warned in advance that both of these choices are bare-bones, but that the more mainstream of the two is decidedly funky Paradise Villas, with units that surround a small swimming pool. On the premises is one of the only restaurants in Abraham's Bay, a partially open-aired affair with meals that cost from $10 to around $18 each, with Bahamian specialties that include the usual roster of fish, goat, conch, and beef dishes. No one on the island accepts credit cards.

EXPLORING THE ISLAND

Abraham's Bay is the main town on the south coast, with an excellent harbor. The other little settlement on Mayaguana is **Betsy Bay,** secluded and lost in time. Wild corn and saucy hummingbirds share this spot along with some little sun-worn cottages basking in the hot sun. At **Pirate's Well,** goats are now the chief residents, although buccaneers used to roam past here. Locals still dream of finding buried treasure.

The best views of the Mayaguana Passage can be had from both Betsy Bay and Pirate's Well.

Fishing is good on the island. Locals will often take you out on one of their boats, but you've got to ask around. In summer and early autumn, temperatures can soar beyond 100°F. Winters, however, are ideal, and it never gets cold here as it can in the North Bahamas.

Mayaguana might be called The Bahamas's "great outback" or "wild west." It's a rugged and salty environment, with no organized activities of any kind. Sailing, deep-sea fishing, scuba diving, snorkeling, swimming, and walking are the main pastimes. If you need rental gear or want to hire a guide for an organized outing, your best bet is to inquire at your hotel; they can usually hook you up with the right person. The island is still too laid-back to have many organized outfitters.

It is a total escapist's paradise, a place amazingly undeveloped off the shores of America. So far it's remained safe and secure from most human intrusion.

6 Great Inagua ⟨★⟩

The most southerly and the third-largest island of The Bahamas, flat Great Inagua, some 40 miles long and 20 miles wide, is home to 1,200 people. It lies 325 miles southeast of Nassau.

This is the site not only of the **Morton Salt Crystal Factory,** here since 1800, but also of one of the largest nesting grounds for **flamingos** in the western hemisphere. The National Trust of The Bahamas protects the area around Lake Windsor, where the birds breed and the population is said to number 50,000. Flamingos used to inhabit all of The Bahamas, but the bird is nearly extinct in many places. The reserve can be visited only with a guide. Besides the pink flamingo, you can see roseate spoonbills and other bird life here.

Green turtles are raised here, too, at **Union Creek Reserve.** Tours here are not well-organized; it's all very informal. You can ask your inn to arrange a tour for you, or call **Larry Ingraham's Great Inagua Tours** at ⓒ **242/339-1862** to ask if he'll set up something for you. They are then released into the ocean to make their way as best they can; they, too, are an endangered species. The vast windward island, almost within sight of Cuba, is also inhabited by wild hogs, horses, and donkeys.

The settlement of **Matthew Town** is the chief hamlet of the island, but it's not of any great sightseeing interest. Other sites have interesting names, such as Doghead Point, Lantern Head, Conch Shell Point, Mutton Fish Point, and Devil's Point (which makes one wonder what happened there to give rise to the name). There's an 1870 lighthouse at Matthew Town.

Little Inagua, 5 miles to the north, has no population and is just a speck of land off the northeast coast of Great Inagua, about 30 square miles in area. It has much bird life, though, including West Indian tree ducks. There are also wild goats and donkeys.

Henri Christophe, the self-proclaimed Haitian king, is supposed to have had a summer palace built for himself here in the very early part of the 19th century, but no traces of it can be found today. (This island is much closer to Haiti than it is to Nassau.) In 1687, long before the coming of Christophe, a Captain Phipps recovered 26 tons of Spanish treasure from sunken galleons off these shores.

ESSENTIALS

GETTING THERE Bahamasair (© 800/222-4262 in the U.S.) flies to Matthew Town Airport from Nassau on Monday, Wednesday, and Friday at 8am.

You can also go by **mail boat,** which makes weekly trips from Nassau to Matthew Town (schedule varies). The boat leaves Nassau on Wednesday and comes back on Sunday. Call the **Potter's Cay Dockmaster** (© 242/393-1064) in Nassau for details.

GETTING AROUND   Taxis (© 242/339-1284) meet incoming flights from Nassau.

If you need a car, check with one of the guest houses, but don't expect the vehicles to be well-maintained. One of the best ways to explore the island is by bike: Call **Pour More Bar** at © 242/339-1659. The cost is $1 per hour.

FAST FACTS   The **Inagua Hospital** can be called at © 242/339-1249. The **police** can be reached at © 242/339-1263.

WHERE TO STAY

The choices aren't great on this island, but most visitors are willing to forgo comfort to see the spectacular flamingos.

Morton Main House   The Main House is owned by Morton Bahamas Ltd., the salt people, whose employees often fill up all the rooms. Only six bedrooms are rented, and the furnishings are extremely modest, though everything is clean. Each unit comes with a small bathroom containing a shower stall. Life here is casual and completely informal. You can order breakfast or lunch here—no dinner. It unfortunately sits near a noisy power plant.

Matthew Town, Inagua, The Bahamas. © 242/339-1267. Fax 242/339-1265. 6 units. $63.60 double. No credit cards. In-room: A/C, TV.

Walkine's Guest House   Set a half mile south of Matthew Town, this simple guest house has a blue exterior and rosy, shell-pink bedrooms. Your hosts are Eleanor and Kirk Walkine, who built their place in 1984 across the road from the beach. Rooms are very modest but spacious, with only racks to hang your clothes in lieu of a closet. Bathrooms are large, each containing a shower stall.

Gregory St., Matthew Town, Inagua, The Bahamas. © 242/339-1612. 5 units, 3 with private bathroom. $65 double. No credit cards. In-room: A/C, TV.

WHERE TO DINE

Cozy Corner BAHAMIAN/AMERICAN   The most consistently reliable restaurant outside any of the guest houses is this lime-green, stone-built house 2 blocks from the sea. Your hosts, Rosemary Ingraham and her daughter, Veronica, maintain a friendly bar, where beer, rum punch, and gossip seem to be the staples of the town. Menu items include a simple roster of mostly fried foods that are almost always accompanied by french fries. Dishes include fried conch, fried chicken, burgers and "whopper burgers," and whatever kind of fried seafood is available from local fishermen on the day of your visit.

William St., Matthew Town. © 242/339-1440. Breakfast $5; lunch $7; dinner $7–$10. No credit cards. Daily 9:30am–10:30pm (closing time could vary).

EXPLORING THE ISLAND: PINK FLAMINGOS & MORE

Inagua, the southernmost island of The Bahamas, and third-largest in the chain, lies just off the eastern tip of Cuba. Partially because of its isolation, it's home to some of the best-stocked bird colonies in the western hemisphere. In fact, the island's vast number of **pink flamingos** ⟨⟨⟨ outnumbers its human population of 1,200. They're so plentiful on Inagua that some of them even roost on the runway of the island's airport, as well as at thousands of other locations throughout the flat, heat-blasted landscape. When seen in a huge flock, they present a surreal vision.

Dedicated bird-watchers who are willing to forgo comforts usually trek inland to the edges of the many brackish lakes in the island's center. About half the island is devoted to a national park; the island's most viable industry involves distilling salt from the local salt flats.

To visit **Inagua National Park** ⟨⟨ to see the birds is reason enough to come here in the first place. Anyone going into the park must be accompanied by a warden, and reservations and a day pass costing $25 per person must be obtained in advance, either through The Bahamas National Trust in Nassau (© **242/393-1317** for information or reservations), or else by contacting one of the local wardens on Inagua, either Randolph or Henry Nixon at © **242/339-1616.** In addition to the park fee, it is expected that you'll offer the wardens a large tip. Figure on about $50 a day, the usual payment. The best time to see our feathered friends is from November until June.

One of the best panoramas on the island is **Southwest Point,** lying 1¼ miles south of the "capital." From here you can see Cuba on a clear day, because it lies just 50 miles to the west. There's a lighthouse here dating from 1870. From it, you can wave at Castro. The reefs off this point are treacherous, as many a captain learned when his ship was wrecked here. The lighthouse is one of the last quartet of hand-operated kerosene lighthouses left in The Bahamas.

Seawater is pumped into the interior of the island and held in dikes. The island's salt ponds, about 80 of them, cover some 12,000 acres. As the water evaporates, it turns into heavy brine. Continuously, the salt solidifies at night and melts during the heat of the day, and a crystallized bed forms at the bottom of the pond. In the final stage, any remaining water is drained, and the salt is bulldozed into bleached white mountains and shipped around the world for processing. As the water evaporates in the salt ponds, brine shrimp concentrate and provide great meals for the flamingos. If you'd like to marvel at salt, you can call **Morton Salt Company** (© **242/339-1300**) and ask if a tour would be possible. They produce more than 1 million tons of salt a year.

You can also visit the **Erickson Museum & Library,** Gregory Street, at the northern edge of Matthew Town (© **242/339-1863**). Exhibits detail the history of the island and Morton Salt. The museum is named for the Erickson family, who came here in 1934 to run the salt company. Hours are Monday to Friday 9am to 1pm and 3 to 6pm.

7 Ragged Island & Jumento Cays

Talk about "faraway places with strange-sounding names." Very few tourists, except for stray people who come in on yachts, visit the area.

The thing that's truly memorable here is the **sunset.** Except in the rare times when clouds obscure the sky and horizon, the sunset bursts forth in some of the most spectacular shades of gold, purple, red, and orange—sometimes with a green flash, reflecting in the crystal-clear waters.

This island group, a mini-archipelago, begins with Jumento Cays off the west point of Long Island and runs in a half-moon shape for some 100 miles down to Ragged Island; Little Ragged Island is the southernmost bit of land at the bottom of the crescent. They constitute the southeastern limit of the Great Bahama Bank.

Ragged Island and its string of uninhabited cays are the backwaters of The Bahamas, since most of them are so tiny and so unimportant they don't often appear on maps. However, visitors who return from this area talk of the remarkable beauty of these little pieces of land and coral.

Sailing in this area in bad weather is dangerous because of the unrelenting winds. Otherwise, the cays would be better known among the boating crowd. In summer, it's usually a good place to cruise the waters.

Like nearly all the islands in this chapter, Ragged Island knew greater prosperity when hundreds of inhabitants worked its salt flats. Today **Duncan Town,** the little village still standing on the island, is all that's left of the island's better days. Its people are hardworking and weather-beaten, and many have a difficult time making a living. Nassau seems to have forgotten this outpost of the nation.

Some of the little cays, from Jumento Cay around the semicircle toward Ragged Island, have names such as No Bush Cay, Dead Cay, Sisters Cay, Nurse Cay, Double-Breasted Cay, and Hog Cay. There's a Raccoon Cay, as well as a Raccoon Cut. A light tower (lighthouse) stands on Flamingo Cay.

Visitors are so rare that anybody's arrival is treated as an event, and the townspeople are eager to help in any way they can. There's a 3,000-foot paved airstrip here, but because it's accessible only to private planes, it's not used much.

A mail boat, **MV *Emmipt and Cephas,*** leaves Potter's Cay in Nassau on Tuesday at 2pm en route to Ragged Island. It returns on Thursday. For details about costs and sailing, contact the dockmaster at **Potter's Cay Dock,** Nassau (© 242/ 393-1064).

Regrettably, there are no hotels for tourists.

11

Turks & Caicos

The Turks and Caicos Islands (or "Turks and Who?" as they're often called) have long been dubbed the "forgotten islands." Sun worshippers discovered them in the early 1990s, however, and now there's talk of a "second Bahamas" in the making. Although they are actually part of the Bahamian archipelago, they are tucked away to the east of the southernmost islands of The Bahamas and governed separately.

Directly north of Haiti and the Dominican Republic, the islands lie at the crossroads of the Caribbean and the Americas. Technically, however, this obscure outpost is not in Caribbean waters, but on the fringe of the Atlantic. *Le Figaro* of Paris once quoted a developer on the Turks and Caicos who said, "These islands will be the only place left where the jet set, tired of Florida and The Bahamas, will be able to take refuge." They're still off the beaten track, and they're not right for travelers who want lots of glitzy facilities or nightlife, but development is beginning. The bustle of construction is underway, particularly in Provo.

Grand Turk and **Salt Cay** (which constitute the Turks Islands) and Cockburn Harbour (South Caicos) are ports of entry, while the major island for tourism is **Provo.**

Many of the islanders today work in the salt-raking industry; others export lobsters (crayfish), conch, and conch shells. But more and more, the citizens of this little country feed off the tourist industry. It's the kind of place where you still greet people as you encounter them walking along the roads.

The average temperature here is 82°F, dropping to 77°F at night. The cooling breezes of the prevailing trade winds prevent the climate from being oppressive.

The Turks and Caicos Islands are a coral-reef paradise, largely shut off from the world, free of pollution and crowds. Even with the advent of real tourist development, the beauty and tranquility of this little island chain are still intact. You won't find the highly refined tourist infrastructure that exists in The Bahamas, but that's the appeal for some travelers.

The inns of the Turks and Caicos Islands, except those on Providenciales (Provo), are small, personally run, and very casual. Entertainment on the islands is most often impromptu. The islands have no TV or daily papers, but there is a radio station. Most visitors who come here are more interested in diving, fishing, sailing, and boating than in shopping or a resort scene. Divers still dream of finding that legendary chest of gold hidden in the coral reefs or underwater caverns.

What's beginning to put Turks and Caicos on the map is amazing scuba diving and an incredible array of beaches—225 miles of beaches, to be precise. Sometimes, the stretches of soft white sand run for miles; others are small, hidden in secluded coves.

AN UNDERWATER PARADISE

A reef system 65 miles across and 200 miles long, a great range of dive sites, playful dolphins who show up unexpectedly, countless varieties of colorful fish and coral—these are the undersea attractions of the Turks and Caicos Islands.

For example, off the northwest corner of the island of Provo is **Smith's Reef,** a walk-in dive to a seascape of brain and fan corals; purple gorgonias; anemones; sea cucumbers; sergeant majors; green parrot fish; long-nosed trumpet fish; the odd, ominous-looking green moray; an occasional southern ray; and a visiting hawksbill turtle or two.

From the shore at **Grace Bay**—a sweep of powdery white beach graced by some of Provo's most highly regarded resorts—visitors can see where the sea breaks along 14 miles of barrier reef. But the reef is much more than the natural breakwater that makes this beach so accommodating; it is also the teeming undersea home of sea life that ranges from swarms of colorful schools of fish to barracuda to large, rotund grouper.

Around Grand Turk, there are miles and miles of drop-off diving. Here you can enjoy one of the underwater world's great experiences: a night dive on a wall where, due to bioluminescence, the colors of the day become the phosphorescent illumination of the night.

Ledge and wall dives are the attractions around South Caicos. Here divers can literally select the level of their vertical descent, then glide horizontally among the multicolored, multishaped corals and drift through schools of trumpets, hamlets, basslets, and more.

Divers can explore the wreck of the **HMS _Endymion_** ⋒ off **Salt Cay,** which went down in a storm in 1790. Two centuries later, Brian Sheedy, a local diver and inn operator, discovered the wreck. Today, while the reef has reclaimed the hull and all else that was biodegradable, divers can still get a close-up look at its cannons and four huge anchors lying about.

But Salt Cay is more than the final resting place of a ghost ship. Between January and March each year, **humpback whales** come here to play. Visitors can watch their antics from shore, boat out among them, or don dive equipment and go below.

To reach the underwater treasures of West Caicos, a handful of dive boats make hourlong transits (each way) from the southern tip of Provo (Sapodilla Bay) several times a week. Once they're below the water's surface, divers are usually awestruck at the 2 miles of sheer coral walls less than a quarter mile from the West Caicos shoreline. The most popular dive sites are **Boat Cove, Sunday Service,** and **Isle's End.**

A LOOK AT THE PAST

The Arawaks first settled the Turks and Caicos Islands. Ponce de León sighted the little chain in 1512, although there are those who believe that Columbus landed here—not at San Salvador (Watling Island) or Samana Cay in The Bahamas. It was not far to the south, in the waters off the north coast of Hispaniola (the part that is now Haiti), that the _Santa María,_ the flagship of Columbus's discovery fleet, sank on Christmas night, 1492.

In recent years, eminent Caribbean historians have endorsed the claim that Columbus landed here. Symposia on the subject have presented supporting data. The assertion is that Grand Turk was the site of Columbus's first landfall, on October 12, 1492, and that he set foot on the island's western shores later that same day. He was supposedly greeted by the native Arawaks, who called the island Guanahani.

The Turks & Caicos Islands

N

15 Miles
15 Kilometers

0
0

Scuba Diving
Airport
Shipwreck

ATLANTIC OCEAN

GRAND TURK

Cockburn Town

TURKS ISLANDS

SAND CAY

SALT CAY

Turks Island Passage

SOUTH CAICOS

Cockburn Harbour

BUSH CAY

EAST CAICOS

AMBERGRIS CAY

SEAL CAYS

Bambarra

Conch Bar

MIDDLE CAICOS

CAICOS ISLANDS

Bottle Creek

Whitby

NORTH CAICOS

Kew

PARROT CAY

PINE CAY

Turtle Cove
Grace Bay

PROVIDENCIALES

FRENCH CAY

Caicos Passage

Northwest Point

Blue Hills

Sapodilla Bay

WEST CAICOS

Abaco

Grand Bahama

Eleuthera

Cat Island

San Salvador

Long Island

Crooked Island

Paradise Island

Andros

Great Exuma

Great Inagua

Cuba

Florida

Turks and Caicos

Pirates marauding the Spanish Main learned of the hidden coves of the Turks and Caicos Islands and used them as refuges when they ventured out to plunder Spanish galleons sailing out of Cuba and Haiti. This nest of cutthroats was called "Brothers of the Coast." The most famous of them was Rackam the Red, an Englishman.

After the Arawaks were removed from the islands to face their doom in the mines of Hispaniola, the islands had no permanent inhabitants until 1678. In that year the Bermudians, who had built ships and were searching for goods to trade with the American colonies, established the salt-raking industry. The Spanish drove the Bermudians away in 1710, but they soon returned and thereafter repelled attacks by both Spain and France. Their ranks were augmented during and after the American Revolution by Loyalists who fled America, bringing their slaves with them.

Bermuda finally lost out in 1799, when the Bahamian assembly in Nassau gave representation to its little island neighbors to the southeast. This attachment to The Bahamas ended in 1848, when the people of the Turks and Caicos Islands petitioned to withdraw from the assembly. They said the Bahamian government had paid no attention to them except to send salt-tax collectors, and that they saw the mail boat only four times each year.

The islands were allowed to break their ties with their northern relatives and to have their own president and council, supervised as a separate colony by the governor of Jamaica. After a quarter century, however, they were annexed by Jamaica as a dependency. It was not until 1962, when Jamaica became independent, that the little group of islands became a separate British Crown Colony.

The Turks and Caicos Islands are mainly self-governing today. Queen Elizabeth selects a governor to be her representative in island affairs; this governor appoints the chief minister, who, in turn, appoints minor ministers.

TURKS & CAICOS ESSENTIALS
GETTING THERE
Miami is the only U.S. gateway for flights into the Turks and Caicos, and **American** (© **800/433-7300**) is the only carrier flying from the U.S. mainland. American offers two daily non-stop flights to Providenciales. The first flight departs Miami at 1:15pm and the second at 4:55pm. Flight time is 1 hour and 39 minutes. Even the early departure is late enough in the day to permit transfers from any of the hundreds of flights winging into Miami from virtually everywhere every day. Return flights from Provo to Miami depart every day at 7:50am and 4:05pm.

Delta (© **800/241-4141**) offers non-stop flights from Atlanta to Provo. From Nassau, you can fly to Provo Thursday and Sunday on **Bahamasair** (© **800/222-4262**). Once on Provo, you can then fly **Turks & Caicos Airways** (© **649/946-4255**) to all the other major islands, including Grand Turk.

Canadians and Brits should fly to Nassau or Miami to make connections with American Airlines or Bahamasair.

GETTING AROUND
Getting around can be a problem. Car-rental agencies, except on Provo, are few and far between (most visitors don't use this means of transport, but see below). Each of the inhabited islands has taxi drivers with just-adequate vehicles.

BY TAXI Taxis can be found at the airports on Providenciales, South Caicos, and Grand Turk. They'll quote you a fixed price to and from the various hotels. They'll also deposit you on an isolated beach and return at a predetermined time to pick you up. Don't be surprised if you end up sharing a ride; the government is trying to save fuel. Ask your hotel to make arrangements for you.

BY CAR   Because Providenciales is so large, and its hotels and restaurants are so far-flung, you might find a car useful there. See individual island listings for car-rental agencies. On the remaining islands, except for Grand Turk, you have to depend on taxis or locals to transport you, although hotels or inns can sometimes arrange rentals with residents who might lease you their house buggy.

Note: In the British tradition, cars throughout the country drive on the left.

BY PLANE   The most leisurely way to explore the outlying islands is by boat, but barring your access to a yacht, you can travel on one of the eight- or nine-passenger propeller planes operated by **Turks & Caicos Airways** (© **649/ 946-4255**). Most convenient are the airline's "patch flights." Eastbound, they fly from Providenciales to North Caicos, Middle Caicos, and South Caicos, and terminate at Grand Turk. Westbound, they fly the same itinerary in reverse. The planes touch down briefly after only a few minutes' flight time at each of the above-mentioned islands, depositing passengers, luggage, and supplies en route. In addition, the airline offers two daily flights between the country's most populous islands, Provo and Grand Turk. The price is $65 each way, or $120 round-trip. Most passengers traveling to Salt Cay arrive by boat, but those who prefer to fly opt for one of the Monday, Wednesday, or Friday flights (two round-trip flights on each of those days) between Grand Turk and Salt Cay. Small islands, such as Pine Cay, are serviced only by prearranged charter flights.

 FAST FACTS: Turks & Caicos Islands

American Express   American Express is not represented anywhere on the Turks and Caicos Islands.

Climate   The islands receive approximately 21 inches of rainfall annually. The Turks and Caicos's mean monthly temperature is 80°F, and the winter water temperature ranges from 72°F to 80°F. Since the climate is largely the same as that in The Bahamas, see "When to Go," in chapter 2.

Currency   The U.S. dollar is the coin of the realm here. There are branches of major banks on Provo, along with a few ATMs; but in the outlying islands, banks and ATMs are scarcer, so bring enough cash or traveler's checks with you.

Customs   On arriving, you may bring in 1 quart of liquor, 200 cigarettes, 50 cigars, or 8 ounces of tobacco duty-free. There are no restrictions on cameras, film, sports equipment, or personal items, provided they aren't for resale. Absolutely no spear guns are allowed, and the importation of firearms without a permit is also prohibited. Illegal imported drugs bring heavy fines and lengthy terms of imprisonment.

Each U.S. citizen is eligible for a $400 duty-free exemption if he or she has been out of the country for at least 48 hours and if a period of 41 days has elapsed since that privilege was last exercised. This allowance may include 1 liter of liquor. In addition, you can mail home a number of unsolicited gifts to friends and relatives amounting to $100 or less per day and not to include more than 4 ounces of liquor or 1 ounce of perfume.

Drugstores   There are clinics on Grand Turk and Providenciales that can provide help and medications, but it's best to arrive on the islands with whatever prescribed medication you think you will need.

Electricity   The electric current on the islands is 120 volts, 60 cycles, AC. American appliances will work; British and European appliances will need adapters.

Entry Requirements   U.S. and Canadian citizens must have a passport or a combination of a birth certificate and photo ID, plus a return or ongoing ticket, to enter the country. The photo ID could be an official driver's license with a photograph or a voter's registration card with a photograph. These entry requirements are subject to change, so always confirm what the latest entry requirements are before heading for a foreign country. We always recommend bringing your passport whenever you're visiting a foreign country. Citizens of the United Kingdom, Commonwealth countries of the Caribbean, the Republic of Ireland, and EU countries must have a current passport. Citizens of all other countries must have a visa in addition to a valid passport. Visas for the Turks and Caicos Islands may be obtained from the British High Commission or various consulate offices in the United States.

Holidays   The actual dates of some of these observances may vary from year to year. If the date of a particular celebration falls on Saturday or Sunday, the actual observance may not take place until the following Monday. Holidays include New Year's Day, Commonwealth Day (Mar 11), Good Friday, Easter Sunday, Easter Monday, Birthday of Her Majesty the Queen (June 15), Emancipation Day (Aug 1), Columbus Day (Oct 12), International Human Rights Day (Oct 24), Christmas, and Boxing Day (Dec 26).

Hospitals   The islands are served by three medical practitioners and a qualified nursing staff. There is a 35-bed hospital on Grand Turk, **Grand Turk Hospital,** Hospital Road (✆ **649/946-2040**), with X-ray facilities, an operating theater, and a pathology laboratory. On Providenciales, there is the **Providenciales Health Medical Center,** Leeward Highway and Airport Road (✆ **649/941-3000**). There are clinics on South Caicos (✆ **649/946-3216**), Middle Caicos (✆ **649/946-6145**), and North Caicos (✆ **649/946-7194**). All the islands are served by one **dentist,** who can be reached at the Providenciales health center. Anyone critically ill is transferred to Grand Turk for hospital treatment or evacuated to Nassau, Miami, or Jamaica for specialist treatment. Should you become ill, your hotel will locate the nearest medical facility.

Information   **The Turks & Caicos Sales and Information Office,** Front Street, Cockburn Town, Grand Turk, BWI (✆ **800/241-0824** in the U.S., or 649/946-2322), is open Monday through Friday from 8am to 5pm. The website for Turks and Caicos is **www.turksandcaicostourism.com.**

Language   The official language is English.

Police   In Grand Turk call ✆ **649/946-2299;** in Providenciales ✆ **649/946-4259;** and in South Caicos ✆ **649/946-3299.** On North Caicos call ✆ **649/946-7261;** on Middle Caicos ✆ **649/946-6111.**

Post Office   The General Post Office is on Grand Turk (✆ **649/946-1334**), and another major post office is on Provo (✆ **649/946-4676**). There are suboffices on South Caicos, Salt Cay, Bottle Creek, and Middle Caicos. Offices are open Monday through Thursday from 8am to 12:30pm and from 2 to 4pm, Friday from 8am to 3:30pm. There is a Philatelic Bureau on Grand Turk, operated separately from the post office, but with the same hours.

Safety   Although crime is minimal in the islands, petty theft does take place here the same as anywhere, so protect your valuables, money, and cameras. Don't leave luggage or parcels in an unattended car. Beaches are vulnerable to thievery, so don't take chances.

Taxes   There is a departure tax of $15, payable when you leave the islands. Also, the government collects an 8% occupancy tax, applicable to all hotels, guest houses, and restaurants in the 40-island chain.

Telephone, Telegram & Fax   It's not too difficult to keep in touch with the outside world, if you really want to. Incoming direct dialing is available from the United States, the United Kingdom, and most countries in the world. Outgoing direct dialing is being introduced slowly.

Most hotels in the country have fax machines. Your hotel's staff can send and receive faxes for you. The international-operator telephone service is available 24 hours a day, and the telegraph service operates from 8am to 4:30pm Monday through Friday from the company's main office on Front Street, Cockburn Town, Grand Turk (© 649/946-2222).

Time   The islands are in the Eastern Time zone, and daylight saving time is observed.

Tipping   Hotels usually add 10% to 15% to your bill automatically, to cover service. If individual staff members perform various services for you, it is customary to tip them something extra. In restaurants, 10% to 15% is appropriate unless service has already been added. If in doubt, ask. Taxi drivers like at least a 10% tip.

Water   Don't drink from the tap and avoid drinks with ice that was made from tap water. Don't even use tap water to brush your teeth. Remember that water is precious on the islands—try to conserve it. Hotels provide safe drinking water.

1 Grand Turk ⟨★

The most important island in the chain, **Grand Turk,** with its Government House, is the capital of the Turks and Caicos Islands and has the largest population (3,500 people). Cockburn (pronounced "Coburn") Town is also the financial and business hub of this tiny nation. The island is rather barren and windswept, and there is little vegetation. Don't come here looking for lush tropical foliage. Do consider Grand Turk, however, if you want a real bargain destination that's excellent for snorkeling and diving, with luscious white-sand beaches.

Many scholars believe that Grand Turk was the site of Columbus's first landfall in 1492. They maintain he set foot on the western shores of the island late on the day of October 12. The native Arawaks were here to welcome him to their island of "Guanahani," although they were later to pay a terrible price for that hospitality, because they were sold into slavery in the Caribbean.

Once this was the teeming headquarters of a thriving salt industry. Today, some folks want to restore the colony's economy by making Grand Turk an off-shore banking center like the Cayman Islands, but that may be problematic with both the British and the U.S. governments.

Chances are, if you come to the Turks and Caicos for your vacation, you'll land at Grand Turk. **Cockburn Town** might remind you of New Plymouth on Green Turtle Cay in the Abacos, but it's a larger, more bustling town. The harbor road is called Front Street. You'll find **Governor's Beach** near—you guessed it—the governor's residence on the west coast of the island. It's the best place for swimming. If you are on your way to another island, at least take time to tour Cockburn Town's **historic section,** particularly Duke and Front streets, where three-story houses built of wood and limestone stand along the waterfront. The 7-square-mile island of Grand Turk has several protected historical buildings, one of which is a hotel: Turks Head Inn. The other landmark buildings include the police station and Government House.

ESSENTIALS

GETTING THERE   See the introduction to this chapter.

VISITOR INFORMATION   The **Turks & Caicos Sales and Information Office,** Front Street, Cockburn Town, Grand Turk, BWI (℃ **800/241-0824** in the U.S., or 649/946-2322), is open Monday through Friday from 8am to 5pm. At this office, the National Parks of Turks and Caicos produces a guide to the marine parks, nature reserves, sanctuaries, and historic sites of the island nation.

GETTING AROUND   Many visitors walk where they are going, or else check with **Dutchie's Car Rental** (℃ **649/946-2244**) if they need a car. Rental prices start at $45 per day.

Taxis are available, but there is no central agency to call. Your hotel can manage to summon you one, or you can find them at the airport when you arrive. The fare is about $15 from the airport to most major hotels.

Another way to get around is by bike. Along Duke Street in Grand Turk, both the **Osprey Beach Hotel** (℃ **649/946-1453**) and the **Salt Raker Inn** (℃ **649/946-2260**) will rent you bikes for about $10 per day or $50 per week.

There's a public **bus system,** but service is patchy. The charge is only 50¢ one-way to any scheduled stop.

FAST FACTS   For cashing traveler's checks and other transactions, try **Barclay's Bank,** Front Street (℃ **649/946-2831**), or the **Bank of Nova Scotia,** also on Front Street (℃ **649/946-2506**).

The **Government Clinic,** Grand Turk Hospital, Hospital Road (℃ **649/946-2040**), can fill prescriptions and provide simple medical assistance. The hospital itself has 35 beds, X-ray facilities, an operating theater, and a pathology laboratory.

Call ℃ **649/946-2299** if you need the **police.**

The **General Post Office** (℃ **649/946-1334**) is open Monday through Thursday from 8am to 12:30pm and from 2 to 4pm, Friday from 8am to 3:30pm. There's also a Philatelic Bureau, operated separately from the post office, but with the same hours.

WHERE TO STAY

As mentioned, hotels add a 10% to 15% service charge, plus an 8% government occupancy tax, to the rates quoted below.

EXPENSIVE

The Arches of Grand Turk *(* Atop the island's North Ridge, these newly constructed town houses—a short walk from beautiful beaches—are the most deluxe way to live on Grand Turk. Bedrooms open onto island or ocean views. At Arches you find two-story town-house units, each linked together and containing two bedrooms with two baths and balconies for taking in those sunsets. Families and couples are especially fond of the complex, and accommodations contain two double beds or queen-size beds. Units are suitable for six guests who make use of a fully equipped kitchen.

Lighthouse Road (P.O. Box 226), Grand Turk, Turks and Caicos, BWI. ℂ **649/946-2941.** Fax 649/946-2941. www.grandturkarches.com. 4 units. Winter $225 double, $300 quad; off-season $150 double, $225 quad. AE, DC, MC, V. **Amenities:** Washer/dryer, storage area for diving equipment, maid service upon request, linen provided, bikes for guests. *In room:* A/C. No phone.

MODERATE

Arawak Inn and Beach Club Set near the extreme southern tip of Grand Turk, this two-story apartment complex was built in 1996 on a sugar-white strip of beachfront. It's largely geared to divers, many of whom book in here on dive packages. Each spacious unit has a separate bedroom and living room, as well as a kitchenette and a private veranda or patio, plus a full-size bathroom with a shower unit. Accommodations are carpeted upstairs and have ceramic tile floors on the ground level.

There's a full bar on the premises, as well as a simple indoor-outdoor restaurant serving moderately priced American food, including a lunch menu of burgers, club sandwiches, and salads. Although there aren't a lot of amenities and diversions on-site, the staff is able to arrange all manner of tours and sports for you, if you want to rouse yourself off those white sands.

c/o Harbour Sands Condominium (P.O. Box 190), Cockburn Town, Grand Turk, Turks and Caicos, BWI. ℂ **649/ 946-2277.** Fax 649/946-2279. E-mail: arawakinn@tciway.tci. 15 apts. $110–$170 double. Rates include breakfast. Children under 12 stay free in parents' room. MC, V. **Amenities:** Restaurant, bar. *In room:* A/C, TV, minibar, kitchenette.

Osprey Beach Hotel *(Kids* The hotel is a landmark on the island, with a white-sand beach that offers good swimming and snorkeling. A family favorite, its bedrooms occupy modern two-story town houses, each with a ceiling crafted from

---

(Kids **Family-Friendly Hotels**

Osprey Beach Hotel *(see p. 301)* A local landmark, this hotel is the family favorite on Grand Turk. Families can prepare simple island meals in the units, which are equipped with kitchens.

Comfort Suites Turks and Caicos *(see p. 323)* In expensive Provo, this is a good, moderately priced choice. Many of the accommodations can house up to six in a family, thanks to an extra sleeper sofa and two double beds. The rooms feel like comfortable, predictable hotel rooms in Florida.

Sibonne Hotel & Beach Club *(see p. 324)* Near one of Provo's best white sandy beaches, these villa-like condos are great for families. Kids like to splash in the freshwater swimming pool.

varnished pine. Some rooms have kitchenettes, but all contain ceiling fans and verandas with a view of the sea, plus small bathrooms with shower units. The rooms on the upper floors benefit from high ceilings and more space. Across the street in the older wing of the hotel is The Courtyard Café, open for breakfast and lunch. Dinner is served at Secret Garden in the Salt Raker Inn.

Duke St., P.O. Box 42, Grand Turk, Turks and Caicos, BWI. ℂ 649/946-1453. Fax 649/946-2817. www. ospreybeachhotel.com. 24 units. Year-round $100–$150 double or suite. Children under 12 stay free in parents' room. Dive packages available. AE, MC, V. **Amenities:** Café/restaurant, pool, laundry. *In room:* A/C, TV.

Salt Raker Inn   A mile from the airport and a short walk from the island's busiest docks, the informal Salt Raker Inn stands across a one-way street from a good sandy beach. It occupies a clapboard house that was originally built in 1810 by a Bermudian shipwright. Its English-colonial style is visible in its front veranda, which overlooks the ocean and a garden filled with bougainvillea. The main house, set close to the road that parallels the sea, contains a wide front hallway, a guest library, the main office, and the three best accommodations. Each of the rooms has a small private bathroom with shower unit, a ceiling fan, and a minifridge; seven ocean-view rooms have phones. The two large suites upstairs open onto verandas that overlook the sea. The downstairs accommodation has a large screened porch. Two motel units, with several other rooms, are spread end to end on either side of the garden.

The **Secret Garden** in the Salt Raker Inn is also one of the most popular dining choices in town (see "Where to Dine," below).

Duke St. (P.O. Box 1), Grand Turk, Turks and Caicos, BWI. ℂ 649/946-2260. Fax 649/946-2817. Sraker@ tciway.tc. 12 units. $90–$150 double. AE, MC, V. **Amenities:** Restaurant, bar, bikes, laundry. *In room:* A/C. No phone in some units.

Turks Head Inn 𝒻   As charming as anything you'll find on the island, this old-fashioned hotel was originally built in 1840 by Bermudian shipwrights, as a private home, with a sandy beach nearby. It has more of a European flavor than any other inn on the island and doesn't really offer resort-style facilities. It was once the governor's private guest house and later the American consulate. Today, most business comes from its bar and restaurant (see "Where to Dine," below), and that's where most of the staff's attention is focused. A handful of bedrooms can be rented upstairs, however, behind a two-level veranda with ornate balustrades painted in bright tropical colors. Two of the bedrooms have access to an open second-floor veranda in front; four have access to the somewhat-more-private enclosed veranda overlooking the back. Each has a private bathroom with a shower unit, a ceiling fan, high ceilings, and antique or period furnishings. All contain queen-size beds, two of which are four-posters. The inn lies in a mature garden with towering trees and a shady terrace with outdoor tables.

Duke St. (P.O. Box 58), Grand Turk, Turks and Caicos, BWI. ℂ 649/946-2466. Fax 649/946-1716. www.grand-turk.com. 8 units. $110–$170 double. MAP $35 per person extra. AE, MC, V. **Amenities:** Bar/restaurant, car and bike rental, baby-sitting, laundry. *In room:* A/C, TV, minibar, coffeemaker, hair dryer, ceiling fans.

WHERE TO DINE

Calico Jack's 𝒻 INTERNATIONAL   This is the island's oldest and busiest pub, a landmark to the many divers, dock workers, writers, and eccentrics living on Grand Turk. Set within the Turks Head Inn, it has a funky tropical indoor dining room, and a thatched-roof annex so you can catch the breezes while you dine.

The well-flavored food is served informally, in large portions, and created from whatever happens to have arrived from mainland suppliers that week. You might find char-grilled sirloin steak, traditional baked grouper in Cajun spices, or smoked chicken and mango with a raspberry coulis. Desserts are the best on the island, especially the banana and coconut mousse or the mango and peach Romanoff. The bar is open every day throughout the afternoon until midnight.

Duke St. © 649/946-2466. Reservations recommended on Fri night only. Lunch platters from $6; dinner main courses $15–$22. AE, MC, V. Daily 7am–10pm.

Regal Begal CARIBBEAN   Located about a 3-minute drive from the center of Cockburn Town, this is one of the simplest and least pretentious restaurants on the island. The name comes from the long-running sitcom, **Three's Company,** starring John Ritter. There's a bar to quench your thirst, as well as a handful of plain tables where you can order lobster salad, several variations of conch, chicken or fish with chips, or pork.

Hospital St. © 649/946-2274. Soups and fritters $2.50–$4; sandwiches and salads $4.50–$8; platters $8–$23. No credit cards. Mon–Sat 10am–3pm and 6pm–midnight.

Secret Garden CARIBBEAN/SEAFOOD   This comfortably unpretentious restaurant remains open throughout the morning and afternoon for anyone who happens to wander in hungry from the nearby sands. Many guests prefer to dine in the rear garden. You can lunch on club sandwiches, cheeseburgers, fish-and-chips, or cracked conch. Evening meals are somewhat more elaborate, with grouper cooked island-style (with onions and peppers), conch Creole, and the house favorite, broiled lobster with butter sauce. You might also try an award-winning version of local Junkanoo-style (spicy) barbecued spareribs.

In the Salt Raker Inn. Duke St. © 649/946-2260. Reservations recommended for dinner Wed and Sun only. Lunch platters $3.50–$12; dinner main courses $16–$28. AE, MC, V. Daily 7:15am–9pm (last order).

Water's Edge BAHAMIAN   Set directly on the sands, close to the center of town, this battered but funky shack manages to transform the simple conch into a surprising number of culinary specialties. Come here for views of the sea, an engaging informality, a short list of standard fish and chicken dishes, as well as "conch burgers," pizzas, curried conch platters, and overstuffed sandwiches.

Duke St. © 649/946-1680. Reservations not necessary. Main courses $9.50–$21. AE, MC, V. Daily noon–11pm.

THE WORLD UNDERWATER: DIVING OUTFITTERS

The Turks and Caicos Islands are home to some of the world's most magnificent underwater life. For years, divers and snorkelers have enjoyed immersing themselves in the countless varieties of brilliant coral and fish that thrive within TCI's nearly 500-mile, pristine reef system. Some of the finest diving in the archipelago happens around Grand Turk.

The dive shops mentioned below will all rent you snorkel gear if your hotel does not supply it.

Blue Water Diver, Front St. (© and fax **649/946-1226**), offers single dives, PADI registration, and dive packages, even running trips to Salt Cay. These people are top rate and will tell you many facts and legends about diving in their country (like the fact that the highest mountain in the Turks and Caicos is 8,000 feet tall, but only the top 140 feet are above sea level!). Scuba divers flock here to enjoy panoramic "wall dives" on the vertical sides of the reefs. A single-tank dive costs $30, with a two-tank dive going for $55; a night dive costs $35. A PADI-instruction resort course is priced at $85.

(Moments A Whale of a Time

From January through April, you might be able to witness the amazing spectacle of some 2,500 humpback whales migrating. Sightings of the mammals, which measure between 40 and 45 feet in length, occur daily, and visitors frequently have a chance to encounter them in the water and from boats.

The waters near both Grand Turk and Salt Cay are the southern terminus for the migration of the Atlantic herd of humpbacks. The whales pass through the 22-mile-wide Turks Island passage on their way to mate, and calve near the Mouchoir Bank in the Turks and Caicos national waters and the Silver Bank, located north of Hispaniola. Throughout the winter, divers exploring the wall reef around Grand Turk can hear the eerie and melodic songs of the male humpback searching for a mate.

You can observe breaching (leaping from the water), tailing (tail slapping on the water surface), and blowing (surfacing for air) from the shores of Grand Turk and Salt Cay or from on board a ship. These antics provide dramatic photographic and video opportunities. The Silver Bank region is only about 100 feet deep, so whales swim closely to the surface. The waters are crystalline, so visibility is extraordinary.

Oasis Divers, located in Grand Turk, offers afternoon whale-encounter excursions three times per week during the winter season. The tours take place from 2 to 6pm. Capt. Everette Freites, a warm and knowledgeable guide, has years of experience approaching and interacting with the visiting whales. Sightings are almost guaranteed. Freites gauges the whales' curiosity about the waiting vessel and approaches slowly, which often leads to a snorkel experience with humpback mothers and their calves. Groups enjoy refreshments on board and return at sunset. This exhilarating experience of a lifetime costs $45. **Oasis Divers** can be reached by phone or fax at © **649/946-1128.**

Visitors looking for a more in-depth experience can join a 16-passenger dive yacht, the Turks and Caicos *Aggressor.* Capt. Peirs van der Walt sets off from Grand Turk for 7 days of thrilling face-to-face snorkeling encounters with magnificent humpbacks. Like an intimate, floating, all-inclusive resort, the *Aggressor* provides private cabins or quads, breakfast to order, maid service, private lavatories, all meals, a hot tub, underwater camera rentals with on-board film development, a video lounge, and morning and afternoon snacks. Participants row inflatable dinghies twice daily for snorkel or boat-based whale encounters. The charters run weekly, departing on Saturdays from January through April, and cost $1,795 per person based on double occupancy. For reservations and information on the Turks and Caicos *Aggressor,* contact **Aggressor Fleet Ltd.** (© **800/348-2628** or 504/385-2628; fax 504/384-0817; www.aggressor.com).

Sea Eye Diving, Duke St. (© **649/946-1407**), is located near the Secret Garden in the Salt Raker Inn, and it's convenient to most other hotels. It offers two-tank morning dives at $55. An afternoon single-tank dive costs $35, and a single-tank night dive goes for $40. Rental equipment is also available. NAUI and PADI courses at all levels are offered. A full certification course goes for $375, including training equipment and boat checkout dives. Dive packages that include accommodations can be arranged at a hotel of your choice. Snorkeling and cay trips are available for non-divers. The owners and operators, Cecil Ingham and Connie Rus, are among the more experienced divers on the island, and they know where to take you to see marine life in a kaleidoscope of colors.

EXPLORING THE ISLAND
SOAKING UP A BIT OF HISTORY

People go to Grand Turk mainly to swim, snorkel, dive, or just do nothing but soak up the sun on those gorgeous white sands. The island, however, does have one major sightseeing attraction, previewed below.

Turks & Caicos National Museum ☆   This is the country's first (and only) museum. It occupies a 150-year-old residence (Guinep House), originally built by Bermudian wreckers from timbers they salvaged from ships that crashed on nearby reefs. Today, about half of its display areas are devoted to the remains of the most complete archaeological excavation ever performed in the West Indies, the wreck of a Spanish caravel (sailing ship) that sank in shallow offshore water sometime before 1513. Used to transport local Arawaks who had been enslaved, the boat was designed solely for exploration purposes and is similar to vessels built in Spain and Portugal during the 1400s.

Treasure hunters found the wreck and announced that it was Columbus's *Pinta,* in order to attract financial backers for their salvage—to guarantee a value to the otherwise-valueless iron artifacts, in case there proved to be no gold on board. There is no proof, however, that the *Pinta* ever came back to the New World after returning to Spain from the first voyage. Researchers from the Institute of Nautical Archaeology at Texas A&M University began excavations in 1982, although staff members never assumed that the wreck was the *Pinta.* Today, the remains are referred to simply as the Wreck of Molasses Reef.

Today, although only 2% of the hull remains intact, the exhibits contain a rich legacy of the everyday (non-biodegradable) objects used by the crews and officers.

The remainder of the museum is devoted to exhibits about the island's salt industries, its plantation economy, the pre-Columbian inhabitants of the island, and its natural history. The natural-history exhibit features an 8-by-20-foot, three-dimensional reproduction of a section of the Grand Turk Wall, the famous vertical reef. You'll also find displays on the geology of the islands and information on the reef and coral growth.

Guinep House, Front St., Cockburn Town, Grand Turk. ℂ 649/946-2160. Admission $5 non-residents, $2 full-time island residents. Mon–Tues and Thurs–Fri 9am–4pm, Wed 9am–6pm, Sat 9am–1pm.

GRAND TURK AFTER DARK

At night, people mainly hang out and drink rum or beer. On most Wednesday and Sunday nights, you can hear pop or folk music at the **Salt Raker Inn** on Duke Street (ℂ **649/946-2260**). Sing-alongs often burst out at the **Turks Head Inn,** also on Duke Street (ℂ **649/946-2466**). Still in search of action? The inaptly named **Nookie Hill Club,** Nookie Hill (no phone) offers occasional dancing.

2 Salt Cay

Just 9 miles south of Grand Turk, this sparsely settled cay is named for its salt ponds, a once-flourishing industry that may someday be revived. In its day it was known for this "white gold," and some 100 vessels a year sailed from here and Grand Turk with their heavily laden cargoes bound for the United States. During the American Revolution, more than 20 Bermudian privateers were running salt on a regular schedule from the Turks Islands past British blockades to Washington's battered armies. (Salt was the chief preservative for the colonial army's meat.)

In 1951 the government took control of the 300-year-old industry and, in 20 years, managed to destroy it completely through bureaucratic mismanagement. Salt Cay fell into a long slumber until 1990, when adventurous guests began visiting the Windmills Plantation (see below).

The cay has a landmass of 3½ square miles, with a beautiful beach bordering the north coast. The National Park Service of Turks and Caicos designated it a historic site. You can walk down to the salinas and see the windmills that once powered the salt business, and you can stroll past the 150-year-old **"White House,"** built by a Bermudian salt raker. In addition, you can visit the ruins of an old **whaling station** and learn how fearless seamen caught whales in the early 19th century. It's also possible to drop in at the local school, where the children are likely to greet you with island calypso songs.

Divers will want to check out the wreck of the *Endymion,* the recently discovered 140-foot wooden hull of an English warship that sank in 1790. It lies just off the southern tip of Salt Cay. The best scuba outfitter is **Salt Divers Cay** (© **649/946-6906**). Charges for a one-tank boat dive are $30, or else $55 for a two-tank boat dive, going up to $80 for a three-tank boat dive that includes a night dive.

Essentially, Salt Cay is peaceful, quiet, and colorful—the perfect spot to get away from it all. Since there are only four automobiles on the island, traffic jams aren't a problem.

GETTING THERE

For a long time, residents of Salt Cay depended on their small sailboats for communication with the outside world, and people still often reach the island by private boat. But a brand-new 3,000-foot airstrip, located 575 miles southwest of Miami, connects the island to the wider world once again. Now you can fly direct from Miami to Provo on **American Airlines** and then on to Salt Cay via **Interisland Airways** (© **649/941-5481**). **Turks & Caicos Airways** (© **649/ 946-4255**) also offers six flights weekly on Monday, Wednesday, and Friday.

WHERE TO STAY

Mt. Pleasant Guest House   This rustic house is the domain of owner/host Bryan Sheedy, who welcomes you as if you were his guest at a house party. There are four mid-size bedrooms in the newly renovated guest house, plus another four quite similar units in an annex next door. The personal touch is evident in the library, which is filled with rare books such as a large collection of the first editions of Eugene O'Neill.

Guests enjoy horseback riding, Robinson Crusoe–style day trips, and walks on nature trails for photography and bird watching. Chef Nettie, one of the island's finest, serves quality meals in an open-air patio with a gazebo bar. At the end of the day you can enjoy an "Iguana Margarita."

Balfour Town, Salt Cay, Turks and Caicos, BWI. © **800/821-6670** in the U.S., or 649/946-6927. 8 units, 1 with private bathroom. Year-round $85 double. 7-night dive packages available. MC, V. **Amenities:** Restaurant, bar, horseback riding. *In room:* Ceiling fans. No phone.

Salt Cay Sunset House (★ (Value) A rare find, this is the most historic B&B in the island archipelago, and it lies near a beach. Constructed in 1832, it was once the home of a shipwright and later salt baron, Skipper Harriott, who ran the oldest salt plantation on Salt Cay. The decades go by, and Michele Wells and Paul Dinsmore arrive to restore this mortise-and-tenon-joined building of cypress planks that has withstood the test of time.

Today its wraparound veranda and oceanside patio dining area is cooled by trade breezes and opens onto panoramic views. Only three bedrooms are available, each spacious and with a full-size bathroom, comfortable double beds, and a day bed. Ceiling fans whir overhead from the 11-foot ceilings. Antique furnishings enhance the mellow atmosphere.

Victoria St., Balfour Town, Salt Cay, Turks and Caicos, BWI. © and fax 649/946-6942. www. seaone.org/eltravel/vacation.htm. 3 units. $35–$45 double. AE, DISC, MC, V. **Amenities:** Café, laundry, basketball court, picnic grounds, TV in parlor. *In room:* Ceiling fans. No phone.

The Windmills Plantation at Salt Cay (★(★ Set amid 17 acres of scrubland beside a white-sand beach on the north side of the island, this hotel was built entirely by local artisans using centuries-old building techniques. Each of the dozen or so buildings within the compound was designed in a different whimsical colonial style, recalling French, English, Dutch, and Spanish plantations of 200 years ago. Their design was the culmination of years of research by architect/owner Guy Lovelace, a man who until recently made a career of designing other people's Caribbean resort hotels. The Windmills Plantation is the highly creative result of a dream come true. Each of the accommodations contains a tasteful selection of antique reproductions (mostly handmade in the Dominican Republic or in Haiti), a veranda, and a cathedral ceiling with a ceiling fan. Four of the accommodations are suites in the great house, two of which have their own plunge pools; all four have four-poster beds, ocean-view balconies, and ceiling fans, plus well-maintained bathrooms with shower stalls.

Meals feature a culinary tour of the Caribbean, with a visit to a different island for lunch and dinner every day. You've got to be a guest of the hotel to dine here, but if you are, you'll enjoy the finest cuisine in this island nation. Pat Lovelace spent 25 years traveling the islands and collecting authentic recipes, often for dishes that have now largely disappeared. She notes that these recipes were originally developed before the age of refrigeration and chemical tenderizers. Meats were shredded, pounded, boiled, herbed, spiced, and blended with vegetables, resulting in an exotic mélange. From the original Indians came corn and seafood; from Africa, root vegetables and herbs; and from the Europeans, beef and the many tropical fruits and spices carried from the East Indies. All this resulted in a unique cuisine that is now almost lost. After years of researching and testing, Pat has married modern kitchen technology with traditional recipes. If you happen to dine at The Windmills Plantation on, say, Haitian night, you'd begin with a creamy peanut soup followed by a *gato-gato* salad (essentially, mixed greens topped with peanut-rum vinaigrette). The main course is a conch curry served over a bed of rice, surrounded by cassava and shrimp crisps. What makes this curry extra special is the plate of sauces that comes with it. Every bite might be different, depending on whether you choose the tomato Creole sauce, the mango chutney, the *kuchela* (a very spicy sauce made with hot peppers and tamarind), or the sugar-syrup sauce made with picante-style peppers. It also comes with grated coconut and raisins, which are great to sprinkle on when your mouth gets too spicy-hot. The meal is topped off with soursop sorbet, also excellent for cooling your taste buds. The hotel bar is open all the time.

The hotel's centerpiece is a trio of dramatically proportioned swimming pools, which include a 50-foot lap pool and a "fun pool" only 4 feet deep centered around a mermaid-shaped fountain.

N. Beach Rd., Salt Cay, Turks and Caicos, BWI. ✆ 649/946-6962. Fax 649/946-6930. www.saltcaysite.com. (For reservations and information, contact **Windmills Plantation at Salt Cay,** P.O. Box 635, Easton, MD 21601. ✆ **800/822-7715** or 410/819-0562. Fax 410/820-9179.) 8 units. $625 double; $725–$775 suite. Rates include all meals, service charge, drinks, and airport transfers, but not tax. AE, MC, V. Closed July–Nov. **Amenities:** Restaurant, 3 pools, laundry service, game room, nature trail, mangrove trail, horseback riding, historic salt tour, bicycles, complimentary gear for snorkeling. *In room:* Ceiling fan. No phone.

3 North Caicos

North Caicos is the most northern of the major islands in the archipelago. This 41-square-mile island is strictly for people who want to get away from it all. Most of the other islands in this tiny nation are dry and rather barren, but this one experiences abundant rainfall, making it much lusher and more verdant.

If you're seeking deserted, soft white-sand beaches and crystal-clear water, then this is the place. It contains miles and miles of uncrowded sandy beaches and is surrounded by a sea teeming with fish—an ideal place for scuba divers and snorkelers. Experienced guides can take you fishing for snapper, barracuda, or bonefish. Beach picnics, boating excursions, and fish cookouts on deserted cays are easily arranged. You can snorkel on a barrier reef or tour the island by taxi. Ask to be taken to **Flamingo Pond,** located south of Whitby, which is a nesting place for these elegant pink birds. You'll also be shown the ruins of old plantations and such tiny hamlets as Sandy Point and Kew.

But go now (and leave your jacket and tie at home). North Caicos is a resort waiting to happen, and the island is slated for development.

ESSENTIALS
GETTING THERE　The local airline, the not-always-reliable **Turks & Caicos Airways** (✆ **649/946-4255**), runs connecting flights to the island's terminal. If you disembark at Providenciales, the flight to North Caicos takes only 6 minutes. It is not necessary to prebook with TCA. When you clear Customs in Provo, you'll also find several reliable local pilots who fly continuously throughout the day from Provo to North Caicos for a price beginning at $25 per person one-way. No advance reservations are necessary.

GETTING AROUND　The best way to see the island is to have your hotel arrange a taxi tour at a rate to be negotiated.

The most fun way to see the island is to rent a bike at **Whitby Plaza** (✆ **649/946-7301**), at a cost of $15 per day.

FAST FACTS　For medical help on the island, call ✆ **649/946-7194.**

WHERE TO STAY
Club Vacanze/Prospect of Whitby Hotel 🖈　This beachside hotel was named after one of the most historic Thames-side pubs of London, the Prospect of Whitby. It is surrounded by vegetation, verdant for the Turks and Caicos Islands, and lies on the expansive white sands of a terrific beach. Each of the half-dozen buildings that compose this complex is painted a soft pink. The

spacious units have a scattering of art, a ceiling fan, comfortable furnishings, a tidy bathroom with shower stalls, and a view of the sea.

The bar and restaurant are popular with yachties, who moor their sailing craft off the expansive north-coast beach on which the hotel sits. The hotel's Italian-born managers imbue the cuisine with a European flair. The managers will help arrange excursions to nearby cays.

Whitby, c/o Kew Post Office, North Caicos, Turks and Caicos, BWI. ℭ **649/946-7119.** Fax 649/946-7114. www.prospectofwhitby.com/reservations.htm. 27units. Dec–Apr and July–Aug $390 double, $500 suite; May–June and Sept–Nov $340 double, $450 suite. Rates include all meals. AE, MC, V. **Amenities:** Restaurant, bar, water sports. *In room:* A/C, TV, minibar, hair dryer.

JoAnne's Rooms & Suites Motel This secluded home away from home is run by JoAnne Selver, the island's most gracious and helpful host, who lives on the premises. A former Peace Corps worker, she has established a beachhead on a good sandy beach. She'll also feed you well at Papa Grunts, which she runs (see "Where to Dine," below). Her private villa shelters visitors from all over the world. Bedrooms are simply furnished but comfortable, with views of the water. Each unit comes with a small bathroom containing a shower stall. Everything is informal and relaxed around here. They also offer all-inclusive snorkeling and fishing packages.

If you're interested, she can also rent you other accommodations, including basic motel rooms at Whitby Plaza with a bathroom, costing $90 for a double; or $100 per night for an executive suite in a second-story location, with a restaurant and bike-rental outlet on the premises.

Whitby Beach, North Caicos, Turks and Caicos, BWI. ℭ and fax **649/946-7301.** www.turksandcaicos.tc/Joannesbnb. 4 units. $90 double, $105 2-room suite, $120 4-room apt. MC, V (for room deposits only). **Amenities:** Restaurant, bikes. *In room:* Ceiling fans. No phone.

Ocean Beach Hotel This simple condo resort sits on a 10-mile stretch of sheltered beach, a 6-mile taxi ride from the airport and a mile from the center (such as it is) of Whitby. You can rent regular rooms or two- and three-bedroom suites. Each suite offers a fully equipped kitchen, a small bathroom with a shower unit, full linen service, and safe drinking water. Sliding glass doors and picture windows open onto an ocean view, and the rooms are cooled by trade winds. Furnishings are in the typical tropical Florida style.

Guests can purchase groceries and drinks at the commissary, or head for the small dining room and lounge, which offer local and international dishes. Sometimes the place takes on a house-party atmosphere, with barbecues, patio dancing, or beach picnics.

Whitby, North Caicos, Turks and Caicos, BWI. ℭ **649/946-7113.** Fax 649/946-7386. www. turksandcaicos.tc/oceanbeach. 10 units. $120–$215 double. Extra person $40. Children under 12 stay free in parents' room. MAP $35 per person extra. AE, MC, V. **Amenities:** Dining room/lounge, pool, tennis courts, fishing, snorkeling, bikes, car rental, scuba diving, beach cruiser charters. *In room:* Kitchen, ceiling fans. No phone.

WHERE TO DINE

Papa Grunts AMERICAN/WEST INDIAN The friendliest restaurant on the island, within walking distance of the Whitby Beach area, this operation is directed by JoAnne Selver, who also operates JoAnne's Rooms & Suites Motel (see above). Other than the hotels, it is the best place to eat on the island and is the only full-service, family restaurant in Whitby. Dine indoors or on a screened veranda. The atmosphere is casual, friendly, and tranquil.

At lunch many visitors opt for the sandwiches made with fresh homemade bread or one of the homemade soups. You can also order conch, fried chicken, and the fish of the day, or else one of the local salads, most often made with conch or lobster. At dinner the choices vary, including the fish of the day or the ubiquitous conch (steamed or cracked). Chicken breast is also served, as are broiled steaks, and even vegetarian platters. Many guests prefer an old-fashioned banana split for dessert. Since JoAnne's husband is a minister, she doesn't serve booze but does offer mixers. Guests can brown-bag it.

Whitby Plaza. ℭ and fax **649/946-7301.** Reservations required for dinner. Breakfast from $6; lunch $3.50–$7; fixed-price 4-course dinners $15.75–$22.50. MC, V. Daily 7am–7pm.

EXPLORING THE ISLAND

White-sand beaches, pristine and uncrowded waters, and endless possibilities for swimming, snorkeling, and beachcombing lure visitors to North Caicos.

The beaches, ideal for shelling, are the main attraction. Offshore waters attract snorkelers, and there are plenty of off-site challenges for the scuba diver as well. Much of the underwater world of the north shore coast remains unexplored. Huge coral hills here rise to 30 and 40 feet high. They are separated by tiny canyons and overgrown with soft corals within ½ to 1 mile offshore. Regrettably, as of yet, no organized outfitters operate on the island. The best place for snorkeling is **Three Mary's Cays**—in the northwestern part of the island, lying to the east of Ocean Beach Hotel.

The fishing here is among the best in the Turks and Caicos, because virtually all water game species abound. There are bonefish by the thousands, as well as snapper and grouper. Most any hotel will help you make arrangements for an outing or set you up with a local guide.

You can observe flocks of pink flamingos at **Flamingo Pond** in the middle of the island, to the west of the airport. There is a constant presence of pelicans and ospreys in the area as well.

To the west of Flamingo Pond is the hamlet of **Kew,** which provides a glimpse of local island life. Here you'll find the local school, a small post office, a church, and even the ruins of old plantations. The trees here are tropical and filled with papaya, custard apples, and limes.

At the far western end of the island lies **Sandy Point,** a small settlement you can reach after passing a series of salt flats. This is another good place for spotting flamingos. Once here you'll find a secluded cove, excellent for snorkeling.

4 Middle Caicos

Called Grand Caicos by some islanders, Middle Caicos is the largest island in the archipelago, consisting of 48 square miles (it's 15 miles long). Secluded beaches and towering limestone cliffs that protrude into the sea along the north coast give Middle Caicos the most dramatic coastline of the islands. Conch Bay, on the north side of the island, offers cathedral-size limestone **caves** once used by the Lucayans. In the 1880s these caves were the site of a thriving guano (fertilizer) export industry. With their clear underground salt lakes, the caves have been called a "natural museum" of stalagmites and stalactites. Nearby wild cotton plants derive from the 18th century, when Loyalists from the former southern colonies in the new United States came to try their hand at establishing plantations.

Middle Caicos men were some of the most expert boat builders in the island nation. They made their vessels from pine taken from the middle island's pine groves. Fishermen used the boats to fish the waters around many of the cays and to gather conchs for shipment to Haiti.

When you visit Middle Caicos, bring an insulated cooler packed with food and supplies (you're likely to land on Provo or to be visiting on a daylong excursion from Provo, so you can stock up there). When you return to Provo, use the cooler to pack whatever fish or lobster you catch offshore or to cart conch shells back from Middle Caicos. The island has about a half-dozen simple mom-and-pop food outlets, but their inventory is limited to dried or canned foods such as cornmeal, flour, sugar, salt, and powdered milk.

Big real-estate plans and wide speculation about major development in this now-sleepy place include a causeway that would link its mangrove swamps and scrub-covered landscapes to the booming developments of nearby Provo.

ESSENTIALS

GETTING THERE   Most visitors come to Middle Caicos on a private-boat tour for a 1-day visit to the caves. Ask at your hotel in North Caicos if any fishing or supply boats will be going here during your stay. Larger boats usually avoid Middle Caicos because of the shallow waters that surround it.

The cheapest and easiest way to reach this largely undeveloped island is to fly to Provo any way you can and then transfer to one of two regional airlines. **Turks & Caicos Airlines** (© 649/946-2455) stops at Middle Caicos several times a day as it island-hops between Provo and Grand Turk. The one-way cost (for the 15-min. flight) to Middle Caicos from Provo is $35.

FAST FACTS   If you need medical assistance, call © **649/946-6145.**

WHERE TO STAY

Arthur's Guest House   The white-sided house that contains these two rental units lies on the western edge of the hamlet of Conch Bar, about 250 feet from the beach. Inside, each of the small units has its own small-scale kitchen, a pastel color scheme, and furniture with lots of cushions scattered over the sofas and armchairs. Stacia and Dolphus Arthur are your hosts. Upon request, Stacia will prepare a meal or two for you, perhaps while you're out fishing or at the beach.
Conch Bar, Middle Caicos. © and fax 649/946-6122. 2 units. $60 double. No credit cards. **Amenities:** Dining room. *In room:* TV, kitchen. No phone.

Blue Horizon Resort   The most appealing place to stay on Middle Caicos was designed as a five-unit cottage complex that lies up a gentle slope from the beach, a 1-minute walk from the water. It's the domain of Mike and Mikki Witt, who retired from Alabama and Florida for a secluded life on a secluded island, a fact that doesn't detract in the least from the warm welcome they extend. Each of their five cottages is painted a bright island color (pink, yellow, or green), and each contains a full kitchen, small bathroom with a shower unit, ceiling fans, and views over the nearby greenery. Other than swimming, there aren't too many organized activities at this resort, although the Witts have added a labyrinth of paved walkways that lead from the core of their resort to nearby sites of panoramic beauty or ecological interest. Some units are air-conditioned and contain TV sets; most do not.

There's a restaurant on the premises, but it serves meals only at dinnertime, and only during the months of December, January, and February. Most of the time, clients buy their supplies at a local grocery store and cook for themselves within their cottages. If you fax a grocery list to the Witts in advance of your arrival, they will stock your cottage with the supplies you requested before you arrive.

Mudjin Harbor, Middle Caicos, Turks and Caicos, BWI. ⓒ **649/946-6141.** Fax 649/946-6139. www. bhresort.com. $150–$225 double. AE, MC, V. **Amenities:** Restaurant, laundry. *In room:* Kitchen, ceiling fans. No phone.

Maria Taylor's Guest House   The bare-bone rooms and general lack of ambience may disappoint those expecting to stay in an old Bahamian-style home, but the price here is the island's lowest. One room has a private bathroom, but the other three share one, and the only TV is in the living room. The nearest beach is about a 5-minute walk from the house. Maria can arrange snorkeling trips for anyone who's interested. Her neighbor (and sister-in-law) does all the cooking, fixing whatever local dish is requested.

Conch Bar, Middle Caicos, Turks and Caicos, BWI. ⓒ **649/946-6161.** 4 units, 1 with private bathroom. $50 double without bathroom, $55 double with bathroom. No credit cards. *In-room:* Ceiling fans. No phone.

WHERE TO DINE

You can ask local homeowners and residents to feed you, family-style. The most likely candidate is **Mrs. Annie Taylor** (ⓒ **649/946-6117**), whose cement-block home in Conch Bar is open to well-meaning visitors who phone and request a meal. You'll discuss with Mrs. Taylor in advance of your visit what you'd like to eat, then agree on a price between $8 and $10 per person. Menu choices usually, but not always, include cracked conch, chicken, and any of several kinds of pan-fried fish. She doesn't serve alcohol, but few other experiences will give you such a rich glimpse of life in a private Middle Caicos home.

EXPLORING THE ISLAND

Giant stalagmite and stalactite caves and fantasy-like underground lakes beckon exploration by adventurous visitors, who arrive via a flight from Provo.

Day-trippers and overnight visitors enjoy other natural sights as well. The 120,000-year-old limestone caves on Middle Caicos are the largest and most dramatic above-water caverns in the Caribbean. Although many have been explored and some are even inhabited, only a portion of this labyrinth of underground chambers and passages has ever been fully investigated. Four species of bats and giant white owls with 5-foot wingspans live here. Visitors can explore these caves with a local guide.

The Indian Cave is a massive cathedral-like space held up by a series of limestone arches. These natural, flying buttresses lie under a hillside of dense tropical vegetation. The roots from this vegetation spiral down some 50 feet into the cave. It is a place of extreme tranquility, almost spiritual.

You can swim, snorkel, and scuba dive just about anywhere along the beaches. Guides help divers explore the magnificent reefs and walls surrounding Middle Caicos and view some of the most colorful underwater life in the Caribbean. Middle Caicos is also a sportfishing paradise, with boats available to some of the best deep-sea fishing spots in the Caribbean.

On-shore shelling on Middle Caicos is spectacular. Few people walk these beaches, so a tremendous variety of shells lie waiting. Some rare and extraordinary shells have been found here.

Visitors should also keep their eyes peeled for artifacts. The Tainos settled here around A.D. 750 and were renamed the Lucayans when explorers discovered the island on the feast of St. Luke's Day. An estimated 4,000 Indians lived here and left behind thousands of artifacts in Lucayan settlement locations, on beaches and in caves. One of the most interesting excavations revealed a ceremonial court that doubled as an arena for a sport that involved rubber balls from the Amazon.

Around the 1640s, the buccaneer Pierre Le Grand captured a Spanish treasure ship near the Caicos Islands, and the age of piracy began. Middle Caicos proved to be a hospitable hideout and the base of operations for such infamous pirates as Calico Jack Rackam, Ann Bonny, and Mary Reade. The caves of Middle Caicos may yet hold some long-unclaimed treasure.

The next inhabitants to arrive around 1784 were loyalist plantation owners from the American colonies who grew cotton. Visitors can explore their plantations, which still seem haunted by this past.

The island terrain includes spectacular cliffs and enticing hidden beaches tucked away at secluded coves with sands that are talcum-powder soft. Many afford visitors the ultimate in privacy.

Flora on the island is varied and includes two interesting species. The Old Man Cactus is easily identified because it stands taller than other plants in its vicinity and has a fuzzy white beard surrounding its top. Another unusual Middle Caicos plant is the stringy yellowish-orange Love Weed. Legend has it that when a boy is interested in a girl, he plants a piece of Love Weed in front of her house. If it grows, love is possible; if it dies, he stands no chance.

5 South Caicos

Some of the finest diving and snorkeling in the Bahamian archipelago is found on South Caicos, an 8½-mile-long island with numerous secluded coves and panoramic coral reefs. Long Beach is a beachcomber's paradise. One visitor wrote, "This is like escaping to another era." Locals are always available to take you sailing, boating, or fishing, for a small fee. Bonefishing here is the best in the country.

Although it is sleepy today, this island was the commercial hub of the archipelago in the 1800s. Owing to its good anchorage, ships transported salt to The Bahamas and the U.S. mainland from here. Salt from South Caicos served to preserve meat for the winter in the fledgling United States and also graced the tables of noble European families. In the early 20th century, vast salt mines opened in the United States, however, and killed the market for South Caicos salt.

The island economy revived again in the early 1960s when it became a popular airplane-refueling stop between Miami and South America. Many American carriers, such as Pan American, also used it as an emergency landing strip. Eventually, divers arrived on the island, seeking giant sponges, mantas, squadrons of eagle rays, and sharks, among other attractions. This industry dried up in the face of a thriving drug industry and the dearth of accommodations. Today islanders can only look to the boom on Provo, hoping some of the tourism there will wash up on its shores. The island does have an excellent resource in Cockburn Harbour, the best natural harbor of the island nation. It is the site of the annual **Commonwealth Regatta** in May.

ESSENTIALS

GETTING THERE   Some 600 miles southeast of Miami and 22 miles east of Grand Turk, South Caicos can be reached by **Turks & Caicos Airways** (© 649/946-2455), which has daily flights. There is a 6,500-foot paved and lit jetport.

GETTING AROUND   Although the island may appear nearly deserted, there are 1,400 permanent residents and what one local described as "about 65 vehicles and a few wild horses and donkeys in the bush." Some of the residents use their cars as taxis and meet visitors at the airport.

FAST FACTS   For medical assistance, call © 649/946-3216.

WHERE TO STAY & DINE

South Caicos Ocean Haven   Overlooking the harbor, this is the island's finest place to stay, although in this remote outpost that's not saying a lot.

Nonetheless, the welcome is genuine, and the small to mid-size bedrooms are comfortable enough, each with a small bathroom containing a shower stall. An attractive feature is the large private sundeck on the upper level. A favorite with divers, the inn offers a full range of PADI courses and dive packages. Our favorite time of the day here is when the guests gather for a sundowner, watching truly spectacular sunsets. The best dining on the island is here, with an array of locally caught fish and shellfish.

West St., Cockburn Harbour, South Caicos, Turks and Caicos, BWI. © 649/946-3444. Fax 649/946-3446. www.oceanhaven.tc. 22 units. Winter $200 double; off-season $150 double. MC, V. **Amenities:** Dining room, pool, dive shop, boating, fishing, ocean kayaks, windsurfing. *In room:* A/C. No phone.

6 Providenciales (Provo) ⭐⭐⭐

Affectionately known as **Provo,** this 38-square-mile island has white-sand beaches that stretch for 12 miles along the northeast coast. It also has peaceful rolling hills, clear water, a natural deep harbor, flowering cactus, and a barrier reef that attracts swimmers, divers, and boaters. The roads may not always be paved, but you'll still find some stores and two full-service banks. The island is served by an airport (capable of handling wide-body jets), a good marina, and diving facilities.

Provo is the most developed island in the Turks and Caicos chain; its discovery began with the opening of the Club Med Turkoise (see below) to the tune of $27 million. Once known mainly to a group of millionaires headed by Dick du Pont, Provo has now developed a broader base of tourism.

The island is undergoing a major growth spurt, and you're sure to see lots of construction around the island from the minute you land at the airport. New resorts are being built, and the real-estate market is booming. Once you reach your hotel, however, it's easy to feel that you've gotten away from it all.

Provo is the headquarters for **PRIDE,** a non-profit organization for the Protection of Reefs and Islands from Degradation and Exploitation. PRIDE assists residents and visitors with conservation education and management.

ESSENTIALS

GETTING THERE   See "Getting There," at the beginning of this chapter. Provo is the mostly easily reached island in the nation, with daily service from Florida on American Airlines.

GETTING AROUND   Taxis meet arriving flights; otherwise, call the **Provo Taxi Association** (© 649/946-5481). Cabs are not metered, but government-controlled rates are posted in the taxi.

Pelican Tours (no phone) operates shuttle buses that run from the major hotels into town about every 15 minutes. Service runs Monday through Saturday from 9am to 6pm only. A one-way fare costs $3.

Because the island is so large and its hotels and restaurants are so far-flung, you might find a car useful on Providenciales. Some local outfits rent cars, but it can be difficult to book advance reservations with them and settle disputes in the event of an accident. A major U.S.-based car-rental agency with a franchise in the Turks and Caicos Islands is **Budget Rent-a-Car** on Providenciales. It's located in Butterfield Square, near the airport (℃ **800/527-0700** in the U.S., or 649/946-4079). Cars rent for $294 to $474 per week; collision-damage insurance costs $10 to $11.95 a day. The local government will collect a $10 tax for each rental contract, regardless of the number of days you keep the car. Because the company's main office lies in the commercial center of the island, a short drive from the airport, a representative will come to meet your flight at the airport if you notify them in advance of your arrival.

Charging comparable prices, **Avis Rent-a-Car** (℃ **649/946-4705**) has also moved into the island. Its main location is on Leeward Highway at Bay View Motors (℃ **649/231-0226**), with a branch at the airport (℃ **649/946-4882**).

If you'd like to try your chance with a local agency, call one of the following: **Rent A Buggy** (℃ **649/946-4158**), **Turks & Caicos National** (℃ **649/946-4701**), or **Provo Rent-a-Car** (℃ **649/946-4404**). Rates average from $37 to $89 per day, plus a $10 government tax.

Note: In the British tradition, cars throughout the country drive on the left.

VISITOR INFORMATION   There's a branch of the **Turks & Caicos Islands Tourist Board** at Turtle Cove Landing (℃ **649/946-4970**), open Monday to Thursday 8am to 4:30pm and Friday 8am to 5pm.

FAST FACTS   Head for **Barclay's Bank,** Town Centre (℃ **649/946-4245**), for cashing traveler's checks and other banking services on Provo. **The Bank of Nova Scotia** is also at Town Centre (℃ **649/946-4750**).

Providenciales Health Medical Center, Leeward Highway and Airport Road (℃ **649/941-3000**), can help if you have a medical problem. All the islands are served by one **dentist,** who can be reached at this number. Anyone critically ill is transferred to Grand Turk for hospital treatment or evacuated to Nassau, Miami, or Jamaica for specialist treatment. Should you become ill, your hotel will locate the nearest medical facility.

Call ℃ **649/946-4259** if you need the **police.**

There's a **post office** in the Town Centre (℃ **649/946-4676**), open Monday through Thursday from 8am to 12:30pm and from 2 to 4pm, Friday from 8am to 3:30pm.

WHERE TO STAY
VERY EXPENSIVE
Allegro Resort Turks & Caicos ⟨ε   Set on 14 acres of flat, sandy scrubland adjacent to a 900-foot beachfront, this resort was taken over in 1998 by a chain of all-inclusive resort hotels based in the Dominican Republic. Nearby competitors, including the Ocean Club, are more glamorous and have better facilities; we like the Allegro but think it's becoming overpriced. It's certainly a good choice for a family vacation if you can afford it. (Always ask about packages and promotional rates.)

With prominent balconies in a modern-hip-roofed design, the buildings are arranged symmetrically around a landscaped garden and central swimming pool. Radical renovations and improvements, completed late in 1998, doubled the size of the pool (it's designed as a series of interlocking ovals), added drama

Provo

ACCOMMODATIONS

Allegro Resort Turks & Caicos **12**
Beaches Turks and Caicos Resort & Spa **16**
Caribbean Paradise Inn **7**
Club Med Turkoise **6**
Comfort Suites Turks and Caicos **10**
Coral Gardens **3**
Erebus Inn **18**
Grace Bay Club **8**

Ocean Club **4**
Ocean Club West **5**
Ocean Point/Chalk Sound Villas **25**
Parrot Cay Resort **1**
Point Grace **13**
The Sands at Grace Bay **2**
Sibonne Hotel & Beach Club **15**
Turtle Cove Inn **17**

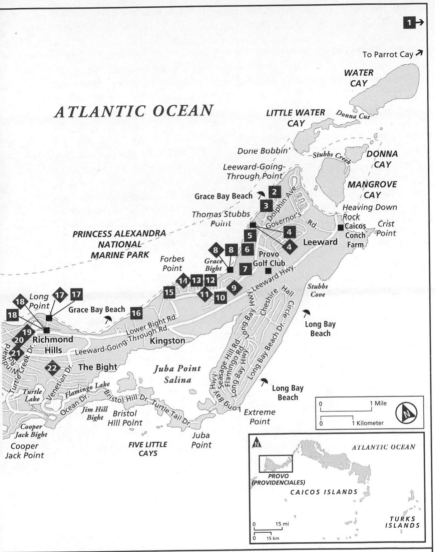

1

DINING ◆

Anacaona **8**	Gecko Grille **4**
Banana Boat Restaurant **17**	Hemingway's Beachfront Restaurant **14**
Caicos Café **11**	Hey José Cantina **21**
Coco Bistro **9**	Sunset Bar & Restaurant **18**
Dora's **22**	Tasty Temptations **23**
Fast Eddie's **24**	The Terrace Restaurant **20**
	Tiki Hut Cabana Bar & Grill **19**

within the public spaces and reception areas, and enhanced landscaping around the somewhat spartan-looking original premises. Each bedroom contains clay-tile floors, wicker furniture, ceiling fans, either a king-size bed or two doubles, plus a full-size bathroom.

All food, drink, official entertainment, and non-mechanized water sports (kayaking, snorkeling, sailing, water polo, aqua aerobics, and windsurfing) are included in the price. Three separate restaurants open their doors to residents. They include an all-purpose dining room, site of an ongoing series of buffets, and two dinner-only restaurants (advance reservations are necessary) that specialize in Italian and Caribbean cuisine, respectively. There's also a disco and nightclub, usually with live music (reggae, jazz, salsa, merengue, or whatever) performed by artists flown in from other parts of the Caribbean. The hotel is also the site of the island's major casino, which is recommended separately.

Grace Bay (P.O. Box 205), Providenciales, Turks and Caicos, BWI. ℂ 800/858-2258 in the U.S., or 649/946-5555. Fax 649/946-5522. www.allegroresorts.com. 186 units. Mid-Dec to Apr $265 per person double; May to mid-Dec $200 per person double. Rates include all meals, drinks, entertainment, and non-mechanized water sports. AE, MC, V. **Amenities:** 3 restaurants; 3 bars; 3 pools, tennis courts, health club, Jacuzzis, concierge, baby-sitting, laundry service, massage, guest activities coordinators, tour desk, scooter and motorcycle rental, free bikes, beauty parlor. In room: A/C, TV, hair dryer.

Beaches Turks and Caicos Resort and Spa 𝒇 (Kids)   This resort is part of the couples-only Sandals chain of all-inclusive hotels, though unlike the policy at most Sandals properties, families with kids are welcome here. This is a luxurious, pampering place, opening onto the luscious sands of 12-mile-long Grace Bay Beach. The $30-million resort's Bermuda-style bungalows, with lovely pink and white exteriors, are gorgeous. The price tag is high, but at least you get a lot for your money here, with a casino, a fine spa, excellent water sports, and good service.

Catering to travelers from Europe and North America, the property features guest rooms that are finely decorated, though they could use more warmth; the one- and two-bedroom villa suites are veritable pockets of posh in the Turks and Caicos. All accommodations have panoramic ocean views from private balconies, king-size or double beds, individual climate control, and full bathrooms. Villa suites also have a spacious living room, a kitchenette, and two bathrooms (one with a Roman tub and separate shower).

The restaurant Reflections offers casual fare for breakfast, lunch, and dinner. Its weekend breakfast buffet is the island's best. Otherwise, it serves burgers and fries and all the standard fare. Some other restaurants offer seafood, Southwestern cuisine, and Japanese food. The Turtles and Iguanas is the spot for an after-dinner drink, and there's another bar and lounge at poolside. The resort's showcase restaurant, Sapodilla's, features Caribbean-influenced international cuisine. A 6,000-square-foot casino opened in 1999.

Lower Bight Rd. (P.O. Box 186), Providenciales, Turks and Caicos, BWI. ℂ 800/BEACHES or 649/946-8000. Fax 649/946-8001. www.beaches.com/be-turksvillage.html. 370 units. Winter $780–$800 double, $850–$1,200 suite; off-season $600–$720 double, $780–$1,120 suite. Rates include all meals. AE, MC, V. **Amenities:** 9 restaurants; 6 bars; free-form swimming pool with rock formations, waterfalls, and a swim-up bar; tennis court lit for night play; spa; fitness center; laundry; baby-sitting; in-room massage; professionally staffed children's center; game room; nearby championship 18-hole golf course; full array of water sports; parasailing; kayaking. In room: A/C, TV, minibar, hair dryer, safe.

Club Med Turkoise 𝒇   Set on 70 acres of sun-blasted scrubland, on a white strip of beachfront overlooking Grace Bay, 11 miles from the airport, this is one of the most popular and successful Club Meds in the Americas. (If you want

more seclusion, you might opt for the Club Med on San Salvador; see chapter 10.) This was the first major resort built on Provo, and although more recent newcomers have already pulled out in front, it remains an appealing oasis of verdant charm and communal fun. Unlike some Club Meds, this one does not particularly go out of its way to entertain children. The ambience is among the most casual of any member of the Club Med chain, a fact that seems to appeal to the laid-back French and North American clientele.

The village-style cluster of two- and three-story, rather-basic accommodations are painted a pastel pink and capped with cedar shingles imported from Sweden. The resort contains simple rooms with twin beds (why?), all designed with beachfront living in mind. Each is equipped with a mid-size bathroom containing a shower stall.

Most meals are served buffet-style and consumed at long communal tables, in a system not unlike that of a grown-up summer camp. Table wine and beer are free at mealtime. Two specialty restaurants have waiter/waitress service and include a pizzeria and a beachfront eatery (the Grill) that specializes in late breakfasts, late lunches, and late suppers. A disco keeps residents active, if they wish, from 11:30pm to at least 3am nightly. All meals are included; drinks, which cost extra, are paid for with bar tickets.

Scuba diving, which is not included in the package price, is offered on a space-available basis. Activities that are part of the package include windsurfing, sailing, snorkeling, and waterskiing. Also at no extra charge, introductory and intensive circus programs teach guests basic and advanced acrobatics like aerial twists, somersaults, and spins.

Grace Bay, Providenciales, Turks and Caicos, BWI. (C) 800/CLUB-MED in the U.S., or 649/946-5591. Fax 649/946-5500. www.clubmed.com. 300 units. Winter (AP) $1,079–$1,984 per person weekly; off-season (AP) $1,099 per person weekly. Rates include all meals, wine and beer at meals, and most activities except for scuba diving. AE, MC, V. **Amenities:** 2 restaurants, 3 bars, 2 Jacuzzis, 8 tennis coursts, water sports, disco. *In room:* A/C. No phone.

Grace Bay Club 🎖🎖🎖   This tasteful Swiss-owned and -managed development is the leading hotel on the island, sitting in the most desirable spot on a white sandy beach. Ringed with about 200 palm trees imported from Florida and Nevis, it lies on 5 landscaped acres of what used to be sun-blasted and barren scrubland on Provo's North Shore. Designed in the spirit of a Spanish seaside village at the edge of a white-sand beach, the hotel is capped with terra-cotta tiles and partially sheathed in sculpted coral stone, and it was built around a courtyard with a splashing fountain in the center. The price is high, but if you can afford it, you'll get great elegance, taste, superb food, and a lot of pampering for your money.

Each accommodation has an eclectic kind of elegance and can be configured as an individual room or as an extended suite simply by opening or closing inner doors. The bedrooms contain king-size beds with carved headboards imported from Mexico, carpets from Turkey or India, tables and armoires from Mexico or Guatemala, artwork from Haiti or Brazil, and ceiling fans. Suites and penthouses each have their own kitchens, washing machines, and dryers. Full-size bathrooms throughout the resort contain hand-painted Mexican tiles and lots of mirrors.

The hotel's restaurant, Anacaona, is separately recommended in "Where to Dine," below. The gracefully furnished bar area contains its own artificial waterfall and meandering stream, and a wide selection of tropical drinks. Live music is presented several times a week. For other types of entertainment, guests can easily walk over to the casinos at Allegro and Beaches (see above).

Grace Bay Rd. (P.O. Box 128), Providenciales, Turks and Caicos, BWI. Ⓒ 800/946-5757 in the U.S., or 649/
946-5757. Fax 649/946-5758. www.gracebayclub.com. 22 units. Winter $635 junior suite, $675–$995
1-bedroom suite, $995–$1,195 2-bedroom suite, $1,395 penthouse; off-season $395–$405 junior suite,
$415–$625 1-bedroom suite, $725–$795 2-bedroom suite, $955 penthouse. Breakfast and dinner $65 per
person extra. AE, MC, V. No children under 12. **Amenities:** Restaurant, bar, 2 tennis courts, room service
(7am–9pm daily), massage therapy, water sports, Jacuzzi, bicycling, bonefishing, deep-sea fishing, boating
excursions, and parasailing. *In room:* A/C, TV with VCRs, hair dryer, safe.

Ocean Point/Chalk Sound Villas ⓡ   Many visitors to Provo prefer the privacy of staying in their own villa on the beach. These two villa compounds lie
on Provo's arid and windswept southern coast midway between Sapodilla Bay
and Taylor Bay. Each building within the compound is constructed of imported
Canadian cedar, fir, glass, concrete, and (in one case) local stone, and blends into
the rocky, scrub-covered landscape that surrounds it. Angled toward sweeping
views over turquoise waters, the villas feature a veranda-ringed design based on
either West Indian or Creole models. Each sits on a half acre or more of oceanfront land, offering a sense of isolation. But grocery stores lie within a 15-minute
drive, and since each unit contains a kitchen, many visitors choose to cook their
own meals. All of the villas boast their own piers; others have serpentine staircases that wind down to the water's edge. Each has a scattering of tasteful furniture and many of the amenities you'll need for an escapist vacation. All have
ceiling fans, and most also have air-conditioning. Each has a full-size bathroom.
All rental arrangements are made through the Atlanta address that is listed
below, and the availability of any particular villa will vary with each individual
owner.

Between Sapodilla Bay and Taylor Bay, Providenciales, Turks and Caicos, BWI. (For information and reservations, write P.O. Box 550509, Atlanta, GA 30355. Ⓒ 404/355-9944. Fax 404/351-2615.) 8 units.
$2,800–$7,200 weekly. No credit cards. *In-room:* A/C, TV, kitchen. No phone.

Parrot Cay Resort ⓡⓡ   The newest hideaway outpost in the Atlantic opened
in December of 1998 on an isolated and very private island with a white sandy
beach that lies north of Provo. It's the work of investors from Asia and London,
some of the hippest designers in London, and the former manager of the
K-Club (Italian designer Krizia's private hideaway on Barbuda).

The compound features 10 white- or peach-colored buildings, each with a
terra-cotta roof and a design by Keith Hobbs, recent creator of such ultra-trendy
London landmarks as the Clarence Hotel and the Metropolitan Hotel. (He's
been referred to by fans and critics alike as "London's designer flavor of the
month.") What he's created is a leave-your-jewelry-at-home kind of place, where
a mostly neutral decor enhances the intense sunlight, turquoise waters, sands,
and greenery.

Spacious rooms each have louvered doors that open onto private terraces or
verandas, stark white walls with dark wooden trim, terra-cotta tiles, and an artful positioning of mosquito netting over four-poster beds. The large tiled bathrooms are beautifully appointed with tub and shower combos and deluxe
toiletries.

All meals, drinks, and most activities are included in the price. The kitchen
strives to produce meals that are elegant and wholesome; they are served in
either the stylish main dining room or your accommodation.

There's a rectangular swimming pool—the largest in the Turks and Caicos—
on-site. Water-sports facilities include access to scuba diving, Hobie Cats, snorkeling, canoes, and waterskiing. A holistic spa has a trio of pavilions with
treatment salons where Eastern-influenced healing and rejuvenating therapies

are applied, everything from yoga to meditation. Despite a large rectangular pool and a low-key water-sports and bonefishing program that's organized, on request, by the staff, the beach is the real draw. If you want to make an excursion back to the restaurants or diversions on the "mainland" of Provo, the shuttle launch will haul you back and forth whenever you wish. It's a completely laid-back place where you can sunbathe topless if you'd like.

Parrot Cay (P.O. Box 164), Providenciales, Turks and Caicos, BWI. ℭ 877/754-0726 in the U.S., or 649/946-7788. Fax 649/946-7789. ww.parrot-cay.com. 56 units. Winter $650–$750 double, 1,350 1-bedroom suite, from 1,650 1-bedroom beach house; off-season $500–$645 double, $850–$870 1-bedroom suite, from $1,150 1-bedroom beach house. Rates include all meals, drinks, most activities, and round-trip airport transfers by car and hotel boat. AE, MC, V. Reached by private boat from landing dock on Provo direct to Parrot Cay, a 30-min. speedboat ride north. **Amenities:** Restaurant, bar, pool, 2 tennis coursts, nature trails, health club, spa, Jacuzzi, free bikes, sauna, laundry, baby-sitting, water sports. *In-room:* A/C, TV, minibar, coffeemaker, hair dryer, safe.

Point Grace ℱℱℱ   This boutique hotel, the most charming and atmospheric on the island, opened in March 2000 on one of the best beaches in the western hemisphere. From exceptional suites to panoramic penthouses, its accommodations are the finest in the country. The motif is British colonial–inspired, and the services and amenities are first-rate, ranging from complimentary Indonesian sarongs to scented oil lamps. The complex features one-, two-, and three-bedroom suites, furnished with Indonesian hardwood and teak, and brightened by Indonesian silk fabrics. Hand-painted tile and mahogany grace the bedrooms with exclusive bathroom amenities. Each suite also has a full kitchen. Point Grace is set in the Princess Alexandra Park, a protected marine reserve on the north coast. The hotel is named for Grace Hutchings, who spent her honeymoon here in a small cottage a century ago. Situated poolside are four replicas of Grace's original honeymoon cottage.

Breakfast and lunch are served poolside, and there's daily afternoon tea. At night, a free private shuttle takes guests to the choice restaurants along Grace Bay.

Grace Bay, (P.O. Box 158), Providenciales, Turks and Caicos, BWI. ℭ 888/682-3705 in the U.S., or 649/946-5096. Fax 649/946-5097. www.pointgrace.tc. 30 units. Winter $435 $595 double, $750–$930 2-bedroom suite, from $1,175 3-bedroom suite; off-season $345 double, $545–$695 2-bedroom suite, from $845 3-bedroom suite. AE, DISC, MC, V. **Amenities:** Restaurant, bar, swimming pool with bar, fitness center, concierge, room service (7:45–10am, lunch noon–2pm, dinner 6:30–10pm), nearby golf, arrangements for water sports, bottom and bone-fishing. *In room:* A/C, TV, minibar, coffeemaker.

EXPENSIVE

Coral Gardens ℱ   A three-story resort of charm and grace, Coral Gardens competes successfully with such stellar properties as Ocean Club and Ocean Club West. In a setting of such tropical flora as pink hibiscus and purple bougainvillea, the resort offers tastefully furnished and spacious condo suites and two penthouses. The decor is especially inviting with Asian accents and upholstered wicker along with wrought iron and glass tables, everything opening onto a view. Bathrooms are full-size and elegantly appointed. Suites come with one or two bedrooms, and also include a fully equipped kitchen.

The property opens onto one of the best snorkeling reefs in Turks and Caicos. The beachfront patio and pool area are enhanced by two manmade waterfalls cascading down the face of each structure.

Penn's Road, Grace Bay (P.O. Box 281), Providenciales, Turks and Caicos, BWI. ℭ 800/532-8536 in the U.S., or 649/941-3713. Fax 649/941-5171. www.coralgardens.com. 40 units. Winter $175–$620 double, $700 penthouse; off-season $135–$500 double, $600 penthouse. AE, MC, V. **Amenities:** Restaurant, bar, pool, snorkeling. *In room:* A/C, TV, hair dryer, kitchen.

Ocean Club *☞☞*   Across from the Provo Golf Club, this luxury condo complex—the best of its type on the island—opens onto Grace Bay, site of the finest beach. Billing itself as a place to "Escape the Stress of Success," the resort community has accommodations available for sale or rent, all spread across a 7-acre piece of landscaped property.

The resort consists of studio suites, deluxe studio suites, and one-, two-, or three-bedroom deluxe suites, all with ocean views and full-size bathrooms, plus fully equipped kitchens, except for the studios, which have kitchenettes. Each suite is equipped with both ceiling fans and central air-conditioning. A series of buildings surround gardens and a courtyard. Except for the studio suite (the cheapest rental), accommodations are spacious and comfortable, with large screened balconies.

The hotel has a grill restaurant that serves international food (see "Where to Dine," below), plus a cabana bar. There is a dive shop that is an annex for Art Pickering's Provo Turtle Divers Ltd. (see the section on snorkeling and scuba diving, below). Dive classes are available at the hotel, but for diving and rental equipment, you'll have to take a shuttle bus to the company's headquarters in Turtle Cove. There's also a daily shuttle-bus service for dining in the evenings and a part-time shuttle bus for daytime shopping, both for a small fee.

Grace Bay Beach (P.O. Box 240), Providenciales, Turks and Caicos, BWI. ✆ 800/457-8787 or 649/946-5880. Fax 649/946-5845 or 302/369-1421. www.oceanclubresorts.com. 86 units. Winter $180–$280 studio suite, $460–$535 1-bedroom suite, $630–$715 2-bedroom suite, $835–$910 3-bedroom suite; off-season $180–$225 studio suite, $315–$335 1-bedroom suite, $415–$485 2-bedroom suite, $550–$600 3-bedroom suite. AE, MC, V. **Amenities:** 2 restaurants, bar, dive shop, baby-sitting, fitness room. In room: A/C, TV, washer/dryer.

Ocean Club West *☞☞*   This is the equally enticing sibling property to the previously recommended, Ocean Club. It, too, is nestled along the shores of Grace Bay with its spectacular beach. Casual but comfortable suites, in various shapes and sizes, surround a tropical setting. Each unit has a balcony or terrace opening onto the view. The range of living options is wide here, suitable for a variety of needs—everything from an efficiency to a three-bedroom accommodation. Accommodations come with fully equipped kitchens or kitchenettes.

Grace Bay Beach (P.O. Box 640), Providenciales, Turks and Caicos, BWI. ✆ 800/457-8787 or 649/946-5880. Fax 649/946-5845. www.oceanclubresorts.com/rates.php3. 90 units. Winter $225–$280 double, from $460 suite; off-season $180–$225 double, from $315 suite. AE, MC, V. **Amenities:** Restaurant, bar, 2 pools, exercise room, dive shop. In room: A/C, TV, coffeemaker, hair dryer, refrigerator, iron/ironing boards, safes.

The Sands at Grace Bay *☞*   Attracting well-heeled beach buffs, this suite-only oceanfront resort is a soothing retreat. Opened in 1998, it is furnished in a plush Caribbean motif with wicker chairs and minimalist glass-and-steel tables. Units have large screened-in terraces and oversize windows. This is upmarket condo living Turks- and Caicos-style. Hardwood from Indonesia and fabrics the color of the sea set the tone of a limited hangout sophistication—nothing overpowering, everything tranquil. There are two- and three-bedroom suites, each with full-size bathrooms with luxurious toiletries.

Hemingway's, the resort's excellent seafood restaurant, overlooks the beach.

Grace Bay (P.O. Box 681), Providenciales, Turks and Caicos, BWI. ✆ 877/77SANDS or 649/946-5199. www.thesandresort.com. 40 units. Winter $220–$785 per suite; off-season $155–$575 per suite. AE, MC, V. **Amenities:** Restaurant, bar, 3 pools, tennis court, water sports, cabana, laundry, car rentals, bikes for guests, massage, baby-sitting. In room: A/C, TV, refrigerators, kitchenettes, safes.

MODERATE

Caribbean Paradise Inn An intimate and cozy inn-style retreat, this hotel overlooks Grace Bay with its beach, which you can see from one of the private balconies at the inn. All the mid-size units have a combined bedroom and living area, with various types of beds, and are furnished like a high-grade motel, containing small bathrooms with shower stalls.

Swimming pools and sundecks are accessible from each unit, and divers are provided with lockable open-air closets to store their gear.

Grace Bay (P.O. Box 673), Providenciales, Turks and Caicos, BWI. ℂ **649/946-5020.** Fax 649/946-5022. www.paradise.tc. 16 units. Winter $135–$238 double; off-season $129–$199 double. Extra person $30. DISC, MC, V. **Amenities:** Pool. *In room:* A/C, TV, minibar.

Comfort Suites Turks and Caicos *(Kids)* This complex, which opened in 1998, seems like a Florida beach hotel. Two three-story buildings with a swimming pool lie across from the Allegro Resort Turks & Caicos and the Ports of Call shopping center. You'll have a traditional hotel stay here—no surprises, but no disappointments either. Rooms have either a king-size bed or two doubles, and a sleeper sofa, so the unit can accommodate up to six people. Each room is modern and streamlined with a number of amenities such as modem ports. Twenty of the rooms have balconies but not necessarily an ocean view. The only views of the ocean are seen from the outer ends of the complex, looking around the taller Turquoise Reef. Bathrooms are full-size with tub and shower combos.

Room service is actually delivered from one of the five dining posts in the Ports of Call; fare ranges from sandwiches to Italian to Tex-Mex. Water sports aren't a specialty here, but you can arrange an excursion to the Conch Farm for snorkeling and full-day dive trips.

Grace Bay (P.O. Box 590), Providenciales, Turks and Caicos, BWI. ℂ **888/678-3483** or 649/946-8888. Fax 649/946-5444. www.comfortsuitesci.com. Winter $175–$195 double; off-season $135–$155 double. Rates include continental breakfast. AE, DISC, MC, V. **Amenities:** Pool, baby-sitting. *In room:* A/C, TV, coffeemaker, refrigerator, safe, hair dryer, iron/ironing board on request.

Erebus Inn Provo's oldest inn, the Erebus, was built in the early 1960s, before the island's boom began. Often renovated since its early days, it occupies a perch on a low cliff above the coastal road, looking down on the Turtle Cove Marina, on the island's northern coast. If you opt for a stay here, your view will be either one of the two swimming pools or the boats bobbing at anchor in the nearby marina. A shuttle is available to haul visitors to and from Smith's Reef Beach, but because it's only a 10-minute walk from the hotel, most guests prefer to walk.

Most of the accommodations are within a low-rise cement-sided building that was constructed in the late 1980s. The others are less conventional-looking, because they were designed as a series of small one-room cottages, each of which resembles a small bird cage, with some tricky trusses and buttressing to keep them on their steep hillside. None has a kitchen, but each is equipped with a small bathroom containing a shower stall. Throughout the complex, accommodations have tiled floors, pastel color schemes, comfortable but slightly battered furniture, and either a private terrace or a balcony. Throughout the property, terraces are ringed with low walls of chiseled stone, which help to create a sense of intimacy and coziness.

The hotel's Sunset Bar & Restaurant, which is separately managed by a newly arrived couple from French-speaking Canada, is recommended in "Where to Dine." Its bar area and terrace are the resort's social center, where guests often gather for drinks.

Turtle Cove (P.O. Box 238), Providenciales, Turks and Caicos, BWI. ℂ **649/946-4240.** Fax 649/946-4704. 25 units. Mid-Dec to mid-Apr $140–$200 double; mid-Apr to mid-Dec $100–$150 double. AE, DISC, MC, V. **Amenities:** Restaurant, bar, 2 pools, 2 tennis courts, dive shop, health club. *In room:* A/C, TV.

Sibonne Hotel & Beach Club ℱ ℛ*Kids*

Set a few steps from the very white sands of the island's eastern beaches, this has an informal, laid-back West Indian style that attracts lots of families who don't want the formality of some of the other hotels. The land on which it sits is rather modest when compared to the acreage of the bigger resorts. It benefits, however, from its location, a 10-minute walk from the Allegro Resort Turks & Caicos; guests frequently walk over to the bigger resort to visit its restaurants and casino. Each accommodation has a ceiling fan and a comfortable but no-frills decor of beachy furniture and Caribbean colors. Bedrooms come with a small tiled bathroom containing a shower stall. There's also a villa-like condominium that sits a short distance from the rest of the hotel. The two-story hotel is painted pink and white, and contains on its premises a curve-sided freshwater swimming pool, a wood-trimmed clubhouse/bar/restaurant with big windows and sea views, and a full array of water-sports options.

Grace Bay (P.O. Box 144), Providenciales, Turks and Caicos, BWI. ℂ **800/528-1905** in the U.S., or 649-946-5547. Fax 649/946-5770. www.wheretostay.com/caribbean/resorts/869-facts.html. 25 units. $205–$250 double, $285 suite; off-season $145–$180 double, $210 suite. AE, MC, V. **Amenities:** Restaurant, bar, pool, water sports. *In room:* A/C, TV.

Turtle Cove Inn ℱ

This two-story hotel, built in a U shape around a freshwater swimming pool, is a favorite with divers and boaters. A few feet away, boats dock directly at the hotel's pier, which juts into Seller's Pond amid the many yachts floating at anchor. Each bedroom is simply but comfortably furnished, with views over either the pool or the marina. All units are equipped with a small bathroom containing a shower stall.

Near the pool lie the tables of the separately recommended Tiki Hut Cabana Bar & Grill. Upstairs, open for dinner only, is the Terrace Restaurant, also recommended below. Although it doesn't have a beach of its own, many guests don't consider this a problem because a shuttle carries them from the hotel's wharf to the sands of a nearby beach.

Turtle Cove Marina, Suzie Turn Rd., Providenciales, Turks and Caicos, BWI. ℂ **800/887-0477** in the U.S., or 649/946-4203. Fax 649/946-4141. www.Provo.net/TurtleCoveInn/. 30 units. Winter $124–$185 double; off-season $105–$150 double. AE, MC, V. **Amenities:** Bar/grill, restaurant, pool, dive shop. *In room:* A/C, TV, minibar.

WHERE TO DINE

In addition to the restaurants recommended below, you may want to check out the options at Beaches Turks and Caicos Resort and Spa (recommended above). The resort's showcase restaurant, **Sapodilla's** (ℂ **649/946-8000**), can be visited by outsiders who purchase a day pass for $85 or an evening pass for $80 valid from 6pm to 3am. Once you have the pass, you can dine and drink anywhere at the resort, including Sapodilla's.

Be aware that the island is undergoing many changes, and the restaurants do come and go. Have your hotel call ahead for you if you're venturing off the beaten path.

EXPENSIVE

Anacaona ℱ MEDITERRANEAN/CARIBBEAN Set in three thatched-roof outbuildings of this luxury hotel, this place is lighthearted, fun, and elegant. It's as good as hotel restaurants get in Provo. You might enjoy a frothy drink in the bar before crossing over a fountain stream to the restaurant. French recipes are combined effectively with Caribbean produce—not always an easy marriage, but here the effect is successful. At lunch you might prefer a classic salade Niçoise or the excellent grilled tuna. In the evening the atmosphere becomes more romantic, with flickering light from the torches and candlelight on the tables. The chef's grilled lobster is among the island's finest dishes. To his credit, however, he also does fresh fish dishes extremely well. Grounded in the classics, he offers such familiar fare as home-smoked salmon or a perfectly executed roast rack of lamb under a mustard and herb crust. His house dessert specialty deserves an award: crème brûlée topped with peaches.

In the Grace Bay Club, Grace Bay Rd. ℂ 649/946-5050. Reservations recommended. Lunch salads, sandwiches, and platters $8–$14; dinner main courses $24–$34. AE, MC, V. Daily noon–3pm and 7–9pm.

Caicos Café ℱ FRENCH/CARIBBEAN   Set on a terrace that's open to the sun, moon, and stars, this 6-year-old French restaurant is across the street from the sea and the entrance to the Allegro Resort. Its charming French-born owners Daphne and Pierrik provide a lot of the magic. Walls are cheerfully outfitted in bright tropical hues and a collection of oil paintings inspired by Caribbean colors and vegetation. The cooking is light and sophisticated, including lobster, Caesar and Greek salads, plus several kinds of sandwiches, a medley of grilled fish and lobster, plus several vegetarian dishes.

Grace Bay. ℂ 649/946-5278. Reservations recommended. Main courses $14–$29.50. AE, MC, V. Daily 6–10pm.

Gecko Grille ℱ FLORIBBEAN   One of the most appealing restaurants at Grace Bay, this place is set in a garden (no sea views) on the grounds of a previously recommended resort. You'll dine beneath a soaring 35-foot ceiling, surrounded by a frieze of cavorting geckos and banana leaves painted by a local artist. Menu items include pastas, salads, grilled steaks, and a roster of snapper, tuna, or wahoo, prepared in any of four ways, with virtually any sauce you want. House specialties include fresh grouper garnished with avocado slices and macadamia nuts, roasted chicken with shredded papaya, and marinated pork chops with chutney salsa.

Ocean Plaza, in the Ocean Club, Grace Bay Beach. ℂ 649/946-5880. Reservations recommended. Main courses $16–$32.95. AE, MC, V. Tues–Sun 6–10pm. Closed Sept–Oct.

Sunset Bar & Restaurant ℱ FRENCH/INTERNATIONAL   A couple from French-speaking Canada runs this restaurant in the Erebus Inn along Provo's north shore. Set on a deck that's cantilevered over the edge of a low cliff, it offers views of Grace Bay and the boats that bob at anchor within Turtle Cove Marina just across the coastal road from the restaurant. (It's a great place to watch the sunset.) Depending on the weather, you can opt for a meal under the stars or within the sheltered (and air-conditioned) interior. Lunch brings pizzas, salads, burgers, and ribs; dinner offers a greater selection of seafood, grilled or fried, and dishes of French inspiration such as boeuf bourguignonne or roasted lamb with rosemary, and steaks with green peppercorns.

In the Erebus Inn, Turtle Cove. ℂ 649/946-4240. Reservations recommended at dinner. Lunch platters $6–$12.50; dinner main courses $18–$26. AE, DISC, MC, V. Daily 7–10:30am and 6–10pm.

MODERATE
Banana Boat Restaurant INTERNATIONAL   The Banana Boat is the most popular restaurant on the island that's not in a hotel. It's not the best, but

it's certainly the most convivial. Since 1981, there's hardly been a yachtie on Provo who hasn't moored here to enjoy an island meal and a potent tropical drink. For a main course, you might try T-bone steak, cracked conch, or some freshly caught local fish. At lunch, favorites include lobster or tuna salads, along with half-pound burgers. Dessert might be carrot cake or key lime pie. No one in the kitchen fusses too much with these dishes, but they are good and full of flavor. A choice seat is on the timber-and-plank veranda that juts out over piers on Turtle Cove.

Turtle Cove Marina. (C) 649/941-5706. Reservations recommended. Main courses $9.95–$21.95; lunch $6.25–$10.95. AE, MC, V. Daily 11am–10pm.

Coco Bistro *&* FRENCH/INTERNATIONAL   The most attractive and appealing French restaurant on Provo lies on a plot of land that was a plant nursery in the 1980s, which has since grown into the largest palm grove on the island. The vaguely Mexican/vaguely Moroccan-looking restaurant is run by a husband-and-wife team from Provence, Yves Coutisson and Dominique Rousset (he tends bar, she cooks). Most meals here are enjoyed in the garden, under the palms. Desserts are all French and homemade. We especially recommend the crème brûlée. Menu items, often Mediterranean in origin, include penne pasta with chicken and basil-infused sun-dried tomatoes; spaghetti in a lobster-flavored cream sauce; grouper in puff pastry; tagine (stew) of lamb or lamb kebabs; or snapper baked in a crust of sea salt, served with a sauce of olive oil, basil, and sage.

Grace Bay Rd. (C) 649/946-5369. Reservations recommended. Main courses $14–$29.50. AE, MC, V. Daily 6–9:30pm.

Dora's *&* *(Finds* AMERICAN/CARIBBEAN   Set in a concrete building on the Leeward Highway, partially hidden behind a larger building, this is a quintessential West Indian hangout, where food abounds, drinks flow, slot machines whir, and jukebox music plays constantly. It's the island's social hub, thanks to hostess Dora Lightburne. Menu items focus on hearty, summery foods like cheeseburgers, chef salads, platters of peas 'n' rice, barbecued ribs, fish and lobster, and earthier foods like goatwater and souse. Every Monday and Thursday, there's a $15-per-person all-you-can-eat seafood buffet between 7 and 10pm. If you don't want to drive, Dora or a member of her staff will arrange taxi pickup and drop-off at your hotel for an additional $7 per person. Beer and frothy rum-laced drinks are the beverages of choice, and on weekend nights, the place rocks to the sound of local bands.

Leeward Hwy. (C) 649/946-4558. Reservations not necessary. Lunch main courses $7–$11; dinner main courses $14.95–$19.95. AE, MC, V. Daily 7am–4am.

Hemingway's Beachfront Restaurant CARIBBEAN/INTERNATIONAL   An instant island hot spot, Hemingway's beachside locale attracts international travelers as well as locals. The selections are inviting and the creations are palate-pleasing. Fresh grouper, for example, is lightly spiced and pan-seared, served with a tequila-spiked veggie salsa with charred onions, black beans, corn, red and green peppers, and carrots. Shrimp is lightly sautéed with a scrumptious pesto cream over penne, and filet mignon is exquisitely grilled with a fragrant red wine mushroom sauce. Hemingway's is also a good lunch choice, serving gourmet sandwiches, hearty salads, soft fish tacos, or fresh vegetable pitas. Finish with fresh fruit crepes laced with a Grand Marnier caramel and fried ice cream. At night, with its torches and candlelight, there's a hint of romance.

At The Sands at Grace Bay. ℭ **649/946-5199.** Reservations required. Main courses $13.95–$22.95. AE, MC, V. Daily 8am–11pm.

The Terrace Restaurant ☞ EURO CARIBBEAN/SEAFOOD Divers,
boaters, and young couples, often guests at the Turtle Cove Inn (previously recommended), have turned this convivial place into Provo's trendiest spot. Trendy would mean little if the food weren't good; fortunately, it is. The setting helps, too: a covered outdoor terrace and an intimate dining room.

Many guests still come here looking for Jimmy's, the restaurant that used to be here, which became somewhat of a legend during its short reign. The Terrace Restaurant is only slightly different. One thing that remains the same is the motto: "Eat, eat, eat—don't go away hungry." The conch ravioli is one of the best we've ever sampled, and a terrific lobster dinner is always waiting. You can also start your meal with a delectable home-smoked salmon. The local catch is invariably moist and tender, grilled to perfection. The pasta dishes are also superb. For dessert, be sure to try one of their ice cream creations.

In the Turtle Cove Inn, Suzie Turn Rd., North Shore. ℭ **649/946-4763.** Reservations recommended. Main courses $7–$28; lunch $6–$12. AE, MC, V. Mon–Sat 11:30am–3pm and 6–10pm.

Tiki Hut Cabana Bar & Grill AMERICAN/CARIBBEAN/PASTA This
open-air, festive cabana-style restaurant arranges its tables beside the pool of an informal inn that sits next to one of the island's biggest marinas. The Tiki Hut serves full-fledged American-style breakfasts; lunches that include salads, fresh fish platters, and sandwiches; and dinners that almost invariably consist of pasta and fresh fish. Culinary specialties include jerked grouper (slow-cooked with spices in the Jamaican style), pan-fried or grilled catch of the day with fresh dill and caper-tartar sauce, and the traditional favorite, English-style fish-and-chips, prepared with your choice of wahoo, grouper, snapper, or dolphinfish. They also serve a fabulous array of specialty pizzas. The house drink is a Banana Slammer. This place is a local favorite, serving solid, reliable fare.

In the Turtle Cove Inn, Turtle Cove Marina. ℭ **649/941-5341.** American breakfast $5–$7; lunch platters $7.50–$12; dinner main courses $11.50–$23.95. AE, MC, V. Daily 7am–10pm.

INEXPENSIVE

Fast Eddie's AMERICAN/CARIBBEAN Set in a beige two-story, cement-
block apartment building, this place lies close to the airport. It's owned by a father-and-son team: Eddie ("Fast Eddie") and his son, Jervon Laporte, who cheerfully welcome visitors into their simply decorated but cozy restaurant. The menu focuses on all-American fare like burgers with fries, apple or cherry pie, and steaks, as well as West Indian staples like fried conch or turtle steak, grilled grouper or snapper, and roasted pork. Note that, for religious reasons, the owners don't serve alcohol of any kind.

Airport Rd. ℭ **649/941-3176.** Reservations not necessary. Lunch items $4.50–$8; dinner main courses $16–$25. No credit cards. Mon–Sat 8am–9pm.

Hey José Cantina MEXICAN/PIZZA/AMERICAN Set in the center of the
island as one of the focal points of a small shopping center, this lighthearted place is run by Steve and Marilyn Mull. Surrounded by burnt orange, green, and yellow hues, you can enjoy the best margaritas in Provo. The parade of burritos, tacos, quesadillas, chimichangas, and grilled steaks and chicken will make you think you've been transplanted to some fiery little eatery along the Tex-Mex border. Also popular, especially with expatriate North Americans who have had their fill of grouper and cracked conch, are the richly topped pizzas. Available in

three sizes, they culminate with a variety known as "the kitchen sink," with virtually everything you can think of thrown into the mix.

Central Square, Leeward Hwy. © 649/946-4812. Lunch platters $8–$10; pizzas $6.50–$20; dinner main courses $10.95–$18.95. AE, MC, V. Mon–Sat noon–10pm. Bar Mon–Sat noon–midnight.

Tasty Temptations DELI   Head here for your morning cup of espresso or cappuccino, bagels with smoked salmon and cream cheese, and about a dozen kinds of lunchtime sandwiches that are perfect for a beach picnic. It's arranged deli style, and you can collect your food on a tray to eat on the outdoor terrace, or get it to go. "Tasty" sells cold cuts and deli foods by the pound. Run by an expatriate from French-speaking Canada, it's a 10-minute drive west of Provo's airport.

In the Butterfield Square Shopping Center, Leeward Hwy. © 649/946-4049. Pastries and turnovers $1–$2; sandwiches $5.50–$7.50; breakfast $2.50–$4. No credit cards. Mon–Fri 6:30am–3pm.

BEACHES, WATER SPORTS & OTHER OUTDOOR PURSUITS
HITTING THE BEACH
Starting at Leeward and running all the way to Thompson Cove, **Grace Bay Beach** ⚹⚹⚹ is Provo's finest beach, stretching for 12 miles of spectacular, powdery-soft white sand. The gin-clear, crystal-blue waters are extremely tranquil and there are no rocks, making it ideal for kids. Many resorts, such as Club Med, have developed along its edge, so you won't have these sands all to yourself. Though there are no public facilities on the beach, the hotels themselves come in handy, because all of them have rest rooms and bars serving tropical drinks. The folks at Condé Nast have rated it "number one beach on the planet."

Grace Bay Beach is so stunning that you might not want to venture anywhere else, but there are a few other beaches on the island. They tend to be less spectacular, but also less crowded. In the east, **Long Bay Beach** lies on the opposite shore from Grace Bay, opening onto Long Bay itself. It begins around Juba Point and extends east to Stubbs Cove, and is virtually free of hotels. The sand here isn't as powdery fine as that of Grace Bay, but you'll have more privacy. The waters here are very sheltered and there are virtually no waves.

If you want to flee the hordes, you can rent a four-wheel-drive vehicle, following Malcolm's Road west to **Malcolm's Road Beach.** Figure a 30-minute drive to reach this beach from Grace Bay, and the last 3 miles of the road are very rocky. But once you reach this beach, it is stunningly lovely, with fine white sands, and nearly always empty. There's good snorkeling, though you'll have to bring your own gear. There are no facilities.

A final choice worth exploring is **Sapodilla Bay Beach** in the west, opening on Proggin's Bay, south of the airport. It's a gem of a white sandy beach with crystal-clear waters. It lies between two 30-foot cliffs at Gussy Cove, stretching all the way west to Ocean Point. This is such a well-protected beach, with fine sands and clear shallow water (even 100 ft. out) that the locals often refer to Sapodilla as "the children's beach."

FISHING
Silver Deep (© 649/941-5595) offers the best fishing excursions, with both half- and full-day expeditions, usually for bonefishing or bottom fishing. Tackle and bait are thrown in.

For those who'd like to venture farther afield—and pay a lot more money—half- and full-day deep-sea fishing expeditions are available, with all equipment included. Catches turn up wahoo, tuna, kingfish, marlin, and even shark.

Moments Hanging Out with the Iguanas

One of the most impressive remaining sanctuaries for rock iguanas is **Little Water Cay,** off Provo, where between 1,500 and 2,000 of these endangered creatures lie. The iguanas that inhabit the otherwise-uninhabited cay are a subspecies found nowhere outside of the Turks and Caicos and the Southern Bahamas chain.

Since Little Water Cay is only a short boat ride from Provo, the potential to love the iguanas to death is apparent. The iguanas are highly sociable and will come down the beach to meet boats and even accept food from visitors. As the number of visitors to the cay began to approach 20,000 per year, a coalition of public- and private-sector organizations assembled to develop a sustainable, ecologically oriented tourist attraction on the tiny island: the **Little Water Cay Nature Trail Program.** A system of boardwalks has been built from the most popular anchorages into the interior, where most of the iguanas live, to allow visitors to observe the iguanas without intruding upon them. Now visitors can see iguanas, their burrowing systems, and their nests without endangering them. Observation towers have also been constructed to provide a higher vantage point for views of the interior of the cay and the beautiful blue waters that surround it. Interpretive signs are located throughout the network.

It costs $3 to visit Little Water Cay, with proceeds used to maintain the trails. Children under 6 are free.

The best way to visit "Iguana Island" is to take one of the excursions offered by **J&B Tours,** located at Leeward Marina on Provo (*✆* **649/ 946-5047**). The cost is $30 per person, and a minimum of two people must sign up.

Arranging virtually the same fishing tours is **Sakitumi** (*✆* **649/946-4065**), at comparable prices. They'll sell you a fishing license for $15. A half-day fishing trip costs $400, a full day $750.

GOLF

Provo Golf Club *✦* at Grace Bay Rd. (*✆* **649/946-5991**), is the only golf course in the country. It was rated as one of the top-10 golf courses in the Caribbean by *Caribbean Travel and Life.* The 6,560-yard, par-72, 18-hole course was designed by Karl Litten, of Boca Raton, Florida, and is owned by the Sheik of Qatar. It is powerfully green and takes an extraordinary amount of water to keep it so, because Provo is one of the driest spots on the globe. Young palms and bougainvillea, as well as rocky outcroppings and powdery sand traps, help make the course a challenge to the serious golfer or a lovely day on the links for the beginner or novice. Four sets of tees allow golfers to tailor a game to their level of expertise. A driving range and putting greens are also available. The clubhouse contains a bar and a restaurant that serves breakfast and lunch. Daily hours are from 7am to 7pm. Greens fees are $120 per person for 18 holes. The price includes the use of a golf cart, which is mandatory. Golf clubs can be rented for $20 to $40 per set.

PARASAILING

This increasingly popular sport is offered by both **J&B Tours,** Leeward Marina (© **649/946-5047**), and **Dive Provo,** Allegro Resort Turks & Caicos (© **800/ 234-7768** in the U.S., or 649/946-5040). A 15-minute flight costs around $60.

SAILING & KAYAKING

Boating in the hard-to-reach islands has become a popular pastime. **Dive Provo,** in the Allegro Resort Turks & Caicos (© **800/234-7768** in the U.S., or 649/946-5040), rents small sailboats for around $25 per hour. This outfitter will even provide beginner sailing instructions for $40 for up to 2 hours. You can also rent an open-cockpit ocean kayak here for $15 per hour for two adventurers. More expensive sailing craft, even with a private captain for half- or full-day excursions, are available from **J&B Tours** (© **649/946-5047**).

SNORKELING & SCUBA DIVING

Dive experts, including the late Jacques Cousteau, have cited Provo as one of the 10 best sites in the world, because of a barrier reef that runs the full length of the island's 17-mile north coast. At Northwest Point there is a vertical drop-off to 7,000 feet.

In order to help protect delicate coral reefs and facilitate conscientious snorkeling, the Turks and Caicos National Trust has recently established snorkel trails on **Smith's Reef** and **Bight Reef** in Provo's Grace Bay.

Unlike offshore reefs where access is limited, and boats visit infrequently, the Bight and Smith's reefs are located just next to the shoreline. Their proximity lends easy access to underwater explorers, and the impact of frequent visits causes significant wear and tear on the majestic, yet fragile, coral gardens. By touching, breaking, or kicking the coral, snorkelers can inadvertently damage or kill these delicate organisms, as each and every impact takes its toll.

The newly marked trails not only lead people through safe areas, but also help educate snorkelers in how to minimize reef impacts. The first underwater signage of its kind, 24 handmade tile signs guide the way, with information baked into the abrasion-resistant square-foot surfaces. Companion beach signs help direct visitors to points of entry and, with internationally understood symbols, rehearse the rules of reef etiquette. Snorkelers are asked to follow trail markers, to avoid touching and kicking sand onto reefs, and to attempt a body-length distance between themselves and the reef. Laminated trail maps, for sale in hotels, restaurants, and tourist and dive shops, complement the beach signs.

Smith's Reef, just outside the channel leading to Turtle Cove Pond, has a total of 13 underwater signs that describe the coral reef ecosystem and the diversity of life that thrives there. Snorkelers can learn about the various creatures camouflaged within the reef, the importance of seagrass beds, and the ways that parrot fish contribute to the environment. The trail follows the perimeter of the reef starting inshore in about 3 to 6 feet of water, increasing to 24 to 30 feet deep. The depth marks a spectacular display of coral creations, colorful schooling fish, and spotted eagle rays; even resident turtles can be found.

Bight Reef is located in the Grace Bay area known as the Bight, just offshore from a large white house. A public footpath leads to the beach, and two marker buoys indicate both ends of the snorkel trail. The Bight Reef Snorkel Trail has a total of 11 underwater trail signs that describe corals and how they grow. Water depth ranges from 3 to 15 feet, and visitors can view mobile species like yellow-tailed snappers, big jolthead porgies, and sand-sifting mojarras.

If you'd like to take a snorkel cruise, consider **Ocean Outback** (© 649/ 941-5810). A 70-foot motor cruiser will take you to neighboring, uninhabited islands for snorkeling. For $85 per person, you are taken to your own private island for the day (9am to 4pm). The cost includes the boat shuttle to your private island (pickup is at 4pm), snorkel gear, a beach umbrella, a picnic lunch, and plenty of cold drinks. **Tao** (© 649/946-5040) has become a favorite for its sailing and snorkeling cruises. It's also known for its sunset cruises. A full day's cruise costs $80 to $135 per person, and that includes lunch and rental of snorkeling equipment.

Art Pickering's Provo Turtle Divers Ltd, Turtle Cove (© 649/946-4232), with headquarters directly in front of the Erebus Inn on the water, is the oldest and best dive operation in the islands, offering personalized service. There are scuba tanks for rent, plus ample backpacks and weight belts. A single dive costs $45, a night dive goes for $50, and a morning two-tank dive is $75. Prices include all equipment. A PADI open-water certification course is $395. Provo Turtle is a PADI training facility, with full instruction and resort courses. An open-water PADI referral course goes for $250. Snorkeling equipment is also available.

Dive Provo, Grace Bay (© 649/946-5029) has one of the best scuba programs on the island. You're taken to unspoiled spots where you see an extraordinary array of marine life. You can dive at the vertical walls of Northwest Point, where sheer drop-offs begin at 50 to 60 feet. Here you'll discover a panoramic array of corals and vibrant gold and purple sponges. Its Grace Bay dive boat leaves the Turquoise Reef pier daily at 8:30am and 2:30pm. Dive Provo also offers PADI open-water certification courses, along with snorkeling trips, glass-bottom boat rides, equipment rental, Windsurfer or sailboat instruction, and sailing excursions. A two-tank scuba dive costs $78, with a PADI certification course going for $395. Snorkeling trips go for $30 for 2 hours, and Windsurfers or sailboats can be rented for $20 per hour.

TENNIS
Many resorts have courts that are lit at night. Some of the best include **Turtle Cove Inn** (© 649/946-4203), with two courts, both lit at night.

The best courts are at the all-inclusive **Club Med Turkoise** (see above), but these are usually set aside for guests. Non-guests can play at many other courts, however, including **Erebus Inn** (© 649/946-4240).

WATERSKIING & WINDSURFING
Provo, with its calm seas and turquoise waters, is ideal for waterskiing. The best outfitter is **Dive Provo** at Grace Bay (© 649/946-5029), which charges $45 for a 15-minute run. This company is also the best outfitter for windsurfing.

EXPLORING THE ISLAND
Chalk Sound, a landlocked lagoon west of Five Cays Settlement, has been turned into a public park. The hamlet of Five Cays itself boasts a small harbor and a modern airport.

Caicos Conch Farm, Leeward Hwy. (© 649/946-5330), is located on the isolated eastern end of the island, amid a flat and sun-baked terrain of scrub and sand. This place was founded in 1984 by a consortium of investors from Miami and Canada. It is a pioneer—the only one of its kind in the West Indies—for the commercial production of our faithful friend, the conch. Its techniques are not commercially viable, but this place could spark breeding techniques that could change the way conch is cultivated worldwide. Its staff will give visitors a walking tour of the breeding basins. For another $3, they will give you a conch after the tour. Admission of $6 for adults and $3 for children includes a tour of the hatchery and the laboratories. In the gift shop, you can buy rare conch pearls, shell jewelry, and commemorative T-shirts. Open Monday to Friday 9am to 4pm.

SHOPPING

You might enjoy browsing through the **Bamboo Gallery,** Leeward Highway (© **649/946-4748**), one of the island's leading art galleries. Its inventories include wood carvings, ceramic sculptures, and the kinds of colorful oil paintings that, if they don't come directly from Haiti, were at least inspired by that island's traditions. The most unusual pieces—to look at if not to buy—are some of the locally made metal sculptures, sometimes created from oil drums or old car wrecks.

   Greensleeves, Central Square (© **649/946-4147**), is the best craft and souvenir shop on Provo, featuring paintings and ceramics by local artists, baskets, unusual jewelry, and sisal mats and bags. A collection of handmade soft toys is also sold. **Paradise Gifts & Art,** Central Square (© **649/946-4748**), owned by the Bamboo Galley, specializes in local art, handcrafts, and navigational and decorative charts. It also carries a line of souvenir and gift items.

   For the best duty-free shopping, head to **Royal Jewels,** Leeward Highway (© **649/946-4699**). It has good stocks in gold jewelry and designer watches, and French and international perfumes—all that standard showcase stuff found on other islands in the Caribbean.

PROVO AFTER DARK

The major center for after-dark diversion on Provo is the **Casino at Allegro Resort,** Grace Bay (© **649/946-5555**), which is one of the few to operate in any British Dependent Territory. It's generally packed every night, with resort visitors playing blackjack, craps, Caribbean stud, roulette, and poker. There are also about 100 slot machines. Casablanca-style fans whirl overhead as waiters serve frosty drinks. Hours are daily from 6pm until 1 or 2am. The latest casino to open is at **Beaches Turks and Caicos Resort and Spa** (© **649/946-8000**), a large casino and the first in the Sandals chain of resorts.

   Many hotels stage entertainment for their guests. If yours doesn't, you can seek some action at **Casablanca** (© **649/946-5449**), next to Club Med. Many Club Med residents flock here when they get bored with the diversions at their own resort. It's a Riviera-like club, with mirrors, music, drinks, and a lot of fun if the crowd's right.

   The bar at the lovely **Gecko Grille,** Ocean Plaza, in the Ocean Club, Grace Bay Beach (© **649/946-5880**), stays open until midnight.

   Reviewed above under "Where to Dine," **Dora's,** Leeward Highway (© **649/946-4558**), is an island hot spot, with casual dining, cold beer and island-style drinks, and a good jukebox. On weekend nights, you might catch a local band.

7 Pine Cay ✯

This exclusive territory, a private island in the West Indies, is owned and managed by members of the **Meridian Club,** who rightly praise its 2½-mile talcum-powder beach, which is among the finest in all the islands.

Pine Cay is one of a chain of islets connecting Providenciales and North Caicos. Two miles long and 800 acres in area, it is a small residential community with a large area set aside for a park. It has its own 3,900-foot airstrip with scheduled local air service, as well as dock and harbor facilities. No cars are allowed, and transportation is by golf cart or bicycle. There is just enough fresh water, and the cay has its own generating plant.

Once a private club, Pine Cay still has members, but they now join the public guests for swimming, sunning, and shelling along the white-sand beach. Snorkeling and diving are possible in an unspoiled barrier reef. Explorers look for Arawak and British colonial remains. There is also a wide range of birds and plants.

There is no place in Turks and Caicos—nor in The Bahamas for that matter— quite so chic as the Meridian Club on Pine Cay. There are no newspapers, no TVs, no radios, no roads, and no cars, and that's how the people who visit here want to keep it. The island is the size of New York's Central Park, but much less dangerous. In fact, it's not dangerous at all. That's one of the many reasons the movers and shakers of the East Coast like to retreat here. They have enough trouble back home, and when they arrive at Pine Cay, they like to leave the world behind. So far, club members have kept the developers at bay, watching in horror what happened to Provo. They even voted against adding more cabanas to their own club, even though they clearly need them. Once you leave the club, the pristine island is yours to explore. If you truly want to see what the islands looked like when Columbus made his landfall (wherever that was!), Pine Cay will give you an excellent idea. Nothing has changed.

To reach Pine Cay, fly to Miami and then take another flight to Providenciales (see "Getting There," at the beginning of this chapter). There, you can arrange for an air taxi to meet you for the 10-minute flight to Pine Cay.

WHERE TO STAY & DINE

The Meridian Club ⊛ This resort is a pricey but environmentally sensitive resort. The main clubhouse faces the beach and a freshwater pool. The club, barefoot elegance at its best, has a delightful dining room, a comfortable library, and an intimate bar with a panoramic terrace for sunset cocktails. A dozen motel-style units are offered, with bed- and sitting-room areas, dressing rooms, outdoor showers, small bathrooms with shower stalls, and terraces facing the beach. You can easily walk the 2½ miles of the fine white sand that stretches out from your back door. The rooms may not have phones or TVs or air-conditioning, but with a beach like this, who cares?

The Meridian Club has one dining room and two bars, one of which is poolside. The open-air dining room offers full American breakfasts, buffet-style lunches served poolside, and dinners by candlelight. The food is usually a Caribbean/continental cuisine. Local produce, especially lobster, conch, and snapper, is used whenever possible. The hotel participates in a visiting chef program, so you may be dining on the unexpected. Guests can enjoy poolside barbecues, a band once or twice weekly, and afternoon tea.

Pine Cay, Turks and Caicos, BWI. (For reservations and information, contact the Meridian Club, c/o Resorts Management, Inc., 456 Glenbrook Rd., Stanford, CT 06906. ☏ 800/331-9154, or 203/602-0300 in the U.S.) Fax 649/941-7010 or 203/602-2265. 12 units. Winter $825 double; off-season $585–$650 double. Rates include all meals. No credit cards. No children under 12. **Amenities:** Dining room, 2 bars, pool, tennis court, room service for breakfast only, laundry, nature trails, snorkeling trips, boat trips to neighboring islands, free tennis rackets and balls, free bicycles, fishing guides, experienced boatmen available. *In-room:* Ceiling fans. No phone.

Appendix:
The Bahamas in Depth

The Bahamas (that's with a capital "T") is one of the most geographically complicated nations of the Atlantic. A coral-based archipelago, it is composed of more than 700 islands, 2,000 cays (pronounced "keys," from the Spanish word for small islands), and hundreds of rocky outcroppings that have damaged the hulls of countless ships since colonial days.

Made of more than 100,000 square miles of dry and sometimes barren land, the archipelago encompasses the islands of The Bahamas and, in the south, the separately governed Turks and Caicos Islands, a British Crown Colony of more than 40 islands and small cays, eight of which are inhabited.

The Commonwealth of The Bahamas came into being in 1973 after centuries of colonial rule. After Great Britain granted The Bahamas internal self-rule in 1964, the fledgling nation adopted its own constitution but chose not to sever its ties with the Mother Country. It has remained in the Commonwealth, with the British monarch as its head of state. In the British tradition, The Bahamas has a two-house Parliament, a ministerial cabinet headed by a prime minister, and an independent judiciary. The queen appoints a Bahamian-general to represent the Crown.

1 The Bahamas Today

As The Bahamas moves deeper into the new millennium, the government and various investors continue to pump money into the tourism infrastructure, especially on Paradise Island, across from Nassau, as well as Freeport/Lucaya on Grand Bahama Island. Cruise arrivals continue to increase, and a more upscale crowd is coming back after abandoning The Bahamas for many years in favor of other Caribbean islands like St. Barts or Anguilla.

When Hubert Ingraham became prime minister in 1992, he launched the country on the long road to regaining its market share of tourism, which under Prime Minister Lynden Pindling had seen a rapid decline, with large numbers of visitors flocking to more hospitable climates. Bermuda, for example, enjoyed a long list of repeat visitors, including many middle-aged couples who visited the island annually ever since their college days. In contrast, exit polls showed that some first-time visitors vowed never to return to The Bahamas under the administration of the notorious Pindling.

Pindling's government had taken over a number of hotels and used them as cash cows without reinvesting in them. When Ingraham took over as new prime minister, however, he wisely recognized that the government wasn't a hotelier and decided to turn many properties back over to the professionals. After a painful slump, tourism in the post-Pindling era is booming again in The Bahamas, and more than 1.6 million visitors from all over the world flock here annually. In the capital of Nassau, for instance, it's easy to see where money is being spent: new air terminals, widened roads, repaved sidewalks, underground phone cables, massive landscaping, sweeping esplanades, an islandwide cleanup campaign, and additional police officers walking the beat to cut down on crime.

Unlike Haiti and Jamaica, The Bahamas has remained politically stable and has made the transition from a poverty-stricken nation under minority white rule to black majority rule with relatively little tension.

You do not see the wretched poverty in Nassau that you see when you fly into Kingston, Jamaica. Many poor people live on New Providence Island, but most of them live in a section called "over-the-hill," which few tourists venture to visit, though the neighborhood is fascinating.

You'd think that a city so close to the U.S. mainland would be overpowered by American culture. Yet except for some fast-food eateries, and American music and films, Nassau retains its traditional British overlay. On the other hand, Freeport/Lucaya on Grand Bahama Island has become totally Americanized. There is little British aura or Bahamian tradition here. Everything is completely modern.

The biggest changes have occurred in the hotel sector. Sun International has vastly expanded its Atlantis property on Paradise Island, turning it into a virtual waterworld. Several new restaurants have opened, replacing older establishments that had grown tired over the years. The Hilton interests have developed the tired old British Colonial in Nassau, restoring it to life.

Grand Bahama Island is in a state of flux. Hotels along the entire Lucayan strip are being either built from scratch or upgraded. The fabled The Resorts at Bahamia in Freeport is having a renaissance under new owners.

If there's a downside to the boom, it's the emphasis on megahotels and casinos and the corresponding lack of focus on the Out Islands.

Most large resort chains except for Four Seasons on Great Exuma have ignored the Out Islands, letting them slumber in their poverty. Disney developed Castaway Cay (the former Gorda Cay), but this will be only for its cruise-ship passengers. Disney will use its private island for 1-day excursions. Four Seasons may open its megaresort with an 18-hole golf course late in 2001 or in 2002. Other developments have been minor, so the Out Islands stay drowsy—but that's how their devotees prefer them. It is the very lack of progress on the Out Islands that attracts the adventurous explorer who shuns megaresorts and glittery casinos, which are at their best on Paradise Island and Cable Beach and a little less sparkly in the Freeport/Lucaya area.

Little change is anticipated until way past the millennium. The rival Turks and Caicos, especially the island of Provo, attract the big spenders and developers. It is a daunting task, however, to make a living on the inhospitable Out Islands, as the plantation owners of yesteryear could testify. For the most part, the Out Islands are The Bahamas "the way they were"—in the 1950s.

Although tourism is bouncing back, many problems remain for this archipelago nation. Some Bahamians are among the friendliest and most hospitable people in the world; but others, including some in the tourist industry, can be downright hostile, an attitude observed by writers for many publications. To counter this, the government is trying to train its citizens to be more helpful, courteous, and efficient. Sometimes this training has taken root; at other times it has fallen on barren ground. Service with a smile is still not assured in The Bahamas.

After a long slumber, the government and many concerned citizens of The Bahamas have awakened to eco-tourism. More than any government in the Caribbean except Bonaire, the country is trying to protect its natural heritage. If nothing else, they realize it's good for business, because many visitors come to The Bahamas for a close encounter with nature.

Government, private companies, and environmental groups drew up a national framework of priorities to protect the islands. One of their first goals was to save the nearly extinct West Indian flamingo. Today, there are nearly 60,000 flamingos living on the Island of Great Inagua. Equally important programs aim to prevent the extinction of the green turtle, the white-crowned pigeon, the Bahamian parrot, and the New Providence iguana.

The government is also casting a leery eye toward Cuba, wondering what will happen to Bahamian tourism if Castro's closed socialist island is reopened officially to the American market.

Drug smuggling remains a serious problem, and regrettably there seems to be no immediate solution. Because the country is so close to the U.S. mainland, it is often used as a temporary depot for drugs from South America that are eventually shipped to Florida. The Bahamas has a long tradition of catering to the illicit habits of U.S. citizens; during the heyday of Prohibition, long before cocaine, marijuana, and heroin were outlawed, many Bahamians grew rich smuggling rum into the United States.

2 What's Cookin' in The Bahamas

There is a bona fide Bahamian cuisine, but you'll have to leave the first-class hotels to find it. In Nassau, for example, head to such old-time favorites as the Travellers Rest or the Bahamian Kitchen for an authentic "taste of The Bahamas" (see chapter 3). On Grand Bahama Island you'll have to look even harder to find typically native dishes. They're best at Fatman's Nephew (see chapter 5). If you'd like to eat authentic Bahamian food, look for the word "BAHAMIAN" in caps under each chapter's restaurant reviews. When you see the word "INTERNATIONAL," know that this is typical fare likely to be offered anywhere, especially at a resort in Florida.

Once you reach the Out Islands, eating Bahamian food is often the only way to go. In some of the remote places, it's the only type of cuisine offered. Of course, the major restaurants have continental chefs, but in many places, especially at the little local restaurants previewed in this guide, you eat as the Bahamians eat.

Cuisine, sad to say, is not one of the most compelling reasons to come to The Bahamas. You can fare much better on the mainland, especially in Florida. Except for some notable exceptions (see "The Best Restaurants," in chapter 1), many restaurants serve fairly routine international fare of the surf-and-turf variety. Local fish and shellfish consist mainly of grouper and conch. When we tour the Out Islands, we often get one or the other every night. More exotic fish is often flown in frozen from Miami, as is most meat and poultry.

The best restaurants are in Nassau, Cable Beach, Paradise Island, and, to a lesser extent, Freeport/Lucaya. The Out Islands are not famed for their cuisine. It's pretty much local fare, or an international dish or two if the hotel is more upscale. That doesn't mean you can't eat satisfactorily in The Bahamas. You can. But chances are you won't be writing any cookbooks or collecting recipes for the meals you are served.

THE CUISINE

SOUP   Bahamian fish chowder can be prepared in any number of ways. Old-time Bahamian chefs tell us that it's best when made with grouper. To that, they add celery, onions, tomatoes, and an array of flavorings that might include A-1 sauce (or Worcestershire, or both), along with thyme, cooking sherry, a bit of dark rum, and lime juice.

Increasingly rare these days, turtle soup was for years a mainstay of the Out Islands. Turtle soup and other turtle dishes still appear on some local menus despite turtles' status as endangered species. However, if you have alternatives, it would be better to choose another dish.

CONCH   The national food of The Bahamas is conch (pronounced "konk"). The firm white meat of this mollusk is enjoyed throughout the islands. Actually, it tastes somewhat bland, at least until Bahamian chefs get their hands on it. Locals eat it as a snack (usually served at happy hour in taverns and bars), as a main dish, as a salad, or as an hors d'oeuvre.

Some people think it tastes like abalone. Conch does not have a fishy taste, like halibut, but it has a chewy consistency, which means that a chef must pound it to tenderize it. Every cook has a different recipe for making conch chowder. A popular version includes tomatoes, potatoes, sweet peppers, onions, carrots, salt pork or bacon, bay leaf, thyme, and (of course) salt and pepper.

Conch fritters, shaped like balls, are served with hot sauce and are made with finely minced sweet peppers, onions, and tomato paste, among other ingredients. They are deep-fried in oil.

Conch salad is another local favorite, and again it has many variations. Essentially, it is uncooked conch that has been marinated in Old Sour (a hot pepper sauce) to break down its tissues and to add extra flavor. This is a tangy dish served with diced small red (or green) peppers and chopped onion.

Cracked conch (or fried conch, as the old-timers used to call it) is prepared like a breaded veal cutlet. Pounded hard and dipped in batter, it is then sautéed. Conch is also served steamed, in a Creole sauce, curried, "scorched," creamed on toast, and stewed. Instead of conch chowder, you might get conch soup. You'll also see "conch burgers" listed on menus.

SEAFOOD   The most elegant item you'll see on nearly any menu in The Bahamas is the local spiny lobster. A tropical cousin of the Maine lobster, it is also called crayfish or rock lobster. Only the tail is eaten, however, and it's not as sweet as Maine lobster. You get fresh lobster only when it's in season, from the first of April until the end of August. Otherwise it's frozen.

Bahamian lobster, in spite of its cost, is not always prepared well. Sometimes a cook leaves it in the oven for too long, and the meat becomes tough and chewy. But when prepared right, like it is at the famed Graycliff restaurant in Nassau, it is perfection and worth the exorbitant cost.

The Bahamian lobster lends itself to any international recipe for lobster, including Newburg or Thermidor. A typical local preparation is to curry it with lime juice and fresh coconut, among other ingredients.

After conch, grouper is the second-most-consumed fish in The Bahamas. It's served in a number of ways, often batter dipped or sautéed, and called "fingers" because of the way it's sliced. The fish is also steamed and served in a spicy Creole sauce. Sometimes it comes dressed in a sauce of dry white wine, mushrooms, onions, and thyme. Because the fish has a mild taste, the extra flavor of the other ingredients is needed.

Baked bonefish is also common, and it's very simple to prepare. The bonefish is split in half and seasoned with a hot pepper sauce (Old Sour) and salt, then popped into the oven.

Baked crab is one of the best-known dishes of The Bahamas. A chef mixes the eggs and meat of either land or sea crabs with seasonings and bread crumbs. The crabs are then replaced in their shells and baked.

PEAS 'N' RICE & JOHNNYCAKE   If mashed potatoes are still the "national starch" of America, then peas 'n' rice performs that role in The Bahamas. Peas 'n' rice, like mashed potatoes, can be prepared in a number of ways. One popular method is to cook pigeon peas (which grow in pods on small trees) or black-eyed peas with salt pork, tomatoes, celery, uncooked rice, thyme, green pepper, onion, salt, pepper, and whatever special touch a chef wants to add. When it's served as a side dish, Bahamians most often sprinkle hot sauce over the concoction.

Johnnycake, another famed part of the Bahamian table, dates from the early settlers, who were most often simple and poor. They survived mainly on a diet of fish and rice, supplemented by johnnycake, a pan-cooked bread made with butter, milk, flour, sugar, salt, and baking powder. (Originally it was called "Journey Cake," which was eventually corrupted to johnnycake.) Fishermen could make this simple bread on the decks of their vessels. They'd build a fire in a box that had been filled with sand to keep the flames from spreading to the craft.

TROPICAL FRUITS   Bahamians are especially fond of fruits, and they make inventive dishes out of them, including soursop ice cream and sapodilla pudding. Guavas are used to make their famous guava duff dessert. The islanders also grow and enjoy melons, pineapples, passion fruit, and mangoes.

Their best-known fruit is the papaya, which is called pawpaw or "melon tree." It's made into a dessert or chutney, or eaten for breakfast in its natural state. It's also used in many lunch and dinner recipes. An old Bahamian custom of using papaya as a meat tenderizer has, at least since the 1970s, invaded the kitchens of North America. Papaya is also used to make fruity tropical drinks, such as a Bahama Mama shake. And if you see it for sale in a local food store, take home some "Goombay" marmalade, made with papaya, pineapple, and green ginger.

RUM, LIQUEURS & SPECIALTY DRINKS   Although rum came north from Cuba and Jamaica, the people of The Bahamas quickly adopted it as their national alcoholic beverage. And using their imagination, they invented several local drinks, including the Yellow Bird, the Bahama Mama, and the Goombay Smash.

The Yellow Bird is made with crème de banana liqueur, Vat 19 rum, orange juice, pineapple juice, apricot brandy, and Galliano. A Bahama Mama is made with Vat 19, citrus juice (perhaps pineapple, as well), bitters, a dash of nutmeg, crème de cassis, and a hint of grenadine.

The Goombay Smash is usually made with coconut rum, pineapple juice, lemon juice, Triple Sec, Vat 19, and a dash of simple syrup.

Nearly every bartender in the islands has a personal version of Planter's Punch. A classic recipe is to make it with lime juice, sugar, and Vat 19, plus a dash of bitters. It's usually served with a cherry and an orange slice. If you want a typically Bahamian liqueur, try Nassau Royale. It is used to make an increasingly popular drink, the C. C. Rider, which also includes Canadian Club, apricot brandy, and pineapple juice.

Index

See also Accommodations and Restaurant indexes, below.

RESTAURANTS

FROMMER'S® COMPLETE TRAVEL GUIDES

Alaska
Amsterdam
Argentina & Chile
Arizona
Atlanta
Australia
Austria
Bahamas
Barcelona, Madrid & Seville
Beijing
Belgium, Holland &
  Luxembourg
Bermuda
Boston
British Columbia & the
  Canadian Rockies
Budapest & the Best of Hungary
California
Canada
Cancún, Cozumel & the
  Yucatán
Cape Cod, Nantucket &
  Martha's Vineyard
Caribbean
Caribbean Cruises & Ports
  of Call
Caribbean Ports of Call
Carolinas & Georgia
Chicago
China
Colorado
Costa Rica
Denmark
Denver, Boulder & Colorado
  Springs
England
Europe

European Cruises & Ports of Call
Florida
France
Germany
Greece
Greek Islands
Hawaii
Hong Kong
Honolulu, Waikiki & Oahu
Ireland
Israel
Italy
Jamaica
Japan
Las Vegas
London
Los Angeles
Maryland & Delaware
Maui
Mexico
Montana & Wyoming
Montréal & Québec City
Munich & the Bavarian Alps
Nashville & Memphis
Nepal
New England
New Mexico
New Orleans
New York City
New Zealand
Nova Scotia, New Brunswick &
  Prince Edward Island
Oregon
Paris
Philadelphia & the Amish
  Country
Portugal

Prague & the Best of the Czech
  Republic
Provence & the Riviera
Puerto Rico
Rome
San Antonio & Austin
San Diego
San Francisco
Santa Fe, Taos & Albuquerque
Scandinavia
Scotland
Seattle & Portland
Shanghai
Singapore & Malaysia
South Africa
Southeast Asia
South Florida
South Pacific
Spain
Sweden
Switzerland
Texas
Thailand
Tokyo
Toronto
Tuscany & Umbria
USA
Utah
Vancouver & Victoria
Vermont, New Hampshire
  & Maine
Vienna & the Danube Valley
Virgin Islands
Virginia
Walt Disney World & Orlando
Washington, D.C.
Washington State

FROMMER'S® DOLLAR-A-DAY GUIDES

Australia from $50 a Day
California from $70 a Day
Caribbean from $70 a Day
England from $70 a Day
Europe from $70 a Day

Florida from $70 a Day
Hawaii from $70 a Day
Ireland from $60 a Day
Italy from $70 a Day
London from $85 a Day

New York from $80 a Day
Paris from $80 a Day
San Francisco from $60 a Day
Washington, D.C.,
  from $70 a Day

FROMMER'S® PORTABLE GUIDES

Acapulco, Ixtapa &
  Zihuatanejo
Alaska Cruises & Ports
  of Call
Amsterdam
Australia's Great Barrier Reef
Bahamas
Baja & Los Cabos
Berlin
Boston
California Wine Country
Charleston & Savannah
Chicago

Dublin
Hawaii: The Big Island
Hong Kong
Houston
Las Vegas
London
Los Angeles
Maine Coast
Maui
Miami
New Orleans
New York City
Paris

Phoenix & Scottsdale
Portland
Puerto Rico
Puerto Vallarta, Manzanillo &
  Guadalajara
San Diego
San Francisco
Seattle
Sydney
Tampa & St. Petersburg
Vancouver
Venice
Washington, D.C.

FROMMER'S® NATIONAL PARK GUIDES

Family Vacations in the
  National Parks
Grand Canyon

National Parks of the American
  West
Rocky Mountain
Yellowstone & Grand Teton

Yosemite & Sequoia/
  Kings Canyon
Zion & Bryce Canyon

Frommer's® Memorable Walks

Chicago	New York	San Francisco
London	Paris	Washington, D.C.

Frommer's® Great Outdoor Guides

Arizona & New Mexico	Northern California	Southern New England
New England	Southern California & Baja	Vermont & New Hampshire

Frommer's® Born to Shop Guides

Born to Shop: France	Born to Shop: Italy	Born to Shop: New York
Born to Shop: Hong Kong,	Born to Shop: London	Born to Shop: Paris
Shanghai & Beijing		

Frommer's® Irreverent Guides

Amsterdam	Los Angeles	Seattle & Portland
Boston	Manhattan	Vancouver
Chicago	New Orleans	Walt Disney World
Las Vegas	Paris	Washington, D.C.
London	San Francisco	

Frommer's® Best-Loved Driving Tours

America	France	New England
Britain	Germany	Scotland
California	Ireland	Spain
Florida	Italy	Western Europe

The Unofficial Guides®

Bed & Breakfasts in California	Golf Vacations in the	New Orleans
Bed & Breakfasts in	Eastern U.S.	New York City
New England	The Great Smoky &	Paris
Bed & Breakfasts in the	Blue Ridge Mountains	San Francisco
Northwest	Inside Disney	Skiing in the West
Bed & Breakfasts in Southeast	Hawaii	Southeast with Kids
Beyond Disney	Las Vegas	Walt Disney World
Branson, Missouri	London	Walt Disney World for
California with Kids	Mid-Atlantic with Kids	Grown-ups
Chicago	Mini Las Vegas	Walt Disney World for Kids
Cruises	Mini-Mickey	Washington, D.C.
Disneyland	New England with Kids	World's Best Diving Vacations
Florida with Kids		

Special-Interest Titles

Frommer's Britain's Best Bed & Breakfasts and
 Country Inns
Frommer's France's Best Bed & Breakfasts and
 Country Inns
Frommer's Italy's Best Bed & Breakfasts and
 Country Inns
Frommer's Caribbean Hideaways
Frommer's Adventure Guide to Australia &
 New Zealand
Frommer's Adventure Guide to Central America
Frommer's Adventure Guide to India & Pakistan
Frommer's Adventure Guide to South America
Frommer's Adventure Guide to Southeast Asia
Frommer's Adventure Guide to Southern Africa
Frommer's Gay & Lesbian Europe
Frommer's Exploring America by RV
Hanging Out in England

Hanging Out in Europe
Hanging Out in France
Hanging Out in Ireland
Hanging Out in Italy
Hanging Out in Spain
Israel Past & Present
Frommer's The Moon
Frommer's New York City with Kids
The New York Times' Guide to Unforgettable
 Weekends
Places Rated Almanac
Retirement Places Rated
Frommer's Road Atlas Britain
Frommer's Road Atlas Europe
Frommer's Washington, D.C., with Kids
Frommer's What the Airlines Never Tell You

Let Us Hear From You!

Dear Frommer's Reader,

You are our greatest resource in keeping our guides relevant, timely, and lively. We'd love to hear from you about your travel experiences—good or bad. Want to recommend a great restaurant or a hotel off the beaten path—or register a complaint? Any thoughts on how to improve the guide itself?

Please use this page to share your thoughts with me and mail it to the address below. Or if you like, send a FAX or e-mail me at frommersfeedback@hungryminds.com. And so that we can thank you—and keep you up on the latest developments in travel—we invite you to sign up for a free daily Frommer's e-mail travel update. Just write your e-mail address on the back of this page. Also, if you'd like to take a moment to answer a few questions about yourself to help us improve our guides, please complete the following quick survey. (We'll keep that information confidential.)

Thanks for your insights.

Yours sincerely,

Michael Spring

Michael Spring, *Publisher*

Name (Optional) _____

Address_____

_____

City_____ State_____ ZIP_____

Name of Frommer's Travel Guide _____

Comments_____

Age: ( )18-24; ( )25-39; ( )40-49; ( )50-55; ( )Over 55

Income: ( )Under $25,000; ( )$25,000-$50,000; ( )$50,000-$100,000; ( )Over $100,000

I am: ( )Single, never married; ( )Married, with children; ( )Married, without children; ( )Divorced; ( )Widowed

Number of people in my household: ( )1; ( )2; ( )3; ( )4; ( )5 or more

Number of people in my household under 18: ( )1; ( )2; ( )3; ( )4; ( )5 or more

I am ( )a student; ( )employed full-time; ( )employed part-time; ( )not employed at this time; ( )retired; ( )other

I took ( )0; ( )1; ( )2; ( )3; ( )4 or more leisure trips in the past 12 months

My last vacation was ( )a weekend; ( )1 week; ( )2 weeks; ( )3 or more weeks

My last vacation was to ( )the U.S.; ( )Canada; ( )Mexico; ( )Europe; ( )Asia; ( )South America; ( )Central America; ( )The Caribbean; ( )Africa; ( )Middle East; ( )Australia/New Zealand

( )I would; ( )would not buy a Frommer's Travel Guide for business travel

I access the Internet ( )at home; ( )at work; ( )both; ( )I do not use the Internet

I used the Internet to do research for my last trip. ( )Yes; ( )No

I used the Internet to book accommodations or air travel on my last trip. ( )Yes; ( )No

My favorite travel site is ( )frommers.com; ( )travelocity.com; ( )expedia.com; other_____

I use Frommer's Travel Guides ( )always; ( )sometimes; ( )seldom

I usually buy ( )1; ( )2; ( )more than 2 guides when I travel

Other guides I use include_____

What's the most important thing we could do to improve Frommer's Travel Guides?

_____

_____

_____

_____

Yes, please send me a daily e-mail travel update. My e-mail address is

_____

Mail to: Michael Spring, Publisher and Vice President, Frommer's Travel Guides
909 Third Ave., New York, NY 10022   FAX: 212.884.5432